JANE BLANNIBUS

In Cahoots!
Nailing Harry

JANE BLANCHARD OMNIBUS

In Cahoots!
Nailing Harry

JANE BLANCHARD

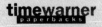
timewarner
paperbacks

A *Time Warner* Paperback

This omnibus edition first published in Great Britain by
Time Warner Paperbacks in 2004
Jane Blanchard Omnibus Copyright © Jane Blanchard 2004

Previously published separately:
In Cahoots! first published in Great Britain in 2001
by Warner Books
Copyright © Jane Blanchard 2001

Nailing Harry first published in Great Britain as a paperback original
by Time Warner Paperbacks in 2002
Copyright © Jane Blanchard 2002

The moral right of the author has been asserted.

A CIP catalogue record for this book
is available from the British Library.

ISBN 0 7515 3640 7

Printed and bound in Great Britain by
Clays Ltd, St Ives plc

Time Warner Paperbacks
An imprint of
Time Warner Books UK
Brettenham House
Lancaster Place
London WC2E 7EN

www.TimeWarnerBooks.co.uk
www.janeblanchard.com

In Cahoots!

For Mum and Dad

acknowledgements

I wrote this book in secret, early in the morning, late at night and mostly in my pyjamas. The handful of friends to whom I entrusted my secret offered me the belief and encouragement that I needed to finish it.

In all the newsrooms I've worked in, if someone announces that they are writing a book it tends to prompt a 'pass the sickbag' reaction or mysterious mutterings about it being 'good therapy'. I was curious to see if I could do it and so secrecy became an added impetus.

When I first told my partner Iain Blair (alias bestselling novelist Emma Blair) that I wanted to write a book, we struck a brilliant deal. He said he would read it only when it was finished and that he would give an honest opinion. Having watched Iain over the past seven years climbing the stairs to his office at nine every morning, I did at least have some idea of the terrain ahead. Forty chapters later, I now know first hand just how difficult but rewarding it is. *In Cahoots!* would not have been possible without his total love and support. Oh, and he really enjoyed the book too.

My other main supporter is my wonderful son Mark who willingly made so many sacrifices during the year it took to write. He had to queue for the computer and he gave me the peace I needed. His cooking's improved too.

I have four fantastic friends to thank as well. Rene

Wyndham, who has spent years nagging me to write, Jane White, Elayne Hoskin and Sally Sedgman, who were also convinced I could do it.

My love and thanks to my agent, Pat White, who bravely took me on based on one chapter and believed in me all the way. A sincere thank you to Barbara Boote at Little, Brown whose encouraging note after receiving the first chapter was pinned up in my office for inspiration. Thanks also to all the team at Little, Brown for their fantastic support and enthusiasm.

And finally, thanks for the inspiration from the Curry Night Girls – Cherry, Judy, Gill, Lizzie, Jean, Jenny, Deirdre and Angie. For more than a decade we've met regularly for a good gossip over a chicken tikka. Long may it continue.

Part One

chapter one

'Why don't you wear that blue dress? You know the one, you wore it at the company dinner and you wouldn't tell me how much it cost.' Roger's voice came rather persuasively from the shower. All that steam must be making his voice shrill or something.

Why the hell have we got to meet your boss on a Saturday? thought Vicky ungratefully. It was the first day of her leave and she'd woken up absolutely whacked. Didn't the boss ever have some sort of life either?

'Oh come on, it *is* the Moathouse. We'll have a nice boozy lunch, a great view of the sea, and it sounds very much like promotion for me. It can't be bad news because we wouldn't be having lunch, would we?' he reasoned. 'Also he wouldn't have invited you.'

Another burst of Niagara Falls. What the hell was he doing in there?

'I don't really know why I have to go,' she shouted from the bedroom. 'If you're being promoted you certainly don't need me making up the numbers.'

Chauvinist twit, thought Vicky. All that sizing up your social cred before you got the next hoick up the ladder. She allowed herself a short nightmare of future dinner parties chez Mr and Mrs Upper Middle Management, all that forced, braying laughter and silent angst about fish knives and forks, do you or don't you? Vicki didn't think the fish would care about the cutlery any more than she did.

Back to reality and Roger was still in full flow under the shower, nagging on about that blue dress. Why is it that men don't understand that women have fat days and thin days? Today might have been Blue Cross day in the high street but it just wasn't Blue Dress day as far as Vicky was concerned. It needed several days of severe dieting to get into that one. And besides, some telltale thread veins were getting a tad too prominent on her thighs. Soon the blue dress would co-ordinate only too well with her legs. Soon, she thought miserably, she'd be too old and too crinkly to venture into Top Shop ever again. Worse than your credit card not swiping in front of a queue of tutting customers.

'I want you to look really great today,' urged Roger. 'It's really important that you create a good impression. And make sure you use some of our products.'

Roger worked for Tressed Out. They made shampoos and hairsprays on a rather dismal industrial estate on the edge of town. He headed up the marketing department where they were all clearly brainwashed (probably by their own products) into thinking of nothing but Tressed Out.

It was one of those firms where everyone refers to each other as Mr Peacock in Packing and Mrs Plum in the postroom. It always reminded Vicky of noisy childhood games of Cluedo. Roger of course had never played anything as silly as Cluedo and thought her remarks rather infantile. He had a serious career ahead of him and here he was, apparently, poised to move up yet another rung and join the World of the Secret Bonus, private health, share options and a better company car.

In fact the blue dress prompted another nightmare about the Tressed Out Annual Ball. She'd worn it there during one of her thin weeks and it had been a great success.

Buoyed up by losing a few pounds and therefore

instantly pissed on a couple of quick glasses of champagne, she'd viewed the whole evening through a wonderful haze. A four-piece band – average age about 103 – had thumped out fifties lounge music as a few brave couples tried to recall the intricacies of the slow foxtrot in an atmosphere of retro mothballs. The high spot was when Miss Scarlett in Sales, resplendent in drawstring Crimplene, tutted loudly that they 'really could have shelled the peas' when a poor waitress turned up to serve the mange-touts. Vicky's uncontrollable giggles had led to Roger doing a lot of meaningful hissing and kicking under the table to shut her up.

Vicky often embarrassed Roger. She didn't mean to but they came from totally different worlds. His revolved around the unit price of shampoo, rival conditioners and styling mousse wars. Hers was all about deadlines, shrieking and shouting across a busy television newsroom.

Vicky worked as a reporter on the local station. Not a high-flying hack bound for ITN – those days were long past – but she was regarded as a 'safe pair of hands', someone who could go out on a news story or a feature and turn in something passable. She knew she'd never be a top-notch journo because she was now forty-three and raw ambition had long since gone. She'd also given too much of her life to her career to make up for a series of fairly hopeless relationships which had gone nowhere. Instead of marriage, kids and roses around the cottage door, she'd had to settle for the endless re-telling of the same old stories, MPs in sex scandals, barmaids bludgeoned to death, or the Curse of the And Finallys – those often painful stabs at humour at the end of a particularly gruesome news bulletin.

This week, as well as three days stuck in a long and boring murder trial, she'd covered the miracle of the skate-boarding dog and the lovelorn camel in the local zoo signing up with a worldwide dating agency for camels. Presumably they'd all given their previous partners the hump.

Vicky also knew in her heart of hearts that she was gradually being given the hump too. Her days on the box were numbered. Jack, the news editor, had tried tactfully to suggest that her pieces would have more impact without her face in them.

'Keep out of vision, love,' he had said, pretending to wrestle with two phones to hide his embarrassment. 'Never let the reporter get in the way of a good story. Know what I mean?'

No, she didn't, especially when there was a different set of rules for Alicia, the young blonde office runner who was already being groomed for future stardom by being sent out on earth-shattering items about hairdressers and horse shows. A secret fan club had started up among the chaps dedicated to the adoration of her bottom. E-mails whizzed back and forth daily around the studio fantasising about the type and colour of knickers she was wearing.

Yesterday, when it was obvious from the outline that young Alicia was wearing a G-string under a very tight pair of trousers, the short message system crashed for a while, losing an afternoon bulletin. The computer support guys knew exactly what the cause was. Most of them belonged to the fan club too.

Oblivious to Alicia's underwear arrangements, Jack, on the news desk, had gone into orbit, blaming everyone for relying on the computer and not printing up their scripts as they were supposed to.

'How do we explain this to the viewers?' he raged to all in range, picking up the phone to find out how many complaints there had been. (Transmission had had to substitute a five-minute standby item which was so old that the people in it were wearing flared trousers the first time around.)

'One complaint flooded in,' replied Shirley the rece,
tionist, coolly. 'But we've had about a dozen calls so far
saying they really enjoyed the other item and in future
could we show more of—'

'Enough, enough,' shouted Jack, slamming down the
phone so hard it promptly bounced out of its cradle,
knocking his coffee all over the desk. Soon there'd be complaints that the people in the flares had died and why
hadn't relatives been told it was being shown. Next thing
they'd all be wanting VHS copies.

Vicky mopped up the mess and brought him another
coffee from the machine.

'Thanks, Vick,' said Jack gratefully, calming down.
'Loved your camels piece by the way. Nice treatment – you
let the pictures tell the story. One shot, worth a thousand
words, etc. Always works best.'

Except when you're a couple of decades younger, thought
Vicky ruefully.

'You're off on leave next week, aren't you? I'll miss you,'
said Jack charitably. 'Doing anything mad?'

'Must be joking,' she replied. 'Roger's taken the same
week off so there's no escape. We're having lunch with his
boss tomorrow and then doing a round of his dreary relatives. Besides, I'm broke so at least I'll get fed.'

'Oh well, as you're not going abroad, don't forget to keep
your pager on just in case we need you. And if it's really
boring, come in and do a shift. I think we could be a bit
stretched next week,' said Jack shamelessly.

'Thanks a bunch,' she grinned back. 'No, I think I'll just
stick with being bored and do the decent thing.'

And that's just the trouble, thought Vicky as she closed
down her computer and threw all the newspapers and
scripts into a nearby bin. She'd been boringly polite all her
life, never wanting to hurt people's feelings, putting their
emotional needs before hers.

As she steered her car out of the studio car park, she pondered on the week ahead with Roger. It loomed rather like a black cloud with the marked absence of a silver lining.

Vicky had met Roger during one of life's many lows. She'd discovered the object of her desire, a rather dashing solicitor called Mervyn whom she'd met during a long fraud trial. He had swiftly become life's great tragedy when she'd caught him red-handed in her flat, in her bed, listening to her CD player, sipping her champagne. With someone else.

Mervyn the Marvellous had secretly been renamed Swervin' Mervyn by her closest friends, Judith and Sarah, who'd guessed what was going on, but couldn't bring themselves to tell her the awful truth. Just in case they'd got it wrong.

Instead Vicky got the full-frontal facts by coming home when an industrial tribunal settled earlier than expected. Vicky never slept in the flat again. She couldn't bear the thought of putting her head on the pillow where the terrible deed had taken place. So she had sold up, packed in her job and stayed with Judith for a while.

Then Sarah, an incurable spendaholic, had persuaded her to go off on a shopping trip to Hong Kong on the basis that 'when the going gets tough, the tough go shopping'. Egged on by Sarah, Vicky did just that and drowned her sorrows in some silk suits and a jade Buddha. It became a permanent reminder of the extremely large dent it had made in her bank balance.

So she'd had to pull herself together and start job hunting immediately. The first job offer sent her to a small regional television station, a couple of hundred miles away from London and her friends. But at least it was miles away from everything that reminded her of Merve the Swerve.

Six months later she'd met Roger. She'd interviewed him

for a story about new jobs in the region. Tressed Out were taking on another sixty factory staff and he'd been the company spokesman that day. He'd phoned her three times a week after that, inviting her out to dinner, and in the end she'd given in. Then he had pestered her to go to bed with him, and again she'd given in.

Vicky had been at her lowest ebb, weak, tired and desperate to find an antidote to Mervyn. She'd hoped, rather ashamedly, that seeing Roger for a while might just numb her grief.

Of course it didn't, but the whole thing had drifted on and now, eighteen months later, she knew she really ought to summon the strength to end it. They just weren't suited.

An only child, Roger had been idolised and over-protected by his parents. He'd worked hard at school, never rebelled, never smoked dope, never bought a porn mag or even had a parking ticket. He planned his life meticulously, paid his bills on time, bought the same shirt five at a time and you could almost see your face in the shine on his shoes.

In short, Roger had never taken a risk in all his forty-five years. He left nothing to chance, he'd never been married, yearned for kids, held impromptu dinner parties or spent all day in bed with the papers. He even took a calculator to the supermarket. Average A levels had taken him to university, an average degree had eased him into marketing. Now he was devoting his life to a steady but decidedly unmeteoric rise up the ladder at Tressed Out.

Rather like the way he'd persuaded Vicky to go out with him, he'd chiselled away rather than adopting a sledgehammer approach. He'd ended all his previous relationships, usually because the women were just too untidy in mind and body, so they did not fit into his disciplined life.

Even sex had to happen on set days at set times to a set

routine. If Roger had been persuaded to light a candle, he'd have consulted the small print of his house insurance first. Passion was something Roger knew nothing about.

Vicky felt guilty. Despite his pedantic ways, she knew that deep down Roger was one of the good guys. The trouble was basically that he was boring. Bastards are so much more exciting. She also couldn't frankly understand what Roger saw in her. She thrived on late-night phone calls to Judith and Sarah, laughs in noisy restaurants, fervent horoscope readings and shopping bags full of retail therapy.

Roger's idea of a holiday was a carefully picked long weekend in a good English hotel, paid for by the credit card which gave him the most bonus points. Vicky was more of a book-today-go-tomorrow-pay-later merchant, armed with her appropriate Lonely Planet guide. Roger thought Lonely Planet must be some sort of dating agency.

It was no good, she'd have to start thinking about ending the relationship. It simply wasn't fair on him.

'What are you doing in there?' queried Roger. It was Vicky's turn in the shower. 'Time's getting on. We mustn't be late. I want to leave dead on twelve.'

Vicky finally emerged in the blue dress, wishing she'd skipped breakfast. This was definitely not one of her thin days but just to please Roger, she'd gone along with it. It was a deep kingfisher-blue silk, long, straight and sleeveless with a mandarin collar. Utterly plain and beautifully cut, with long slits at the sides, it was one of her favourite buys from the Hong Kong trip.

At least when we're sitting down I won't look so fat, thought Vicky. *And no one will see my thread veins under the tablecloth.*

Roger had already brought his car round to the front of his house. Now he was fretting about locking the windows and doors. He seemed nervous, thought Vicky. Obviously this lunch was really important to him. She must make an effort not to swear or laugh too loudly.

Soon they were heading into the centre of Plymouth. It was that moment in August when the leaves start to look dusty and rather tired – as if they know autumn is not all that far away. *Rather like me*, thought Vicky. *Dusty and tired.* What she would have given for a week in Spain rather than a week touring round Roger's dreary relatives. For a Saturday, the city was relatively empty, tourists were either on their journey home or they'd gone to the beach to catch the last of the summer sunshine.

They were close to the Moathouse now as Roger looked nervously at his watch. He really was on edge. Vicky was suddenly gripped with fear. Could this be the big elbow rather than the step up he yearned for? Was this going to be a pay-off rather than a promotion? Had she been invited so that she could pick up the pieces and drive a distraught Roger home? Oh hell, she could hardly leave him after all that – at least not for a while. His whole life revolved around bloody Tressed Out.

Lost in these thoughts, Vicky never noticed that they'd actually driven past the Moathouse and were now pulling into a car park. She was already mentally rehearsing soothing phrases and advice. He was overdue for a job change, should think about brushing up the CV, time to take on a new challenge, what about seeing a headhunter, and so on. All those platitudes you trot out in times of crisis.

'Why are we parking here?' she queried, realising with embarrassment that she'd not been paying attention.

'Never you mind,' said Roger rather harshly. 'Just take my arm.' He almost frogmarched her up some steps.

The soft red brick building had a sense of familiarity about it, but in her sudden confusion, Vicky failed to read the plaque 'Register Office' on the wall. Once inside, she was aware of a large foyer in soft pink colours, a sea of faces and then, suddenly and strangely, a round of applause.

'What the hell is . . .' she faltered. Some awful truth was beginning to dawn.

'Darling,' said Roger with a forced smile. 'We're getting married. Right now. This is our wedding day.'

Vicky started to keel over, her mouth went dry, her vision blurred. Waves of shock rose from deep within and she felt suddenly and very violently sick. She blinked and the room went abruptly back into focus. She scanned the line of people standing there, clapping and smiling at her. Roger's parents, his widowed aunt from Eastbourne, another aunt and uncle with their two obnoxious children. She looked again. Half the marketing team from Tressed Out seemed to be there too, along with Roger's boss, Roger's secretary and even Roger's cleaner.

They were all in on the act. All except her. Shock gave way to panic.

'Just a simple ceremony and then out into the garden for photographs. Then the cars will take us all up to the Moathouse,' said Roger. He started to outline details as if he were ticking them off on an imaginary clipboard for a military operation.

'We'll be in a white limo. I knew you'd like that . . .'

'Just hang on a minute,' spluttered Vicky. Tears of anger were starting to course down her cheeks. This was Roger who never took risks, Roger the boring, the predictable, the self-control freak.

'What about me? Don't I get a say in this? How dare you,' her voice started to rise, 'how dare you assume, just bloody assume that I'll go along with this.'

'Keep your voice down, darling, we don't want a scene. Let's not spoil our big day,' said Roger smoothly. 'We've been together a long time and you've always gone on at me for not being spontaneous so here we are. I'm being spontaneous. It's what we both want, isn't it!'

'Well it's looking pretty one-sided from where I'm standing. Most normal people ask . . .' Vicky stopped and glanced down. She realised she was holding a bouquet. Someone must have handed it to her.

The shock brought her to her senses. She must get out of there and fast.

'Of course, darling. It's a bit of a shock. So I will ask you, in front of these witnesses.' Roger grinned nervously in the direction of the assembled guests.

'Vicky, will you do me the honour of becoming my wife?'

With a sob that came up almost from the ground beneath her, Vicky turned and fled. Down the steps, out of the building and into the sunshine.

Dropping the bouquet as she went.

chapter two

Vicky was horribly aware of being stared at. Shoppers stood back in her wake as she ran as fast as she could through the crowded streets, silent tears streaming down her face. *Please, please let there be a taxi at the rank.*

She'd been aware of Roger following, but mercifully he'd given up after a couple of blocks. She prayed her legs wouldn't buckle under her and she'd be hauled back into unholy matrimony. Why oh why hadn't she worn a decent pair of trainers and a sports bra? At least she was reasonably fit from a bit of swimming.

Within the safe confines of a cab, she burst into hysterical sobs.

'Something wrong, love?' enquired the cabbie with all the understatement in the world.

'Just get me home.' She gabbled out her address.

'Here's some tissues,' he replied, tossing over a box from the glove compartment. 'Don't want to let your massacre run, do you.' He laughed at his own joke. Freda Payne's 'Band of Gold' was blaring from the radio. *How bloody ironic*, thought Vicky.

The taxi passed the end of Roger's road. The very recent memory of all the lies about meeting the boss and insistence on the blue dress came flooding back. They headed

out of town towards the small commuter village where
Vicky rented a tiny cottage.

'Haven't I seen you on the telly?' queried the driver,
looking at her sceptically as she scrabbled in her handbag
for the fare.

'Well maybe in a previous life,' she muttered, and fled
inside, embarrassed that she didn't have enough to give
him much of a tip.

As the door slammed shut behind her, Vicky sank to the
floor in the hallway. A mixture of shock and humiliation
engulfed her and she started to shake violently. *A drink,
that's what I need*, she thought. As she went in search of
some gin, she half ran around the cottage instinctively
drawing all the curtains as if to shut out the world.

Two minutes later, nursing a very large gin and some
rather flat tonic, she calmed down a little. *Must ring Judith*,
she thought. *Please let her be in*. Oh God, she was praying
again.

'Shit,' muttered Judith. 'Why does the bloody phone always
ring at the wrong time?' She put down the supermarket
bags, raced to the phone and it promptly stopped. *When
I've unloaded the boot, I'll ring 1471*, she promised herself. A
minute later, laden with the next load of bags, she heard it
ring again.

Grabbing the phone, baguettes flying and Beaujolais
bottles clanking, she noticed a scrawled note from her
teenage son Simon, to the effect that he'd emptied the
fridge. Thank goodness she'd done a huge supermarket
run.

'Judith,' sobbed a tiny voice. 'It's Vicky. The most terrible
thing's happened . . . Roger and I . . . it was just awful . . .
they were all there . . . how could he!'

'For Chrissake, what's happened, Vick? Calm down and
tell me.'

'I don't believe it, I just don't believe it. What an insensitive plonker, how fucking dare he,' Judith finally pronounced when Vicky had sobbed her way through some brief headlines of the day's events.

'I'm sorry, Vick, but at least I can tell you now. We all thought he was a total pillock. He was never right for you, I mean, we all knew he was a bit of a rebound jobbie for you after Merve the Swerve. But he was just so boring and predictable. Mind you, how wrong we were on that last bit. Whatever possessed him to pull that sort of stunt? For a start, we all want a bit of notice for that sort of thing. I'd need at least a year's advance warning for the diet and the plastic surgery alone. Also the bastard never even invited me. And anyway I hate his bloody shampoo!'

Judith was making a brave but fruitless stab at making Vicky laugh. But that was clearly off the agenda for the moment.

'Oh shit.' Vicky lowered her voice to an urgent whisper. 'There's someone at the door.'

She instinctively started to cower at the kitchen table over her drink. Who the hell was this? The bell rang persistently. Please let it not be Roger. She was too exhausted for a showdown. Thank God she'd drawn the curtains.

'Hello, hi! Anybody in?' said a cheerful voice. It wasn't Roger. Relief engulfed Vicky. She was still holding the phone.

'Vicky, we'd like to talk to you. It's Sam from the *Mirror*,' came the smooth, confident tones through the letterbox.

'Shit, Judith, what am I going to do?' Vicky whispered into the phone, all that journalistic calm-in-a-crisis deserting her in a nano-second. 'It's Sam Spencer, he's the *Mirror* man down here. Christ, if he's on to this, the whole pack'll be here in a minute.'

'How do you know that?' asked Judith.

'Normally I'm one of the pack.' The irony hadn't escaped either of them.

'Now listen carefully. Don't answer the door,' said Judith urgently. 'Keep out of sight and find somewhere quiet to talk to me where you can't be overheard. You call me back in one minute. I won't ring you because they'll hear the phone being answered. One minute, you call. OK? Bye.'

Aiming for the stairs, Vicky fell on to her hands and knees and crawled back out into the tiny hallway to avoid being spotted through the letterbox. She suddenly felt as if she were auditioning for some absurd game show. With an imaginary clock ticking and a slick suave host in a loud jacket urging her on, she knew what prize she wanted most. It wasn't the fondue set, the cuddly toy or two weeks in Torremolinos. All she wanted right now was to be somewhere, anywhere but here. Right now she'd settle for the sanctuary of upstairs. At which point there was a rat-tat-tat of the door knocker.

Before the minute was up, she allowed herself a good slug of gin and a tiny peek out of the bathroom window through the foliage of a rather tired Swiss cheese plant. A small gaggle of journalists and photographers was begining to form up at the garden gate and, worse, some were standing in her tiny front garden, looking for a chink in the curtains.

Suddenly all hell seemed to break loose. The door bell went again in long angry bursts and she could hear shouts from the garden calling her name Then the phone sprang to life. Vicky was not usually one to leave a phone ringing. It was her job to answer it and turn out on some life-or-death story. News was no respecter of sleep. But this time she froze. Instinctively she shied away from it as if it were a venomous snake. If she answered and it was them, she was doomed. Caught like a rat in a trap.

She peered out again through the large waxy leaves of the Swiss cheese. A rather familiar Land Rover Discovery was just pulling up on the verge opposite the cottage. It was Jonathan, one of the cameramen from work. What the hell was he doing here? Same as the others, she reasoned.

The phone stopped, the door bell ceased and the pack resumed their babble of conversation, comparing notes on what they'd found out so far. Vicky was tempted to sit there straining to hear what they were saying. But instead she decided to use the chatting as a shield to ring Judith on her mobile.

'Now this is the plan,' said Judith. 'I've got a good two hours' drive ahead of me so you've got to tough this one out. Don't answer your house phone, don't move or do anything to give away any clues. Pack a bag if you can, without arousing suspicion, and stay upstairs. Switch off your mobile to save the battery. Now, make sure you've got your pager and I'll issue instructions on that. OK?'

Vicky nodded dumbly into the phone, realising she needed to say something. 'Yes, I've got it,' she whispered, hastily filling the silence. 'I really appreciate this,' she added somewhat inadequately.

The pager jumped to life, vibrating and chirping at the same time and waking Vicky from a troubled slumber. She'd somehow dozed off, probably caused by the gin she'd polished off on an empty stomach. She glanced around her bedroom, momentarily wondering why she was there. The suitcase, packed and standing at the end of her bed, brought her sharply back to reality and the ghastliness of the register office. She wondered briefly what all the dreadful people from Tressed Out were doing right now. Not discussing dandruff control, that was certain. Probably wolfing down copious amounts of wine and food at the Moathouse at Roger's expense, dining out on the story that they were likely to dine out on for years to come. *I hope it chokes them*, she thought.

She psyched herself up for another look out of the bathroom window. Two television reporters, including Randy
Old Rob from her studio, were clearly getting their early
evening story together by making statements to camera
and handing back to their respective studios. And there
were other reporters there – people she didn't recognise as
the usual Plymouth crowd. She still couldn't quite believe
they would be so interested in what had happened. Well it
was Saturday and it was August, traditionally a quiet news
month.

Then it dawned on her why Sam and the pack had
arrived on her doorstep so swiftly. There'd been another
story at the register office that day, she'd seen it on the
prospects list in the newsroom computer. A chap of seventy-
nine was due to marry a girl of twenty-four. A little digging
by the newsroom research team had shown up that he was
quite rich and somewhat confused and that she was
blonde, bright and broke.

There'd been a spot of banter about it in the canteen earlier in the week, with bets placed as to whether the
marriage would take place. Would the girl turn up, just
how confused was he, was he marrying her for her knock-
ers, had he changed his will, would she flush his vital
tablets down the loo thus ensuring him a reserved seat in
God's waiting room? Could this be a Viagra success story,
with the subsequent heart attack from too much shagging?
The speculation had been endless. It was a good old-
fashioned sex-and-shopping story.

Why couldn't they have stuck with that story instead of
clogging up her front garden and her life? It was strange
being on the other side of the tracks.

A sudden anger overtook her. How dare Roger assume
she'd marry him, how dare he . . . No, later, she checked
herself. Let's get out of this first and then have a really
good rant.

So what did Judith have planned? Her message came in several instalments, interspersed with increasingly stroppy messages from the newsdesk to phone in, demanding that she switch on her mobile. Some hope.

DON'T ANSWER THE DOOR. HAVE MY MOBILE NUMBER READY. AT CODE WORD VICTORIA, CALL ME ON MY MOBILE. IGNORE WHAT I SAY ON PHONE. WAIT FIVE MINUTES. LEAVE BY BACK DOOR AND WAIT IN REAR LANE.

Almost on cue, Vicky heard a disturbance outside her cottage. A quick peek through the Swiss cheese confirmed the stake-out was very much in evidence. There was still quite a contingent from work as well as most of the usual media pack. Alicia, the office runner, was busily dispensing coffee in plastic cups to all and sundry out of the back of Jonathan's Discovery. There was clearly a bit of bonding going on between her and three of the photographers who were happily applying for membership of the newly formed SAAB, the Society for the Adoration of Alicia's Bottom.

All of a sudden, the luvvies' laughing and joking evaporated. They were sworn enemies again as they sensed something was happening.

'Excuse me, do you mind. I am entitled to be here,' declared Judith at her most bossy. 'Would you be so kind.' She pushed past two photographers who'd set up tripods and huge lenses by the front gate.

Judith turned to the throng. 'I've no idea why you're here but I'm visiting my friend, and I can tell you for nothing, she won't take kindly to you lot trampling all over her geraniums.' She started to knock ostentatiously at the cottage door.

Vicky, sensing escape within her grasp, nearly forgot her

instructions as she became overwhelmed with the urge to throw open the door and be saved by her friend.

A barrage of questions was being fired at Judith. Were you at the register office, were you in on the surprise wedding, how long has she known the groom, what's happened to Vicky, have you spoken to her? It all came out like machine-gun fire.

'I think you should all mind your own bloody business. Haven't you got anything better to do? Why not get a life,' shrieked Judith indignantly. 'Or better still why not have lunch at the Moathouse? From what you say, it sounds like they've had one or two cancellations there today.'

'Well, obviously Victoria isn't in,' she proclaimed, emphasising the name that Vicky never used. 'So why don't you lot all naff off.'

The code word jolted Vicky into action. No one ever called her Victoria except her mother. She dialled Judith's number as instructed. Judith answered almost immediately. That was another shock for Vicky. Her friend normally spent at least ten minutes grappling with her bag and its dense jungle of keys, Filofax, make-up, notebook, leaking biros, first aid kit, corkscrew, superglue. You name it, Judith carried it.

'Hello, Victoria! Thank God you've phoned. Where are you?' She paused for an imaginary reply. The pack fell silent, unashamedly listening. Judith lowered her voice to a stage whisper just loud enough to be heard.

'Right, OK, OK. You're going to the studio. Thank goodness, I've been so worried about you. It's OK, Security will let me in. I'm on my way. I'll see you there . . . Yes, yes, of course he's a total bastard,' she added for effect.

Please, please let them swallow this one, prayed Judith. She paused, fiddling with her mobile, waiting to see the reaction to her 'call'. Nothing. It seemed an age. She couldn't go on delving into her bag for ever. Then suddenly, in unison, they started packing up, ready to follow this new scent on the story.

She tried not to show her relief as she walked briskly back to her car. The great rush was now under way, so much so that she couldn't have driven off immediately anyway. Pretending to fume, she was able to sit at the wheel of her car while they all hurtled off in the direction of the studio, mobiles buzzing as they told their respective news desks of the latest developments.

When she was absolutely certain they'd all gone, Judith drove gently to the end of the lane, took a sharp left and down a narrow alley which skirted the back of the terrace of cottages. Halfway down she stopped and waited. Almost immediately the figure of Vicky emerged from the back door, running, waving, tripping, clutching a large battered suitcase.

'Where to, miss?' joked Judith.

'How's about Hell?' Vicky replied with a wan smile. 'No, silly me. I've just come from there.'

Nee nah nee nah nee nah, the sound of a police siren and a nudge on the elbow woke Vicky from her slumber. Judith was pulling into a layby followed by a police car, blue lights flashing.

'I'll do the talking, you just nod. OK?' said Judith quietly.

'Did you realise you were doing eighty-nine mph back there?' queried the uniform now peering into the car and taking in Vicky's dishevelled state and puffy eyes from all the crying.

Judith was instantly into an apologetic stream of excuses, sun on the dashboard, stress, etc. She was just beginning to warm to her theme of tragic family news, cancer, a last-minute dash to a death bed as a favour to her distraught friend in the passenger seat.

'Any points on your licence?' interrupted the officer.

'No, none,' she replied, truthfully.

'Well that *is* a surprise. Now where's this sick auntie?'

'Southampton General,' replied Judith, amazed at her own quick reaction. And only twelve miles from home, she thought thankfully.

'Follow me and we'll get you there as fast as we can.' He began radioing ahead to someone in his traffic control room.

The two cars sped straight on to the fast lane, zipping past a typical summer Saturday afternoon contingent of caravans, campers, trailers and cars packed to the gunwales with everything including 'BRAT ON BOARD'.

'What happens now?' queried Vicky, wondering how many more shocks she could take in a day.

'Leave it to me, just go with the flow. Don't forget we're in a stonking hurry to visit your Auntie Maude who's about to gasp her last. So we don't hang about when we get to the hospital. Just be grateful the copper didn't ask her name so he could start checking out the ward. That would have killed the story stone dead.'

Soon they'd reached the hospital grounds and were pulling into a car park. Judith got out, rushed straight over to the startled policeman and flung her arms around his neck.

'I don't know how to thank you,' she gushed. 'Now come on, Vick, let's get to see Auntie Maude before it's too late.' Together they rushed dramatically through the hospital entrance and into the main foyer. For the second time that day, Vicky found herself regretting not wearing trainers and a sports bra. At this rate of rushing around, she'd have lost a couple of stone, her boobs would bounce a little less and she'd be planning a new career as a supermodel. Well, perhaps a supermodel's youthful grandmother . . .

'What happens now?' She turned to realise Judith had momentarily disappeared. 'Where the heck . . .'

A grinning Judith was emerging from a nearby flower stall, carrying a bunch of rather garish gladioli.

'Here you are, these are for Aunt Maude. You know she loves her gladis and she's a big fan of Dame Edna Everage.'

Vicky looked puzzled. It was all beginning to get too much.

'The cop car's still outside.' Judith indicated behind her. 'He's chatting to some of his mates in the ambulance bay. Come on, we're still acting. Let's find your sick auntie.'

And with that, she pushed the gladioli into Vicky's arms. With a wave of sadness, Vicky realised it was the second time that day someone had handed her flowers.

This time she hung on to them.

chapter three

Sarah Franks was feeling extra specially fat. And for once she didn't care all that much.

In her depressed mood, she thought of that silly song about nobody loving a fairy when she's forty. Never mind forty, hello forty-three. And if she'd been a fairy, she'd have been much too fat to fly, she thought ruefully.

But Sarah wasn't really depressed about feeling fat: she knew deep down why she was fed up. Alan, her husband, was due home the following week after a three-month stint working in the Middle East. And she was dreading it.

The marriage had reached that farcical state where both parties knew it was a complete sham but neither had the courage to do anything about it. Besides, they'd produced a son and daughter, both in their early twenties, whom they both desperately loved. The only trouble was that Sarah and Alan had long since ceased to love each other. More to the point, they'd developed an unspoken loathing of each other.

The marriage had survived undoubtedly because of the long separations. If they'd had a nine-to-five marriage, P45s would have been issued long ago, but the continual separations caused by Alan's job in shipping had merely prolonged the agony.

So the marriage was in its death throes. Sex had ceased,

she'd long since given up trying to arouse him. She couldn't remember the last time he'd even kissed her.

Over recent years, she'd had the odd affair – nothing emotional, just a good romp in a posh hotel, usually with a doctor from the private clinic where she worked. Sarah discovered to her delight that hotels were quite a turn-on. But what made these have-it-away days even more delicious was that for once in her life, she was spoiled. Champagne, a candlelit dinner, the usual old chestnut preliminaries about 'my wife no longer understands me' and 'we no longer have sex'. If only men realised what a boring old overworked script that was. Then on to the main event, a night of unbridled passion, doing things that Alan had never ever been interested in, things which Sarah, in a long marriage spanning almost twenty-five years, had learnt about. She soon discovered that there was nothing more irresistible than a sex-starved doctor, especially a generous one. So, although Sarah felt cheated in her marriage, she balanced this by a bit of cheating of her own.

Sarah had had none of the companionship of someone to come home to and cuddle up with every night, someone to discuss the kids with, pay the bills with. She'd done it all virtually alone, except when Alan came home and took over in his dictatorial way, giving her no credit at all for what she'd achieved in his absence.

But worst of all, Alan was tight. Tighter than a duck's arse. In fact, during a jolly evening over an Indian take-away and several bottles of vino collapso, Sarah and her friends had nicknamed him Bostik Pockets. Because, they concluded, he must have glued them up.

What Sarah's friends knew for sure, but never discussed, was that Sarah had problems with money. Handling money, that is. Whatever was in her wallet had to be got rid of as quickly as possible. It didn't just burn a hole in her pocket, it set fire to the whole damned coat. The problem was, to some extent, the result of Alan's meanness. Any cash she secretly accrued had to be spent in case he found out and started carping again.

And so the foundations of ruin were laid. She'd grown accustomed to lying about money. Salary rises and bonuses at her job in the clinic were never mentioned. It was the only way Sarah could buy those little luxuries she felt were her due – and of course which Alan thought were completely unnecessary. She always lied about the price of anything she bought, particularly clothes. As a rough rule of thumb, thirty pounds was mentally knocked off the price of a dress, and sixty off a suit. Stuck out on a ship in the Middle East, Alan couldn't understand that a new bottle of perfume could lift your spirits on a rainy day. Or that a Jaeger jacket was simply the only thing to pull together all the rather useless bits of your wardrobe. And as for a bargain, Sarah could not resist. At that price, she reasoned with herself, she couldn't afford *not* to have it.

The advent of credit cards had been a further disaster. If Sarah didn't have the cash, she just flashed the plastic. Fortunately, with Alan away most of the year, he was unaware of the bills and the juggling Sarah did to avoid firms taking legal action. Catalogues were paid off at a fiver a month. She'd already got herself on that downward slide where she was borrowing cash from one card to pay off another.

Yet somehow Sarah always slept soundly at night. In her way, she was compensating for her marriage. It was part of the paying back for the treatment she received. So the bills belonged to the World of the Never Never. She was far more concerned with her next shopping fix.

Anyway, today was Sunday, one of her last days of freedom before Alan came back from Bahrain, and she'd decided she was going to relish it. Tea and the Sunday papers in bed, she planned, then perhaps a little minimalist housework before Sunday lunch in the pub with her friend Anita from the clinic. Then an evening call to her children, Roz and Daniel, to see how they were getting over their respective après-weekend party hangovers. And finally some total slobbery on the sofa watching TV before another week at work. And of course the prospect of Alan's return. She shuddered again at the thought. They had recently discussed putting their house on the market when he returned from this trip. It was far too big now that the kids had moved out and she was on her own there most of the time, rattling around. Perhaps this was the moment to start talking about divorce too, she wondered.

She threw on a dressing gown and a pair of mules and wandered downstairs to make her tea. *God, this place is much too big*, she mused, flip-flopping around the huge kitchen noting that the floor needed a good wash. In fact the whole place needed a good scrub-up, she realised rather guiltily. At one time it had been a proper family home, with Roz and Daniel often bringing their friends back to stay. With five big bedrooms, theirs had always been the most convenient house for the overnighters. How she'd enjoyed those years with the place bursting with laughter, loud music and noisy meals, especially when Alan was away. But now she felt overwhelmed by its emptiness. There just wasn't as much incentive to keep it looking clean, tidy and inviting. Not just for her. Definitely time to move on, she thought. And move on from her marriage too.

Enough of that, she pulled herself up. She mustn't spoil the day. Picking up the newspapers in the hallway, she grasped them under the tea tray and padded back upstairs to her bedroom. She was just settling down to a comforting sip of Earl Grey with the duvet wrapped around her when she spotted it.

'Oh my God,' she breathed out loud, spilling most of the

tea in the saucer. 'Oh no, please no.' She felt the colour drain from her face.

There, on the front page of the *News of the World*, next to the main story about a footballer's wife enjoying several of his team mates, was a picture of a shocked Vicky running down some steps under the headline 'HERE *GOES* THE BRIDE'.

Sarah's hands trembled as she moved on to page five for the full story. There was Roger's angry face glaring out of the page with another headline, 'I DO – BUT SHE WON'T'. Plus another unflattering photograph of Vicky's departing rear. *She won't like that one*, thought Sarah immediately. *It does make her bum look a tad big.*

She tipped the spilt tea from the saucer back into the cup, took a sip and lit a cigarette. She had to calm herself down before she could read the full story.

It was a case of wedding BILLS rather than wedding BELLS for one would-be bridegroom yesterday after his bride fled from their surprise wedding.

Romantic Roger Smith went for the BIG ONE when he lured his girlfriend to Plymouth Register Office on the pretext of meeting the boss for a business lunch. He'd booked the ceremony, bought a ring, and organised a limousine to take his new bride to a reception for forty relatives and friends.

All local television reporter Victoria Chadwick had to do was to say, 'I do.' But to the embarrassment of marketing manager Roger, she said, 'I don't.'

One of the guests, Mrs Isabelle Stokes, Mr Smith's aunt, said, 'We'd travelled all the way up from Eastbourne for this. It must have cost Roger a fortune. I don't know what possessed her to run off. Disgraceful display of manners.'

Another guest, Mrs Patricia Plum, who works at
the would-be groom's hair products company
Tressed Out, said, 'We had no idea it was a surprise.
We'd even had a whip-round at work and bought
Roger a trouser press as a wedding present. But
when they arrived, she didn't seem to know what
was going to happen. He then proposed and she
said no. I don't really blame her. It must have been a
dreadful shock. Then we realised he hadn't invited
any of her relatives or friends.'

But jilted Roger was unrepentant. 'I've spent a
huge amount of money on this and she's made me
look a fool in front of all these people. No I don't
want her back after all this. I wouldn't marry her
now if she was the last woman on earth. This is the
worst mistake of my life.'

Victoria, who's thirty-nine, regularly reports news
and current affairs for a regional television station.
Colleagues at her studio said they had no idea she
was getting married, but thought the couple had
been seeing each other for about a year. It's believed
neither of them has been married before.

The three-thousand-pound reception went ahead
without a bride. Guests tucked into crepes with
forest mushrooms and rocket salad, boned quail
with lemon and sage risotto and roasted vegetables,
followed by a chocolate mousse with summer
berries and Drambuie. But the champagne toast,
speeches and wedding cake were cancelled.

One guest, who didn't wish to be named, said the
atmosphere was more like a wake than a wedding.

Meanwhile reporters and photographers, including a TV crew from Victoria's own studio,
converged on her cottage eight miles outside
Plymouth, but there was no sign of anyone at

home. A woman friend called Judith visited the
house later in the afternoon but went away again.

Miss Chadwick's parents, who live in Swindon,
knew nothing of the ceremony. Her father Tom
would only comment, 'We've only met Roger once
and that was ages ago. I never got the impression he
was the love of her life. And it certainly doesn't
sound like he is now.

'We are very proud of our daughter and angry
that someone would treat her in this way. But we
will hear the story from her before passing judgement.'

Mr Chadwick said he expected his daughter
would get in touch soon.

But Mr Smith's mother, Elizabeth, saw things differently. 'Thank goodness this happened,' she said.
'By now, that appalling woman would have been my
daughter-in-law and a member of our family. My
son has been hurt and humiliated. He has spent a
lot of money on this wedding but at least we now
know she wasn't worth it. I have to say I never took
to her. It's a blessing in disguise.'

Sarah reached for the phone and dialled Judith's
number. The answering machine kicked in with one of
Judith's typically jolly messages. This time it was a voice
welcoming her to the Opera Crisis Line. 'Are you bored
with Bizet or pissed off with Puccini?' queried the voice
over a background of Pavarotti singing an excerpt from
Rigoletto. 'Then just sing a few notes of any well-known
aria. And we'll call you back – p'raps.'

Sarah was *not* in the mood for singing or any operatic hi-
jinks that might have ensued. She left a message begging
Judith to call her back as soon as possible.

Sarah then re-read the story. She still couldn't quite take

it in. Roger's angry face, his unspeakable mother, a wedding reception without a bride, a trouser press. Now that bit had made her smile. It really was just the perfect present for Roger, boring old finicky Roger with his shiny shoes, meticulously ironed shirts, and soon to be joined by even more immaculately pressed trousers. She was not a Roger fan.

She also smiled at the mention of Vicky's age. Thirty-nine was certainly very flattering but a little economical with the truth. Someone at the studio was being kind. She knew damned well how old Vicky was. They were all forty-three, she, Vicky and Judith – they'd all been at university together all those years ago.

The phone interrupted her thoughts. It was Judith.

'You've seen the papers, I take it,' she said with under-statement.

'Only the *News of the World*. That was enough,' replied Sarah. 'Is it in the others?'

' 'Fraid so,' said Judith grimly. 'The bride's hiding out here with me. You might as well come round and join in the fun. We've got the hangovers from hell.'

chapter four

Vicky stopped reading the newspaper coverage of her 'wedding' after the first paragraph in favour of the horoscopes. If I were an aircraft's black box, I might have survived all this, she decided.

'Another G and T?' Judith interrupted her thoughts.

'Silly not to,' replied Vicky. 'I don't know about the hair of the dog, I think I'm more in need of the leg of the dog. Anyway I've got to psych up to ringing my parents in a minute. They wouldn't dream of reading the *News of the World* or any of the small'n'smutties for that matter, but sure as hell half their snooty neighbours do.'

'Why don't you get that over with before Sarah arrives,' shouted Judith from her kitchen. Invigorating smells of garlic and tomatoes were beginning to waft their way into the sitting room. It was only just lunchtime but they both needed something to soak up the alcohol. After a brief coffee and croissants, they'd plunged back on to the gin and tonics in anticipation of lunch. There'd been a lot of late-night drinking and chat about the wedding, the police chase and the impromptu hospital drama.

Judith had thought it best to keep Vicky up as late as possible so she would collapse into a deep sleep. In the event they'd polished off the best part of a bottle of gin and only vaguely heard the phone ring, followed by Sarah's message this morning.

The newspaper coverage had brought them sharply to their senses. Vicky'd even made the *Sunday Times* – albeit a tiny piece on the front page. In some papers she shared a page with the original story all the snappers had been hoping to cover at the register office. The seventy-nine-year-old who was supposed to be marrying twenty-four-year-old Miss Tasty Bits. Except that she'd had the sense not to turn up. What a lucky escape they'd both had. His wallet was still intact and she didn't have to endure unflattering pictures of her departing bottom all over the front pages. Except that she was probably some blonde size-10 stick insect and her bum was probably pert and perfect, thought Vicky. Her head was pounding too much to care a great deal.

An old Volvo tottered up on to the driveway outside Judith's neat little modern end-of-terrace. As it spluttered to a halt, the driver's door was flung open and Sarah emerged sporting leopardskin leggings and a large black T-shirt. She was bearing flowers and several carrier bags which clanked ominously.

'Dahlinks,' she shrieked in delight. 'Vot a vunderful surprise.' Sarah had always drawn a crowd with her bleached blond hair, generous figure and celebrated impression of Zsa Zsa Gabor. 'I lurve veddings even ven ze bride does ze bunk. Vun must alvays find excuse to celebrate, yah? For vonce, ze bride ees not me.'

The air was rent with mwah mwahs as they all air-kissed frantically and went into the house. Judith dispensed huge drinks in the kitchen.

'Brilliant to see you both,' said Sarah. 'Anyone told you how dreadful you both look?' Actually that was a half lie. Judith was her normal immaculate self, wearing a pair of stone chinos and a blue cotton shirt. But Vicky looked as if she was auditioning for a walk-on in a horror movie. Her dark brown curly hair was dishevelled, heavy bags under her eyes contrasted with sallow skin. No make-up and a scruffy old navy track suit completed the look.

Sarah, who was well used to dealing with people in various states of appallingness at the clinic, hid her surprise with her broadest and most professional smile.

'So this is what the Bride of the Year is wearing,' she joked. 'Great trousseau, kid.' She stopped abruptly, seeing Vicky's eyes welling up.

'Right,' said Judith, sensing the situation. 'Sarah and I will get lunch sorted. Meanwhile, Vick, why don't you call your parents and get that over with and then we can all relax. Use the phone in the other room.'

Vicky did as she was told and wandered into Judith's sitting room. It was a real home, she mused, unlike the temporariness of the cottage she'd been renting. The piano stood in the corner, strewn with sheets of Gershwin and Chopin all vying for attention. Judith was a good pianist but, as with many of her attributes, she had no idea quite how talented she was. Then there was the CD player with hundreds of discs, a widescreen television and video with piles of tapes. A rack stuffed with newspapers and magazines, whacky paintings on the walls and three large squashy burgundy sofas. It was a combination of taste and comfort. She found the phone half hidden under a pile of surfing magazines – obviously the current passion of Judith's son, Simon.

'Victoria? Oh, thank God you've phoned,' said her mother, answering on the first ring. Did she sit on the phone in case it hatched? 'Of course we've seen the papers. We had some frightful people ringing us up about it all yesterday. We tried to get hold of you. Why on earth didn't you let us know about all this?' she added pompously.

'How could I, Mum? I didn't know myself, did I,' wailed Vicky. 'It was a shock to me too, remember?'

But Vicky's mother wasn't really listening. She was back into full flight. 'Well your father dealt with it of course. We were going to a cocktail party at the Hendersons' last night but I just couldn't face it after all this. It was all too much and I went to bed with one of my migraines. Of course the Hendersons just had to stick their oar in – they were on the phone this morning at eight o'clock telling us you were in all those frightful Sunday papers. At least I was able to say we didn't read that sort of newspaper. I had to send your father out to the next village to buy them to find out. It's all so embarrassing. The whole street will be talking about it. I don't know how I'm going to face everyone after this. Now if you'd got a proper job in the first place, this would never have happened. Anyway speak to your father.'

Thank you so much, God, thought Vicky. She and her mother had always had an uneasy relationship. Frances Chadwick had made the fatal mistake of trying to live her life through her daughter. Except that the life she had wanted for her only child was marriage to a suitable young man with the right connections who drove a Range Rover with matching towbar, rode to hounds and roughshod over everyone else. A decent sort of chap, who could plough a furrow, dance a foxtrot and came complete with Coutts bank account, stuffed with old money. Frances allowed herself the occasional fantasy of her daughter on the arm of some suitable young buck flickering across the pages of Jennifer's Diary.

But Vicky didn't see life that way at all. She wanted a career and independence. To Frances's horror, she'd always hung around with the noisiest friends, waltzed through university, and ended up working as a television reporter. No marriage, no babies, no connections and certainly no Coutts bank account. Frances had never liked any of her daughter's boyfriends. They'd all been far too Bohemian for her tastes, except Mervyn the solicitor. At least he wore

sharp suits and had a respectable job. Vicky had spared
her mother the gory details of their parting. She felt that
the account of catching Mervyn in her flat with his pinstripe trousers well and truly down would have been too
much of a shock. Roger had made an impression too but
only because he was different to all the others. Boring,
fanatically tidy and punctual, these were not qualities usually associated with Vicky's choice of partner. But 'doing
something in marketing shampoo' was not likely to
impress the Hendersons.

'Hello, darling.' It was Vicky's father Tom on the phone.
'You must have had a terrible time. I tried to call you last
night but I realised you would have gone to ground. Is
there anything I can do? Are you OK?'

Vicky adored her father. He was the complete antithesis
of her mother. A retired headmaster, he was steady as a
rock and didn't give a stuff about the Hendersons or
anyone else come to that. So long as his beloved daughter
was all right.

'Dad, I'm sorry you got those calls from the papers. I
didn't realise till I read them this morning. You must have
been so worried.'

'No, well not really. You're a sensible girl. I knew you'd
be in touch. Now where are you?'

'At Judith's place in Southampton. Sarah's just arrived.
It's like old times, they're being great, so please don't worry.'

'Oh I'm not at all. It's just your mother. You know what
she's like,' said her father. Lowering his voice, he continued, 'I'm very proud of you, my girl. You did all the right
things, got the hell out of that. Was it as ghastly as it
looked?'

'Yes, and heaps worse,' replied Vicky. 'It was like watching a film about an operation and then realising that you're
the patient. The irony is that I was thinking of finishing
with Roger anyway. So I suppose it spared me that. Mind

you, it's not all over yet. I'm expecting repercussions and I'll just have to face up to them.'

'Well I hope I'm not going to upset you by saying this, but he wasn't your type at all,' he said. 'Anyway, enough of that. What are your plans for the next few days? You know you're always welcome here.'

'Thanks, Dad, but I've got a week off work anyway so I'm going to lie low here at Judith's and have a think about things.'

'Sounds like a very good idea,' he said. 'Now one final thing. Don't worry about your mother. I think she's secretly beginning to enjoy all the attention. Difficult one for the Hendersons to top, eh!'

Vicky walked back into the kitchen feeling a whole lot better. Her head had cleared, lunch smelt good and her two best friends were there in support. Suddenly for the first time in twenty-four hours, the world felt like a friend-lier place.

Lunch was a triumph. Judith had put on quite a feast. Juicy beefsteak tomatoes, mozzarella and avocado to start, fol-lowed by tagliatelle with a wonderful sauce of tomatoes, mushrooms, bacon, garlic and herbs. Plus ciabatta straight from the oven, washed down with lashings of soft fruity red wine. She was just whisking up an impromptu zabaglione when Sarah announced the first in a series of toasts.

'To Vicky on surviving the most famous day of her life.' They raised their glasses and drank.

'To Roger for successfully retaining his title as Plonker of the Year. Let's hope he and his trouser press will have many happy years ahead of them.' They clinked again.

'And to us. For being the bestest friends for ever.' Another gulp and a slight pause of emotion.

Sarah then decided it was time to steer the conversation

away from the 'wedding'. She felt Vicky had been through enough. She entertained them with hilarious stories about all the goings-on at the clinic, who was doing what to whom and why they shouldn't be.

'This all sounds a bit edited,' said Judith suspiciously. 'And are you involved in any of this extra-curricular stuff?'

Judith and Vicky were aware of Sarah's occasional little adventures with doctors at the clinic. And they understood why she did it. They both loathed Alan and couldn't quite fathom why she stayed with him now that the kids had left home.

'Well I'd like to be,' said Sarah. 'There's an extremely promising bit of tottie starting in Dermatology next week but I can't do anything about it.'

Why's that?' asked Vicky, cheering up by the minute. 'I've got you under my skin . . .' she started singing.

'Bostik's back on Thursday,' said Sarah dully. 'And to put it bluntly, I'm in a mess.'

chapter five

Sensing a new crisis on the agenda, they delayed for a few minutes, making coffee and settling down on the sofas.

Sarah lit a cigarette, took a long deep puff and began. 'Well I'm just dreading him coming home. The thought of having to get into bed with him makes me feel physically sick.'

'I thought sex was definitely off the menu anyway these days,' said Vicky.

'It most certainly is, but it's just the sheer physicality thing. I've been dreading Thursday for weeks and weeks, in fact ever since the moment I waved him off last time. Isn't it terrible when you realise you loved someone so much and now you loathe them more than anyone else on the planet?'

'Well I know about that too,' said Judith. 'I think if I read about Malcolm's death in the papers, I'd probably just flip on to the lottery results.'

Judith's marriage had been brief and fairly brutal. The one good thing it produced was her son, Simon, whom she adored. But Malcolm had taken no interest in Simon and even less in Judith. His finest contribution was to have an affair when she was in hospital giving birth, and spend the next five years criticising everything Judith said, did or cooked. Eventually Judith had called time on the marriage, and had concentrated on bringing up her son and making minor documentaries and low-budget travel programmes.

'Yeah, I loathed Malcolm and still do,' she continued. 'But I loathe him because of his complete disinterest in Simon. No birthdays, Christmas presents, not so much as a fiver in child maintenance. That's what I loathe. With you, though, it's different. Bostik loves the kids and maybe he loves you, but if he does, he has a funny way of showing it.'

'Well the word I'm trying to get out, girls, is divorce. Yes, D-I-V-O-R-C-E. The D-word,' said Sarah. 'After more than twenty years of marriage, I've realised that's what I want. A divorce.'

'What prompted this?' asked Vicky. 'I mean, we've always known you've been unhappy with old Bostik but I suppose I thought you'd always stick with him, to pardon the pun. Is it because the kids have finally left home?'

'Well, sort of,' replied Sarah. 'The house is too big, I'm rattling around in it on my own most of the time and we'd decided to put it on the market when he comes back. I was lying in the bath one night last week thinking about the sale, estate agents, solicitors, all that stuff and then I thought, why not get a divorce at the same time. One-stop shopping, so to speak.

'Anyway, the more I thought about it, the more I realised that's what I really wanted. I've thought of nothing else since.' Sarah paused to light another cigarette from the butt of the outgoing one.

Vicky looked at Sarah and realised, with a shock, how haggard she looked when her guard was down. Sleepless nights, too much gin and too many cigarettes.

'Yes, I know I'm smoking too much,' said Sarah, reading Vicky's thoughts. 'But I'm so psyched up for Thursday that I'm going off my head.'

'How will you tell him?' asked Judith, thinking back to the terrible, final scene with Malcolm all those years ago.

'Fuck knows,' said Sarah. 'They didn't teach us that at university, did they.'

'Surely he must know you're unhappy,' said Vicky. 'I mean, your marriage hasn't exactly been one long shagfest, has it.'

'No it hasn't. Bostik was always mean in that department too but, do you know, I was trying to remember the last time he just kissed me, and I couldn't. I don't think he knows what his cock's for, to be honest. Nothing in that department for years now, not remotely interested. It doesn't even bother to pop up in the morning,' Sarah added.

'Well, if you take my advice, you'll tell him quickly, as soon as he gets home,' said Judith. 'Otherwise you're going to stress yourself into oblivion, just thinking about it.'

'Yes, you're right. I can't go on like this. I'm living the life of a nun. Having none, getting none,' she managed to joke. 'I might as well take holy orders and give all my worldly goods to the poor.'

'What do you mean, give all your worldly goods,' Judith joked. 'You haven't paid for your worldly goods yet! I don't think the poor would appreciate being bequeathed your credit card debts.'

'Well no, I suppose not, but that's another point. If Bostik wasn't so mean, I wouldn't be in this mess.'

'Which particular mess?' asked Judith.

'Well, I did buy a lot of clothes recently. I had to, because I was going away for a weekend with . . . Oh hell, do you think Bostik knows about my, er, little adventures? Would he drag that up in court?'

'If he knows, he's obviously not been bothered about it up to now,' reasoned Judith. 'Anyway, the court only has to decide if the marriage has broken down. Who did what to whom doesn't matter these days. If he's any sense, he'll go quietly, split the proceeds on the house and you can both go off and live happily ever after. Preferably on opposite sides of the planet.'

'Sounds reasonably painless,' said Sarah.

'No, it will be total hell and you will come out the other end battered, bruised and broke,' promised Judith. 'But you will be free. And you won't have to spend the whole of the rest of your life dreading next Thursday.'

The phone rang. Its shrill tone made them jump. Judith went out to the kitchen to pick up the call. Within seconds, she was back.

'*Bella* magazine on the phone, Vicky,' she said. 'They want to talk to you about your thoughts on holy matrimony.'

Vicky looked aghast. Oh hell, it was all starting again. 'What did you say?' she asked.

'I told them to rearrange two of my fingers into a well-known phrase or saying,' said Judith.

'How did they know I was here?' asked Vicky.

'Oh come on, don't be naive. You're in the media. I'm in the media. It's a small world. We've all got bulging Filofaxes. It only takes a few calls to get a result. There could be more of this over the next few days so I suggest we get up a game plan.'

The phone rang again. Judith went out to take the call. Who was it this time? The *Sun*, the *Mirror* or the *Mail*? When would they all move on to something else?

'It's Roger,' said Judith simply. 'Do you want me to fob him off?'

Vicky felt her heart pounding and the pit of her stomach doing somersaults. She had to face this and get it over with.

'I'll speak to him,' she said. 'Give me the phone.'

The others tactfully withdrew into the kitchen, making signs that they would make up another round of gin and tonics.

Vicky picked up the phone. This wasn't going to be a cosy chat. Roger started off calmly enough but he soon whipped up to what could only be described as a tirade.

'I will never recover from this,' he ranted. 'I've been made to look a complete bloody idiot. And not just in front of my relatives and friends. Not just in front of everyone at work. Oh no! Thanks to your low-life media friends, I've been dragged across the front pages of the gutter press. The whole world now knows about this, and the whole world's roaring with bloody laughter.

'Imagine having to go to your own wedding reception on your own. Just imagine, if you could get that into your thick head. And that's before I tell you the price of all this. That meal cost a fortune, they drank for Britain. All at my expense. Then there were the flowers, a cake, a photographer. Well I needn't have bloody well bothered with that. Plenty of pictures taken by your appalling friends, thank you very much.

'I can tell you now. My mother will never get over this. Imagine her embarrassment in front of all the family. And then I've got to face everyone at work next week and won't they be gossiping. They even gave me a trouser press as a wedding present. It's brilliant, I've always wanted one. But now what do I have to do, give it back? And they'll say, "Oh poor old Roger, please keep it." What? As a memento? I thought this was what you and I both wanted. I assumed—'

'Well you assumed wrong,' said Vicky, finally getting a word in. 'If you'd only stopped assuming and just asked, you would have saved yourself a lot of expense and hassle. If you choose to wine and dine your relatives, that's your problem. I notice you didn't invite any of mine. And if they chose to drink themselves under the table, then good on them. I hope they had a nice day. I certainly didn't, in fact it was probably the worst day of my life. Now I come to think about it, it would have only been made worse, if that's possible, by me making the biggest mistake of my life and marrying into your bloody awful family. I hope you and your bloody trouser press will have many happy years together.'

Vicky was shaking with rage, her voice now high-pitched and her palm sweaty as she gripped the phone with intensity.

'I now wonder what I ever saw in you,' said Roger, going for the jugular. 'I must have been off my head to ask you out in the first place.'

'Ditto,' cut in Vicky. She was beginning to realise how cathartic this was becoming. She could feel some of the tension in her body releasing.

'We had nothing in common,' she continued, 'as I think yesterday illustrated perfectly. What you did was cruel, calculating and smug. I didn't want to marry you yesterday, and I certainly don't want to marry you tomorrow, next week or any other time come to that.'

'Good, I'm glad we agree on that. So you just walk away as if nothing happened, and I'm left with a bill of several thousand pounds.'

'Well, just think of all those bonus points on your bloody credit cards,' she replied icily. 'I'm sure you worked that into the equation. What are you expecting me to do? Chip in on this? Get real.'

'Well that's exactly what I'm going to do,' Roger cut back in. 'Get real. Our relationship is over and I'll send your stuff round to the studios in a taxi. Oh, and don't worry, I'll pay.' He slammed down the phone.

Vicky sank back into the welcome contours of the sofa and breathed a sigh of relief. At least that was over and done with.

Judith and Sarah came in from the kitchen bearing gin and tonics and huge grins.

'Well done, Vick. We couldn't help but hear some of the highlights,' said Judith. 'Didn't realise you were such a tiger. Cruel, calculating and smug. That just about sums him up. Well, it's over now. Here, drink this.'

Vicky accepted the glass. She realised that her mouth

had gone dry from the strain of the phone call. The sharpness of the tonic was a welcome relief and she could feel the gin settling her trembling stomach.

'Well it's not quite over yet,' she said after that first gulp. 'Our evening news programme will carry something tomorrow night. Don't forget I had half the world's camera crews camped outside my house, including one of ours . . .'

The phone rang again. They all tensed. Could it be Roger wanting a return match?

Judith reappeared trying not to laugh. 'It's for you, Vick. Would you like to be a judge on a Bride of the Year competition?'

'Not bloody likely,' replied Vicky, managing to laugh. 'Oh, when will all this stop?'

'Gawd knows,' said Judith. 'One day we'll laugh about it.'

In fact, they laughed about it that night. And they laughed about loads of things, reminiscing about their university days all those years ago. Leaving home for the first time, learning how to use the laundrette, eking out their grants, and of course men. Loads of them, outnumbering the women students by four to one. They might have been short of money but they were never short of boyfriends. It had been an artificial lifestyle though. All the chaps you met were roughly the same age, of guaranteed intelligence and most definitely single. Sex had beckoned from every corner of the campus.

Sarah had been the first to succumb. She'd always been more upfront than the other two, and calmly announced what she'd done with Tim in Chemical Engineering the night before. The others had been shocked but not surprised. They both felt their moment was nigh too and had sensibly got themselves 'sorted out' at the family planning clinic up the road from the halls of residence, where, to their great embarrassment, they'd bumped into what seemed like most of the girls from their block all there for the same reason – the Pill.

Sarah had continued to shock them all through her time at university. She'd been caught in the men's showers one night and photographed. Whenever there was a scandal, Sarah was in the thick of it. She soon gained a reputation for being a bit of a goer, and privately she didn't like it. But she craved attention and this was the quickest way to get it. In her final year, Sarah started going out with Alan Franks in Maritime Studies. He seemed to have a calming influence on her, but eventually Judith and Vicky discovered the real reason. She'd fallen pregnant because she'd been too careless about taking her pills. Pressure was brought to bear by her family and Alan's and so up the aisle they went, Sarah clutching a large bouquet to hide her six-month bump. Instead of celebrating at her graduation ceremony, Sarah was up in the wee small hours bottle feeding and changing her son's nappies. It was an abrupt end to a misspent youth.

Judith and Vicky had none of Sarah's panache. They envied her boldness and yet it frightened them. They'd both come from strict and very exam-geared grammar schools and kept their heads firmly down in their books at first. That initial taste of freedom away from home and prying parents had come as quite a shock. Suddenly they could party till late, get drunk and stay out all night without having to report in. It was a frightening prospect to a couple of girls who'd led rather sheltered lives. Vicky's parents had wanted her to find some sensible and moneyed young man, snap him up and settle down. Judith's just prayed she'd not go off the rails, and would work hard and get a worthwhile job. Teaching perhaps.

So from those impoverished but heady days of jelly parties, re-using teabags and hitching home without telling your parents, they'd all gone their separate and somewhat unexpected ways.

They all thought Sarah, the sex bomb, was destined for some glittering career which would keep her in the headlines. Instead she'd had to settle for earlier than expected motherhood, marriage to Alan and instant domesticity.

Judith began her career in the fast lane. Instead of the teaching route favoured by her parents, she'd landed a job in the music business and thought she'd gone to heaven. Unlike many of the empty-headed girls working in the offices at her record company, Judith really did know about music from her years of piano playing. Soon she was on the fast track through the company, whizzing from the art department to production to the press office, where she surprised herself at her own dynamism and motivation. She rubbed shoulders with the daft and the dazzling, the famous and the infamous, attending awards ceremonies, launches, parties and first nights. It was a dream job and she loved every minute of it.

Too soon, she met Malcolm, a photographer, fell madly in love with him and gave it all up. Her job, her life in London, her friends and all the fizz and buzz that she'd thrived on. That couldn't go on forever, she told herself, opting instead for a dream of domestic bliss in the country with Malcolm, ravishing children and a cottage with roses around the door. The reality was different. Once the ring was on her finger, Malcolm turned into a monster. The affairs began when she was pregnant and continued throughout the marriage. Malcolm was a control freak who reduced the once bubbly Judith to a constantly apologising shadow of her former self. He despised everything she did or said, and triumphed when he reduced her to tears. Having insisted they have children, once Simon was born, he announced that babies were boring and she could just get on with it on her own.

He kept her short of money, starved of self-esteem and devoid of love.

Judith could never understand why he didn't leave her. After all, he'd had so many affairs. Surely one of these women wanted to take him on. But Malcolm was lazy. He wanted it all. The excitement and illicitness of the affairs turned him on and he had someone to kick around when he got home. So why not have it all?

Finally Judith fought back, but it took her virtually eight years to rebuild herself. Firstly, she started working from home, writing short features for any magazine who would pay her. Secondly, she made certain she could not be pregnant again from the rape-style encounters that Malcolm occasionally inflicted on her. And thirdly, with an end to the pain in sight, she had a brief affair with a colleague of Malcolm's. She was shocked at how guiltless she felt, and equally shocked to find that someone found her attractive enough to go to bed with her, and more importantly, someone who listened and valued what she had to say.

When she finally delivered the ultimatum to Malcolm, she thought he would be relieved to be offered an escape route from the sham of their marriage. But instead, he went berserk, threatened suicide several times and then belittled her for what he called 'stamping her little foot'. But Judith kept 'stamping her little foot' and within a year, she was free and exhausted but well on the way to recovery.

After the subsequent divorce, Malcolm did exactly what she would have expected. He rubbished her to everyone he knew, took little interest in his son and even less in his welfare. After a couple of maintenance payments, the cheques started bouncing and Malcolm's rubber cheque book became the subject of a flurry of bank manager's 'please represent the cheque' letters until Judith simply gave up.

She concentrated on emotional recovery, bringing up her son, and earning a living to support them both. Having had such a bashing from Malcolm over a decade, she had no idea of her own abilities and was always surprised at everything she achieved. Here she was now making documentaries for a small television company, and still wondering when she'd be rumbled. No amount of praise would give her real confidence. Sadly it was the same problem with men. Why would any man be interested in her? Malcolm's constant mocking had had its effect. If anything, men were put off by her because she was bright and talented and, they assumed, snapped up. Judith was not a beauty but she made the most of herself, always dressing smartly because it bolstered her confidence. Her other great talent, apart from her music, was an extraordinary ability to think on her feet. That was why she took to television like a duck to water, and why friends turned to her in their hour of need. Like poor Vicky after the register office fiasco yesterday.

Of the three of them, Vicky was the one who was supposed to get married, have kids and live happily ever after. She was the late starter with an ambitious mother who didn't really see the point of university if her daughter was going to marry the right chap, have babies, and live in a house plucked straight from the pages of *Country Life*. Vicky was far too spirited and clever for that. After graduation she'd opted to become a journalist, starting on a local newspaper and working her way up. She'd clawed her way up and into television the hard way, first as a researcher and then as a reporter. Not the Blondes-on-the-Box route. Vicky wasn't pretty enough, or blond for that matter. She had got there by sheer graft and determination. A safe pair of hands – as all her news editors had always described her – the three Ps, punctual, polite and professional, but not a ground breaker.

Somehow Vicky had never met the right man at the right time. If she met Mr Totally Gorgeous, he was still busy looking for Miss Devastating. Or sometimes, as in the case of Mervyn the solicitor, Mr Totally Gorgeous had been caught busily attending to the needs of Miss Devastating. So no marriage, no babies, certainly no house from *Country Life* for Vicky.

Close friends though they'd always been and always would be, they all quietly envied each other. Vicky and Sarah envied Judith her talents, her modesty and her calm in a crisis. Judith and Sarah envied Vicky her freedom, especially during their years of child rearing. And Vicky and Judith envied Sarah her sex appeal and devil-may-care approach to life.

Which of course only goes to prove what they knew anyway, that you can't have it all.

chapter six

Here we go then, another fun week at the Pleasure Dome, thought Judith as she strode purposefully into her office. *Another day, another douleur!*

Yes, it was going to be a bit of a battle today, she thought, recalling her horoscope over breakfast. 'Same Shit, Different Day,' greeted her computer with a list of reminders she'd tapped in the previous Friday. 'Oh God, I lead such an interesting life,' she murmured, looking at the list, which included notes about dry cleaning, dental appointments and her car MOT, mingled with fixing an interview with Dame Edna Everage and a chat with the big boss about a documentary idea in Romania. *Perhaps I should change that greeting to, 'Different Shit, Same Day,'* she mused.

Her e-mails were equally varied and mostly out of date or of no interest. People trying to sell props from previous programmes, or borrow props for forthcoming programmes, and the usual plethora of flats and cars for sale. Judith hit the delete button and reached for her coffee cup. 'Let's get on with it,' she muttered, clicking open a file marked 'Wedding'.

It was one of the most bizarre stories she'd ever worked on, and in fact she'd been intending to discuss it with Vicky. But the ironic events of the weekend had overtaken that. This particular wedding had taken place all right, with no expense spared. Or rather no expense whatsoever. The couple had pulled off the seemingly impossible – a lavish wedding with all the trimmings for next to nothing. They'd not paid for a thing. The other factor in all this was that the bridegroom was about seventy-five and the bride just pushing seventy. If Judith made a programme about this, would public sympathy go with them? Were they deliberately conning everyone or were they just a confused old couple? She knew she'd have to tread carefully.

'Hello, Judith Fielding,' she answered her phone briskly.

'You don't know me,' started the male voice unpromisingly, 'but I was given your name by the woman at the flower shop, Rosemary's. She said you might be interested in this. You see, I'm a photographer and I didn't get paid for that old folks' wedding . . .'

'Ah ha,' replied Judith, getting excited. This could be the breakthrough she needed. 'You don't by any chance have a copy of the photographs, do you?' she asked.

'Better than that, love. I've got a video too. I didn't get paid for either and so I didn't hand them over. Would you like to have a look?'

'Not half,' said Judith, grinning to herself. So the list was getting longer. The happy couple hadn't paid for their reception, an evening party, cabaret entertainers, a brass band, the flowers, nor, it seemed, the photographs and a video.

She dialled the number of the rectory. Within two rings, the Revd Peter Robson answered.

'Yes, Mr and Mrs Trafford, of course I remember them. It was a rather last-minute booking,' he said, when Judith had explained what she wanted to know. 'Well, off the record, I do slightly know these people and I'm afraid I was aware that they have a . . . well . . . certain amount of credit around the town, shall we say. So I insisted they pay up while they were signing the register. After all, I have to pay the organist and choir's expenses. And then there were the bell ringers.'

'How did they pay?' enquired Judith.

'Cheque, I'm afraid,' replied the vicar, trying to hide the embarrassment in his voice. 'Need I say more, it was returned in my post this morning.'

'Oh I am sorry to hear that,' said Judith. She replaced the phone. At least that Slug of the Century Roger had paid up for his 'wedding', unlike this pair.

The dispatch rider arrived with the eagerly awaited photographs and the video. Sensing this could be something of an occasion, Judith called in her assistant, Lizzie, who'd been working on the story.

'Come in here, bring in some coffee. It's showtime,' she said, shoving the video into her machine. They settled down to watch. Soon they were wiping their eyes with laughter as the Traffords were joined in holy matrimony.

The bride was in full white regalia, satin dress with sequins, huge veil of tulle with a tiara. The groom was in a white tuxedo complete with a spangly bow-tie. They both looked about 103 and quite grotesque.

As they staggered back down the aisle, tiara and bow-tie slightly askew, they shouted to the bemused guests about the venue for the reception. The next scene on video was outside the hotel, where a brass band played in the sunshine and all the guests stood around clearly wondering whether to laugh or cry.

On then to the hotel reception where tables groaned with fresh salmon, tiger prawns, salads, turkey and sides of beef. A small band played with gusto 'If You Were the Only Girl in the World' as guests tried to make some sense of it all. After the cutting of the cake, during which the happy couple were obviously having a quiet row under their breath, the band struck up once more and the newly-weds took to the dance floor to the somewhat ironic choice of 'I Could Have Danced All Night'.

Taking her cue from the song and grappling with the huge skirts of her dress, the elderly bride gamely launched into a sort of a jig, lifting up her petticoats to reveal not sexy stocking tops or a traditional garter but a pair of tan-coloured pop socks.

Judith and Lizzie were uncontrollable by this time. They laughed till they cried, till their mascara ran. People from other offices drifted in and begged for a repeat performance so the pop socks scene was shown again and again.

'The trouble is,' said Judith, sobering up from all the laughter and clutching an aching stomach, 'that the photographer has lost his business over this, the hotel is about three grand down and even the vicar, the choir and organist didn't get paid. Not to mention all the others – and that brass band. Let's find out who they are and whether they got paid. We'll have to find someone who can identify the uniforms. Silly question probably but it must all be checked and double-checked.'

The phone rang. It was Vicky.

'What's going on there, a party?' She could hear background laughter in the office.

'Well, sort of,' said Judith. 'We've just been watching the funniest thing I've seen in ages.'

'What's it about?' asked Vicky.

'A wedding, and before you get upset in view of the weekend's circumstances, this is one to show you what a lucky escape you've had. I'll bring it home tonight. I promise it will make you laugh. Now, are you OK?'

'Oh absolutely fabulous, sweetie,' said Vicky with irony. 'I've just had a call from *Hello!* magazine. I thought they only interviewed married people who then got the *Hello!* curse and divorced. Seems I've got in there a tad early.'

'What did you say?' asked Judith.

'Well actually I took a leaf out of your book and pretended I was the Swedish au pair. Impressed or what?'

'Yeah, you're learning,' said Judith.

'But I thought you ought to know in case they ring you at work. So this is me tipping you off.'

'Thanks,' replied Judith. 'They're bound to. I've got several old mates who work for them on and off. So just fill me in on the details. How long have you been in England and what's your name?'

'My name ees Helga, three weeks am in dees country and only leetle English,' said Vicky, shifting promptly into a cod Swedish accent. 'By the way, I'm cooking all week since you're slaving over a hot computer, so how's about spag bol tonight?'

'Brilliant. It's Simon's favourite too. And I think he'll be in tonight, so make tons as he eats his own weight in food every day. There's loads of stuff in the freezer and the cupboards. Just raid them. Fortunately I did a supermarket sweep on Saturday just before I made that mercy dash to you.'

They rang off. Sandra on the switchboard called immediately to say that Judith had had two calls from someone from *Hello!* magazine and did she want them put through if they called again? Might as well get it over with, thought Judith. She knew from experience, the more people avoided journalists, the more suspicious they got.

'Hello, Judith Fielding?' a smooth, confident voice half enquired. 'Just wonder if you could help us about the wedding.'

'Perhaps you'd care to tell me who you are and which particular wedding you're referring to,' said Judith, grinning to herself. Pop socks or Roger the Trouser Press? What a choice! If only they'd known.

'We're following up the story about the runaway bride

from Plymouth. We understand from the bridegroom that she's an old friend of yours and is staying with you.'

'Well I'm not in the habit of talking to people who don't introduce themselves but I half expected a call from you. My au pair Helga rang me just now. She's Swedish and only been in the country for three weeks, so her English is limited.' She was reading what she'd noted on a pad. 'Fortunately one of the few words she has learnt so far is "Hello" so I'm putting two and two together and guessing that's you, right?'

'Oh all right then. Give us a break. We're desperate to talk to her. It's such a brilliant story.'

'Sorry, can't help. She went abroad this morning. I don't expect to hear from her for several days. Now, I've got calls stacked up here, must go.

'Please don't strike me down, God.' She gazed out of the window at the bright blue sky. 'These lies are in an extremely good cause.'

Monday, thought Sarah gloomily, as she sat at her desk in the clinic. The last three days of freedom before Alan came back. It felt worse than waiting for major surgery. Then she had a sudden pang of guilty conscience. On her screen was a list of people waiting for exactly that. *I bet they all have loving partners to go home to*, she compensated.

Her eyes started to mist up as she gazed across the banks of bright red geraniums and deep blue lobelia outside. Then she remembered the sort of thing she went home to: the rows, the occasional punches, the nights when she craved affection and sex and he just turned his back on her.

Back to reality as her computer bleeped to tell her she'd received a new e-mail. It was from Vicky, sending her a message from Judith's home computer.

It read: *Still being bombarded by the world's press! If you ring me at Judith's, I'm the Swedish au pair. OK?!*

Sarah picked up the phone and dialled.

A pseudo Swedish voice answered.

'Hi, is that Helga, the au pair?' Sarah enquired jokingly. 'Fancy being on *Des O'Connor Tonight*?'

'I don't fancy being on anyone tonight,' replied Vicky, dropping the Swedish immediately. 'Anyway, apart from the odd call from the world's press, I'm enjoying being here. It's like being a proper housewife. I've done four loads of washing, I'm cooking dinner and then I shall immerse myself in ironing and daytime telly. How's things at the cutting edge of surgery?'

'You don't have to be incisive to work here, but it helps,' replied Sarah in kind. 'Actually, there's going to be the usual kerfuffle here today.'

'Why's that?'

'We've got the Abominable Slowman on today,' said Sarah lowering her voice.

'Who the hell's he?' asked Vicky.

'One of our general surgeons, Henry. Lovely guy but terribly slow. He sends everyone to sleep. The patients like that aspect of it, but the guys in theatre don't. He always does too long a list and then tempers start to fray. I tell you, I wouldn't risk my tonsils being tinkered with at the end of one of Henry's days.'

'Anyway, what about the new bit of talent from Planet Top Totty in Dermatology?' said Vicky. 'Surely he'll cheer you all up.'

'Not a chance,' replied Sarah. 'Seriously scrummy but lots of competition lining up already in that direction. Anyway I've got D Day on Thursday, remember. My last three days of peace before war is declared.'

'Ooops, sorry. Nearly forgot,' apologised Vicky. 'Though it's more like D Day in reverse, isn't it?'

'Not in this instance. D stands for divorce and I've got to do this,' said Sarah ruefully. 'Already my heart's drumming and my head's splitting with the tension. I can't sleep or think about anything else. He should be there when I get back from work on Thursday.'

'Quite a week for both of us, isn't it?' said Vicky. 'You're getting out of your marriage after a couple of decades and more. And I didn't even manage a couple of minutes.'

'Just think what a lucky escape you've had. I'm now worrying about what the kids will think, our parents will think. I don't give a bugger about what the neighbours will think though. Which reminds me. I'm putting the house on the market today. Might as well strike while the iron's hot. We'd planned to anyway so I'm going to get them to measure up hopefully this afternoon and get the whole thing going.'

'Listen, you know where I am,' said Vicky. 'Actually you're one of only a handful of people in the world who know where I am at the moment, but call if we can do anything. And call as soon as you can after Thursday. We'll be worried sick.'

'Promise. You'll be the first to know.'

'And Sarah, thanks for everything. It's my turn to help you now if I can. And Jude too.'

Sarah put the phone down and stared out at the geraniums again. Three days to go, until all hell broke loose. She dialled the estate agent's number.

Judith sat at her desk, musing. The Traffords' wedding story was coming together quite satisfactorily. She was now certain they weren't just a confused old couple, but a pair of determined fraudsters. She'd started to get angry when she heard the sorry tales of people not being paid, in some instances, quite large sums of money. It would soon be time to make the fateful call. Invite Mr and Mrs Trafford to explain it all.

'Reception here, Judith. There's a couple here who'd like

to talk to you. A Mr and Mrs Sinclair. Say they might be able to help you on a wedding story. Ring any bells?' Sandra laughed at her own joke.

'Very funny. Absolutely. I'll be right down to see them,' said Judith. *Good*, she thought, *obviously more people owed money by the newly weds*, as she picked up a small notebook and pen. They were coming in their droves now. When would it end?

As she scampered down the stairs to reception, she thought ahead to the spag bol Vicky was knocking up at home. What a treat to go home to a meal on the table instantly. Her mouth started to water and her stomach rumbled. She rounded the corner into the large softly lit reception area with its pale cream leather sofas and chrome furniture. For once, it was crowded with people and equipment. Four film crews had arrived at the same time, complete with stacks of silver flight cases of gear.

'They're sitting over there,' said Sandra, indicating the far corner. Judith peered through the throng and stopped short. She looked again and turned back to Sandra.

'What did you say their name was?' she asked.

'Sinclair,' read Sandra from her clipboard. 'Anything wrong? You've gone quite pale.'

Judith wended her way through the crowd and the boxes of gear.

'Mr and Mrs Sinclair? How do you do,' she shook them warmly by the hand, turning on her broadest smile. 'Now how can I help you?'

'Well,' started the woman a little nervously, looking at her husband. 'We heard you're doing a programme about Mr and Mrs Trafford and we thought you ought to know something important.'

'I don't normally discuss any future programme plans,' said Judith smoothly. 'It's not company policy to reveal programme content to members of the public. Also we find people get rather disappointed if the programme doesn't eventually get made.'

'But we've travelled here from Winchester and we've some important information to tell you,' said the man. 'You see Mr and Mrs Trafford aren't in the best of health. Mrs Trafford particularly. She's got heart trouble, takes a lot of tablets and shouldn't be put under any stress.'

The woman continued, 'We just thought you ought to know, as we heard you might be doing something on a programme about it. Mr Trafford's not a well man either. He's had a bad stroke and can't get about much. So you really shouldn't do this sort of thing. It might kill them.' She smiled benignly at Judith.

'Well it's kind of you to come all this way and tell me,' said Judith. 'I'll certainly pass on this information. Now I'd better take a note of your details and a contact number.'

'We're Mr and Mrs Sinclair,' said the woman, dictating a number. 'And we're very old friends of the Traffords. That's why we know about their health problems.'

'So you must have been to the wedding?'

'Oh yes. It was a lovely day, so lovely for them. But as I said, they're both really quite ill so if you did this little programme, it would be very distressing for them.'

'Yes of course. Quite understand. I'll pass on your comments. Thank you for coming in, Mr and Mrs Sinclair.' Judith paused, reading from the note she'd just made in her book. 'I'll see you out. Goodbye and thanks again.'

Judith stepped outside and watched as they climbed into a gleaming old silver Mercedes. She waved them off, noting the car number in her book and the fact that it bore a taxi plate.

Back in reception, she picked up an internal phone and called Lizzie.

'Come down here now. It's nearly six. We've done quite

enough for one day. We're going for a drink. I've got something very interesting to tell you.'

Sipping large glasses of chilled Chardonnay in Cahoots, the wine bar next door, Judith unleashed her bombshell.

'My visitors just now were the Sinclairs, dear friends of our wedding-on-the-cheap couple. Came to warn me about the shock our programme would have on their health,' said Judith seriously.

'Oh bum,' said Lizzie with instant disappointment. 'Does this put the skids on what we've got so far?'

'Far from it,' said Judith, breaking into a smile. 'My visitors obviously know Mr and Mrs Trafford really well. In fact, nobody on the planet could possibly know them any better.'

Lizzie looked blank.

'They were none other than Mr and Mrs Pop Socks themselves. My visitors just now were the Traffords doing a little play acting!'

chapter seven

The alarm went off abruptly. The radio started blaring. Sarah woke up with a start as if she'd been hit over the head by a hammer. She'd had little sleep, tossing and turning into the wee small hours about the day ahead. Now it seemed that she had just finally dropped off when it was immediately time to get up. She felt like a piece of chewed string.

She staggered into the bathroom and winced at what she saw in the mirror. Blonde hair askew, yesterday's smudged mascara, and puffy eyes from last night's consoling gin and tonics.

It was D Day. The day she'd been dreading now for months. Her heart started to hammer again and last night's headache was already creeping back as if to remind her what lay in store. She felt sick with nerves.

How would Alan react? Would he go berserk, would he hit her? She'd had one or two black eyes and bruising from him in the past when he'd gone into uncontrollable rages. Would he actually be relieved to get it over with? Perhaps this was what he wanted but hoped she would open the batting? Would he react at all?

Sarah knew she had to be prepared for anything. She suspected he'd go through the whole spectrum at some stage. She was realistic enough to expect anything from a battering to suicide threats, even derisory laughter. She shivered in anticipation, knowing it had to be done. In six months' time, she told herself, she'd be over the worst, rebuilding her life. No more of Alan's rages, no more rejection, no more criticism. Freedom with a capital F. And who knows, even Fun. It didn't feel much like fun right now.

She lobbed a couple of tea bags into a pot, poured on some boiling water, and while that was stewing, she fetched the morning paper up off the mat. Settling with her tea, she flicked straight to her horoscope. 'Every silver lining has a cloud.' Well, you could say that about the whole marriage. Perhaps Alan's reaction would be something she hadn't anticipated. Well he'd be home by around six, if the plane landed on time. In about eleven hours, she'd find out.

She deliberately diverted herself by turning to a fashion article about cashmere coats, her eyes drawn to the bottom of the page and the stockists. She could feel a purchase coming on. The trouble was, in her current mess, cashmere was more likely to be creditmere. Her store cards were all up to their limit and beyond.

As if to remind her, a flutter from the letter box indicated the post had arrived. Oh dear, thought Sarah, as she padded out to the hall to collect it. Two letters which looked ominous. Probably credit card bills or 'unless' letters. The other was a plain white envelope.

I'll go for the plain white first, she thought, stuffing the two others in a drawer for later. Inside were sale details of the house sent by the estate agent for her approval. Mr Oliver from Oliver, Bath and Emerson (known inevitably as OBE) had done a good job. The house, 'spacious family home with five good-sized bedrooms in this sought-after village', sounded great. Flattering photographs taken in Monday's glorious sunshine gave the house a real touch of class. The details waxed lyrical about the American ash kitchen, secluded garden with its range of unusual shrubs,

Victorian-style conservatory, inglenook fireplace, well-appointed bathrooms and so on.

Good job it didn't highlight the iffy plumbing, the panes slipping on the greenhouse, the constant damp in the corner of the main bedroom and the intermittent valve problem on the water tank in the attic. These were things Sarah had got used to dealing with when Alan was away.

'Well I'd buy that,' she muttered, putting down the details. 'I'll ring Mr Oliver this morning and approve it.' Sarah also heartily approved the price too. Just under two hundred thousand pounds, more than she had expected. Once they'd cleared the mortgage and paid the conveyancing fees, they'd have nearly one hundred and sixty thousand pounds clear. To split fifty-fifty, she supposed, once today's thunderbolt had been delivered.

It was full steam ahead on the pop socks wedding story. Satisfied that Mr and Mrs Trafford were not confused crumblies, and smart enough to pretend to be friends of themselves, Judith and Lizzie were busily setting up interviews with all the aggrieved. After a morning of phone bashing, they decided to reward themselves with lunch in Cahoots wine bar.

They opted for a dark corner where they could survey everyone who came in, without appearing to stare. Judith and Lizzie loved people-watching, especially in Cahoots, which had a bit of a reputation for being a place where the couples conducting illicit affairs met for casual lunches as if by coincidence.

Judith loved its dark oak tables, benches and chairs, French countryside scenes on the walls and its soft green lighting. It had a real oasis feel about it. Calm, cool, refreshing. The menu matched the atmosphere. No heaped-high plates, no Black Forest gateau, no prawn cocktail here. And positively no chips. It served what the camera crews called dismissively frilly lettuce. All that girlie grub, was how the young lads in the postroom described it. But they weren't mature enough to realise that not every girl's idea of eating out was a doner kebab served through a window.

Judith and Lizzie consulted the menu in token fashion. They'd already mentally decided. Couscous with roasted vegetables for Judith and mushroom stroganoff for Lizzie. They plumped for a bottle of modest Rioja to wash it all down with. As the waiter scurried away with their order, they settled down to watch the human circus performing before them.

Several tables were already occupied. A group of young accountant types had already abandoned their jackets and were having a spirited discussion about the forthcoming football season. Two women, triumphantly clutching holiday brochures, took up another corner. Within seconds, they'd papered the table and spare surrounding chairs with glossy pictures of endless hotel and apartment blocks while they thrashed out whether it was to be Greece again next summer or, more adventurous, the Gambia. Meanwhile a rather unhappy-looking couple in their late thirties was installed next to one of the stained-glass partitions.

'They must be married. They look pretty miserable,' joked Lizzie.

'Hey now, don't get cynical,' said Judith. 'You're tying the knot next year. You're not expecting to be miserable, are you?'

'No, 'course not,' replied Lizzie. 'It's just that everyone I know who gets married seems to end up totally miserable. I sometimes wonder if Paul and I'd be better off just living together.'

'Now come on, not everyone makes a muck-up of it. Paul's a lovely guy, you both adore each other and you both want to make a commitment. That seems to be perfectly simple and straightforward. You've known each other a long time. Anyway you can't change your mind now because you've bought the frock!'

'Well that's settled then,' laughed Lizzie. 'I do want to get married but . . . now don't be offended, Jude, but I do see what happened to you.'

'Look, I just got it badly wrong. I didn't know Malcolm for long enough, looking back. There were warning bells in my head at the time, but I stupidly ignored them. But I can't possibly regret marrying him.'

'Why ever not? He was a pig,' Lizzie declared.

'Oh yes, a complete low life. But I wouldn't have had Simon and he's simply the best thing that ever happened to me. So no, I don't regret it.'

'But it's put you off men, though, hasn't it? I can't remember the last time you went on a date,' said Lizzie.

'Well, to be honest, they're a bit thin on the ground. Look, you're twenty-six, I'm forty-three. When I meet a man I might possibly fancy, he's usually married. And the outrageously funny ones, the ones you know you'd have a rip-roaring evening with, are quite often gay. Somewhere in between that, you get the odd Mr Walking Wounded.'

'Who the hell's he?' enquired Lizzie.

'He's just out of a marriage or relationship and desperately seeking something, anything, anyone so he can unpack all his unhappiness and get a hot meal at the same time. He's Mr Big Time Rebound and he's usually quite boring. And then occasionally, if you're really, really unlucky, you get Mr Ego-On-A-Stick.'

'Go on, I'm enthralled,' urged Lizzie.

'Well he's probably married but you don't find out till later, or he's been recently dumped but it may have escaped his notice. And that's because he's in love with himself. Oh c'mon, you must have had those evenings, where the conversation goes something along the lines of "Me, me, me, me, let's talk about me" and then when you get to the coffee and mints stage, it suddenly dawns on him that you're sitting there too and so he generously says, "Well that's enough about me. Now what do *you* think about me?"

'Frankly, Lizzie, I'd rather spend an evening at home tickling the ivories or reading a good book,' concluded Judith. 'Now that's quite enough about me, ha ha. That couple over there are definitely *not* married 'cos they're talking.' She indicated over her shoulder.

They certainly were becoming intense, heads together, whispering. The woman started to cry gently and the man took out a handkerchief to dry her tears. Judith found herself rather ironically envying them their obvious distress and passion. She wondered whether she'd ever feel that intensity ever again, whether she'd ever experience the sheer physical joy of feeling someone's naked flesh against hers, the going to bed and waking up wrapped around the same wonderful person.

Her thoughts were interrupted by all the young suits getting up and putting their jackets on. There was so much scraping of chairs and continuing banter about the forthcoming footie that she didn't notice Alan coming in.

The couple in the booth were cheering up now and surreptitiously consulting their Filofaxes for their next illicit meeting. Judith and Lizzie finished the last dregs of the Rioja and decided to order coffee before heading back to work. As Judith glanced around to attract a waiter's attention, she spotted him.

'Bloody hell,' she half whispered.

'Who, not Mr Right by any chance?' said Lizzie, instantly intrigued.

'Far from it. Mr Absolutely Wrong. He's married to my friend Sarah. You've heard me talk about her. We were at university together. And today is D Day.'

'What are you on about?' said Lizzie, now totally puzzled.

'Well that's Alan Franks, and he doesn't know it yet, but

tonight Sarah is going to tell him it's all over after twenty-odd years. Today is D Day. She wants a divorce.'

'Why? What went wrong?' asked Lizzie.

'Just about everything really,' said Judith. 'He's a deeply unpleasant man, foul-tempered, treats Sarah like shit, no sex for years and he's mean. We nicknamed him Bostik Pockets years ago. It was a shotgun jobbie, Sarah got herself pregnant in our last year at university. And the rest, as they say, is history.'

Lizzie started to laugh at the nickname but stopped herself. Judith was clearly troubled.

'What else?' said Lizzie.

'Well I know this sounds daft,' said Judith, her brain really buzzing now, 'but he's not due home until tonight. He should be still on the plane right now.'

'Won't Sarah be meeting him at the airport?' asked Lizzie.

'Oh no, he never lets her meet him. Says it's silly and schmaltzy and that she shouldn't take time off work. I wonder if I ought to tip her off. She's psyching up for this and if he turns up early . . .'

Judith stopped and stared. So did Lizzie. So did every other woman in the wine bar. A beautiful young man had just joined Alan. Tall and slim, with sun-streaked blond hair swept back, he was fashionably, lightly tanned and wearing what was clearly a very expensive cream linen suit with a white open-necked shirt. He could have been a model.

As if by an invisible signal, all the women looked away again. He was too impossibly beautiful and, as most of them clocked immediately, he was not available. Not at least to women.

'D'you think . . .' started Lizzie.

'Yes I do,' replied Judith immediately. 'And it would explain just about everything. Now I have two major problems here. One, do we wave and say hello as casually as we can? And two, do I tell Sarah?'

'No to both, I'd say,' said Lizzie.

'Yes,' said Judith in agreement. 'You order the coffee so I won't accidentally catch his eye. And let's face it, we're only guessing. We've hardly caught them with their trousers down, have we. I think Sarah will have enough to cope with tonight. Funnily enough, several of us suspected this over the years but never felt we could broach the subject with Sarah.'

She glanced back over to Alan and his beautiful friend. *Unless I'm mistaken*, she thought, *the heat's coming off them in waves*. She also realised with a jolt that she'd never seen Alan so happy before. He was always such a miserable git, she couldn't recall ever seeing him really smile. Now he seemed a man transformed.

Sarah paced the floor, round and round the coffee table, her breath coming in short bursts, her stomach heaving and her head fit to burst. Perhaps this was how it felt when you had a heart attack. It was now seven o'clock, he was already an hour late.

She'd had a hell of a day at the clinic, for which she'd been pathetically grateful. It stopped her from constantly rehearsing what she had to say. She'd made up for it in the car driving home, though, muttering her speech out loud and drawing strange glances from other drivers at the traffic lights.

She heard the key in the lock. *This is it*, she thought, her heart sinking further and further. *I have to do this. I have to do this. I must. I must.*

She heard the sound of bags being dragged through the front door. Then it slammed shut.

'For God's sake come and give me a hand,' Alan shouted angrily from the hall. 'Terrible journey, terrible plane, two hours late.'

He came into the sitting room. 'Christ, you look a mess. What's up with you? Get me a drink, will you. Something decent. Large whisky'll do.' He collapsed into an armchair.

'Nice to see you too,' muttered Sarah under her breath. No kiss or cuddle, this was the norm.

'What are you mumbling about?' said Alan.

'Oh, nothing.'

He took a slug of whisky and lit a cigarette. After a couple of minutes, the alcohol had its effect. Some of the tension in him began to ease a little.

'Nearly didn't recognise the place,' said Alan. 'Thrown by that board outside.'

'What board?' Sarah asked nervously.

'For God's sake, Sarah, the estate agent's board. For a nano-second I thought I'd pitched up at the wrong house. Unless I am in the wrong house.' He glared at her.

'Sorry, Alan, I didn't notice,' replied Sarah, realising that in her wretched state tonight she just hadn't seen the board when she came home. 'I . . . I thought I'd put the house on the market as we agreed b . . . b . . . but I didn't think it would all happen quite this quickly.'

Her heart was really hammering now and she clasped her hands to stop them shaking.

'Mind you, I don't know why you put it on with that firm, OB something or other?'

'Oliver, Bath and Emerson,' prompted Sarah.

'That's it, OBE. Other Buggers' Efforts. Very apt. Never known them shift anything much around here. D'you remember the Bishops next door? They ended up selling theirs to a distant cousin and still had to cough up OBE's considerable fees. And the head honcho, what's his name, Oliver. Couldn't run a bath, let alone a business.'

'Well obviously I can't do anything right. Which brings me on to another subject.' Sarah tried to stop her voice quivering. 'Now I'm not sure how to tell you this but I think it's time we had a serious talk.'

'Not now, Sarah, not now. Look, I've had a long journey,

I don't want to discuss anything until I've had a large drink or three, a good night's sleep and then we'll discuss your little idea in the morning, whatever it is.'

Here he goes again, treating me like a fool, she thought. *I can't wait until tomorrow, I'll go off my head.* She'd already made up a spare bed with fresh sheets ready for the inevitable separate bedroom syndrome she was sure he would welcome.

'Now get me another drink,' he barked.

The phone rang and he snatched it up immediately.

'Oliver? Oh, Oliver . . . OBE. Yes, I saw the board when I came back tonight. What? You're kidding. Absolutely. Say yes and I'll get solicitors on to it tomorrow morning.' He put down the phone triumphantly.

'Well, well. Mr OBE's managed to get us a buyer, a cash buyer. Offered the full price – one hundred and ninety thousand crisp spondulicks. Marvellous.'

'That's t . . . t . . . terrific,' stammered Sarah, any last ounce of confidence she had now shot to pieces.

'I take back what I said about OBE,' Alan acceded. 'Now that's what I call a sale. Brilliant. Now I can pack in my job.'

'W . . . w . . . what?' Sarah thought for a moment that she'd been shot.

'Well, I'm fed up with all the to-ing and fro-ing in the Middle East. Too much unrest. Also much too much like hard work. Anyway I have lots of irons in the fire over here and now I've suddenly got the money to back my new business venture.'

'What business venture?' asked Sarah. This was all going horribly wrong.

'Never you mind,' said Alan. 'The sooner we can get this house sold, the sooner I can get a move on. We'll rent somewhere for the time being.'

Sarah wept silent tears for most of the night.

chapter eight

Alan awoke from a blissfully deep sleep, the first he'd had in weeks. The travelling had long since ceased to be a novelty and now that he had Charles to come home to, the journeys seemed even more of a nuisance. And then there was the strain of keeping their relationship a secret. His long-standing routine of insisting Sarah did not get involved in airport hellos and goodbyes had given him the freedom to come and go a little more as he pleased. He'd actually been back in the UK for four days this time before he had to pitch up home. Pity, but there it was.

Those four days had been extremely useful too. Meeting influential friends of Charles, who could open the doors to some sort of export consultancy, had given him the impetus to think seriously about ending his marriage. What would the kids think? Well, they were grown up now and homosexuality was not the disgrace it once was. He was sure Roz and Daniel had plenty of gay friends. They'd accept it soon enough. Sarah had her job at the clinic so she wouldn't need supporting. He allowed himself the brief fantasy of waking up every morning with Charles. No more lies, no more deceit. How Sarah would react he had no idea, and had long since ceased to care. As long as he wasn't landed with any more of her debts.

The thought of money brought him sharply out of his

early morning reverie. The house had been sold last night, or was he dreaming? Did he have one whisky too many or had he spoken to that stupid estate agent about a matter of nearly two hundred grand?

'Sarah, Sarah, where the hell are you?' he shouted. But there was no reply. Ten o'clock, his watch informed him, so the bitch must have gone to work. Oh well, at least he could have a leisurely chat with Charles and tell him of the new developments.

'Sarah? It's Judith. How did it go, did you tell him?'

'No I didn't.' Sarah bit her lip. 'It all went horribly wrong. I just can't believe it. I'd just got to the crucial bit and the phone went. And would you believe it, the fucking estate agents phoned up to say they had a cash buyer for the house. Prepared to pay the whole whack. So that was it, he was instantly on the whisky, celebrating. And then came the real belter.'

'And what was that?' asked Judith, dreading what was coming next.

'He's packing up the Middle East and starting up some sort of mystery business using the proceeds of our house.'

'Shee-eet,' said a stunned Judith, relieved that Sarah was being spared the outing of Bostik. Well, for the moment anyway. She wondered if the beautiful boy in the wine bar had anything to do with this 'mystery business'.

'Well you're entitled to half the value,' she reasoned. 'Surely you don't have to hand that over.'

'Alan fully intends to use every penny,' replied Sarah, 'and knowing his wily ways, he'll manage it somehow.'

'Well, you mustn't let him.'

'Easier said than done,' shrugged Sarah. 'He's watched the finances like a hawk since I got into a bit of trouble a year or two ago. He goes through all the statements with a fine-tooth comb. If I start withdrawing money, he'll spot it immediately and go off his head. Believe me, Jude, it's not a pretty sight.'

'What you need, my girl, is some legal advice,' said Judith. 'You shouldn't have to plough your future nest egg into some dubious company that Alan wants to set up. The very least is that he should discuss it with you. After all, half that money's yours.'

'Yeah, I know,' said Sarah. There was a defeatist tone in her voice. 'But when Alan's made up his mind about something, he'll do it, you wait and see.'

Sarah said her goodbyes, promising to ring Judith again very soon for an update, and inevitably another pep talk.

Judith produced two glasses and a bottle of wine. She poured out generous amounts and handed one to Vicky. They'd decided to settle in for the night and were each outstretched on one of her sofas.

Judith had already updated Vicky on the Adonis in the wine bar, the house sale and Alan's mysterious business plan.

'I think she'll bottle out of the divorce,' said Vicky. 'I'm pretty sure Sarah's actually terrified of Alan. He's a terrible bully and a moody sod. And if he's got his mind set on whatever this mystery business plan is, then she will not shift him. And if it all depends on him using all the house proceeds, then he will. You mark my words.'

'I wish I could contradict you, but I think you've got it in one,' agreed Judith. 'I just don't know what we can do to help.'

'One way and another, you've had a bit of a bucketful from the pair of us this last week, haven't you?' said Vicky ruefully. 'First me, the reluctant bride, and now Sarah, the reluctant divorcee. I think I can see why *your* life is in such control. No men. No problem. Must be so much easier not to have all this hassle. Actually, I can't even remember when you last went on a date.'

'Don't you start,' said Judith, laughing. 'I had a session of this from Lizzie in Cahoots yesterday. First of all, I got chapter and verse on why I should be more adventurous and start going out again. And then I got the addendum on whether she should get married or not as it always seems to end in tears.'

'Well, my brief foray into marriage *started* in tears,' said Vicky. 'I don't think either of us is exactly a fully qualified expert on this one. But she has a point. Why haven't you been on a date?'

'Simple. Nobody asked me,' said Judith. 'And don't forget, I'm rather engulfed in holy matrimony at the moment. I'm working on that story about the crinklies' wedding. You know, the couple who had a dream wedding for next to nothing.'

'What's on the cards when you've done that?' asked Vicky.

'Well I'm glad you brought that up because I've a suggestion to make. Let's have another glass of wine and I'll tell you all about it.'

The car sprang to life on the first turn of the key. *Pity I'm not so keen to get going*, thought Sarah as she swung out of the car park and headed home. *Last night I was all set to get a divorce. Tonight, I seem to be about to lose my home to some stupid business idea.*

She felt rather like a boxer after ten rounds, punch-drunk, dazed and confused. She'd psyched herself up so much for the divorce confrontation that it had totally drained her. Perhaps she'd over-rehearsed it and therefore been wrong-footed. All her instincts told her Alan was up to something. He'd always been rather a mystery but she'd put that down to the fact that he had another life working away, another world to which she did not belong. Her little flings and spending sprees had been her pathetic way of getting back at him. But this time the ground rules had changed and the stakes were much higher.

'Sweetie, heard you come in the gate. Poured you a glass of wine.' Alan smiled as he handed her a drink. Instantly Sarah was on her guard. Smiling was not usually on Alan's agenda, and he only ever called her sweetie when he wanted something.

'Had a good day at work?' he enquired, not waiting for her reply because, of course, he was not the slightest bit interested.

'My goodness, what a busy day,' he continued. 'Phone never stopped. Got the house sale underway. Instructed the solicitors. They're straight on to the case. Seems the other lot want to move in pretty damn quick, which suits me fine. You did so well choosing OBE to do the sale. You were right, sweetie, I was wrong. Certainly not Other Buggers' Efforts this time. And they've come up even more trumps. Found us somewhere to rent for the time being, just a small flat, quite sufficient.'

'Just a small flat?' quivered Sarah.

'Absolutely. Going to have to live modestly until things get going.'

'Alan, stop a minute. What exactly are "things"? You still haven't told me what it is you're going to do.'

'Of course, sweetie. Just give you a top-up first.' He refilled her glass with aplomb. Alan was obviously in cele- bratory mode, while Sarah just felt as though she'd gatecrashed a funeral.

'In a nutshell, I'm setting up as a partner in an export consultancy with special emphasis on the Middle East. There's a huge market out there just waiting to be tapped. I could make a lot of money, sweetie.'

'Except that we'll apparently have to live in abject poverty first, by the sound of it,' Sarah interrupted.

'Anyway this house sale couldn't have come at a better

time,' continued Alan, ignoring her concern. 'Just the right capital I need to get started.'

'And supposing I don't agree,' said Sarah, her voice shaking.

'Oh you will, you will,' said Alan firmly. 'Well actually, Sarah, to put it bluntly, you don't have any choice. The house is in my sole name, remember, so what you think about it doesn't actually amount to diddley squat.'

Sarah left the room biting back the tears.

Judith topped up their glasses and then announced her proposition.

'I'm going to Romania to make a documentary. Probably in a couple of weeks' time. I've done some number crunching and I could afford an assistant. What do you think? It wouldn't exactly be a five-star tour.'

Vicky was speechless.

'It's only a suggestion,' Judith continued. 'I just thought you might not want to go back to Plymouth for a while, not with all the embarrassment of Roger. It's not a permanent job or anything but I thought it might put a bit of space between what happened last weekend and the next step in your life.'

Vicky still couldn't speak.

'It would be a bit rough, in fact that's an understatement. The idea is to go to make a film about some orphanages up in the mountains. The kids were found hidden in filthy cellars after the revolution. Those who'd survived, that is. These kids have been to hell and back. Some of them have Aids. I think it will be traumatic, and personally I'm scared shitless.'

'It would certainly get me away,' said Vicky finally, with understatement. 'My first instinct is to say yes. I think it would do me good, but it does sound scary.'

'I don't want an answer now. Think about it over the

weekend, ask questions and I'll try and fill in any gaps. I went to Romania years ago as a tourist and I have to say it's never been high on my holiday wishlist since.'

'What's the food like?' said Vicky, realising it was a frivolous question the moment she'd uttered it.

'Cold pork and chips,' said Judith with emphasis.

'Just cold pork and chips? Surely there's some interesting local cuisine we could investigate.'

'Nope, that's it. Cold pork and chips. And by the way, the chips aren't just lukewarm, they're stone cold.'

chapter nine

Judith opened the post while she waited for her computer to boot up. One letter stood out from the rest. Out of the crumpled, cheap envelope came the inevitable lined paper and small mouse-like writing. It was from Mr and Mrs Trafford. This time they'd decided to be themselves and were clearly making one last-ditch effort to stop the programme.

They'd had a change of direction since their 'visit' and had since given an interview for the programme where they defiantly suggested that as 'everyone else' owed them money, it was perfectly all right for them to do the same. Judith hadn't been present at that interview. She thought it might prove embarrassing for them so she'd stayed away.

The letter listed a series of even more amazing illnesses from which the Traffords claimed to suffer, and how the showing of this programme could prove to be fatal. 'We do not wish this programme to be broadcast,' they wrote, 'and, by the way, we fully expect you to rot in hell for the evil you have caused.'

Judith fired off a reply.

Dear Mr and Mrs Trafford,
    Thank you for your letter. I was sorry to hear about your various illnesses and hope that you will

both fully recover soon. The programme for which you have been filmed, *What Price A Wedding*, will be transmitted on Thursday at 9.30 pm.

May I take this opportunity of thanking you for putting your side of the story. I do totally understand your sentiments about me rotting in hell.

Yours sincerely,
Judith Fielding
Programme Producer

PS I must add how delightful it was to meet you both the other week here at the studio. So kind of you to make the journey from Winchester.

Just wanted them to know, thought Judith in a rare moment of pomposity. This was at least a subtle way of letting them realise she knew who they really were when they'd visited the studio that ridiculous day last week.

Judith now turned her attention to Romania. There was a long list of things to do: travel arrangements, visas, health aspects, booking the right crew. It was going to be tough and very distressing. But Vicky had already said yes, and Judith knew she really wanted to go. Vicky'd also had a quiet word with Jack, her news editor in Plymouth, who had guessed she wouldn't be returning to work on Monday morning.

'We'd already decided to offer you a bit of gardening leave,' he told her.

'What's that, for chrissake?' asked Vicky.

'Management speak for you staying away for a while in everyone's interests. It doesn't involve you running around with a Flymo.'

'Oh, thank God for that. By the way, thanks, Jack,' said Vicky gratefully.

'Well it's the least we could do. You had a rough time,

love. We all felt for you, especially as we had to run the story. No choice, I'm afraid. But I know you'd understand, being an old pro. And, by the way, you did the right thing. I knew Roger was a bit of a nobber, but even I underestimated him. Lucky escape, love. Now give me a ring in a month and we'll have you back after that.'

So the way was clear for the trip to Romania. 'It's gonna be even zanier in Transylvania,' she announced gleefully to Judith. So it was a good idea, after all.

Alan couldn't believe his luck. He was already sensing victory where Sarah was concerned. He'd soon have his hands on nearly one hundred and sixty thousand smackers, and then, once installed in a grotty rented flat, he was certain Sarah would pack in the marriage. By then, all the money would allegedly be invested in the business (and in the luscious Charles) and she'd have a real fight on her hands if she wanted anything else. After all, she had a job, and he would deliberately pay himself a small salary in the first year of set-up so he didn't have to pay her any maintenance.

That would be real revenge for all the debts she'd run up over the years. And the kids? They'd believe his story, he was certain. Yes, the future was suddenly looking quite rosy. He poured himself a large slug of whisky and toasted his success.

'I'm going to take a long lunch hour,' Sarah announced to a colleague. 'I'm going to pop into town.'

'Buy yourself something,' shouted Jonathan, one of the porters. 'You've had a face like thunder for days. Go on, give yourself a treat. Buy something sexy and give us all a thrill.'

Jonathan secretly fancied Sarah. She might be ten years older than he was, but she had real sex appeal. He loved her bleached blonde hair and slightly tarty make-up, her short skirts and tight blouses. Sarah had a proper woman's figure and she didn't mind showing it. Not for her the stick-insect look of the catwalk.

Sarah headed for town. She'd been awake most of the night, thinking, tossing and turning, thinking some more. Downstairs for a drink, a cigarette, a cup of tea. Thinking and plotting. Sarah was frightened of Alan but now she was angry. He'd totally wrong-footed her. She'd forgotten about the house being in his sole name, for tax reasons some years ago, he had been advised. Suddenly the whole thing stank. She'd just accepted it at the time, although she had taken a dislike to the accountant who came up with the advice. And what about the solicitor who'd transferred the property to Alan's name? Was he in on the plot too? At the time she'd not suspected a thing. After all, what was there to worry about, she'd surmised, she and Alan would be stuck with each other for ever, for better, and mostly for worse, because of the kids, because of more than two decades of marriage. Nothing was going to change. Well, hadn't it just!

Cashmere, the word made her drool. Yes, I'll start with a cashmere coat. And the perfume-laden air of the department store beckoned her in.

'Where the hell is she?' Judith berated Lizzie. 'I've been trying to ring her all weekend and no dice.'

'She's apparently gone into town shopping,' said Lizzie. 'She should be back any minute.'

Oh dear, thought Judith to herself. *I don't like the sound of this one tiny little bit*. Warning bells were going off in her head. *Oh please, God, don't let her start again*.

'Shall I leave a message for her to call you?'

'Yes please,' said Judith. The phone range immediately. 'Miss Fielding?' a voice enquired.

'Yes, that's me.'

'I'm Ben Jarvis from the Official Receiver's office. I wonder if we might have a chat. It's about a matter concerning a Mr Trafford.'

Here we go again, thought Judith. *What this time?* He insisted he could not discuss the matter over the phone and they made an appointment for Friday, the day after the programme. At least it made a change from being invited to rot in hell.

Judith turned her attention back to Romania. She and Lizzie were full steam ahead. There wasn't a moment to lose because the likely first transmission date for the programme was December. That didn't leave much time. And also there was the weather to consider. From October onwards, there were likely to be power-cuts and frozen pipes. It wasn't conducive to working and it was going to be a difficult enough shoot as it was. Judith had fixed a detailed meeting with two organisers from the charity they were travelling with to thrash out the final details. That was for Friday, along with the meeting with the Official Receiver and the inevitable reaction to *What Price A Wedding*. Busy day, thought Judith with understatement.

Sarah went back to the office feeling a whole lot better. Safely wrapped in layers of tissue paper in the boot of her car was a beautiful ivory cashmere coat. Yes, it was impractical, yes, it would need dry cleaning after almost every wear but yes, it was totally gorgeous and she'd felt a million dollars in it. In fact she couldn't believe how much better she'd felt, given the current circumstances. It was like the most glorious fix.

As she'd signed the credit slip on one of their joint cards, Sarah felt some invisible weight lift from her shoulders. Still on a shopping high, she decided she must have some shoes in the softest beige suede to complement the coat.

That, of course, led to the handbag to match and then some very expensive sheer tights to do the shoes justice.

Her confidence bolstered by the fact that she'd done something practical, if vengeful, Sarah picked up the phone and dialled Judith's number.

'Thank God,' said Judith. 'I heard a nasty rumour you were out shopping. Anyway, how are you and what's the latest on Bostik?'

'Can I come over tonight?' asked Sarah.

'Of course, come and eat. My galley slave will prepare supper!' Vicky was, of course, still doing the cooking.

'Great. I'll tell you the whole lot later then. Bye.'

Sarah immediately rang Alan and said she wouldn't be home until late. His feigned disappointment didn't fool Sarah at all. What was really going on?

Good, thought Alan. *An evening without her*. He could take Charles out to dinner without too much suspicion. Can't cook, wife out with friends, that sort of well-worn shrugging excuse if he bumped into anyone.

It was all looking good. The house sale seemed as though it was in the bag. There was no chain, so unless the survey came up with some sort of problem, they could complete in three weeks, his solicitor reckoned.

Alan walked around the house, wandering from room to room. God, he'd be glad to say goodbye to this place. He never felt he belonged here, partly due to working away most of the time, but it had so many unhappy memories over so many years. Now that Roz and Daniel had grown up and moved on, the place seemed so hollow and somehow pointless. He'd never taken an interest in the place, avoiding DIY like the plague. He equated it with huge electricity bills, a constant battle with the garden, which seemed to turn into a jungle the minute you turned your back, noisy plumbing and a driveway with more grass fighting its way through the tarmac than there was on the back lawn. No, it had not been a happy home, at least not for him, anyway.

Mustn't knock it too much, he thought, pondering on the money which would shortly be winging its way into his bank account. Again he congratulated himself on being ahead of the game. He'd already seen his solicitor about a divorce, the same one who'd managed to get Sarah to sign over the house to his sole name a couple of years back. It's a tax dodge, he told Sarah, whom he knew had not the slightest interest in financial matters, other than getting into the changing rooms of the most expensive boutiques as fast as she could. She'd really swallowed that one, and the same solicitor, whose scruples were perhaps not the most squeaky clean in town, had advised him to get the house proceeds into his new business as fast as he could before Sarah realised what was happening. His income would drop overnight to whatever level he decided to pay himself and, with luck, the court would take that as the ballpark figure for any maintenance arrangement. Then the bitch could start paying her own bills and finding out the hard way about her excesses. He couldn't wait for the day when he could shut down the joint accounts and credit cards.

'Are we going to tell Sarah what you saw in Cahoots?' shouted Vicky from the kitchen, where she was briskly chopping up chicken, onions, mushrooms, red peppers and broccoli for a stir-fry.

'What? You mean about Mr Beautiful But Very Possibly Gay?' replied Judith. 'I'm really not sure about this. It sounds so naff in the telling. Oh by the way, I saw your husband in Cahoots – literally – with a really good-looking man. He might be gay, they might be having an affair, and we thought we ought to tell you. Just in case it's true.'

'Well, they *were* in Cahoots,' grinned Vicky.

'Yeah, ha ha. And I'm sure they probably still are, and I could go on by telling Sarah that I'd never seen old Bostik smiling like that before, and at the very time when he was supposed to be mid flight from Bahrain. There could be the simplest explanation, something we've totally overlooked.'

'But we can't think of one,' interrupted Vicky. 'You're right, we could be so wrong, so we'd better shut up. Sarah's got enough on her plate right now, by the sound of it. And by the sound of it,' she paused, hearing the familiar sound of Sarah's rattling Volvo, 'that's her right now.'

Judith went to answer the front door. Through the frosted glass she could see Sarah's familiar figure seemingly wrapped in something cream.

'Good God,' she muttered as Sarah swept through the door.

'Dahlinks, vot do you zeenk of zees?' Sarah was doing her Zsa Zsa Gabor again, twisting and turning on an imaginary catwalk.

'Vunderful, dahlink,' replied Judith 'but take that off pronto before one of us spills something down it.'

Vicky emerged from the kitchen to admire the coat. It was truly wonderful, luxurious to touch and beautifully cut. Vicky thought it looked terrific on Sarah but immediately noticed the clash between her confident body language and the sad message in her eyes. This was not a happy lady.

'It's great, but get it off now,' said Vicky hastily.

'I wish the heavenly number in Dermatology would say that,' sighed Sarah, savouring the moment before the coat was consigned to Judith's little cloakroom.

'Here, get this down you,' said Judith, handing her a glass of Chardonnay. 'Now let's sit down and eat and then you can tell us how much it cost.'

chapter ten

After the stir-fry, during which Sarah confessed that she'd spent eight hundred pounds on the coat, and Judith and Vicky had done a spot of silent choking, Judith went into her sitting room and sat down at the piano. She played a little mellow jazz while the other two loaded up the dishwasher.

'God, I really envy Jude,' said Vicky, 'just playing away like that. I really wish I'd plugged away at violin lessons at school.'

'You played the violin?' queried Sarah, laughing.

'Well more like the vile din, if you asked my parents,' replied Vicky. 'My mother thought it a very suitable thing for a young gel to learn but didn't quite bank on the unspeakable noise I would make for hours on end. Not helped by the fact that I hated the lessons. And if I'm being truthful, I played deliberately badly in order to really, seriously annoy her. Actually that wasn't difficult, thinking back, it came sort of naturally. Come to think of it, I've been doing it ever since. I just used to love annoying her snooty friends, so if she made me play something, I'd saw away for hours playing all the repeats until they begged me to stop!'

'And I thought I was the rebel among us,' said Sarah, grinning.

'Oh I don't know about that. My mother had this natural ability to make me do exactly the opposite of what she wanted. Over everything really. She was obsessed with me marrying the right sort of chap. Bit ironic really. And she used to drop the most horrendously unsubtle hints about men she deemed "suitable" and who "mixed in the right kind of circles". Now some of these blokes were quite nice, but the minute they got Mother Approval, that was the kiss of death. They instantly grew horns and a goatee beard and appeared in a purple anorak.'

'Not to mention socks and sandals. Talking of nerds, what did your mother think about Roger?' asked Sarah.

'Ironically, I think she quite liked him,' said Vicky. 'Says it all really, doesn't it? Do you know, I never thought about that until now. I should have listened to the old antennae. Now what about your folks? Did they ever like Bostik? Or did he bowl them over with what he learnt at the Attila the Hun Charm School?'

'Difficult to say. When you've been married all this time, you grow immune to it. I think when the shit hits the fan, they will perhaps come out about it all. Deep down, I know they dislike him, but they're very loyal. Whatever I've done, they've tried to support me. I suspect I'm about to find out just what brilliant performances they've been giving all these years.'

'And just when *is* the shit going to hit the fan?' asked Vicky. Sarah nodded meaningfully, indicating she would reveal all over the coffee. She carried in a tray of cups, saucers and a cafetière and set them down on a low table. Judith rounded off her Cole Porter medley with a flourish, and the other two applauded, enviously.

They then sprawled on the sofas and Sarah elaborated on Alan's weekend bombshells: the house sale, the mystery business and now the proposed move into a small rented flat.

'I can't even face going to view it,' said Sarah, beginning

to feel her throat tighten with hysteria. 'It's all such a mess. I really thought we'd have been starting a divorce by now. Instead I seem to be subsidising a mystery business and about to live in a Dickensian-style hovel. Come to think of it, I feel like the proverbial mushroom, kept in the dark and fed on shit.'

'Now come on, it might not be that bad,' said Judith calmly. 'It might be Bostik's way of starting afresh. New business, new home, new start for both of you.'

'Old tricks from an old bastard,' interrupted Sarah. 'Sorry, girls, I smell a total rat. Same old routine, not a kiss or a hug, just a rather sickly smile when he wants something. And it certainly isn't what I want. What I need right now is a damn good screw, but that's about the last thing on *his* mind.'

Do I tell her about Alan and the beautiful man in Cahoots? thought Judith, agonising privately. She decided not. One glance at the disturbed look in Sarah's eyes clinched it. She was far too upset to cope with another new facet of this doomed relationship. Judith met Vicky's eyes momentarily, asking the same unspoken question about Alan's companion. They exchanged the most fleeting of looks, both agreeing to stay silent. For now.

'So what *are* you going to do about it?' asked Vicky. 'I think you ought to get some legal advice, especially as the house is now only in his name.'

'Well I am going to, but I'm also trying to find ways of accessing some of the money before it's too late. At the moment we don't have a joint bank account, only joint credit cards, so I'm going to sting him a little bit. And maybe then he'll take other people's needs into consideration, preferably mine.'

'Are you sure this is wise?' asked Judith. 'I thought you'd only just got out of one financial mess. Your plastic isn't elastic, you know.'

'Well yes, but it may be my last fling. I'm very tempted to skin the bastard alive. Then he'd have to prise open those bloody Bostik pockets and pay up. I just know he's going to keep all the money himself. It'll disappear somehow, you watch out. Ugh!'

Sarah shuddered. She thought of the credit card bills she'd stuffed in a drawer at the weekend. Alan would be livid but she was beginning to realise she wanted a showdown. She'd been so psyched up for the divorce scene that the fear and the adrenalin had not deserted her. She'd wanted the row, the tears, the screamings and possibly the hurling of crockery as well. She needed to end this mess. Yet at the same time she knew she had to bide her time. *I'll punish him, in my own time and in my own way*, she resolved bitterly.

As Sarah drove home, she thought about the evening she'd spent. The warm and cosy atmosphere of Judith's house, with its fresh flowers stuffed into vases, the colourful bits and pieces Judith collected on her travels, the piles of newspapers, magazines and books, music gently filling the rooms and the fridge always filled with tasty nibbles. Yes, Judith had really made a proper home for herself and her son. And yet no man in her life, not for a long time. The trouble was she was probably now too independent for most men, who tended to be attracted to helpless fluffy bunny types. Fluffy bunny Jude was definitely not.

As Sarah coaxed her old Volvo up the slope to the driveway she noted with relief that the lights were out. Alan was either in bed or perhaps he was out. She crept into the kitchen, made a cup of tea and then discovered that he wasn't at home. She wondered fleetingly where he was and with whom. At the same time, she realised she didn't care all that much.

Sarah woke up early – disturbed by a car alarm blaring

and the milkman clanking bottles noisily on the doorstep. She padded out to the bathroom and heard snoring coming from Roz's old bedroom. So he had come back after all. Was this a new regime of separate bedrooms? she wondered.

She went downstairs, put on the kettle and picked up the post. There were two letters, one from OBE to say that the buyers were adamant that the deal had to be completed on the house in under three weeks. The other from the solicitors indicating that the proceeds of the house would be safely lodged in Alan's bank account on the day of completion. Sarah noted bitterly that both letters were addressed solely to Alan. She was nowhere in this particular race. What was he really up to? she wondered for what seemed the hundredth time in a week.

Alan phoned her mid morning at the clinic. She could hear him keeping his temper in check as he demanded to know why she'd opened his post.

'I always open the post,' she retorted. 'Remember, you work in the Middle East for eight months of the year. Remember, I'm the mother of your children, I run the house most of the time. Remember, I've spent years opening your post. What's different now? And by the way, where were you last night?'

'Oh, out with friends, discussing business,' said Alan rather too swiftly. 'Nothing for you to worry your little head about.'

'Well I think there's everything to worry my little head about. You're about to sell our home in three weeks' time. What happens then? Are you expecting me to enjoy being homeless and rush out selling copies of the *Big Issue*?'

'Of course not, sweetie,' said Alan, trying to control his temper. Must keep things on an even keel to get that deal through and keep Sarah well away from a solicitor's office.

'No, no, it's all going to be exciting. I could make lots of money when this whole thing takes off.'

Like hell, thought Sarah. She knew she should be making an appointment to see a solicitor as Vicky had suggested. But she knew that would be terribly depressing because she suspected she'd be told a few home truths. No, today she would have another treat, then tomorrow she would make an appointment. Her credit cards almost jangled in her pocket.

Sorry, Alan, I'm going to have at least some of my share, she thought as she swung through the doors of Winchester's most expensive boutique.

As Sarah eyed the rails of horrendously expensive clothes, the sales assistant, a very corseted woman in her fifties with her hair swept up in an elaborate chignon, was assessing Sarah's cashmere coat. Probably could afford our clothes, she thought, and homed in for the kill.

Sarah twirled in front of a huge mirror in the luxurious dressing rooms. The blue pin-striped suit with its long-line jacket and wide trousers looked terrific. It gave her gravitas and class. *Just the sort of thing to wear in a divorce court as the heartbroken wife*, she thought. Then she tried on a couple of skirt suits, one with a short straight skirt and boxy jacket in black and white tweed with glorious brass buttons. *Very Chanel, very me*, she thought. The other was in loden green, a mid-calf-length skirt with a split front and back, together with a long jacket with deep pockets and a velvet collar. Mrs Chignon suggested that the matching trousers would give the jacket a longer life, and then showed Sarah some tailored black trousers which would team with the black and white tweed jacket. Soon silk tops and co-ordinating scarves were being added to complete each look.

'I do love silk,' murmured Sarah. Picking up her cue immediately, Mrs Chignon brought out a beautiful silk suit consisting of straight trousers and a simple jacket with a mandarin collar in a deep petrol blue.

'Now this would go anywhere,' she purred. 'You really could wear this to work, then to the theatre or dinner. It is such a classic. Would never date. And of course it's completely lined in silk so it's terribly comfortable to wear.'

Sarah was desperately trying to decide which suit to buy. Of course she wanted them all because they each had different moods. She had also come to the startling realisation that she was in fact re-inventing herself. This was not the slightly brassy, sexy Sarah of old, but a new classy model staring back from the mirror. She remembered all those endless magazine articles about women changing their hair or their clothes after a relationship break-up. *Well, I need a new image too and I like the one I'm seeing in the mirror*, she thought.

Meanwhile Mrs Chignon was also in seventh heaven. She was mentally calculating the commission she might be raking in from this deal. Should she go for the jugular, push for another sale and risk an attack of total indecision, or quit while she was ahead?

'I don't know if you're thinking of buying any evening wear, but we do have a stunning new range. Some marvellous new pieces came in only this morning. I know they'll be walking out of the shop, they're so gorgeous.' *Actually they've been in the stockroom for a fortnight but we couldn't be bothered to get them out*, she thought.

'There's one outfit that I think would look stunning on you.' She tried to sound casual. 'I'll just pop out and get it to show you.'

She re-emerged carrying something long and black over her arms. Sarah disappeared back through the curtains like a lamb to the slaughter. Mrs Chignon was right, the dress was total heaven. It was made of the finest black crepe, long and straight, which skimmed her hips and just brushed her ankles with a split up one side. The bodice was of black satin softly pleated with cross-over shoestring straps and cut low at the back. It was every woman's dream because its brilliant cut gave her a great cleavage *and* made her hips look slim. The jacket was made of the same crepe with satin lapels in a soft tuxedo style and just reeked of class.

'Gorgeous, isn't it?' said Mrs Chignon, clapping her hands with delight in the anticipation of even more commission. 'It just combines glamour with class, so versatile.'

Sarah saw herself on the arm of some young stud attending a flash-popping première in Hollywood. Well she'd even settle for the annual Christmas bash at work.

'I'm going to have them all,' she announced emphatically, trying to keep the wobble out of her voice.

'Wonderful. I know you won't be disappointed,' replied Mrs Chignon, fingers rippling over the till and trying to give the impression that she made this sort of sale every hour of every day. Then there was a flurry of tissue paper and carrier bags as various suits, tops and scarves were carefully packed and ready to go.

As Sarah scurried back to the car park, clutching her expensive carrier bags, she was suddenly overcome with a fear of being mugged. Understandable, as she'd just spent nearly six thousand pounds.

chapter eleven

The reaction to *What Price A Wedding* was unprecedented. Judith and Lizzie spent most of the morning fielding calls. It seemed half the population of Hampshire was owed money by the Traffords. And not just as a result of their wedding. As well as a newsagent, a greengrocer, a tailor and a video shop, it seemed they'd had a couple of birthday parties at restaurants in Southampton and failed to settle the bill. It was the same old familiar tale, with people's businesses suffering as a result. The meeting with the Official Receiver would be even more interesting than Judith had thought.

The calls prompted loads of office banter, particularly among one of the film crews whose job had been shelved because of the heavy rain. They were all hanging around the office, waiting for opening time, because they'd already decided that as it was Friday, they'd begin the weekend early with a long lunch in Cahoots.

Ben Jarvis, the Official Receiver, reminded Judith a little bit of Vicky's ex, Roger. Boring grey suit, boring tie, and carrying the world's most boring briefcase. The week's events were beginning to catch up on Judith and she had great difficulty in disguising several yawns.

However, Mr Jarvis was full of surprises. As the discussion got underway, he warmed to his theme. Judith showed him a list of all the Traffords' creditors, which had now stretched to three pages, since the broadcast last night. He was clearly impressed at the detail and the numbers and amounts involved.

'Do you think they have any obvious assets?' he asked. 'Anything we could sell to recover some of the debts? It looked as if the interview was conducted at their house.'

'Well I can't help you on that bit because I took a decision not to be at the interview,' Judith explained.

'Oh, I thought you'd met them,' replied Mr Jarvis.

'I certainly did but it was under, let's say, unusual circumstances.' Judith explained how the Traffords came to her office and did their now infamous impersonation act in a bid to warn her off broadcasting anything.

'I think I now understand a little more of what I'm dealing with,' he said. 'Very clever, I must say. Now one last thing before I leave you in peace. The taxi business, did you know about that?'

'No, that one escaped me,' said Judith, intrigued.

'Well it seems that Mr T runs a taxi business. I describe that in the loosest possible terms because he has neglected to apply for the necessary licence plate so he's therefore not insured. But that wouldn't surprise you, would it?'

'Nope,' said Judith. 'But I can offer a car number. They left here in a rather old silver Mercedes and, come to think of it, it did have a taxi plate.' She reached in a drawer for her notebook and gave him the number she'd noted when she'd seen them off the premises.

'Brilliant, I'll start running checks on that immediately,' said Mr Jarvis, shutting the world's most boring briefcase and shaking her hand. 'You have been the most fantastic help, Miss Fielding.'

'Oh, one last thing,' said Judith. 'Only sheer nosiness, but you know how we all work on this need-to-know basis.

What were they up to before all this wedding and taxi business? I can't believe they've only just recently given up the
straight and narrow.'

Mr Jarvis paused and told her, a twinkle in his eye.
Perhaps he wasn't quite so boring after all.

'Lunch,' shouted Judith out of her office door to Lizzie.
'Another bombshell on the Trafford case.'

Sarah had finally made an appointment to see a solicitor.
She'd been recommended to a firm in Winchester by the
new dish in Dermatology. No flicker of interest from him at
the mention of divorce. Oh well, she had enough to cope
with at the moment.

With a reluctant heart, she'd dialled the number, knowing
the call was the final seal on her fate. She'd been strangely
pleased because Mr Barnes couldn't see her until early next
week. It felt like a short reprieve, but of course she knew she
was deluding herself. All she was buying was more shopping
time, and by next week, the damage would have been done.

Since the big spender bender of Tuesday, she'd naturally
had to buy accessories to go with all the new outfits. Staff
at the local branch of Russell and Bromley thought
Christmas had come early. Sarah had swept in to buy boots
and shoes to go with all the suits, plus, of course, the
matching handbags.

Then she'd had quite a hunt for just the right shoes for
the silk suit. Eventually she'd found them in a tiny boutique without prices to match. The shoes alone, exquisite
though they were with delicate seed-pearl trim, came in at
a tad over three hundred pounds, and the bag just on four
hundred. They were of course just totally gorgeous. The
same shop had come up with just the right strappy sandals
for the black tuxedo outfit. So they too were snapped up,
together with a little jewelled evening bag that the woman
assured her was a classic. Something that would be handed

down through the family, having carefully established that
Sarah had a daughter.

If Alan finds out about this, he's more likely to hit me
about the head with it, Sarah had thought. The word classic
had clinched the deal, and yet another boutique assistant
totted up the commission on the sale and dreamed of
Mauritius instead of Minehead for her next holiday.

Any qualms Sarah had had earlier in the week had been
swiftly dispelled. Alan was obviously spending as well.
Gone was the old Ford Mondeo he used to run around in
when he was home from the Middle East. Without a word
of explanation, he'd turned up on Tuesday night in a dark
green Mercedes convertible, its sleek lines gleaming in the
drive. He seemed to have acquired a mobile phone, which
was apparently Superglued to his ear, and she noticed an
obviously expensive sand-coloured suede jacket slung
casually over the passenger's seat.

As she pushed open the jeweller's door, a delicate peal of
bells cued in an assistant, who as yet didn't know his luck
was in. A necklace and matching earrings for the evening
outfit, two strings of delicate pearls to go with the silk suit,
a couple of dress rings, cameo brooch and a Rolex watch.
Well, why not? she thought. It's hardly in the same league
as the Merc, and half that money's mine, she reasoned,
smiling sweetly at the man behind the counter, who was
busily wrapping the purchases and fantasising about
having Sky Sports installed after all.

'Well, well, don't leave me in suspense,' said Lizzie as they
were safely installed in their favourite corner of Cahoots.
The place was packed out, mostly by the cancelled film
crew, who were already three bottles of wine into a very
noisy lunch, destroying the usual calm of the place. A
debate about chat-up lines had moved on to noisy accounts
of 'how I lost my virginity'.

Lizzie and Judith winced as the superstuds regaled each other with their instant sexual prowess.

'Well come on, Jude, you've made me wait ten minutes now. What did the Traffords do before they got married? It's obviously dreadful. What is it?' Lizzie was desperate to know.

'Well you're never going to believe this,' said Judith, milking the situation as much as she could.

'Why not try me?' retorted Lizzie.

'Oh all right. Well apparently,' she paused for a fit of giggles, 'they ran a sort of old folks' knocking shop. A sort of daytime club for crumblies with a few fringe benefits.'

'What sort of benefits?' asked Lizzie.

'Well, apparently they'd lay on a few girls for the blokes and vice versa, show some blue movies, and sell a few bits and pieces.'

'Like what?' asked Lizzie, totally gripped.

'Blow-up dolls, that sort of thing. In fact that, according to Mr Jarvis, is how they were rumbled in the first place. It seems they supplied this doll to one old chap in a wheelchair. He got it home and found it had a puncture so he complained to the Traffords. They told him it was nothing to with them and he'd have to take his complaint to the manufacturers. And do you know what happened?'

'No, I can't imagine.'

'The manufacturers sent him a standard sort of postcard, not a letter, a postcard, saying something like "Dear Mr So and So, we acknowledge the return of your inflatable doll, model Sharon, and our customer service section is examining it and will be in touch again when they have completed tests." And, in the process, we'll let your nosy postman and all your mates at the sorting office know as well, natch.

'Of course, the old boy was too embarrassed to follow it up, because this firm apparently did all their business by postcard deliberately to put people off. Then the old boy discovered that the Traffords owed the firm heaps of money, surprise, surprise, so he reported it quietly to his local trading standards department.

'Somewhere along the line, the Traffords eventually closed down their little sideline after local pressure, and turned their attention to juggling a little bankruptcy problem and getting married on the extremely cheap.'

Lizzie laughed until she ached, tears running down her cheeks. Judith made valiant attempts to keep herself in check. She had an important meeting about the Romanian trip to attend in the afternoon that would be a serious affair. But in the end, she had to give in. The pair of them couldn't speak for laughing. So much so that the film crew, who by now had moved down their packed agenda from tattoos to body piercing and being at the birth, stopped mid flow and demanded to know the reason for all the laughing.

When Judith finally told them, they launched into a flurry of jokes about it.

'What was it called, this knocking shop? Help the Aged?' joked Colin. 'I suppose it did really.'

Trevor picked up an air guitar and started to sing Cliff Richard style: 'Got myself a walking, weeping, talking, sleeping blow-up doll!'

'Another bottle, sir?' The wine waiter in his long white apron hovered expectantly. 'Another Châteauneuf-du-Pape?'

'Yeah, why not,' growled Colin. 'More Chateau Naff de Poop coming up, lads.'

Judith and Lizzie left them to it.

chapter twelve

The sun finally broke through the showers, drying the pavements and washing the dust off the August leaves. Too late for the lads in Cahoots. Their shoot had been cancelled and they were now much too full of French wine and food to focus on putting a tape in a camera.

Judith returned to the office for the Romania briefing. She was filled with trepidation but desperate not to let it show. She was also vastly relieved that Vicky was going too. Somehow it wouldn't be so bad if she was there. Funny how when you get to your forties, all your priorities change. Would there be a minibar in the room, decent towels and sheets, enough hot water to wash your hair every day? Would the telephones work, would there be a signal on the mobile? In your twenties, none of this mattered a jot. Now, creature comforts and instant communications became life's essentials.

Vicky was waiting in Judith's office.

'Sarah's been spotted in Gems, the jeweller's,' she reported. 'And I can't believe it's to counsel the staff about their forthcoming hip replacements.'

'Oh well, we'll find out later,' replied Judith. 'Now let's get a game plan up for this meeting. We must get through the logistics so I can start a shooting schedule and a rough script. One thing that's really important is the filming permit for Bucharest. Otherwise we could get snatched by the Securitate and never be seen again. Remember, I got arrested there years ago for taking a photograph of the wrong thing so I don't want to find we spend a week filming and then get our tapes seized. Difficult to explain that one to the management.'

Reception informed Judith that the two charity representatives had arrived so they all made their way to a small meeting room at the quiet end of the building. Everyone shook hands. Paul Morrison, in his forties, tall, dark and not very handsome but with a quiet, confident manner, was introduced as the volunteers' organiser. And Stephanie Bannister, also in her forties, plumpish and friendly with a mop of blonde-going-grey curls, was the charity's treasurer and secretary.

Judith heaved a mental sigh of relief. Neither looked particularly fit nor the type who'd enjoy roughing it. Perhaps it wouldn't be so bad after all.

They spent two hours going through checklists of flights, connections, visas, customs clearance, interviewees and interpreters so that Judith could get her all-important timetable together. Then they talked about the orphanage they were to visit up in the Transylvanian mountains. Both Paul and Stephanie spoke very affectionately about the children. It seemed they had been found in filthy underground cellars after the revolution. The tale was horrific. The pre-revolution regime had insisted that all couples produce at least five healthy children. Weak or disabled children could be drowned in buckets at birth. But those who'd somehow survived that cull had been hidden away in the countryside in the hope that they would just die. The children in the orphanage were the survivors of that particular nightmare.

'You might get bitten or scratched and you'll certainly get your pockets picked,' said Stephanie cheerfully. 'A lot of the children sit rocking all day because they've been so traumatised and many have their heads shaved because they have nits. It's our only way of controlling it.'

Judith and Vicky exchanged anguished glances. This was going to be a terrible ordeal.

'The hotels in Bucharest aren't too bad,' warned Paul, 'but up in the mountains, it's a bit more primitive. I suggest you think of it more in terms of camping. Anything you need for your own personal comfort, you're best taking with you.'

'Like what?' asked Vicky.

'Oh, towels, loo roll, sheets, that sort of thing,' he replied casually. 'At least you're going in September. Once the winter sets in up there, they can have power cuts for up to a fortnight and all the pipes freeze.'

Thank you, God, for September, thought Judith, counting small blessings. At least they'd be able to charge up the camera batteries.

The meeting drew to a close. Next time they met would be at Stansted airport in a week's time.

'Bloody Nora,' said Judith, slumping back in her office chair. 'This is going to be tough. Are you sure you still want to do this?'

'Can't back out now,' replied Vicky. 'My name's on the ticket and you'd never speak to me again anyway. Oh come on, it'll be all right. Those two seem to manage and they're no spring chickens. It'll make a change from the usual punch-ups outside Crown Court that I'm used to.'

'I suppose there's that,' sighed Judith, who was already making mental lists of nit and scabies lotion for all of the crew, a travel kettle, tea, coffee, Cup a Soups and enough hot chocolate to see them through the next couple of millennia.

'This will appeal to my mother,' Vicky consoled herself. 'She's buried up to her armpits in *The Lady* and hangs around with all those ghastly types who "do lunch and charidee". It might get me some brownie points and at least she'll dine out on it for a while, talking about her daughter who did "some simply marvellous work with some simply marvellous children up in those mountains where that simply fascinating chap, what was his name, Dracula, hung out". I can hear her voice droning on about it already. It will be fun for us too, well, retrospectively.'

'OK, I've got an awful lot of work to do on this before next week, but before that, let's find out what Sarah's been up to. I could do with a diversion after all that lot. It was desperately worthy but also desperately depressing.'

She dialled Sarah at the clinic.

'Is that the Head of Credit Scoring?' she joked. 'Detective Inspector Fielding here. You were spotted coming out of the most expensive jeweller's in town. Now, you've either won the lottery, got engaged and had the cheek not to tell us, or you're up to something. I suspect the latter and I want your signed confession in Cahoots, in about an hour's time. Can you make it?'

'Yeah, of course,' said Sarah, her voice instantly a dead giveaway. She sounded totally deflated. 'Anything's better than going home.'

Oooops, thought Judith. *Not a happy bunny*. Perhaps I shouldn't have made such a joke. What with trying not to mention weddings in Vicky's presence, she felt she'd been treading on eggshells for the past fortnight.

Judith and Vicky were back in their favourite corner of Cahoots when Sarah swept in. They almost didn't recognise her. Gone was the slightly tarty short skirt, tight half-unbuttoned shirt and lashings of large, chunky jewellery. Instead came an elegant woman with newly coiffed hair in a navy pin-striped suit consisting of a long lean jacket and matching trousers. A whisper of a plain white silk shirt under the jacket and some simple pearls completed the outfit.

'Bloody hell,' whispered Vicky. 'What a transformation.'

'So what brought this on?' asked Judith when they'd settled down to gin and tonics. 'What's happened to the Zsa Zsa collides with Marilyn Monroe look? We've only just come out of therapy after the cashmere coat.'

'Bostik, basically,' said Sarah, flatly. 'He's gone absolutely berserk spending. The house is being rushed through and completes in less than two weeks now. I still know nothing about this supposed business plan he has. He just refuses to discuss it. But I sense in every bone in my body that I will end up with nothing.'

'Have you seen a solicitor?' asked Vicky.

'Next Monday is the earliest appointment I could get but, honestly, I think it's all a lost cause. The house isn't in my name, so it's all over my head, basically.'

'No, it's not,' said Vicky, quickly, grateful for the few things she'd learnt from her relationship with Mervyn the solicitor. The thought of him suddenly made her wistful. She pulled herself up sharply again. 'You will definitely have a claim to the house, mark my words. But you've got to act fast.'

'Trouble is, he and I are now having an unofficial spending competition,' confessed Sarah. 'At this rate there'll be nothing left once the house is sold. Just debts to clear.'

She gave a brief résumé of the Mercedes, the mobile, the new clothes, new golf clubs, mystery comings and goings, the long-haul holiday brochures and yachting magazines lying around.

It certainly didn't sound at all like Bostik, thought Judith, who was again agonising over whether to tell Sarah about the beautiful young man they'd seen here in Cahoots. He must be something to do with all this. But it was not the time for a lecture on spending, she reasoned.

She deliberately changed the subject to Romania and gave Sarah a brief account of the afternoon's revelations.

'Now we're off next Friday for a fortnight on this shoot and I'm going to give you some spare keys to my house. Just in case things get iffy, you'll have somewhere to go. I've just realised that your house will be sold slap bang in the middle of our trip and we won't be around. Also you can do something for me.'

'Anything,' said Sarah, suddenly overwhelmed by the kindness around her.

'You could keep an eye on Simon for me,' said Judith, knowing it was likely to be the other way around, Simon being wise beyond his years. 'You know what all kids are like, six-packs converging the minute your car turns the first corner, and next thing, they're frantically flipping through Yellow Pages searching for that French polisher in the ads. Or worse.'

'Thanks,' sniffed Sarah. 'I don't know what I'd do without you two.'

That weekend Judith and Vicky turned out their wardrobes, trying to find the impossible. Clothes that would be comfortable, practical and look reasonable even if you slept in them for a fortnight. No black and red, the two charity workers had warned them. You might be mistaken for gypsies, and Romanians regarded gypsies as sub-humans.

'Trouble is,' said Vicky, 'half my stuff is in Plymouth, either still in my house or at Roger's if he hasn't chucked it out or set fire to it yet. The other half is black. Well actually, if I'm honest, all my stuff's black 'cos black is so bloody slimming.'

They raked through piles of jeans and sweatshirts that hadn't seen the light of day for years. The massive trying-on session continued for hours, with both of them realising that they couldn't get into most of the clothes. Time had taken its toll on their waist measurements.

'We're bound to lose weight on this cold pork and chips lark,' said Vicky optimistically.

'I very much doubt it,' replied Judith, 'because I think we'll be seeking consolation in alcohol. But we could take some of this stuff for the kids at the orphanage.'

'Brilliant idea,' said Vicky, trying to squeeze herself into a pair of Judith's old jeans. 'Oh to be thin again. Actually that's a lie. I've never been thin, I've just got a lot fatter over the years.'

'Haven't we all,' laughed Judith. 'There's a bit of me that looks longingly at all the supermodels and wishes my thighs were just thin, tanned and endless. But there's another bit of me, or perhaps rather a large chunk of me, which says that nibbling on a lettuce leaf every other Thursday isn't a life.'

'Well you're not as bad as me,' moaned Vicky. 'I'm straining at the size-sixteen seams here. At least you're still a small fourteen. I just don't have any will power. And any that I might have had got killed stone dead two weeks ago at the proverbial altar.'

Vicky did look a bit of a mess, Judith thought to herself. She'd put on a very brave face after the register office fiasco, but the shock had given way to a tiredness of body and soul. Her hair had lost its lustre, her skin looked sallow and rather blotchy, and her shoulders seemed to sag from an invisible burden. A fortnight in endless tracksuits had done nothing to brighten up her mood or her muscle tone. Perhaps Romania would snap her out of this. She hoped so.

'Are you all right, Vick?' enquired Judith, gently. 'I mean, really all right?'

'No, not really,' she replied, a single tear snaking its way down her cheek. She made no attempt to wipe it away. 'No, I'm not. Roger did more damage in a way than I'd realised. Here I am, fat, forty-three, and maybe I've just passed up my only chance of marriage.'

'Is that what you want, marriage?' queried Judith, somewhat surprised.

'Well, I'd never thought about it much before, except where Mervyn was concerned. We did go through a stage of skirting around the m-word. I was so totally potty about him that if he'd shouted "jump", I'd have just asked "where from?". There's no doubt he was the love of my life. The trouble is, staying here's reminded me of what I've missed out on. It's a proper home and you have Simon. I know you've brought him up on your own, but at least you've had him and you've given him a good home and a decent upbringing. It's too late now for me for anything – kids, des res, matching saucepans, washing the car on Sundays and all that stuff. I've spent years thinking I was still mentally about twenty, but I'm not any more. I could be on my own for the rest of my life now. I might never have sex again.'

'Don't be daft, of course you will.'

'Who'd want me the way I look and feel at the moment? If I met someone tomorrow, I'd have to live my entire life in candlelight so he wouldn't see any of my cellulite.'

'You should try stretch marks,' said Judith, trying to lighten the conversation.

'At least you've got stretch marks, at least you've had a baby,' replied Vicky, her voice becoming taut as she fought back tears. 'All I've got is cellulite, and more bloody, bloody cellulite.'

'We all get it sooner or later,' said Judith. 'I'm surprised women don't cheer each other up during mid-life crises with gifts of candles or twenty-watt light bulbs. Now if it's any comfort, there won't be many light bulbs in Romania, if my memory serves me well, so who knows, you could pull! We both could!

'So stop feeling sorry for yourself and let's get an Indian

from the takeaway. It could be one of our last hot meals for a while. And maybe we'll pack some condoms just in case.'

'Yeah, as if!' Vicky surrendered to a small smile. 'It would be a rather sad state of affairs if Roger was the last sex I ever had.'

'Oh it won't be,' said Judith, appalled. 'Now in the meantime, why not while away the time until your Next Good Shag with a chicken tikka, sag prawn, vegetable bhaji, pilau rice and a couple of poppadoms apiece!'

chapter thirteen

The solicitor's office was predictably depressing. The wait-ing room was painted an uninspiring green with a selection of maroon leather chairs hugging the walls. Two large and straggly Swiss cheese plants dominated one corner, looking suspiciously as though they were trying to obscure a damp wall. Sarah shivered as she perched on one of the maroon chairs that had long since given up any promise of comfort.

A coffee table was piled up with property supplements, conveyancing magazines and various missives from the Law Society. Sarah had already sifted through them in the vain hope of a *Cosmopolitan* or *Hello!* magazine peeping through the pile. In desperation she picked up a very worthy but extremely dull leaflet giving step by step advice on buying your first house. Why give away trade secrets in the waiting room when you could be rooking your clients in one of the offices? One swift look answered that ques-tion. It all looked so monumentally dull, she decided, no wonder people were prepared to cough up the fees to avoid wading through that lot.

Her thoughts were interrupted by a rather portly woman in her late fifties, who peered over her glasses to announce that she was Miss Adelaide, Mr Barnes' secretary. Sarah fol-lowed her dutifully up two flights of rather noisy, dusty stairs to a large landing, on to which there converged a mass of old oak doors. Miss Adelaide had clearly given her life to the firm. Devoid of make-up, grey hair scraped back in a rather severe bun and wearing a floral dress with unflattering pleats, she almost bowed to Mr Barnes as she ushered Sarah through an office door. No first names here, Sarah noted.

Mr Barnes turned out to be much more friendly than Miss 'Stately as a Galleon' Adelaide. Thin and grey-suited, he had a crinkly smile and not a lot of hair. Just a grey layer around the back and sides with one of those absurd partings just over one ear and a long piece combed over the top to tone down his bald pate. *Why do men do that and whom do they think they're kidding?* thought Sarah. One of the consultants sported that look at the clinic, where he was known as 'You're Never Alone With a Strand'.

Mr Barnes shook Sarah's hand warmly, invited her to sit down, ordered coffee, and in a stroke he'd dispelled her initial nervousness. Sarah glanced quickly around the room. The sunlight was streaming in, mercilessly exposing the smeared windows and dust on all the bookshelves, but it had a cheery air in the circumstances and she relaxed.

'Now, Mrs Franks, I'm not quite clear what you'd like me to do,' said Mr Barnes, gently. 'It's a question of a property and your husband. Just take me through it step by step and in your own time.'

Sarah started to outline the events of the past two weeks, omitting her initial plans to divorce Alan. She began with his return home, the quick sale of the house and her discovery that the house was no longer in her name. Mr Barnes listened intently without writing a single note. There were two things that puzzled him. Why had she signed over the house ownership so readily and why was she so opposed to the house sale when she said she had put it on the market?

Sarah opened her handbag, took out a tissue and dabbed

her eyes. She couldn't hold back the tears any longer. Was this how marriages ended, in dusty offices talking to complete strangers about your private life? It all seemed such a shabby contrast to the hope and happiness she'd felt, bouncing down the aisle with Alan on that sunny day. Sure, she'd been pregnant, but it was what they'd wanted. Or was it? She didn't know any more. The man she'd married was long since gone. Now a total stranger had taken his place, a stranger who now struck terror in her heart every time she heard his car draw up.

Mr Barnes was obviously well used to people snivelling in his office. Unembarrassed, he prompted her to continue.

'We'd been going to sell the house. It's too big now that the children have left home,' she finally explained. 'Our marriage has been a bit of a sham, to be honest, these last few years. It's survived longer than it should have done because Alan's always worked away. But this time I'd been just dreading him coming back and I began to think about us splitting up at the same time as selling the house. It sort of made sense, you see.'

She paused to dab her eyes again.

'Yes, I do,' he nodded. 'So you put the house on the market and, bingo, there's a buyer.'

'That's exactly it,' said Sarah, feeling relieved that she'd got through to him. 'And before I can broach the subject of divorce, the house is sold, he's talking about some mystery business which he's ploughing the money into, and then he reminds me that my name's no longer on the deeds.'

'OK, so that explains one bit,' said Mr Barnes. 'Now forgive me for asking, but did you seek legal advice when the deeds were changed?'

'Well, er, no.' Sarah stared down at her fingernails, embarrassed. 'I know I should have but – oh I might as well be honest – I'm not very good with money, Mr Barnes. And I'd got us into a bit of debt. Alan was always saying we'd lose the house if I went on spending, and there were lots of arguments about it. Also he came up with some stuff about tax breaks and things which I didn't understand. In the end, I agreed to it for a quiet life. I know I should have known better, so it was, to some extent, my fault. I can see now that he had the upper hand and he played on that.'

She glanced up at him shamefacedly. It was the first time she'd truly owned up to her own problems with money.

Mr Barnes then quietly explained that she did in fact still have a claim on the property and he'd investigate the progress of the sale as a matter of haste.

'There's one other thing I ought to tell you,' said Sarah, faltering. 'He's behaving very out of character. Apart from this mystery business, he's spending money like water.'

Bit ironic, thought Mr Barnes wryly to himself. *A touch of the pot calling the kettle black.*

'In what way?' he prompted.

'New car, mobile phone, new clothes, golf clubs, you name it he's either bought it or he's got the brochures. Even my friends have remarked on it. Bostik's always been famous for his meanness.'

'Bostik?' queried the solicitor.

'Oh, sorry. My friends nicknamed him Bostik Pockets. Because he's so tight, they always reckoned he glued up his pockets,' said Sarah, miserably. It sounded so silly in the telling.

Mr Barnes privately thought it was the funniest thing he'd heard in ages, but he managed to control his laughter, as Miss Adelaide, easing her corseted frame though the door, brought in a tray of coffee.

'Anything else, Mr Barnes?' she boomed, setting down cups, milk, sugar and biscuits, and then smoothing down her sunray pleats with fat fingers.

No rings, thought Sarah. *Bet she's never had sex either. But there again, she's not the daft one, sitting here like me. At least she's been spared all this.*

'No, that's fine, Miss Adelaide. Thank you very much.'

Sarah swore she noticed Miss Adelaide blush in a girlish way as she stately-galleoned her way out of the office. Perhaps he was her secret pash.

'Now where were we?' said Mr Barnes, who by now was making detailed notes with a fountain pen in impeccable handwriting.

'I think we've dealt with the property for now. But there's one other matter which I need a little enlightenment on.' He cleared his throat. 'You mentioned divorce just now. Do you wish to begin divorce proceedings?'

Sarah took a deep breath. 'Yes,' she said. 'I do. And the sooner the better.'

The supermarket trolley was piling up. Tea bags, coffee, powdered milk, drinking chocolate, instant soups, in every flavour known to man, chocolate bars, glucose tablets. *Enough to feed an entire Romanian marching army for a good couple of months*, thought Vicky, going through Judith's list.

'Don't forget, anything we don't use, we'll give to the orphanage and the volunteers,' were her words. 'None of this will be wasted.'

Next on the list were socks, handkerchiefs, soap, tights, scarves, hats and gloves. Items which could be welcome gifts to anyone who eased their path, from the poorest villager to the highest-ranking official. 'Bribes by any other name,' said Judith.

All the camera gear, tripod, lights, batteries, chargers, sound mixer, microphones, cables and tapes, had been carefully weighed in their silver flight cases for customs clearance and excess freight charges.

The visas had arrived safely, declaring they were all doing humanitarian work for a charity. The explanation would be that the film would help generate funds for the orphanages, show the world that the Romanian people really did care for their children and that they were grateful for Western aid.

Judith, meanwhile, had been busy cleaning the house from top to toe, filling the freezer, clearing all the ironing, giving Simon his final instructions, lists of emergency phone numbers, and, of course, generally fretting. Simon was busily trying to conceal his delight at the prospect of having the house to himself for a fortnight. A little entertaining of the opposite sex was on the cards, but definitely not a party. Not his style. He couldn't seem to convince his mother otherwise.

'Too much hassle, Mum. Can't be bothered,' he'd tried to reassure her, to no avail. He'd get some booze in once she'd gone. After all, there was plenty of time. A whole two weeks of not having to make the bed, get moaned at for leaving his wetsuit soaking in the bath, leaving lights on, leaving lights off. Two weeks feasting on takeaway food – Indian, Chinese, pizza, kebabs, fish and chips. Simon had already worked out that the money Judith was leaving behind would rule out any bother of cooking. He'd have the kitchen as immaculate as she'd left it. No sweat! It would do Mum good, too, he reasoned. She enjoyed a challenge and she might even meet a new bloke. Instead, he'd enjoy a break from all the Beethoven blasting out of the sound system. In the meantime, he was hoping to employ super seduction services on his new girlfriend Lucia. *Let's hope she hates Beethoven*, he mused. *It would be just my luck.*

'I've got Mr Barnes for you.' There was no mistaking Miss Adelaide's brisk telephone manner.

'Hello, Mrs Franks. It's Howard Barnes here. Is it convenient to talk?'

Sarah sensed bad news.

'I'm afraid the house purchase has already gone through,' he said. 'Contracts were exchanged on Monday and completion is on Friday of next week. I must say it was rather swift. Now, don't worry, because this isn't the end of the matter. When your divorce goes through, there has to be a division of assets in the marriage and of course the proceeds of the sale are still very much part of that consideration.'

'But there won't be any assets,' said Sarah slowly. 'Because I think we've both already spent them.'

Mr Barnes realised immediately that he'd not only delivered a shock, he'd received one back. How many more skeletons were there to come out of this marital cupboard? They made another appointment for two days' time.

Sarah sat looking blankly at her computer screen, all colour drained from her face. If only she'd got to see Mr Barnes earlier, if only, if only.

'As usual, too busy bloody shopping,' she muttered to herself. If only she hadn't filled last week with trips to the hairdresser, manicurist, make-up artist, acupuncturist, aromatherapist. Instead of all that, she should have got her head together and gone to a solicitor. *Too late*, she thought. *And it's all my fault.*

Judith was still in a flurry of packing and cleaning as Vicky came off the phone.

'Stand by for a crisis,' she said. 'That was Sarah in a right old state. Seems as though Bostik's managed to get the house sale through already. My God, the grass doesn't grow under that man's feet, does it? Anyway, she's on her way.'

'OK,' said Judith. 'I think I've just about finished the packing so we could reward ourselves with a drink. By the way, I've packed those horrible purple shell suits we found. Yes, I know they're totally naff but they're probably high fashion in Romania, and by the sound of that place we're staying in up in the mountains, we'll probably end up sleeping in them.'

'I just can't imagine you ever buying them in the first place,' said Vicky. 'I've always thought of you as the pinnacle of good taste.'

'I must have been ill,' Judith cut in. 'Anyway, we won't meet anyone we know when we're wearing them. Look at it like this, hon, they don't crease, they won't need ironing and we can always throw them away if the locals get sniffy about them.'

'We could get deported for wearing them,' said Vicky. 'God, I can just see the headlines: Two Girls Deported by Fashion Police.'

'Yeah, yeah, yeah,' drawled Judith. 'Now calm down, we're not shooting inserts for *The Clothes Show*, you know.'

Sarah's old Volvo pulled up outside. Within seconds they were raising glasses of gin and tonic, shoes off, feet up on the sofas, while Vicky and Judith wrestled with mental estimates of what tonight's new and devastating outfit cost. It was another drop-dead-gorgeous suit, dark green this time with a beautiful matching devoré scarf. They caught the name 'Manolo Blahnik' on the shoes, casually tossed into the middle of the room. Big bucks, they both concluded.

'I've got to see my solicitor again on Friday,' said Sarah, 'and he's asked me to think about what grounds I should go for in the divorce. I want to ask you two some rather basic questions, and please, I do want truthful answers, not the ones you think I'd like to hear.'

'Fire away,' said Judith, bracing herself for something unpleasant. She and Vicky exchanged the most subliminal of nods. If she asked, they'd tell. It was too late now for white lies.

Sarah took a deep breath. 'I know I've not been exactly

Goody Two Shoes over the past few years, but you know the reasons why. Alan hasn't been interested in me sexually for years and years. Not so much as an inflection, let alone an erection. I want to know if he's been seeing other women. If you do know anything, please tell me.'

Judith and Vicky exchanged glances again. Vicky took the lead.

'Well, we have speculated, I must be honest,' she said slowly. 'We couldn't understand why your sex life died. Especially yours. I know lots of women go off sex after babies but you've always been a randy little git, ever since we were at university. I'm sure most blokes would be only too pleased to have their wife at home permanently on heat and dying to get into their trousers the minute they were through the door.'

'So what's gone wrong? What's wrong with me?' asked Sarah, the colour in her neck rising.

'Well, our opinion, for what it's worth,' Vicky was picking her words carefully, 'was that we thought perhaps Bostik, I mean Alan, must be gay. You know, a sort of closet camp. He's always been in all-male environments, except when we were all students. Public school, away in the Middle East on ships, all blokes together.

'God knows this is so difficult, Sarah. We could be so totally wrong, but we've always had a sneaking suspicion, Jude and I. Somehow it just made sense, a missing piece of the jigsaw, that sort of thing, but then the week before last I think Jude stumbled on another piece.'

She stopped and bit her lip. Was the wine bar incident just a case of them putting two and two together and coming up with *soixante-neuf*?

'Go on, the week before last. Come on, Jude, I need to know.' Sarah was desperate.

Judith took up the story. 'I was in Cahoots with Lizzie the day Alan was flying back, except that he was already there. You were expecting him in the evening but he was in Cahoots, quite literally, larger than life at lunchtime.'

'Who with?' came the inevitable question.

'A young man. A very beautiful young man. A real head-turner, a serious bit of male model type tottie. But I think every woman in the place realised immediately that he'd never be interested in any of them,' Judith finished lamely.

'Did Alan clock you both?' asked Sarah.

'No, he didn't, Sarah. The truth is he had eyes only for this boy. They seemed engrossed in each other.'

chapter fourteen

'It's not all personal stuff,' Judith explained away the size of her suitcase in comparison to the others as they met up at Stansted airport. Always immaculate, Judith found it impossible to travel light and was slightly embarrassed about the fact.

'It's stuffed mainly with all the food, drinks and presents for the trip,' she explained, hastily.

'So's mine,' chipped in Vicky, trying to get on the same excuse bandwagon.

Cameraman Colin Matthews and sound recordist Ron Bradley grinned to each other. They knew women, all that hair mousse and matching shoe palaver. Both believed in travelling light. After all, they were both used to lugging tons of gear around the world. Anything other than absolute basics did not see a suitcase.

Despite the ribbing about the cases, they held Judith in great respect. They knew that if they turned in the goods, she'd transform it into a great documentary.

Soon they had loaded up four huge trolleys with all the gear and luggage. Customs clearance was straightforward, their carnets stamped as required. So far so good.

Next Judith was introducing everyone to Paul Morrison and Stephanie Bannister, the two charity representatives who were going to accompany them on the trip. She noted with relief that they too seemed to have mountains of luggage. Perhaps they were official suppliers to that Romanian marching army too.

As she fastened her seatbelt, Judith had that familiar pang. It always got to her when she was going away without Simon. It was simply a mother's wrench from her son. She prayed silently he'd be all right while she was away. Next thing she knew, the plane was making its steady ascent, heading for Bucharest. There was no turning back.

Mr Barnes was talking Sarah through the various legal procedures that could be explored if she wished to continue living in the house.

'I'm sorry, Mr Barnes, but I don't think I can face going through all that,' she said finally. 'I want out as much as he does. And as I explained, we've already spent most of the proceeds, so we might as well jack it in.'

She was horribly embarrassed about having to explain her spending spree over the past two weeks.

'No, I'll move out. I can't face that court order business, but thank you for going through it all. I can stay at a friend's for a while, until I've sorted myself out a bit. I just don't think I can spend many more nights under the same roof as that man.'

Mr Barnes nodded in agreement. She looked at the end of her tether. Next item on the agenda was the divorce itself. He outlined the various options, including a two-year separation, which he said was often the most painless.

'Of course, if there is a third party involved – in other words, adultery – then this can make things simpler and cheaper if everyone agrees,' said Mr Barnes delicately. 'I'm afraid I have to put this to you. Do you think your husband is having an affair?'

'Yes, I do,' said Sarah bluntly. 'I've no proof yet but, as sure as hell, I'm going to get it. You see, Mr Barnes, I think my husband is gay. I think he's having an affair with a bloke.'

The flight was unmemorable except for the food. As if offering a taste of the many culinary lowlights to come, a piece of lukewarm pork the consistency of plastic, accompanied by some warmish chips and very dubious gravy, was served up. Even with the roar of the jet engines, the passengers were briefly silenced by the awfulness of the food.

'I knew I should have packed a microwave,' joked Vicky. 'We could have improved this lot with a quick zap.'

'I think Romania needs Delia Smith,' replied Judith. 'I'll be straight on to her agent's office when I get back.'

'I think I'll be straight into Cahoots when I get back,' said Vicky, grinning. 'Wonder if Bostik will still be straight by then. Anyway, this talk won't help. Our stomachs are going to have to get used to this. Not to mention the service.'

Politeness and tact had clearly not been on the agenda at the Charm School for Romanian Air Stewardesses. They marched up and down the aisle in their ill-fitting uniforms with faces like thunder, their unflattering court shoes thumping as if they were wearing jack boots.

'Hey, that was great,' said Colin, mischievously, handing back his plastic tray to one of the stewardesses. 'Any chance of seconds? No? Oh, shame!'

They all hissed under their breath at him, but it appeared not to register with her at all. Not a flicker on the immovable face. Obviously irony, humour and 'the customer is always right' ethos hadn't made it to their training programme either.

The crew all settled into magazines and papers, the plane being too old to boast any sort of in-flight video or entertainment service. Soon they were bumping down at

Bucharest, straining to take in the landscape as they came to a halt. Grey, grey and more grey were Vicky's first impressions. An endless horizon of utilitarian blocks of flats and the criss-crossing lines of old-fashioned trolley buses. It was like stepping back into the fifties. Paul and Stephanie swung into action as soon as they entered the terminal.

'We'll be meeting Josca, who's our guide, here,' said Stephanie. 'He will get you through all the controls. Just follow his lead and have some dollar bills handy.'

Almost on cue, a lean, dark-skinned man in black leather jacket and cap swaggered towards them. He flashed them a toothy half-smile and with a swift nod indicated to them to follow him. He seemed to know most of the armed soldiers standing around the forum.

The crew fell silent. Documentation, passports, visas and carnets were handed over, inspected and re-inspected, checked and re-checked, only punctuated by the odd grunt between all the uniforms. It was getting tense. Then suddenly, as if someone had flicked an invisible switch, Josca got the nod and they were through.

Sarah was busily scanning the Yellow Pages in between typing up lists of operations. *I don't know why I'm bothering*, she thought. The surgeon on duty was the Abominable Slowman again. *He'll never get through this lot in a week, let alone a day.*

Aha, that one looks promising. She ringed a number in the phone book, checked that the coast was clear and dialled the number with her pen top. Since the visit to the manicurist last week for the fixing of a set of glamorous talons, she'd had difficulty using her keyboard and dialling telephone numbers.

A friendly male voice answered almost immediately. 'Spies R Us Detective Agency, how can we help?'

Sarah outlined her request, constantly scanning the office in case someone came near enough to eavesdrop.

'Well if it's any comfort, it's not the first time we've investigated this particular type of case. Can you pop into the office, say at lunchtime, and we could get things sorted fairly quickly. I get the impression there's a bit of haste involved here. No time like the present, then.'

Someone had taken a dislike to the Hotel Bucharest. Either it was in the last stages of concrete cancer or it had been shot at. The crew decided the latter. There were bullet holes everywhere and on the building opposite. It must have been quite a shoot-out.

Reading their thoughts, Josca explained in his limited English that the hotel had played host to some of the terrorists who had brought about the revolution more than a decade ago. Josca, Judith noted, did not give away any opinion on the revolution. Whether it was a good or bad thing, he was not betraying as much as a flicker. He just related the facts without feeling. *My God, they must still be so repressed*, she thought, remembering all the rumours about hotel lobbies being bugged by the secret police, the Securitate. The thought made her shiver. No wonder he was non-committal.

In its heyday, the hotel must have been quite grand but now the old dowager duchess had resigned herself to a very faded glory. Huge glass chandeliers hung in the large reception area, but they were very lacklustre affairs, each one boasting only a couple of tiny light bulbs and in desperate need of a good clean. A graceful, wide sweeping staircase dominated the area, curving its way majestically to the next floor. Yet the carpet was so threadbare that any decipherable pattern had long since worn away. *What an entrance you could have made, wafting down those stairs in a knockout frock*, thought Vicky.

Beyond the staircase was a rather spartan bar area with some thirty small tables and chairs. Plain and utilitarian, in its heyday it had probably been Bucharest's equivalent of Cahoots. The place to be and be seen, to meet and be met. Today it was full of lunchtime drinkers, yet there was no jollity, raised voices and shared laughter. The conversation level was low and sombre. It was really quite spooky.

'Didn't see any mention of comedy clubs in the guide book,' said Colin, grinning. 'Don't think this is quite the place to start my new career as a stand-up.'

Staff in cheap uniforms covered in brass buttons wandered aimlessly up and down behind the huge polished wooden reception desk. No smiles, no welcome, no 'have a nice day'. Instead, another session of the Romanian national sport of form filling.

Considering this was supposed to be one of Bucharest's top hotels, the rooms brought a new meaning to the word basic. Judith took in the thin sheets, rough blankets, the single pillow, shabby nylon carpet and lopsided curtains. A huge television dominated the room, which was an unexpected comfort. The tiny, windowless bathroom was difficult to evaluate because it did not have the benefit of a light bulb. She'd sort that out later. But at least it was reasonably clean and bright. The main thing was to ring Simon. No bedside phone, but thank goodness her mobile worked.

'Hi, Mum. Bet you're whooping it up already! Lucky you,' came his cheery voice down the line. She decided not to contradict him.

Time to meet downstairs for lunch and then work. Another uniformed charmer clanked shut the ancient lift doors, Judith indicated the ground floor and they were soon making their descent. Lost in thought, she walked out of the lift as a small group were entering. As the doors shut again, she realised she had alighted too soon – on the first floor. *Oh well, I'll just swan down that enormous staircase*, she thought.

As Judith picked her way down the stairs, in her imagination she could have been Gloria Swanson in *Sunset Boulevard*, or the heroine in the last scene of a Gene Kelly movie. Halfway down, she became aware of the ground-floor bar they'd spotted when they arrived. Two more steps down and she realised that the bar was still full. Another step, and they all fell totally silent. One more step, and they were blatantly staring.

What the hell am I doing wrong? thought Judith, panicking inside but determined not to let it show. She braved the last few steps and headed purposefully for the front of the hotel.

'Did you get the big freeze from the bar?' she asked Vicky and Colin, who were already waiting.

'What on earth do you mean?' said Vicky.

'Well I got out of the lift a floor too early so I came down that big staircase and everyone in the bar just shut up and gaped. I felt a right twit.'

'Perhaps they think you're Gwyneth Paltrow,' said Colin unhelpfully.

'More like Glynis Pultroon's ageing mother,' shrugged Judith.

They agreed to try out a new pizzeria which Josca had apparently recommended. Anything to put off the on-slaught of cold pork and chips. Settling down with menus, they all ordered different toppings, while Vicky tried to guess their star signs from what they'd chosen.

'Ham and pineapple, a perfect combination of tastes. You must be a Libran, Colin,' she announced. 'And Ron's chosen the prawn and tuna topping. Very interesting. Two fish. You must be Pisces.'

'That's incredible,' said Colin, mocking. 'That's just totally incredible.' He paused. 'And totally wrong. Anyway I don't believe in horrible-scopes.'

After what seemed a lifetime and two fairly decent bottles of local red wine, the pizzas arrived. The expressionless waitress, helped by Josca, matched the orders to the customers. Once she had retreated through the tatty curtain to, presumably, the kitchen, they could control their laughter no more. Despite the loving descriptions on the menu and the palaver of serving, they'd all been served exactly the same pizza, lukewarm and rubbery.

Ever the gentleman, Ron launched into a routine of offering sample tastings of his pizza in exchange for the others. But they couldn't really contain themselves. Even Josca, who'd obviously been sufficiently Westernised to appreciate their sense of humour, laughed with the best of them.

'Unbelievable,' gushed Colin when the dour waitress returned to collect the plates. 'I can honestly say I have never tasted anything like it.'

chapter fifteen

Sarah slowly checked up and down the street before she nipped through the door and up the stairs to the first-floor offices. Spies R Us, she winced at the sign on the door. At least the girls would have a laugh over this.

The office was predictably scruffy. The half a dozen chairs were well past their sell-by date, a huge spider plant in one corner was clearly in its death throes. The walls were covered in an ancient flock wallpaper which was coming away from the walls. It had the feel of a run-down Chinese restaurant. You could almost smell the mono-sodium glutamate, oozing from the plaster.

Spies R Us supremo Fred Grover introduced himself and ushered Sarah into his office with a confident air. However, the air itself was more along the lines of a kip-pering plant. Mr Grover clearly smoked for Britain and it was difficult to see across the small room for the smog. Unperturbed, Sarah fished out a packet of cigarettes from her bag without needing to ask if there was a smoking ban. She'd been gasping for one since leaving the office, and since all the recent strain, she'd given up lunch in favour of coffee and ciggies.

'I don't have much time,' she explained as calmly as she could. 'A week today our house is being sold and I've got to know what my husband is up to. He's become very secretive since he came home from the Middle East. My friends think he's seeing someone else. Er, but that someone else is, well they think, it's possible, although of course they could be wrong, but I've always suspected and they said they always had, but we could have the wrong end of the stick and just be imagining things,' she finished lamely.

'From my experience, Mrs Franks, if women suspect their husbands are playing away, they probably are,' said Mr Grover, casually lighting another cigarette from the butt of the previous one. 'On the other hand, when we suggest to men that their wives might be seeking, er, comfort elsewhere, they invariably throw their hands up in total disbelief. Believe me, Mrs Franks, nothing surprises me in this game. We're unshockable here. You name it, we've seen it,' he laughed, exposing a set of yellow teeth.

'Now give me what clues you can. I'll need his car details plus any idea you have of his movements.'

Sarah took a last drag on her cigarette before stubbing it out in the red plastic ashtray in front of her, where many had so obviously gone before. 'I think he's seeing a bloke,' she said simply. 'A boyfriend. What I'm trying to say is that I think he's gay. I need to know and I've got to know by the end of the weekend.'

That was all she could afford, two days of surveillance at Mr Grover's rates. But she was convinced he'd get a result in that time. Alan was now being so secretive and so bizarre that she too was fast becoming unshockable. She had no idea where he was going after next Friday. The subject of the flat they were supposed to be moving into had been conveniently dropped. Alan had taken absolutely no interest in her arrangements.

She gave Mr Grover Alan's new car details and briefly outlined what Judith and Lizzie had seen in Cahoots. They shook hands to clinch the deal, with him assuring her through his nicotined grin that all his staff were fully trained and discreet. Somehow Sarah got the impression that there were no other staff. That Mr Grover was just a one-man band with delusions of grandeur. What the hell, so long as he did the job.

As she strode down the pavement and back to her car, Sarah knew she should have felt sad and ashamed of what she had been reduced to. But the fact that she'd done something positive somehow boosted her and she went back to work feeling a little happier.

Bucharest was busily unveiling her charms on a sunny afternoon. After initial reserve, Josca turned out to be quite an illuminating guide to his native city. But the English sense of humour completely baffled him.

'I think we'll start with a quick nervous,' said Judith.

'Good idea,' replied Colin, loading up his camera and setting the time codes.

'What is a nervous?' queried Josca, sensing trouble.

'Just short for nervous recce,' said Colin. 'Nervous wreck, nervous recce. Recce short for reconnoitre, geddit?'

The joke, of course, got lost in the telling. The two charity workers' grasp of Romanian only extended to ordering from the menu, directions and bartering for petrol. Then Judith tried to explain it in French to Josca, who spoke a little. They all resorted to miming but that didn't work either.

'Where's Clive Anderson?' joked Colin. 'We could do an episode of *Whose Line Is It Anyway?* at this rate.'

'All you need to know, mate,' intervened Ron, indicating Judith, 'is that when she says, "Let's do a nervous," that means we'll have a look around first.'

'OK, OK,' grinned Josca, the ice finally broken. 'Now we do the nervous. I show you the city of Bucharest and where you can safely make your film.'

They piled into two battered cars and moved off in

convoy around the city. Josca pointed out the television station where the revolution had more or less started. He took them to Bucharest's answer to Paris, the Arc de Triumpf – a replica of Paris's famous landmark, and set in the middle of a huge roundabout.

The highlight of the tour was the Palace of Parliament, built by the evil dictator Ceauşescu to house his burgeoning empire of henchmen. The third largest building in the world, it made Buckingham Palace look like very small potatoes.

'There are more than a thousand rooms in that building, with a big car park in the basement,' said Josca, as they all gazed at the magnificent cream building with its tall windows and elegant contours.

'What was here before the palace was built?' asked Judith. Josca did not reply. She'd noticed that he had an attack of selective deafness when an awkward question was asked, and this time she was testing. She actually knew the answer because she'd read it in a guide book. Ceauşescu had simply torn down some very old and beautiful buildings to make way for this ostentatious display of wealth and power. But Josca was playing safe. She didn't blame him. He must have been here in Bucharest during those terrible days of the revolution and who knows what atrocities he'd witnessed? For all they knew, he'd lost some of his family in the crossfire. Whatever it was, it was not up for discussion.

Back at the hotel, Judith sat down with Colin and drew up a shot list. They plotted a route around the city for filming the next day, taking Josca's advice on traffic and parking. The flight and all the form-filling earlier in the day were beginning to take their toll. By majority vote, everyone agreed to have a late afternoon snooze and then eat at the hotel in the evening.

The afternoon sun gone, Judith's hotel room was getting

dark. The one light bulb was soon going to be submitting overtime sheets, commuting from the bedside lamp to the bathroom. The solution to all this was staring her in the face. The television. Remote controls hadn't yet penetrated Romania but the old set sprang to life once she had found the correct switch. *Let's see what Bucharest's favourite buttons have to offer*, she thought, expecting to scan through at least two or three stations. Oh dear, no *Supermarket Sweep* here. Just shash, she tutted, gazing at the endless snow scenes on all the channels. At least it was enough to light the room. The solitary light bulb could now take up permanent residence in the bathroom.

The euphoria of Sarah's brief brush with the world of espionage had worn off. The weekend was now before her, beckoning like the talons of a wicked witch to a bubbling cauldron. She'd made no plans, her friend Anita at the clinic was doing La Grande Bonque Parisienne experience with a new boyfriend. Meanwhile Judith and Vicky were now probably having the time of their lives in Bucharest. It was the last weekend in the house, and the last weekend of her marriage.

Her instincts were to get away, especially with Mr Spies R Us snooping around. But where? She still hadn't told the kids anything, other than warning them that the house was on the market. She had no idea if Alan had spoken to them. He'd not so much as mentioned Roz or Daniel in any of his brief conversations about his 'business plans'. It was as though they didn't exist. Sarah was now certain she was in that category as well. Filed under 'forgotten but not forgiven'.

Sarah walked through her front door and knew she did not want to be there a moment longer than necessary. Still in her coat, she dialled Roz's number, using her car keys as she remembered the size of her manicure bills. She prayed

Roz would be in for once, her daughter being a bit of a party animal.

'Darling, it's Mum.' She breathed a sign of relief at the familiar voice on the end of the line. 'How are you?'

'Fine, Mum, but you sound harassed.' Roz's chirpy tones came down the line.

'No, I'm absolutely fine, fine,' said Sarah, trying to take the agitato out of her voice. 'I was just wondering, er, you know the house is, er, up for sale and it's all a bit of a mess. I just wondered if you were around over the weekend. I know it's short notice and I expect you've plans with Pete so you can just say no because I wouldn't want to be a gooseberry and . . .'

'I've no plans with Pete,' said Roz flatly, her voice changing. 'Not this weekend or any weekend ever. I dumped the skunk last night. Actually, Mum, I'd really, really love you to come. We could go spit on his car and post muddy stones through his letterbox.'

'Oh dear, love, what's happened? What's he done?' Sarah had rather liked Pete, the one and only time she'd met him. He'd been a bit older and more mature than most of Roz's previous boyfriends.

'You name it, he's done it,' snapped Roz. 'I couldn't possibly afford the phone bill to give you chapter and verse so I'll tell you when I see you. By the time you get here, I will have finished my first book, *The Compleat Bastard*. Oh by the way, Fiona's away this weekend. She won't mind you having her room, so don't book a hotel or anything.'

Just as well, thought Sarah, whose fistful of new credit cards was starting to be refused.

'Oh, Mum, bring something nice to wear. I've got some free tickets to the opening of a new wine bar tomorrow night. We'll have to tart up just in case that skunk turns up.'

The Hotel Bucharest's restaurant had the most magical

atmosphere, with its chandeliers and crisp white table cloths. Although the light bulbs weren't in abundance here either, somehow the dimness seemed quite appropriate. There was a faded glory about the place. If the wood-panelled walls could have talked, they would have certainly told tales of scandal, plotting and indiscretion involving royalty, power and politics. Waiters in long white aprons presented them all with leather-bound menus, which lovingly listed the various dishes on offer. Trout, salmon and prawn dishes, roast meats and accompanying vegetables. They all chose fishy starters and studiously avoided pork for their main courses.

'I'm beginning to think this tale we've all been sold of cold pork and chips is just a load of old Horlicks,' said Vicky, perking up after a couple of sips of red wine.

'Don't count your chickens,' warned Ron. 'No pun intended. Honest.'

A ten-piece orchestra at the far end of the restaurant suddenly struck up. They played a selection of what Judith guessed were Romanian folk tunes, jolly, toe-tapping numbers. The soaring gypsy violins reminded her of Romania's musical heritage and its unhappy relationship with its Hungarian neighbours. She must record some of this for the programme, or find a music shop selling CDs tomorrow.

Soon all the crew, Paul and Stephanie and even Josca were clapping and swaying to the infectious music.

'Can't believe I'm enjoying this,' said Colin. 'I'm more of a Status Quo fan myself. But they're really good.'

The chief violinist broke away from the orchestra to tour the tables, serenading the diners. It was terribly corny, but given the atmosphere, it somehow worked.

Judith was quietly having a quick guilt trip about Simon. She'd been wondering what he would eat tonight. Probably a pizza from the freezer, while here they were, about to enjoy some of Romania's finest cooking. She hoped he'd eat sensibly, remember to turn off the taps and not leave the Internet running.

The waiter interrupted her thoughts. He quietly explained in respectable but very limited English that several of the dishes they'd ordered were not available.

By now, though, the wine had been flowing, along with the music, and everyone was in a good mood. The waiter couldn't believe he'd got off so lightly. He went back to the kitchen with a pronounced spring in his step.

As the orchestra struck up once more, a wooden trolley made its approach to their table. Plates of vivid red salami and goat's cheese were unloaded.

'So much for the scallops and smoked trout,' said Colin, laughing. Silence descended as they tucked in. In deference to Josca, no one said much. The salami was tough, the cheese mushy and the bread stale.

'Unbelievable,' pronounced Ron, clearing his plate.

'Incredible,' offered Colin.

The squeaky wheels of the wooden trolley approached again. As one army of waiters scooped up the empty plates, another lot served up the main course.

'Thank goodness,' said Ron. 'How did they know? This is my all-time favourite. Pork and chips! Brilliant, and they've got it just how I like it – not too hot.'

'Great meal,' said Vicky sarcastically when they had finished. 'I shouldn't have opened my big mouth about the pork and chips. You never know, I could lose a bit of weight at this rate. I've never been a salad fan but after twenty-four hours of this junk, I fell on that old bit of tomato garnish. I could learn to love lettuce at this rate.'

'Or not,' said Judith. 'Here comes the pudding menu.'

Again the waiters brandished leather-bound menus which described everything from apricot torte to zabaglione. Once again, orders were taken, and a few minutes later, once again apologies were expressed. There was a little vanilla ice cream but only enough for three. The guys valiantly insisted that the three women should be the lucky ones. They rounded off the meal with coffee.

'Hmm, delicious,' murmured Colin, laughing. The coffee tasted as though it had been brewed hours ago. It was virtually cold.

Vicky looked across at Colin and felt a momentary pang. He was too young for her and she was too old for him. But he was fun, full of stories and he seemed to make the best of everything. For a brief few moments, she imagined she was in bed with him, feeling his warm and comfortable body up against her and doing wonderfully despicable things to her. She felt herself blushing. It was more than a month since she'd had sex with Roger. And that had been about as passionate as watching paint dry.

When it was time to go, they waved cheerily to the orchestra. Back out in the hotel foyer, the chandeliers had taken on an eerie aspect with their sparse light bulbs. As they waited for the ancient lifts to crank their way down to the ground floor, they were all puzzled by the sound of young high-pitched voices, all chorusing, 'Hello, hello.' In unison, they looked across to the bar area, and in unison, they all looked away again. It was full of girls, some as young as fourteen, all vying for attention. They wore almost a uniform of short skirts, cropped tops and smashed-on make-up that made them look rather grotesque.

'Oh God,' murmured Colin, the first to clock the situation. They all gazed straight ahead at the lift doors, willing them to open. Two sinister-looking pimps started to make their approach.

'What's the Romanian for S and M?' asked Ron, trying to make light of the situation.

'Gawd knows,' retorted Colin. 'Anyway, I'd have put you down as more of an M and S man.'

'That's why you got all that silence from the bar when you came down that big staircase this morning,' said Ron quietly to Judith. 'They must have all thought you were a brazen hussy on an overnight.'

As the lift doors mercifully opened, there was a virtual stampede inside. When they turned to face the closing doors, they were confronted by the pimps, who had reached the lift entrance and were holding up signs on which was scribbled in English: 'Special offer. Two for one price.'

'Bargain,' proclaimed Ron, joking. 'Do you give air miles as well?'

With perfect timing, the doors immediately closed and they made their way up to a decent night's sleep and dreams about cold pork and chips.

chapter sixteen

'Bloody hell, Mum, you look amazing,' gasped Roz at Sarah standing on her doorstep. 'What the hell have you been up to?'

'I'm dying for a cigarette and a drink and then I'll tell all,' replied Sarah, pecking her daughter on the cheek.

Roz led the way up the corridor and into the small kitchen. It was a typical rented London flat, a little unloved and frayed around the edges. *Like me*, thought Sarah bitterly. The kitchen was the predictable bombsite of any young girls' flat. Not much evidence of nutrition going on but loads of candles in empty wine bottles and the obligatory week's worth of washing up.

'Don't bother,' said Sarah, realising Roz was rooting for a bottle of wine in a chaotic larder cupboard. 'Just get two glasses and I'll do the rest.'

She produced a bottle of Chardonnay from her shoulder bag while Roz hastily washed up two glasses from the pile on the draining board.

'It's not chilled, but who cares,' she said, fumbling in her bag for a lighter.

'Where's the bloody corkscrew?' muttered Roz. 'I bet that twonk's put it somewhere stupid.'

'Twonk?'

'Cross between a total twit and an absolute plonker,'

explained Roz. 'That's Pete. I'll tell you about all that later. Oh God, Mum, you look dreadful.'

'Hang on a minute. You said I looked amazing when I walked in.'

'Well, you look different somehow, and I love your hair and that suit – it's terrific – but you don't look well.'

The strip light in the kitchen was not the most conducive to the 'just dumped' look. All the weight Sarah had lost in the last three weeks had gone from her face.

Sarah was examining her daughter too. Swollen eyelids and sallow skin indicated a prolonged period of sobbing.

'Look, love, you look pretty dreadful too,' replied Sarah. 'Let's find somewhere more flattering away from this bloody strip light to sit down and you can tell me your news and I'll tell you mine. Why not light some of those candles and we'll both look a damn sight better.'

They moved off into the communal lounge, which was another après holocaust experience. In order to sit on the sofas, they cleared off various sweaters and kicked aside several pairs of impossibly high-heeled shoes. A pair of boxer shorts bearing the legend 'Oh, go on then' was hastily shifted together with a pile of old *Hello!* magazines, so ancient that at least two of the marriages featured on the front were well and truly into injury time. Due to a lack of springs, no life left in the cushions and, Sarah suspected, loads of late-night grapplings, they both sank in unison almost to the floor.

'Sorry about the mess, Mum,' apologised Roz. 'It's not always like this.'

'Well it always was in my student flats,' said Sarah. 'We all hung our clothes on sky hooks, so don't worry. Now let's get this out of the way. What's wrong with Pete and why is it all over? Do you want to talk about it?'

'There's not much to tell,' said Roz, gulping her wine. 'In fact there's bugger all to tell. I must have been so stupid.'

'What?' said Sarah, trying to keep the urgency out of her voice. 'Come on, darling, you're not stupid. What happened?'

'Silly, silly me. Only the mobile phone number, never went to his house, always the excuse, always meeting in out-of-the-way places, never on a Saturday night. I'm just kicking myself for being so utterly thick. I found out yesterday that the bastard's married and his wife is very, very pregnant.'

'Oh shit,' said Sarah, her heart inwardly sinking. 'Now come on, darling, he deceived you. You weren't to know. It happens to loads of people. At least you've found out sooner rather than later. How did you find out, by the way?'

'A real own goal. She rang me up. She'd obviously checked the phone bill or did that last number redial thingy. We had an illuminating little chat. I don't think she believed me when I said I had no idea he was married.'

'What did you do then?'

'I phoned the bastard on his mobile and left the equivalent of a "Dear John" message. He hasn't phoned back. I hope he's being beaten to a pulp at home. He certainly would be if he ever turned up here.'

Sarah topped up their glasses and offered Roz a tissue to catch the tears now starting to trickle down her face.

'Next time, there won't be a next time,' she soothed. 'You'll be much more on your guard. There's no harm in that. Men can get desperate for a leg-over especially when their wives are pregnant. Some men get very frightened about pregnancy. They see the woman they married become the size of a number-ten bus. This wasn't your fault, you trusted him. But next time, you'll know the warning signs.'

I wish I'd spotted them myself, thought Sarah bitterly. *Then I wouldn't be in such a mess either.* Funny how you can see the solution to other people's problems but never your own.

'Now let's have another glass of that Chateau Blotto and then sort out something to eat,' said Sarah brightly, fumbling for another ciggie in her bag. 'What's the best takeaway around these parts? I'm too tired to cook after that drive up here and trying to park. And so are you, by the look of you.'

Actually Sarah couldn't face wading through the mess in the kitchen but her daughter was not in the right frame of mind to be told that.

'Chinese is the best and they deliver,' said Roz, rummaging for a menu.

'Thank God for that, because that Chardonnay has gone to my head. I'd be done for drink walking.'

Saturday afternoon and it was time to leave the city for the mountains. Josca said his farewells at the airport. He'd done all the wheeling and dealing to get the crew through customs. This time it had needed bribes to get their tickets accepted. But they were all getting used to this routine now. Nothing was simple or straightforward in Romania, nothing at all. Stern faces and grunts were clearly the national sport. In fact there'd been a competition going among the crew to try and make someone in uniform smile. They'd nearly succeeded during the x-ray stage when two solid women built like brick powder rooms had waved what resembled crude table-tennis bats all over them. The table-tennis bats made loud squeaks, rather like farting noises.

'Must give the baked beans a miss tomorrow,' joked Colin.

'You'll be grateful for some baked beans after a few days of where we're going,' warned Stephanie. She and Paul had begun to loosen up with the crew now they'd all got to know each other. They were quietly impressed at the way everyone worked and had a laugh along the way. The worse the conditions, the more the jokes flew. The next stage, however, would be a real test of humour.

Now they were bound on a short flight to Oradea, up near the Hungarian border. Ron and Colin were suffering from secret hangovers they'd acquired from drinking too much Pinot Noir the night before. It was the only decent thing they'd tasted so far and they'd had rather a skinful. At least it helped you to sleep, even if it left you feeling sick with a thumping headache in the morning. They'd both skipped breakfast and were desperate not to let the side down. Colin concentrated on the portly air stewardess in an attempt to stop himself feeling queasy. As she squeezed herself up and down the aisle, distributing dry biscuits and cold coffee, he tried to imagine what she'd look like in the buff. A fright, he decided.

Ron immersed himself in a computer magazine in an attempt to divert himself from his heaving stomach.

'Not exactly a ripping read,' commented Judith, looking across from the next seat.

'Waddya mean?' said Ron.

'You've been on that same page for at least three quarters of an hour,' grinned Judith. 'It must be un-put-downable. Bags I borrow it next.'

Meanwhile Vicky decided to read the book on Romania she'd brought with her. She turned to the phrase section in an attempt to pick up a few useful words. It was all basic stuff, directions, meals and homage to the state.

'Several pages about restaurants, I see,' commented Colin, who'd now perked up next to her. 'I'm amazed there are so many words for food in this country. I wonder who made them all up. Is there one of those crazy emergency sections?'

'No,' said Vicky, checking the index. 'Obviously they don't have emergencies here. I've always wondered what it would be like the other way round. What sort of phrases they'd put in English books for foreigners.'

'Oh they'd have to have things like, "Please feel free to queue", or "For the convenience of passengers travelling to Waterloo, the bar and buffet is now shut",' said Colin. 'Or there'd be a section of phrases for when you appear on television game shows. Things like, "P please Bob," or tips on appearing in *Stars In Their Eyes* with phrases like, "Tonight Matthew I'm going to be Glen Miller."'

'Glen Miller?' queried Vicky.

'Yeah, Glen Miller. You go into those clouds and you don't come out again.'

Vicky roared with laughter. Colin was so easy to talk to, even over the din of the aircraft. What a difference to boring old Roger and the tedious world at Tressed Out. Colin instinctively liked Vicky too, although he wasn't attracted to her. He thought she could have done with losing a stone but he'd never have said so. He knew how neurotic women were about their weight. All she needed was a bit of an overhaul, he thought, and she was wearing some rather appalling clothes.

I wish I was thinner, thought Vicky. *I could do with someone like Colin*. She began to wish she and Judith hadn't packed all those old clothes for the trip. And they hadn't even brought out the purple shell suits yet. Now there'd be a fair amount of ribbing about those. They were real show stoppers.

Sarah'd never really known what it was like to be a single twenty something. She'd been pregnant and married at the end of her university days so she'd never had the chance. Roz's Fulham lifestyle wore her out. After a slow start, getting out of bed at around eleven, they'd had a token breakfast of coffee and cigarettes and were then hurtling off round the corner to the tube station.

Sarah had almost forgotten the grime and debris of the

metropolis. The smells, the sounds, the multi-cultural atmosphere, picking their way across old cabbage leaves from the street market as the stall holders shouted their wares, anxious to close up and get into the pub.

Like worms, they slithered underground and on to the tube. Like ants, they bustled out at Oxford Street for an afternoon session of retail therapy. Cheering up Roz had helped Sarah put her own problems aside. Roz was so pre-occupied with her own misery that she hadn't even asked after her father or about the house sale. That suited Sarah for a while. She wasn't sure she could trust herself not to spill out the entire story, which would not do Roz any favours just now.

They were searching for the perfect outfit for Roz to wear to the opening of the new wine bar later that evening. Roz was convinced that Pete would be there, and she wanted to show him what he was missing. In and out of Miss Selfridge, Top Shop and any number of boutiques selling minuscule dresses, Sarah thought her feet were about to give up and die. Finally, the perfect outfit was spotted in a boutique called Let's Go Clubbing. A short black slip dress that Sarah had to admit really did suit Roz.

'Just got to find the shoes now,' said Roz, steering her mother through the traffic and the crowds across Oxford Circus for what seemed the umpteenth time.

'At least we could sit down,' replied Sarah, wilting by the minute. They spent half an hour in Shelleys along with what seemed like half the population of London, where Roz tried on endless pairs of shoes, none of which Sarah would have given house room. Eventually the right pair was found, four-inch heels in black suede, wrapped and paid for. Roz was happy now.

She takes after me, thought Sarah. *She finds shopping as therapeutic as I do. Just hope she doesn't get herself into the mess I'm currently in.*

'You haven't bought anything, Mum,' exclaimed Roz, suddenly finding her social conscience.

'Oh don't worry about me, darling. I've had a bit of a spree recently. But I'll tell you what I am going to buy.'

'What's that?'

'Lunch.'

They found a little Italian restaurant just down a side street with cheap and cheerful check tablecloths and a waft of garlic so strong that it could have stripped paint. They ordered fizzy water and a bottle of house red while they studied the menus.

'We'll both have the fettuccine,' said Sarah to the hovering waiter.

'Would you like garlic bread with that?' he enquired. She nodded.

'Silly not to,' grinned Sarah, after he'd scurried off. 'We're going to absolutely pong of the stuff anyway.'

Roz took a sip of red wine, a drag from her cigarette, and came straight to the point.

'All right, Mum, what's up? You've got a problem and it's written all over your face. It's Dad, isn't it?'

Sarah put her glass down and looked Roz in the eye.

'I can't lie to you, love. Yes it is your dad and it's everything really,' she blurted out. 'The house has been sold and I have to move out next Friday.'

'You said "I". What about Dad? Where does he fit into all this?'

'To be truthful, I just don't know. Your dad seems to have a different agenda. Oh look, Roz, it's no good beating about the bush. I think our marriage is over. I can't think of any other way of telling you.'

'Oh Mum.' Tears started trickling down Roz's cheeks. She got up and rushed off in the direction of the loo, colliding with the waiter bearing huge, steaming plates of fettuccine.

Several minutes later, she returned looking shame-faced.

'Sorry, Mum.' She hugged Sarah before she sat down again. 'That wasn't fair. You must be having a dreadful time.'

'Don't be silly, darling, it's just as difficult for you. I've also given you a terrible shock. Your dad and I have grown apart over the years and what's happened to us happens to lots of couples when their kids leave home. They're suddenly flung together all the time and realise sadly it's not so good any more.'

'Oh come on, Mum. Dad was never there anyway. When Dan and I left home, we both felt awful because we knew you'd be on your own. We talked about it quite a lot. It's funny, although I was so shocked just now when you told me, I'm not really surprised, now I start to think of it. You two never seemed to get on, but as kids we just assumed that's what all parents were like. It's only since I left home that I realised how unhappy you probably were. By the way, does Desperate Dan know yet?'

Roz secretly adored her elder brother but would never admit as much. They'd had their ups and downs as children, with Roz always jealous that Dan seemed to do better in his exams with apparently no effort whatsoever. She'd had to slog for her mediocre grades.

'No, I don't think so. I certainly haven't told him. I don't know whether your father has,' said Sarah. 'Dan's away on a business trip at the moment and it's not the sort of thing you leave on a message machine, is it?'

'No,' replied Roz. 'So what's happening about the house?'

'Well, the sale completes on Friday, and your dad was talking about giving up the Middle East and putting the funds into some sort of new business. There was talk of us renting a flat for a while but that seems to have gone by the board. So I'm going to stay at my friend Judith's house in Southampton for a few days. You remember her, we were at university here all those years ago. And then I'll have a bit of a think.'

'And what about Dad? Where's he moving to?'

'I don't know, love. You'll have to ask him that yourself. He's being very cagey. He's just got himself a mobile phone so I'll try and get the number for you.'

'Sorry, Mum, I hate to say this but I think he's having an affair,' said Roz, with her new-found worldly wisdom. 'There are all the signs. It's all sounding very furtive to me. Now you tell me he's bought a mobile phone. Well that's a turn-up for the books. He was always such a mean sod.'

Sarah smiled inwardly. In less than twenty-four hours they'd done a complete role reversal.

'So what are you going to do about it?' demanded Roz, getting heated. 'I hope you're going to confront this floozy and tell her a few home truths.'

If only she knew the real truth, thought Sarah. Even now the head and only honcho from Spies R Us was probably trailing Alan to some sordid little rendezvous with his beautiful toyboy.

'No, darling,' she said firmly. 'I've had enough. I'm tired of it all and I'm going to make things as easy as possible. He's still your father, you know.'

'Well I think he's being a total shit. Anyway, talking of total shits, we'd better get a move on. We've got to get back to the flat to tart up for the wine bar opening tonight. Pete might be there and I want to look drop-dead gorgeous.'

'Are you sure you want me to trail along?' said Sarah. 'Honestly, I'd be quite happy to watch telly while you go out. I don't want to let you down.'

'Mum, you never let me down. I really want you to come. Besides, you seem to have brought a bag full of amazing new clothes so you'll look terrific anyway.'

'I didn't buy them at Let's Go Clubbing, that's for sure,' said Sarah, fingering her credit card ready to pay the bill. *Let's hope this one doesn't get refused.*

chapter seventeen

The new wine bar, Corks Away, sounded ghastly, Sarah decided, thinking wistfully of Cahoots for a moment. But the weekend was certainly having the desired effect. She had stopped dwelling on her problems and was concentrating on Roz's current grief.

Understated, she thought, *that's how I want to look tonight. Understated, so nobody will notice me.* She donned charcoal grey trousers, pale grey silk top and a beautiful embroidered lilac pashmina, remembering with a shudder what it had cost. *I might be losing my home, but at least I'll have some decent clothes to wear for a while.*

Sarah was still wrestling with her new more sophisticated hairdo and make-up, but even she had forgotten just how long it took someone of Roz's age to get ready. She was coiffed, perfumed and dressed, had watched an entire episode of *Blind Date* and had a reasonable stab at the *Daily Express* crossword before Roz emerged in the new black dress and shoes.

'You look fantastic,' she exclaimed as her daughter whirled around the tiny lounge. 'Mind you, you could be done for manslaughter if you kick anyone with those shoes. I love heels but even I'd have to admit defeat over those. I'd get vertigo wearing them. Or maybe I'd get done for wearing an offensive weapon.'

'Thanks a bunch, Mum,' replied Roz, flashing newly varnished rouge noir nails. 'Now let's get a cab and then get bladdered.'

Oh God, thought Sarah. *This is definitely all going to end in tears.*

They baled out twenty-five minutes later in Chelsea, where revellers at the opening night of Corks Away were already spilling out on to the pavement. The happy hour was in full swing as they elbowed their way to the bar. Minutes later, clutching glasses of Chilean red, because they'd read in the paper that day that it stopped you getting cancer, they buffeted their way back out to the relative quiet of the pavement.

'If we drink this muck, does it mean we can still have a cigarette and it doesn't count?' queried Sarah, fishing one-handed into her bag for a packet and her lighter. 'I feel like I've done ten rounds already.'

'You forget what London's like, Mum. It's always a scrum wherever you go.'

'I'm beginning to feel like my own grandmother,' said Sarah, lighting two cigarettes and handing her daughter one. 'I hope I'm not embarrassing you. I do seem to be the oldest here by several decades. And I note that I'm also the only woman in this bar not wearing a skirt up round her knickers.'

'Don't worry, Mum, if you were embarrassing, you wouldn't be here. But I think you're right. You're most definitely the oldest.'

'Thanks a bunch.'

But Roz had stopped listening. She was straining to see through the crowd and the gaps in the stained glass window. She'd gone horribly pale.

'He's here, the bastard,' she hissed. 'I was right, he couldn't keep away. Especially if there's cheap drink on offer.'

'So what's the plan?' said Sarah, wondering what those

etiquette books would have said was the form for meeting your daughter's married ex-boyfriend. Hit him with your handbag, denounce him in public or swap e-mail addresses?

'We do nothing,' said Roz. 'He's clocked us. If he's any sense he'll avoid us like the plague. Or else he'll have a major scene on his hands.'

Sarah glanced back through the door at the packed wine bar. It rather resembled a cattle market. The corks were certainly away tonight. Everyone seemed to be pouring huge glasses of wine down their throats and leering at each other as if it were going out of style. Salsa music boomed out incessantly, which meant that any conversation inside consisted of shouting. Was this what she had to look forward to in her new single life? At this rate, roll on a good book, a spot of needlepoint and a night in with a couple of Sanatogen slammers.

Seeing the agitation in Roz's eyes, Sarah scanned the crowd for a man she'd met once, quite liked but would never in a million years have picked out in an identity parade. They could have taken bookings for the pavement, it was filling up so fast. It was elbow to elbow even out on the street.

'I bet he'll be playing breast cricket tonight,' hissed Roz half under her breath.

'Breast cricket, what the hell's that?' asked Sarah, appalled. 'I've heard of topless darts but not breast cricket.'

'It's blokes' stupid idea of a bit of fun in crowded places like this. You get one run for a brush past, four runs for a full elbow and a six for hands on,' explained Roz, as if it were the most normal thing on the planet.

'Do men really do that these days in public?' said Sarah, even more appalled.

'When they're a bit pissed and cheered on by their mates, they do.'

'What are we coming to, whatever happened to respect?' said Sarah, now totally appalled.

'Wasn't it a song years ago by Aretha Franklin?' replied Roz. 'You'll get used to it, Mum, in your new single life. In fact I've got a friend who got so badly screwed up by various boyfriends that now she only goes out with people she doesn't fancy. That way she gets the rumpy pumpy but not the pain. When you see dorks like this everywhere, you can understand why. Let's get some more drinks.'

'Do you want me to keep our pitch here?' said Sarah, stubbing her cigarette out on the pavement with her foot.

'No, come in with me. I might need moral support. Or there again, you might need to resuscitate the bastard. How's your first aid?'

They began the slow struggle to the bar, Roz pushing and shoving ahead with Sarah trying to keep up. They were ten deep at the bar with the music getting louder by the minute. Roz had just finished paying for another couple of glasses of the Chilean red when she felt a hand go up under her skirt and tug at her G-string. She wheeled round in a fury, took in Pete's inane grinning face and neatly raised her knee in the direction of his crotch, simultaneously spilling most of the wine down his shirt. It all happened in less than three seconds.

'Out of here,' shouted Roz to her mother. They pushed and shoved their way out of the wine bar, through the crowds on the pavement and away a few yards up the street. The September air now had a very pronounced autumn pinch to it. Both of them shivered, feeling the contrast after the sweaty atmosphere in the wine bar.

'I gather that was Pete,' said Sarah. 'I wouldn't have recognised him.'

'You won't need to again,' said Roz, shaking with emotion. 'It all happened so fast. I can't believe I just did that.

He'll have a bit of explaining to do when he gets home. Bastard deserves it.'

'Back to the flat?' said Sarah.

'Nope. Too soon. The night is young, madness is a broad! Or even two broads. We'll get a cab back to Fulham and have a drink in the Irish pub near my flat.'

Fifteen minutes later, they were ensconced in a corner of the dimly lit pub, scanning the mostly pensionable age clientele and sipping more glasses of Chilean red.

'Cheeky little number,' joked Sarah, sniffing the wine and taking a sip. 'It certainly travels well.'

'Especially did down that bastard's shirt.'

'Exactly.'

A small Irish show band struck up with a rather ragged version of 'When Irish Eyes Are Smiling' and a fat woman in a salmon pink satin dress, so tight it must have been sprayed on, took the mic and sang. What they lacked in musical ability they certainly made up for in enthusiasm.

At least you can get a drink, a seat and a conversation here, thought Sarah. Beats all that salsa, and shouting. And no breast cricket either.

Sarah awoke with a start. For a few moments, she couldn't remember where she was. Then she heard a bus go past the window, and then the diesel rattle of a taxi. She could hear the voices of revellers spilling out of the cab and on to the pavement. Of course, she was still in Fulham.

She realised her head was pounding. That Chilean red might keep cancer at bay but it was absolutely bang on for hangovers. The pain concentrated over her right eye. Her watch said seven o'clock, but which seven o'clock?

As she peered through the strange yet familiar curtains, it all came flooding back. She and Roz had chatted and drunk wine into the wee small hours, cursed the male species generally and put the world to rights. But now it was Sunday, time to go home and face the music. Time to find out for certain what Alan was really up to. She shivered with nerves and then felt very queasy. *Mustn't be sick*, she told herself, *not here*. She took some deep breaths and concentrated hard on the artex pattern on the ceiling. *God, that's really naff*, she thought, realising the moment of sickness had passed.

The events of the previous evening came to her in a series of flashbacks. Poor Roz had been so distraught about Pete but they had at least had some fun with the knee-in-the-crotch and the wine-down-the-shirt.

'I hope it never washes out,' Roz had declared defiantly. 'I might be out of his head and his heart but I'll always be the stain on his shirt.'

Sarah wandered into the kitchen. She found two mugs among the piles of dishes and washed them thoroughly under the tap. The teapot had a garden growing in it, so she just popped a tea bag into each of the mugs. At least the milk was fresh. She'd bought it yesterday.

Clutching her steaming mug, she sat down at the tiny kitchen table, lit a cigarette and began to think of the week ahead. There'd be the results from Spies R Us on Monday, followed by the sale of the house and moving into Judith's on Friday. Not exactly a run-of-the-mill week, she noted.

Her thoughts were interrupted by Roz, a dishevelled figure in a navy towelling dressing gown, a far cry from the high-heeled disco goddess of last night.

'Sorry, darling, I suffer from strange bedroom syndrome,' said Sarah by way of explanation. 'I couldn't sleep, woke up wondering where I was and with a thumping hangover. I didn't mean to wake you.'

'Don't worry, I wasn't asleep,' replied Roz. 'Couldn't really sleep either. Any of that tea going?'

'Of course, I've already made you some. Wasn't quite sure whether to bring it in and disturb you.'

They sat at the table nursing their mugs, trying to cheer one another up and disguise their own particular heartache.

'By the way, Mum, it's absolutely not up for discussion. I'm coming down to Hampshire at the end of the week to help you move. You can't go through all that on your own.'

'Oh, darling, you don't have to. I'm sure you've got better things to do. I'll manage.'

'No you won't. Your two best mates are whooping it up with the vampires in Transylvania or somewhere. Anyway, I want to see Dad. I want to know what's going on and I think he owes me an explanation.'

Sarah knew that look in Roz's eye. Her daughter was a very determined woman with a strong sense of right and wrong.

'If you do find out, perhaps you'd let me know,' said Sarah meekly. She still hadn't told Roz about Alan's gay lover. Somehow, until Spies R us confirmed the awful truth, it wasn't a problem. Until then it would not exist.

By Monday, though, it just might.

It was pitch black when they finally landed at the tiny airport in Oradea. As the plane taxied around, they caught sight of a dimly lit shed-type building. This was clearly where the next round of officialdom would be waiting for them. Judith had dollar bills ready in her pocket as Josca had instructed. Bribery was becoming a way of life.

This time, though, it was not needed. A handful of soldiers were sitting at a table passing a bottle of clear liquid around, each pouring themselves measures into shot glasses. They grunted at the passengers, indicated the exit with a flick of the head, and carried on with their drinking.

Soon they were out in the cold night meeting their next guide, a tall, lanky lad who introduced himself as Dinu. He was obviously popular with Stephanie and Paul, who greeted him like a long-lost son. He pointed to two battered old identical Dacia cars being guarded by the other driver, Andrasi, who was wearing the obligatory black leather jacket and beret, and dragging heavily on a roll-up. They all began the laborious process of loading up the kit. It was rather a feat, squeezing everything and everybody in, especially in the darkness.

Eventually the cars set off, spluttering their way through the town and off up into the mountains. No street lights, no road signs, noted Judith. But then there probably wasn't very much in the way of nightlife.

The journey up to their hotel would take about an hour, Dinu assured them as the cars pitched and rolled through the potholes. They all fell silent, concentrating on the pain of being squashed in with boxes and kit bags balanced on their knees. When Andrasi's car spluttered to a halt, there was almost a wave of silent relief from everyone. At least they'd be able to get out and stretch their aching limbs for a few minutes.

Dinu and Andrasi seemed completely unperturbed about the breakdown. It was obviously a regular occurrence judging by the condition of the cars. They scratched their heads as they casually peered under the bonnet. Somewhat scarily, they lit matches to see what they were doing.

The night air had a vicious nip in it. Although they couldn't see a thing in the darkness, the crew were aware of being high up in the mountains simply by the cut in the air. Judith and Vicky exchanged worried glances but didn't say anything. They didn't want to appear too girlie.

Suddenly the old engine came to life once more and they all piled back in, trying to remember which way to twist their arms and legs. The tortuous journey continued its bends and twists. Everyone fell into silence, dreaming of a decent night's sleep.

Four hours later, the two old cars finally pulled up outside a dark and almost derelict-looking building. Not a light on in the place, it was surrounded by trees creaking and groaning in a persistent wind. This was truly Dracula country. They were right in the heart of Transylvania. The place looked so bleak, you almost expected a hump-backed old butler to answer the door.

Dinu led the way through a set of double doors in dire need of paint, glass-panelled with moth-eaten and filthy net curtains hanging behind. He walked knowledgeably through the hallway to a small window, rather like a serving hatch. He spoke a few words of greeting and, to everyone's amazement, a grubby curtain was swept back and in the dim light provided by a waning moon, a voice spoke back.

'The hotel has a power cut,' he explained to the rest of the group. 'You must fill in your forms first. I have some matches.'

Vicky and Judith couldn't believe it. Form-filling at this time of night, and after the journey they'd just completed. Everyone was too dead beat to argue. They lined up rather like children to sign in and be given a key.

'At least I have some candles and matches in my bag,' said Judith, grateful to provide something that justified her huge suitcase. Mercifully she found them quickly, without having to delve through two weeks' worth of knickers. Then they all shuffled off down the dusty corridor, trying to make out the room numbers. As each found their number, they muttered their goodnights and disappeared inside.

Vicky put her key in the lock of No 10, and the door creaked open. She put down her case and lit her candle as quickly as possible. The scene was appalling. She could just pick out a single bed, a small chest of drawers, a chair and a window with a moth-eaten curtain that went nowhere towards covering the window. Wiring was looped around the walls, and the smell of damp was overwhelming. She took her candle into the tiny bathroom. All she could see was some old tiling coming away and a shower filled with building masonry, presumably from the crumbling walls.

'Well I'm not unpacking and I'm going to sleep in what I'm wearing,' she declared aloud. She clambered into the bed, feeling the thin sheets and coarse blankets as she settled down. Her last thought was that, for the first time in years, she hadn't cleaned her teeth before she went to bed. The bathroom looked too risky for that. She'd inspect it in the morning.

Meanwhile, in the next room, Judith had just hit the same pain barrier. She'd found an old grey dish cloth and realised that it was supposed to be a towel. Thank God she had insisted they all bring sheets and towels. Not trusting the bed in case it was crawling with indescribable nasties, Judith fished out her sheets and one of the dreaded shellsuits from her case. *Perfect*, she thought, putting it on. *I never thought I'd be saying that about a purple shell suit.* And within seconds, she was sound asleep.

Judith found her way to breakfast in the dining room. It wasn't difficult because it was the only public room in the hotel. As she crossed the shabby entrance hall, she saw the tiny hatch where they'd signed their forms the previous night and collected their keys. Daylight certainly did not become it.

The woman behind the hatch just pointed gruffly to a door with a crude knife and fork sign on it. The dining room was massive, with at least forty tables, Judith estimated. However, it wasn't difficult to find the rest of the crew, as they were the only ones there. And they were huddled at one end, where there were a couple of working light bulbs.

'Good job we booked,' Colin greeted her. 'Good old Jude. You know how these great little places get discovered and snapped up by the glitterati. It'll get overrun by food-ies before you can say hey pesto!'

'Don't worry, we've ordered for you,' Ron joined in. 'What's the Romanian for muesli, Dinu? You know how all women love chomping their way through hamster drop-pings for breakfast.'

Even Dinu's linguistic abilities didn't stretch that far. Very seriously, he explained to Judith that there wasn't a menu but there would be something simple, probably coffee and toast. Judith was busily taking in the filthy table-cloth which must have once been white, the old crumbs and the chipped and grimy salt and pepper pots.

'Great rooms,' continued Colin. 'Mine's so terrific I'm going to insist on it again when I rebook for a holiday.'

'I don't know how they do it for the money,' joined in Ron. 'Any chance of us having an overrun, Jude?'

'Oh shut up, you lot,' interrupted Vicky. 'My room's the pits. So if yours are that good, I might make you swap with me. What's yours like, Jude?'

'Your every worst nightmare,' replied Judith. 'By the way, did you all find those red worms in your bathroom?'

chapter eighteen

'Red worms?' they all chorused in disbelief. It had been quite a show stopper.

'Yes, red worms,' said Judith. 'When I went to have a shower this morning in my bathroom, if you can call it that, there were these tiny little red worms crawling all around the shower tray. It was just disgusting. That's why I was a bit late getting down here.'

'Oh we'll soon sort that out.' Colin and Ron suddenly recalled the age of chivalry.

'How did you manage?' said Vicky incredulously.

'I took a couple of the loose bricks around the shower tray and sort of balanced on them,' explained Judith, who was looking her normal immaculate self. 'Well I had to have a shower and wash my hair. I just can't function unless I do. But I couldn't face standing there with them crawling around my feet.'

'I thought it was bad enough cleaning my teeth in water from the filthy taps,' said Vicky. 'If only we'd packed some bleach and scrubbing brushes.'

'I know what we'll do,' said Ron, ever practical. 'We'll get a couple of bottles of that cheap Pinot Noir they serve up and clean up your bathrooms with that. Alcohol's the next best thing and the worms will think they've had a jolly good night out before they wiggle their last, so to speak.

What a great way to go! Pissed as a newt, or even a worm, and then straight down the plug hole!'

'Brilliant,' pronounced Colin. 'That man's a genius. Oh good, at last here comes breakfast.'

An elderly woman emerged through the swing door from the kitchen carrying a large tray. Without a single word or a flicker of expression on her face, she set down some chipped cups, saucers and plates, a large pot of coffee, a small jug of milk and a bowl containing some very dusty old sugar. Finally she placed before them a plate of toast and a small square of butter. As she returned to the kitchen, she muttered something in Dinu's direction.

'No jam,' he explained to the expectant faces all turned towards him.

The coffee was thick and strong but it was almost stone cold. The bread must have been virtually stale when it was toasted and the butter did not stretch very far. Nobody touched the grubby sugar bowl, Judith noted, wondering why the woman had let the coffee go cold before she'd brought it out. It must have been hot at some stage in its life. Thank God she'd packed a travel kettle.

'I think we'll all have a hot cup of tea before we set off,' she announced. 'In fact if you come to my room, you can meet my red worms.'

'Even better,' said Ron triumphantly. 'You can make the introductions and then we'll kill them with your hot water. Sorry, worms, wine's off!'

Sarah's heart had started to pound again as she turned into her road late on Sunday night. The start of possibly the most difficult week of her life lay ahead and she felt desperately alone. She'd been preoccupied with Roz's anguish over Pete, exhausted to the point of limping from shopping and then had her hearing shot to pieces in the wine bar, not to mention a slight hangover this morning. But that was now done, dusted, and belonged to yesterday. What lay ahead she didn't know, but one thing she did know. It frightened her.

Alan's new car was not to be seen. Relief surging over her, she rushed into the house, made a quick cup of tea, phoned Roz to say she'd arrived and then got herself into bed, lights out. At least then she could feign sleep when he came back.

He didn't, of course, come back.

My last Monday morning in this house, she mused, getting herself ready for work. The new wardrobe was cheering her up but it was only a question of a few days now before the credit card bills would be dropping on the mat.

Today, though, Sarah was more concerned with the call she had to make to Spies R Us. What time should she call, should she wait until she was at work or risk phoning from home and Alan walking in? Her office would be the safer option, she decided, knowing that she was also buying herself a little bit more time.

When she got to work, she opened the post, checked her e-mails, counted to ten and dialled the number. Mr Nicotine himself answered the phone on the second ring, almost catching her by surprise.

'Mr Grover?'

'Yes, that's Mrs Franks, isn't it. Recognised your voice.'

That's because it's shaking, thought Sarah.

'I have already prepared my report so I can fax or post it to you. Do you wish me to give you details over the phone?'

Most clients asked for the results over the phone. They were invariably the ones for whom he had bad news. That was his theory anyway.

'Yes please.'

Oh dear, right again, thought Mr Grover, awarding himself another cigarette.

'Well I'm afraid it looks like being what you suspected, Mrs Franks. Do you want me to elaborate?'

'Yes please. Just tell me. What's going on?'

'Obviously you appreciate I only had two days to carry out my investigation, but I can tell you that your husband spent two nights with another man at the, um, Queens Hotel just outside Winchester. A four-star establishment where they shared a double room ensuite at one hundred and twenty-five pounds per night. I took the liberty of checking with the night porter – who happens to be a friend of mine – and he told me that your husband's, er, young friend was described as his son. They ate dinner at the hotel on Friday night but had an Indian meal in Winchester on Saturday. They also had lunch earlier on Saturday in the wine bar which you mentioned, Cahoots. Seems they've been there a few times. One of the barmen there – who also just happens to be a friend of mine – said they were occasional customers there. He remembered them because they always drink the most expensive wines. And they're never joined by anyone else.'

Sarah, who'd been listening intently, started to quiver with anger, aimed at Alan but misdirected at Mr Grover.

'But this doesn't prove anything, does it,' she stated, raising her voice and realising immediately she'd be attracting attention around the office. She lowered her voice again hastily. 'Sorry, Mr Grover. I didn't mean to shout at you. You're just doing your job.'

'Absolutely, Mrs Franks. And I quite understand your distress, but I am still quite certain that your theory is correct.'

'Oh, how can you be so sure? I need to be absolutely certain.'

'Well, this is a bit delicate. As I said, the hotel night porter is a friend of mine. And as you probably know, chambermaids do talk. Often about the state of the sheets if you get my drift.'

'Oh God,' whispered Sarah, wondering if she was going to be sick.

'And of course, photographs are all part of the service,' continued Mr Grover.

'Photographs?' Sarah thought she was going to faint. 'Surely not. Oh no, not that.'

'Well not quite, Mrs Franks. We have to be completely above board here. No, I simply took some pictures of them with a long lens by the Water Meadows on Saturday afternoon.'

'And what were they doing?' Sarah was now gripping the phone, aware that her palms were slippery.

'Well I managed to get a shot of them kissing. On the lips.'

The travel kettle was already earning its weight in gold. As well as making a decent hot cup of tea for everyone before they set off, it had delivered the death knell to the red worms. Now the real trial beckoned, the reason they were all there. It was the first day of filming at the orphanage. Everyone fell silent as they loaded up the cars with all the equipment. There was clearly some mental preparation going on.

Fifteen minutes later, having bumped their way down the hillside, they rolled up in the middle of a small mountain village. In awe, they realised what they had missed on the dark journey the night before: the scenery was simply breathtaking. Soft green slopes, pretty little farmhouses with red tiled roofs, wisps of smoke coming from chimneys, straw piled high in cone shapes rather like witches' hats; it was like looking at pages from a Hansel and Gretel picture book. The mountain air had a different quality about it, still and calm with just the soft tinkle of cowbells and the odd cockerel proclaiming another conquest. A handful of villagers seemed to be going about their business, the women in sombre black skirts and with scarves tied firmly under their chins, the men in tweedy jackets and corduroy trousers. Some were outside their houses, tending their small plots of land, others trudging up the steep hillsides to begin their day's work. Another couple unloaded a cart full of straw, their pitchforks almost making a gentle rhythm as they went about their task.

Colin was in raptures. He saw life through a lens and this was going to make great pictures.

'Oh dear, I think we're the talk of the town,' said Ron quietly, bringing everyone abruptly out of their own private reverie. They realised that they were being watched by small groups of villagers who'd gathered on street corners. They smiled and waved a greeting but the villagers just carried on staring.

'Not many cars, not many foreigners come here,' explained Dinu unnecessarily.

Stephanie looked at her watch. 'In about five minutes, some of the older children will be setting off to school,' she said, indicating a large grey concrete building across the road. Surrounded by a tall wire fence, the orphanage was built on three storeys with a steep flight of steps up to the main door. Judith thought it looked like a prison, it was so bleak and soulless.

She nodded to Colin and Ron, who started setting up the tripod ready for the shot.

Suddenly the grey doors opened, and about fifty dark-haired children swarmed noisily down the concrete steps and headed straight for the gate. Soon faces were being pressed against the wire fence, small hands shoved through the gaps as they eagerly called to Stephanie and Paul on the other side. The couple were obviously great favourites and seemed to know all their names.

'Now calm down, calm down, because you're off to school in a minute,' said Paul, trying to create some sort of order out of the chaos.

A woman in a white coat appeared from behind them, spoke sharply in Romanian and then opened the gate. The swarm took no notice of whatever the instructions had been, and surrounded Stephanie and Paul, touching them, nudging them, begging to be picked up. It was a case of the survival of those with the sharpest elbows, so the rest of the pack then turned its attention on the crew. It was like being attacked by locusts. They were everywhere, grabbing, begging, nudging, desperate for some affection. Sensing a possible disaster, Colin and Ron quickly unhooked the camera and sound gear, and headed off the few yards towards the cars. With the equipment locked away, they returned for the tripod that was fast becoming a climbing frame.

Suddenly the woman in the white coat spoke again sharply and they reluctantly let go of their new-found friends and loped off to school.

'Don't worry,' said Stephanie to Judith, 'they'll soon get used to you. The novelty will have worn off by tonight. They love visitors and new things, but their attention span is short. You'll soon be part of the furniture.'

'Hope so,' said Judith, still slightly shaken from the whole experience and having her empty pockets thoroughly picked as well. 'Otherwise it'll be difficult to film anything.'

Sarah packed in work at lunchtime and went home. The stress of everything had wrecked her concentration. Her manager, sensing the turmoil in her head and the weekend written large on her face, suggested she took the afternoon off. She turned into her road and nearly drove straight out again. Alan's gleaming new Mercedes was parked in the driveway. It sat there menacingly, like an enemy tank.

She parked behind it. As she walked past the Mercedes to get to the front door, she noticed that the driver's door was slightly ajar. She couldn't resist having a look inside. It really was a luxurious car, she had to admit. It smelt gloriously of leather. And an aftershave she couldn't place.

She quietly shut the car door and went up to the porch. As she eased open the front door, she could hear voices, men's voices, coming from the sitting room. Within seconds of her shutting the door, Alan was in the hall, white with anger and waving some pieces of paper.

'What the hell are you doing here and what the fuck have you been up to?' he ranted at her.

A strange calm came over Sarah. She couldn't believe her steady voice in reply.

'In answer to your first question, I live here, if you remember. Although, I grant you, not for very much longer. And regarding your second question, I could ask the same about you.' She turned to walk away towards the kitchen. But Alan was across the hall, grabbing her by the shoulder and wheeling her round to face him.

'This, you bitch. What the fuck's all this?'

Sarah could now see he was waving some credit card bills and statements.

'Yes, I've spent some money. But so what? There's a very expensive motor sitting outside which I wasn't consulted about.'

'It's none of your business. Nothing to do with you.'

'Oh yes it is. You've done the dirty on me over the house. Got me to sign it away all that time ago. Well I'm getting my own back. Seeing as you're getting the house, you can pay those bloody bills. Why shouldn't I get something? After all, I've cleaned the bloody place all these years.'

'Do you know how much you've spent in the last month?' he ranted. 'Have you any idea? No, I didn't think so. There's at least thirty grand's worth of crap bought on these cards and I suppose it's all gone on your back.'

And there's a whole lot more to come, thought Sarah, with

a secret smile. She was beginning to enjoy this. Revenge was supposed to be sweet, maybe this was how it felt.

'Well, put it this way, I'd have sued you for half the house but at least this way there's no arguments, no court battles. It's spent and that's that. You've got your car and God knows what else and I've got a new wardrobe. I think that's fair. Saves us bothering to go to court, doesn't it. And the rest you can put into this mystery business you won't tell me about. You won't tell me about it because it doesn't exist.'

She turned to walk in the direction of the sitting room. What she needed right now was a large gin and tonic to steady herself. Before Alan could stop her, she was through the door and confronting a stranger sat on one of the sofas.

'Oh hello,' she said sweetly. 'Sorry you've picked the wrong time to visit. My husband and I are getting a divorce and right now I'm getting myself a gin and tonic.'

Before she could reach the cocktail cabinet, Alan, red-faced with anger and embarrassment, hastily introduced her.

'This is Charles Jefferson, my business partner,' he said. The beautiful young man jumped up nervously. She was suddenly down wind of the same aftershave.

'How do you do?' he said, shaking hands. 'I'm sorry if I'm here at a difficult time. I had no idea.'

'Oh that's quite all right,' said Sarah smoothly. 'Actually, I'm certain I've seen you somewhere before.'

'Probably a film. Charles has done a bit of acting in the past,' interrupted Alan, who was now doing a fair impression of a cat being threatened with a bucket of water.

'Maybe that's it,' said Sarah, pretending to sound puzzled. 'No, it's something more recent. Have you been on telly over the weekend?'

'No, sorry, not me,' said Charles. She had them both jumping now.

'Hang on, it was a photograph.'

'I don't think so.'

Sarah paused and smiled at the pair of them. 'I know so. It was a photograph taken in Winchester last Saturday afternoon. See, I knew it would come back to me.'

'I don't know what you're talking about,' said Alan, sensing danger.

'Oh yes you do. In fact you're in the photograph too. It was in the Water Meadows and you two were kissing. How very romantic.'

'Stupid bitch,' Alan started, but Sarah was now in full flow.

'In fact I've got the picture in my bag. I thought I might frame it and show it to the kids. I must say, Alan, many congratulations. You fooled us all. We never realised your little secret. Anyway, it has certainly cleared up a few mysteries for me.'

Tears of anger spurted from her eyes as all the pent-up emotion of the discovery was finally released. She paused and took a gulp of gin and tonic. Alan seized the moment to grab at her handbag.

'No point. There's a copy on its way to my solicitors,' she declared. 'Now are you going to tell the kids, or shall I?'

chapter nineteen

Sarah met Roz at Winchester station on Thursday evening. They hugged briefly and then got into Sarah's old Volvo. The journey took ten minutes but not a word was spoken between them. Sarah knew full well that her daughter was nervous about meeting her father for the first time since the recent bombshells.

'I've had all your stuff and Daniel's packed up in boxes ready to move,' said Sarah as they pulled up in the driveway. 'Judith's letting me store some stuff in her garage for the time being. The furniture van's coming at eight tomorrow so we can help load up and then follow the van over to her place.'

'What's Dad doing?' asked Roz.

'I haven't the foggiest,' said Sarah wearily. 'I haven't spoken to him since Monday. We had a bit of a showdown unfortunately.'

She still hadn't had the courage to tell Roz about her father and his toyboy, or that she'd employed a private detective. She'd rehearsed some sort of explanation in front of the bathroom mirror several times but still couldn't get anywhere near to delivering it. It all sounded so tacky and so ridiculous in the telling. Probably better to spare Roz all that anyway.

They went inside, Sarah breathing a sigh of relief that,

yet again, Alan was not in evidence. They sat down in the kitchen to the Chinese takeaway they'd bought on the way home from the station. Sarah's excuse was that she'd already given the kitchen its final clean-up. Roz then took herself quietly off on a nostalgic trip around the house. Sarah left her alone, realising she was saying goodbye to all the rooms which had been so much a part of her childhood.

'How long do you think you'll stay at Judith's?' she asked when she returned to the kitchen.

'Only a week or two at the most,' replied Sarah. 'Then I'll have to find somewhere to rent while I sort myself out. I can leave my stuff in the garage a bit longer than that. I don't know what I'd have done without Judith. She's been such a good friend . . .'

She started to sob. Roz was instantly by her side, putting an arm around her shoulder.

'Please don't cry, Mum,' she comforted. 'You've always been so tough, you're one of the survivors. Don't give up now. I'm sure Dad will come to his senses and realise he's made a terrible mistake.'

Neither of them had heard the car arriving in the driveway, the front door key in the lock and the door opening. Alan stood motionless in the kitchen doorway, glaring at them with a face as black as thunder.

'Hi, Dad,' said Roz.

'What the fuck are you doing here?' he demanded.

'Nice to see you too, Dad,' replied Roz grimly. 'I've come to help Mum out seeing as you can't be bothered. Anyway, Mum's told me the whole thing.'

Alan went white.

'You bitch.' He lunged at Sarah. 'Couldn't wait to open your fucking mouth.'

'She doesn't know, Alan, honestly, she doesn't,' screamed Sarah. He slapped her repeatedly across the face, causing her to fall backwards against the kitchen cupboards. Roz remained transfixed to the spot, frozen with fear. As her mother crumpled to the floor, blood pouring from her mouth, Roz suddenly sprang to life, raining blows with her fists on her father's back without making the slightest impact.

Alan turned to her, his face now purple with rage.

'You tell your bloody mother to get out tomorrow,' he hissed. 'I'll be back at noon and I expect her to be gone.' Without a further word, he turned and walked out.

It was the last Sarah would ever see of him.

'That's a wrap for today,' said a tired Judith to the crew. The shoot was going well and the children had soon got used to them, just as Stephanie and Paul had suggested. But it had taken much longer for them to get used to the children. The shaved heads, the constant rocking of the more disturbed youngsters, the ever-present smell of pee, the endless diet of tasteless and colourless soup and mashed potato.

Vicky had surprised herself by taking to it all like a duck to water. She'd instantly fallen in love with all the children and spent any spare time between filming playing football around the orphanage grounds, feeding the tiny ones and helping the more able ones to splosh paint on to paper in the cause of art. Tonight, now that they'd finished work for the day, she was organising an outdoor disco. She'd found a rather ancient ghetto blaster hidden away from the children's grasp and fished out some tapes from her bag. Soon they were out dancing on the steps in the late afternoon sunshine, the music echoing off the mountainside. All the crew and volunteers bopped away with the children, some of whom were mean dancers. Even those in wheelchairs or on crutches managed some sort of rhythm.

I'd like to bottle this feeling, thought Vicky. *These kids*

*have been through so much, and now they're teaching us how
to live for the moment.*

'They all adore you, you know. You should have been a
mum,' Colin said to Vicky, as they drove back up to their
horror hotel for the nightly cold pork and chips.

'Couldn't track down a father,' replied Vicky, sardoni-
cally.

'Well, it's a shame, if you don't mind me saying,' persisted Colin. 'I think there'll be quite a few tears when we
finish up here.'

'Yeah, probably on both sides,' agreed Vicky, wistfully.
She was already dreading the goodbyes.

'I sometimes wonder if I missed out on kids,' said Colin.
'Got cleaned out in the most expensive divorce on the
planet and been running scared ever since. How about you,
Vick? Have you ever been married?'

'No,' snapped Vicky abruptly. She should have seen this
one coming.

'She's got more sense,' interrupted Judith, who did not
want the wedding-that-wasn't raked up again. She hadn't
seen Vicky so happy since the heyday of Swervin' Mervyn
and she was determined to try and keep it that way.

Back at Hotel Horrendous, the cleaners were making
their annual visit. Two women in tatty old aprons were
busy with brooms, buffing up the corridor that led to their
rooms. All they'd succeeded in doing was creating a thick
dust cloud and a no-go area. Presumably in another year or
so, they'd stir it all up again.

'No jokes about letting the dust settle!' declared Judith.

'Blimey, Dyson would mop up here,' said Colin, chuckling. 'Wouldn't mind the vacuum cleaner concession for
Transylvania. We can't get through that lot without oxygen
tanks, so let's go and get the pork and chips out of the way.'

They sat down at their usual table under their usual
twenty-watt light bulb.

'Twenty-five pints of lager and a vindaloo,' said Ron cheerfully to the waitress, who'd emerged stone-faced from the kitchen. 'Gotta lose weight the natural way.'

Ordering the meal via Dinu was, of course, just a charade. There was no menu and no choice, but as the nights went by, they'd developed a game of Fantasy Food.

'I think I'll have the steak tonight.'

'Polenta and roasted winter vegetables for me.'

'I'm going for the tagliatelle.'

'How about moules marinières to start?'

'Y-eeesss,' they all chorused.

Dinu held up a hand to silence them. 'She says she's got some fish tonight.'

'Whaaaat?' They were dumbstruck.

'More Pinot Noir,' commanded Colin. 'We're all in shock.'

Several bottles later, the kitchen door creaked open and the stone-faced woman emerged carrying plates. Silence descended around the table. The fish were about the size of very small goldfish, two each, with a small pile of chips, served Romanian style, in other words, stone cold.

'Oh well, I think it'll be Cup a Soup in my room after this,' said Judith, thankful yet again that she'd brought all the back-up rations.

Next day the weather turned. The hot sunshine, particularly around the middle of the day, had gone, and was replaced by grey skies and a biting wind. It was definitely the Day of the Purple Shell Suits.

'We might as well get this over with,' whispered Vicky to Judith while they were waiting for the others at breakfast. 'We might not be fashion victims, but at least we'll be warm and dry.'

'I already know. I've been sleeping in mine since we

arrived because my room's so damp and cold,' replied Judith.

The purple shell suits drew a round of applause when they all met up outside the hotel. Colin whipped out his camera from the boot of the car and filmed a mock catwalk sequence with Ron giving a commentary.

'Perfect for the Christmas video,' said Colin.

However, it was a different story when they reached the orphanage. Purple shell suits were clearly big fashion news in Romania and they were instantly mobbed by all the teenage girls, each begging to be given one.

'You see,' said Vicky, triumphantly. 'Where we lead, others follow. I'm glad we didn't throw them out.'

Colin was busily filming all the kids milling round, obviously another scene for the Christmas video. Judith could only imagine the commentary. 'Fashion triumph for middle-aged frumpies. Crowd hysteria as shell suits take Eastern bloc fashion pundits by storm. Meet Judith Fielding and Victoria Chadwick – Transylvania's new It girls.'

Because the weather had changed so dramatically, none of today's exterior shots would match. So Judith decided they would attempt to film some scenes in the one and only village shop. Dinu had gone off for the day with Stephanie and Paul on an interpreting mission involving adoption papers for one of the children. So getting themselves understood would be a problem.

'What's your mime like?' Judith asked Colin.

'Oh, I always tune into the Marcel Marceau channel,' he chipped back.

'Right then, motor mouth, let's see how good you are.' She commandeered him into the shop. It was, as an estate agent might describe, deceptively spacious. Masses of wooden shelves right up to the ceiling, but the vast majority were empty. There was no food, no fruit, no vegetables, no sweets or drinks. Just a faint smell of must and dust. At one end there was a small collection of goods, too incongruous for words. Two slotted spoons, a packet of Omo, several packets of red buttons, two pink zips and about a dozen pairs of extremely tarty red leather strappy shoes with ridiculously high heels.

Stephanie had warned them about the secret delights of the shop. Villagers grew all their own food, except bread that they could get from a small van. Harrods Food Hall it was not.

A woman of about sixty, headscarved and dressed in black, appeared from a back room and glared at them, muttering and cursing under her breath.

Judith tried English and French to no avail.

'Come on then, Marcel Marceau, it's your turn,' she said to Colin. He immediately swung into action, flashing his broadest smile.

'We would love to film,' he indicated a rolling camera, 'in your wonderful shop.' He flung open his arms expansively. 'Hey, babe, terrific shoes. Wow! And red buttons. My mum just loves red buttons. Gotta buy some of them. Mother's Day is only ever just around the corner,' he gushed.

The woman started to melt but she was still nervous. *Socks*, thought Judith suddenly, *socks. That will do it.*

'Just getting something out of the car,' she half whispered to Colin. 'You carry on. You'll be fixing up a date at this rate.' She scurried out, leaving Colin in full flow. He appeared to be batting seriously for a Bafta.

She returned with a Tesco carrier bag containing several pairs of socks. The woman's face lit up.

Colin sounded as though he was auditioning for *The Price Is Right*. 'See. Everyone's a label junkie, even here. Who needs a Prada bag, sweetie, when you can have a Tesco!' He turned back to the woman, who couldn't wait to get her hands on the bag. 'Hey, Tesco. It's my favourite too. And socks. Wow!'

The woman's happiness was complete. To clinch the deal, Colin grabbed a pair of the tarty red sandals and slapped down a five-thousand Romanian lei note on the counter.

'For my mother,' he grinned as he bore them off to the car and returned with the tripod.

The woman was now putty in his hands. She even roped in a friend from the mystery back room to play the part of a customer, as they were obviously a bit thin on the ground.

'I'm amazed those sandals haven't been snapped up,' said Ron, laughing. 'They're just the job for tottering up and down the mountains.'

'I think they're what we call in the trade fuck-me pumps,' replied Colin knowledgeably. 'I bet there's quite a demand in a backwater like this.'

'Well, your mother will love them,' said Judith. 'I'm sure she always wanted to be a tart. At least you've managed to buy something. Souvenirs are a bit thin on the ground. I don't think Simon would appreciate a packet of Omo. He's too young to remember it anyway.'

The weather had closed in so they adjourned next door to the village's only bar. To their surprise, it was heaving. There was not a seat or table to be had so they congregated at the bar.

'I thought we'd get the silent treatment,' said Judith, surprised that their entrance went almost unnoticed.

'I think you'll find that's because they're all somewhat refreshed,' answered Ron.

'But it's only eleven o'clock in the morning,' said Judith.

'Correct. But there's bugger all else to do here,' said Ron.

They huddled at the bar, wishing Dinu was with them to help order drinks. In desperation, they pointed to a nearby table where a group of forestry workers were huddled around a bottle of clear liquid.

'We'll have some of that,' said Colin, miming to the man behind the bar. A similar bottle and four shot glasses were produced.

'Cheers,' announced Colin as they all clinked glasses. The silence was followed by spluttering and coughing. It tasted like firewater.

When they'd recovered, they realised that everyone in the bar was laughing at them.

'Palinka!' shouted an old man. 'Palinka!'

'Of course, it's that local spirit they make themselves. I think it's made from potatoes,' said Judith when she'd recovered a little. 'Might as well take up fire-eating.'

'Well I'm totally palinka-ed,' said Vicky, wiping her eyes. 'Never again. That was painful. I felt that go all the way down. Just hope it doesn't come up again.'

The rest of the day continued in the same vein, except that it got colder. Judith shivered in her room that night. She'd had a terrible attack of homesickness. She was missing Simon, although he'd sounded cheerful enough on the rare times she'd managed to reach him on her mobile. She worried about Sarah, who had been moving out that day. And she fretted about the documentary and the responsibilities that went with it. That they had the shots she had no doubt. But would she do it all justice and turn in a cracking script? She was still terrified that the Securitate would suddenly turn up and seize the tapes. Just to underline her insecurity, a car had roared up outside the hotel earlier that evening. A huge, menacing-looking man had got out, together with three black-leather-jacketed, equally unpleasant henchmen. Convinced that they'd been sent to ask awkward questions, she'd nervously prompted the crew to remember that their visas stated they were in the country on 'humanitarian work'. To her great embarrassment and subsequent ribbing, it transpired they'd come to install a new central-heating boiler.

chapter twenty

It was the last day. The last day for loading up the old cars, the last day for everyone squeezing in, the last day to see the children, and the last day to breathe in the beautiful scenery before they made their descent down the mountains to the airport in Oradea. At least the luggage was a lot lighter. Judith and Vicky had donated all the remaining coffee, tea and packet soup plus most of the clothes they'd brought, except what they stood up in.

There had been tears at the orphanage, mostly from Vicky, who'd been dreading the moment so much. She hugged each child in turn, fighting her emotions. She was only momentarily distracted when she realised that her absolute favourite, a show-stopping eight-year-old little rascal called Bujorel was nowhere to be seen. With the crew now waiting for her to extricate herself, she reluctantly waved farewell and climbed into the first car. In the back, screwed up into the tightest ball he could make himself, was Bujorel, grinning at his own naughtiness but still hoping to be taken home with Vicky.

'Sorry, darling, you can't come,' she said, hugging him tight, 'but I'll come back one day, I promise. I'll come back as a volunteer one day and see you.'

'Cool,' replied Bujorel, who'd picked up all the essential

words in life. 'Come back soon. Sony Walkman. Bye, bye, Mama Vicky.'

Vicky turned her head away from the rest of them so they couldn't see her tears as the old cars trundled their way down to the airport. It was the nearest she'd ever get to motherhood.

Dinu tried to suppress his yawns. He'd been up half the night, bargaining enough diesel from local farmers to make the journey back down to Oradea. He'd not told Judith and the crew because he knew they would have been mortified about it. Besides, he'd had such a great time with them all and he knew he was going to miss all the laughs, their bizarre sense of humour and the camaraderie of film-making. Like Josca in Bucharest, he'd picked up some of the in-jokes and the jargon.

'Now I will help you get your equipment through customs and then you must have your passports and forms ready,' he announced as they finally spluttered through the airport gates.

Another team of the regulation fat women with their squeaking x-ray table-tennis bats was waiting for them. The women's po-faces never flickered, even when Judith quietly slipped them each some Romanian lei.

The plane-sized portion of cottage pie and tinned carrots tasted like manna from heaven after two weeks of cold pork and chips.

Judith sank back in her seat and tried to take stock of the whole trip. She was glad it was over, relieved that all her careful planning had paid off. She was certain they'd come back with some fantastic and very moving material but she also felt the invisible cloud of Romania's oppression lifting. She was also desperate to see Simon and sleep in her own bed.

'What will you miss most?' said Vicky to Judith as they sipped gin and tonics in tiny plastic glasses.

'Oh, being issued with two small sheets of Bronco-type loo paper every time I needed to use a public loo,' she quipped. 'My morning glass of palinka, the red worms, oh I could go on and on, How about you?'

'Oh, the kids,' said Vicky wistfully. 'I just loved Bujorel. He was so utterly gorgeous. And all of them really. They were so innocent and yet so streetwise. But I won't miss that filthy hotel or their rotten food.'

'Ditto. Oh well, at least we'll dine out on it, so to speak. That's the trouble with filming abroad – it's always retrospective fun. It's a hoot in the telling, but shite at the time. Mind you, I think we'll have some fresh drama when we get back. Don't forget Sarah's been at my place for a few days. Simon's been a bit enigmatic about it when I've spoken to him, but I gather she's in quite a state.'

They drifted off into their own reveries, Judith pining for her piano and decent sheets, Vicky fantasising about living in a cottage with roses trailing around the door, greeting Mr Wonderful with a cordon bleu dinner and two ravishing, dark-haired children just like Bujorel at her side.

'Welcome to the Shock Exchange,' proclaimed Sarah, coming out of the front door to help them bring in their bags. 'Don't ask. I'll tell you all later.'

Even the delicious smell of a casserole wafting out of the house could not distract them from Sarah's bruised face. One week later and she was still having splitting headaches from the whack on her head and the stitches to a head wound. Her face was only just starting to go yellow from the bruising. She looked as though she'd done ten rounds with Mike Tyson.

Vicky and Judith were open-mouthed in horror. They had half expected some sort of confrontation to happen between Alan and Sarah, but it was still dreadful to see their friend in that state. No one spoke of it until after the meal, which they ate in grateful and comfortable silence, Vicky and Judith thankful to eat something decent and wholesome, Sarah glad to have friends back who would understand.

'Well, come on then. What happened? It's up to you if you want to tell us,' said Judith finally, opening their third bottle of wine.

'I think it's called ending your marriage,' said Sarah.

She gave them a brief résumé of her trip to Spies R Us, the ubiquitous Mr Grover, his photographs, the confrontation with Charles the toyboy and the fight.

'Well if it's any comfort, if this is what nearly twenty-five years of marriage means to Bostik Pockets, then you're well shot of him,' said Judith vehemently. 'Look, Sarah, you've had a rotten time ever since day one, as far as I can tell, so the only way is up. Any time you question whether you're doing the right thing, just remember the bad times. Just remember now, and how this feels.'

'I think it'll be pretty difficult to forget,' said Sarah, feeling her face gingerly. 'Let's change the subject. I want to hear all about your trip. But first, I have a surprise.'

Can we cope with any more? thought Judith.

'I think my daughter and your son are an item,' said Sarah.

'Good grief, how did that happen?' said Judith.

'Roz came down from London to help me move out last week. She was pretty fed up because she'd just been dumped by the current boyfriend. She hadn't seen Simon for years. I think the last time they saw each other, it was a case of pigtails and short trousers. Well, they've had a bit of a rethink.'

'He never even hinted when I spoke to him on the phone this week, the crafty little monkey,' said Judith. 'Well, well, it just goes to show, you turn your back for five minutes, it's all change. I do hope it won't all end in tears, for both our sakes. He said he'd be in late tonight. I hope I can stay awake long enough to pull his leg about it. I must say, I think they both have impeccable taste.'

They chatted late into the evening about Romania, amusing Sarah with tales of the red worms and the hotel prostitutes.

'And I thought working in telly was supposed to be so glamorous,' said Sarah. 'At least you got shot of those dreadful shell suits. I suppose we have to be thankful for some small mercies. I'm amazed you weren't deported for fashion evasion.'

'Not much chance of that,' replied Judith. 'I'm surprised we weren't barred entry for having too many clothes. It's not exactly a place where you can shop till you drop.'

'I should move there instantly,' said Sarah, smiling properly for the first time that evening.

Part Two

chapter twenty-one

Sarah was the first to arrive. They'd booked a table for dinner in Cahoots to fill in that rather iffy time between Christmas and the New Year. That time when, if you're in with a social swing, it's one long round of boring drinks parties, constant hangovers and a panic attack every time you clap eyes on a turkey sandwich. But if you're as out as yesterday's milk bottles, you wonder why the shops are selling ball gowns, seeing as you haven't been invited to anything remotely festive, and then resolve to be nicer next year to potential party hosts.

Sarah lit a cigarette and surveyed the scene. Cahoots was filling up rapidly with an odd mix of people. Not the usual evening crowd, but people hell bent on escaping whatever Christmas crisis they were facing.

Minutes later, Judith and Vicky burst through the door and the trio greeted each other noisily. A waiter bore in a top-hat-shaped ice bucket containing a bottle of champagne and they raised their glasses to the New Year.

'Resolutions, then,' declared Judith. 'What's yours?'

'To get a decent job,' said Vicky, promptly. Since Romania, she'd been freelancing for a local television station, doing all the really bum early and late shifts and weekends. She'd never returned to her old job in Plymouth but instead stayed on at Judith's. She was helping out with the bills but feeling guilty that she wasn't quite earning enough to move out and rent her own place again.

'To get my divorce,' said Sarah, firmly. Alan had finally agreed through his solicitor to admit adultery with 'an unnamed person', pay off her credit cards and give her five thousand pounds from the proceeds of the house sale. In return, she had agreed off the record not to press charges after he'd thumped her.

'We'll have to have a bit of a party when your divorce goes through,' said Vicky. 'When's that likely to be?'

'February, my solicitor reckons, about the same time as I'm completing on the flat,' replied Sarah.

Judith had read Sarah several sections of the Riot Act on spending the five grand wisely. For once, where money was concerned, she'd listened and put it down on a very small garden flat on the outskirts of Southampton. A far cry from the huge house she and Alan had lived in, but at least it would be home.

'Well you're being a bit quiet, Jude,' said Vicky. 'Come on, what's your New Year's resolution, or will it be a revolution this year?'

Judith considered for a bit. 'Next year I want to have sex.'

'Bloody hell, that's a bit much, isn't it?' joked Vicky. 'Anyway, I thought you'd given up all that.'

'Well, you thought wrong. Everyone else seems to be getting it, so why can't I? It's been so long since I did it that I've forgotten what goes where. Actually, if a man walked over now and offered his body, I'd be terrified. But yeah, that's my resolution.'

'Well it's right up the top of my wish list too,' said Sarah wistfully. 'When was the last time you got any?'

'Old Passion Pants Roger, back in the summer,' said Vicky, rolling her eyes. 'Before my brief arrest by the marriage squad.' Over the past few months, she had grown to see the funny side of that episode. 'I suppose you could say we just got stuck on the pre-marital sex. And then of course I did my well-documented runner.'

They laughed and refilled their glasses.

'At least if I die tonight, I can honestly say my last time wasn't with Alan,' said Sarah emphatically. 'In fact it was so long ago with Alan I cannot actually remember when we did it. But I did have a rather gorgeous weekend with a totally scrummy throat specialist way back along.'

'How way back along?' asked Vicky.

'Oh shit, it was last spring. That must be the longest I've ever gone without sex.'

'Well in my case, it would be a question of which spring are we talking here,' said Judith. 'No, seriously, I'll tell you what's prompted all this. Roz and Simon. All the phone calls, the meetings, the partings. It's so romantic, and I've realised I'd like a bit of that myself.'

Roz and Simon were still going strong, meeting most weekends at Roz's flat in Fulham. Now they were planning a holiday together in the spring.

'Quite where I'm going to find Mr Gorgeous, I haven't worked out,' continued Judith. 'But if you two stumble across anyone remotely decent next time you're shopping at Blokes R Us, let me know. In the meantime, let's drink to the success of my documentary. Here's to hopefully good reviews and ratings.'

Judith had finished editing the Romanian documentary, now titled *Forgotten But Forgiving*, just before Christmas. She was quietly pleased with it, believing it to be the best thing she'd ever done, but aware that she was much too close to it, especially after two solid weeks in an edit suite.

'Here's to *Forgotten But Forgiving*,' said Sarah, raising her glass again. 'May it rate itself senseless, and give you the recognition you deserve. And may it lead to you getting a really serious shag.'

As they raised their glasses to toast the New Year, the song 'It's Raining Men' wafted across the wine bar.

'That's exactly what we could do with,' said Vicky, 'a good old downpour of men. Let's pray for a mansoon.'

'I don't know about a mansoon,' said Sarah. 'But I couldn't half do with a man soon. How about you, Jude?'

'Me? Oh, right now, menwise, I'd be out of my depth in a puddle,' she replied.

They giggled uncontrollably until the fish fajitas they'd ordered arrived, together with another bottle of champagne.

'I do have one other resolution,' said Sarah when they'd finished eating. 'And that's to get myself better organised with money.'

The other two made fainting gestures, pretending to revive themselves with their napkins.

'And how are you going to do that?' said Vicky, taking in yet another fabulous outfit. 'With respect, Sarah, it's not quite your thing, is it? I remember that shopping trip we did in Hong Kong. It was great fun but, well let's be honest, you did go berserk, especially when you discovered Marks and Sparks over there took credit cards.'

'OK, you two can laugh but I am trying to be careful,' said Sarah, trying to maintain some sort of dignity out of all this. 'Anyway, I've got a bit of a strategy.'

The others leant across the table conspiratorially, as though shielding the whole of the clientele in Cahoots from this revelation.

'Well for a start, we three are going to resolve to make more effort to find new men,' said Sarah, sensing the others' disappointment the moment the words fell from her lips.

'Now how on earth are we going to do that?' asked Judith suspiciously. 'We're not going up the married men route, for God's sake. It's never worth it, Sarah. Statistically, they never leave their wives. You know that.'

'No, not the married ones,' announced Sarah, triumphantly. 'No, we're all going to resolve not to turn down
opportunities, invitations.'

They raised their glasses solemnly in promise.

'We're not going to chicken out and opt for Delia Smith
repeats when we could be out and about meeting new
people,' continued Sarah. 'And, besides, I've signed up to a
singles club and I've signed you both up too.'

'Oh puleeze, not one of those rooms full of life's greatest
misfits,' dismissed Judith.

'Yep, and don't get all stroppy on me. Everyone does
this sort of thing these days. Why do you think Teletext
and the ads in newspapers are full of messages? People
aren't meeting people any more. Oh, sure, they meet office
lechers and all the creeps imaginable, but decent totty,
absolutely not. No, it's got to be a singles club and we're
going next week. I've already fixed it.'

'Don't be ridiculous,' said Judith. 'You wouldn't catch
me there if it was the last place on earth.'

The last place on earth, Judith discovered, was in fact the
car park at the rear of the Brickmakers' Arms the following
week. She and Sarah had already had a bout of hysterics on
the journey in Sarah's car. They then proceeded to corpse
once more as they stood just outside the entrance to a side
bar which proclaimed 'Meeting in Progress'.

'I don't believe I'm doing this,' said Judith, desperately
holding back and praying her mobile phone would go off
so she could pretend to rush off. Silence from her handbag,
the phone refused to ring. If she'd had any sense, she
would have asked someone at work to ring at a given time
to give her an escape ticket. She'd also been deep down
convinced that Sarah was somehow joking and that they
wouldn't go through with it. Wrong.

'In we go,' urged Sarah enthusiastically. And they made

their entrance into the rather drab bar and found themselves being roundly stared at. Fifty pairs of eyes bored into them and they stood, momentarily dazzled by the attention.

A man in a green baggy sweater and brown cords homed in on them immediately.

'I'm Kevin,' he announced, giving them a warm smile and a rather limp double handshake. 'So good of you to come.'

It felt like being welcomed into the church by a vicar trying to drum up trade among an ailing congregation. Sarah and Judith could not make eye contact. They knew it would be fatal and that the giggles would start again out of sheer nerves and embarrassment.

Kevin, meanwhile, was the perfect host. He patiently introduced them to everyone in the room, giving pencil sketches of all the members and their interests.

'This is Pat, she's widowed sadly and thoroughly enjoys patchwork. And this is Steve, he's terribly good at ten-pin bowling when he's not plastering, or should I say plastered. Ha ha, just my little joke. Ha ha. Now Nigel here, he's our steam engine buff, and Marion over there. Well, what Marion doesn't know about cake decoration isn't worth knowing. Do you know she once made a cake in the shape of a mobile library? It was marvellous, it had all the detail, but that's of course because she works at the local council, you know. Now this is Phil, he's a painter. Not paintings, just walls of houses!'

It was almost like a spoof programme called *Blind Hate*. Once they'd completed the circuit, Judith insisted on buying Kevin a drink.

'Oh lemonade would be lovely if you don't mind,' said Kevin. 'Don't want to make the room start rocking, do I.'

I wish it bloody well would, thought Judith sadly. If this was the first foray into coupledom, a night in alone watching paint dry was looking like a more attractive option. Before she could make any silent plea to Sarah to get them out of this hellhole, Phil the painter had pounced on them. Hemmed into a corner, with nowhere to go, they all sat down resignedly. Phil was obviously a very sweet man in his thirties, hard-working, earnest, caring and not bad looking. But his specialist subject for the evening? His wife's funeral.

'Never, never, never again,' muttered Judith as they rushed to the car. 'I now know how to organise a funeral, plan the cortège, a seating plan, knock up the bridge rolls for the buffet and even choose the bloody hymns. All I need is the body.'

'Somehow it sounded like he'd enjoyed it,' said Sarah. 'Reading between the lines, his apparently perfect wife sounded like a rather bossy cow, so perhaps the funeral was his chance to be centre stage. He didn't sound all that distraught, seeing as his wife had died so suddenly in a car crash. But he can obviously run a helluva tight funeral.'

They drove home in stunned disbelief. Did people really meet their future partners at something like that? Nobody had appeared to drink much either. Sarah and Judith were sufficiently embarrassed at apparently being social outcasts that they'd passed off their gin and tonics as fizzy water.

Over coffee at Judith's, they began to see the funny side.

'Vicky would have loved it,' said Judith, flopping into a sofa and kicking her shoes off. 'Pity she couldn't make it. Anyway she'll be back soon so we'll find out how she got on.'

Vicky had had the perfect excuse. She'd been asked to give a talk on Romania to a businesswomen's club in Winchester. She'd met the organiser while covering a planning protest against a new housing development. It was one of those protests that had looked great on the news-room prospects list for the day, with organisers predicting several hundred angry protagonists and plenty of banners. The thirty or so mostly ladies-who-lunch types had turned up, huddled under designer umbrellas in their Puffa jackets on a rather bleak Friday afternoon. It hadn't made for much of a story so it had been relegated from a news package to a short read by the presenter over three shots of the 'crowd'. Vicky and her cameraman had had to bunch them all up together to make it look busy. The organiser had apologised profusely to Vicky about the lack of turnout, mysteriously blaming it on the weather, an old Robert Redford film on the telly and the latest crisis in the Balkans.

Afterwards she'd insisted on dragging Vicky off to a nearby tea room for a pot of Darjeeling and some cellulite-defying cream cakes. Still recovering from her pork and chips regime, Vicky had abandoned all hope of toned thighs and tucked in. The talk had got around to Romania, with Vicky becoming passionate about the children and all the experiences they'd had. Before she knew it, she'd been persuaded to give a speech on the subject.

'I can't do it,' she'd wailed to Judith afterwards. 'I've never done this sort of thing before. I'd be hopeless.'

But Judith had assured her otherwise. 'Just put down some bullet points and speak from the heart. Make them laugh, make them cry. I think you'll be great.'

Vicky had had sleepless nights about it, but she knew deep down she wasn't going to back out of it, no matter how many excuses she created. It became a sort of compulsion, rather like going to the dentist. You loathe the idea, but if you don't go, your teeth might just fall out.

A car pulled up outside. It was Vicky back from her talk. Please let it have been a success, prayed Judith. She needs a boost of confidence.

'Well?' they both shrieked at her. 'How did it go?'

One look at Vicky's face and they didn't need to hear the answer. Her grin stretched almost from ear to ear.

'I think it worked,' she said, 'I honestly think it worked. I was so nervous, I've not been so nervous since my driving test. Well, the first two of them, anyway. And when they introduced me, I wanted to crawl under the table. But it's funny, once I got going, it was great. I know this sounds naff, but I really got a buzz from it. Also they loved your red worms, Jude, and you being mistaken for a prostitute.'

'Oh I *am* pleased they derived so much pleasure from my little discomfort,' said Judith, laughing.

'And what's more, I've been booked again. I've been asked to speak at a business club dinner. And this time I'm being paid! Anyway, enough of me. What happened at the singles club? I suppose you two have come home with bulging Filofaxes.'

'Er no,' said Judith. 'But we've had a crash course on how to organise a funeral.'

'Oh hell, was it that bad?'

'No, just infinitely worse.'

chapter twenty-two

It was becoming a regular nightmare. Roger looming out of the mist, Roger on the doorstep, Roger leering through her car window, Roger sneering at her supermarket trolley contents. And the worst, Roger an irritatingly smug contestant on *Countdown*. Occasionally the nightmare included Mervyn. Not the beautiful Mervyn she'd so adored, but the cheating Mervyn Vicky'd caught in flagrante in her flat. Except that in this particular nightmare, when he got up out of bed, he turned into Roger.

Vicky woke up, sweat dripping off her, confused and exhausted from violent and vivid dreams. Why couldn't she dream about the good times with Mervyn – the blissful holiday they'd spent in Menorca, sunning themselves by day, seafood lunches overlooking crystal-clear waters, followed by cool evenings with shared laughter as they worked their way through the hotel's cocktail menu followed by passionate sex half the night? Why couldn't she get the irritating Roger out of her head? She'd tried to analyse it and came to the conclusion that although she despised him for what he'd done, she still felt somehow guilty about leaving him in the lurch. Vicky was going through a typical woman's phase of blaming herself. It was her fault that she didn't guess about the wedding plans, she should have realised he wanted to marry her and therefore not hurt his feelings. Then there was her own very private sadness about never being married, not that she'd wanted to marry Roger, but realising that probably nobody else would ever ask her.

She slid out of bed, for once glad of the lonely reality, shoved on a dressing gown and went downstairs. Judith was already bustling about, washing machine and dishwasher churning and a welcome smell of coffee and toast coming from the kitchen.

'Great timing,' she said. 'Shit, you look dreadful.'

'Sorry, Jude,' said Vicky, scraping back her dishevelled hair. 'Bad night. Another nightmare about Roger.'

'Grab this.' Judith handed her a large cup of coffee. They settled in silence to breakfast and the papers.

'And about bloody time too,' exclaimed Vicky suddenly, slamming down the *Daily Mail*. 'At last they're looking at changing the way people book weddings at register offices. In future, both parties would have to meet the registrar in advance to do all the paperwork. They've quoted some chap saying they do have surprise weddings occasionally but none of the unsuspecting parties has ever backed out. Huh, well I know someone who did.'

'Yeah,' said Judith grimly, 'and you'd better read on because you get a mench in that piece. Sorry, hon, but you might as well know.'

Vicky scanned the paper frantically. There were a couple of paragraphs near the end of the piece, detailing 'Victoria Chadwick's dramatic escape from her own wedding at Plymouth Register Office'.

'Will I ever escape from all this?' she asked despairingly.

'Doubt it,' said Judith unhelpfully. 'Just be grateful they didn't sign you up afterwards to advise our Olympic athletics hopefuls on their finishing speed. Better to just put it out of your head. That's what ultimately counts.'

The phone rang. It was Sarah, who'd read the piece in the *Mail*.

'It's all right,' said Judith, 'she's seen it, but thanks for warning me. You what? You're kidding! You've got a date? Get me a powder. Trust you to be the first of us this year – I'll be lucky if I manage within the decade.'

They hung up.

'Well whaddya make of that?' said Judith, still staring at the receiver.

'To put it crudely, I think she's looking for a nine-inch wallet,' said Vicky. 'I know Sarah's trying to be good with money but she isn't succeeding. She's had a reality bypass where that's concerned. Did you know she's ordered a top-of-the-range kitchen for this flat she's buying? And she's spent a small fortune ordering curtains?'

'No I didn't,' replied Judith. 'But it doesn't surprise me. They might as well have dedicated "Hey Big Spender" to her. She's been up this particular alley so many times before. Unlike you and me, Sweet Charity doesn't have sleepless nights about her bank balance. She's always been hopeless with money and I suppose she always will be. The only thing that would change her is the right chap with a Fort Knox style security system on his finances. He'd have to cut off all access to telephone ordering and bonk her senseless to keep her out of the shops.'

'Don't I know it,' said Vicky ruefully. 'I'm still recovering from the Hong Kong shopping experience last year. Those silk suits, when I have a thin enough day to get into them, were an absolute bargain, but what I saved I paid for in the interest on my credit cards. Sarah knew she'd be in deep trouble with Bostik when she got back, but she still carried on. It's almost as if she's trying to get one up on the banks. It's just absurd.'

'Anyway, we're just jealous because she's got a date and

we haven't,' retorted Judith. 'Mind you, if it's one of those singles club misfits, then she's welcome. You've got to admire her confidence though. If that were me, I'd be terribly nervous. Also there's all that body maintenance stuff. Waxing your legs, getting your roots done, plucking your eyebrows. It's all basic pain. Then there's the clearing out of the handbag so you don't look like a slut. Picking the right music for when they arrive, putting erudite books in the loo just in case he has a brain. No, on the whole, I've got far too lazy, and anyway there wasn't anyone remotely worth the bother at that terrible club.'

Vicky glanced up from her coffee. 'Do you think I'll ever have sex again?' she asked.

'Don't be ridiculous, of course you will. I bloody hope so. It's just a question of meeting someone, quick coup de foudre and then suddenly you're in the sack. Just like that.'

'Yeah, but where are we going to meet these six-pack sensations?' asked Vicky.

'Well not at the Sad Plonkers and Lonely Losers Club,' said Judith brightly. 'Look, not so long ago you were worrying yourself senseless about giving that talk. Now you're a star with another booking. Who knows where this could lead? You could have a whole new career ahead of you. There's big bucks to be made out of this, you know. You don't have to be a celeb necessarily and it's one of those things most of us just can't do. Remember, after death, divorce and being done for drink driving, public dinner speaking is the thing most people dread.'

'Yeah, just sneaks in above the holocaust, second-hand car salesmen and shampoo marketing executives,' replied Vicky, cheering up a bit.

The doorbell rang. 'Anyway,' continued Judith as she headed for the hall, 'who knows what could await us on the front step? Remember our evening in Cahoots at Christmas, we did all resolve not to turn down invitations.'

She came back a couple of minutes later looking perplexed.

'So was that Dream Boy in his *An Officer and a Gentleman* white jacket and gold braid?' said Vicky.

'Er no. Boot's on the other foot, so to speak,' said Judith. 'That was the local amateur theatrical society. They're short of a pianist, desperately. And wondered if I could help them out.'

'And you said yes, I hope.'

'Well, I said I'd have to look at my diary.'

'Right, Judith Fielding,' announced Vicky defiantly. 'If I can risk all by standing up on my feet for forty minutes and giving a talk, you can bloody well get down there and play the piano. You play brilliantly and I know what's in your diary at the moment. Sod all. Just a couple of dreary corporate videos at work. You've got to say yes and, who knows, in a fortnight we could be snuggling up to Harrison Ford and his long-lost twin brother. Remember that resolution you were talking about just now. No more having to trawl supermarkets, scan the personal ads and saddos on Teletext, making up the numbers at dreadful dinner parties.'

'I suppose we might have resorted to that eventually,' replied Judith. 'Oh, all right, it's only fair. I made you do that speaking gig, I'll call them up and say yes.'

Vicky indicated the phone on the kitchen table. Judith dutifully picked it up and dialled a number from a slip of paper she'd been given.

'I'm going to have to get my skates on,' she said after she'd spoken to the society's chairman. 'There are only two weeks of rehearsals left and they haven't even started on the songs. It'll be chronic, but I start tonight.'

'Well, how did it go?' All eyes were on Sarah. She paused, milking the situation for all it was worth.

'Hm, well, William picked me up in his BMW. Leather

seats, by the way. And we went out for dinner down at that Spanish seafood place near the Docks.'

'Then what?'

'We had dinner, prawns, oysters, that sort of thing, expensive bottle of wine.'

'Then what?'

'We went back for coffee.'

'Where?'

'My flat.'

'Then what?'

'Well nothing really. We had coffee, a bit of a snog and then he left.'

'OK, so was he a good kisser and are you seeing him again?' Judith and Vicky almost chorused in stereo.

'He says he'll phone. He's given me his mobile number too,' she finished triumphantly. 'Now how about you two? How's the new world of showbiz?'

Judith paused while the waiter produced a huge plate of nachos. They'd decided to celebrate Sarah's date, and Judith and Vicky's new ventures, with a meal in Cahoots.

'Well I don't think Cameron Mackintosh needs to re-arrange his diary. His pulse certainly won't be racing to get this one into the West End, if that's what you're all hoping,' said Judith. 'It's a revue basically with a cast of people, some who can sing and some who *think* they can. There are a few sketches and they want me to play some stuff between them. And then there's the Explicit Sextet.'

'Whaaaat? Didn't think local am dram was that raunchy,' said Sarah.

'No, sadly not. Appearances are mercifully deceptive. Apparently their wardrobe mistress preys on the recently widowed and helps them turf out their attics. Well the cold spell's obviously killed off a few because they've acquired a collection of tailcoats and some very glam thirties evening dresses. From that, they got the idea of putting on a Fred

Astaire/Ginger Rogers type of routine. So they're doing a medley of Irving Berlin and Cole Porter numbers.'

'Why the Explicit Sextet?' Sarah was intrigued.

'Quite simple, really. There's six of them.'

Judith went on to outline the evening's rehearsal. No, there wasn't anything interesting in the potential totty department. Mostly bearded anoraks, a couple of suspected walking wounded and some definitely-married-but-looking-for-discreet-adventure types. But it had not been anything like as horrific as the singles club.

'After the final show, there's a posh party that I don't think I can get out of,' said Judith. 'I'd appreciate a bit of support. Why don't I get you tickets for the last night, and then you can have a good laugh at my expense – literally.'

She told them the date. Unfortunately it clashed with Vicky's next after-dinner speech.

'Oh I'll come,' said Sarah. 'Remember our resolution. No invitation refused, no stone unturned.'

'Well I think this will be more of a case of no turn unstoned,' smiled Judith. 'Anyway, what about your new bloke? Would you want to subject him to this? I know how fast you work, Sarah Franks. You two could be an item by then.'

'Hmmm. Doubt it.'

'It sounds promising to me,' said Judith. 'You've obviously started the ancient mating ritual of swapping phone numbers.'

'True,' said Sarah. 'But there's a bit of a problem.' She paused, nervously. 'I think William wears a wig.'

'What do you mean, you think?' gasped Judith, willing herself not to laugh. 'Didn't you run your fingers through his hair, check it for nits, hairspray, mousse, that kind of thing?'

'Well I didn't. You see I'm pretty sure it's a wig so I didn't want to touch it somehow. It's a bit early days for that sort of confessional.'

'If it's that blindingly obvious, is there any need to discuss it?' said Vicky. 'Mind you, I have to say I've never been out with a man in a rug, so I can't speak from experience.'

'Ditto,' said Judith.

'Well I just want him to handle it in his own way,' said Sarah, feeling herself go crimson. 'He had one of those rather jaunty tweed caps and a Barbour on when I met him. Now I understand why.'

'And where did you meet him?' asked Vicky.

'We were parked next to each other in the car park at the clinic,' said Sarah. 'I'd got hemmed in and he helped me out. It was bucketing with rain and, very romantically, he held an umbrella over me while I dropped the entire contents of my handbag all over the ground. He might have a wig but he has a gorgeous car.'

'I hope he's not a LOMBARD,' said Judith, suspiciously.

'LOMBARD? What's that?'

'Loads Of Money But A Right Dick,' said Judith, grinning.

Abba music was blaring out of a small ghetto blaster as Sarah leapt about her flat, paint brushes flailing as she joined in the chorus of 'Mamma Mia'. Miraculously, her last credit card had swiped at the local hardware shop and she'd come back with several pots of paint. Hair unwashed, no make-up on and wearing an old pair of leggings and a T-shirt that even the poorest nation would have turned down, Sarah was rather enjoying herself. The flat was dark and gloomy and needed a quick facelift. She was just beginning to slap on the lime green in the bathroom when she heard a knock at the door.

Must be a salesman or a misrouted parcel, she thought, wiping her hands. *Nobody knows I live here yet*. The roller had left a fine spray of lime green on her face, hair and clothes.

On the doorstep stood William the Wig. *Oh shit*, thought Sarah. *I couldn't have looked more dreadful if I'd tried. Did I clean my teeth this morning and oh why didn't I start this earlier?*

William thought Sarah looked incredibly sexy despite the paint. He saw her full figure and dishevelled blond hair and a sort of wildness that many men would happily pay for.

'Well you have caught me on the hop,' said Sarah, praying that in her next life she'd look permanently like Cindy Crawford. 'I don't always look like this.'

'I know that,' replied William. He seemed nervous. 'Look, can I come in? There's something I need to tell you. It's really, really important.'

'Of course,' she said awkwardly. Even a quick trip to the bathroom couldn't salvage this one. 'I'll make some coffee.'

In the privacy of the kitchen, she tried to scrape off some of the paint from her face with kitchen roll but only succeeded in making it worse. Instead of spots, she now had stripes. But William seemed much too distraught to notice. She laid down two cups of coffee, a jug of milk and a sugar bowl.

'I don't quite know how to tell you this. I've rehearsed it in my head endlessly, I've talked myself out of telling you and then talked myself into telling you because I really like you, Sarah, and I think you ought to know. It's only fair.'

'What's only fair?' said Sarah, her mind whisking through various possibilities. Clap, Aids, terminal cancer, impending holy orders, appearance on *The Cook Report*, gay? Oh no, not that one again. Anything would be better than that.

'It's no good, it's deeply personal but I've got to tell you. I owe it to you.' William hung his head as if in shame.

'What is it?' she asked gently.

'I just hope you don't react the wrong way, but I need to tell you that I wear a wig.'

Sarah started to quake inwardly. How could she begin to tell him that she and her two best friends had giggled for the best part of an evening about it? That she'd guessed immediately and had had to make conscious efforts to stop herself from running her fingers through his hair when they'd kissed?

She fought hard not to let the sense of let-down show.

'Most people don't realise,' William continued, 'but I just thought I ought to let you know, especially if we're going to see more of each other. I'd like that if you would, but I would totally understand if this, er, bombshell might put you off.'

'No, William, it doesn't. Of course it's a bit of a surprise.' Sarah couldn't quite look him in the eye, her voice quivering slightly with contained laughter. 'When we get to our age, we don't always have everything in place, so to speak. I mean, I'm sure you could interpret great works of art on my thread veins. Middle-aged dating is a bit like that. We're not all supermodels any more.'

'I hoped you would accept it,' William exclaimed joyfully. 'I just felt I had to tell you early on. It would have been terrible for you to find out at a more, er, crucial time.'

He sipped his coffee and seemed to relax. Sarah, having now found some inner control, warmed to him as she thought of the luxury leather interior of his car and took in the expensive cut of his dark suit. I bet his house is full of tastefully expensive things too, she mused, imagining herself standing at the doorway of some wonderful country house with two perfectly groomed Afghans by her side, being photographed for *Hampshire Life*.

'How about dinner again later this week then?' he said hopefully. 'There's a little French place I know in Southampton that is very good. Do you fancy that?'

'Could do,' answered Sarah. 'Or we could go to my absolute favourite Italian in Winchester? I know you'd love it.'

William shook his head. 'Sorry, sweetheart, bit too close to home.'

'What do you mean? Bit too close to home?'

'The wife. Don't want to be spotted, do we,' said William. 'Must be discreet.'

'The wife, what wife?' Sarah stopped in her tracks. She glared at him, forgetting that she was still covered in smears of lime green paint. She was shouting now.

'Do you mean to tell me that you've come all this way to do the "hey, big confession, Sarah, I wear a wig, hope you don't mind" and then just drop in the "oh, by the way, I'm married."'

'I, er, thought you realised. I'm married but I'm not really married, if you know what I mean,' William spluttered.

'Married but not married. It's all so bloody clear now why I only got your mobile number, why you did a forty-mile round trip to take me out to dinner and come back here for coffee. Well, don't tell me, I know what you're going to say next. "My wife doesn't understand me, we don't have sex any more. Oh, and I can't divorce her because she owns half my business."'

'Yes, yes, that's all true,' said William, astounded.

'Of course it's true,' snapped Sarah. 'It's a rusty old record all you married creeps trot out when you get found out. Anyway, there's the door, why don't you bugger off home to the wife who doesn't understand you. Try having sex with her for a change and then you might stop bothering people like me.'

'Sorry, Sarah, I'm sorry, I thought you realised.'

'Sorry is just the silliest word ever invented. In fact it's so silly, it must have been invented by a man. Now fuck off and leave me alone.' She was now out in the hallway holding the door open. William got up without saying another word.

'Bugger off,' she shouted after him, incandescent with rage. 'And by the way, I knew it was a bloody wig anyway. You could have saved yourself a trip.'

Two workmen digging a hole on the opposite side of the road burst into applause.

'Well done, love,' they shouted. 'He wasn't worth it.'

'No, he bloody wasn't,' said Sarah aloud, banging the door behind her. She caught sight of herself in the hall mirror and laughed. The green streaks made her look like an alien passed over at a casting for *Star Trek* for being too alien.

Pouring out a glass of wine with one hand, she dialled Judith's number with the other.

'Hi, it's me,' she said. 'Just had a cosy little chat with Wiggy.'

'Oh dear, this sounds ominous.' Judith immediately picked up the tone in Sarah's voice. 'What now? Don't tell me we're talking dentures and glass eyes as well?'

'Well, he might as well have, for all I care,' said Sarah sarcastically.

'Ooops,' said Judith, trying not to laugh. 'Let me guess, he's got a wife who doesn't understand him.'

'Got it in one. The usual script.'

'And we thought it was just that he was a bit challenged in the follicle department. I'm sorry, Sarah.'

'Well I'm not,' she raged. 'He came all the way over unannounced to make this huge confession about wearing a wig. And then happened to mention, like you do, that he's got a wife as well.'

'Oh well, hair today, gone tomorrow,' said Judith. 'Come round and I'll crack open a bottle of hair restorer.'

chapter twenty-three

By the time she'd reached Judith's house, Sarah had calmed down and was already beginning to see the funny side. She was also anxiously watching the fuel gauge on her car, worried that she might not have enough petrol to get there and back. Her last remaining credit card was about to retire, due to a terminal case of overswipe. Judith took one look at her, burst out laughing and indicated the bathroom door.

'I know we're all trying to save the planet by going green but you're taking that a bit far,' she said. 'Get scrubbed up and I'll pour you a G and T.'

Ten minutes later, and now pink rather than green, Sarah emerged from the bathroom in one of Judith's dressing gowns.

'Well it wasn't a good start to the Chinese Year of the Big Date, was it?' said Judith, handing her a glass. 'Let's drink to the Year of the Rat. And there I was, thinking we'd all be meeting this new hot pair of trousers at the party after my show next week. You'll still come, won't you? I'd still like some moral support.'

'Of course, Jude. Don't forget our resolution – every invitation, every opportunity could lead to a shag. The trouble is, when you've been married for so long, even to the pits of the world like Bostik, you do get used to going to things together. It'll be strange going without a partner.'

'It's exactly the opposite for me,' replied Judith. 'I'm used to turning up on my own and making animated small talk over the canapés with the only single man, who's usually come to the party dressed as Quasimodo. Actually what really bothers me is that there *will* be some single men at this bash. And I can assure you they're definitely not from Planet Top Totty. They've got their own hair all right, but they've got the bushy beards, sandals and socks to match.'

'Hmm, we'll have to do something about that,' pondered Sarah. 'I've an idea. Which you won't like much.'

Tempers were beginning to fray at rehearsals. Time was running out, lines hadn't been learnt, and the director, a skeletal guy called Steve, had walked out in a tantrum. Judith was secretly enjoying it all. It was such a change from work, where professionalism and deadlines were the stuff of life. Here at the village hall, chaos was king. The stage creaked, the curtains had an obvious tear, the piano looked as though someone had chucked battery acid all over it, and it was so cold, you could see your breath in the hall. Judith played in fingerless gloves, coaxing the cast through their songs, and pleading with them to learn the words. Even the Explicit Sextet were getting their knickers in a twist. Irving Berlin and Cole Porter weren't just turning in their graves, they were on the waiting list for pirouette lessons.

'Why can't you play in tune with my singing?' demanded one woman in the sextet, whose voice sounded like a sheep having a particularly difficult birth. And as for a simple dance routine, choreographed to 'Steppin Out With My Baby', it soon became apparent that Les Dawson was to piano playing what the Explicit Sextet were to hoofing.

'Step, step, step, ball change,' shrieked the choreographer, a well-preserved woman in her fifties with a wardrobe of endless chunky sweaters, leggings and half a ton of cheap jewellery. 'Come on, Connie, kick that leg. Think Ginger, think glamour. You're in a long slinky dress, dancing on the arm of a devastating man.'

'I don't know about dancing on his arm, I might be tempted to trample all over his face,' came the forceful reply from the stage. 'How can I be poetry in motion with this blob beside me? And you've eaten garlic again, you bastard. Turn your face away from me when you sing. I don't suppose Ginger Rogers had all this bother.'

'No, I don't suppose she did,' scowled her partner. 'At least Fred Astaire was luckier. He had a partner two stone lighter with some sense of rhythm.'

It's only for a fortnight, Judith told herself, *only two weeks and then I can bid farewell to the Explicit Sextet, the fingerless gloves and all the shouting.* But she didn't regret joining the show. Sarah was right. Every invitation, every opportunity, no stone unturned. It was fun in the loosest sense of the word.

Vicky was getting ready to give her talk. She was nervous all over again, as if it was the first time. She kept reading and re-reading her notes. She'd rehearsed in front of a mirror, but the more she practised the more it sounded like nursery rhymes. This time, though, she'd remembered to wear something comfortable. She'd felt fat, standing up in front of an audience last time, and got fatter as her talk went on. She couldn't concentrate on what she was saying and hold her stomach in at the same time. This time she'd opted for one of her Hong Kong silk suits with some hidden help underneath in the form of what lingerie departments politely call 'tummy control'. It always sounded like pest control. Same difference really, she supposed. Flab isn't exactly fab, after all. Vicky didn't even have the other two's excuse of having had children. Her bulges were all her own work.

Sarah and Judith were also busily getting ready for their big night out at the village hall. Because all three of them were going out, reminding each other about 'no stone unturned', they'd drawn up a rota for the bathroom. Judith was last in, so Sarah and Vicky, already tarted up, were allowing themselves a glass of wine to steady the nerves while they waited.

'That'll be my taxi,' said Vicky, getting up to the door-bell. She went out to the hallway.

'There must be some mistake,' Vicky was saying to some mystery people on the doorstep. Sarah followed her out quickly.

'No, no, they're expected,' she butted in. 'Do come on through. Have a seat and I'll get you both a drink. White wine OK? We've only just opened it.'

Vicky sat gobsmacked as two white-tuxedoed young men sat down on the settee and were handed glasses of wine. Judith emerged from the bathroom and put her head around the door.

'Oh hello,' she said, puzzled at the two strange men sat on her sofa. 'Who are you two? Friends of Simon? I'm afraid he's in London this weekend with his girlfriend.'

'No, no,' said Sarah, grinning nervously. 'They're here for us. Meet Tristram and Giles. They're our escorts for the evening.'

The show was a nightmare, but the audience seemed to love it. Heckling was obviously expected and actually appeared to be welcomed by the cast. Forgetting lines induced hysterics from the audience. Judith soon discovered how the cast overcame their learning difficulties on the night. Most had found ingenious ways of having their lines in front of them. There were loads of previously unre-hearsed newspapers on stage with scripts Sellotaped inside. Words written on wrists, on props, anywhere. And of course the best laughs were won when one actor revealed his particular secret to the audience, a script taped to a table, immediately causing his fellow actor to dry.

The audience helpfully went to the local pub en masse at half time. The forty-five-minute interval was apparently a tradition which made the second half go with extra zing.

But the night belonged to the Explicit Sextet. Tottering on for the grand finale in their evening dresses and tail-coats, they looked ridiculous. They totally mucked up the words of 'Top Hat, White Tie and Tails', getting all the items of clothing in the wrong order so that the lyrics didn't rhyme. Then they proceeded to murder 'I've Got My Love To Keep Me Warm', by singing it about a semitone flat. 'Oooch,' cried the audience, cheering for more.

But the real moment came when Connie and her partner went into their big number, 'Steppin' Out With My Baby'. Frightened of forgetting the words, they'd arranged idiot boards on either side of the stage so they could read each line as they did their routine. The first verse went like clockwork. Unfortunately the back stage crew, now several beers into the performance, decided that there was some fun to be had. So the boards miraculously appeared in front of the tabs for verse two. Fred and Ginger were well and truly shown up as they tried to sing and dance. For the final verse, the boards were turned upside down. Judith could have been bashing out a Mozart sonata in the style of Mrs Mills, for all it mattered.

The audience was on its feet, cheering and whistling. Clearly this was what they'd expected and enjoyed. Sarah, sitting with Giles and Tristram, was terrified they'd think it really naff, but they'd entered into the spirit and were wiping their eyes from laughing.

'What did you think?' said an exhausted Judith, as she emerged from the piano.

'Fat, flat and very, very funny,' Sarah summed it up. 'The

lads loved it too. Actually they've been great sports. Cor, I wish I were twenty years younger. I'd snap up the pair of them. They're students at the uni so they've even got brains as well.'

Judith had taken the escort shock in her stride. Sarah gambled on her being too wound up about playing to worry unduly, and she'd been right. But now the moment of truth had to be faced. It was party time for the cast, and the hall had been transformed into nightclub mode – now candlelit, with tables, a disco, a buffet and a bar. It was time to brazen it out. Did they come clean about Giles and Tristram being escorts or did they pass them off as boyfriends? Sarah had already decided the latter and busily gave Judith a crash course on the subject in the ladies' loo.

'You're with Giles, he's a microbiologist and you've been seeing him for a couple of months. He's then introduced me to Tristram, who's studying accountancy. I must say I'd like to study their chemistry and see what sort of fizzle we could create.'

'Sarah!' said Judith, appalled. 'They're young enough to be our sons.'

'Oh come on, Jude, I'm only kidding. It's only a bit of fun. Everyone's going to be pissed anyway by the look of things and at least we're spared the advance of the knitted yoghurt brigade you've warned me about.'

'Oh give me some anabolic stair rods,' said Judith. 'I'll need something to get me through this.'

She needn't have worried. Giles and Tristram turned out to be terrific fun at the party, invited them to dance, constantly refilled their glasses and plied them with food. Their effect on the rest of the company was mesmeric. They watched their new pianist with fresh eyes, while the beard and sandals set made mental notes to hire white tuxes next time. It obviously had the desired effect.

'Why do you two do this?' said Judith as soon as she could find a quiet moment to ask.

'To supplement our grants,' said Giles. 'It sure beats the hell out of shelf-stacking in Sainsbury's. You get invited to all sorts of do's and it can be quite fun. Actually we were both saying just now, this is the best night we've done so far. That show was a blast. I've never seen anything quite so naff. It was just total pants.'

'Pants?' queried Sarah.

'Just means rubbish,' whispered Judith. 'I get updated on life in the office.'

'Do you ever get propositioned?' said Sarah. Judith shot her a warning look. *Don't you dare*, she told her silently. Sarah retaliated with a *don't be stupid* look in reply.

'Sometimes,' said Tristram. 'But it's always easy to decline. We just plead pissed, brewer's droop. Then nobody gets upset. Also, present company excepted, we often escort women old enough to be our mothers.'

'But we could be your mothers,' exclaimed Judith.

'Well, neither of you look old enough.'

'Flattery will get you all over the place,' said Sarah. 'If you two have girlfriends, then I envy them.'

'Too busy doing this and studying,' said Tristram. 'Anyway, it's not often you get front-row seats for the Explicit Sextet.'

Judith glanced around the hall. 'Do you think they've guessed?' she asked him.

'No, not this lot,' said Tristram, casting an experienced eye around the crowds. 'Far too pissed. Also, with respect, you two are out of their league. You both look terrific, you've both got good careers, you're bright and intelligent. We're both surprised you needed to hire us tonight.'

'Nice of you to say,' said Judith wistfully. 'But no, neither of us has exactly been snapped up. That's the trouble with our age group. Most men aren't as enlightened as you two.

They still want some blonde bimbo on their arm. It's a bit like men and cars really. They want the latest model that goes like the clappers, and then after a bit of mileage, they want a no-fuss trade-in deal on a newer version every couple of years.'

'There are some sad plonkers around,' nodded Tristram in agreement. 'I really hope you find somebody who's good to you.'

'Finding somebody full stop is a major problem,' said Judith, the drink plunging her into a confessional mood. It was ridiculous talking to this chap, young enough to be her son, but he seemed to understand.

She continued: 'Sarah's made us promise to accept all invitations this year. That's our New Year resolution and we've promised to keep each other to it. Actually she's right. I would have chickened out of tonight otherwise, but I've had a ball. In fact, if you were thirty years older, I'd proposition you here and now. Don't panic, because I'm not going to, but tonight has made me realise I've got to get out more, have some sort of life.'

'Good,' said Tristram. 'Go for it.'

Two hours, three bottles of wine and some frantic disco dancing later, Judith and Sarah sat in the kitchen, slumped over a coffee pot and the dregs of a bottle of white wine. Sarah lit a cigarette and took a deep drag.

'Have you forgiven me?' she asked.

'What for?' replied Judith, staring at the bottom of her coffee cup, too tired to reach for a refill.

'For hiring the guys. I thought you'd be livid.'

'No, it was a shock. I thought I'd be appalled but I had too much on my mind at the time. And then it was fun. I learnt a lot tonight.'

'Phew. It was a terrible gamble but I thought it might be a laugh.'

'You were right. I've been avoiding life. I've got to start taking a few risks again. And not just work. One day, work might not be there, Simon will have left home and then what? A lonely old life, stuck in night after night, scanning the *TV Times* with a marker pen planning my nightly viewing. A glass of sherry over a microwave supper. Nope, there's got to be more to it all than that.'

'Yeah, there has,' replied Sarah, stubbing out her cigarette and pulling a face. 'Bloody hell, my head's hurting already. I thought hangovers were supposed to start the next day. Mind you, I'd still rather have a bottle in front of me than a frontal lobotomy.'

'Oh very funny. I'm not feeling too special either. I think we'll have to write off tomorrow.'

'Funny you should say that, because we've got some writing to do tomorrow,' said Sarah, rallying a little.

'Oh hell, not another of your mad schemes. What is it this time?'

'Wait and see,' said Sarah, tapping her nose.

chapter twenty-four

Speech number two had been a success, despite a disastrous beginning. Vicky's host and chairman at the dinner had committed the cardinal sin of hitting the pre-dinner drinks too enthusiastically and been of no help and support whatsoever. When Vicky's time to speak approached, he rose to his feet, steadying himself perilously with the tablecloth, banged the table vigorously with a spoon and announced, 'I'd like to introduce our speaker for the evening. I can't remember what her name is and I haven't a bloody clue what she's going to talk about. So here she is. I thank you.'

Everyone laughed and settled back in their seats. Except for Vicky, whose nerves were not in any way helped by the introduction. Thank goodness she'd made them laugh in the first couple of minutes and soon she had them gripped. Again her passion about her subject had won over her audience and she'd come back, exhausted but fulfilled, with three more bookings in her diary, including compèring a fashion show.

She'd been long since in bed and asleep before Judith and Sarah had practically fallen out of a taxi and crawled up the path. So they had to compare notes over Sunday morning breakfast. Except that the look of their green faces said it all. While Vicky tucked into a bowl of muesli, the others could only watch in disgust.

'Ugh, the sight of that gerbil food is making me feel sick,' said Sarah.

'I take it you had a great night out then?' replied Vicky between mouthfuls. 'So you won't be wanting a cooked breakfast, then?' The other two made retching noises.

'So how come, Sarah Franks, your eyes look like two piss holes in the snow?' Vicky continued cheerfully. They gave brief headlines on the evening in between much moaning and head holding.

Vicky collapsed with laughter when she heard about the show and the Explicit Sextet. 'Oh hell, I could have done with one of those guys last night,' she said, regaling them with some of the horror of her evening out. 'I'll make you both some coffee. Or is there any other hangover cure you'd like? A raw egg, some brandy or a little hazelnut yoghurt, perhaps?'

More retching noises.

'So what's the next thrilling instalment of Three Try To Get Laid?' continued Vicky. 'Come on, Sarah, it was your idea. What's the next step? We've now exhausted the worlds of singles clubs, after-dinner speaking and amateur dramatics. Where do we go from here?'

'Right here,' said Sarah, plonking the *Sunday Times* down on the kitchen table with a thud. She and Judith winced at the noise. Immediately a handful of leaflets offering insurance, car loans and catalogues fell out.

'Why do they load a perfectly good newspaper with half a rain forest?' said Vicky, scooping them up and depositing them in a bin. 'And give the paper boy a bad back. Anyway, what's the next cunning stunt? Careful how you say that one, you two, in your current state of health.'

Sarah picked out one of the supplements, flipped through several pages and read aloud to them.

'*Tim, own hair, teeth and business, late forties, GSOH, bored with bimbos, WLTM striking woman 35–40 for wining, dining and who knows what else. No fatties, no kids, no pets, London area only.'*

'Oh shame, that's me out of the running,' said Judith sarcastically. 'He sounds unspeakably vile with an ego so large it needs its own postcode. By the way, what's GSOH stand for? Gorgeous Specimen On Heat?'

'No, dippy. Good Sense Of Humour. WLTM is just the short form for Would Like To Meet,' explained Sarah. 'There's loads of them. Look, columns and columns of them. All we've got to do is reply.'

'Hell's teeth,' muttered Judith. 'I can't believe we're even discussing this.'

But Sarah went one better. She announced that each of them would have to reply to at least one ad. And, to make sure no one ducked out, she would post the letters on the way home to her flat that night.

Judith secretly scanned the columns for the least offensive and the most truthful. It was difficult as most of the *Sunday Times* readership appeared to be mostly millionaires offering yachting holidays in the Mediterranean. Eventually she plumped for an advertising executive from London hoping to hear from someone over 40 who enjoyed drinking wine and skiing.

'I'll pass on the last bit. The nearest thing I get to a downhill slalom is watching *Ski Sunday*. I'd probably be good getting off piste so I could help him out on the wine drinking. And at least I qualify on the age count,' she added. 'I don't mind handwriting the letter as he asks, but he's not getting a photograph. He'll have my phone number, first name and that's it.'

Vicky opted for a businessman from the Midlands, a good distance away from Hampshire so he wouldn't bother to follow up her letter, she decided. The man said he was a youthful fifty, whatever that meant, and enjoyed country pubs, DIY and the theatre.

'It's funny how a few of them list DIY as one of their hobbies,' she observed. 'I personally don't know any men who do any DIY, let alone enjoy it. They obviously think it's a big totty magnet. You can see the logic. Women read it and think, oh hell, he may well bore me senseless but he might just be able to put up shelves.'

Sarah was the last to declare her pick. Predictably, she'd made the most adventurous choice.

'*Englishman, 48, divorced and living in Spain, WLTM English rose for friendship and wherever that may lead. I enjoy wining, dining, art, Spanish culture and sunshine. You are 30–50, intelligent, preferably blond and voluptuous, with no ties. Write to me and, before you know it, we could be sharing our life histories over a glass of Rioja.*'

'Well that's you settled then,' said Judith. 'I'll get the paella in ready to throw at your wedding.'

A leaving card was doing the rounds of signing at Judith's office. Fred Stone, one of the world's great miseries, ran the stores, grudgingly parting with the stationery and pens as if they were coming out of his own pocket. By some minor miracle he'd been offered a better job in a firm of estate agents, clinched, everyone suspected, by a deliberately glowing reference from the bosses.

'I hate being hypocritical by writing something gushing, but he's always been so rude to me,' said Lizzie. She passed the card on to Colin, who was waiting for his new filming schedule to be spat out of a computer printer.

'How do you spell riddance?' joked Colin, pen in hand.

'Two d's. I've just looked it up,' replied Judith, laughing. 'By the way, I've got a transmission date for Romania. It's in just over three weeks' time in a good slot. It's had a couple of advance reviews which I've been told are really good.'

'Brilliant,' said Colin. 'So some of my stuff was in focus after all, then.'

'Well it was a struggle,' joked Judith. 'But I managed to salvage something. Also it's being entered for some awards, so you never know, it could be good news for our CVs. By the way, did you know, Vicky's reinvented herself as an after-dinner speaker, thanks to our trip.'

'Yes, I had heard a rumour. We'll have to book her for the rugby club bash then,' said Colin. 'Does she take her clothes off as well?'

'Only if you're very, very good,' replied Judith, picking up the ringing phone.

'Hi, Vick. We were just talking about you. Colin wants to book you to bare your soul and other bits and pieces at his rugby club do. What's that? Oh right, I'll pass it on.' She held two fingers up to Colin.

'I think that'll be a "no" then,' said Colin. 'Pity. The committee would have been so impressed if I'd hired a stripper with a brain.'

But Judith was no longer paying any attention to Colin. She was listening intently to what Vicky had to say.

'She's what? Bloody hell. And you've heard too. No, I haven't. Story of my life. Tonight, in Cahoots, eight o'clock. Tell Sarah. Brilliant, see you then.'

They'd booked a table in a small cubicle, knowing they'd want a good gossip and no eavesdropping. The Hangover from Hell a couple of weeks ago was now forgotten. All those resolutions about no more alcohol, drinking plenty of water to flush out the body, get slim, fit and have a stab at looking like Kate Moss had evaporated like the morning mist. They compared notes on the *Sunday Times* column.

'Well I haven't heard from my wine-quaffing free-style skier,' said Judith, 'so that lets me off.'

'Oh no it doesn't,' retorted Sarah, who was wearing another of her expensive power suits. 'You'll have to write to another one.'

'Well, I've heard from my Midlands businessman,' chipped in Vicky. 'He was quite persistent, he'd apparently rung me at work several times, and because I'm on dreadful shifts at the moment, he only caught me today. Thank God he didn't leave any messages. If it had got out at work, I'd have had my leg pulled forever.'

'What does he sound like?' asked Sarah.

'Frightful, to be brutally frank,' said Vicky. 'He's supposed to be a youthful fifty and into DIY. He sounded more like a hundred and fifty and making his own zimmer frame.'

'So what did you say?' the others chorused.

'Not a lot. He caught me rather on the hop. I had to rush off into editing some packages for the mid-morning bulletin so I had a really good excuse to fob him off. I just hope he got the message. Sorry, girls, the answer's a big no. He sounded really creepy.'

'So come on then, Sarah. When are you off to Spain?' said Judith, curiosity coming on in waves.

'Well,' said Sarah, pausing for effect, 'I've had a letter. His name's Leo, because he was born under the sign of Leo, and he lives just outside Malaga. He's divorced, doesn't appear to have or need a job, and lives in a villa out in the countryside. He lets some rooms in converted barns but that's about all I can tell you.'

'There must be more than that. How old is he, why is he divorced, does he have kids, what's the catch?' The questions were coming thick and fast.

'He says he's forty-eight, seems very well-educated, judging by the writing and spelling. No mistakes. I don't know about kids or the divorce. Look, I wasn't checking him at the local Child Support Agency, remember. He said he'd had loads of replies to his ad, about sixty, he reckoned. But he liked my letter because I sounded sincere and he approved of my job.'

'Oh, and what did you say about your job?' said Judith suspiciously.

'Well I just said I worked in this marvellous private clinic. Perhaps he thinks I'm a very caring person who's dedicated her life to the sick and needy.'

'Or perhaps he thinks you're some fantasy nurse in a kinky uniform,' said Judith.

'Anyway,' continued Sarah, undeterred, 'he's given me his address and we're going to send each other photographs. So I've brought along a few and I want you both to pick out the one which looks best.' She fished into her handbag.

'Shit, Sarah, these were taken years ago,' said Vicky, appalled at the pictures now being laid out on the table. 'That's a bit unfair, isn't it?'

'I daresay he'll do the same. How do I know he'll send pictures of himself anyway? OK, I was a bit thinner then and my hair was a bit more blonde.'

'Also your roots didn't need doing in that photograph,' observed Judith. She instantly regretted saying that when she caught the anguished look on Sarah's face.

'Well I'm a bit broke at the moment, what with moving and everything,' she explained, biting her lip. 'I haven't had time to get them done. I've also just had the bill for my divorce. And it was bad news.'

'Well tonight's nosh is on me then,' said Judith, hastily trying to make up. 'How much was it?'

'Well put it like this, if I'd known, I wouldn't have been having the new kitchen.'

'Didn't you ask how much it would be?' said Judith.

'Well no, you know me and money, if it's not in my head, it's not happening.'

'Look,' said Judith, gently, 'just how bad is your situation?'

'Not spectacular. I've got a wardrobe to die for and an

award-winning overdraft. And I'm already getting hassle from the mortgage people. Don't they realise you're broke when you've just moved? They bloody well should do, that's what they do all day.'

'For God's sake, Sarah, be careful. You don't want to lose that flat, do you. Just buy things when you can afford them. I know you don't want us to mention him any more but you don't have Alan's salary now to pick up the bills.'

Sarah shot her a glance. She always winced now at the sound of Alan's name. Not a word, not a letter, not a phone call had she received from him since the divorce. It was as if he was missing, presumed dead. She sensed he'd been in contact with Roz and Daniel but that they would not say, for fear of causing her any more upset.

'Death by cholesterol, that's what I should have done,' said Sarah, coming out of her thoughts abruptly.

'What?' said the other two.

'Death by cholesterol. Alan was always stuffing himself with chocolate and I always used to ration him. Now I wish I hadn't bothered. I might have been better off.'

'Ouch,' said Judith. 'Does it still hurt that much?'

'Yes, I suppose it does,' said Sarah. 'In fact it hurts very bloody much. I could have much more accepted him going off with another woman, but not a man. And then the bill for the divorce was just the last straw.'

chapter twenty-five

The letter sat defiantly on the mat, standing out from the bills and junk mail. From the stamp, Sarah knew immediately whom it was from. Good, strong handwriting, she thought. *Let's see what he looks like.*

The enclosed photograph showed a man in his late forties, with brown wavy hair, crinkly brown eyes and a friendly smile. He was wearing a casual light green shirt which set off a healthy tan. *First impressions are so important*, she thought to herself, *and so far so good*. Not a huge 'phwoar', nor a stirring from within, but a pleasant reaction all the same.

The letter was just as pleasant as the first one. Leo wrote about his life in Spain that appeared to be a simple, quiet existence. He'd worked in the city for a merchant bank, made enough money from an early redundancy payment to quit the rat race and live in the country he'd always loved. He'd now been there for five years, mixing a little with the ex-pat community but keeping largely to himself. He now found he missed certain things about living in Britain: good books, fog, Marmite, Cheddar cheese, *Top Gear* and the *Guardian*. What he loved were the open spaces, the views from his villa, bougainvillea spilling from all the balconies, simple fresh food and no hassle, no traffic queues, shrieking phones or constant stress.

Sarah folded the letter and put it in her handbag. She'd get the girls to give the photo the once over before she penned a reply. In the meantime, there was a day at work to contend with, plus an interview with her bank manager, who'd be asking some awkward questions. She smiled to herself, fingering the letter in her handbag once more. You never knew, this could be the answer to an overdrawn maiden's prayer.

The interview at the bank was worse than she'd expected. The manager, a stern young man – young enough to be her son, she suspected – told her in no uncertain terms that he was taking away her cheque book and guarantee card. In future she'd have to come into the bank to draw cash. Sarah felt as if she'd been stung by a very large insect from outer space. She'd explained about the divorce bill, which had been well over one thousand pounds, thinking this would get a huge sympathy vote. But the bank manager had done his homework and been through the very extensive file of letters to the former Franks household, which all featured the word 'unless'.

She begged and pleaded with him to be more lenient but he was adamant, saying it was for her own good. But as she walked out into the street, her quivering bottom lip gave way to tears and she fled back to the office.

'Jude? It's Sarah. The bloody bank manager's taken away my cheque book and cards,' she half whispered down the phone, not wanting the rest of the office to know. 'It's all right for people like him, sitting in judgement with their fat pay cheques and swanky BMWs. What about me and my pittance here and my grotty old Volvo? I feel like taking my overdraft elsewhere. Somewhere they'll appreciate it and be glad to have it.'

'Sarah, don't be daft,' said Judith soothingly. 'It'll be the same wherever you go. You've just got to get better organised. Do a few sums now and again, get yourself straight.

Then you'll get your cheque book and cards back. In the meantime, stay out of the shops, chuck out all those catalogues and just thank God that you don't have access to the shopping channels.'

Judith was right, of course, but Sarah was not in the mood to hear the truth. She was still enraged about the confrontation with the bank manager. Bloody men, all the bloody same. If it wasn't the bank manager, it was her divorce lawyer or Alan himself. All fleecing her, giving her grief one way or another. She opened her handbag to reach for a tissue and saw Leo's letter. She redialled Judith's number as a complete change of mood came over her.

'Jude? Me again. Sorry about that just now. You're right, and I was a bit sharp. Listen, I've had another letter from Spain. Yeah, really nice. Good piccie too. I want you and Vicky to give it the once over before I reply. Don't want to bugger this up. Later in the week's fine, but best if you come over to me. Slight lack of petrol. Just enough to get to work this week. Great, see you both then.'

She allowed herself a quick re-read of Leo's letter. Maybe, just maybe, the sun was coming out.

To avoid adding any further dents to Sarah's finances, Vicky and Judith insisted on bringing wine and a Chinese takeaway with them. By the time they got there, the whole car reeked of monosodium glutamate.

'God, that stuff smells good,' said Vicky, taking a huge sniff from the brown paper bag. 'There must be some kind of drug in it. Makes you go back and order another one. No wonder there's a takeaway on practically every street corner. Got to keep your E numbers up.'

They settled around Sarah's new kitchen table and admired the new cupboards, split-level oven and smart new Roman blind at the window. She'd picked Mediterranean tones of yellow, blue and green as the flat was rather dark. It certainly did look terrific, *but not so terrific if you can't afford to put on the oven*, thought Judith.

'Let's use chopsticks so we slow down our intake,' said Vicky. 'That way we might lose weight.'

'What planet are you currently on?' asked Judith.

'Oh, Planet Calorie Count. You should see my thighs at the moment. They shouldn't be allowed. I think they're almost an arrestable offence.'

'Don't particularly want to,' replied Judith. 'Anyway, what makes them so criminal?'

'Oh just a whole new intake of cellulite,' replied Vicky. 'Horrible puckered bits and thread veins. I'm beginning to thank my lucky stars I bombed with the man from the *Sunday Times*. Too many takeaways, too much wine. It's all catching up, I couldn't possibly get my kit off, even if Harrison Ford rolled up outside in a Ferrari and whisked me away. Anyway, that's so unlikely I might as well carry on. Come on, dish up, and for Chrissake, let's have a drink.'

'That report from our consumer correspondent, Will Power. And now back to the main studio,' said Judith, laughing.

Over the sweet and sour prawns, fried rice, Singapore noodles and pork chow mein, they all read and re-read Leo's letter avidly and assessed his photograph.

'Pity we can't see his hands,' said Vicky. 'You can learn so much about a man by his hands.'

'Whaddya mean, size wise?' asked Sarah anxiously.

'Well, there is that theory of course,' said Vicky. 'In my last newsroom, though, they reckoned feet were the better indicator. Big in the feet department means big in the bedroom.'

'And is it true?' asked Sarah.

'Well I can't speak from personal experience because at the time I was seeing the ghastly Roger and he was very much Mr Average in every department. Except when he talked about Tressed Out. Then he scored very high on the old bore-ometer.'

Sarah and Judith both laughed, trying not to spit out noodles, as they nodded to her to continue.

'But the biggest feet of all were owned by a chap called Den, who was one of the studio floor managers. All the girls got quite excited until he got the sack for ringing up gay chat lines and racking up a huge bill. We had a quick whip round for his leaving present and someone slipped in a BT phone card. Bit cruel when he opened his presents in front of us, but we did all have a laugh.'

'Well perhaps I could ask Leo to send me a photocopy of his hands,' said an unperturbed Sarah, 'and then I could send it off to a clairvoyant I know. She does readings off photocopies, she's absolutely brilliant. It's only twenty quid . . .' Her voice tailed off.

'Nope,' said Judith, emphatically. 'Not at the moment. You've got to start watching your cash. Get your debts paid off first and then you can dabble with half the clairvoyants in the northern hemisphere for all I care.'

While Sarah made some coffee, they each took time out to re-examine Leo's latest letter. It was impeccable, good strong handwriting in ink on good-quality notepaper, no spelling or grammar mistakes. Yet it gave away nothing other than the words on the page. The photograph too was non-committal. A fairly good-looking chap, wearing quite well and enjoying what seemed like an enviable lifestyle.

'Sorry, Sarah, can't find anything to help you,' said Judith. 'He doesn't look or sound like a psycho, if that's what you want us to tell you. There must be some normal blokes out there, although between us, we haven't exactly dredged up anything special so far.'

'He doesn't look like the slug of the century to me,' said Vicky. 'Why don't you just keep writing and take it from there. If he writes again, you could then suggest having a chat on the phone. It's no big deal at the moment, is it?'

Oh yes it bloody is, thought Sarah bitterly. *If they knew what financial shit I'm in, they'd realise that Mr Costa del Sol could be the answer to everything.*

The kitchen plunged abruptly into darkness. Sarah feigned annoyance at a power cut but she knew exactly what had happened. She'd run out of electricity and would have to get her key meter topped up. But she wasn't about to admit this so she fished out some candles and rammed them into the empty wine bottles.

'What a pity, I was enjoying the photo session,' joked Judith. 'Now Vicky's got a bit of news, haven't you, Vick?'

'Well yes, I've got another speaking gig. Well actually it's much more fun than that. I've been asked to compère a fashion show. It's for charity with local models and boutiques. It won't be Prada, sweetie, but it might be quite fun. And of course I haven't forgotten our resolutions. No invitations declined, no offers refused. So I've said yes.'

'Well done,' the other two chorused.

'And now your turn, Jude,' said Vicky, acknowledging imaginary applause. 'You've got something good to report too, so spill the beans.'

Judith paused, always embarrassed when she had to mention her own achievements. 'Oh all right, well my Romania documentary's now got a network slot and it's being entered for some awards.'

'Brilliant,' the other two chorused.

'Well I haven't won anything yet,' protested Judith.

'OK, point taken,' said Sarah, 'but you might meet some devastatingly tasty bit during one of the ceremonies and that'll be that. I can just see it. "And the award for the most outstanding documentary goes to . . ." and the spotlight falls on your empty chair at the table but you're of course underneath, snogging your socks off with a gorgeous hunk.'

'I've obviously led a sheltered life,' replied Judith. 'No Mr Perfect would keep me from grabbing that award. Anyway, calm down, you two, let's keep things in perspective. Now, about that fashion show, Vicky. Don't forget how to walk on the runway. Just imagine walking up and down with a pencil stuck between your buttocks, that's the posture.' She demonstrated an exaggerated catwalk movement plus angry young supermodel scowl on her face.

An hour later, Judith and Vicky said their farewells. Heading back home, Vicky quietly remarked how strange it was that Sarah's had been the only place in the road to have had a power cut.

'You noticed as well then. I think she's on a key meter and it had run out but she was too embarrassed to say anything,' said Judith.

'You're right. I think she's in big trouble financially,' said Vicky. 'I've seen that look of desperation in her face before. Like on the plane back from Hong Kong after she'd been on that spender bender. And did you notice, she's started smoking roll-ups.'

Sarah blew out the candles and groped her way upstairs. How dare they do this to me, she swore under her breath at the electricity company. She'd go to the key meter during her lunch hour and recharge her key. Then she'd go to the second-hand jewellers and see what they'd offer for her hardly worn white gold necklace and matching bracelet.

Tomorrow night, though, will belong to Leo, she decided, cheering up immediately at the thought. She'd spend the evening writing a long and chatty letter to him. Nothing too heavy, just friendly with perhaps a slight undertone of 'we could take this further if you ever thought of suggesting the idea'.

Sarah knew full well she was investing too much in these two letters from a stranger but she couldn't stop herself. She felt at her lowest ebb, as low even as when Alan had hit her. She always shivered when she thought of their fight. So much pent-up emotion, and yet so much release.

Perhaps she'd have to sell some earrings as well.

chapter twenty-six

The minute Vicky turned up at the school to compère the fashion show, she knew she'd made a big mistake.

For a start, the organiser, a well-padded woman called Mrs Sweet and definitely no Christian names, was evidently not a paid-up member of the fashion police. Fat bordering on obese, with thin greying hair scraped unflatteringly back, she had a booming voice to match and was sporting a large-check gathered skirt with a beige body warmer, which combined to lob on an extra three or four stone illusion to her already generous weight. Presumably she'll change for the big night, thought Vicky, who'd borrowed one of Sarah's spectacular suits, dieted frantically on cabbage soup all week to get into it and was now terrified of farting. Thank God for all that modelling stuff about sashaying up and down the catwalk with the imaginary pencil between your buttocks. The same technique might just work for the avoidance of rogue raspberries.

Vicky met the models, mostly local teenagers who were well into overdrive with excitement, convinced that the entire population of talent scouts employed by Storm, not to mention every fashion photographer on the planet, would all be in the audience.

Even the clothes were a nightmare, provided by boutiques from a bygone age. It was as if it were just a question of time before Crimplene was to make a comeback. Clutching a huge file to her ample bosom, Mrs Sweet fussed and fretted about the lighting, the music and the running order.

'I'll need some sort of script,' stammered Vicky, feeling desperately out of her depth. If someone had committed suicide during the show, the Queen had decided to take up modelling or the hall had been bombed by a mystery guerilla group, she'd have felt on home ground. But this was different and it definitely wasn't her territory.

'Script,' queried Mrs Sweet imperiously. 'What do you mean, script?'

'Well, just notes on the clothes, prices, that sort of thing,' burbled Vicky. 'Won't the audience want to know where to buy them?'

Mrs Sweet shot her a look of pure contempt. Sweet was turning very, very sour.

'I very much doubt it. You must realise that the audience here tonight won't be the slightest bit interested in fashion,' she boomed. 'They're just here to see and be seen and to patronise a worthy cause.'

'I see,' replied Vicky, not seeing at all. 'So what would you like me to say?'

'Oh you'll think of something. I thought you people knew how to do this sort of thing.'

Vicky nodded in defeat. She was still trying to get her head around the concept of people attending a fashion show who were not the slightest bit interested in fashion. Or in her case, they'd booked a compère who was not really a compère and they wanted her to speak but they didn't care much what she said.

The rehearsal was a shambles, owing mainly to a dip in the middle of the makeshift catwalk that had been built out into the body of the hall. Every wannabe Naomi Campbell or Jerry Hall managed to trip, no matter how many times they walked up and down. If they remembered on the way out, they got lulled into a false sense of security and forgot on the way back. If they tripped on the way out, they got so nervous they tripped again in anticipation on the way back.

Without any thought to the ages of the models, some young girls had to parade in outfits more fitting to the mother, even grandmother of the bride. Young lads of sixteen were made to look like dusty old civil servants approaching retirement. The music, played through a state-of-the-ark sound system, would have done a Debenhams lift proud. It kept stopping abruptly, leaving the poor model to carry on sashaying in enforced silence, usually punctuated by another slip-up on the catwalk while the tape was hastily changed or rewound. The lighting would best have been described as suitable for a supermarket checkout.

Vicky knew she had to make the best of it. She felt sorry for the kids having to do the modelling. If they could put on a brave face, so should she.

Sarah kept walking past her kitchen drawer, eyeing it as if a poisonous snake were about to slither out and bite her. She'd been storing up bills for over a fortnight, too afraid to open them. She sat at the table, rolled a cigarette, lit it and took a deep drag. One by one, she opened the letters and placed them neatly in a pile. There was an assortment of Visa bills, water rates, and final demands for her council tax, gas and telephone bills. She sighed and put them back in the drawer. Then she went upstairs and opened her jewellery box. A diamond solitaire ring, bought during her 'End of Bostik' spree, that she'd hardly worn would now have to be sold to help pay the bills. The Gucci watch she'd so proudly bought and worn once would have to follow suit. She sighed again, forcing herself not to cry.

Then she turned to the letter on her dressing table

and re-read it for the umpteenth time. It was another letter from Leo, just as delightful as the others. Evidently he'd written back almost by return, as far as Sarah could make out from the rather blurred postmark. Now he was suggesting that they swapped phone numbers and had a chat.

'Can't risk starting that,' she said aloud to herself. 'At the rate I'm going, I won't even have a phone.'

But she knew she'd do it anyway, and impulsively she reached for some writing paper and a pen and began another letter. This time she added her phone number at the top of the sheet. She detected her hand shaking as she stuck down the envelope and wrote Leo's address.

Nothing ventured, nothing gained, her grandmother used to say. She grinned inwardly at the memory of a feisty white-haired woman who'd advised her as a young teenager to 'love 'em and leave 'em, dear'. 'Get out there and have a good time before you settle down,' Nan had said before she died. *A woman ahead of her time*, thought Sarah. And what a pity she'd been too stupid to take Nan's advice. And what a pity she'd got pregnant.

Next thing she knew, she'd braved the wind and lashing rain to post the letter. *Too late now*, she thought as she stared at the red box. *I'm committed. Can't get it back now. My arms aren't long enough to reach into the box.*

With twenty minutes to go, Vicky was a bag of nerves. She sat in a room behind the stage, scribbling notes on what she'd seen of the clothes during the rehearsal in the hope of making a reasonable commentary.

She stopped when she heard Mrs Sweet 'n' Sour's distinctive boom down the corridor. The door swept open and there she stood, still in the unflattering check skirt and body warmer from the afternoon. Fashion was one of those concepts that had obviously passed Mrs Sweet by.

The ensemble was clearly in for the long run. Even a hint of an iron might have helped. Not a trace of make-up, not even a brush of lippy. Mrs Sweet would probably much rather have spent time mucking out stables than hanging around cosmetic departments. Suddenly Vicky felt strangely sorry for the woman, who seemed incapable of making the best of herself. Then again, she was puzzled. How could anyone be so arrogant as to swan around looking such a mess? Supreme confidence, a complete absence of mirrors and a refusal to attend regular eye tests, Vicky supposed. To look somewhat reminiscent of an old Russian bag woman *and* organise a fashion show needed very, very serious bottle.

'Ah, Victoria,' she brayed. 'I'll say a few words of introduction and then it's all yours. Have a good show. Enjoy. Enjoy.'

'Absolutely,' replied Vicky, thinking anything but. She took a deep breath and followed Mrs Sweet towards the stage, where a microphone had been rigged up.

Mrs Sweet boomed so loudly that the microphone was quite unnecessary. She probably didn't need a phone either, thought Vicky.

Then it dawned on her why she'd taken such a dislike to the woman. It was more than just the appearance factor, there was a touch of her mother in Mrs Sweet. That obsession with meeting the right people, being a slave to social climbing, desperate to be seen at the right events. But curiously, having secured the invitation, she didn't see the need to look the part as well as act it. Having bought the chic house from the pages of *Country Life*, she couldn't be bothered to clean it or keep it tidy.

Vicky took her place at the microphone. She took a deep breath, tried to remember all her telly training, and pretended that they were going live to her at some earth-shattering event. Speak clearly and think gravitas, she told herself. You know something they don't. Inform and entertain in that order.

'Good evening, ladies and gentlemen. My name's Vicky Chadwick and I'm your compère for this evening. We have a stunning fashion show for you tonight staged by a team of international supermodels. They've come all the way from behind that door over there.' She paused, relieved that the audience laughed. 'So put your hands together and let's welcome our first models on to the catwalk. And I think you'll agree, this is the look for spring.'

The applause mercifully activated the man on the music, who'd been dreaming of a decent pint in the pub over the road, to press the button and they were off.

Vicky had done her homework. In spite of Mrs Sweet, she reeled off prices and availability, complimented the young models and managed to crack a few jokes during the gaps in the music. She even persuaded the audience to cheer when the models tripped on the dip in the catwalk. As a result they were soon remembering where it was and many managed their outward and inward journeys without any mishap. They were then rewarded with even more applause. During one painful gap in the music, she led the audience in a brief bout of community singing until the next tape got going.

It was a great success, with the audience swarming around afterwards to Vicky to get repeat details on some of the outfits they'd seen. She caught Mrs Sweet sending her invisible hate daggers from the back of the throng. So the audience wasn't interested in fashion! Huh, well she'd shown them.

A grey-haired man in his late forties and dressed in a very sober dark suit, with an incongruously loud Deputy Dawg tie, shook hands with Vicky and introduced himself as the chairman of the charity.

'Absolutely marvellous,' he said. 'Best we've ever had.

You must, must promise to do it all again next year. Everyone loved all the details. You really did your homework. I know Mrs Sweet can't wait to book you again. Now come and join us for the champagne and nibbles.'

With that, he elbowed her firmly through the crowd to the back of the hall where caterers had laid out huge trestle tables and starched white tablecloths. Waitresses were now weaving in and out of the crowds carrying huge platters of canapés. Waiters busily plied everyone with champagne. There was a moment of almost total silence as everyone juggled with handbags, programmes, cigarettes and lighters so that they could miraculously produce two available hands to eat, drink and smoke simultaneously.

'My name's David Bletchley,' he told her. 'This is our biggest money spinner of the year so I can't tell you how grateful we are to you. Also because you did such a marvellous job, it'll be easy to persuade the boutiques to stump up their frocks next year.'

'Oh that's funny because . . .' Vicky stopped herself. Why rot up a good evening by slagging off Mrs Sweet 'n' Sour? Might get some more bookings, she thought to herself. Mustn't forget the girls' resolution, accept invitations, follow every avenue, leave no stone unturned. She shuddered, thinking how it could have all gone so dreadfully pear-shaped.

'Sorry?' said Mr Bletchley.

'Pear-shaped,' replied Vicky absentmindedly, her thoughts breaking into the conversation. 'Sorry, I was just thinking it could have all gone pear-shaped. You see, this is the first time I've done this sort of thing.'

'Good grief, I'd never have guessed. Also, if I may say so, you really look the part. You should have modelled that outfit. It really suits you.'

It should do, thought Vicky. *I've starved myself all week to get into it and it must have cost Sarah the best part of a grand.*

It was in soft buttermilk silk, parallel-leg trousers and a simple long-line jacket. Sarah had lent her all the accessories as well to finish it off. It had certainly done Vicky's confidence wonders even if it couldn't drown the noise of her rumbling stomach and the constant urge to break wind.

'I must say I was caught by your tie,' she said politely, thinking it was the height of naff. 'It's a bit of a show stopper, isn't it.'

Mr Bletchley nervously fingered Deputy Dawg. 'Just a little stab at fashion.'

'Where did you get it, don't tell me, Ties R Us?' she said cheekily. She was beginning to unwind from the tension of the evening.

They both laughed. Vicky took a gulp of champagne from her refilled glass. The hall appeared to lurch, momentarily.

'I seem to have swapped phone numbers with someone I hardly know,' confessed Vicky, more than a little the worse for wear. 'I kept remembering our resolution. Mustn't turn down any invitation, don't know if there was any invitation, but I seem to have this phone number on a piece of paper.'

Judith groaned and filled the cafetière. 'What was he like?' she asked.

'Can't remember,' said Vicky, hiccuping. 'The whole evening was a nightmare, I was so nervous, then it was all over, hic, and then there was this champagne. I think it was Sarah's suit that did it.'

'Did what?' queried Judith.

'Well I've got lots more, hic, bookings and I seem to have given away your, hic, phone number. Oh shit, Jude, I'm sorry.'

'Don't be. This guy sounds nice, actually, reading between your hiccups. If he calls, do you want me to fob him off?'

'No, hic, well yes, oh, hic, I dunno.'

'Glad we're clear on that one.' Judith smiled to herself. It was ages since she'd seen Vicky enjoying herself so much.

'It's for you.' Judith covered the receiver with her hand. 'Didn't let the grass grow under his feet, did he?'

'Oh shit, what do I say?' said Vicky helplessly.

'Can't help you there, hon. Up to you.' She grinned, handed over the phone and left the kitchen.

'Well?' she said a few minutes later when a red-faced Vicky poked her head around the sitting room door.

'Thursday night,' said Vicky. 'Oh shit, why did I agree to this?'

'Because you fancy him. And Thursday night is a good one.'

'Why?'

'Well it's not Monday or Tuesday, which are naff nights, and it's not Friday or Saturday, which are the serious biggies. Thursday night's cool. It's non-committal night. It implies you have better things to do at the weekend, but you could just fit him in between all your other commitments.'

'So how do you know all this, seeing as you claim to have given up on men?' said Vicky accusingly.

'Read it in *Cosmo*,' replied Judith, laughing. 'Seriously, think about it. Friday and Saturday are super seduction nights. Sunday is sacred. It's either slobbing out with whoever you spent Saturday night with or it's a bit of culture, an art exhibition or trendy concert with someone intelligent of either sex, or it's a face pack/toe nails/pilates jobbie for the week ahead.'

'What about Monday, Tuesday and Wednesday?' said Vicky, now totally confused.

'Well if you're having torrid sex at weekends, then you'll need a top-up early in the week. Or you're busy moving and shaking at work. Or you might be soaking up the latest movies, books and plays. So that only leaves Thursday. So as I said, it's a smart choice.'

'I'm not so sure a man in a Deputy Dawg tie is that smart a choice,' pondered Vicky.

chapter twenty-seven

'Something soft but smart, not too officey but not too casual,' counselled Sarah. 'A soft jacket with a hint of silk underneath. Trousers, perhaps, rather than a skirt. After all, he fancied you rotten in trousers, so that's his image of you at the moment. You need to recreate the magic. And if you're really, really interested in him, exfoliate everything that moves and wear seamless underwear. No zips, buttons or fiddly bits. You don't want any nasty marks.'

'Bloody hell, Sarah. We're only having dinner. This isn't the Big One,' protested Vicky down the phone.

'You never know, it might turn out to be,' said Sarah, warming to her theme. 'Just imagine, you're having a candlelit dinner and then, phwoar, you're struck by sexual lightning and decide this is it. Except that it can't be because you realise that you're wearing a pair of pants which should belong in a museum and you didn't shave your legs.'

'The way I'm feeling now, after nearly two weeks on cabbage soup, is, well, to put it bluntly, shite,' said Vicky. 'A plateful of alfalfa sprouts seems like quite a serious feast from where I'm coming from right now. Anyway, talking of hot dates, how's your man from Malaga?'

'Well, we've had a chat,' said Sarah, desperately grateful to be able to talk about it at last. 'He sounds really nice. We nattered for nearly an hour. It was very relaxed. I think we'll talk again.'

'I'm sure you will, when you've recovered from the phone bill,' retorted Vicky.

'Fortunately he phoned so he paid for the call. But I'll have a problem if he thinks I can reciprocate. Because I can't.' She was fingering another ring, this time a rather showy ruby ring that she knew full well would have to go. She couldn't quite bring herself to tell Vicky that she could only take incoming calls. BT had sensibly realised that they were going to have a problem extracting much money from Sarah and had put her on an incoming calls basis only. So far no one had rumbled her, because she was making her outgoing calls from work.

But she couldn't swing calls to Malaga, unless by some stroke of fate someone set up a transplant business on the Costa del Sol. Unlikely, she concluded wisely.

Vicky had arranged to meet David Bletchley in a rather smart wine bar at Ocean Village in Southampton. Not Cahoots, she mused, that was more like home and much too intimate for a man she hardly knew. No, this one was neutral territory, bright, jolly and usually packed so if they ran out of conversation they could fall back on the ancient art of people watching.

Vicky was as nervous as if it had been her first ever date. A step into the unknown, an evening out with a man she could hardly remember, probably wouldn't recognise if she tripped over him. How did she manage to get herself into this situation? She remembered her first date with Mervyn. They'd gone into the West End to see what turned out to be a rather dreary thriller. They'd had so much to say to each other in the interval that they'd guessed the ending and not bothered to return for the second half. Instead they'd gone to Joe Allen's for dinner, picked at it and talked into the night. Vicky still missed their shared jokes and endless conversations. She shivered, her eyes misting up at the memory. When would she ever get over Mervyn?

Vicky shivered again with nerves. Right now she'd have opted for a quiet night at home in front of the box. Anything vaguely edible out of a tin and a video would have been the perfect option. But then she remembered their New Year resolutions yet again and jammed the car decisively into first gear as the lights changed.

She'd borrowed another of Sarah's outfits, this time a black jacket and trousers with a fuchsia pink silk top underneath. Might as well go for it having lost all that weight, and of course there was nothing more slimming than black. At this rate David Bletchley would think he was buying dinner for a stick insect, that is until she took her clothes off, then he'd find out, shock horror, Cellulite City! *Hang on a minute*, she thought, *we haven't got to that bit yet, you're jumping the gun a bit here, gel.* He might find her so totally repulsive that leaping into bed with her would be the last thing on his mind. In which case, she could enjoy her dinner tonight, give up the cabbage soup, get fatter again and nobody'd ever know. Except Sarah, who wouldn't be able to lend her any more outfits.

In between all the soul searching about whether to stay slim or be fat and happy, Vicky found herself in the wine bar car park with the engine turned off. Funny how journeys go so much quicker when you're nervous. She applied a quick bit of lippy and powder in the car's rear-view mirror (no more squirts of perfume because that would smack of desperation) before taking a deep breath and stepping out. Why do humans put themselves through the pain barrier of first dates? she thought as she strode up to the entrance. There again, if there hadn't been people brave enough to go on first dates, the human race would have died out years ago.

All her fears were dispelled. David was more or less as she remembered over those desperate glasses of champagne at the fashion show. He had lovely eyes, she decided, and he made a real effort to entertain her. He'd also presumably left Deputy Dawg in a kennel, thank God, and traded him in for a more casual look. Open-neck dark blue shirt, navy blazer and chinos. The conversation started with the inevitable re-run of his thanks for her compèring effort but then he moved on to her work in television, asking some sensible questions and appearing to make an effort to understand. It was certainly a change from the old 'self self self' routine that most blokes, particularly of his age, practised.

She asked him about his work, remembering vaguely that he did something quite important with the local council. It turned out that he was a trading standards officer, which sounded like death on legs to Vicky. All that boring legislation about toys, road testing pushchairs and being the most unpopular chap in the pub because he came in to check all the measures. A touch of the Rogers, she thought grimly. She could just imagine David enjoying a long winter fireside evening relishing the small print of his car insurance policy. But there was a charm about him which she found endearing.

David's choice from the menu was reasonably adventurous for a man who shut down pubs for a living. He opted for lamb with couscous and roasted vegetables and picked a good bottle of red wine. Vicky chose a monkfish kebab, reasoning that it wouldn't leave her reeking of garlic or with bits of spinach or herbs stuck to her teeth. Wrong on both counts. You could smell the garlic before the kebab left the kitchen. And when she went to the loo and checked her appearance, sure enough, there were the lurking remains of some oregano. She managed to remove them with a pen top and she found an old packet of Polos that she hoped would help deaden the garlic.

They moved on to the pudding, both giving in to a raspberry mousse, while Vicky, now relaxing by the minute, regaled him with tales of her old days of radio and telly. The pissed announcer who introduced a concert of the works of Purcell 'featuring one of his most famous pieces, Dildo's Lament'. Another who, during a long-running seamen's strike, persistently read news items about a Cross Flannel Cherry Service. And then there was the night they ran a Hollywood-style mini-series with one whole reel missing.

'In one scene, a chap was proposing to this girl. But straight after the commercial break, in the next scene, there they were in the final stages of divorce,' explained Vicky. 'Now I know it's a bit whistlestop in Hollywood, but do you know, not one viewer clocked the fact they'd missed a whole reel. Not one letter or phone call of complaint. Even the engineers couldn't understand why they were packing up about twenty minutes early.'

Their laughter was interrupted by a waiter, bringing their coffees.

'Have you ever been married?' said David, suddenly changing the mood.

'Er no.' Vicky was taken aback and started concentrating on stirring her coffee. 'Got a bit close to it once but no, it wasn't quite for me.'

'Been there, did ten years at the coal face and then got out,' said David. 'Two grown-up children now and an even bigger mortgage than when we were together.'

'Any regrets?' asked Vicky, anxious to get away from the subject of her own brief brush with wedlock.

'No, not really. I adore the kids but my ex-wife, having traded me in for a younger model, got greedy and took me to the cleaners. Do you wish you'd had a go?'

'Nope. All the married ones I know seem to end up on the Sketchleys route as well. I just started out single and stayed that way. I'd have hated all that aftermath stuff, fighting over the ashtrays and custody of the breadbin. Anyway . . .' She made to go, glancing at her watch.

'OK, I'll settle up, but before we go, I just wanted to say how much I've enjoyed tonight. Can we do this again? Don't say anything now. I'll call you in a few days.'

'Well. Well. What happened, what did you eat, what did he say, what did you do afterwards and were you overcome by an attack of pure lust?' asked Sarah impatiently

'My God, it's like being turned over by the Passion Police,' said Vicky, laughing. Sarah was clearly desperate to know but there wasn't much to tell.

'It was a very pleasant evening, the meal was great, your suit was much admired,' said Vicky.

'Is that it?'

' 'Fraid so.'

'What's his zodiac sign?'

'God knows.'

'What sort of car does he drive?'

'No idea.'

'What size were his hands and feet?'

'Oh for God's sake, Sarah. I didn't notice.'

'Did you play footsie under the table?'

'Don't be daft.'

'What does he earn?'

'He didn't say.'

'Did you snog him?'

'Nope.'

'Are you seeing him again?'

'Probably.'

'Whaaaaat?' Sarah had been caught off guard.

'But only if he rings.'

'Oh, he will,' said Sarah. 'This one means business. When blokes boast about the size of their pay packets, it's usually to get themselves on fast forward into the bedroom. And he didn't snog you either. Sees you as a class act. You've cracked it, babes.'

Vicky wasn't sure she wanted to. Anyway, he might have found her boring. He might not ring.

He did. Five days later, just at the point when Vicky had mentally begun to cross him out of her Filofax. True to his word, he hadn't been pushy. He repeated how much he'd enjoyed their evening and hoped they could do it again. Caught off guard, Vicky found herself saying yes and then afterwards wondering why she had agreed. *I feel nothing for this man*, she thought, *I don't react in any way shape or form. My stomach doesn't churn, my heart doesn't leap. He's pleasant but I don't fancy him. I'm not repulsed by him either*. She explained all this to herself in the bathroom mirror and then to Sarah on the phone.

'Brilliant, brilliant,' she exclaimed. 'Roz was telling me recently about a friend of hers who always went out with blokes she didn't fancy. That way she reckoned she'd never get disappointed.'

'What happened to her?' asked Vicky, only half interested.

'Oh I think she's succumbed now, just like the rest of us. Met this bloke, and then wham bam, bed, babies, the whole business.'

'I'm not sure this is for me,' said Vicky. 'Having said that, I didn't exactly jump over the moon when I met Roger. He pestered and pestered and in the end I just gave in. Maybe this is the same, except that this man can't possibly have a mother as Godzilla-like as Roger's.'

'Not possible to have two on the planet,' counselled Sarah. 'Look, don't bother about his mother. Use this as a springboard. You've already told me that he's got you some more speaking gigs. Well, he might have some devastatingly interesting friends too, and then we could all get fixed up. Don't forget our resolutions.'

'OK, OK,' said Vicky, feeling a little battle weary from it all. 'Anyway, how's Our Man in Malaga? Any more love letters or phone sex?'

'Well yes and no in that order as a matter of fact,' admitted Sarah, dying to talk about Leo again. 'We had a lovely chat a couple of days ago and I had a letter this morning.'

'What's wrong then?' asked Vicky, detecting a note of tension creeping into Sarah's voice. 'You've been thrilled with every letter so far.'

'Oh, he wants me to think about visiting him, says the weather is perfect this time of year, spring flowers out and so on, but I can't.'

'Isn't this a bit previous?' said Vicky. 'I mean, you don't know this guy. OK, you've written and talked but you've never set eyes on him. Anyway, apart from the fact that he could be some crazed psychopath who got lucky on community release day, why can't you go?'

'Because I can't afford it,' said Sarah, miserably. 'I've tried every which way but I've sold virtually all my jewellery now just to try and pay the bills. I just don't know how I'm ever going to get straight. I've had a look around for a better-paid job, but there's nothing that pays anything like as much as I'm getting now. I'm now psyching up to selling my engagement and wedding rings.'

Sarah started to cry softly down the phone.

'Surely they don't mean much to you now,' said Vicky, trying to be helpful.

'It's what they *did* mean. That's what they mean to *me*,' explained Sarah. Vicky didn't understand, but she did mentally agree that Bostik was at least, well, mean. Sarah would not have appreciated that joke. She sounded distraught.

'Anyway, they've got to go,' continued Sarah. 'They've put me on a key meter for my electric so I have to keep traipsing off to get the key topped up every time the lights are about to go out.'

'Could be quite romantic,' said Vicky, trying to keep the mood light, and realising she was not succeeding.

Judith flung off her coat and shoes and slumped on to a sofa. She'd been filming away in Birmingham all week and she was exhausted. The shoot had been difficult, the crew awkward and the subject, a corporate video, had been a nightmare. The clients, a double-glazing company who were taking their first steps into the world of moving picture, thought they were the world experts on video production and made Judith shoot all sorts of terrible things she'd never have dreamt of doing.

For a start, the boss of the company had decided he was going to be the star. Unfortunately a speech impediment came between him and a burgeoning career as a future television presenter. He insisted on wearing a very tweedy jacket, thinking the country/reliable/trustworthy look was more important than the fact that the jacket strobed like hell on camera. And they'd had to shoot a tedious session with various workmen saying why they liked working for the company and how good the product was. Their conviction wouldn't have persuaded flies within miles of an open jam pot.

An hour later Vicky staggered in after her shift.

'Hi, how was it?' said Judith.

'Oh, a ferry aground, a fire at a firework factory which went up like a rocket, ha ha, and a crash probe which concluded that the plane flew too low. A packed programme! How about you?'

'Weary, but I'm cheerfully consoling myself that I'm now a fully fledged expert on double glazing,' boasted Judith. 'I am now in the enviable position of being able to quote you approximately on just about every window combination. It makes rocket science seem positively gripping.'

'Why?' asked Vicky unnecessarily.

' 'Cos it's boring. But it pays the bills.'

'Talking of which,' Vicky paused, 'I think Sarah's having trouble in that department. She seemed very down when I spoke to her on the phone earlier on.'

'What seems to be the problem?' asked Judith. 'Or do I need to ask?'

'No you don't. The usual. Money and how to spend it faster than you earn it. She can't even keep up with her normal bills. Do you think she'd be offended if we tried to help her organise herself better?'

'That's a thought. I've also been thinking about lending her some, but I don't think that would solve her problem. She'd just go out and spend it on some little expensive something by Prada or blow it all on a swanky dinner to thank us.'

'You're right,' said Vicky.

'I've an idea to cheer her up but I need to know what you think. It's her birthday coming up next month and I've got a suggestion to make.'

chapter twenty-eight

'Would you come away for a weekend?' said David, forking up the last of his boeuf stroganoff. 'I know a lovely hotel in Torquay, overlooking the sea. It would only take us a couple of hours to drive down there. It's beautiful in the spring, not too busy and some good restaurants around.'

Vicky was praying he'd do his 'don't answer me now, just think about it' routine, but he didn't. He wanted an answer there and then, and he plainly wanted her too. She pushed a stray mushroom around her plate, trying to decide whether the idea was absurdly flattering or just absurd.

'I'd have to see if I could get some time off,' she muttered. 'You see, as a freelance, you get all the bum shifts so I often work at weekends. And there's my speaking dates too . . .'

'It doesn't have to be a weekend, just two or three days whenever you want. It doesn't have to be Torquay either. We could go somewhere else, Bath perhaps, Brighton?'

'OK,' said Vicky, taking a deep breath. 'That would be lovely.'

No it won't, she thought, *it'll be hell*. Going to bed with someone for the first time was so scary. Undressing in front of a virtual stranger, wondering if he'll recoil at the sight of your body. And wondering what's underneath his clothes.

Will he have a spotty back and nasty underpants? Will the room be lit for a film set so that there's no escape from a good view of your thread veins? Also holed up in a hotel room without your normal diversions like endlessly putting on the kettle, cranking up the stereo if you can't think of anything to say and escape routes like your friends ringing up at given times.

'Are you sure about this?' said Vicky. 'I mean, we hardly know each other, and two or three days together non stop might be a disaster. We don't know very much about each other, do we?'

'Ask away. What would you like to know?' He smiled at her with crinkly blue eyes. Vicky did detect a slight flutter in her stomach. Maybe, just maybe this could be lust. It had been a while since Roger.

'Well, we've never been to each other's houses,' she said. 'We don't know each other's musical tastes, films or anything. I don't even know what car you drive.'

'A BMW, Stravinsky and *Good Morning Vietnam*. And you?' There was that disarming smile again.

'Oh heck, the Beatles, *Sleepless in Seattle* and a very, very old Citroën.'

'How old, your Citroën?'

'Oh, Hercule is very elderly.'

'Hercule, why Hercule?'

'Because he's air-cooled,' explained Vicky.

David started to laugh. 'Do you want to do favourite colours, cities, songs, newspapers, best holidays?' he asked. 'Or are you really saying, hang on a minute, we haven't even kissed properly and now this man's inviting me away for a few days?'

'Er yeah, that's about it,' said Vicky, lamely, casting her eyes down to her empty plate, wishing there were a few more mushrooms to play with.

'Look, don't worry. I can book us separate rooms if you

like. Just tell me when you can get away, where you'd like to go and I'll sort it. Just one thing though.' He paused.

'What's that?' said Vicky, who'd now been lulled into a false sense of security.

'I'd like to kiss you goodnight properly when we leave this place.' David looked into her eyes.

'Yes, I'd like that,' said Vicky. And she realised that she meant it.

Vicky carefully hung up Sarah's navy suit and sighed. Two serious meals with David were taking their toll on her waist-band. She'd soon be back to her own wardrobe and at this rate it would be straight to the Fat Days section. Either that or get back on to the cabbage soup or low-fat lettuce leaf routine.

En route to the kitchen she stopped and studied herself intently in the hall mirror. She heard a key go in the door and Judith swept in.

'What are you staring at?' Judith laughed.

'Just checking out my wrinkles,' said Vicky, slightly embarrassed. 'Actually my grandmother used to say women didn't have wrinkles or crow's feet, they had laughter lines.'

'Well, nothing's that funny!' said Judith.

'All right, Miss Smart Arse. I don't suppose you have any.'

'Of course I do, but this quick-drying concrete's a marvellous investment,' said Judith. 'Anyway, talking of concrete, are you cementing your relationship, how was your date, get the kettle on and we must talk about Sarah.'

'My date was fine,' shouted Vicky over her shoulder as she headed for the kitchen. 'We're going on a dirty weekend.'

'Bloody Nora,' exclaimed Judith. 'This *is* progress. What brought this on? I didn't think you were all that keen on him.'

Vicky related the evening's events over a pot of Darjeeling.

'I think that's brilliant,' said Judith. 'What have you got to lose, Vick? Hardly your virginity. He does sound like the sort of chap who grows on you and that's much better than Wow! Kerpow! and followed by, "Oh shit, he's lean, mean and married."'

'Yeah, I know, but it's the whole agony of getting your kit off for the first time and wondering what the hell he's going to do to you,' said Vicky, anxiously. 'The irony is that Sarah, the one who's been married most of her life, is much better at all this first-time-in-the-sack stuff. It doesn't seem to faze her. She's champing at the bit to visit this Leo guy in Spain. And here am I, worried sick about two days in Torquay, in separate rooms if I say so. I wish I had her confidence.'

'If it's any comfort, I wish I had *your* confidence,' said Judith quietly. 'I've been thinking about sex since that evening with the escorts. They were terrific chaps actually, bright, witty and intelligent. And they couldn't understand why Sarah and I didn't have blokes. Now they might have been lying, but it made me realise how much confidence I've lost. I'm fine at work, hiding behind my job. But when I go out as me, on a scale of one to ten, my confidence is slipping down the minuses, big time.'

'You'll just meet someone when you're least expecting it,' replied Vicky soothingly.

'Anyway, I'm glad David's asked you to go away with him,' Judith continued. 'It will do you good, and of course we have our resolutions to think of. Talking of men, don't tell Sarah this, but another reason why I keep remembering the evening with the escorts is that her cheque to the agency for our Dream Boys bounced. They've now sent me the bill and I'm going to pay it. But not a word to her. She's very, very down. I think our birthday surprise for her will help.'

*

They dragged a protesting Sarah from her flat.

'I don't want to celebrate,' she said ungraciously. 'I'm just too miserable.'

'Oh shut up and have a treat, for God's sake,' said Vicky as they bundled her into the car. 'We've booked a table in Cahoots and if we don't turn up, they'll send out a search party.'

The after-work gin and tonicers were just filtering away, reluctantly picking up their briefcases and laptops as they downed the last dregs, and it was a little early for the main dining traffic. Soon the three were settled in their favourite corner so they could survey the scene.

'It's all arranged so we don't need to order,' said Judith mysteriously. A waiter appeared with three glasses, a bottle of champagne and an ice bucket.

'First a toast,' said Judith, brightly. 'Happy Birthday, Sarah. Well done on surviving forty-four years.'

'Yeah, well, dip the volume on that last bit,' said Sarah, anxiously. 'Listen, girls, this is lovely of you. I really appreciate it, but if I appear a bit harpy it's because I'm a bit down at the moment.'

'Gosh, we hadn't noticed,' said Vicky, laughing. 'Oh come on, Sarah, I know you've got money problems, but forget them tonight. This one's on us.'

Sarah gulped some champagne. Despite yet another stunning outfit, a dark green silk dress and pale green jacket, she looked terrible. She'd lost even more weight so the beautiful clothes just hung off her. Her eyes looked empty, her face drawn, she had an air of total defeatism about her.

'Sorry folks,' she said, her blue eyes filling with tears. 'It's just been a bad week all in all. The money thing is really getting to me now. I suppose it's because I had Bostik around all those years to sort it out. And now I don't. I've just been through an extra specially bad time about him this week.'

'Anything in particular to trigger that?' enquired Judith gently.

'Yep. I had to sell my wedding and engagement rings yesterday to pay off some of my bills. I never thought it would all end like this. You know, I still remember the moment that Bostik gave me that ring and asked me to marry him. I felt like a bird taking flight. I was so happy I thought I could conquer the world.'

'Well, there was also a slight matter of pregnancy,' said Judith, trying to bring the conversation down to earth.

'Yeah, all right, I was up the duff, but it was still very romantic.' She paused for a moment, lost in old memories.

Then she brightened. 'Funny thing is, at the time he told me it had cost him a fortune and that it was some very fancy cut of diamond. Turns out it wasn't anything like, according to the jeweller yesterday. So the bastard was at it even then.'

They refilled their glasses and drank a mock toast to 'The Bostik Diamond'.

'Right,' said Judith, rubbing her hands in a businesslike fashion. 'Enough of this sentimental pop psychobabble clap-trap. Vick and I have a surprise for you. Tonight is a themed night, as you're about to find out.' She motioned to a hovering waiter. He produced a bottle of Rioja and three fresh glasses.

'Clue number one,' she said. 'Clue number two follows shortly.'

Out came three plates of charcoal-grilled prawns together with a bowl of aïoli sauce.

'Anyone planning to have sex tonight?' said Judith. 'Best not, because you'll pong of garlic.'

Clue number three, swordfish steaks with a Mediterranean salad.

'Any idea what this is about?' asked Judith, who was enjoying the suspense.

'No, except that perhaps it's a gentle leg pull about Malaga Man,' said Sarah. 'By the way, he phoned tonight just before you lot dragged me here, and wished me a happy birthday.'

'Oh, that's nice,' said Judith. 'Because that brings me to the main event of the evening.'

A small birthday cake crammed with candles made its approach to the table. All eyes were now on Sarah as she half rose from her seat to blow out the candles. There was polite applause from other diners and hovering waiters.

'Now,' said Judith, crisply. 'There's an envelope been sat on this table for the best part of an hour now. And you've not mentioned it, Sarah Franks. Not like you, you're normally so nosy, you'd put Pinocchio out of a job.'

Sarah shook her head. She'd vaguely noticed it but she was basically too miserable to care about anything much. She really must get a grip.

'Well it's for you,' said Vicky, handing her the pale pink envelope.

'What's all this about?' said Sarah, her hands shaking as she opened it. Inside was a birthday card from Judith and Vicky plus another smaller white envelope.

'Well,' said Judith, adopting Cilla Black *Blind Date* speak. 'Tonight meet Sururh, she's from Southampton, she's a health administrator and she's totally gorgeous. And she's picked a blind date to Malaga!'

Inside the white envelope were two hundred and fifty pounds' worth of travel vouchers. Sarah thought she was going to faint.

'And here's our Graham with a quick recap,' continued Judith. 'Remember number one, she's the birthday girl who wants to see if the rain in Spain really does stay on the plain.'

Sarah just sat staring at the vouchers, her mouth dropped open in shock.

'Stop looking like a goldfish,' said Vicky. 'It'll at least pay for the flight, and if you decide not to go, then just use the vouchers another time.'

'I, er, you shouldn't, er, I don't . . .'

'. . . know what to say,' finished Judith. 'Don't say anything. We just thought you badly needed a treat and we figured this was the one thing that would buck you up. I hope we've done the right thing.'

'Oh you have,' said Sarah, finally finding a voice. 'I just don't know what to say. This is too much, I can't take it all in.'

'We figured that you should be able to get a flight to Malaga for that so it's up to you. Don't worry, Vick and I raided our piggy banks.'

'I still can't believe this,' said Sarah, still aghast. She rose slightly from her seat and flung her arms around Judith and then Vicky to thank them. There was a ripple of applause from the other tables, all of whom had been enjoying the scenario.

'I must go to the loo and repair my face,' she muttered, realising tears had trickled down her face.

'I hope we've done the right thing,' said Vicky as she watched Sarah's departing back.

'I've never seen Sarah as depressed as I have this week,' replied Judith. 'At least we've cheered her up. Don't worry, Sarah's perfectly capable of looking after herself in that sort of situation. She's spent a lot of time chatting to this guy on the phone. And you learn an awful lot about people from letters too.'

Somehow Vicky wasn't quite so convinced.

chapter twenty-nine

Sarah was taking a fag break at work, casually leafing through a book on southern Spain. She took a packet of ten Benson and Hedges out of her handbag and lit one. She was smoking roll-ups at home but couldn't quite bring herself to do that at work. Not quite her image. It wasn't anyone's business that she was on her uppers.

She was determined to mug up on the area, just in case she and Leo ran out of things to say. Or do. *Even if he's drop-dead gorgeous, we can't bonk all day*, she reasoned. *At least I'll be able to make some intelligent conversation about our surroundings.*

Leo had sent some more photographs recently of himself and his villa. It looked elegant in a sort of faded glory way, not brand spanking new like some German-invaded tourist resort with symmetrical strands of bougainvillea spilling over uniform balconies, overlooking symmetrical rows of sunbeds, bagged, of course, by Germans at dawn. The pictures were already curling at the edges because she'd hawked them around so much in her handbag, showing them to anyone remotely interested.

Two weeks to go and she'd be in those pictures. She was so excited and so nervous she could hardly sleep. What to wear and what to take were the next big hurdles. Thanks to her big spend, she was spoilt for choice. But somehow everything seemed a bit formal for a week in Spain. She'd take a few silk suits to wear out in the evenings but also she'd need some casual stuff, shorts, chinos and tops. Sod the bills, she'd have to have a tiny fling after pay day next week. Also, she reasoned, she'd be saving by buying duty-free fags on the way out and back. That way she could afford to buy a couple of bits and pieces.

Last night she'd had a dress rehearsal in front of her mirror. It had been a shock to see some of her suits hanging off her, she'd lost so much weight. Also she'd have to do something about her hair. It just hung limp and lifeless. The new style she'd been so pleased with needed quite a lot of maintenance. She'd lash out on a sesh at the hairdresser's just before she went.

'Because I'm worth it,' she trilled to herself, twirling in the mirror, trying to look like Jennifer Aniston in that silly shampoo ad.

Also, the bod was looking a bit lacklustre, she decided. It certainly lacked lust all right but she might be able to put that right in less than a fortnight from now. She was beginning to pay for the sedentary lifestyle, too many ciggies and not enough fresh air.

Fake tan, that's what I need, she realised, and started rooting through the bathroom cupboard. She found some left over from last year and started slapping it on her legs. At least she'd be able to wear shorts if her legs weren't too white.

It reminded Sarah of her school days when the first fake tans appeared on the market. Something called Tanfastic had been *the* thing to give you that 'sun-kissed look'. Except that it was more of a 'collision with a terracotta pot' look. That year, the future of the Lower Sixth was orange, but more of a streaky orange.

Her reverie about life in the sixth-form common room

was interrupted by the phone. It was Vicky, wondering how she was feeling in the countdown to the big day.

'Excited, nervous, oh everything really,' she said. 'I've been working out what to wear but everything's hanging off me.'

'Huh, you should be so lucky,' tutted Vicky. 'I've finally given up on the cabbage soup now. They were thinking of including methane warnings on our weather forecasts. I was so bloody hungry that I started dropping off everywhere and losing my concentration. Last night I committed the cardinal sin of writing a story for the late news about people being evacuated from a fire.'

'What's wrong with that?' asked Sarah, not really paying full attention.

'Journo clanger number one. Buildings get evacuated, not people. Otherwise they'd make a terrible smell. Rather like the cabbage soup effect, I suppose.'

'Talking of which, have you made up your mind where you're going on your dirty weekend?' said Sarah.

'Torquay. Corny I know, but I've always loved it. I quite miss the West Country actually, especially this time of year. Hopefully it's just removed enough from Roger's old haunts so I won't run into him. And also if the whole thing's a total lulu, I can hop on a train back to Southampton.' Vicky regretted saying that the second the words had fallen from her lips. But it was too late. Sarah was quick on the draw.

'Well I won't have that option,' Sarah replied. 'I'm there for the week, come what may.'

'Are you sure you'll be OK?' said Vicky. 'I hope we haven't pushed you into this. We just thought it would cheer you up.'

'Honestly, I'll be fine. I'm taking lots of stuff to read, I've brushed up on my emergency Spanish and I'm now an expert on the Alhambra Palace. If the romance bit falls to shit, at the rate I'm going, they'll be snapping me up as a guide.'

'I have to say, Sarah, I think you have enormous guts.'

'I think you do too. Excuse me but I think you're doing virtually the same thing as me.'

'Well I'll have even bigger guts if I carry on eating like I am,' said Vicky. 'I think it's because I'm nervous, and then I'm even more nervous because I feel fat so I get hungry because I'm nervous. Are you with me?'

'Yeah,' said Sarah wryly, 'sort of. By the way, do you want to borrow anything for Torquay?'

'I'd love to but I think I might have a problem defying nature. Also I've done some calculations and I think I'm due to come on just after our trip so I'll be nicely bulging even more with fluid retention, thank you so much, God.'

'There's one thing worrying me about all this,' said Sarah. 'I have a terrible feeling that your trip to Torquay is going to be a great success, I am going to fall madly in love in Spain. And you know what that leaves, don't you?'

'Yeah, Judith,' said Vicky. It had crossed her mind but she wasn't as optimistic about David as Sarah clearly was about Leo. 'Let's cross that bridge when we come to it. Go on, get back to your packing, Señora.'

'Hasta la vista,' said Sarah, replacing the phone. She glanced at her hands. They'd turned a lurid orange. She'd forgotten to wash them after putting the fake tan on her legs.

'Oh well, the future really is orange,' she muttered to herself. 'Bloody Tanfastic. Now where's the bloody bleach to get this off?'

The flight was only three quarters full and Sarah had the luxury of sprawling (well, that wasn't quite the word) over two seats. She'd agonised for so long over what to wear that, in the end, she'd panicked and gone for a comfortable look. Stone-coloured chinos, a pale blue cotton shirt and a navy cotton sweater draped over her shoulders.

In the interests of looking wonderful when she stepped out at the other end, she'd pored over a magazine article at the hairdresser's about how stars managed to look so marvellous when they appeared at Heathrow. It seemed to involve either having your own personal jet, or travelling first class, natch, and having a complete change of clothing. One helpful magazine tip was to put your feet in brown paper bags. This was supposed to avoid swollen ankles. Sarah and her hairdresser had been reduced to shaking hysteria over this one, but both agreed that on a two-and-a-half-hour flight it probably wasn't necessary.

So Sarah had ditched the paper bag idea and settled instead for a small spray of Evian (as advised by various beauty columnists) with which she managed, in her nervousness, to drench her shirt. Fortunately the stuffy cabin atmosphere soon dried it out. In an attempt to calm her nerves, she'd ordered a large gin and tonic and then wine with her meal. She checked her watch, an hour to go. She settled back, regretting that she'd not put her toothbrush and paste in her flight bag. Just before the descent, she'd go to the loo and tart up a bit.

Her mind drifted back to the packing. She'd remembered what a head hunter had once told her. That interview panels make up their minds about you in the first thirty seconds. So first impressions count. A lot. She wondered what messages the clothes she'd packed would send out to Leo. If he was gorgeous, then she'd want to look sexy. If he was lovely but not lustworthy, then she'd want to look presentable but not wanton. And if he was just the pits, then she'd want to wear armour.

Unfortunately she couldn't pack armour. But she had packed a few bits of interesting lingerie just in case he fell into the 'gorgeous' category. Stockings, suspenders and a basque. Funny things, basques. Hers had been bought by one of the doctors at the clinic who claimed he was kept awake at night having constant fantasies about her wearing one.

Basques always reminded her of the Basque Separatist Movement, which sounded really rather painful. Were basques simply designed as a form of torture to lift and separate? Or perhaps members of the movement were closet transvestites who all secretly wore basques under their uniforms. Sarah didn't know but she was certain they'd been invented by a man. And the same went for G-strings, again created by a man. No bloke in his right senses would subject himself to buttock floss.

An air steward announced, bing bong, that the plane was beginning to make its descent, bing bong. Too late to visit the loo, so she settled for a quick comb, brush of lippy and squirt of breath freshener where she sat. Only a few more minutes and the suspense would be over. Her heart started to pound, just like it did the night she tried to tell Bostik it was all over.

Judith had only had the briefest of chats with David Bletchley when he came to collect Vicky, but it was enough to make her uneasy. He seemed very pleasant, very polite and definitely very keen on Vicky. But there was something, something she couldn't quite pinpoint. And she certainly wasn't going to agonise over it to Vicky. She was surprised that he hadn't wanted to examine Vicky's house, or rather *her* home, a little more closely. Why wasn't he more curious?

Probably because Vicky and I are on this constant need-to-notice basis, she thought, we love to snoop around other people's houses just to get clues about their personalities from their clutter. Journalists often say they can learn more about someone in thirty seconds on their doorstep than a half-hour interview in a hotel lobby of your choice. But, she kept reminding herself, not everyone was as bloody nosy as she and Vicky. Probably David Bletchley was only interested in other people's premises if they were licensed and he might be involved in shutting them down. Whatever it was, he just didn't look quite right for Vicky.

Anyway, it wasn't her problem. At least Vicky had eye-balled David and had spent a couple of evenings chatting to him over dinner. Sarah's situation was much more of a minefield. She wondered how it was all going. Sarah would have just touched down at Malaga by now. How would the meeting go? She could hardly wait to hear. Sarah had promised to ring within twenty-four hours to say she was OK. Judith had suggested a code on the phone so Sarah wouldn't feel too compromised if she were over-heard. It wouldn't be all that cool to pour out all your reactions and be overheard by the person you were dis-cussing. Like, he's got a big nose and he's terrible in bed, but I love him. Typical of Sarah, though, she had gone into overdrive and come up with a list of phrases with double meanings.

The paella's absolutely brilliant – I can't get enough of it. (He's great and we've already shagged ourselves senseless.)

Wonderful scenery – I'm having a good look around. (We haven't yet, but it's only a question of time.)

I've spotted this marvellous place to eat – he's taking me there tonight. (Tonight's the Big One.)

I must brighten up my flat with a bit of bougainvillea when I get back. (He's ever so nice but boring.)

The sangria's been giving me a terrible hangover. (Get me out of here pretty damn quick.)

Sarah had also been trying to mug up on some basic Spanish and had pored over a phrase book. She'd read out a few phrases phonetically to Judith, who was suitably impressed until she asked what they meant.

'Help, help. There's an escaped prisoner hiding in the hotel gardens,' Sarah had translated.

'What the hell do you want to know that for?' Judith had exclaimed. 'It does make me wonder who writes these books. Can you imagine the gathering local crowd being rendered speechless in all this or unable to speak their own native tongue? They have to wait for a foreigner to organise it all.'

'All right, point taken. I am just making the effort,' Sarah had retorted. 'I never did Spanish at school.'

'OK, but let's hope you don't have to use any of that stuff.'

Sarah recalled that conversation as she waited anxiously for her luggage by the carousel. Only a few more minutes and she'd know her fate. Leo had said he'd carry a bunch of flowers and hold a card bearing her name. Her heart was now beating so heavily it sounded like an old central heating boiler in desperate need of a service. There came her case, loaded on to a trolley, through customs and the point of no return.

She scanned the waiting faces by the barrier. No flowers, no card with her name for all to see. She kept on going, the faces a blur, mostly taxi drivers hoping for a fare into town or travel reps all called Tracey in their gaudy suits, busy shirts and court shoes, nursing closet hangovers, brandishing clipboards and flashing painted-on smiles.

Sarah felt her throat go dry. Was this all a mistake, just a big wind-up? Had she come all this way for nothing? Had her friends wasted their money? Had she come on the wrong day?

There he was, just behind a group of taxi drivers. Sarah gave an inner gasp and found herself doing a mental check list. Six foot one, yes, slimmish, yes, brown eyes, yes, clothes, acceptable. Closer still, hair a bit longer and

lankier than in the photographs. Makes him look a bit
seedy. Teeth, oh hell no. The camera had been generous, or
perhaps he'd kept his mouth shut. Leo clearly didn't see a
trip to the dentist as an essential part of life.

First impressions, though, six out of ten, because he
gave her a warm welcome, a brief hug and peck on the
cheek, and he'd brought the most beautiful bunch of flowers. He swept her straight out of the airport and to his car,
an old Seat parked nearby.

'It's been a lovely day here so I thought, if you didn't
mind, we'd go into Malaga, have a drink and a walk along
the seafront. Then we'll have dinner whenever you want
and after that we'll head home.'

Sarah nodded her approval, still getting used to the face
while knowing the voice so well. A slight wave of disappointment overcame her because she knew immediately
she'd never in a million years really fancy Leo. It wasn't just
the lanky hair and the grotty teeth, there was something
missing, that indefinable something that makes you want to
delve into someone's soul, and probably their underpants.

Sarah shivered, overcome by a sense of anticlimax, and
then remembered what he'd emphasised on the phone. 'No
pressure, we're just friends. We'll take things as they come.'

They parked near the seafront and walked along the
palm-fringed Paseo del Parque. Sarah could feel the
warmth of the late afternoon sun seeping into her bones.
She noted the smiling faces everywhere, people strolling
without seemingly a care in the world. Small children
having fun in a small playground. No language barrier to
playing in a sandpit. It felt so good.

They stopped at a bar for a drink. Leo ordered a jug of
sangria without consulting her.

'First couple of days, I'll do the ordering so you don't
miss out on anything here, and then after that it's up to
you,' he said, smiling with those horrible teeth again. 'As

you haven't been here before, there are some things you mustn't miss out on. Carlos, here, makes a mean sangria.'

He certainly did. Sarah was feeling a little pissed already and knew she needed to get a grip. Leo might not quite live up to his photographs but he was a fantastic host.

They checked in at their seafront hotel in Torquay. Vicky thought she'd turned up in paradise. Their suite had the most heavenly view across the bay. The sun danced like sequins on the water, and a bottle of champagne and a basket of fruit lay on a table waiting for them. They sat out on the balcony, drinking in the view, and the champagne.

'I've always adored Torquay but I've never stayed here,' said Vicky, overawed by the whole occasion, and slurping the champagne with gusto. 'You don't when you live near Plymouth. This is total paradise.'

'We can eat here or anywhere else,' said David, delighted that he'd got things so obviously right.

Thanks to the cabbage soup diet, two decent gulps of champagne had rendered Vicky somewhat pissed and desperately randy.

'I want to eat you,' she said, rather over-directly.

'Whatever you want,' said David, quietly pleased with himself. Funny how hotels were such a turn-on for older women.

As the sun finally sank from view, Sarah wiped her mouth with her napkin and sat back in her chair. They'd just eaten an amazing meal. The best *gambas a la plancha* in town, the best paella, the best Rioja, the best coffee, according to Leo.

'Bit clichéd, having paella and Rioja, but your first night on the Costa del Sol should be like this,' said Leo. 'Now we go home, you must be tired.'

Sarah nodded. She was absolutely knackered. Even if she'd fancied Leo, she doubted she'd have been capable of anything much. She sat back in the Seat, happy to be transported to his villa, relaxed in the knowledge that she didn't have a care in the world.

The drive took the best part of an hour, snaking around bends through the countryside that, of course, she couldn't see in the pitch black. They finally pulled up in a darkened courtyard. Sarah came to her senses and stumbled out, yawning. It had been a long day.

Leo took her bags from the boot of the Seat and led her through a large, creaking wooden door. Sarah's first impression was that there were no lights. She followed him into a stone-floored kitchen. As she sat dumbly at the large table, he busied himself making coffee and pouring liqueurs.

'Now,' he said, smiling through those horrible teeth again. 'This should stop those yawns for a little bit longer.'

Sarah nodded dumbly. She was exhausted. If Richard Gere had shown up, she'd have waved him away. She was suddenly aware that Leo was saying something important. Something about sharing rooms, how it would be so much warmer in bed with him than in the spare room. No, her head told her, this wasn't what they'd agreed. She must say something.

'No, please, Leo, we agreed. We've only just met, we talked about this, if you remember,' she burbled, praying this would make sense and sound forceful enough.

'Absolutely,' said Leo. 'Sorry, querida, if I'm sounding a bit familiar. I've just had such a fantastic day with you. I'm getting a bit carried away. Also I keep forgetting, you've had a long journey. I'll show you to your room. And tomorrow, you decide how we spend the day.'

With that he ushered her upstairs and along a corridor. She had a vague notion he was pissed, but she was too tired to register very much. He showed her into a beautiful room with a huge double bed, polished wood floors with rugs and shuttered windows.

'Your bathroom is just through there.' He pointed to an equally polished wooden door. 'And I promise you, the view in the morning will take your breath away. Goodnight, Sarah. Sleep well.'

And with a brief peck on her cheek, he was gone. Sarah dispensed with any attempt at cleansing, toning and all that skin routine stuff. She just fell into bed, fully clothed.

chapter thirty

Sarah stirred, paused for several moments, wondering where the hell she was. It all came back in a flash. Of course, she was in Spain, in Leo's villa. She stumbled out of bed, realised she was still wearing yesterday's clothes, and padded towards the shutters. She threw them open and gasped. The view was just incredible. She stood for several minutes in awe. Beyond the palm-fringed garden, and blood-red geraniums spilling from her balcony, stretched soft rolling hills terraced with vines, olive and almond trees, all vying for attention. The sky was the purest blue and the sun shone with a vengeance, as if for the very first time.

Sarah felt she had been reborn. All her debts, all her hang-ups about Bostik and how he'd finally rejected her, their fight and the terrible bruising, everything seemed to cancel out in that wonderful moment. It suddenly felt good to be alive, to be here. Thank God for Judith and Vicky sending her here. Thank God, too, for Leo. He might have grotty teeth and greasy hair but he was a good friend and he'd brought her here. Already she could feel the early morning sun's heat on her skin.

She turned back and surveyed the room. It hadn't made much impression last night, but now in daylight it looked quite dramatic. It was furnished in typical sparse

Andalucian style, with polished floorboards, leather chairs, dark wood furniture. Simple but stylish. She was ashamed to realise that she'd missed a huge bowl of deep pink hibiscus in a clear glass bowl on top of a chest of drawers. In front of the bowl was a small white envelope. Probably a welcome note from Leo. She wandered across the room to open it by the window.

> Dear Sarah,
>   You may not like this note, but on the grounds of scrupulous, horrific honesty, it needs to be written.
>   As an ex minor public school boy, I have to tell you that I have been 'left' with the need for regular, properly administered discipline. To wit, at least six of the best, given as and when appropriate. I am not unique. I am not proud of this, but it would be foolish not to say so.
>   You will therefore find a small whip hanging inside your wardrobe. Should this be offensive or unacceptable, just put it outside your door and it will be removed and never mentioned again. Please accept my apologies in advance.
>   But if you could see your way to helping me out, then I'd be most appreciative and very grateful!
>   Yours sincerely,
>   Leo xxx

Sarah put down the note and wondered whether to be violently sick.

The balcony from their room had one of the best views across to Torquay. Not wanting to miss a second of the view, Vicky proclaimed she'd like to breakfast alfresco even though the weather was a typically iffy April morning, temptingly warm one minute, and freezing the next. David, relishing her abandoned enjoyment of the whole setting, rang room service and ordered smoked salmon, scrambled eggs and buck's fizz.

They sat out on the balcony, wrapped up in towelling robes, lost in their thoughts from the previous night. Sex had been, well, rather typical first-time sex, nervous and fumbly, if Vicky had been honest with herself. But their eagerness for each other had made up for the fact that it hadn't lasted very long. *Not the world's greatest lover*, she thought, *but a little bit of training in that department might work wonders*. She was cross with herself for thinking briefly about Mervyn and how fantastic he'd been in bed. He could play her like a cello, the bastard. But that particular sonata, she checked herself, was over. Her thoughts meandered back to New Year's Eve and the night of the big resolutions. Sarah had been right. Accept all invitations, you never know where they might lead. Well this one was certainly leading in the right direction. But for that night, and the vast Mrs Sweet at the fashion show, she wouldn't be here now, enjoying this wonderful view, being spoilt by a man she was becoming alarmingly fond of. She thought back to last night and the feeling of sheer relief when David had entered her. She hadn't realised how much she'd missed the physicality of sex, even if it was rather brief.

'You've gone quiet on me,' said David's voice softly. 'Are you regretting what we did last night?'

'Not in the least. In fact I was hoping for a repeat performance after breakfast,' said Vicky cheekily. 'I was also thinking about how my friend Sarah's getting on in Spain.'

She outlined the trip to Spain, how she and Judith had clubbed together to give Sarah the air ticket as a birthday present. She omitted the details about the *Sunday Times* ad, thinking he'd find that bit really tacky.

'And your friend's in Spain staying with a man she's

never actually met beforehand,' said David, gravely. 'She's a brave lady.'

'Yep. I'll say that for Sarah, she's got guts. She'd make the best out of any situation. I bet she's whooping it up. We'll all be sick as pigs when she comes home, all tanned and relaxed.'

This will be the last time, Sarah promised her stomach as it heaved once more. Shock had by now given way to sheer panic and the realisation that here she was, in the middle of nowhere, no old familiar Volvo parked outside, no consoling girls' evening in Cahoots within a phone call's reach. She was alone in the house with a man who'd just become a monster. And, remembering last night's journey and today's view, they were miles from anywhere.

Confront him, I must confront him. I will have this out, talk about it, understand why he's like this and make my excuses and leave, she told the mirror in the bathroom.

Just as a precaution, she jammed one of the leather-backed chairs against the door handle. At least it would give her a bit of notice if Leo barged in. She had the quickest shower on record, then got dressed as fast as she could so she'd feel less vulnerable.

Hang on a minute, she reasoned with herself. *The guy's only asked me to whip him.* OK, so she'd never come across this sort of thing before, but if that was all he wanted then perhaps it was harmless. But Sarah knew in her heart of hearts that it wouldn't stop there. Would he want to whip her? Would these games go too far? Was this why Leo lived alone? So that he could carry on his sordid little games in splendid isolation?

She gazed out of the window and across the courtyard and garden beyond. If only the walls could talk, they'd have filled several months' worth of the *News of the World*. They'd probably send out a planeload of honeytrap reporters who would 'make their excuses and leave' at the critical moment, scurrying back to the airport to tap tap tap out their stories on laptops while they waited for the first flight out of Malaga.

Despite the sunlight streaming through the window with its promise of the heat throughout the day, Sarah shivered as she picked out her most demure clothes, burying the basque, suspenders and stockings at the bottom of her case just in case he went through it. So much for the Basque Separatist Movement, she harrumphed as she strode purposefully downstairs, her heart beating like a pair of castanets.

Leo was in the kitchen, feet up on the polished wood table and smoking a cigarette. He was drinking a cup of coffee as he pored over a local newspaper.

'Buenos días, querida,' he exclaimed, jumping to his feet, and flashing those disgusting teeth. 'Sleep well? Like your room? Coffee?'

'Yes to all three,' said Sarah carefully, trying to keep her stomach in check. She sat down opposite him at the table and waited until he'd set the large cup and saucer down in front of her.

'I read your note,' she blurted out. 'I read your note just now. Why, Leo? Why do you need this? And why drag me into it all?'

She just managed to stop herself crying. She must stay in control. She stirred her coffee intently so that she didn't have to make eye contact with him.

'I thought my letter explained it perfectly,' he said, his tone suddenly clipped. 'I thought I made it perfectly clear.'

'But why bring me all this way? Surely you could get someone, er, someone to do this for you locally,' said Sarah, still stirring her coffee.

'You mean pay someone? Is that what you mean? Well yes, I have done that, but the brutal truth is they, er, the women, have to travel a fair way and it's expensive. I'm out in the wilds here and it's not economic for them.'

Sarah was already beginning to wish she hadn't started this. But she somehow had to find out the real reasons. She ploughed on.

'So why take an ad in the *Sunday Times*? What was that all about?'

Leo took his feet off the table, slowly lit another cigarette and glared at Sarah. His teeth were beginning to look more Dracula-like by the minute.

'I had sixty-seven replies to that ad, and you're the eighth to visit so far,' he announced coldly.

'And what happened to the seven other poor sods?' said Sarah, now briefly and rather ridiculously enraged to find that she was not alone in this mess.

'They all reacted in the same way that you did. Except for one who, I suspect, was barking. After we got back from the airport, she started taking her clothes off as we crossed the courtyard. Within a few days, she got on my nerves and I asked her to leave.'

'Well I must have been barking to come here. I'm sorry, Leo, but I can't do what you ask. I'm going upstairs now to pack my things and go. I'd like a lift to the airport, please.'

Upstairs in the relative sanctuary of her room, Sarah quietly placed the chair against the door handle and began a flurry of packing. She'd find a way out of Malaga, even if she had to camp at the airport for the rest of the week until her flight. When she'd repacked her case and zipped it up, the chair she'd jammed against the door started to move. Leo finally flung the door open and barged in, kicking the chair aside. He was red-faced with fury.

'What did you do that for?' he bellowed. 'How dare you?'

'I, I, you frightened me,' stammered Sarah, starting to cry.

Leo immediately seemed to soften. 'I'm sorry, Sarah,' he said, 'I shouldn't have sent you the note but I'm a driven man. I don't ask for much in life but I do ask for this. It's the only thing that satisfies me. It's why my wife left.'

'Oh I *am* surprised,' sobbed Sarah, relieved that the flashpoint was past. 'I just can't believe this. It's like a bad dream. After all these weeks, our letters, our phone calls and you never mentioned this.'

Leo hung his head. 'If I'd told you, you wouldn't have come,' he confessed. 'I just really hoped that you might be the one to help me out, but I was wrong. I'm sorry. Please forgive me.'

For a few long seconds, there was an awkward silence between them. Leo broke it with an offer of rolls and coffee for breakfast and a promise not to mention the matter again. Desperately grateful for the respite, Sarah nodded in agreement as she dried her eyes.

Downstairs, Leo was back to his genial self, humming as he busied himself making the coffee.

'Now what would you like to do today?' he asked. 'Let me suggest we leave the coast for today and go up into the mountains for lunch. There's a beautiful little place I know, not too far from here, and they do the most wonderful gazpacho.'

In the end, they didn't have sex after breakfast. Vicky was too shy to remind him, just in case he either couldn't manage another performance or perhaps just didn't fancy her enough. Any doubts on that one were dispelled when another 'perfect' day was planned. A brisk walk on Babbacombe Downs, a stroll on Meadfoot beach, followed by lunch at a harbourside wine bar. Then, David proposed, an early return to the hotel for, as he put it, a lie-down. Vicky thought she was dancing on air. Too good to be true, this man makes me laugh, he's good company, a good listener, an interesting life, challenging mind. *I deserve this*, she told herself, *I really deserve this*, especially after all the heartbreak over Mervyn and that shit at the register office with Roger. Vicky was still faintly worried that she'd bump into Roger. It would be just her luck.

The gazpacho proved to be everything Leo had promised. The mountain scenery was beautiful, the villages unspoilt and the sun quite relentless. Yet the minute they stepped into the little farmhouse converted into a small restaurant, it was like walking into a fridge. Ice cool and definitely built for this climate.

Sarah's stomach had not recovered from the shock of the letter so she stuck to mineral water but Leo ordered a big jug of local red wine and drank with gusto. By the time they drove back to the villa, he was clearly drunk. The car started to weave menacingly on the windy roads. The fear in Sarah's heart that she had desperately tried to suppress returned with a vengeance. Not only was his mood changing rapidly, but they were in danger of driving off the side of the road and down a steep slope. She offered to drive.

'No, absolutely not,' snarled Leo. He'd reverted to his black mood of earlier, fuelled by the wine. 'You sit there and shut up. I drive around here.'

They sat silent for the rest of the journey, Sarah aware that her knees were practically knocking and her teeth were certainly chattering. She wanted to be anywhere but that villa, away from civilisation, and stuck with a monster.

Leo strode straight into the kitchen and poured himself a large glass of Rioja.

'I suppose you're not going to join me,' he growled at her. She shook her head, fearful that her teeth would drop out in fright.

'I'd like to phone my mother,' she stammered, hoping

he'd believe her. 'She's not very well and I'd like her to know I got here all right.'

'Suit yourself,' he shouted, indicating the phone with a nod of his head as he refilled his glass and then strode out into the sunshine. Sarah dialled the number with shaking hands, praying that Judith would be in.

Ring, ring, ring, ring, *oh please answer it*, she prayed. *I'll let it ring another five times, no, ten times, no, fifteen times and then I'll give up.*

'Jude? It's me.'

'Brilliant. Thank goodness. You're OK? I'm just dying to know. How's it all going? What's he like? Have you . . .?' Judith's voice was full of enthusiasm. It made Sarah want to weep.

'Er no, it's the sangria, no, the bougainvillea, oh I don't know really,' stammered Sarah.

Judith immediately clocked some of Sarah's code words, albeit mixed up. With her usual resourcefulness, she immediately took charge of the conversation.

'OK, I'll do the talking and you say yes or no. First of all, is he within earshot?'

'No, no, not at the moment.' Sarah's voice was wobbling. 'You're my mother and I'm phoning you 'cos you're ill.'

'OK. If he comes back in, just ask when's the operation?'

'OK.'

'Right. What's gone wrong? Just tell me briefly.'

Sarah started to cry. 'He's got horrible teeth and he's got this wardrobe. Oh shit, Jude, it's awful. I just want to come home.'

'Well he probably can't help the teeth but what's wrong with the wardrobe?'

'There's a whip in it,' sobbed Sarah.

'Oh, I see,' said Judith, not seeing at all but already fearing some terrible kidnap and torture scenario. 'Right, now keep calm, the story's this. I'm your mother, I'm going in for an emergency operation and I'm going to get your flight changed and get you back on the earliest one I can. It's probably too late now today but I'll be straight on the case tomorrow first thing and I'll call you. Now this whip business. What's all that about? Has he hurt you?'

'No, no. He wants *me* to hurt him. He's pissed again and aggressive. Oh Jude, it's all so hideous.'

'In that case, why don't you just get in a taxi and go to the airport and ring me from there.'

Sarah started to cry again, this time tears at her own stupidity.

'I haven't got enough money for a taxi,' she stammered. 'We're absolutely miles from anywhere and he's drunk. I couldn't even hitch. I was so convinced that this was it that I didn't think I'd need much. I spent my little bit of pocket money on some shorts and sexy underwear before I left. Oh Jude, I've been such a fool.' She broke down totally.

'Now listen, Sarah,' said Judith firmly. 'Pull yourself together. If he sees you in this state, he'll have the upper hand. Take control of the situation. Come on, you're a strong girl. Put him in his place, don't play the victim. Look, when men get pissed, they either get amorous or aggressive. Recognise that and take control. Stop him in his tracks and—'

'So when's your operation?' interrupted Sarah, hearing the door open behind her. 'Of course, I'll come as soon as possible. I'm sure I can get my flight changed.'

'OK, he's there. I'll call you first thing tomorrow. Remember, make him the victim. Take control.'

Sarah replaced the phone and wheeled round to find Leo, red-faced and fuming, in the doorway.

'Planning our escape, are we?' he menaced.

'No, Leo, I'm not,' said Sarah firmly, a new calm coming

over her. 'My mother has to have an emergency operation, a heart bypass, and I'm afraid I'm going to have to go back as soon as possible.'

'Pity,' he spat, disbelievingly.

'Well thanks for that sympathy vote,' said Sarah, not quite believing the new firm voice coming out of her mouth. 'In fact I was going to ask whether you would give me a lift to the airport tonight. There might just be a spare seat on a plane.'

'Not now, darling.' He grinned through green teeth. 'Much too much vino tinto. Too risky. We don't want to be having an accident, do we?'

'Well, tomorrow then. My mother's phoning in the morning after she's been on to the travel agent to change the booking. I daresay I'll get a flight quite easily.'

'How come your bloody mother's able to run around sorting out your flight when she's supposed to be having a heart bypass?'

'Well, you don't know my family. We're tough and we get on with things. Mind you, a bypass is a serious operation and that's why I should be with her,' she finished defiantly.

The nearest her mother had ever got to a bypass was the one they'd built near the family home years ago. It had knocked thousands off the value and her mother had never stopped whingeing about it. Sarah prayed hard to keep the wobble out of her voice and that someone up there would forgive her all these lies. Stay in control, Judith's words kept coming back. Turn the tables on him.

'Right,' she said brightly. 'I'll cook tonight.' She started banging saucepans around as she hijacked the kitchen. Soon one pan was bubbling away with smoked ham, tomatoes, peppers, onions, garlic and fresh herbs, while in another some pasta was just reaching the al dente stage.

'Pour me a drink,' she commanded. Leo obliged quick as

a flash, handing her an enormous glass of red wine and refilling his own.

A change of heart, he detected, pleased that she seemed to be getting stuck into the wine. *Maybe, just maybe I'll be in luck later on,* he thought to himself. Maybe this was the one who'd help him out with his 'problem'.

Slug of the century, thought Sarah, surreptitiously tipping large quantities of the wine down the sink or into handy plant pots when he wasn't looking. *Bastard thinks I'm going to get pissed and out of control. Well I'm cracking the whip around here, but not in the way he wants.*

It was just before midnight when Vicky arrived back from Torquay. The weekend had surpassed all her expectations. She felt relaxed and truly happy for the first time in ages. Even in the halcyon days with Mervyn, she'd never felt totally at ease, constantly worrying because he was so attractive to other women. Of course history had proved itself rather bluntly.

She flopped down on a sofa, desperate to tell Judith about it.

'Well, I can tell you've had a good time,' said Judith as she brought in a cafetière and cups from the kitchen.

'Why? Is it that obvious?'

'Yep. You're wearing that "just shagged" look. And it suits you. Was it great, the weekend, I mean.'

'Absolutely brilliant. Lovely meals, walks, fresh air, beautiful hotel.'

'And a jolly good seeing-to, I hope,' said Judith.

'Well now you come to mention it, yes, we did manage that.'

As they sipped their coffee, Vicky glanced through the steam from her cup and realised that Judith was preoccupied.

'Something wrong? You look tense all of a sudden.'

'Yeah, there is. Sorry, I didn't want to spoil your home-coming. It's Sarah. She's basically in deep shit.'

'Oh no, what the hell's happened?' asked Vicky, instantly on a guilt trip because she'd had a great time.

'Let's just say that Leo hasn't turned out to be a very friendly lion,' said Judith.

'Oh no. Is she OK? Is she coming back? What's happened?'

'Well, put it like this,' said Judith blankly. 'I never read *The Lion, the Whip and the Wardrobe* at school.'

chapter thirty-one

It was almost two weeks before Sarah could really speak about what happened in Spain. When she'd finally got back to her flat, she'd phoned in sick to work, taken herself off to bed, slept and cried alternately until there were no tears left and she was totally fed up with the bedroom wallpaper.

Much of the time, she unplugged her phone, only reconnecting in the evenings in case her children called. She cursed the fact that she still couldn't ring out. Damn BT – it wasn't good to talk, not at their prices. Daniel rang to say he was off on another business trip to the States. Roz phoned to say she was still madly in love with Simon and that they were thinking of getting a flat together. Both were so wrapped up their lives that they just accepted her excuses of a 'mystery virus' picked up during a short break in Spain.

She'd also promised to tell Judith and Vicky the whole story but only when she was ready. They had the sense to leave her alone, assuring her that they were there whenever she felt ready to talk.

Sarah finally emerged from her abyss, ten pounds lighter and her wallet a little heavier, thanks to her self-imposed exile from the high street. No petrol, no food, no lunches, no parking. At least there was something to be said for practically having a nervous breakdown. She cautiously opened her bedroom curtains to find that spring with its blossoms had blown away and summer was beginning to take a hold. It had been raining, the road glistened and everywhere summer bedding plants were bravely perking up after a drenching. It'll soon be June, she thought, the Derby, Wimbledon, strawberries and cream, barbecue sets outside supermarkets. I haven't read a newspaper in weeks.

She plugged her phone back into the wall, praying someone would ring. Nobody did, sod them. She staggered into her tiny bathroom and surveyed the nightmare that greeted her in the mirror. Sallow greasy skin, limp greasy hair, nail varnish which had gone halfway up her nails and a body that was now so sunken it could have been snapped up for crowd scenes in *Tenko, The Remake*.

'Bollocks to all men,' she told the mirror, poking her tongue out at her reflection. She stepped gingerly into the shower and emerged a few minutes later feeling much better, if a bit wobbly. She then wrapped herself up in a large bath towel and wandered into her kitchen, switched on the kettle, lit a roll-up and thumbed through all the junk mail that had piled up on her mat over the past weeks.

'Straight in the bin with that lot,' she said out loud, no more temptation to buy anything. She stubbed out her cigarette and made a pot of tea. After days of sipping water and not bothering about herself, it tasted like nectar. Simple pleasures, she reflected, were the best. No more sex and shopping. She was going to get herself straight in her head and in her wallet. That meant a ban on anything remotely retail and absolutely nothing whatsoever to do with the male gender other than work.

The phone rang. *Please let it be someone nice*, she prayed. It was. It was Judith.

'You sound better,' she said. 'Heaps better. Look, Vick's

free tonight, she's tuning up for a seriously big speech in London. So I thought we might all go out for something to eat, my treat by the way, to get a decent meal down you and take her mind off the speech.'

Sarah started to protest, but her stomach won that particular battle. She was suddenly ravenously hungry.

'Get yourself up and dressed and we'll pick you up at about half six and have an early nosh in Cahoots before the riff-raff go in.'

'Now remember, no ordering anything vaguely Spanish,' Judith warned Vicky as they drove over to Sarah's place. 'Rioja, paella, sangria, tapas, Viva España, even Julio Iglesias and the bloody birdie song, they're all off the menu tonight. And although we're dying to know what the hell happened over there, we say nothing. Nada. OK?'

'Si, si,' replied Vicky, grinning.

Sarah was hovering at her front door when they drove up. She was so gaunt that if she hadn't put on some make-up, people might have accidentally walked through her.

The other two managed to disguise their shock at her appearance as they set off for Cahoots. No more the striking blonde with the statuesque body. All they saw was a skeletal figure whose roots badly needed doing. It was as though there'd been a power cut in Sarah's head. She looked completely defeated and it made conversation difficult. Vicky felt she couldn't wax lyrical about her relationship with David or talk about whether she should spend a weekend at his house. Judith didn't think it all that tactful to mention Simon and Roz's plans, even though it was Sarah's daughter. In the end they stuck to safe work subjects like Vicky's forthcoming after-dinner speech in London and Judith's new series, a commission for ten network discussion shows.

The conversation drifted on to the subjects of the shows:

marrying in prison, dobbing on your neighbour's tax evasion, banning of stag nights and so on.

'Why don't you do a programme about the dangers of blind dating?' said Sarah abruptly. 'I'll take part.'

The other two were caught out well and truly. Their jaws practically hit the table, both momentarily lost for words.

'I said, why not do something about dangerous blind dates?' repeated Sarah.

'Er, right,' said Judith. 'Great idea.'

'Look,' said Sarah, taking a deep breath and lighting a roll-up at the same time. 'I've got two things to say, and I want to get them out of the way. Firstly, don't blame yourselves for what happened in Spain. It was terrific of you to buy me the ticket. I really appreciated it, but none of us could possibly have anticipated what would happen out there. It just didn't work out, that's all.

'Secondly.' She paused. They both stopped themselves leaning forward in an attempt to disguise their desperate curiosity. 'I need to tell you both all about it but I'd like to eat first because for the first time in the best part of a month, I've realised that I'm starving. It's a long story and I need some fuel.'

They both sank back into their chairs, knowing they'd have to wait just a little longer.

Penne siciliana arrived with a green salad and a bottle of chianti classico. Judith and Vicky had agreed to stick to Italian to avoid unnecessary grief. Keeping the mood, they then all plumped for a zabaglione followed by espressos. The setting down of the small white coffee cups prompted Sarah to begin her tale.

She related the events of her first impressions of Malaga and Leo's ghastly mouthful. She described their first day together, the sites of Malaga, good food and the feel of the sun on her face. When she reached the bit about finding

the letter, she fished into her handbag, dug out a rather battered white envelope and handed it to them without saying
a word. The other two read the letter together. Their gasps
of horror broke the silence.

'You poor, poor angel,' said Judith. 'Stuck in the middle
of nowhere, no wonder you were gibbering when you rang
me. What happened then?'

'Well it went from bad to worse. As the day wore on, he
got more and more drunk, I was stuck there for at least one
more night before you could change the flight and I was
beginning to think he'd rape me. You could see he was
building up to some sort of great crescendo and there was
no lock on my bedroom door.'

'Oh shit,' they both mumbled in support.

'Well I started to shake with fright. He was just turning
into a monster and those teeth were beginning to grow
into fangs and turn green. But then I remembered what
you'd said.'

She turned to Judith, who looked back at her blankly.

'You told me to take control. Your words kept ringing in
my ears. And then it dawned on me that if I could get
bossy with him, he might just cave in. A sort of shift of
power. So I tried it.'

'So what did you do?' asked Judith, totally intrigued.

'Well, for a start I tried to be really friendly instead of
frightened and kept accepting drinks. I just pretended to
get merry but I was tipping them down the sink, out of a
window or into any old plant pot I could find. He thought
I was just getting into a better mood and I suppose it
occurred to him that if he got me pissed, I might give in
and give him what for, so to speak. So I had to change tack
a bit again.'

'So then what?' asked Vicky, who could feel goosebumps
up her arms just at the thought of it all.

'Again your words came back, Jude, so I took control. I

told him he was a total dweeb, a useless piece of shit and that I'd rather spend a week in a dark cupboard with piles than hear him droning on.'

'How did he react to that?' asked Vicky.

'That backfired too because he obviously got some kick out of being abused. The more I told him off, the more he seemed to derive some sort of pleasure from it. So in the end, I gave in.'

Sarah stopped and finished the last of her chianti.

'You didn't,' gasped Judith.

'How awful,' breathed Vicky.

'Yes, it was. I simply worked out that if I did what he wanted, I'd probably get a decent night's sleep and a fighting chance of getting out of there the next day.'

'So what exactly did you have to do?' asked Judith tentatively.

'It was obvious. It was all in the letter. So I offered to whip him. I couldn't actually believe it was me doing it, but deep down inside I was so scared that it sort of took my mind off my fright. And I really walloped him hard, which made me feel better.'

'God knows what sort of pleasure he derived from that,' said Judith. 'I have to say I've never equated pleasure with pain.'

'Well, you know what they say, different strokes for different folks,' said Sarah, managing a slight smile. 'I now know what that really means. He got an enormous kick out of it. He pulled down his trousers and lay down across the sofa. He had one of those horrible podgy, wobbly, spotty bottoms. Really nasty. And I whacked him with the whip and tried to pretend it wasn't really me there but a tacky movie I was watching. It seemed to go on for ever and the big blobby arse turned from white to red raw. Then he gave an almighty shudder, and I realised he'd come. Then he tidied himself up, packed it all away and, in a schoolboy sort of way, told me he'd never ever be naughty again. It was just the worst thing that's ever happened to me, but it did take the heat out of the kitchen, so to speak. He was instantly calm and he didn't bother me any more that night.'

Sarah, still weak from her self-imposed exile, began to cry slow, silent tears. The others were transfixed with horror on hearing what she'd been through.

'So when I rang you the next morning about the flight change, you'd already done the bizzo,' said Judith, incredulous.

'Yes, I had,' said Sarah through her tears. 'He drove me to the airport the next morning and, as you know, I hung around for the best part of two days waiting for the flight. It was worth it, just getting away. Mind you, the bastard had the gall to say it was a pity I was going back and could I "help him out" again in a quiet corner of the airport car park.'

'Did you?' asked Vicky, still open-mouthed.

'Oh puleeze. No, I was out of that car as fast as I could. Thank God he never followed me in and checked the flight times. And there are one or two things I've learnt from all this.'

'Oh yeah, and what are they?' asked Judith.

'Well, apart from discovering the Airport Diet—'

'Wassat?' interrupted Judith.

'Well, you hang around an airport for two days with a few hundred pesetas in your pocket, lose loads of weight and end up feeling terminal.'

They both groaned.

'The other thing is that from now on I shall be in total denial of whips, wardrobes and wallets. In other words, I'm giving up sex and shopping. Neither of them is worth it.'

They all noticed that their coffee had gone stone cold.

*

Leo,

I have arrived home safely. This letter is to inform you that I do not ever wish to hear from you again. I will not be answering any of your letters and if you call, I will put the phone down.

The other purpose of this letter is to beg you not to put any more women through the ordeal I suffered last week. If you need to advertise for people to help you satisfy your particular habits, then perhaps next time may I suggest you insert the word 'discipline' into the ad. I think most people would get the drift of what you required and then others would not suffer as I have done.

Sarah

chapter thirty-two

Vicky's after-dinner speaking career was beginning to take off. A big gig in London had netted her several hundred pounds and she was starting to think in terms of getting herself an agent. Her repertoire had now extended from experiences in Romania and compèring fashion shows to anecdotes from her career in television. Some of the incidents she'd related to David over the weeks that had made him laugh were now worming their way into a speech which so far had gone down a storm wherever she'd delivered it.

She was also learning the tricks of the trade. If you don't get them laughing within five minutes, then break off and really go for it.

'OK, let's stop for a minute and I'll answer all the questions you're dying to ask me. How old am I, how much did my clothes cost and how did I wind up doing this?'

She was also learning to her cost that whatever people booked you for, they always added on things when you got there. Running a raffle, suddenly being the compère for the whole evening, judging a competition, even having to join in a terrible karaoke session, all these had been thrust on her. She'd learnt the art of looking animated even when she was bored senseless.

Most of the work was now in London, involving fraightfully rich people who didn't answer their own front doors.

Women who 'did lunch and charidee' and were, in some cases, so wealthy they didn't really know what planet they were on. Only that it was a 'fraightfully naice' planet. Vicky was beginning to know every blade of grass on both sides of the railway cuttings up to Waterloo. She'd also invested in some non-means-testable clothes from a tiny boutique in Winchester, which were smart and classless.

The net result of all the speaking was that she was cutting down her shifts at the television station and not seeing very much of David. In a bizarre way, Vicky rather liked this. She knew she was a bit too keen on him and it was a way of keeping him at arm's length so she couldn't get too involved. But after several futile attempts in one week to book himself into her Filofax, she'd agreed to spend a weekend at his house. Vicky thought it unfair to invite him to stay at Judith's so this suited her too.

She smiled to herself as she flung a few things in a suitcase. Since the Torquay weekend, all the mystique of cellulite, wobbly bits and those bloody thread veins had at least been dispelled. Although she thought her body was worthy of a decent-size prison sentence for neglect, David apparently didn't seem to mind. Perhaps his contact lenses needed updating.

David picked her up in his BMW after work on Friday night. It was one of the longest and warmest nights of the year so they drove to his house just outside Winchester with his car roof down, enjoying the cool of the evening.

By the time they pulled up outside an end-of-terrace cottage, it was almost dark. The small front garden looked more like a jungle, with weeds and flowers jostling for space. It desperately needed a decent haircut. David had warned her that he hadn't done much to the place since he'd moved in. They could have done with a machete to hack their way up the garden path. He opened the front door and ushered her in.

Whatever Vicky had been expecting, it was not this. She wasn't daft enough to imagine it to be an exquisite little place, straight from the pages of *House Beautiful*, reeking of polish with fresh flowers at every window and a fridge full of delicious food and drink. But what she didn't expect to confront was a lounge crammed with furniture that even the homeless would have rejected and a kitchen dating back to the Norman Conquest.

Worst of all, you couldn't exactly flop into the old leather Chesterfield because balanced across each arm was a huge piece of hardboard with a five-thousand-piece jigsaw in progress. To the right, about half of it was completed, a picture of a couple of tall ships under full sail, and to the left, all the unplaced pieces had been put into neat colour-coded rows.

'I'm a jigsaw aficionado,' explained David, sensing her shock. 'Now how's about a drink and then we'll get to bed.'

Lying in bed that night, Vicky contemplated the ceiling while David slept peacefully beside her. She'd found herself contemplating the same ceiling during the brief sex they'd had earlier. She really would have to speak to him about that. Foreplay just wasn't in his repertoire. It was still two minutes tops, beginning to end. At this rate, the only way she'd keep him up half the night was by snoring.

She wriggled slightly, trying to get comfortable. The bed could have been the main event on the *Antiques Roadshow*, it was so lumpy and uncomfortable. And the sheets, pillow cases and duvet covers might as well have been picked at random like National Lottery numbers. Peach flowers, purple stripes and pistachio green leaves all vied for attention. It was an instant migraine.

But the pièce de resistance was the staircase, or rather lack of it.

'I really must get around to sorting that out,' David had

said amiably as he motioned her towards an old paint-stained wooden ladder reaching up to a hole in the ceiling.

Sarah had been as good as her word. She'd agreed to talk about her experience on one of Judith's programmes. That particular programme had been titled 'The Lion, the Whip and the Wardrobe' with Sarah as the main guest. The commissioning editor had been drawn to it instantly and had decided that programme would make a really strong opener for the series. Judith and her researchers were now working hard to get together an audience of people who'd all been on blind dates through newspapers, radio, agencies and the Internet. Because the show was live, there was to be a phone-in element too, plus an agony aunt to provide sensible advice.

'My advice?' Sarah had said. 'Don't. Stay at home and read a slushy book instead. It's safe, it's cheap and you're guaranteed a happy ending.'

Judith was really impressed at Sarah's determination. She figured that it was probably good therapy for her to talk about it, particularly as there was a genuine motive. Sarah seemed determined that no other woman should be conned by Leo again. Judith also privately knew it was going to make great telly. She made a mental note to warn Sarah yet again about the effect her appearance on the show might have on her friends and colleagues at work. Also the story might just get picked up by national newspapers.

She ran through some of the researchers' notes. They'd dug up some really good stories but none was in the class of Sarah's. When it came to measuring shocks on the Richter scale, she was in a league of her own.

Some of the stories would have been comical if they hadn't been so sad. One woman talked of a date with a man whose life obsession was car coats and who had brought one along for her to wear for their evening out. Another described her date's obsession with Gibbons' *Decline and Fall*, insisting she read it in advance so they could discuss it over dinner. One man bragged all night about how much he earned and then promptly did the well-worn 'I must have left my wallet at home' routine and left her to settle the bill. Another man very bravely produced two albums of photographs of all his ex-girlfriends, mostly nude or dressed in minuscule bits of strategic rubber. 'Hey, you could be in here too,' he had offered to his stunned dinner date.

Vicky was sitting in David's dreary local pub, hearing yet another story about this previous girlfriend or that one. Now firmly on home territory, he'd relaxed and another side to him was emerging. Boring and insensitive were a couple of adjectives that sprang to mind.

'I'd been at a party and this girl gave me the Big One,' he recounted. 'Well, I drove her home and on the way we stopped in a quiet lane and one thing led to another. Trouble was, when she took her shoes off her feet really smelt so I just got her to poke them out of the car window while we got on with the business.'

Wouldn't have taken long, thought Vicky, who was contemplating yet another ceiling. Ironic that a man you've been so keen on turns out to be crap in bed. With all the practice he seemed to have had, he should have got the idea of it by now, she thought bitterly. Maybe that was why he seemed to have got through so many women. None of them could be bothered to put him right. Her disappointment in him was beginning to hurt. She'd been so keen on him, how could she have got this so terribly wrong? Where was the man with whom she'd spent a heavenly time in Torquay?

Now she was almost fighting back tears of anger when

he launched into another tedious account of some other escapade from his youth.

'Excuse me,' she said, interrupting him mid sentence, and then almost barging past him, 'I must go to the loo.'

Once in the sanctity of the ladies', she pulled out her mobile and rang Judith. She then allowed herself a few bitter tears, powdered her nose, squirted on some perfume and ran a quick comb through her curls.

Back at their table, David picked up his tale mid sentence where he'd left off. Vicky went back to her ceiling.

'You don't seem to talk about ex-boyfriends?' he finally enquired.

'No, I don't think it's cool to talk about your exes,' she replied tartly.

'Totally understand,' said David, totally misunderstanding. 'Although I bet you've had a racy life. After all, there aren't many women who've got to your age without some sort of stab at holy matrimony.'

Oh no, not this one again, she thought, recalling Roger's red-faced fury at the register office. Then she had a sudden pang. Mervyn, the love of her life, hoved into view in her imagination. Not the nasty Mervyn caught with his trousers well and truly down in her bed with somebody else. But the gorgeous Mervyn she'd loved so much. The Mervyn who'd made her laugh, made her feel special. That was what she wanted and that was what she'd hoped for with David. Not this sad scenario with him boring on about ex-girlfriends while she sipped a glass of disgusting hock piped direct from a wine lake.

David was now launching himself into yet another very un-side-splitting account of some ex-girlfriend when her mobile rang.

'Hi, it's your friendly rescue service,' came Judith's welcoming voice.

'It's the office,' Vicky mouthed to David, holding her hand over the receiver. 'What's happened?'

'He's boring for Britain and the only way to shut him up is to commit murder,' suggested Judith.

'A murder? Have they got anyone yet?'

'Only a question of time till they track you down.'

'Is there a motive?'

'Absolutely.'

'OK, I'll get David to drop me off at the studio and start making the calls.' She glanced across to David for approval. He nodded, looking disappointed.

'I nearly died there,' said Vicky, collapsing into Judith's car as they headed home. 'How could I have been so wrong? What on earth did I miss?'

'I don't know but you're well out of it by all accounts,' replied Judith. 'Was his house really that bad or was it just typical bachelor scruff?'

'Oh it was worse. Listen, we've been to Romania and roughed it, remember, but that place was just too creepy. Apart from the lack of staircase, the appalling bed and the jigsaw syndrome, the kitchen should have been condemned. I found six sausages sat on the grill pan. He said they were for our lunch the next day. Well at that point I realised there couldn't be a next day.'

Judith laughed, but secretly she was so disappointed for her friend. This relationship could have been just the thing to cajole Vicky back to life after Mervyn, not to mention Roger. But it had seriously backfired.

Vicky continued: 'I suddenly realised I was with a right old meanie. Too tight to get his house fixed. I mean, frankly, most of us would have hotfooted down to the building society and got a loan to sort it out. It was just the pits. But it didn't seem to bother him, said he'd do it all himself when he had time. Well I couldn't live like that. Yet in other ways he was a right old woman. The jigsaw was immaculate with all the pieces in sick little lines. It reminded me of that crazy husband in *Sleeping With the Enemy*, the one who tries to track down his wife and hangs all the bath towels up in a certain way so she knows he's on her trail. Spooky wasn't in it.'

'Home territory, love,' said Judith soothingly. 'Don't forget, he was on his best behaviour for a few weeks. Then he's back on home territory, and bingo. Reverts to type. Some women are the same. First few weeks, it's a stampede into Janet Reger underwear and nibbling carrot sticks, but six months down the line, we're back into Marks and Sparks and stuffing ourselves with carrot cake. Look upon it as a lucky escape. From the sound of it, his house wasn't exactly the Stairway to Heaven. Six months down the road you'd have been really seriously upset. Ooops, sorry, you are.'

Tears had started to trickle down Vicky's cheeks. Tears of anger, and now humiliation.

'Now look on the bright side,' continued Judith. 'All this is grist to the mill for an after-dinner speaker. Why don't you speak about prats you have known. God knows, we could knock up a few between us. Enough to make a decent speech. It would go down a storm at women-only lunches.'

'Trouble is,' said Vicky in between recovery sobs, 'I'll be included now in all those boring speeches he makes about previous girlfriends.'

'Well, think of it as being nearly famous,' said Judith. 'Let's have a Pimms and drink to your Next Great Speech.'

'Better than my Last Good Shag,' said Vicky, who was beginning to see the funny side. 'And it wasn't with him either.'

'That was fairly obvious.'

chapter thirty-three

Sarah surveyed the buttons in the carpeted lift. Various accountants' offices and firms she'd never heard of were listed. The fourth floor proclaimed Corporate Recovery. 'That's what I could do with,' she muttered to herself. Then she found what she was looking for. Blair Financial Services on the sixth floor. At least she'd pass through Corporate Recovery and perhaps she'd gain some of their aura.

It had been Judith's suggestion that she sit down with a good financial adviser and sort out her money problems. John Blair had been a consultant on a couple of money programmes she'd made in the past, and she'd got him to promise not to flog Sarah any insurance or pensions in the process. This was just a friend calling in a favour. Judith also doubted Sarah would be interested in buying something that didn't come wrapped in tissue paper and a chic carrier bag.

Sarah was ushered into a small office with a pale grey table and dusky pink chairs. She gratefully spotted an ashtray – hurrah for a smoking office – took out a cigarette from her bag and lit it. She'd bought a packet of ten Benson and Hedges, still desperate to keep up appearances. Roll-ups were for home only. She felt nervous and rather foolish. All her own fault, she reminded herself, and now she had to put it right. No sex, no shopping. That was the new rule.

In came John Blair, followed by a woman carrying a tray with coffee. They shook hands and settled into their seats. As he poured the coffee and handed her a cup, she noticed her hands were shaking.

'Now before we begin, Mrs Franks, I wonder if you would mind one of our trainee managers sitting in on this interview,' said Mr Blair gently but in a tone which did not expect a refusal. 'What we discuss is totally confidential of course.'

'No I don't mind,' stammered Sarah, still desperately grateful for being able to smoke. 'Of course not.'

Mr Blair rose from his seat, opened the door and spoke a few words to someone in the outer office. A young blond-haired man in a sharp blue suit entered, shook hands and sat quietly in a corner.

Sarah fished into her bag and brought out a file of papers. It contained the pathetic and sorry state of her life, she thought sadly to herself. Details of her mortgage, the bills, the overdrafts, the threatening letters, the 'we will cut you off unless you stump up some cash' letters, plus the paperwork surrounding her divorce.

Mr Blair was a good listener. He had a gentle way of gaining her confidence and soon Sarah was unpacking most of her life and the reasons for the mess she was in. If he was shocked or appalled, he registered nothing. He just listened sympathetically, took brief notes occasionally and gave her the odd prompt. Sarah began to feel better for unburdening herself, describing the end of the marriage but omitting Alan's dubious sexuality and their final ugly scene. She felt she might even see the light at the end of the tunnel, if they didn't cut off her electricity before then.

Two hours, three cups of coffee and almost all her precious ten fags later, they'd been through everything from her one and only premium bond to her pension prospects. Sarah felt wrung out and was glad of the silence while Mr Blair did some calculations.

'Right,' he said gently, 'here's the scenario. You've got quite a big mortgage on your flat and the main priority is to keep that going. Your utilities, gas, electric, etc. They're also a priority. The rest, the kitchen company, credit cards, catalogues and so on, we'll write to them and make offers of repayment. Small amounts to start with.

'Now you have to make some sacrifices, even to meet these small payments. You've been very honest and owned up to your weaknesses. I don't normally have these sorts of discussions with clients but we're on a different basis here. Clothes seem to have been your biggest problem, so obviously you're going to have to stay away from the shops. Your credit cards have been cancelled so there's no temptation there. And now that you don't have a cheque book, you'll have to budget carefully and withdraw enough cash each week to live on and stick to it.'

Sarah nodded dumbly. He was right of course. House of Fraser shares would plummet at this rate.

'Could you work all this out for me?' she asked, feeling foolish. 'I just can't trust myself any more.'

'Of course I can,' said Mr Blair, smoothly. 'In fact I was going to offer. But there is one item you are going to have to give up in order to make any of this work.'

'What's that?' said Sarah, steeling herself for a shock. She seemed to have so little left.

'Your car,' he said bluntly. 'It's either that or move somewhere cheaper. And for the costs involved, I'd suggest you stay where you are and sell the car.'

Sarah felt as though she'd lost the will to live. Her car, how on earth could she manage without it?

'You've already told me you live on a bus route to work. I think you'd find that a bus pass would work out considerably cheaper than running your car. I know your Volvo's old and paid for, but it's thirsty and it could easily become a liability. You're spending a great deal on petrol, then there's the insurance that's due soon. You don't have that sort of money, even for third party. Then there's the motor tax. It all adds up.'

Sarah blushed. Her car tax had run out just before she'd been to Spain and she hadn't had the money to renew it. So she'd been carefully parking in side streets or in the relative safety of the clinic car park, with the windscreen pointing towards the bushes.

He was right. She couldn't afford it. And she certainly couldn't afford a fine if she got caught.

'OK, the car goes,' she said, a small tear trickling down one cheek. She hoped Mr Blair wouldn't notice. She managed to sweep back her hair and wipe her eye at the same time. Her head was spinning, brain working out how she'd manage without transport. She thought enviously of Alan's swanky Mercedes with its leather seats. Mr Blair gathered up his notes as a signal to close the meeting.

'Now I'll get a letter off to you detailing all the things we've discussed and then it's up to you. If you want to review things at any time, then you know where to call.' He offered a handshake. 'Tristram here will see you out. Good luck. I'm sure you can do it.'

Sarah shook hands with him and turned to the young man in the sharp suit she'd almost forgotten about. He'd not uttered a word during the entire proceedings. There was something vaguely familiar about him. As soon as Mr Blair was out of the room, he smiled at her.

'You don't remember me, do you?' he said, gently.

'I know your face but I can't place it,' she replied, scanning his face, her mind racing.

'Look, I won't tell if you won't. Remember the Explicit Sextet? I was your escort to the amateur theatrical society show that night.'

'Oh shit,' gasped Sarah, hand to mouth in utter horror.

'Hey, listen, don't be upset. We had a great night. I'll never forget laughing so much. You and your friend were such good sports. Giles and I said it was our best escort job. We've both graduated now so we don't do it any more.'

'Oh good,' said Sarah, now puce with embarrassment and wondering what to say. 'Sorry, but you did give me a shock. Not only do you know I'm pathetically single and an old has-been, but I don't possess a bean either. Well I'm more into the minus beans.'

'You'll soon get straight. Blair's a really good bloke. He'll help you sort it. And as for being a has-been, I'd be very surprised if you're not snapped up soon.'

If only you knew, thought Sarah ruefully, casting her mind back to Leo and his wardrobe arrangements. Not bloody likely.

Tristram escorted Sarah out to the lift and insisted on seeing her out of the building. When they reached the ground floor, he planted a kiss on her cheek and wished her good luck.

Sarah stepped out into the sunshine, and for an old has-been, she felt decidedly better.

The car didn't take long to shift. One ad in the local paper produced five callers all offering the one thousand pounds asking price. Not bad for a car that had been around the clock once already. Sarah gritted her teeth, accepted the highest bid and insisted on cash. She waved the buyer away, a young lager type with hideous spots, and put the money into a kitchen drawer. He'd soon find out about the slow puncture in one rear tyre, the windscreen wipers that packed up during heavy downpours and the constant thirst for oil.

She'd treated herself to a bottle of wine and a packet of cigarettes in advance to celebrate/commiserate the departing car. It was a sunny Saturday afternoon so she took a chair out into her tiny garden and settled down with a large glass of chilled Chardonnay and the luxury of an instant fag. No fiddling with papers, tips and tobacco today. The money would be spent on paying off her mortgage arrears as suggested by Mr Blair. He'd had quite an effect on her. She couldn't let him down because she knew she'd not only arrived at the Last Chance Saloon, she was already in there, running up a tab.

'It's the big one,' Vicky phoned to tell Judith, yanking her out of a meeting. 'It's my big break in London. If I get this right, my diary could be full for a year. I could give up telly. Just think, no more "Plane Flew Too Low, Crash Probe Told", or "Prostitutes Appeal to Pope".'

'Brilliant,' said Judith, sounding about as excited as turkeys at the prospect of Christmas.

'I thought you'd be pleased,' said Vicky, rather hurt at her lack of reaction. 'It means I might be able to give up the telly freelancing, earn some decent money and get my own place.'

'No, no, sorry, hon, I'm really thrilled at your news but I'm just up to my eyes with the new series. It's really getting to me. I keep having nightmares about going to a musical at the theatre and it's such a crap show that I come out humming the set. Then I wake up thinking it's all a terrible omen.'

This wasn't like Judith, the calm Judith who coped with everything so effortlessly.

'Sorry, Jude,' said Vicky, instantly apologetic. 'I didn't realise you were under so much pressure.'

'Well it's always the same. You're only as good as your last piece of work. And in my case it was Romania and that's up for several awards. I've now convinced myself the only way up from now on is down.'

'Oh rubbish,' said Vicky. 'Of course it's going to be great, especially with Sarah on it. Come on, you know as well as I do that she's got an incredible story. All I'm worried about is that it'll all blow up in her face.'

'Anyway, what are you going to talk about at this bash?' asked Judith, changing the subject deliberately and making an effort to sound more enthusiastic.

'Well, I'm speaking at a lunch for lots of public relations people so my "Reality of Local Telly" speech is tailormade for that. I've got it off to a fine art now and I can customise it a bit.'

'Sounds good to me. Hey, listen, I'm sorry I didn't ask how you are,' said Judith. 'You know, life after Jigsaw Man.'

'OK I suppose. He'll be great material one day but a bit too close to home at the moment. I still haven't quite got over the mess of his house. I really thought he and I were going places, but the only place he ought to be heading for is B and Q.'

'Trouble is, men are lazy gits when it comes to the home,' said Judith. 'They get struck down by selective hearing and impaired sight when it suits them. In David's case, he was obviously too mean to get it all fixed. Or too busy finishing that bloody jigsaw.'

'Oh, but he'll never finish it,' said Vicky emphatically.

'But it sounded like his life's work from what you say,' said Judith.

'No, he can't possibly finish it,' said Vicky triumphantly. 'I was so angry with him harping on about all the ex-girlfriends, I flushed two pieces down the loo.'

They were only half an hour away from recording the first show. Guests were being led from the green room to the set to take up their seats while the cameras were racked, last-minute adjustments were made to light and focus, principal guests were mic'd up. And the first episode of *Get Out of That One* was about to begin.

The floor manager, an old hand called Dave, warmed up the audience with quips about all the cameramen, telling outrageous stories about what they all did in their spare time. Nervous laughter gave way to chuckles and guffaws. Even Sarah felt herself relaxing a little, although she'd felt sick from the moment she'd woken up that morning. If it hadn't meant letting Judith down, she'd have chickened out. But now she must go through with this, knowing that the programme's success was to some extent riding on her.

The lights dimmed, the floor manager indicated applause, up came the music, and the presenter, an up-and-coming chap in his thirties called Jim Bryant, made his entrance.

'Hello and welcome to *Get Out of That One*, a brand-new live series about real-life problems. Over the next few weeks we'll be meeting people who've faced up to all kinds of strange or terrifying situations and hearing how they've reacted. We'll be finding out what it's like to marry in jail, discover you've been the victim of fraud, or that someone's stolen your identity. We'll be meeting people who've had to read their own obituaries and others who've tried to fake their own deaths. But in this first show, we're dealing with the twenty-first-century way of meeting and mating. Now just a few years ago, the idea of going to a dating agency, answering a newspaper ad or surfing the Net for a partner would have been sniggered at. Not any more. Everyone knows someone who's done it. In fact, everyone in our audience here today has tried one of these methods of meeting people. For some it's worked out, but for others, it was just the start of a nightmare. Ladies and gentlemen, meet our first guest – Sarah Franks.'

Through the applause, Sarah sensed all the cameras focused on her. Jim Bryant smiled and held his stick mic towards her. She swallowed hard and began her tale.

'It was just coming up to New Year's Eve and we were all sitting in this wine bar, making resolutions . . .'

By the end of the programme, three women had phoned in saying they too had answered an ad in the *Sunday Times*, been to Malaga and had the wardrobe experience with Leo. Sarah felt totally wrung out, having relived the story and then having to come to terms with hearing the voices of others who'd been through what she'd endured. It was all too much. She fled to the loo, locked the door of a cubicle and wept.

When she emerged, Judith was waiting patiently outside.

'Sorry, hon,' she said simply. 'I didn't realise you'd suffer so much.'

'My fault, not yours,' sniffed Sarah. 'It was my idea, I agreed to come on the programme so it's my fault.'

'Come and have a drink in the green room,' said Judith. 'In fact, have several and I'll get you a taxi home afterwards. Anyway, you were the star of the show. It was wonderful telly.'

'Oh good,' said Sarah, wondering whether to be absurdly pleased or book straight into a convent. 'Did I come across all right?'

'Total magic, if you want to know the truth,' said Judith honestly. 'And the fact that we got three phone calls from other women who'd been through exactly what had happened to you. That was more than we could have hoped for.'

Sarah powdered her nose, put on some lipstick and gave herself a squirt of perfume. She picked up her bag, ready to face the fray.

'Come on and meet your fellow guests properly now,' said Judith, taking her arm and leading her back to the green room.

The frantic buzz of conversation dipped as Sarah entered the room, and as if from nowhere, applause broke out until the whole room was clapping her. There were even muffled shouts of 'bravo'. A smiling man in his late forties and dressed in a rather lurid Italian blue suit came towards her, offering to get her a drink.

'Gin and tonic, please,' she whispered. 'Make it a large one.'

'Coming up,' said the man. 'I'm Barry, by the way, and I think you're bloody brilliant.'

He turned to fetch them both a drink from the bar and returned promptly.

'Here, Princess.' He handed her a glass, his hands laden with jewellery. 'You could do with that after all you've been through. What a terrible story! Mind you, I'm surprised someone like you needed to go all that way to meet someone. I can think of loads of blokes who'd snap you up, no trouble.'

Sarah muttered an embarrassed contradiction. *Where were they all when I needed them?* she thought to herself bitterly.

Within just a few minutes, Sarah realised she was pissed. Barry had been very diligent, fetching gin and tonics, and now they'd caught up with her. Aware that she was losing the plot, she vaguely heard Barry offering to drive her home in his Rolls Royce.

'Oh do me a favour,' she said sarcastically, now much the worse the wear for drink. 'I bet you don't have a Rolls Royce, hic. Well I don't, hic, have a Lear jet either. So that makes us, hic, quits.'

chapter thirty-four

Much to Sarah's acute embarrassment, Barry did, in fact, have a Rolls Royce. *I must be mad*, she thought, climbing into the car and sinking back into its luxurious cream leather seats. *After what I've been through, I must be potty.* In her haze of gin, tonic and despair, she muttered a speech about going straight home, no hanky panky and that she would not be inviting him in. He just nodded without protest. All he insisted on was taking her phone number, then pecked her on the cheek and left her on the doorstep.

Sarah slumped into bed, still half dressed, and fell asleep immediately. Barry, on the other hand, sat up all night fantasising about Sarah naked and giving him the blow job of the century, while he lounged on a sofa watching Man United on his widescreen boomaround-sound telly, stroking her blonde hair with one hand and a can of Castlemaine 4X in the other. Bliss. His nether regions twitched with longing. He hadn't seen a cracker like that in a long time. He'd make it his mission to cheer her up after that bastard in Spain. Leave it two days, he told himself. Let her get over the stress of the programme and then begin his assault.

Sarah was woken by the phone, its shrill sound boring into her head. The mother of all hangovers had set in. She felt queasy and her head felt like a rehearsal room for a band competition. She reached for the phone, assuming it would be Judith. Wrong on that one. It was a journalist asking for an interview following up the programme. Unfortunately the act of reaching for the phone triggered a bout of gagging, and she had to scurry to the bathroom to be sick. When she finally returned to bed, feeling totally wretched, she noticed that in her haste she'd left the phone off the hook. She replaced it and it rang again immediately. Same chap with the same request.

'How did you get my number?' she shrieked at him.

'The phone book,' he confessed, making her feel extremely silly. Of course she was in the book and surprisingly there were very few Franks listed. Certainly one less since Bostik had left town.

In the end, the journalist talked her into giving a short interview. She was too weak and hungover to protest but at least she held out from revealing Leo's full name and phone number.

Sarah replaced the phone and instantly regretted what she'd done. Now she'd have to tell the kids. She'd been careful to suss out that Daniel would be out of the country and Roz was away in Cyprus on yet another holiday with Simon. She was going to tell them both about the programme when they got back. But now it might make the papers, she'd have to forewarn them. With no car, no outgoing calls and only a hangover for company, it would be difficult.

The phone rang again. Please let it be Judith, not another slime-ball journalist. She answered in her old Zsa Zsa Gabor accent.

'Allo, ees zat you, dahlink?' she whispered cautiously. 'Oh thank gawd it's you. I've had a bloody reporter on the phone.'

'Don't worry,' said Judith's soothing voice, disguising the

fact that she was indeed worried about Sarah. 'I'm taking a day off so I'll come over and pick you up.'

'Thanks, hon. Actually I need to ask you a favour. When we get to your place, can I use your phone? I must try and get in touch with the kids to warn them about this. They're both abroad and I never got around to telling them about the telly thing.'

'Do they know about Spain?' enquired Judith.

'Er no. They don't know anything much about anything much really, especially Daniel. He doesn't know his father is gay. If Roz does, she hasn't talked about it. She was there when Bostik decked me if you remember, but we never discussed his boyfriend. I think she's frightened of facing up to the truth.'

'Don't blame her,' said Judith. 'Not a pretty sight. Especially in Bostik's case. Anyway, I'm on my way. Listen, it's a sunny day. Fancy lunch at Cahoots? We could sit out in the garden at the back.'

Sarah thought wistfully of all the times they'd sat out in the little Mediterranean garden, with its palms, geraniums and terracotta pots. Then she shivered, memories of Malaga, and her stomach heaved.

'Er, well actually I've got the hangover from hell. I don't think I could cope with that, sorry. In fact I'm just about to call God on the great white phone again.'

'Good job God didn't cut that one off,' said Judith. 'I'm on my way.'

Sarah dropped the phone for another mercy dash to the loo.

Sarah was rather relieved to have told her kids everything. There was a certain cleansing aspect to it all, but also the *Daily Mirror* ran the story the next day. 'The Lion, the Whip and the Wardrobe,' shrieked the headlines.

Sarah had phoned in sick. There was no way she could

face everyone at work looking the shade of pea green she'd adopted. She just wasn't up to being the centre of attention she knew was inevitable. Judith suggested she lie low at her house for a couple of days, put a little distance between the programme and going back to work. Although Sarah had insisted on appearing on *Get Out of That One*, Judith still felt it was to some extent her fault. She could have talked Sarah out of it, but she hadn't. It had made great telly and that was her job. At least she could offer Sarah some sanctuary until it all blew over.

'Bit like a re-run of poor old Vicky,' said Sarah the following morning over her breakfast coffee and cigarette.

'Yeah, I do seem to specialise in providing havens for friends fleeing from the press,' said Judith. 'Maybe this is my next career move. Running a safe house.'

'Ha bloody ha,' said Sarah, taking a deep drag on her cigarette. 'Listen, I'm sorry about this.'

'Absolutely not your fault. More mine.'

'No, I was the one who met the slug of the century and it was me who volunteered to be on your programme,' said Sarah very firmly. 'And now this is me breaking my New Year resolution. I've already had to give up shopping, and now I'm giving up sex.'

Vicky arrived at the smart West London hotel white-lipped and shaking. She spent ages fumbling with change to tip the taxi driver, who was beginning to tut. At this rate he'd have already spent the money on diesel. She ran up the marbled steps, past the top-hatted doorman, into the foyer and made straight for the ladies'. Once inside, she calmed down a little. Its cool marble and deep green vases full of cream lilies had an instant, tranquil effect. She inspected her no-nonsense long navy skirt suit, checked her make-up, reapplied lipstick and another squirt of perfume and gave her hair a vigorous brush. Deep breath, count to ten, she emerged with a new calm. This wasn't the Big One, she told herself, it was just another speech. She'd done it before, she'd do it again, she psyched up as she strode across the foyer to meet her host.

Her mind flashed back to the early days of her new career, talking to women's groups and local business people. She'd come a long way since then. Memories of Mrs Sweet, the fat bag lady at the fashion show, came flooding back. Her bitchy comment that the audience wouldn't be the slightest bit interested in fashion. Well, Mrs Sweet clearly wasn't but the audience certainly had been and she'd wowed them. Unfortunately she'd also wowed Jigsaw Man too. She wondered how he was getting on with those five-thousand-piece tall ships minus the two vital pieces.

Her thoughts were interrupted by a woman in her early thirties, a young Grace Kelly, blonde hair swept up in a chignon, who introduced herself as Clare Sanders from the company organising the lunch.

'We've got lots of super people here,' said Clare enthusiastically. 'Some major press and about twenty PR companies have taken tables and brought some of their clients.'

'What sort of accounts do they handle?' asked Vicky, doing her homework. 'Anything unusual?'

'Well there's the usual round of accountants and lawyers, run-of-the-mill stuff, but there are some film, theatre and music PRs here too. Nice mix. There'll be a lot of networking and client poaching before the afternoon's over. Should be fun. Come on through and I'll get you a drink.'

Vicky followed Clare through to a huge room where drinks and canapés were being dispensed by scurrying waiters, who, sensing the clientele, all looked like male models or resting actors. The air hung heavy from personal grooming and overdoses of Calvin Klein and Tommy.

'Just an orange juice for me,' said Vicky firmly, remembering her own rules of guest speaking. The three Ps, she called them. Polite, punctual and not pissed.

Clare wafted off to track down a Brad Pitt wannabe while Vicky surveyed the scene. All the men in sharp suits, bright shirts and ties, the women also mostly in dresses or suits but in this summer's pastel colours. Everyone clutched huge bags, presumably stuffed full of their electronic life support systems, poised for some instant networking. Everywhere there were signs of VPL (Visible Phone Line) bulging from jackets and pockets. The general hubbub of 'mwah mwah' air-kissing was interspersed with the trill of mobile phones going off everywhere. There was certainly a whole lotta moving and shaking going on.

Clare returned, followed by a Brad Pitt body double carrying a tray of drinks. They both sipped orange juice and ironed out the details of the proceedings, who would introduce who and so on until it got to Vicky's speech.

'About fifteen minutes would be just right,' said Clare. 'My colleague has never stopped talking about your speech last month. Said it was totally fabbo and that they were all creased up.'

'That's very kind,' murmured Vicky, trying to keep her stomach in some sort of shape. 'I hope I can do a repeat performance.'

'I'm sure you will,' said Clare, leading the way into the banqueting hall, which consisted of one long top table on a podium and twenty circular tables each seating ten people. *Good*, thought Vicky, *half the room will have their backs to me*. It was a stunning sight, the room resplendent in deep reds and greens with magnificent fruit and flower arrangements on the tables and in every alcove.

Clare and Vicky wove their way through the crowds now milling into the hall and headed for the top table. As they passed through the throng, a group of men were laughing at the tail end of some uproarious joke. There was something familiar about the laughing, she couldn't quite put her finger on it. Before she could get a handle on it, they'd all moved on to another gag.

Vicky and Clare took their places at the table. Vicky glanced at the menu, rather a blur. She'd long since discovered that no matter how hungry you are, if you're the turn, the meal tastes of nothing.

After a plea for phones to be switched off and a quick thanks to the Lord for lunch, the hubbub dipped slightly as two hundred people descended on a vegetable terrine with leaves, followed by brill with a veronique sauce. Vicky used the process of the meal as an excuse to go over her notes mentally. It would soon be time. She checked her watch. Pudding, serving coffee and then she'd be on her feet. Twenty minutes to air, well hot air anyway.

Clare's boss, a slim and expensively suited forty something, rose to his feet. He reiterated a request for phones to remain switched off, paid his compliments to the chef and then expressed a wish that the gathering would be the first of many.

'Now I'd like to introduce you to our guest speaker. And I'm sure she won't mind me saying that she's from the other side of the tracks. We in public relations want to get our client, product, concept into the public's minds, wallets and shopping baskets. So we bombard those with the power to give us coverage. But what about those on the other side of the fence, those who get the brunt of our efforts? Well today we're going to hear first hand what it's like to be bombarded. From the world of television and also an accomplished public speaker, please welcome Victoria Chadwick.'

Applause broke out plus the shuffling of chairs as those facing away from the podium at the circular tables turned their chairs around to watch.

Vicky rose from her seat and placed her one page of

bullet points in front of her on the table, just in case. She took a deep breath, psyched up like an athlete who's made the Olympic finals.

'Good afternoon, everyone. My name's . . .' she faltered into the microphone.

The audience, fuelled by lorryloads of claret and Chablis, burst into hysterical laughter and small outbreaks of applause, assuming this was part of the act.

Vicky stood horrorstruck. There, staring up from the table right in front of her, sat an equally thunderstruck Mervyn.

'I, I, er, I'm sorry, I feel terrible. I can't do this,' she said, looking desperately to Clare for support. There was none forthcoming. Clare stared blankly back at her, like a rabbit caught in car headlights.

'Gotta go,' she muttered, grabbing her bag and pushing back her chair. As she hurtled past the blur of faces all trained on her, she was aware of the official photographer chasing after her, flash gun popping.

Out into the sunshine and mercifully a cab outside.

'Waterloo,' she shrieked at the driver, tears spurting from her eyes. After a few minutes of merciful escape, she grappled in her bag for her mobile.

'Hello, Safe Havens,' joked Judith answering.

'What? Jude? Is that you?' Vicky's voice trembled.

'Yeah, of course. Sorry, Sarah and I were just joking about me running a safe house. Hey, how's it going? I thought you'd have been on your feet doing the speech right now.'

'I've done a runner,' snivelled Vicky. The cabbie perked up and started unashamedly earwigging her conversation through his half-open window.

'I couldn't do it,' she continued. 'Mervyn was there.' She burst into uncontrollable hysterics.

The cabbie spent the rest of his day convinced he'd

carried a big-time thief and wondering what it was that she'd stolen. He found his answer in next morning's red tops. There was his fare, pictured running from the hotel he'd picked her up from, with the headline 'Keep On Running – Again'.

chapter thirty-five

Sarah's couple of days at Judith's house extended to the best part of a week. The effect of the programme had so deeply distressed her that she didn't feel she could handle the newspaper interest as well. Judith was now such an expert at fending off the media, seeing as she was one of them, that her hideaway was the perfect answer.

'Oh shit,' said Judith, over her breakfast coffee the day after Vicky's disastrous speech. 'She won't like this one bit.'

'Wassat?' said Sarah, drawing deeply on a cigarette. Judith handed her the *Daily Mail*. There it was on page three.

VICTORIA IS NOT AMUSED – AGAIN!
TV reporter cum public speaker Victoria Chadwick has taken flight again. Due to address a meeting of public relations movers and shakers yesterday, Victoria did just that. She looked decidedly un-amused as she rose to her feet and then moved pretty rapidly – straight out of the door.

It's the second time in a year that the forty-year-old journalist has done a bunk in front of a large audience. Last time it was at her own wedding. In August last year, would-be bridegroom Roger Smith was left with egg on his face and a huge bill after

she bolted from the surprise wedding he'd planned.
But this time there appeared to be no surprises.
Victoria was due to speak at an inaugural lunch for
some of the country's top PR agencies and clients.
But something mysterious happened that caused
her to make a run for it.

'It was as though she'd had some kind of shock,'
said one guest. 'She got up and introduced herself
but got confused about her own name. We all
thought at first that it was rather a hoot but next
thing, she was doing a runner out the door.'

Another guest commented: 'It was strange.
Almost as if she'd seen someone or something
which triggered an attack of some kind.'

Whatever Victoria's attack of nerves, her bosses
at Hartford Independent Television could provide
no clue as to the cause. A spokesman from HIT
said, 'We don't expect to see Victoria here until next
week. What she does in her spare time is her affair.
She's a freelance journalist.'

Her whereabouts are now a mystery too.
Colleagues at HIT said they were aware she'd been
staying with a friend for several months but have
not received any calls from her since yesterday.

'She's popular, always turns out and does all the
unsociable shifts here,' said one member of staff.
'But we didn't know she was of Olympic running
standard. Perhaps she ought to move over to the
sports desk.'

Judith tossed aside the paper. 'Well at least this time no
one thought to trace her to her parents' house,' she
grinned. 'I suppose at forty – and I bet she'll be chuffed at
that bit of maths – you're not always expected to have a
mum and dad, let alone go home to them.'

Sarah lit another cigarette and poured out some more coffee. 'I suppose one overnight celebrity in the house is enough to cope with,' she said dolefully.

'Oh don't be daft. If Vick were here, I'd just be fending off the same hacks chasing both your stories. You'd both be on a sort of special offer, two for one. Anyway Vick hasn't been home in yonks and her dad will be brilliant over this. Her mother will have a fit wondering what the neighbours will say. It's the perfect scenario. It'll keep her mind occupied, juggling plates on sticks, keeping both parents happy.'

Judith sipped her coffee and pondered for a moment.

'Tell you what,' she said. 'Let's give her a ring in a while and see how she's doing.'

'Why not now?' asked Sarah.

'Oh if I know Mrs Chadwick, she'll have been up since dawn, buying the papers under cover of darkness, Dior shades and a Hermès headscarf. And by now she'll be tearing her very expensive perm out in tufts over what the neighbours will think.'

Judith had cooked a really delicious lunch. They'd had grilled tuna and green salad followed by raspberries and crème fraîche. She and Sarah were now flopped on sofas ready for the afternoon Fred Astaire movie.

'What a fabulous life that must have been,' drooled Sarah. 'All that champagne, floaty dresses, music played by real live orchestras, flash cars and men who could really dance.'

'Yeah. We've come a long way from *Top Hat* to dancing around your handbag like we did at university,' said Judith wistfully, 'although God knows why we guarded our bags so jealously. I don't know about you but there was sod all in my bag in those days.'

'I don't think it's even that civilised any more,' said Sarah. 'These days there seems to be a competition to see

how little you can wear when you go out. You should have
seen some of the get-ups that weekend I went up to see
Roz. Mind you, what she wore you'd have blinked and
missed. It was almost subliminal.'

She rubbed her feet, still remembering the pain from
walking the length and breadth of Oxford Street that weekend with Roz.

'Actually our two seem to be going strong, don't they,'
said Judith. 'I was a bit worried that one would get hurt and
that would put a strain on our friendship. You know, if
one treated the other one badly. But I have a feeling it's the
Real Thing, don't you?'

'I think you could be right,' said Sarah. 'If Roz and
Simon got together, we'd each be the mothers-in-law.
Perhaps that would make us mothers-in-law-in-law to each
other. That sounds ancient, doesn't it? Well at least if they
do get married, we can make sure we don't wearing clashing outfits.'

'That's bloody typical of you,' said Judith. 'Get the shopping organised. Even if you were pregnant, you'd shop till
you dropped.'

'Not much chance of either,' laughed Sarah, sounding like
her old self. 'No more sex and shopping for me, remember.'

The phone burst into life. Judith went into the kitchen
in search of the cordless.

'Judith Fielding?' said an imperious female voice.

'Yes, who is this?' asked Judith, knowing full well who it
was.

'This is Victoria's mother, Mrs Chadwick,' she boomed
down the phone. Judith shuddered. She might have
expected this. Somehow it would all be her fault.

'Victoria is here staying with us. She needs to be kept
away from all these nasty journalists,' she declared, conveniently forgetting that both her daughter and Judith were
members of that apparently obnoxious profession.

'And,' she boomed, then suddenly lowered her voice, 'that lawyer fellow with the silly name, Mervyn, rang here, asking for Victoria. Well, I sent him away with a flea in his ear. He might wear a pinstripe suit and drive some sort of fancy car, but I'm not fooled. He's nothing but trouble and I don't want her hurt any more. So if he gets in touch with you, then I demand that you say nothing, especially to Victoria.'

'He's not likely to, he has no idea where I live,' said Judith sweetly.

'Oh these sweet-talkers have a way of finding out. We haven't told her that he's telephoned. And I don't want him making contact with her via you. Understood?'

Judith returned to the sitting room.

'You'll never believe this,' she said. 'That was Mrs Chadwick in all her glory. And guess what, Merve the Swerve is on Vicky's trail. Now that spells trouble.'

'T-R-O-U . . . Sorry, can never resist that one,' said Sarah. 'What a bloody cheek after what he did to her. Men have this most amazing combination of brass nerve and short-term memory loss. I thought Vick's mum approved of Mervyn because he had a sensible job, as she saw it. You know, professional job, briefcase, pinstripe suit and Range Rover with the colour-co-ordinating tow bar.'

'I think he was, but he went a writ too far when he got caught with his trousers down in her flat,' replied Judith. 'Mind you, I doubt very much Vick would have told her mother all the gory details. Otherwise Mrs C would have been hotfoot down there and handbagged him straight into the nearest casualty department.'

'Anyway, we have a problem,' said Sarah. This turn of events was snapping her out of her own problems. 'Just supposing Merve rings here, what do we say? Do we warn Vicky or not tell her?'

'Nothing to the first and pass on the other two,' replied

Judith. There was a knock at the door. 'Oh hell's teeth, that could be him now.'

She strode purposefully to the door. The flash gun momentarily blinded her.

'Any chance of a chat with . . .?'

'Absolutely not,' said Judith, slamming the door shut, drawing the hall curtain and returning to the sitting room.

'What was all that about?' asked a suddenly nervous Sarah.

'Just some jolly hacks on the trail,' said Judith. 'Trouble is I don't know who they were after, you or Vicky.'

Within twenty-four hours, Wapping interest had thankfully waned on the Olympic prospects of the runaway speaker and the victim of 'The Lion, the Whip and the Wardrobe'. They'd all moved on to a motorway pile-up, a short-lived celebrity wedding and yet another Cabinet love child.

Within forty-eight hours, there'd been no call from Mervyn either. Judith allowed herself to relax, believing that the crisis was over. Sarah was moving back to her tiny flat, and Vicky had had quite enough of her mother. They all agreed to get together for dinner in Cahoots, to mark the return to normal life. Judith made it clear that the meal was to be her treat. She was secretly having a huge guilt trip because she'd got a small bonus as a result of the early rat-ings success of *Get Out of That One*.

It was a hot evening so they decided to eat out in the garden. Too hot for wine, so they ordered a pitcher of ice-cold beer and then opted for ribs and various salads. Ordering done, they all sat back in their chairs and sipped their beers.

Sarah lit a cigarette. 'Do you know,' she said after the first satisfying drag, 'this is a bit like a re-run of our epic meeting here at New Year.'

'How can we forget!' chorused the other two.

'Sorry, girls. All my fault. It didn't really work, all that chasing men and accepting all invitations,' said Sarah apologetically

'Nope,' said Judith. 'I resolved to have some sex, and what have I had, bugger all. In fact bugger nothing.'

'I resolved to get a decent job,' said Vicky. 'Well I very nearly got one and then I did a bunk. So I've failed miserably.'

'Now hang on. Some of us have achieved something,' said Sarah. 'I resolved to get my divorce, which I did. I resolved to get better with money. Well I had no choice there. However, I have totally bombed where the sex is concerned. Willie the Wig turned out to be married and then there was Mr Whippy in Sunny Spain. He had sex but I didn't, so it doesn't count really, does it?'

'Well I had sex with Jigsaw Man but it was so brief it doesn't count either,' said Vicky. 'I wonder if he ever worked out what happened to those two missing pieces.'

'And there we were, all praying for a mansoon,' said Judith. 'Seems to me we're better off Sexless in Southampton.'

Judith dropped Sarah off at her flat. Sarah stood on the pavement and waved until the car was out of sight. She took a deep breath.

'Back to reality, back to work tomorrow,' she muttered to herself, grappling for her key. As she opened the door, she could hear her answering machine beeping away.

Some hope, she thought. *I can't ring them. They'll all have to call again.* Anyway, none of them could be important. She'd just said goodnight to her best friends, and she'd spoken earlier that day to Roz and Daniel on Judith's phone. There was also a nasty pile of letters, ominously window envelopes. She decided it was either the bills or the messages tonight. John Blair's words of financial wisdom echoed in her head, 'Open the bills, face up to

things, hiding them away only piles on the interest.'
Impressed with herself, she started to go through the post.
Three letters were from magazine journalists begging her to
contact them to discuss her story and hinting at payment.
They all had flimsy reasons for justifying themselves. One
said that her story would target a sympathetic audience,
and highlight the enormous risks of answering lonely
hearts columns. Conveniently forgetting that the same
magazine carried several pages of people desperately seeking someone, anyone. Another letter claimed her story
would definitely halt the increase in date rape, Britain's
fastest-growing crime. Bit optimistic, thought Sarah, hesi-
tating for a nano-second at the thought of payment and
then filing them in the bin.

She made a coffee, rolled a fag and settled down to go
through the rest. Mostly bills and statements. But her new
financial routine was slowly beginning to pay off. It would
take at least a year, possibly two, but she'd do it. Then who
knows, perhaps she'd not have to roll her own. Maybe
she'd be able to buy another car.

Among the envelopes was a small delivery note from a
local florist. Someone had sent flowers and left them with
the people in the flat above. It was too late to bother them
now, and too late anyway, judging by the date. Five days
ago. They'd be pretty well dead by now, especially in this
heat. Who the hell were they from? She'd have to wait
until morning.

The phone rang. Absentmindedly, Sarah picked it up on
the second ring, not thinking for a moment that it might be
a journalist.

'Hello, Princess,' said a male voice.

'Look, I don't know who you are but I'm sorry, my story
has been told once and once only, it's not for sale and please
don't bother me any further. Anyway, how did you get this
number?' she demanded hotly.

'Because you gave it to me,' said the friendly voice, unperturbed by Sarah's reaction.

'Who is this?' she shrieked.

'It's Barry.'

'Barry who?'

'Barry from *Get Out of That One*. Barry with the Roller.'

'Oh yes, sorry. Look, I was pissed that night, upset. I'm sorry, but thank you again for the lift.'

'Hey, Princess, I didn't mean to upset you. I just wondered if you'd like to go out to dinner with me this week.'

'Sorry, I'm busy that night,' replied Sarah, hastily trying to regain her cool.

'I haven't said which night,' said Barry smoothly.

'Oh shit,' said Sarah, embarrassed at being caught out. He wasn't the slightest bit ruffled.

'I have tried to ring you before but I guessed you'd gone away for a few days. Why don't you think about it, and perhaps I could call you again tomorrow night. No pressure, Princess. I promise.'

Grateful to be got off the hook, Sarah mumbled goodbye. She found an old bottle of cooking sherry at the back of the kitchen cupboard, poured herself a large glass and rolled another ciggie.

'How do I bloody well do it?' she muttered aloud. 'I'm getting like Shirley Valentine now, talking to the bloody wall.'

Next morning she played back the messages. They were mostly from Barry, asking how she was. She remembered the florist's note and managed to catch the people in the upstairs flat before she caught the bus to work. They handed her an enormous bunch of flowers that had seen better days, a mixture of pink roses and lilies now shedding petals profusely. A card attached read: *Hi, Princess. Hoping these will help you forget Mr Whiplash. Love Barry*.

chapter thirty-six

True to his word, Barry phoned Sarah the following evening. All her prepared statement about doing a Greta Garbo and wanting to be left alone went out of the window. He was persuasive but not pushy. Weakened by her first day back at the clinic since *Get Out of That One*, and aware of all the silent sniggers, Sarah had come home mentally exhausted. It had been hot in the office, the air con had packed up and the Abominable Slowman had been operating that afternoon so tempers had frayed. Suddenly the prospect of a meal in a restaurant of her choice, and no hanky-panky as Barry had faithfully promised, sounded appealing.

He'd pick her up on Thursday, three days from now, and would book a table at her favourite Italian in Winchester.

Sarah stared at her phone when she'd hung up. 'Why did I do that?' she asked it. 'Why on earth did I agree?'

Later that evening, relating the conversation to Judith, she found herself secretly looking forward to the evening. Now that alarmed her.

'Well I think it will do you good for two reasons,' said Judith. 'Firstly, you don't fancy him so that's easy. No involvement, no disappointment. Enjoy the evening as a couple of friends would. And secondly, it might take you a step nearer to recovery from Mr Whippy. You might just be able to distance yourself from him a bit more and remind yourself that there are still some decent men on the planet.'

'I hate you, you're so bloody sensible,' joked Sarah. 'I'm not doing the very thing I promised myself I would, i.e. give up men completely. And now you turn it around to make it sound like therapy.'

'Well it'll probably work out cheaper than a week at the Priory or the Betty Ford Clinic.'

'Ah, Vicky, I want a word with you.' It was Harry Hampton, the head of news at HIT. There was no missing the menacing tone in his voice.

Vicky went into his office. Harry was from the old school of management, act mean, keep 'em lean, tell 'em nothing. As a result, he had a newsroom full of under-achieving journalists scared of going the distance on their stories because of their insecurities. Claret fat, with a flushed face and a footballer's perm now flecked with grey, he'd never stopped being the playground bully.

Harry indicated to her to sit down. Again the old trick, the chair was much lower than his, giving him the height advantage. He tapped a pile of cuttings on his desk. Vicky knew immediately what they were about.

'Not good news, I'm afraid, Vicky, is it?' He leered at her. 'We can't have this sort of publicity. How can the public take you seriously as a reporter when you resort to this sort of caper?'

'It won't happen again,' said Vicky, trying not to let her voice wobble.

'It definitely won't be happening again,' Harry hissed. He was positively enjoying this. 'In fact I wanted you sacked but the press office wouldn't hear of it. Even though you're freelance, they said the resulting publicity wouldn't do the company any good at all.'

He paused to prolong her agony.

'So you stay on, but on two conditions. One, you give up this public speaking lark, if it hasn't already given up on you, and two, I'm taking you out of vision. From now on, you stay off screen and write bulletins, geddit?'

'I'd already decided to jack in the speaking anyway,' Vicky stammered. 'Don't worry. I've got the message. I'm sorry for the trouble I've caused.'

She upped and left the office, knowing he was right, but angry that he still had the effect of making her quake whenever they had any sort of conversation. How she longed for the whackier atmosphere in Plymouth where good old Jack, the news editor there, was Premier Division compared to Fattie Hampton's Conference League performance. Jack also had a much kinder way of telling you that you were crap.

She went back to her desk, logged in and gulped at the barrage of e-mails awaiting her. She waded through the predictable list of cars for sale, flats for rent, and got to the new rosters. Her name was already listed in the sub editors section. Fattie Hampton had worked swiftly to get her desk bound. Oh well, perhaps it was just as well. It was getting harder and harder to look good, windswept, soaked or freezing cold, doing a piece to camera these days. At least she wouldn't have to agonise about what to wear any more.

She continued clicking down the list of e-mails. There were the usual legal reminders, pleas for missing tapes, forthcoming computer upgrades. And a message from reception. A man had called several times for her over the past few days but had refused to leave his name.

The speculation list was endless. It could be David Bletchley asking for his jigsaw pieces back, or Roger from Tressed Out, whingeing about the non-wedding story being resurrected. Perhaps the PR people had decided to sue her for non-delivery of her speech. Or more requests for interviews from half the journalist population in Britain.

She called Judith at work.

'I nearly got the sack,' she whispered down the phone. 'Mad axe man Hampton nearly gave me the chop. I was only saved by the press office because they said it wouldn't look good for the company to get rid of me in the circumstances.'

'Oh how awful for them,' said Judith sarcastically.

'I've had to promise to give up my speaking career,' said Vicky. 'Well that wasn't difficult. I've blown that one anyway. But the fat controller's taken me out of vision. I'm back on the production desk. Still, I'm probably very lucky to have a job, and a low-profile one's probably best.'

'Poor you,' consoled Judith. 'Never mind, at least my wardrobe won't get raided so often for emergency story jackets.'

'Yeah, that's true,' conceded Vicky, allowing herself a little chuckle. 'But some mystery man's apparently been ringing and refused to leave a message. You don't think it could be Roger all stroppy again, do you? In a way, I don't blame him, having the story raked up again. It isn't his fault this time.'

'No. It's probably a sports wear manufacturer asking you to endorse their running shoes,' replied Judith cheerily. 'I can just see you in a pair of swanky trainers with the slogan, "For the Run of Your Life". Seriously, it might be some more journalists on the trail. Can you get anyone to filter your outside calls now that you're on the production desk?'

'I'm sure one of the lads would answer them for a few days if I mentioned pints of beer after work,' said Vicky, cheering up. 'I'll get a huge sympathy vote after the bollocking from the fat bastard so I'll start negotiations right now.'

Judith hung up. She was convinced she knew who was making the calls. Mervyn couldn't have failed to see the regurgitated newspaper coverage and now knew exactly where Vicky was working. The net was closing, she'd have to think this one out.

She turned her attention back to episode five of *Get Out of That One*. The guest list was shaping up well considering it was such a difficult subject. People who'd either written their own obituaries, read their own obits thanks to a newspaper blunder, or had their identities stolen in deception cases. Judith's assistant Lizzie and her researchers had come up trumps yet again. She sank back in her chair to re-read the research notes on the guests so far firmed up.

She was still absorbed in them when the phone rang again. It was Jack, Vicky's old news editor in Plymouth.

'Sorry to bother you, still had your numbers in the Filo from when Vicky had her, er, lucky escape last summer,' he explained. 'It's just that we've had a man ringing up trying to trace Vicky and he's been quite persistent. We don't obviously ever give out phone numbers but in the light of her latest, er, problem, I thought I ought to check it out with you.'

'That's very kind,' said Judith. 'So who is this guy?'

'At first he wouldn't give his name, but in the end they put him on to me and I got rather bolshy with him for time-wasting. At first I thought it was that appalling creep who was trying to marry her but it wasn't. A chap called Mervyn. Ring any bells?'

Judith sat bolt upright in her chair. It was a surprise but then again it wasn't.

'Can I pass on your numbers to him?'

'Absolutely not,' said Judith. 'Please don't. She's had enough to cope with lately.'

'Well we couldn't help but notice,' Jack continued tactfully. 'Do hope she's OK. We all had a soft spot for Vicky when she was here. Very sorry to see her go, especially in those circumstances. Do pass on our best. And tell her

there's always a job here for her any time. I'm surprised
she's stuck it at HIT with Fat Bastard Hampton for so long.'

It was a small world in television. Everyone tended to
meet everyone else either on the way up or the way down.
Bad reputations circulated faster than e-mail.

'Yeah, he's giving her a rough time,' conceded Judith.
'For a head of news, he makes a very good colour ser-
geant. She'll be pleased to hear what you say though.
Listen, thanks for that. This Mervyn guy, he's bad news.
He treated her appallingly and I don't think she ever got
over it.'

Judith drove home, enjoying the cool of the evening, but
her mind racing. It was Sarah's date tonight with Barry. She
hoped it would be pleasant and uneventful. *Please let him
not jump on her*, she prayed. *It's the last thing she needs at the
moment.* Her other dilemma was Mervyn. Ought she to tell
Vicky that he was on her trail, or should she hope he might
just give up? She decided to leave it to fate.

Relieved at coming to some sort of conclusion, however nebulous, she poured herself a glass of chilled
Chardonnay and strolled into the garden. The hot weather
of the past few days was now having its effect on the roses.
Where they'd rambled enthusiastically all over her fence,
they now looked tired, worn out and dusty. She rigged up
her hose and gave the tiny garden a good drenching. The
effect was instantaneous. All the flowers seemed to perk up
and look their best again.

Quick fix, lucky them, thought Judith. She was really
feeling the strain of *Get Out of That One*. It was rating
extremely well, but at a price. The hassle of finding guests
with the right story, and then persuading them to take
part in a live programme, was taking its toll on her and her
team. The subjects were ambitious but it was working
well, with only one no-show so far – a woman journalist

who hadn't checked her facts properly, and had written an obituary of a local dignitary only to find him featured very much alive, on another page in the same newspaper, presenting a cheque to a charity. Great story but she'd ducked out at the last minute.

Judith sat down at her garden table, sipping some more of her wine. She was enjoying the solitude. Vicky had phoned earlier to say she was working an extra shift because someone had gone sick. She'd thought it best to show willing, after her little 'chat' with Fattie Hampton.

Summer's nearly over, she thought sadly. *I could do with a holiday, but I've no one to share it with.* Simon had long outgrown trips abroad with his mum. She missed the extra closeness they'd enjoyed during their holidays together. Now all his plans revolved around Roz. Sarah was not in any sort of financial shape to go anywhere for quite a while to come. And Vicky was currently hanging on to her job by the scruff of its neck. Not a good time to take leave, especially as a freelance.

Suddenly she had an idea. Her Romania documentary *Forgotten But Forgiving* had been entered for various international television competitions. If it reached one of the finals, she'd treat herself to a trip to wherever it was being held.

Absurdly pleased with herself, she went back into the house to refill her glass. She was just stepping outside again when the phone rang.

'Is Vicky there?' demanded a male voice, curtly.

'No she's not,' said Judith, realising immediately who it was, and imitating the abrupt tone.

'Probably just as well,' continued the clipped voice, loaded with restrained anger. 'I suppose she's out gallivanting somewhere and getting herself into another mess.'

'Do you wish to leave a message or would you like me to cut you off?' asked Judith, pleasantly.

'This is Roger Smith.'

'I know,' said Judith, appalled at his rudeness. 'I'd recognise that phone manner anywhere.'

Taken aback, Roger harrumphed for a few seconds.

'Well I'd just like to know when this humiliation is going to end. Yet again, my name is dragged through the newspapers thanks to her exploits. It's wrecked my career prospects at Tressed Out. I could have had another ten grand and a decent-sized Volvo by now. Not to mention private health and a very nice share option package, thank you very much.'

'Well if you'd asked her to marry you *prior* to the wedding day, then you'd have avoided all this,' said Judith sweetly. 'She'd have said no, you'd have saved squillions of pounds and you'd have been driving your decent-sized Volvo, probably with the go-faster stripes and the Carlos Fandango tyres on it by now.'

'Well that's typical of you women. You all side with each other. It's never your fault.'

'It wasn't Vicky's fault she didn't want to marry you. It was your idea and she didn't fancy it too much. Good decision, I'd say. Anyway, she can't help what appears in the papers. Even us nasty journalists, the scum of the earth, can't always control what makes the headlines.'

Roger harrumphed some more, his temper gathering like storm clouds.

'Well listen, scum of the earth,' he hissed. 'Just tell her I'm fed up with constantly reading about myself in the papers. It's fucking up my career.'

'Language, Timothy,' tutted Judith. 'I'll pass on your fondest wishes to Vicky when I see her.'

'Fondest wishes, my arse,' shrieked Roger. 'And another thing. I've even had some bloke on the phone to me at work trying to get in touch with her.'

'Some bloke?' said Judith, taken aback.

'Yes, can you believe it, saw the story and has been pestering me at work. So tell her I'm not her bloody secretary.'

'Wait a minute, Roger. Who was this guy?'

'Malcolm, Melvyn, Mervyn, some stupid name. He's rung several times, bloody nuisance, and I told him to piss off.'

'Thanks, Roger.'

'Oh the pleasure's all mine. I've passed on your number. You can have the hassle of him now.'

He slammed down the phone.

chapter thirty-seven

The net curtains twitched, the Venetian blinds parted and passing cars slowed down to an indecent crawl. The people in the upstairs flats craned their necks out of hastily opened windows to catch snatches of conversation.

There was no doubt about it, if you want to get ahead, get a Roller.

Barry arrived on Sarah's doorstep in a loud blue suit, clashing shirt and tie, rings on every finger and clutching an indecently large bouquet of roses, delphiniums and gypsophila.

'Here you are, Princess.' He handed them to her with a grin. 'To make up for the ones that never made it.'

'How lovely,' she exclaimed, privately realising, hell's teeth, she'd have to invite him in while she put them in a vase.

'Great place,' he enthused, casting around the kitchen. Sarah had managed, on her meagre means, to make her tiny flat look quite stylish, but she was ashamed of having fallen on hard times. It could never compare in any way to the large house she'd lived in with Bostik. She saw it as a riches-to-rags home.

Barry saw none of this. All he saw was Sarah. He thought she looked like Marilyn Monroe with her blonde hair, red-painted lips and a proper womanly, curvy figure.

He also thought she was looking particularly luscious in a deep green silk dress and pashmina. Class act, he decided.

As Sarah stepped into the Roller, she was aware of all eyes from the street upon her. Thank goodness she still had a magnificent wardrobe of clothes to plunder. No car, no outgoing phone and roll-ups behind closed doors, but enough silk to rival Singapore.

The restaurant was half empty, the hot weather having killed trade. Sarah was relieved, feeling that even if the evening were a complete disaster, not too many people would bear witness, or worse, recognise her from *Get Out of That One*.

A waiter led them through the black and white marbled restaurant to a quiet table in a corner alcove, where a bouquet of orange and yellow genistas had been placed.

'Not more flowers,' said Sarah. 'You shouldn't have.'

'It's about time you were spoiled,' grinned Barry, ordering them two kirs. They sipped them while consulting the menu. Sarah had to admit she was beginning to enjoy this.

Over their meal of salt cod with artichokes and porcini, they chatted, the conversation becoming more relaxed as the evening went on. She'd been dying to ask how Barry had come to be so filthy loaded, but couldn't bring herself to raise the subject. He eventually supplied the answer. He'd won four million on the lottery, given up his job as a pub manager and had been pretty miserable ever since. He was such jolly company, she couldn't imagine him sad.

'It's simple, Princess,' he explained over the pudding, the most delicious panna cotta with raspberries. 'All my mates are frightened to speak to me now 'cos they think I'll think they're after my money. And then you get a new set of friends whom you wouldn't cross the road to piss on if they were on fire. They're not friends at all, they're just looking for a sub.'

'But surely, if you stick with your old friends, you're OK,' said Sarah.

'No, it doesn't work like that. Money throws everything out of synch. We all meet for a few beers and then who pays? If I pay, it's smug bastard with all that dosh. If they pay, there's a competitive thing.

'It's the same with women. I've never had so many advances since I won. They've all been coming out of the woodwork. I've even had letters from some celebrity ladies as well. But they're all looking for the main chance. It was as if the jungle drums were sounding. So how do I know they want to be with me or my wallet?'

'So why did you appear on the programme?' said Sarah, suddenly embarrassed that she might fall into that category.

'Well I tried some dating agencies so I could meet women without them knowing about the dosh,' said Barry.

'And did you?' she grinned, thinking all his jewellery was a dead giveaway.

'Nah. They were all dogs.'

They laughed.

'I answered an ad to appear on the programme. Thought it might be fun. But I didn't get to say anything.'

'Did you mind?'

' 'Course not. Met you, didn't I.'

Sarah giggled again. The wine had finally hit home.

'Anyway,' he said, 'I want to know why you appeared on the programme. You were very upset afterwards.'

'I know this sounds like a total cliché, but the producer is a very good friend of mine. She and another pal bought my air ticket to Spain as a treat. The rest, of course, is history. I went through a stage of anger about it and decided that I ought to warn other women.'

'Was it worth it, appearing on the show?' Barry asked gently.

'No, but I wouldn't tell my friend that. All the publicity

afterwards was horrid, and going back to work this week was just total embarrassment. I don't think I'd really thought it through. But the appearance fee came in jolly handy.'

She reached for her cigarettes. 'I've been through a pretty bad time one way and another,' she said, tears suddenly filling her eyes.

Without leaving her gaze, Barry silently handed her a napkin to dab her eyes.

'Sorry,' she muttered, 'I have to pull myself together.'

'Why? If you've had a bad time, then allow yourself a wallow. We can't all cope all of the time, you know. Give yourself some credit for surviving what you went through in Spain.'

She looked at him through her damp lashes. She'd misjudged him, thinking he was just a flash bastard with a Roller. There was a very kind and sympathetic man sat there.

With minimal prompting from Barry, it all tumbled out. Bostik and his legendary meanness, discovering he was gay, his and hers spending, the divorce, the New Year resolutions, and the ill-fated trip to Spain.

'Now I'm broke, I've had to sell my car and I can't even make outgoing calls on my phone. I only smoke these,' she tapped her cigarette packet, 'in public. At home it's jolly old roll-ups. I'm just a total saddo.'

'On the contrary,' said Barry brightly. 'I've had the best fun tonight I've had in ages. I think you're terrific and I hope we can do this again.'

Sarah dried her eyes and managed a smile. 'I've had a lovely time too. Sorry I rotted it all up just then. I do feel better for talking to you about it. The meal was lovely and so were the flowers.'

'So will you see me again?'

'Yes, I'd like that, but . . .'

'But you don't want me to pounce on you.'

'Yeah. Is that OK? I just couldn't hack that at the moment.'

'Of course it is,' he assured her, wishing his cock would subside under the table. He really had the hots for her but he would have to play it very slowly or she'd run.

Barry settled up and guided her out of the restaurant and into the Roller. True to his word, he dropped her off at her flat, pecked her on the cheek and dropped something into her bag.

'What's that?' she asked.

'Don't look until you get inside, use it as much as you want.' And with that, the Roller purred off down the road, amid another frenzied burst of quivering net curtains.

Judith unplugged her phone. She needed to tell Vicky what was going on before Mervyn had the chance to ring. She didn't even want to hear his voice on her answering machine until she was sure of Vicky's feelings about him. She poured another glass of wine and took to her piano for consolation. She felt troubled, knowing that what she had to say would throw Vicky into a quandary, and one in which she couldn't help her.

Judith adored her music and was soon lost in some of her favourite classical pieces. She was so involved in a fiendish piece by Liszt, which was going quite well considering the drink, that she didn't hear Vicky's car roll up.

'Don't stop, it's lovely,' said Vicky, flinging down her bag and flopping on to a sofa.

'Bloody Nora,' Judith exclaimed, glancing up at the clock. It was not far off midnight. 'I must stop, otherwise I'll get bricks through the window from the neighbours. I'll get you a drink, you must be knackered after an eighteen-hour day.'

She emerged from the kitchen with two glasses, the last of the Chardonnay in them.

'How was it?' she asked.

'Well I did earn a few brownie points by doing the extra shift tonight,' said Vicky wearily. 'So hopefully that will keep Fatman Hampton off my back for a while. Also those mystery calls have stopped. Not one all day.'

'Ah yes, now there's something you need to know,' said Judith, taking a deep breath, 'and I've spent most of the evening wondering how to tell you this.'

'What's wrong?' demanded Vicky, sitting bolt upright, her tiredness now forgotten.

'Have a large glug of that wine and I'll tell you,' said Judith.

'Is it something to do with these mystery phone calls?'

'Yep. Got it in one. The mystery caller has been calling you at HIT. He's called you at your old studio in Plymouth. The reason I know this is because I had a call from Jack today, who, by the way, sends his love and says there's a job there any time.'

'Oh that's sweet of him,' said Vicky. 'Go on.'

'Now it gets worse. Our mystery man's called your mother, who told me in no uncertain terms not to tell you he'd called. He has also been pestering Roger at Tressed Out. How do I know this? Because I had a telephonic earful from him tonight. Don't worry, it's been dealt with. Our mystery caller desperately wants to get in contact with you and now he has this number so I'm certain he will call. Don't panic, I've unplugged the phone so that I could tell you first and then you can decide whether you want to speak to him. The mystery caller, I'm afraid, is Mervyn.'

Vicky went white. For a second, Judith thought she was going to faint. She sat stock still, then took another gulp of wine.

'How did he get this number?' she stammered.

'I'm afraid it was Roger's revenge. He gave my number to Mervyn. I'm sure he'll ring. Now you have to decide whether you want to speak to him because as sure as hens lay eggs, that phone'll ring the moment I plug it back in the wall.'

'I need to think about this. Why do you think he's ringing?' Vicky mumbled, now showing signs of distress.

'Well it's blindingly obvious to me. He saw you do your runner from the PR lunch, and realised he was the cause of it. So we can assume that he's either ringing to apologise or he's realised what he's lost. My vote, together with all the Eurovision juries, is for the latter.'

'Oh shit,' was all Vicky could say.

'Well I suggest you sleep on it, have a good long think about whether you want to speak to him and, if so, what you want to say. If he rings tonight or first thing tomorrow, I'll fob him off. But ultimately, Vick, you're going to have to face up to this.'

'What do you think I should say?' she asked pathetically.

'I can't help you there, but I ought to plug this phone back in, just in case of emergencies with the kids.'

She got up and went into the kitchen to reconnect the phone. She came back with another opened bottle of Chardonnay.

'Let's have one more and then call it a day,' she said, refilling their glasses.

The phone rang. They stared at one another in a moment of panic.

'I'll go,' said Judith, regaining her calm. She disappeared into the kitchen. It was Sarah, back home and dying to tell them what a lovely evening she'd had with Barry.

Judith went back to filling the glasses.

'Hey, hang on,' she said, startled. 'How come Sarah rang here? She still can't make calls from home.'

She dialled 1471 and got an unrecognisable number.

She then rang Sarah's home number and Sarah answered immediately.

'How come you managed to ring out?' asked Judith.

'I knew there was something I forgot to tell you. As we said goodnight, Barry slipped something into my bag. When I got into the flat, I discovered he's lent me a mobile phone.'

chapter thirty-eight

Vicky emerged from the sitting room and burst into tears. She'd been on the phone to Mervyn for a good half an hour.

'Well?' said Judith, looking up from the ratatouille she was stirring.

Vicky sank on to a chair at the kitchen table and put her head in her hands.

'Of course I'm still potty about him. I've never got over him,' she said, between sobs. 'But I just can't go through all that again, finding him like that in my flat, in my bed with some other woman.'

Judith put a cup of tea in front of her and offered a tissue. Vicky gratefully took a sip and mopped her eyes.

'It was bad enough just seeing him in London the other week. God knows, I treated the tabloids to another great story about my new running career. But then I hear he's been trying to track me down, and now I've heard his voice again. I feel I'm back to square one in the grief stakes. I'm just hopelessly in love with him and terrified of going through all this hurt stuff again.'

'Good,' announced Judith, brightly.

'What's good about it?' asked Vicky.

'It's good. Very good. I thought you'd jump back in with both feet. I presume he wants to see you again, after all this detective work.'

'Yes, he does. Says he made the biggest mistake of his life.'

'And what did you say?'

'I said I'd think about it.'

'Good girl. Tomorrow's Saturday. Let's go shopping. But don't tell Sarah. We can't have her rotting up her new regime.'

Date number two with Barry happened sooner than Sarah had expected. Barry had called to say the mobile was fully charged but would only last a couple of days. So he craftily suggested delivering the charger and combining it with a trip to the cinema and supper afterwards.

This time, to Sarah's amazement, he turned up in a dark green MGF with the roof down.

'Nice weather, shame to miss it,' he said. They zoomed off up the street to the further intrigue of her neighbours, who couldn't now decide whether Sarah had several boyfriends or a boyfriend with several cars.

The cool of the evening and the wind in her hair as the car raced into Southampton felt quite intoxicating. They arrived at the multiplex in Ocean Village.

'You choose the film, I get the popcorn,' Barry grinned.

Sarah gazed at the movies on offer. Oh God, this was fraught. If she picked a romantic one, he might get the wrong idea, if she picked an 18, any steamy sex scenes might be misconstrued as a hint. Plump for a sci fi and he'd probably love it but she'd be bored to tears. In the end she played safe and chose a fringey film billed as a comedy thriller. It proved to be not the remotest bit funny nor exciting. It raised not a guffaw, nor a goosebump.

'Got that a bit wrong, didn't I,' she said, over tacos and ice-cold beers in a nearby Mexican restaurant afterwards. 'In fact I think it almost defied the Trade Descriptions Act. Perhaps we should apply for a refund.'

'Good to see crap,' said Barry. 'Makes the good films seem even better. You can always tell it's going to be a rub-bishy film. You're in for a bit of a lulu when someone escapes through a town and joins in a passing St Patrick's Day parade, no matter what time of year it is.'

'And kitchens never have light switches,' chipped in Sarah. 'At night everyone just opens the fridge door and creeps around by that light instead.'

'The police chief always suspends his star detective at the most crucial moment.' They were having a competition now.

'All houses in Paris have a view of the Eiffel Tower.'

'And all grocery bags have at least one stick of French bread.'

'You'll get through the war but not if you show someone a photograph of your girlfriend back home.'

'In sci fi films, the villain who wants to rule the world always wears a mask and gauntlets and suffers from asthma.'

'You can always get around any strange building secretly via the ventilation system.'

'Lipstick never comes off, even when you're scuba diving.'

Sarah collapsed into giggles. 'OK you win, I can't think of any more,' she laughed.

The arrival of coffee signalled the end of the evening. Both of them started that silent mental process about whether the other one would want to see them again.

Barry spoke first. 'Princess, I've had a great time. Can we do this again? What I'm really trying to say is, can we do this a lot?'

Sarah hesitated. There was something she needed to say. She lit a cigarette first.

'You know you talked about women being interested in you because of your money,' she began. 'Well you now know that I'm on my uppers so you could assume that I'm after your wallet too. I know it's impossible to prove otherwise, but I'm not. You're a very nice human being, especially compared with all the shits I've hung around with.'

Barry smiled and looked into her eyes, trying not to betray how desperate he was to get her into bed.

'You've already proved it, Princess. When I told you I had a Roller, you refused point blank to believe me. And to put it crudely, if you'd been after my bank balance, you'd have been flat on your back by now, going like a rabbit.'

Sarah blushed and took another drag on her cigarette. Before she could speak, Barry continued, 'Now I hope one day that you will let me take you to bed, but I know what you've been through and I've promised not to pester. It's your shout.'

He glanced in the direction of his crotch. 'Down boy!' he half whispered.

Sarah blushed again. 'Thanks,' she said simply. 'I've had a smashing evening. And yes, let's do it again.'

The night was still warm enough for them to drive back with the roof down. After drawing up outside Sarah's flat, Barry went round to the boot of the car. Inside was a carton of two hundred Benson and Hedges.

'Can't stand the idea of you smoking roll-ups,' he grinned, handing them to her. 'If you must smoke, then smoke something decent.'

And, with a peck on the cheek, he zoomed off into the night.

As all women will testify, there's nothing more exciting than the prospect of a sunny Saturday morning, the first since pay day, and you're being summoned to appear before High Street magistrates by your best friend.

Vicky wandered into the kitchen bleary-eyed to find Judith knocking up bacon and eggs.

'Sustinence for the mission ahead,' she announced, flipping over mushrooms with one hand, and pouring hot water into a cafetière with another.

'Smells wonderful,' said Vicky, positively drooling as she laid the kitchen table. It tasted fantastic. Vicky realised she hadn't eaten properly since her latest chronicled exit.

'It's good to see you tucking in,' said Judith. 'You've begun looking like the winner of a bean sprout lookalike contest.'

'Oh c'mon, I'll never be thin. I've got my mother to thank for my water retention and big bones.'

'I don't know your water arrangements, hon, but we're seeing a little too much of your cheek bones. You're too thin in the face. It doesn't suit you.'

'I've been able to get back into my Hong Kong wardrobe though,' said Vicky triumphantly.

'Well you might look sleek in your silk numbers but they won't look good topped off with the face of an anorexic sparrow.'

'I suppose so. But I was always desperate to be thin. You see these young girls around now with cropped tops, pierced navels and little thongs. I'm not saying I want to be like them but let's face it, your navel is never going to look good pierced if you suffer from water retention. I'd like to be thin enough to wear a thong.'

'Not good news unless you live permanently in a gym or subscribe to *Tight Bum Monthly*,' replied Judith.

'Anyway, where exactly are we going today?' asked Vicky.

'I'll reveal all as we go along,' said Judith mysteriously, scraping the plates and putting them in the dishwasher.

They drove into Southampton, parked near the top of the High Street and began their assault. They drooled at the dresses, hankered after the handbags and slavered over the scarves.

'We're showing remarkable restraint,' said Judith, ten

shops later, several try-ons and still not a purchase in sight. 'But that's OK because we're going to have lunch now in Café Rouge, and then *you* have an appointment!'

'What for?' said Vicky.

'Hair cut and blow dry, followed by a make-up session,' said Judith bluntly. 'All booked and on me. My treat to cheer you up after what happened in London. Call it an advance birthday present.'

'Is there a sub plot here?' said Vicky suspiciously. 'Anything to do with Mervyn, by any chance?'

'Well, ever so slightly if I'm honest. If you do decide to meet him, then you'll want to look good, even if it's for yourself. Some years ago, an ex-boyfriend, whom I'd been dead keen on, moved with his wife just up the road. So I had to tart up every time I went out for a paper just in case. I just didn't want to bump into him wearing my grabbed-the-first-thing-out-of-the-wardrobe look, no make-up and grotty hair. And him having the satisfaction of thinking, "Phew, lucky escape. Didn't she let herself go." Just pride I guess.'

'OK, you win,' conceded Vicky. 'Only on one condition, that I buy the lunch.'

Chicken, polenta and roasted vegetables, a bottle of white burgundy and two cappuccinos later, Vicky went off for her makeover.

She looks terrific, Judith thought, when they met up again an hour and a half later. Vicky's wavy brown hair often pursued a life of its own, but she'd had quite a sharp haircut which made her look very chic, very French. The new make-up complemented it.

'Gorgeous, dahlink,' said Judith as they air-kissed. 'Now back to the shops. I've done a little homework while you were being transformed and I've found you the perfect outfit.'

It was. A long straight black linen dress with side splits and a matching bolero jacket. Very plain, very understated and very slimming. Judith was right. It looked terrific on Vicky. She hotfooted to the cash desk, credit card a-quiver. Meanwhile Judith had found a pale blue trouser suit with a long-line jacket that was pronounced divine.

The two of them left the shop, several hundred pounds lighter and giggling at their extravagance.

'Now you're ready for him, whether you want him or not,' said Judith as they drove home.

Sarah hit the red phone button once again on Barry's mobile. No reply from Judith, only her answering machine with another of her nutty messages.

'Welcome to Judith's instant psycho service. Leave a message after the tone or choose from the following multiple choice menu. If you want to be alone, press 1. If you're schizophrenic, press 2, if you're indecisive, press 3, 4 and 5.'

What number do you press if you're a total space cadet? thought Sarah, ruefully. Saturday morning, and perhaps Judith had gone shopping. Lucky sod. Paying homage to the shrine of John Lewis would have to wait for at least another year. *Quick shower and then I'll have a coffee and a decent cigarette*, she planned mentally.

Standing under the gushing water, she recalled how much she'd enjoyed her evening at the cinema with Barry and wondered when he'd ring again. At what stage would they take future dates for granted? When would she be classed as a girlfriend or refer to him as a boyfriend? Was a man in his late forties a boyfriend? Or did you have to call him a partner? And more crucially, when was the right time to go to bed with him?

These had never been questions needing answers during more than twenty years of marriage with the odd dalliance on the side. She'd have to get advice from the girls.

Wrapped in a red towel, hair in a turban, eyes smeary from last night's mascara, she was just settling down to search for the answers in an old *Cosmo* over a cup of coffee and a cigarette when she heard the doorbell. *It's either Jehovah's Witnesses or a doorstep salesman*, she decided. The perfect outfit to fob them off, she thought, fag dangling from her mouth. The way I'm looking, I'll probably scare them away.

She opened the door several inches and nearly slammed it shut again. On the doorstep was Barry, grinning from ear to ear and carrying a supermarket carrier bag.

'Great outfit, babe.' He roared with laughter. 'Lady in Red.' And he started to sing. Sarah blushed the colour of the towel.

'Ever seen that Rita Hayworth film, *You Were Never Lovelier*?' he joked. 'Thought not.'

'That's killed any mystique I had stone dead, hasn't it,' she said, mentally working out how she could salvage her appearance in the bathroom in record time. She was already regretting that her naffest dressing gown was the only one hanging in the bathroom.

But Barry had read her mind. He waved the supermarket bag. 'I've brought our breakfast,' he said. 'You get yourself sorted and I'll cook.'

With that, he busied himself in the kitchen. Soon the combined smells of crispy bacon, coffee and freshly squeezed orange juice were wafting through to the bathroom. Sarah, meanwhile, was all fingers and thumbs, trying to rake a comb through her hair, remove the travelling mascara and generally get her face in a straight line. She was in the tatty old dressing gown, just about to bolt into her bedroom to get dressed, when he announced that it was ready and escorted her to a chair. There was no hiding place.

They sat down at the table. He'd even brought a couple of pink roses and plonked them in a small vase.

'A peace offering in case you got stroppy with me for turning up unannounced,' he admitted.

They ate in silence but it was a comfortable silence, broken only by the birds singing their hearts out in the tree outside the kitchen window.

'Barry, that was totally delicious,' she said, getting up to clear the table.

'You're not cross about the surprise then?' he asked, knowing the answer.

'Of course not,' she said, smiling. Impulsively she went over to plonk a kiss on his forehead. How it happened, Sarah couldn't explain, but suddenly they were locked in the most passionate embrace.

The cordless phone sat in the middle of the kitchen table like a prize leek at a gardening show. Judith and a very subdued Vicky had been sitting opposite each other for the best part of an hour, sharing a bottle of wine and discussing the call Vicky was or wasn't going to make.

'You don't have to call him, you know,' said Judith gently. 'Remember, you owe him nothing. He hurt you, he betrayed you. Totally. Let him wait in all evening, all week, the rest of his life. It's not your problem.'

'Yes, I know.'

'But on the other hand, if you don't call him tonight, tomorrow night or sometime soon, you might regret it in ten years' time.'

'Yes, I know.'

'Or you could toss a coin. Heads you call, tails you don't,' said Judith.

'That'll do me,' said Vicky, springing to life. 'Fate, let fate decide.'

She scrabbled in her handbag and produced a fifty pence coin. 'Heads I call, tails I don't.'

She flicked the coin into the air, missed it on the descent

and it rolled into a corner. Scurrying to pick it up, she groaned.

'Tails,' she said dejectedly. 'I don't call. How's about best of three?'

'Then you've answered your dilemma. Call him now and I'll be in the sitting room,' said Judith, and with that, she upped and left the kitchen, shutting the door very firmly behind her.

chapter thirty-nine

'Cahoots next Thursday at seven. He's driving down from London and he's sure as hell paying,' said Vicky, relieved to have got through another conversation with Mervyn without crying.

'Sounds sensible and at least you know the menu,' replied Judith, who'd been on almost as tenter tenterhooks as Vicky. 'This is the time to make new ground rules.'

'I'm nervous already and it's only Saturday. Thank God, I know what I'm going to be wearing. I don't think I could cope with all that stuff as well. My new black will be very appropriate. Chic, understated, every season's perfect colour. And if we have a rotten evening or a row, it can symbolise mourning for the dregs of our relationship. I still don't know if I'm doing the right thing. My stomach's going topsy-turvy.'

'You'll only regret it if you don't,' said Judith. 'I'd hate to see us plonked in wing chairs in some old folk's home in thirty years' time, eating tripe, drinking Horlicks and discussing what might have been. At least it's not a first date with someone you may or may not sleep with at some stage. So all the standard magazine advice crap is irrelevant.'

'What sort of advice is that?' queried Vicky.

'Oh you know, wear clothes with velcro fastenings so they don't leave marks. Avoid eating anything with garlic, spinach or basil in it. And don't order red wine because it makes your face flush and your accent slip.'

'Well, that'll be why I have had such rotten luck in the past, then. It's a relief not to have to do all that lot.' Vicky grinned, her sense of humour returning. 'I'll have to map out some non-offensive topics of conversation and for the moment I have sort of hinted that there might be a boyfriend in the background.'

'Oooh, fascinating,' said Judith. 'Give me a quick sketch on him just in case Mervyn does some sort of Rumpole impression and starts cross-questioning me down the phone.'

'Well let's see,' said Vicky. 'His name is Tyro, he's just a run-of-the-mill Raybanned sex god, he's ten years younger than me, works out daily and has an enormous dick, a six-pack and a Lotus Elise.'

'Got it,' said Judith. 'They're on every street corner, hovering at every supermarket deli counter.'

'Don't forget, though, the one thing you can't do with a solicitor is pull the wool over his eyes.'

'Not unless you're hurriedly removing his sweater,' replied Judith cheekily.

'No chance.'

'My theory,' said Judith with a twinkle in her eye, 'is that either it will be a total disaster – you will decide that he's a complete dickhead and you'll wonder why you wasted these past two years weeping and wailing for him. Or you will be struck by lightning and the magic will rekindle. Either way you're ahead of the game.'

'How do you work that one out?' asked Vicky.

'If the test of time shows him up to be a complete dickhead, there's no better instant therapy. You can draw an end to the mourning, and move on happily to the afternoon! Or, if you are hit by that bolt, and he certainly has been, judging by his persistence, then you're still in the driving seat. 'S easy!'

'You make it sound far too good to be true,' said Vicky reflectively. 'Here I am poised for the very thing I've always wanted, thought would never happen, even in my wildest dreams, and how do I feel? Absolutely scared shitless.'

'How do you think he feels? Probably akin to being a total louse. He was caught pants down, well and truly. There's no defence, and as a lawyer, he should know that better than anyone else. Don't panic. I'll get that.'

Judith disappeared into the kitchen to pick up the call. Moments later she was back in the sitting room.

'Well there's a turn-up for the books. Sarah's succumbed. She's been to bed with Barry the Bank. So we can now rename him Barry the Bonk! Champagne, I think!'

They rummaged for glasses and shoved a bottle in the freezer for a quick chill.

'Three toasts,' announced Judith when their glasses were filled.

'Here's to Sarah and Barry's first bonk! Here's to your date with Mervyn next week. May you knock him sideways, one way or the other. And here's to me. Romania's got to the finals, to be held in New York next year, and I'm going too!'

'Dark horse, you didn't tell me,' said Vicky, ashamed that her own problems seemed to have taken centre stage yet again.

Sarah spent Sunday morning agonising, over a pot of tea and twenty chain-smoked cigarettes, about the fact that she'd slept with Barry. Would he chuck her now that she'd succumbed? Would she be relegated to the Easy Lay Department he'd referred to when they first met?

Her agony didn't last long. Barry emerged bleary-eyed from her bedroom, looking ridiculous – wearing one of her more unflattering dressing gowns, his hair all dishevelled – but as always wearing his crinkly smile.

'You all right, Princess?' he queried. 'What's bothering you? Why are you up, and not in bed cuddling me?'

'I . . . I don't . . .' faltered Sarah.

'I know,' said Barry, taking in the worried face and sitting down at the kitchen table next to her. 'You're worried that now we've had sex, I'll move on.'

'Y . . .yy . . . esss, I suppose so. You talked about these women you met who were easy lays because they were after your money. I'm frightened you'll think I'm one of them.'

'Look, Princess, I'm not interested in easy lays. They're chickens with loose morals as far as I'm concerned. The only thing I'm interested in is you. I'd do anything for you, babe. I'd even crawl over broken glass for you. And by the way, when can you get time off? I want to take you on holiday.'

Sarah was overwhelmed. She got up and flung her arms around his neck. She couldn't remember the last time she'd felt so happy.

Thursday loomed closer and closer. Vicky wondered how quickly Prozac kicked in, if you started taking it. She'd been working hard at the studio too, volunteering for some more extra shifts to keep her mind occupied and Fattie Hampton off her back. What she didn't know was that Judith had had an illuminating conversation with Mervyn. He'd phoned her at work to ask about his chances of Vicky taking him back.

'Zilch, I'd say at a conservative estimate,' replied Judith. 'You really were the Slug of the Century. It's bad enough finding out that your bloke has been unfaithful, but to have had a ringside seat! It's what we call, in the trade, the pits.'

She could tell Mervyn was hanging his head, telephonically. 'It was a complete aberration,' he said. 'Losing Vicky was the biggest mistake I've ever made. I've been through hell these past couple of years. I just missed her so much, but I couldn't ever have expected her to forgive me.'

'Dead right, and maybe she still hasn't,' said Judith, who was warming slightly to his confessional.

'It was only when I saw her at that lunch and realised she'd run out because of me that I thought there might be some hope after all. Either she was completely repulsed by me or perhaps there was still some glimmer of feeling. I had to find out, that's why I made so many phone calls to try and trace her.'

'Well, you certainly made friends and influenced a few people along the way,' said Judith. 'For a start, Vick's mother is not exactly running your fan club. I was told in no uncertain terms not to tell Vick you'd called. And then of course Roger of Tressed Out doesn't count you as his best pal either. I got a pile of bile from him too.'

'Sorry, Judith. I'm truly sorry. By the way, can I ask you something? Is Vicky seeing anyone at the moment?'

'You'd better ask her that,' said Judith, secretly laughing at the image of sex god Tyro.

'Anyway, I'm terribly nervous about Thursday. Wish me luck.'

'Yeah, you'll need it,' she replied, replacing the receiver.

Judith and Vicky were privately rather sceptical about Barry. He seemed too good to be true, yet there was definitely something endearing about him. He certainly had the gift of the gab, thanks to his previous life as a pub manager. It was the flash cars, overblown jewellery and naff clothes that put them off. What he lacked in class he certainly made up for in brass. The jury was still out, as far as they were concerned. But they were beginning to concede that he was certainly making Sarah very happy.

Sarah, on the other hand, had gone from one extreme to the other. After a lifetime's love affair with spending, she was so anxious not to appear interested in Barry's money that she asked for nothing, expected nothing. She was still sticking rigidly to her financial routine, determined to get herself straight. She occasionally wondered what Alan was up to. One thing was for sure, he wasn't going straight, not if that Charles character had anything to do with it. She shuddered at the thought of her previous life and realised how happy she was with Barry. Not only was he kind and thoughtful, but he was good in bed too.

She was busy packing for their week's holiday. Barry refused to tell her where they were going, other than that the weather would be hot. She couldn't afford to buy any new clothes so she dug out all the outfits she'd bought for the ill-fated trip to Malaga. At least there would be no whips in wardrobes wherever they were going. All he'd promised her was that it would definitely not be Spain. Too many nasty memories.

Vicky stared at Mervyn across the table. Her eyes roved over every detail of his face, as if trying to commit them to memory just in case she never saw him again. He was slightly older, the lines were more pronounced than she'd remembered, but he was the same Mervyn, tall and rangy with a shock of dark brown hair flecked with grey and deep brown eyes. She caught a whiff of his aftershave, Givenchy Gentleman, her favourite. He was wearing an open-necked white shirt, stone-coloured linen jacket and chinos. He was still irritatingly one of those people who could pig out and stay as thin as a rake.

Ordering the food had helped distract them from their nerves. But now the menus had been collected, and the wine poured, there was nothing to do until the food arrived. Vicky realised she couldn't even remember what she'd ordered, only that it was the same as his. She fiddled with a huge teardrop of wax that had slowly crawled down the side of the candle flickering between them. It reminded her of all the thousands of tears she had shed over him.

'Vicky,' he said, his eyes boring into her, hardly blinking, 'I've been so nervous about tonight, I haven't slept all week.'

She half smiled at him, flinching slightly at his gaze.

'I can't believe my luck that you're sitting here opposite me after what happened, what I did,' he pressed on. 'It was the biggest mistake of my life and I've spent every single day of the past two years regretting it. When I saw you at that lunch, I decided it was fate. Except that I wasn't sure why you ran away. Was it because you couldn't bear to be in the same room as me, or was there some flicker of hope? I had to find out.'

'I must say you were very thorough in your enquiries,' she replied. 'But then, it is your stock in trade.'

'Why did you run away, Vicky? Do I have any chance of a place in your heart? I know I don't deserve it.'

'That's true,' she said, thoughtfully. On one hand she was slightly enjoying his agony, and on the other, she was frightened.

A waiter appeared with their seafood salads, stalling the conversation once more.

'I know I don't deserve it but could you ever see your way to forgiving me?' he begged, when they were left alone again.

'No, I don't think that's possible,' she said firmly.

'I don't blame you,' said Mervyn, crestfallen. He was losing her, he knew it.

'You broke my heart over what you did,' she said slowly. 'I couldn't possibly trust that sort of man again. I have a different life now, higher standards. And then there's Tyro.'

'Tyro? Who's he?' said Mervyn, looking agitated.

'Well, let's say he's a teensy bit younger than me.' She tried not to burst into giggles.

'Sorry, it's none of my business. I have no right to ask. I'd just desperately hoped that because you ran away that day, because we spoke on the phone and now you've agreed to meet me here tonight, there was some hope for me. That you'd perhaps agree to see me again?'

'You should never go back, you can't wipe out the past,' she said slowly. 'The man I knew then turned out to be a complete bastard and I could never forgive him for what he did. He betrayed my trust. He was just a lying, cheating piece of pond life.'

A devastated Mervyn hung his head.

'However,' she said brightly, raising her glass, 'the man sitting opposite me looks like quite a different prospect.'

Mervyn couldn't quite believe what he'd just heard. He made her repeat it.

'I would like to see you again, but there are some new ground rules,' said Vicky, amazed at the resolve in her own voice. 'I've changed a bit since we last saw each other. I seem to have adopted a tendency lately to do a runner whenever photographers are present, but I am not the doormat you used to know.'

She couldn't recall Mervyn ever being stumped for words. Eventually he regained his composure.

'Let's order some champagne,' he suggested, eagerly.

'Nope,' said Vicky, firmly. 'Slowly, slowly this time. Be warned, I'm not rushing into anything and you've got to drive back to London tonight.'

It was the last night of Sarah and Barry's holiday. They'd spent the most idyllic week in a quiet romantic hotel on the Algarve, hurtling around the countryside in an open jeep. They'd walked, swum, sunbathed, relaxed, eaten simple Portuguese meals and enjoyed every minute of it. Tonight they'd revisited their favourite restaurant of the week. They were tinkering with garlic prawns and chicken piri piri.

'I don't want to go back tomorrow,' said Sarah. 'I shall probably cry on the plane and embarrass you. I've had the most fantastic time, the best. I don't know how to thank you.'

'I want to make your holiday even more memorable,' said Barry, suddenly serious, his grin deserting him. Sarah was immediately on her guard. He fished into a jacket pocket and produced a small box. He opened it and placed it on the table in front of her. Inside, nestling in dark blue velvet, gleamed a huge diamond ring.

'Will you marry me, Sarah? Please make me the happiest man on the planet?'

Sarah was totally gobsmacked. In her confusion, she knocked over all the glasses on the table, most of which then smashed noisily on the floor. The eyes of the entire restaurant, diners and waiters, were upon them. But Barry didn't seem to notice.

'Princess, you can smash up the whole restaurant for all I care. I love you. I want to spend the rest of my life with you.' He was now down on one knee, among the broken glass. The whole restaurant ground to a halt, totally gripped by what was going on in the corner.

'I love you too,' she whispered, her eyes filling up. 'Yes, I'd love to marry you.'

A resounding cheer went up, flowers and champagne were borne in by waiters as Sarah and Barry kissed.

'Did you really think I'd say yes?' she asked, when she'd regained her composure and all the glass had been swept up.

'I desperately hoped so but I never thought I'd actually have to crawl over broken glass to ask,' he grinned. 'I had wanted to take you to the Caribbean this week, but I thought we might save that for our honeymoon.'

chapter forty

The wedding was the following spring. A small, very private affair, because neither Barry nor Sarah wanted a big fuss. As a church wedding was out of the question and they didn't fancy the conveyor belt atmosphere of a register office, they found a beautiful hotel right in the heart of the Hampshire countryside that was licensed for weddings. It meant that guests could stay at the hotel if they wished, and drink to their hearts' content. And then the newly-weds would be only an hour from Heathrow and the Caribbean honeymoon Barry had promised.

Sarah wanted only Vicky and Judith to be at her hen night. They discussed various fanciful ideas about going to Paris or Amsterdam but then, because of Judith's work schedule, they opted for the obvious. It had to be Cahoots Wine Bar, because it had been the scene of so many of their tears and triumphs. The manager, Philip, came out to offer his congratulations to Sarah, and to offer them champagne all evening on the house as Cahoots regulars and as a wedding present to Sarah.

Consequently, by the time the starters had been cleared away, they were all a little the worse for wear.

'Now what are you wearing?' said Judith. 'We want to know every detail, and is it white?'

'Don't be daft,' retorted Sarah, lighting a cigarette. 'White's for virgins and washing machines.'

'Whaddya mean?' asked Vicky.

'Think about it,' said Sarah, taking a puff. 'All domestic appliances come in white. And I'm definitely not condemning myself to be one of those for the rest of my life.'

'Good girl,' said Judith. 'Now, if you two will permit me, I'm going to make a speech.'

They all charged their glasses again, giggling like teenagers.

'We all sat here nearly a year and a half ago, remember, and vowed to accept all invitations and leave no stone unturned. Well it's been a fairly rocky road since then! And, if you recall, we all made resolutions. Sarah resolved to get her divorce. Well she finally got rid of dear old Bostick, and after getting the whiphand briefly in Spain, here she is about to tie the knot. If anyone deserves happiness, it's you.

'I'll be honest and say that Vick and I weren't sure about Barry to start with but he's more than proved himself in our eyes. We've never seen you look so happy.'

They clinked glasses and took another slug. Judith continued with her speech.

'Then look what's happened to Vicky. She resolved to get a better job. Although her new career in public speaking disappeared without trace, it brought her back together with Mervyn. And by all accounts, we can't call him Merve the Swerve any more. She's looking happier than I can remember.'

They clinked glasses again.

'And then there's me. Well I resolved to have sex, but that was last year, I didn't get any so it doesn't count. I'm still hoping for this year. But fingers crossed that the Romania programme wins a prize in New York.'

They clinked for the third time.

'And finally, here's to us. I don't know about you two but I couldn't have better friends.'

It was midnight when they finally crawled out of Cahoots, all praying they wouldn't throw up in the taxi back to Judith's house.

Sarah's wedding day was blessed with warm spring sunshine. The sun poured through the windows of the room where the marriage was to take place. Daffodils and tulips vied for attention in huge arrangements. The room hung with the sweet scent of hyacinths.

Sarah, having refused to say what she would be wearing, drew gasps of admiration in a black suit with pencil skirt and nipped-in jacket with white lapels, cuffs and buttons. She wore a huge black silk hat trimmed with black feathers, and black and white high-heeled shoes to match. It was total glamour.

'She's obviously got Barry sorted,' whispered Judith to Vicky. 'He's looking the smartest I've ever seen him.' Barry had been persuaded by Sarah to tone down the bright colours and give up some of the jewellery. He was wearing an immaculate Armani charcoal grey suit with white shirt, and, by Barry's standards, a very sober tie.

The wedding was short but very meaningful. It was only at the part of the ceremony where Sarah had to declare that she would share all her worldly goods with Barry that she had an attack of the giggles. Judith and Vicky, sitting directly behind, shook silently with laughter as they thought of Sarah's now dwindling overdraft situation. Barry calmed the situation by turning and announcing ad lib to the assembled throng that, as far as he was concerned, she looked like a million dollars to him. The registrar grinned, sensing most of them knew something he didn't, and just carried on with the vows. Everyone then applauded raucously and the newlyweds snogged for so long that it was almost indecent.

Three hours, champagne, duck pâté with spiced pears, saddle of lamb with spring vegetables and mango sorbet later, everyone went outside to wave Barry and Sarah off to Heathrow.

'We could do this if you'd like,' whispered Mervyn in Vicky's ear as the car scrunched away on the gravel.

'What do you mean?' Vicky wheeled round, thinking she'd misheard what he'd said.

'We could get married, if you'd like to,' he said, nervously.

Vicky thought for a moment, her mind whirling around a romantic notion of her and Mervyn taking their vows in front of all their friends. Her in a fabulous outfit, him resplendent in a morning suit; wedding cake, confetti, champagne corks popping, speeches, flowers and photographs. That last bit made her wince.

'No, I don't think so,' she said slowly, remembering the newspaper pictures of her running away from Roger that made her bottom look so big. 'I did get a taste of my own wedding, if you recall, and I didn't like it very much. Anyway, you and I haven't been back together that long yet. You might be a bloody solicitor but you're still on trial.'

'I'll wait,' he said. 'I'll wait for as long as it takes.'

She kissed him tenderly on the cheek. 'Come on,' she said, slipping her arm through his, 'let's go in and have some more of that champagne. You never know, you might get me so pissed, I could change my mind.'

Judith sat back in her seat as the aircraft crew prepared to run through the safety procedures. She'd enjoyed New York, marvelled at the art galleries, loved all the landmarks and thrilled at all the street and place names which had inspired so many song titles. There was a buzz to the place that she'd adored. The all-night delis and diners, the dispatch riders weaving their way precariously through five

lanes of traffic, Trump Tower with its over-the-top opu-
lence, Central Park, Empire State, Battery Park. She'd
passed the diner where they shot *When Harry Met Sally*, the
house they used for *The Cosby Show*, Madonna's flat,
Strawberry Fields, the famous Apollo Theatre in Harlem.

The only thing missing had been someone to share it
with. She thought wistfully of the holidays she'd spent with
Simon, sometimes roughing it, sometimes in good hotels
when she could afford it. She'd passed on a real travel lust
to him. But that was the end of an era; he and Roz were
about to get engaged, much to everyone's delight.

Holidays would probably be a lone experience from now
on. She fell into a deep sleep for most of the journey, grateful for an upgrade to a more comfortable seat.

'Excuse me,' said an American voice. 'Breakfast is on its
way, I thought you might not want to miss it.'

She opened bleary eyes to the man across the aisle smiling at her.

'Thank you,' she said. 'I probably am quite hungry.' She
came to feeling rather fuzzy, with a mouth like the bottom
of a bird cage. She tottered off to the loo, splashed her face
with cold water, cleaned her teeth and ran a comb through
her hair. That was as good as it got, she thought.

She returned to her seat. The man opposite smiled
again. He looked familiar. As if reading her thoughts, he
immediately answered her query.

'The TV festival. I saw you at the festival,' he said. 'Pity
about your film. I thought it was great. Mine didn't win
anything either. I'm Ted Colson, by the way.'

They shook hands awkwardly across the aisle.

'Yes, I was a bit disappointed,' she said. 'I'm sorry you
didn't win either.'

He shrugged in a good-natured way. 'Hey, at least we can
be great losers.'

Judith looked at him and smiled back. He had a neat

greying beard, very tanned skin and the most twinkly blue eyes. His face positively lit up when he smiled.

'What brings you to England?' she asked, surprised at her curiosity in his reply.

'Drowning my sorrows at not winning, celebrating my recovery from the most expensive divorce on the planet. That sort of stuff.'

Somehow the next two hours seemed to go faster than the Boeing 747 they were aboard. By the time the cabin crew announced the descent, Judith and this stranger had exchanged most of their life histories, hopes and aspirations.

'I'm beginning to think losing was actually the best thing that's happened to me in quite a while,' said Ted, smiling again. 'If we weren't stacking over Heathrow, I think I'd be asking you to dance.'

How did you explain these things? She didn't know. Only that sometimes they did happen. Her voice cracked slightly.

'If we weren't stacking over Heathrow, I think I'd probably accept.'

Nailing Harry

To Iain
With all my love

acknowledgements

If you don't know me personally, please feel free to skip this bit. It's that small but very important section where I get to say a sincere thank you to those who matter.

OK, so they didn't sit down in my office and type the story, fret over the characters, and drink enough coffee to turn Brazil into a world money-player.

They were simply – there. They said all the right things at the right time: my partner Iain Blair, who spelled out the pitfalls of the 'second book syndrome', my son Mark, who persuades all his mates to buy my books for their mums, my agent Pat White, whose down-to-earth New York humour and advice I so value.

Then there are the fab folk at Time Warner Books – Barbara Boote, Joanne Coen, Tamsin Barrack and Alison Lindsay, who dispense cheerful encouragement and support just when you need it.

Wonderful friends including Rene, Jane, Elayne, Sally, Kathy, Cathy, Janet, Judith and of course the Curry Night Girls. Also colleagues at Carlton past and present who wanted to share in my excitement at being published the first time. Thank you all for being so supportive.

And finally to all the Harrys of this world. Please read this book and then feel free to eat my words!

chapter one

It was an all-too-familiar sight. Val Hampton had begun the evening, her usual scene-stealing self. But as the minutes ticked into hours, she turned into a time bomb. Her speech began to slur, cigarettes were lit and stubbed out almost immediately and her voice started to rise above those of the rest of the diners in the restaurant.

Val was a very striking woman, her thick blonde hair swept up in a chignon, and tonight wearing a fuchsia-pink suede suit, with long nails and spiky heels to match. At thirty-two, she was whippet-thin and well able to carry off the outfit. But it was always the same. Once the drink took hold, she somehow managed to transform herself from supermodel into supermonster.

From hovering attentively, providing a light for her frenzied stream of cigarettes, and constantly refilling her glass with aplomb, the waiters began to hold back, wondering if their overeagerness with the wine bottle was now perhaps the cause of the mayhem. Having taken in the Rolex, the expensive jewellery and perhaps caught a glimpse of Val's new shiny red top-of-the-range Toyota MR2 flashing into the restaurant car park, they thought they were in line for the Big Tip. But now their prey for the night was on the verge of losing them tips from just about everyone else in the restaurant. For Val was well into what the girls referred to as her 'pointing mode'. It always signalled the transition from her general irritation with life to restaurant rage.

'You see, Janet,' she boomed, pointing a dark pink talon in her direction, 'you'll never get another man if you don't make a bit more of yourself. I mean, you're actually looking quite nice tonight. That green is almost your colour. Not quite, but almost. Mind you,' she paused, taking another huge slurp of wine, 'you're no spring chicken, let's face it. How old are you now? Forty-eight? Forty-nine?'

'Forty-two actually,' replied Janet, a mixture of appalled and amused because she'd heard it all before.

'I'm sure you'd find someone if you did something about your hair,' continued Val unabashed. 'I'll give you the name of my stylist in London. Trained by Nicky Clarke, of course, so he's absolutely marvellous but not nearly as expensive. He'd sort it for under two hundred. That's what you need. A really good cut.'

And what you need is a really good smack, thought Janet. She rose from the table.

'Well, thanks for the tip, Val, but I must take myself and my overdraft off to the loo.'

Now far too pissed to take in the irony of what had been said, Val turned to the rest of the table and lowered her voice a couple of decibels. At least only the waiters would now be able to hear, instead of the entire kitchen staff.

'Of course, that's why Janet's husband left her,' she announced, taking another slug of wine. 'You can't expect to keep a man if you let it all go. You remember what Jerry Hall said, that thing about being a lady in the

2

bedroom, a maid in the drawing room and a tart in the kitchen.'

The others smiled, trying not to laugh.

'I think it was slightly the other way round, wasn't it?' ventured Nina, trying to suppress her giggling. 'I think the tart's supposed to be in the bedroom, not the kitchen.'

Val, now in a complete alcoholic haze and only picking up key words, continued: 'You see, Nina, that's exactly your trouble. Tart. Too much pastry. If you could cut down on your carbohydrates, you'd lose weight and live happily ever after.'

Nina, who, at twenty-eight, was fourteen years younger than Janet and much more sensitive to Val's bitchings, found herself coughing to cover up the sob she wanted to utter after hearing that remark.

'Back in a mo,' she muttered, also heading for the loo.

'Such a pity,' drawled Val, turning away from watching Nina's departing backside. Now there was only Liz left at the table. 'Such a pity she's got such a big bum. I'm sure it's down to binge eating. Detox, that's what she needs. Look at Carol Vorderman. Completely reinvented herself. All it takes is will-power and determination.'

Like your drinking, Liz thought desperately. Rescue came in the form of Janet returning from the loo.

'Funnily enough, I was reading a piece in the *Daily Mail* the other day and realized exactly what my problem is,' Janet announced with a twinkle in her eye.

'Yeah, like what?' drawled Val, inspecting her perfect pink nails.

'Anorexia,' declared Janet, trying not to laugh. 'I'm convinced I've got anorexia.'

'Don't be ridiculous,' shrieked Val. 'You're a good two stone overweight. Look, I know about these things. When

3

I was modelling, lots of the girls in the agency had anorexia or bulimia. Or both if they were really lucky. That's how they stayed slim.'

'Exactly,' Janet replied with a half smile. 'I've got the classic symptoms. When you've got anorexia, you look in the mirror and think you are enormous. I look in my mirror and think "omigod I'm fat" so therefore I must have anorexia.'

'But you ARE fat,' shouted Val, shoving back her chair and jabbing another nail in Janet's direction to emphasize the point. 'And you should do something about it. Do you really want to spend the rest of your life sneaking into Evans Outsize shops? You should eat less and exercise more. It's all a question of balance.'

Fuelled by far too much wine and too few lettuce leaves to register on any sort of calorie count, Val ignored her own advice and lost her balance completely, falling backwards into a pink suede mound on the floor. Conversations instantly hushed as waiters ran from all directions to help her up as fast and as inconspicuously as they could. It was not the sort of place to be falling down drunk. Sickeningly, Val still managed to look stylish, even when sprawled in a heap.

'Yes, balance, Val. You're so right,' said Janet, winking at the others. 'Anyway, let's not spoil a good meal by bringing up bulimia or any other eating disorders for that matter. Here comes Nina so I'll have a quiet word with her and see if she's a fellow anorexic. Then I suggest we order some coffee – sugar-free sugar and no-fat milk – and call it a night.'

Val, helped by a waiter, hobbled off to the loo to repair her make-up and check for bruises. Safely out of earshot, the other three breathed a sigh of relief.

4

'What a bloody nightmare,' said Liz. 'The minute any of us goes to the loo, we get slagged off. I have to say, I could see which way it was going tonight, and I've been sitting here crossing my legs. I didn't know I was capable of so much bladder control. I'm actually in pain right now, but if I disappear to the loo, God knows what she'd come out with about me.'

'I wouldn't worry too much,' said Janet. 'Whatever she says, none of us will believe it. It's very easy for Val to sit there, ex-model, wonderful wardrobe, loads of money, and finishing-school fingernails. And then pontificate when she's pissed, on everything from botox from detox.'

'Detox?' queried Nina. 'Is that what she calls her wine-only diet?'

'Wouldn't put it past her,' replied Janet wryly. 'What hacks me off is that we'll all have to be up and at work tomorrow. Val can lie in bed all day and savour her hangover. Different ballgame.'

'I don't know why we put ourselves through these evenings,' sighed Liz.

'Yes, you do,' answered Nina. 'We do it because we've done it for years.'

'We feel sorry for her despite the money and the looks,' said Janet. 'She's lonely and she's run out of friends. We're the only bunch left and let's face it, we're not exactly running her fan club.'

'Not surprising really,' said Liz. 'Especially given the way she slags us off behind our backs.'

'Oh come on,' said Janet. 'We all know why we really feel sorry for her. Because she's married to Harry.'

Janet, Liz and Nina sat huddled around a table in the tiny staff canteen, mulling over the previous night. They all worked in various capacities for Hartford Optimum Television, known locally as HOT. The company specialized in corporate television production, public relations, marketing and advertising. Selling Starts Here was the company's mission statement. Great things begin with a little ssh . . . was the office joke.

'Bit epic last night, wasn't it?' said Liz. 'What a waste of a great restaurant. I'll say that for Val, she does insist on taking us to some fantastic places. The bill she picked up would have paid my mortgage this month with change left for a few winning lottery tickets.'

'Yeah. I thought that monkfish thingy was fantastic,' said Nina. 'I wish I could cook properly. That might tip the balance with Sam.'

Sam in Accounts was the love of Nina's life, except that he didn't know it yet. She worshipped him from afar, convinced that one day, once she'd shed a stone, found the perfect outfit and learned to cook something wonderful that didn't come out of a box or a packet or involve a microwave, he would fall madly in love with her and transport her into eternal paradise. She had taken to flipping through bridal magazines at the hairdresser's, fantasizing about a long cream satin dress with medieval sleeves, a bouquet of blood-red roses and a trail of little bridesmaids all carrying hoops of flowers and behaving impeccably. The fantasy had moved on to her being the Bride of the Year, with Sam adoringly at her side and looking absolutely devastating in a morning suit, kissing her passionately at the altar before whisking her off on a never-ending honeymoon to Barbados. They would then, of course, live happily ever after in a beautiful thatched cob cottage, probably tucked away somewhere romantic in Devon, where they would raise beautiful and perfectly behaved high-achieving children, fed on candlelit gourmet meals. It was all up for grabs, if only she could stick with the Weight Watchers quick-start programme.

Nina was snapped out of her reverie by another woman joining the table.

'You missed a great night, Sue,' said Liz. 'The compliments flowed almost as much as the wine – straight down Val's throat.'

Sue was one of the gang of four usually invited to Val's restaurant evenings. Happily married with two young children, Sue worked as the head receptionist at HOT. She had not been able to get a babysitter and besides, one of the kids had been extra tearful, obviously going down with a cold.

'What happened? Don't tell me. The usual, I suppose,' said Sue, sipping her coffee. 'Let me guess. Val got drunk, starting pointing and shouting. Got rude and fell over.'

'More or less in that order,' replied Janet. 'Apparently my ex left me 'cos I'd let myself go. The mere idea that I asked Crippen to leave because of his horrendous temper had nothing to do with it. Oh, and by the way, I'm suffering from chronic anorexia. But that was my idea, not hers. Ha ha.'

'What about you, Liz? What's your current fatal flaw?' enquired Sue.

'Surprisingly, I got off very lightly this time,' replied Liz. 'I've come up with a new concept of crossing my legs, not going to the loo all evening and therefore sparing myself a whole load of grief. At the rate I'm going, I'll never need to do pelvic-floor exercises if I get pregnant. I was doing them all last night in the restaurant.'

Liz, newly turned thirty, and the clock ticking noisily on the nursery wall, was desperate to become a mother.

The search for a suitable father was on the verge of taking second place to just getting herself pregnant. Every man she met was vetted for possible fatherhood, and in her job as a researcher she certainly met loads of men. Trouble was, most were unsuitable. She'd just finished working on a series of advice videos for pensioners, so there hadn't been much pulling potential there. Her previous project had been on men's medical problems – mostly the 'down belows', as she put it – so that didn't exactly drum up any totty either. Just lorryloads of old men with prostate trouble. Every time Liz had sex, she did a pregnancy test afterwards. And even if there wasn't a boyfriend on the horizon, she sometimes did a test anyway. Just in case. She'd become quite adept at fiddling with spatulas and peeing into small containers.

'The trouble is,' said Janet, 'there are times when I feel really guilty about Val. I know she's rude and embarrassing, and says terrible things behind our backs. In a way, we're guilty of doing the same now. And she's the one who picks up the tab when we go out.'

'But then it's always her idea to go to expensive restaurants,' said Nina. 'I know what you're saying, but I am pretty sick of jibes about my bum. It's all very easy when you can sit there, stick thin and thirty-two, with bugger-all else to do every day except paint your nails, sit under a sun bed and spend money. I'm not surprised she doesn't have any friends any more. I should think she has difficulty keeping a cleaner.'

'Look, Val's got a major drink problem, let's face it,' said Janet. 'I'm certain she's on the pop through the day. She talks blithely about eating disorders. Well, she *is* an eating disorder. She eats nothing. You saw last night what she actually had; it was just a few bits of low-calorie lollo rosso and a fat-free cherry tomato. The rest was solid Chablis. When we meet her in a restaurant, unlike the rest of us, I suspect she's been on the wine all day, so she's just topping up. That's why she gets so pissed so quickly.'

'So what do we do about it?' asked Nina.

'Well, we can hardly tell Harry,' said Janet. 'He'd go ballistic. I'm pretty sure they have the most monumental rows a lot of the time. He's a big enough shit as it is. I'd love to know what state their marriage is in. She never ever talks about it. All I know is that Val is one very unhappy lady. It comes off her in waves. I don't how she puts up with him.'

'I don't know how we do either,' said Nina grimly.

Harry was their boss.

chapter two

The sun had been up for several hours before Val finally surfaced. Harry had long gone to work. The empty bed and the trail of dressing gown, slippers and yesterday's socks were testament to that. She dragged herself into the bathroom and groaned at the sight in the mirror. Her mascara had crept right down her cheeks, her skin was blotchy and angry-looking. She scowled at her reflection and stepped grudgingly into the shower. The hot jets reminded her that she had a real head-banger of a headache. She massaged the shampoo into her scalp, hoping it might deaden the pain. It didn't.

Downstairs she made a cup of tea and swallowed two paracetamol. There she took in another of Harry's trails. He'd made tea and toast, read the *Daily Mail*, smoked two cigarettes and opened the post. She cursed him aloud, resenting the fact that she had to clear up after him.

'Bastard,' she harrumphed at the kitchen mirror. 'That's what he is, a bastard. Oh dear, and you're not looking too terrific, yourself,' she told her reflection.

There were three things in life that Val Hampton would never accept. Firstly that she had a drink problem. That only happened to old blokes in doorways, fading matinée idols and stressed-out stock market traders, not women of thirty-two. Anyway, she dismissed, everyone drank the same amount that she did. Those silly units of alcohol thingies that doctors bleated on about were only for alcoholics, not people like her. Secondly that she ran the risk of being breathalysed. Again Val considered that driving around drunk was what everyone else did. The police were out looking for real villains, not people like her. And those who did get caught had it coming because they drove naff Ford Cortinas with furry dice and go-faster stripes. Lastly Val did not want to make the connection between thumping headache, roller-coaster stomach and several bottles of Chardonnay. To her, wine was an instant pick-me-up and if you drank enough it killed your appetite, thus keeping your ex-model figure eternally slim. Same deal with cigarettes. Handy appetite suppressants, never mind that they clogged up your lungs and arteries and put you at risk of heart disease. Again that sort of thing only happened to the old guys in the doorways, stressed stockbrokers and has-been actors in government health ads.

In fact, anything nasty only happened to other people as far as Val was concerned. Totally spoiled from the day she was conceived, Val had been educated at the best schools, where she, along with the other young gels, was told she was special. She only had to snap her fingers for a pony and there it was, as if by magic, bounding around a paddock. Her every wish was granted, her every whim attended to. She had inherited her model figure and looks from her mother, but again she'd made no effort. She didn't need to spend hours in a gym honing a perfect body. Even when she did a spot of modelling, it wasn't the ambitious, cut-throat sort of modelling, but more a touch of an 'It' girl of the day doing a sashay down the catwalk in aid of some jolly good cause. It wasn't for the money either, because Val didn't need any. Daddy had loads of it in Coutts.

Such an easy passage into adulthood did not do Val any favours. She could not understand the concepts of failure, being short of cash, doing without, or sharing. Val thought the idea of people doing their own cleaning and gardening rather quaint and archaic. The fact that they had no choice in the matter hadn't really occurred to her.

Some of the blame lay with Val's mother Sheila, who, despite just nudging sixty, was still a real beauty. Sheila had grown up in an ordinary middle-class existence where people did their own dusting, bought their cars on HP and saved up all year for a fortnight in Fuengirola. But she'd been catapulted up a couple of rungs by marriage. Keith Mortimer, a self-made millionaire several times over had been captivated by her, pursued her for a year and bombarded her daily with flowers, and in the end Sheila had agreed to marry him. Keith wasn't exactly the most devastating-looking man on the planet. He was short, stocky and bearded, with a rather inane grin. But Sheila saw a lifestyle she aspired to and grabbed the chance. From this rather doomed start, the marriage had surprisingly become a success. Keith couldn't quite believe his luck at what he'd landed and set about making Sheila's life as wonderful as possible. They lived in a beautiful Georgian mansion in the quiet Hampshire countryside, stuffed with antique furniture and fine paintings. It was also a far cry from the nature of Keith's business. He'd made his fortune from waste disposal, which they both felt privately did not go with their image.

Naturally the locals all knew about it and, behind their backs, referred to Sheila and Keith as Lord and Lady Muck. To their circle of friends, mainly drawn from other big houses in the area, they were Beauty and the Beast.

One of the factors that clinched the surprising success of the marriage was sex. Perhaps because Keith had not had much success with women before his marriage, he'd grabbed every opportunity for a legover as if it were his last, and had learned how properly to please a woman. As a result, despite the fact that they were approaching an age when most people would have packed it in and taken to tutting when sex scenes came up on the telly, Sheila and Keith were still at it like rabbits.

The marriage had been blessed early on with the arrival of Val, who proved to be the only child. The proud parents were even more delighted when they realized that Val had inherited her mother's looks, and so they idolized her and spoiled her. But in doing so Sheila conveniently forgot her own roots, and what life had been like before her marriage. So Val grew up not knowing what it was like to struggle. Keith, meanwhile, was pinching himself. He not only had a beautiful wife, but an equally gorgeous-looking daughter, now following in her mother's pretty footsteps and doing a bit of modelling.

Whereas Sheila had married Keith at twenty-five and had immediately been ensconced as lady of the manor, Val hadn't met and married Harry until she was twenty-eight. By then, most of her boarding-school friends had long since trotted up the aisle and into maternity wards, though not necessarily in that order. She suddenly found she had nothing in common with them. It was all baby talk, and in some cases, already divorce talk. Val's pampered existence had become boring. Even shopping,

13

manicures, hairdressers, shiatsu massage, sessions in flotation tanks had become boring. What she needed was people, a job, a purpose. Except that she couldn't see that. Instead Val found a new friend, a friend who was always there, who never answered back or bore a grudge. Her new friend was wine. And as the friendship was forged, their meetings became scheduled earlier and earlier in the day, until a glass after breakfast became the norm. Granted, breakfast for Val was when most people were having lunch, so of course, it didn't count.

When Val met Harry, she had reached rock bottom with boredom. Boyfriends had come and gone, unable to satisfy her demands, embarrassed by her behaviour and her vacuous outlook on life. But when Harry set eyes on Val, it was almost like a repeat of her parents meeting. Harry was captivated, and although he was twelve years older than Val, and divorced, he pursued her relentlessly, just like her father had done her mother. So the circle was complete . . .

Except that Harry and Keith were like chalk and cheese. Where Keith had missed the boat where height and looks were concerned, Harry had fared better. He was tall and well built, though the muscles built up by an earlier rugby career were rapidly turning to fat, and too much claret had left him rather red-faced. Harry, however, thought he still looked gorgeous and that all women fancied him. Val married Harry because she was bored and a bit desperate, and because she wanted to be part of the glamorous world of television. She also assumed, wrongly, that Harry would be able to provide her with the kind of lifestyle that her father had done for her mother. Sure, there was a gleaming Mercedes that came with the job, the very respectable six-figure salary, private health care, share options and loads of first-class foreign travel. But Harry was not a multi-millionaire.

There was one other big difference between Val's marriage and that of her parents. Sex. Val had grown up knowing her parents were always busy in bed. From an early age she'd heard them humping away behind a firmly closed door and thought this was normal. So when she married Harry, she fully expected a similar amount of rumpy-pumpy. But Harry saw Val as a ticket to social cachet, and most of all as a possession. A very beautiful one, but a possession nevertheless. There was no onus on him to make any effort in bed. She was lucky to be there, that was his view. The fact that he was a fairly rotten and selfish lover would never have even crossed his arrogant mind.

With the ink barely dry on the marriage certificate, Harry discovered that Val was going to be a disappointing wife. The chances of his new bride turning into a domestic goddess were about as likely as spotting the Queen buying a lottery scratchcard. So the magic had soon worn off, the babies had not arrived and now, four years on, thanks to a well-stocked wine cellar, Val was not good news to come home to.

There was one silver lining to Harry's job. It had brought Val some new friends. She'd latched on to Janet, Sue, Liz and Nina at the first HOT Christmas party she'd been to. So desperate was she to meet up with them and fill some of the hours in her tedious life, she had taken their phone numbers, rung them up and insisted on taking them out for a meal. The phones had been hot that night, with everyone comparing notes and deciding that they had no choice but to accept an invitation from the boss's wife. And so the pattern had been set and was destined to be repeated several times a year. Val saw it as giving them a treat, doing them all a favour in granting them a glimpse of a lifestyle they couldn't afford. It never occurred to her that they might have been doing her the favour by turning up and putting up with her drunken rages and insults in public places.

Val bent down a little too quickly to reach for a coffee cup and saucer. All of a sudden, her head reminded her that it was hurting. With a brief lurch of conscience, she recalled the previous night and how she'd fallen over. Had she been over the top generally? She knew she'd delivered a few home truths to the girls, but was there a faint chance she'd embarrassed them? She picked up the phone to dial Janet's direct number, just to test the water. It started to ring. She changed her mind and slammed the receiver down again after four rings. Don't be ridiculous, she told the kitchen mirror. The girls thrived on her advice, looked forward to it. And her falling over was due not to too much wine, but to not enough practice on a new pair of Jimmy Choo heels.

'Get me the file on the Hartford tourism project,' shouted Harry Hampton from his office. Geraldine Taylor, his personal assistant, jumped to attention. The file almost at her fingertips, she was straight into Harry's inner sanctum quick as a flash.

'Good. Excellent. Coffee as well, Geraldine,' he bellowed, as he almost snatched the file from her hands. Geraldine scuttled off in the direction of the small kitchen down the corridor. She was used to Harry's manner and accepted it as par for the course. Geraldine had been brought up in a naval family where if anyone commanded

'Jump!' Geraldine's only query would have been 'From which window?' Well, at least that was the production office joke.

Harry sat back in his chair and flipped through the file. This would be an easy killing. Hartford Council's previous video was so old that everyone was in shoulder pads and practically humming the theme from *Dallas*. No wonder all the hotels, B and Bs and theatres were having such a hard time of it. HOT could create a really classy campaign that would put bums on seats, bodies in hotel beds and cash in the HOT coffers. But it was the same old question. How much would the council be prepared to pay? There was an old saying at HOT: What's the difference between a thirty-thousand-pound campaign and a sixty-grand one? Answer, nothing.

He reached across his desk to phone Janet. As he did so, he noticed that his shirt was a mass of tiny creases and cursed Val for the hundredth time that day. Considering the lazy cow did bugger-all, day in and day out, she could at least attempt a bit of ironing. Harry hadn't forgotten his northern roots where men were men and went out to work, while women stayed home, kept house and had babies. He allowed Val a gardener once a week and a cleaner twice a week but he expected her to do the rest. Sod the fact that she came from a wealthy background; she was his wife and should be doing all that stuff.

And as for babies, well, nothing seemed to be happening on that score. Perhaps it was just as well. He couldn't honestly see Val up through the night changing nappies. It would wreck her nails and she'd need an even longer lie-in than usual. Still, he couldn't deny, Val on a good day looked terrific on his arm. It had not done his position at HOT any harm at all.

'Janet? Two minutes in my office. Now.' He banged down the phone imperiously. He liked to keep them on their toes. Treat 'em mean, tell 'em nothing, that was his motto. Gave him the upper hand every time.

'I've been summoned to the bollocking room,' said Janet grimly to Liz. 'You'd better get the tumbrels ready. I wonder what the sod wants this time.'

Janet made her way out of the production office, down a short corridor and into the executive suite where Harry's office was situated. As she walked, she concentrated on deep breathing to help her relax, reflecting on how those telephone calls always instilled fear in her, even after all these years. It annoyed her that Harry could still make her quake. He rarely hinted at what any meeting was about. You never knew whether it was going to be a punch-up or a pay rise. And statistically it tended to be the first, rather than the second.

'Ah, Bancroft, take a seat,' he bellowed, not even glancing up from the open file on his desk.

'If I must,' Janet muttered under her breath. The visitors' seats in Harry's office were pitched a good few inches lower than his chair, all designed of course to give him a psychological advantage. Janet usually preferred to stand, giving her the temporary height advantage, but she'd learned over the years that if he shouted 'Sit!' it was probably in her best interests to do just that.

'Right, your name's on this one,' he barked. 'Hartford Council want a new tourism campaign. Their previous one's state-of-the-ark. I want something zappy, good script, and really grabby pictures.'

'What's the budget?' asked Janet, sensing a poisoned chalice.

'Cheap,' sneered Harry, 'and none of your business. But it's got to *look* expensive. That's why I pay you to run that production office. So get going. I want a draft script and a running order by close of play today. That's it. Scram.'

Without replying, because she knew well enough that Harry did not expect or encourage a response, Janet rose from the low chair, turned on her heel and walked out of the door. She half smiled to herself as she returned to her office.

'"Your name's on this one" my arse,' she muttered to herself. She had long got over the frustration of writing, producing and directing videos and programmes only to find Harry insisting his name be the only one on the end credits. Pays the mortgage, she endlessly reasoned with herself. Why make your life a misery, it's only a name on a caption roller, it's only rock and roll, not brain surgery.

But of course it mattered, it mattered a lot. Janet had learned that if you wanted to survive under Hampton's despotic regime, you kept your head down and just heaved a sigh of relief when the money arrived in the bank at the end of the month. Television was a shrinking market, and at the age of forty-two, as Val constantly reminded her, she was no spring chicken.

chapter three

The day was rapidly going from bad to worse. HOT had made the shortlist for the contract to produce a huge campaign for an insurance company, but they'd been pipped at the post by a rival. Nearly half a million pounds' worth of business had been lost. Harry stomped around his office, incandescent at the news.

'Get Simon and Joe in here immediately,' he shrieked at Geraldine, who, realizing that some blame-storming was about to take place, tactfully left her desk and went down the corridor to warn them. Although fiercely loyal to Harry, she did occasionally feel sorry for those who suffered at his hands.

Geraldine herself was one of the great HOT mysteries. No one could really work her out, or what went on inside her henna-bobbed head. She kept herself very much to herself behind the severe gold-rimmed glasses. She never gossiped, never commented or let slip the slightest whisper about her private life. She could have been anything from a lapsed nun to an ex-lap dancer, for all anyone knew. She seemed completely ageless and sexless. Life hadn't been all that kind either when the female bits and pieces were being given out. Geraldine was a sort of thin

20

cylinder shape and didn't help the cause much by wearing no make-up and incredibly dreary clothes.

Geraldine also had no idea how much mirth she caused around the company. Her problem was language. She mixed her metaphors, got her words confused and would have given Mrs Malaprop a jolly good run for her money. Her daily pronouncements were known as the G-spots and were widely circulated on e-mail. Thanks to the computer world of grammar and spell-checkers, Geraldine had no problem in producing immaculate letters, reports and memos for Harry. It was just in the rare moments when she actually spoke that she opened her mouth and put her foot in it. It had all started when someone had joked about a new blonde secretary being the company's latest 'It' girl, and Geraldine had remarked that she seemed awfully young to be running the computer department.

Now Geraldine put her head round the production department door. Obviously some huge joke was in progress because everyone was creased up laughing. As, one by one, they clocked Geraldine, the laughter died away, except for Ray, the young office runner, who was still oblivious and in mid-flight on his joke.

'And then he said "A hard-on doesn't count as personal growth," so she said . . .' Ray faltered, suddenly aware that the laughter had stopped. 'Oh, shit.'

The silence was awful. Nobody trusted Geraldine, because she was so quiet and nondescript and because they assumed she was Harry's answer to MI6.

'Ehm, Joe and Simon, Harry wants to see you,' she announced in strident tones. 'I thought I'd better warn you, he's not best pleased. In fact, he's in a state of high dungeon.'

A gale of silent laughter whipped around the room,

with people desperately trying not to burst. As a result, most sat shaking silently at their desks.

Joe and Simon left the office, looking like prisoners going to the gallows.

'Wonder what the hell they've done,' said Ray, still smarting with embarrassment. 'It'll be me next, hauled over the coals by Harry for lowering the tone.'

'At least we got a good G-spot out of it,' said Fiona, one of the production secretaries. 'Must get that one out on e-mail.'

'Yeah,' agreed Ray. 'Good old Geraldine, she comes up with some corkers, doesn't she?'

'Just hope Joe and Simon aren't getting it in the neck,' said Fiona, looking extremely worried.

The row in Harry's office could have been heard in five counties. Despite the door being closed, the raised voices and swearing went on for what seemed like hours. A couple of producers took it in turns to wander down the executive corridor on various excuses just to monitor the situation. In desperation, they then pretended they were having a whip-round for someone's leaving present and got horribly embarrassed when various secretaries actually dipped into their purses to contribute. The racket from Harry's office was becoming very ominous. Faces got longer and longer when Joe and Simon did not return to their desks. What on earth was going on?

It was only hours later, when everyone in the production office gave up and plodded out through the main doors to go home, that Sue on reception quietly told them that Joe and Simon had left the building much earlier that afternoon.

'Sacked,' she whispered. 'Not allowed to return to their desks. I think you'll find them in the GX.'

The GX was HOT's local pub. Overlooking Hartford's historic waterfront, it had been a grain store for centuries, but a decade ago it had been bought by a brewery chain who'd converted it into a popular watering hole. Its real name was the Grain Exchange, but from day one it had been renamed the Groin Exchange, or the GX for short. During the day and straight after work, most of the HOT staff went in there for comfort, sustenance or a jolly good gossip. But from about nine in the evening it had earned a reputation as a pick-up joint for the truly desperate.

Joe and Simon were huddled in a corner, four pints and a few vodka chasers into a rest-of-the-day session. They had already moved down the agenda from shock mode to anger.

'What took you so long?' Joe looked up from his fresh pint.

'We've only just heard,' said Ray. 'The others are getting the drinks in. What'll you have?'

'A screwdriver would be great,' said Simon bitterly. 'Then I could stab the bastard.'

Ray and the others finally sat down with Joe and Simon, waiting expectantly.

'We were sacked,' said Joe bitterly. 'We were sacked because Hartford bloody Optimum bloody Television didn't get that big insurance project. The company got to the shortlist but the Fat Controller got a call to say the job had gone elsewhere. So the big bucks flew straight out of the window. I suppose this affects Harry's bonus and his legendary ability to creep to the board. I must say I'm gutted for him.'

'So why did you take the rap?' asked Fiona.

'Quite simple really,' continued Joe. 'A case of wrong

place, wrong time. Simon and I were involved in some discussions about the pitch for the insurance job. We threw in a few ideas, but uncharacteristically Harry insisted on writing the actual document. Makes a change, because he usually gets us poor sods to do all the work and then passes it off as his own. Well, this time, just for once, he wrote it, we never even saw it and it didn't get the deal. So guess who gets the blame – us.'

'But he can't just sack you,' said Fiona. 'There are supposed to be procedures, rules . . .'

'Since when has Harry played by any rules?' Simon interrupted. 'No, this is Harry's Game. Our contracts were up for renewal in a few weeks' time, so he'd have got rid of us then anyway. He told us we were incompetent and therefore in breach of our contracts so we were out. He also threatened to rubbish us around the entire industry if we didn't shut up and go quietly. In the end we decided it wasn't worth putting that to the test. So we said our bit and left.'

A shudder went around the table, followed by mutterings of sympathy. This wasn't the first time people had left the company too hastily for a leaving present.

'He had it all sewn up,' Joe continued. 'He paid us up to the end of the month on condition we left the building without returning to our desks, and put a gagging order on us. No cosy chats with the local media. We'd done enough damage to the company's reputation, he said.'

'Also helps to keep his slate clean with all the suits on the board,' replied Fiona.

'Oh yeah, it's brilliant. He's squeaky clean and is seen as a tough manager because he shovels all the shit on our heads. Easy life!'

*

'Janet? It's Sue. Sorry to ring you so late. Have you heard the news?'

'No, what? I've been out filming most of the day.'

'Harry's been at it again. Sacked Simon and Joe to cover up for the fact that we didn't get some big insurance job.'

'What? I can't believe it. They're brilliant, those two. The most creative people we've hired in ages. A lot of people had high hopes for them. God, he's a bastard.' Janet shivered involuntarily. Morale always dipped for weeks after something like this.

Sue continued: 'Also, Val rang up during the row and insisted on Geraldine putting her through. Said it was life and death.'

'And was it?'

'Was it heck. You know what a drama queen Val is. She'd broken one of her nails on the oven door and was demanding Harry bring home another one.'

'What, a nail or an oven?'

'Come on, you know what Val's like. Which is more expensive? Actually, I'm surprised she knew where the oven was in the first place. Anyway, do you know, he interrupted all the shouting and got Geraldine on the case. It's being delivered tomorrow. I know, because I got caught up in the calls to arrange it.'

Janet was still absorbing all the news. 'It's strange, isn't it? Harry's the biggest bastard that ever walked the televisual earth and yet when Val shouts, he jumps. What does this woman have that we don't?'

'A complete inability to keep anything shut, I should imagine,' said Sue wryly.

Janet was right. Morale next day took a nosedive as the news of Joe and Simon's demise went swiftly round the building. HOT employed around sixty people, some of whom – mainly in Accounts, Marketing and Development – were on the permanent payroll. In production areas, however, they hired as and when required, so the majority of Janet's team, for example, were on short-term contracts. The climate was such that people did come and go on a regular basis, but not usually in the manner of Joe and Simon.

Harry swept in with a real smirk on his face. He positively relished the effect sackings had on the staff. Being the archetypal bully, it gave him even more of the upper hand. Also, last night, he'd been granted a legover with Val and had given her a good seeing-to. It never occurred to him that Val, having been on the pop all day, and delighted that her demands for a new oven had been met so swiftly, had decided to give in. It was Harry's usual self-centred, brief performance, followed by snoring. Val was then left wondering why she'd put up with all that just for a sodding oven.

His self-satisfaction increased later that morning when the company chairman, Sir James Patterson Cripps, called him in to say that the Hartford tourism video was in the bag, thanks to the old-boy network. He expressed brief concern at losing the insurance job, but praised Harry's tough stance with the staff.

'Well done, Hampton,' said Sir James, pausing to puff on a huge cigar. 'Lead by example. Glad to see you remember the company mission statement. Selling Starts Here.'

Back in his office, confidence now brimming over, Harry summoned Janet to tell her the good news about the tourism campaign.

'They liked my treatment, then,' said Janet firmly.

'Nonsense, woman. They didn't have to bother to read it. It was my reputation that clinched it. When will you women ever learn: at my level it's all about contacts, contacts, contacts. In fact, most decent business these days is conducted on the golf course and in the boys' room.'

'Well, that lets me out,' said Janet sarcastically. 'And talking of letting people out, why on earth did you sack Joe and Simon? They were two of my best producers in ages. Those two had real promise, good ideas and knew how to implement them.'

Harry shot Janet a rather world-weary look to hide his sudden unease. She was trouble, this one, a bit too long in the tooth to be fobbed off. She was also brilliant at her job, managing the day-to-day production at HOT. He knew he couldn't do without her but he'd never admit that to her.

'Quite simple. It was a big job, they wrote the pitch, they got it wrong and we lost a good half-million pounds' worth of business. Not to mention losing the chance to expand our client list. So they were out.'

'But they didn't write the pitch,' said Janet, trying to keep the wobble out of her voice. 'They would have discussed it with me.'

'Oh, they wrote it all right. On my express instructions, they kept it confidential. That's the nature of this business, Janet. I'm sure I don't have to remind you. Too many prying eyes and ears in this place. Anyway, you might rate them, but unfortunately our potential client didn't, so tough shit. We can't afford to employ no-hopers.'

Janet knew when she was beaten. She was well aware of the true state of affairs, because she had spoken to Joe late last night, but she also knew when to keep her head down. It was a case of survival.

'Okay, back to the tourism video. So do I go ahead, on the basis of the treatment I gave you?'

'Absolutely. Now get out.'

chapter four

Janet made her way back to her office, fed up to her back teeth and muttering under her breath. She was so angry that she almost collided with Geraldine, who was taking Harry's mid-morning caffeine in on a tray.

'If only I had a handy cyanide pill to pop in that coffee pot,' Janet remarked bitterly, forgetting momentarily that her comments might just go straight back to Harry.

'Come, come,' tutted Geraldine, unamused. 'These things happen. We must accept them. It takes two to tangle, you know.'

'Or even to tango. But your existence here doesn't depend on your marks in the Latin American section, nor on you getting every single spelling right one hundred per cent of the time,' said Janet crisply. Nor on your attempts at saying the company chairman's name, she thought. Sir James Patterson Cripps had, in Geraldine-speak, been transformed into Sir Pitterson Crapps on more than one occasion, amid silent hysteria.

'No, of course not,' said Geraldine huffily, 'but I hope those two young men aren't making out that they're escape goats over that insurance project.'

At the mention of escape goats, Janet completely lost it

and fled up the corridor, tears of laughter rolling down her face as she hotfooted it back to her office to tell her team the latest G-spots. That might cheer them up. She then had the unpleasant task of sorting out Joe and Simon's personal stuff and sending it on to them.

'Right, Liz, I want you to get started on the tourism job,' she said. 'I know we live here, but visitors don't. What we want is not just "this is the museum and oh look, that's the harbour". I want anecdotes, stories that bring the history to life. We have to persuade people watching the video to want to come here because it looks fascinating, even if it's raining cats and dogs. Which it is now.' Janet glanced out at the rain hammering against the windows.

'What's the time scale and budget on this?' enquired Liz.

'To echo the words of our führer, quick and cheap. The short answer is he won't say, so you can bet your Jimmy Choos – or probably Val's – there's loads of money washing around but we don't get to spend it. I would reckon on five filming days tops to do a reasonable job. Then we'll try and squeeze the system and spend a bit on post-production to make it look nice.'

'Shall I go and get a budget code then?' asked Nina, hoping for an excuse to visit the accounts department.

'Yeah, if it makes you happy,' laughed Janet. 'Go and see your beloved Sam. Don't pick up the phone, like the rest of us.'

Nina smiled her thanks, picked up her handbag and headed for the loo. She wanted a last-minute powder, touch of lippy and spray of perfume before going to see the object of her desire. Thank God she was wearing a black suit with a long-line jacket which minimized her bum.

Janet was just returning to the task of emptying Joe and Simon's desks when Ray the office runner came bursting through the door.

'You're unaccountably energetic this morning,' she said sarcastically, 'considering you were the life and soul of the GX last night.' Ray was known for his legendary hangovers.

'Sorry, Janet,' he said. 'I'm trying to get lashed only at weekends. Although I must say I got off quite lightly after that sesh with Joe and Simon. Anyway, guess what, I've just heard from the dreaded Geraldine that Fattie Hampton's having an office refurb.'

'What sort of refurb?' Janet was always nervous when HOT spent money on anything unnecessary or frivolous.

'Very swanky new desk and chair. Must have cost squillions,' replied Ray. 'Leather-top desk, looked like mahogany. And a big black leather chair.'

Make Harry even loftier, thought Janet bitterly. What a charmed life he led.

'This I must see,' she said, and made her way up to the executive corridor. She had long since dropped any pretence of defending Harry to her team. There was no point. She had to manage a roomful of intelligent people. They'd all worked him out and would have thought her daft if she'd stuck up for him. Everyone knew he was short on talent and big on getting bungs and bonuses. But it was Harry's reign of fear that they couldn't crack. Most got angry with themselves that he scared them so much. Janet was the only one who went some of the distance, but even she had to admit defeat most of the time when the going got tough.

'I've come to see the new furniture,' she said, sweeping past an open-mouthed about-to-protest Geraldine and into

31

Harry's office. 'Hmm, very nice, Harry,' she said, trying not to laugh. The chair was straight out of *Mastermind*. She could just imagine Magnus Magnusson's voice intoning: "Harry Hampton, controller of production. Your specialist subject is bollocking and your time starts now."

'What did you do to deserve this?' she asked him.

'Goes with the job,' he smirked. 'Sir James felt it was my due, so here it is. The paintings are arriving later on. Looks good, eh?'

Janet sat down in one of the new visitors' seats, which were even lower than the previous ones. The new desk was certainly a beautiful piece of workmanship. It was long and lean and very minimal. But there was one problem. Janet found herself sitting at direct eye level with Harry's crotch. Was this a new deliberate intimidation tack, or was Harry advertising something?

'I thought,' she paused, wondering whether to avert her gaze, 'you might like to view the catering college series today before it's dubbed. Would you like me to pop in the tapes now? Or would you prefer me to come back after the men from the Tate?'

'Sarcasm doesn't suit you, Janet. You must remember, I entertain important clients in here. We have to impress them and show them that we are a prestigious company with a big track record.'

And then you rook them rotten by charging them the earth for a poxy campaign we could put together for a quarter of the price, thought Janet.

'Bring those tapes in,' he barked. 'I'll look at them now.'

Watching the catering college videos from the comfort of his new chair, Harry reflected once again on the fact that Val did not live up to his job description for a wife. Why couldn't she cook, like other women? Or like the students in the videos, for that matter? Keep house like other women? Again because of his northern upbringing, he'd refused point blank to let Val have an allowance from her parents, reasoning that she'd just spend it on domestic help, leaving her to become even more dippy with nothing to do. The real reason, though he would never admit it, was that keeping her a bit short gave him the upper hand.

As the brief end credits rolled on catering college episode one, Harry thumped his new desk in temper.

'Get that Bancroft woman in here immediately,' he barked at Geraldine. Geraldine didn't accord Janet the favour she'd done to Simon and Joe by tipping her off. She didn't like Janet much, in truth, because she was one of the few who stood up to Harry, and Geraldine saw that as insubordination. She just dialled Janet's number and briskly told her to come in.

'Oh heck, I'm off to the bollocking room again,' said Janet. She left to the rest of her team humming the theme music from *Mastermind*.

'So how was Magnus?' they all chorused when she returned white-faced exactly two minutes later.

'I started but I didn't get to finish,' she half joked. She was secretly livid and trying not to show it. Morale was still too low after Joe and Simon's demise for her to have a real public go about Harry.

'Just a discussion about the end credits,' she whispered to Liz, who was her number-one confidante. 'The usual routine, off with my name as producer/director, on with his instead. I've got to get the graphics redone now so we can deliver. By order of the Third Reich.'

'The bastard,' said Liz. 'I doubt he even knows where the catering college is, let alone how to boil an egg.'

33

'That'll be why he and Val have a lot in common, then,' said Janet. 'I feel lunch at the Groin Exchange coming on. Fancy the idea?'

Over steak-and-ale pies and heaps of naughty chips, Liz and Janet surveyed the scene in the GX. There were solicitors out between adjournments, relaxing in the sure knowledge of receiving their fees, while in other corners, their clients sweated it out. City types who'd already made their money that day and might just not bother to return to the office, given a couple of large gin and tonics and a bit of gentle persuasion.

'Not much talent here,' observed Janet drily. 'They're either too young or too old.'

'Or too infertile,' said Liz too involuntarily for Janet's liking.

'What do you mean by that?' queried Janet.

'Well, look around,' said Liz. 'Those around the thirty mark. They're all drinking too much, smoking too much, overweight and unfit. It's bound to affect their fertility rate.'

'Do you have to view all blokes as baby-making machines?' asked Janet, fascinated. 'Are you always running open auditions for sperm banks?'

'Not exactly,' said Liz, lowering her head sheepishly. 'I just desperately, desperately want a baby. I can't seem to meet anyone. I've almost given up on that. They're either too young, too old, or too pretty. So I'm beginning to think I'd be better off sticking with the idea of having just the baby.'

'Aren't you cutting out the middle man a bit here?' asked Janet. 'I mean, wouldn't it be nice at least to start conventionally?'

'I'm not sure any more. I spent five years with Steve, we

talked about marriage, and then after all that he announced he didn't want babies. End of story. I mean, what's the point of having sex? That was what it was designed for.'

'Don't you think you're a bit young to be thinking this way? After all, you just picked the wrong guy with Steve.'

'Yeah, but every time I meet a new man – which let's face it is getting rarer and rarer, because they're so thin on the ground – I can hardly issue a questionnaire on attitudes to smacking, pocket money and feeding on demand.'

'Don't be daft,' replied Janet, trying not to laugh, because she knew Liz was in deadly earnest. 'All I'm saying is don't give up on the conventional route yet.'

'Well, you don't have kids; don't you ever regret it?' asked Liz.

'No, I can honestly say I don't. They never happened and with hindsight it was just as well. I was never one to coo into prams or kiss babies. So that ruled out a career in politics. No, in the circumstances, the choice was relatively easy. Anyway, Crippen wasn't into babies. He was more into having an Olympic-sized temper and other women's knickers.'

Janet never referred to her ex as anything other than Crippen so that she wouldn't have to utter his name. Clearly her marriage had had the most devastating effect on her, because she'd not been known to have a relationship since. Even Liz, who'd come to be good friends with her, sensed not to ask. She got the distinct impression that Janet had walked out with just the clothes she stood up in.

'Now, changing the subject,' as Janet always did when her marriage came up in conversation, 'the Hartford tourism job. I think it's time we raised your profile. You've been an ace researcher here for a couple of years and I think you're perfectly capable of putting it together yourself.'

'Whaddya mean?' Liz was stunned.

'What I mean is that I think you should take at least an assistant director role. I'll be in the background for any help you need, but I know you'll do a great job.'

'Bloody hell, Janet, are you sure?' Liz stuttered.

'Absolutely. Good, you're agreed,' grinned Janet, rubbing her hands together in delight. 'All I need to do now is formalize it. I'll pick a good moment with the Fat Controller. He'll probably want to have you in for a brief chat to pretend he had the idea himself, and then . . . Liz, are you all right?'

Liz had gone white, and slumped over her drink.

'No, I can't. I can't do that,' she pleaded. 'Please don't ask me because I won't do it.'

'What, go and see Harry? Look, we all know he's the World's Biggest Bully, but he really rates your work. Honestly, you're absolutely on home ground on this one.'

'No, I can't do it.' Liz's eyes filled with tears. 'And please don't ask any questions.' She fled to the loo, leaving Janet wondering what on earth was wrong.

Janet didn't raise the subject again. They returned to the office to find Nina checking into the Inn of the Sixty-Sixth Happiness. She was still reeling from the thrill of spending five minutes talking to Sam in Accounts about the budget code. And she'd nipped home at lunchtime and weighed herself. She'd lost a pound since breakfast.

If only the rest of it was that easy, sighed Janet to herself.

36

chapter five

'They were on my desk last night, honest, Harry,' pleaded a shaking Nina, close to tears.

'Well, if they were, they've grown legs and walked off into the bloody sunset,' roared Harry, thumping his new desk at the same time. 'You realize that if we . . . no, let me rephrase that . . . if YOU don't find them, that's four days' worth of editing down the fucking pan.' He paused, stabbing at the nearby calculator. 'That's not far short of four grand and that's just for the edit suite. That's before I pay for some poor mug to sit there and put it all together again.'

'I'm sorry, Harry, they were on my desk, ready to box up, and . . .'

'SORRY isn't good enough. SORRY is a STUPID word. You are STUPID,' he roared again. 'Well, I tell you this, if those tapes don't turn up by lunchtime, the cost of re-editing will be coming straight out of your salary.'

Nina went white. That was about three months' money after tax on her salary as a production secretary. She opened her mouth but no sound came out.

'Now get yourself and your fat arse out of this office and start looking.'

Tears now streaming down her face, Nina fled out of the room, colliding with Geraldine, who'd been eavesdropping outside. The files Geraldine had been carrying took flight and landed in a mess on the floor.

'Oh, you stupid girl,' wailed Geraldine from beneath her hennaed bob. 'You should watch where you're going. You'll have to help me clear this up and sort it out. Sir Pitterson Crapps is expected any minute.'

'Well, tough shit then,' replied Nina, as she carried on running down the corridor, heading for the ladies' loo for a good cry.

The office jungle drums were working overtime as usual. The row over the missing catering college tapes soon reached Janet's ears and she tracked down a distraught Nina barricaded in one of the cubicles and crying her eyes out.

'He said I had a fat bum and that I'd have to pay for it,' she mumbled through racking sobs.

'You what?' said Janet, wondering for one bizarre moment whether HOT were suddenly offering their staff free liposuction. 'Come on, hon, let's go and have a quiet coffee and you can tell me about it.'

Janet coaxed Nina out of the loo and into the tiny staff canteen, which was mercifully empty. They chose the most obscure corner and Janet gently persuaded Nina to go through what Harry had said.

'Now, I can assure you there's no way you'd be paying for re-editing. That's complete nonsense. He has absolutely no right to say that. We'll find the tapes, I promise you, even if we have to call in the cavalry. I'll get everyone on the case, even Interpol if I have to. The tapes exist. They're there somewhere. So don't worry about that.'

The other subject was a more difficult issue. It would be a complete sham for Janet to pretend Nina didn't have a big bum. She'd have to have been registered blind to be unaware of it, and besides, Nina discussed it constantly. She was always on different diets, different exercise regimes in an attempt to reduce it. It was one of those hereditary features over which she probably had no control. The sad thing was that Nina was an extraordinarily pretty girl, with lively blue eyes and a personality to match. She had her pale blonde hair cut in a short, sharp style that really suited her. From the waist upwards she was a size 12. But from the waist down she was a 16 and counting. Because she was a cockney, the chaps in the production office had nicknamed her the London Derrière. When Janet found out, she made them swear on pain of death not to let her know. Nina would have been devastated.

'If I find any one of you so much as whistling the Londonderry Air or anything else for that matter, I'll have your guts for garters,' she'd warned them. 'You'll think Harry's a real soft touch after I've finished with you.'

Nina had begun to calm down now as Janet spelled out a plan of action to find the missing tapes.

'As for Harry's remarks about your bum, just remember that his isn't as pert as it used to be. Ray told me the gossip is that the company had to buy him that new chair because he'd got too heavy for the old one and they couldn't get the parts to repair it.'

Back in the production office, Janet told the team what had happened and announced a full-scale search.

'Down tools, folks, just answer the phones, but please go through every drawer, filing cabinet, folder, nook and cranny until you find them.'

This was no mean feat for thirty creative people who weren't the tidiest on the planet. Janet began on her own filing cabinet. She pulled out the top drawer and looked in. Was she imagining something or was it not quite as she'd left it? The next drawer looked normal, but there was something about the bottom drawer that made her wonder.

Ray, the office runner and oracle of all gossip, came over in 'have you heard' mode.

'It might be nothing,' he said conspiratorially, 'but several people have said they think their stuff's been got at. Not quite as they'd left it, things moved around, that sort of thing. One or two who leave their computers on all the time have found some of their e-mails have been opened.'

'Hmm,' said Janet, half to herself. 'I wonder, I just wonder.' She looked back at Ray. 'We could all be getting paranoid. Well, even more than usual. Anyway, Ray, let's just find those tapes and worry about this other stuff later.'

Her phone rang, bringing their conversation to a convenient end. Janet did not want to go any further down that particular road. It was the dreaded Geraldine, tutting down the phone.

'I've been trying to ring you for ages,' she said. 'I wish to lodge a complaint against one of your team.'

'I'm very sorry, Geraldine, but we have a crisis on here at the moment. We have some tapes which have gone walkabout and we have to find them,' said Janet sharply. 'That's much further up the urgent list than sitting at my desk awaiting your call. Anyway, briefly, what's your problem?'

'I think it is more *your* problem. Nina Blake came out of Harry's office at great speed, ran straight into me and all my files went all over the floor. That was bad enough, but we were expecting Sir Pitterson Crapps at any time. It would have looked terrible. And she was extremely rude.'

'I'm sure even Sir Crapperson Pitts would have totally understood,' retorted Janet, taking a leaf out of Geraldine's book and scoring another hit for the G-spotters. Predictably it passed straight over Geraldine's head. 'Anyway, I know Nina would not have done it on purpose,' she continued. 'What exactly did she say to you?'

'"Tough shit",' said Geraldine. 'That's what she said, "tough shit".'

'Sounds a fair assessment to me,' retorted Janet and slammed down the phone. Serve the stupid cow right.

A cry of triumph went up. The tapes had been found in the bottom drawer of Joe's now empty filing cabinet. Janet smiled grimly to herself. She'd personally cleared out his cabinet completely the previous day. The tapes had been planted. Ray was right. There was something up.

Janet drove home that night with a heavy heart. Something was going on but she couldn't pinpoint what it was or make much sense of it.

As she put the key in the front door of her modest little terraced house, she made a decision to treat herself to a takeaway. Sod cooking tonight, she thought. I'm too mentally exhausted.

She phoned through an order of chicken biryani and a couple of poppadoms and opened a bottle of Beaujolais while she waited for the delivery boy. The events of the past few days were rattling around in her head. She could at least understand Harry's twisted motives for sacking Joe and Simon. They'd just been treated like cannon fodder to protect his skin. But why was Liz so terrified at the

41

thought of talking to Harry? Was it that she was afraid to be on her own with him? Something must have happened to make her feel like that. And why had the tapes gone missing and then been planted in an empty cabinet, a cabinet she'd been the last to use? Was there someone in the department trying to undermine her? It definitely wasn't Nina or Liz, which narrowed it down to a possible fifty-odd others to choose from. A hopeless task. Or was it Harry on yet another of his control-freak kicks? Could he be capable of sneaking into the production office after they'd all gone home, running the risk of being spotted moving tapes from one place to another or having a rummage through her desk? For the life of her Janet couldn't imagine why he'd go to all that bother.

She glanced at her watch. Eight o'clock. Sue might just be home by now. She'd been working the late shift this week. Janet picked up the phone and dialled.

'Sue, it's Janet. Am I interrupting meals and stories?' She could hear small voices in the background.

'No, it's all right, Jon always sees to the kids when I'm on lates. What's up?'

'Oh, fairly shitty day, that's all. Lost tapes, lost tempers. That sort of stuff. Also a couple of mysteries I'm trying to unravel. Can I pick your brains for a minute?'

'Of course. Fire away.'

'What time did Harry leave the building last night? Can you remember?'

'Oh, that's an easy one,' said Sue brightly, 'because it was unusual. He went way after you lot. In fact it was just minutes before I left at seven thirty. I remarked on it as he went through reception. He muttered something about being overworked. He's normally out on the dot of six. You can almost set your watch by it.'

'Interesting,' said Janet. 'And one other thing that puzzles me. Liz seems absolutely terrified of him. I only really discovered that today.'

'I think we're all terrified of him in one way or another,' replied Sue.

'No, this was different. Real paranoia. Can you think of any reason why?'

'No, I can't, not at all.' Sue was usually the soul of discretion. 'You know I tend to keep my mouth shut. It's better in my sort of job, but in this instance, if I knew anything I would tell you. Liz has never said anything to me. I did hear on the jungle drums that there had been some kind of mega row today.'

'Oh, that was the saga of Nina and the missing tapes. Harry also told her she had a big bum. Nice one, eh?'

'I'm afraid I heard about that too. Mind you, he can't talk. Have you seen him squeezing himself into that Mercedes these days? Shoe horn wouldn't come amiss.'

'Oh, must look out for that! Thanks, Sue. See you tomorrow.'

Over the solitary takeaway and the Beaujolais, Janet pondered some more. Was Harry searching the office, planting tapes? Was he trying to undermine her?

She was just dozing through a rather dreary Hollywood thriller when the phone rang. It was Sue.

'Want the good news or the bad?' she said.

'Go on, whatever.'

'Val's just called. Booked us all in for dinner in a couple of weeks time.'

'Oh, shit,' said Janet. 'It only seems like a couple of lifetimes ago that we had the last fiasco. I wish she'd stop this.'

'Me too. With that amount of notice, I'll not be able to

43

use the "let-down-by-the-babysitter" excuse like last time. Nina and Liz have agreed to go. But then, you say yes to anything when there's a pistol planted against your temple.'

'Let's hope it's a more mundane evening than the last one.'

chapter six

'Smirk alert, smirk alert,' warned Ray as Janet sat down to wade through the morning post and her e-mails.

'What is it this time?' she queried, only half listening.

'Harry's been reported looking very pleased with himself,' said Ray conspiratorially.

'And to what do we owe this underwhelming pleasure?' said Janet vaguely, gazing at her computer screen and deleting all the junk mail with one definitive click.

'Well, strictly *entre nous*, it sounded like some sort of holiday freebie,' said Ray.

'How come I'm head of this department, have been here for years and yet know nothing? And you're the office runner, been here five minutes and you know everyone's blood group?' said Janet, now giving him her full attention.

'Thought it was in my job spec,' grinned Ray. 'I was in really early this morning to deliver the post. Harry's office door was a couple of inches ajar and I caught a few key words.

'Like what?'

'Like "Algarve", "five star", "first-class seats", that kind of thing.'

'Maybe he was just booking a holiday,' said Janet.

'Nah,' said Ray. 'It just didn't sound like that. Not at eight o'clock in the morning It seemed a bit too clandestine to be legit. More like a favour being called in.'

'And you have a very fertile imagination,' Janet sighed. Except he was probably right. Harry had a terrible reputation for being King of the Freebies. She'd stumbled on it herself first hand when HOT had won a contract to make a video series about old family-run boat yards. An old sea dog at one of the yards had let slip that the big white yacht down the end was being built for a 'Mr Hampton'.

'Now put your overly busy mind on the back burner and tell all those here that I want to hold a short meeting in about five minutes.'

'Sure thing,' replied Ray, saluting. Good lad, she thought, bright, hard-working and worth giving a break if she could create one.

Janet sipped a coffee and pondered again on the missing tapes episode. It couldn't really be Harry. Okay, he'd worked unusually late, but what would he gain by searching the office and moving tapes about? He had absolutely no motive whatsoever. Granted, he was a control freak, but this was just damned stupid. No, it must be someone else; perhaps there was some petty jealousy going on that she hadn't clocked.

'Okay, folks, this won't take long.' She addressed the troops, perching on the end of her desk in the style of a Channel 5 newsreader. 'I wanted to thank you all for helping to make a thorough search for the tapes yesterday. Much appreciated, especially by Nina, and we got the result we'd hoped for.'

There was a small round of mock applause.

'But it does throw up some serious issues. First of all, yesterday's search reminded me what a messy load of idiots we are. Tapes, files, notebooks, just general stuff strewn everywhere. Empty coffee cups, plates, yoghurt pots, plastic spoons, pizza boxes. I can't believe you all go home at night and make stuff off *Blue Peter*. So the message is, stop collecting the bits to make Tracy Island, clear up your mess and keep your desks tidier, then if something goes AWOL again we've a fighting chance of finding it. And I won't have to call in the Thunderbirds.'

'Now the second thing is more sinister. A number of you reported to me that you thought your stuff had been moved about a bit, desks rearranged or filing cabinets searched. Not quite as you'd left it, was the phrase. There were too many reports for it to be a coincidence. It saddens me to think that someone here is intent on mischief-making, and I must warn you that if it happens again and I find the culprit, then it'll be the loyal order of the boot. Make no mistake, we cannot and will not tolerate someone hell-bent on a sabotage mission. They will be sacked.'

A shudder, followed by low-voiced reaction, went around the room.

'So I urge you to keep a closer eye on your belongings. Anyone with information is welcome to talk to me or e-mail me in confidence. But I have to say, I think it's a very sad day that I have to stand here and say this. Okay, folks, back to your looms.'

As the morning wore on, Janet received ten jokey e-mails all citing Geraldine as the culprit, with motives ranging from 'her desperate ambition to be a contestant on *Whose Tape Is It Anyway?*' to 'her subconscious desire to write a book entitled *Pronunciation is the thief of time*'.

47

'Starting a business called Say It With Flour' was another cruel suggestion, with a footnote adding that it should be wholemeal flour to match her dreary outfits.

By lunchtime, Janet was convinced it was not an inside job. Someone would have squealed, or at least dropped a hint. However, she still hadn't got to the bottom of Harry's unusual state of happiness. He was obviously up to some sort of mischief, but supersleuth Ray was now out on a shoot for the rest of the day, so that source of information had dried up. She arranged to meet Sue for lunch in the canteen. She'd know.

'Any idea why Harry's allegedly cock-a-hoop?' she asked.

'Yep,' said Sue, triumphantly. 'Free holiday. He's going on a jolly.'

'Where's he going?'

'The Algarve.'

'Look, it's only supposition. How did you get to hear?'

'Ray told me on the sly. Perhaps he's been chatting up Geraldine.'

'Doubt it. He can't stand her. But he always knows the gossip, that lad. He's not usually wrong either.'

'Anyway, trust Harry to get something for nothing, the jammy sod. Wherever it is, the food will be better than this muck.'

They were wading their way through a soggy vegetarian lasagne and some garlic bread in which the bread was very much the side order to the garlic.

'Blimey, they'll smell us coming,' said Janet. 'Good job I'm not planning to have sex tonight. I'd knock some poor sod out from a mile away with this breath.'

'Is there a man in tow? Is there something you've not told us?' asked Sue, straight on the case.

'No, don't be ridiculous. I was only joking. I gave up men years ago, or rather they gave me up. More trouble than they're worth.'

'I don't think you should generalize too much,' said Sue softly. 'I know it's easy for me to sit here knowing I've got Jon and the kids to go home to, but isn't it worth taking another risk, to find someone special?'

'Oh, I dunno any more,' said Janet, suddenly looking wistful. 'I dreamed of all that happily-ever-after stuff and where did it get me? Precisely nowhere. At least now I have my own home, car, hair and teeth and I can sleep easily in my bed, albeit alone. At least I can't kick myself out, or two-time myself. Okay, I'll admit I get lonely sometimes, but I've discovered there are times when chocolate really can solve all your problems.'

'Can't convince you then, can I?' said Sue, laughing.

'Nope. And by sheer coincidence there was one of those blindingly obvious surveys out last week. You know, the sort where they discover after years of painstaking research and squillions of spondulicks that in fact half the married population is female. Well, last week's little bombshell was that they've discovered that more women prefer chocolate to sex. Again obvious. We all knew that one. No fear of pregnancy, no grunting, no wet patch, no post-bonk snoring either. And you get the whole bed to yourself. Look on the positive side. With chocolate, you can take as long as you like or just have a quickie nibble and save a bit for later. It's much cheaper than condoms and there's no risk of cheating.'

'But there are down sides to chocolate,' retorted Sue. 'You get spotty, you get fat, so you need a new wardrobe of clothes, which requires you spending all your money. So suddenly a Cadbury's Flake or a Fry's Chocolate Cream is

49

looking like a major investment. Talking of which, shall we go mad and have some of that chocolate cheesecake for pudding?'

'Might deaden the garlic,' agreed Janet. 'Anyway, you don't need chocolate. You could crawl all over Jon tonight if you felt like it.'

'Not after a day's shift here and two small children to read a bedtime story to. I doubt I'll be bodice-ripping material after all that.'

For the third night in a row, Janet drove home deeply disturbed by events at work. What a terrible week it had been, what with the sacking of Joe and Simon, followed by the catering college graphics row, the missing tapes mystery and now the office poltergeist. And on that one, she was becoming more and more convinced that the culprit was not from the production department at all. There were those who had their differences, didn't speak to each other or were ex-lovers. But not one single person had squealed or even come up with a possible suspect. She also wondered what Harry was up to. Normally he crowed to her about anything interesting he was doing, especially if it involved a little boasting. One of his favourite tricks was to collect an award in, say, New York, and then allow the person who'd actually done the work to meet him at the airport and have the thrill of driving him back to the office while he delivered a blow-by-blow account of the ceremony, the frantic networking and the glorious champagne piss-up afterwards. So why wasn't he boasting about the freebie week in the Algarve? On the other hand, with his six-figure salary Harry could afford to go to most places he fancied. So what was so special about this trip?

Janet shrugged to herself as she popped a pizza in the oven. While she waited for it to cook, she thought a little more about her chat with Sue on the subject of men and chocolate. She thought enviously of Sue and her cosy lifestyle. She'd be home now with Jon, tucking up the children, and then they'd be sitting down together in front of the television over some delicious snack. Sue was one of those domestic goddesses who effortlessly conjured up all sorts of delicious morsels out of nothing very much, whereas Janet's cooking had collapsed and promptly died in the seventies. She could rustle up a prawn cocktail, steak and chips and pass off a Black Forest gateau out of a box as her own. But she'd lost the cooking plot when she left Crippen and couldn't keep up with all the celebrity chefs mucking about with bits of lemon grass and ten different types of olive oil.

Perhaps that was why she hadn't met a man since. Perhaps Crippen had e-mailed the entire male population and warned them about her cooking. Perhaps there was something in the old adage that her grandmother had always trotted out, that the way to a man's heart was the way you braised his kidneys. She'd have liked to cook Crippen's kidneys all right, that at least she did know. But the rest of the time, cooking for one was no fun at all.

Thank God it's Friday, thought Janet, as she swung into the HOT car park. Morale might perk up after a decent weekend. The day's agenda included a meeting with Harry on the subject of the Hartford tourism project. She and Liz spent an hour going through the treatment, the budget and a draft script before making their way to the executive corridor, Liz as white as a sheet.

The ever-faithful Geraldine was sitting, expressionless, at her desk outside Harry's office, clicking away on her computer. What went on behind those severe glasses?

wondered Janet. Probably not a lot. There was definitely less to Geraldine than met the eye.

'Geraldine's looking a triumph of taupe today,' whispered Liz as they swept past. Geraldine's dress sense, or rather lack of it, was a constant source of amusement in the production office.

'Right, siddown,' barked Harry, indicating two chairs in front of his desk. Janet had warned Liz about the new seating arrangements and the eye-line view of Harry's undercarriage.

They outlined the way the video and the website would look, showed Harry some storyboards and went through a rough budget sheet.

'Right, leave this stuff with me. I'll get on to the council,' he snarled.

So you can get all the kudos with your important friends in Hartford, thought Janet.

'And you can save money on this budget by getting the bloody graphics right first time,' said Harry with his usual thump on the table. 'My name only as executive producer on the end credits. Company policy. No one buying this video will give a shit who shot it, lit it or made the tea. Geddit?'

If it's not that important, you pillock, why are you making such a fuss about it? thought Janet.

'Is it company policy to have only Harry's name on end credits?' asked Liz as they walked back to their office.

'Is it heck,' replied Janet. 'He just made that up. Anyway, did you like the new seating arrangements? All designed to distract us, I suppose. There didn't seem to be very much going on down there. The way Harry swaggers around, you'd think he was hung like a donkey. Looked more like a hamster from where I was sitting.'

Liz looked shocked. 'Sorry, Janet, I didn't dare look. I felt too embarrassed. I just hate going into his office at the best of times.'

Hmm, thought Janet. She really is frightened of him. I wonder if I'll ever get to the bottom of it.

'Still no mention of the freebie,' she continued. 'Unlike Harry not to take the opportunity to gloat. Very odd.'

'It could be quite simple,' said Liz. 'Perhaps he wants to give Val a surprise and thinks we might blow it. After all, he knows we see her socially from time to time. Or anti-socially, depending on how you look at it.'

'Perhaps he wants to kid her that he's paid for the trip. It could be just that. I'm beginning to think I'm reading too much into too little. I must chill out over the week-end. Are you doing anything exciting?'

'I'm going to stay with my sister,' said Liz.

'That sounds nice. But I hope you're not going to get all broody and miserable seeing her kids,' said Janet suspiciously. Liz's younger sister had twin daughters of eighteen months.

'No, no,' she replied. 'But I did read this week that one of those supermodels borrowed somebody's baby and held it for a day and then got herself pregnant.'

'Most people find sex is a bit more reliable. C'mon, Liz, it will happen to you. Probably when you're least expecting.'

'That's the trouble, I do want to be expecting,' said Liz wistfully. 'I'm frightened it will never happen to me.'

As they reached their office, Janet couldn't fail to notice the baby and parenting magazines sticking out of Liz's bag on the floor next to her desk.

chapter seven

The great thing about inviting people over to dinner, mused Janet, was that it forced you to get the vacuum cleaner out. She'd spent all Saturday morning at the supermarket and now she was on a dust-busting mission. The place now reeked so violently of bleach and polish that two spiders who'd quietly set up home in the bathroom decided it was time to move on.

It was a beautiful May morning and whilst the sunshine streaming through the windows was a welcoming sight, it did show up how badly everything needed a good scrub. At least it would be almost dark by the time her guests arrived.

Janet was now knee deep in cookery books, trying to knock up some potted shrimps to start, followed by a chicken chasseur-type casserole (the sauce by arrangement with a packet). She'd already burned her fingers twice on the oven door, so she put on some cheerful music to stop herself getting into a temper over it all. Unfortunately Dire Straits' 'Sultans of Swing' proved to be too uplifting when the pan with the cheat's chasseur sauce was accidentally thrown in the air. Oh to be Delia Smith, live in that wonderful conservatory and make millions writing cookery books. If I were Delia, Janet mused, I'd spend the proceeds on a resident chef. If I were Delia, I'd also employ someone to scrape the sauce off these cupboard doors.

With fifteen minutes to blast-off, Janet lit the candles and oil lamps placed around her sitting room cum dining room. She stood back to admire the effect. I might not be able to cook, she thought, but my God, I can light a candle. At least they made the table look good. She'd just poured herself a glass of Merlot as a reward for all her efforts when she heard the doorbell.

Joe and Simon stood on her doorstep, grinning and clutching carrier bags full of bottles and cans.

'Your local off-licence had a sale on,' said Simon. 'We couldn't resist. I wonder if they do reward cards there if you spend loads.'

'I should know,' replied Janet, kissing each of them lightly on the cheek.

'Hey, nice place, Janet,' said Joe. 'Something smells fantastic. Oh, it's me,' he added, sniffing his armpits. 'Only joking. We're starving, now that we're the newly impoverished. The nouveau pauvre as opposed to the nouveau riche. Or as Geraldine would put it, the niveau rouche.'

Janet poured them huge glasses of wine as they made a beeline for the table.

'Let's not do all that Bombay mix foreplay stuff, let's just get stuck in,' said Simon.

'Phew, I'm fresh out of Bombay,' grinned Janet as she disappeared into the kitchen.

'I know just how you feel, ducky,' said Simon.

'So how's your week been since Harry sent you on your way?' said Janet, returning with the potted shrimps and a basket of French bread.

'Well, we've tried mugging, ramraiding, joy-riding, begging and extortion. Only the tame stuff so far,' said Joe. 'No, seriously, I've got an interview upcountry with a small indie production house. Rubbish area but the money's good. And I'd be nearer my girlfriend. So double whammy.'

'And what about you, Simon?' asked Janet, already clearing away the first lot of plates and marvelling that the mountain of bread had almost completely disappeared.

'I've got a mate in London who's trying to fix me up in an ad agency. So fingers crossed.'

'I'm really pleased,' said Janet. 'And don't forget what I said about references. I'd be delighted to write glowing accounts about you both.'

'Well, that certainly wasn't on offer from Harry. All he threatened to do was rubbish us around the entire industry if we didn't leave quietly. More importantly, the HOT-heads would have started asking questions. This way Harry keeps a clean sheet and we're sent like lambs to the slaughter.'

'A case of Silence of the Lambs,' said Joe. They all laughed.

'Well, you'll get great references from me. Might be worth giving my home address and telephone number rather than work, though. I don't want anybody snooping. I keep thinking I'm imagining things, but there's something going on in that building. I can't put my finger on it.'

Over the chicken chasseur à la packet and plates of steamed vegetables which Simon and Joe pronounced 'mental', Janet outlined the mysterious goings-on since they'd left the company.

Joe and Simon looked at each other and started to laugh. They laughed until they almost doubled up, tears rolling down their cheeks. Janet found herself laughing too, but hadn't a clue why.

'I just wonder if the fat sod actually believed us,' said Simon, still spluttering.

'If it's true, then it was worth being sacked,' replied Joe, wiping his eyes with his napkin. 'Well, almost.'

'Put me out of my agony, for goodness' sake,' said Janet, now on the edge of her seat with curiosity. 'No pudding until you tell.'

'Right, right, of course we'll tell you,' said Simon, calming down immediately. 'It started during the big row. I suppose that was the moment when we knew we had nothing to lose.'

'What started?' urged Janet.

'Well, I guess we egged each other on,' continued Simon. 'It was really only a parting shot, but we implied that a secret file was being kept on Harry's activities and we told him we knew what he was up to.'

'We kind of pretended we knew he was involved in all sorts of stuff.' Joe took up the story. 'We muttered mysteriously about backhanders, sexual harassment, that sort of thing. We rounded it off by saying he was a lousy boss and that everyone had zilch respect for him, and that it was only a matter of time before the board heard about it and demanded the file.'

'And how did he react?' asked Janet.

'Well, he was shouting and thumping the desk, but that's the norm with Harry. But then he demanded that we named names; he wanted facts.'

'A bit odd if he's nothing to hide,' said Janet.

'Exactly,' said Joe. 'But it was as though we'd stumbled on something. By time we knew we were out of a job anyway and we wanted our little bit of mischief before we left. Mind you, I'm sure Harry's capable of all that sort of stuff, but why on earth would he bother to get upset? Anyway, now we've told you, it's time for your part of the bargain. Where's that pudding?'

'Oh wow, retro food,' shrieked Simon in delight as a Black Forest gateau à la Sainsbury's freezer cabinet, customized with dollops of double cream, appeared on the table. 'Blimey, you're clever, Janet.'

She'd deliberately left the washing-up until the morning. Joe and Simon had offered but she'd turned them down. They'd been ridiculously brilliant guests, considering her cooking. She'd enjoyed their company enormously, but she'd enjoyed even more hearing how Harry had got a slight bit of comeuppance.

As she stacked the plates and filled the sink, she thought some more about what Joe and Simon had said. It did somehow make sense. Harry'd got the wind up about a file on him. That was why desks had been searched. Maybe the planting of the 'missing' tapes had been his revenge against the whole department. Or perhaps it was a simple case of him trying to justify the sackings. If anyone was going to keep a file, he would inevitably suspect the production department. They bore the brunt of his anger and his ego, day in and day out. In that office he had a whole marching army of enemies. Joe and Simon had hit the nail on the head when they said that no one had any respect for him. Harry also hated not being in control. The idea that someone might be keeping tabs on his affairs would have sent him into orbit. Was Janet the prime suspect? After all, she was one of the few who stood up to Harry. She'd better watch her step.

*

58

The staff at Hartford Optimum Television had finally declared it summer. The weekend sun had decided to stay on for Monday morning. Winter sweaters and dark jackets had been abandoned. Everyone seemed to have dug into their wardrobes and come out wearing last summer's sale disasters.

Ray came bouncing in to inform the general populace that Geraldine had finally become a fashion victim.

'You're not looking too clever yourself,' tutted Liz, trying to stick up for Geraldine, although she couldn't for the life of her think why. Ray was wearing a bright floral shirt in black, tan and yellow. She bent down to her handbag and fished out some dark glasses.

'Cor, that's better. You look like a walking migraine in that shirt,' she said.

'If you think that, then keep those glasses on when you see Geraldine,' said Ray. 'It's bye bye boring old beige and hello hot pink. She must have had a bunk-up at the weekend or undergone some kind of irreversible brain surgery. She's looking like a camouflaged blancmange.'

'This we must see,' said Liz. 'Perhaps boring old G-spot is becoming a fashion statement after all.'

'Don't worry,' said Janet, grim-faced. 'I'm on the case. I'm heading that way. The Fat Controller's just summoned me.' Everyone started humming the *Mastermind* theme.

Janet was just musing about what a rotten start to the week it was to have an audience with Harry and his crotch, when she was stopped in her tracks. Geraldine, sitting at her desk outside his office, truly did look like a camouflaged blancmange. The dress was a sort of voluminous purple and pink concoction, wild by anybody's standards, and completely off the Richter scale by Geraldine's.

Steeling herself not to say anything, Janet swept past and into Harry's office. Yet again, she found herself angry that her heart started pounding the minute she crossed the threshold.

'Good news, Bancroft,' Harry crowed, motioning her to sit down and leaning back in the *Mastermind* chair. 'Clinched a good deal. A series of video shorts with Hot Breaks For Heartaches, plus a really whizzy website. They do singles holidays for saddos. They want ten fifteen-minuters on various holidays, mostly the unusual ones that need more of a hard sell. Your team will love it, something to get their teeth into. Murder-mystery weekends, photography weekends, rambling, line dancing, that sort of stuff.'

Why is the bastard telling me all this? thought Janet, as she smiled sweetly at him. It was Janet who had initially gone to see the people at Hot Breaks For Heartaches and persuaded them that they badly needed some promotion work. She had made the contacts and written the pitch. Harry was now so bound up in his own lies, he'd forgotten what had happened and thought he was still talking to the board.

'Are we confining it to the breaks in this country, or are we including some of the foreign stuff, like the two-week watercolour course in Tuscany and the Provençal cookery weekend?' asked Janet sweetly. Not that I know anything about this company, she thought to herself. Like hell!

'Nope,' said Harry, completely missing the irony. 'Sorry, just the UK stuff. Beggars can't be choosers. Anyway, shove off and get your best people on to it.'

Janet rose, picked up the file Harry handed her and made to leave. At the doorway, she turned back with a mischievous look in her eye.

'Oh, by the way, did you know the catering videos turned up?' she said. 'Would you believe, they were *exactly* where we'd left them. Just some confusion along the line. Mind you, I have had a word with the troops about keeping the office tidier. Shouldn't happen again.'

And with that she swept out, colliding with the ever-eavesdropping Geraldine.

'All you people go round at such a rate of knocks,' she tutted.

'Wow, great frock, Geraldine,' Janet replied. 'That's quite a statement.'

She could have been mistaken, but she thought she saw Geraldine blush for the first time. Perhaps there was a pulse beating under there somewhere after all.

Sue and Janet picked a quiet corner of the GX and sat down. They were both starving, and waited impatiently for their broccoli and Stilton soup and fresh bread.

'I've got to tell you this out of the office and it's totally confidential,' said Janet. 'At least the ashtrays probably aren't bugged here.'

'Okay, understood,' said Sue.

Janet outlined Joe and Simon's visit at the weekend and their invention of a secret file on Harry's alleged activities. She then explained her theory that Harry had moved the tapes the night he'd stayed late.

'I hope I wrong-footed him this morning, because I told him the tapes had turned up in exactly the same place after all,' finished Janet.

'How did he react?' asked Sue.

'He shot me a rather strange look, but I was already on my way out and I didn't want to give the game away.'

'So what happens now?'

'Firstly, I want you to tell me that I am not totally para-noid and reading things into all this that don't exist. And secondly, if you say I'm not paranoid—'

'Which you're not. Your theory makes perfect sense to me.'

'Well then, secondly, it occurred to me that if Harry thinks there's a file on him, perhaps we should create one.'

chapter eight

Over the soup, Janet told Sue about Harry's latest trick, passing off the Hot Breaks For Heartaches triumph as his own.

'It's pretty sick-making, isn't it? I find a brand-new client, persuade them they need a campaign, suss out what they can spend, come up with a treatment and a reasonable budget—'

'And then Harry has an attack of instant Alzheimer's, thinks it was all his idea and gets the glory,' finished Sue.

'Yep,' said Janet. 'That's about the size of it. And then of course he has to have a jolly good crow to those poor souls who came up with the idea, about how it's done. It makes me furious.'

'I'll tell you what would make you even more furious,' said Sue.

'Wassat?'

'Maybe this is the source of the holiday freebie rumour. What Ray told me was all based on what he'd overheard when he was delivering the post early morning down the executive corridor. Harry was on the phone with the door slightly open, and he caught a few cryptic words.'

'Cor, Val's in for a treat then,' said Janet. 'Although it's a bit wasted on her. I suppose one sunkissed holiday beach is the same as another if you're blind drunk.'

'Don't forget we're having another blind-drunk evening with her ladyship later this week. We could mention it then.'

'Or not. Maybe Harry's gone all romantic and he's keeping it as a surprise for her,' said Janet. 'If it is a freebie from this holiday company, then he's not likely to sound off about it, is he?'

'Absolutely not.'

'I don't know why, but I have an overwhelming instinct that we should say nothing about this,' said Janet.

'I think you're right,' conceded Sue.

'Now, changing the subject, I thought I might put Liz on to the Hot Breaks project. They specialize in singles holidays, so maybe there's a chance she'd meet a new man. Do you think it's a bit unsubtle? I mean, do you think she'd automatically think that we're trying to sort out her love life?'

'In a word, yes,' said Sue cheerfully. 'Of course she knows damned well we want her to get married and live happily ever after in Mothercare. Subtlety doesn't come into it. And, come to think of it, we haven't been to a good wedding, or even a christening, in ages.'

When Janet got back from lunch, Nina was positively skipping around the office, much to the amusement of Ray.

'I've lost five pounds this weekend, and two inches off my bum,' she announced.

'Marvellous,' said an unimpressed Ray. 'Must be a weight off your behind, I mean, mind.'

'Don't be sarky,' answered Nina. 'Look, this skirt isn't tight any more. I did it all with a seaweed wrap.'

'Fabulous,' replied Ray, as Nina demonstrated her swirling skirt. 'Wouldn't be any good for me, though.'

'Why not?'

'I don't look good in green.'

'Oh gawd, don't be ridiculous, Ray. Now, be honest, does my bum look less big than it did on Friday?'

'Yes, absolutely. In fact I spotted it across the car park this morning,' said Ray, quite truthfully.

'What?' Nina was agitated. 'My bum or the fact that it's a bit smaller?'

'Oh, everything,' said Ray vaguely. Women, he'd never understand them; they were a constant mystery, apart from being expensive, moody and invariably late.

'Do you think Sam will notice?' pursued Nina.

'Bound to,' Ray lied, trying to redeem himself. 'If I can notice the difference from across the car park, Sam will definitely clock it.'

Nina happily skipped off up to Accounts on some bogus excuse to see the object of her desire.

'One day, Ray,' said Janet, 'you will understand why women are so obsessed with their appearance. We're all convinced that one day we'll be the perfect shape, find the perfect outfit that'll make us look like Audrey Hepburn, and then life will be sublime.'

'Who's Audrey Hepburn?' he asked.

'Before your time,' tutted Janet. 'She was an actress, very beautiful, very elegant and very gamine.'

'Gamine for anything?' asked Ray, suddenly interested.

'No, not where you're concerned. She had more class. For a start, she wouldn't have even allowed you to collect her milk bottles dressed in that shirt.'

Ray glanced down at his multicoloured floral number and grinned.

'Does my head look big in this?' he joked, pretending to model in a mirror.

'Yes, and it will become even more swollen by the time I've beaten you senseless with my handbag,' laughed Janet. 'Now bugger off and do some work.'

Janet went off to view a rough cut of the Hartford tourism video Liz had been working on. They sat in the darkened edit suite waiting for the tape to be spooled back to the right time code.

'Will Harry want to view at this stage?' said Liz, trying to keep the wobble out of her voice.

'No, doubt it,' said Janet. 'Look, I know it's none of my business, but you really mustn't get so scared about Harry. God knows, I shake in my shoes sometimes, but he's just a shit, basically. And not even a talented shit at that.'

'Hmm,' said Liz, more than a tad meaningfully. One day, thought Janet, I'll find out what's happened there. One day.

'Now, the good news,' she said out loud, 'is that we've won a contract to produce some short films about various types of holidays.'

'Oh, brilliant,' said Liz, immediately fantasizing about locations from Florence to Florida.

'Sadly, not all that exotic, I'm afraid,' replied Janet. 'What's your line dancing like?'

'Fat Controller calling, Fat Controller calling,' said Janet in mock station announcer voice. 'Don't worry, Liz. He just wants to thank you for the Hartford tourism video. No hidden agenda, just savour the moment. He likes what you did. Most of the time he thinks we're all pond life. This is our rare chance to surface.'

'I can't go in there,' Liz mumbled, close to tears. Ashen

and shaking, she fumbled for her handbag under the desk.

'Look, I'll come with you if you like,' soothed Janet. 'He's only a great big fat chauvinist bully. Nothing more than that.'

'I don't care what you say, I won't go in there. Anyway, I've got a splitting headache, I must go home.' And with that, Liz picked up her bags and made for the door.

Janet steeled herself to go up to Harry's office.

'Where's Liz?' barked Harry, hardly looking up from the report he was reading.

'Gone home with a splitting headache,' said Janet. Was she imagining it, or was he not the least bit surprised? Perhaps she was reading more into this than met the eye.

'Women's problems, I suppose,' he growled. 'All you women are the same, you and your bloody PMT.'

'That's not very PC, Harry.'

'I don't give a bugger about being PC. The only PC I'm vaguely interested in comes in boxes from PC World. And that's a world away from you lot and your stupid girlie problems. You specialize in messing us all around by getting pregnant, and then it's full speed ahead for the Big Skive.'

'Big Skive? What on earth do you mean?' asked Janet, feeling herself beginning to boil.

'Relaxation classes, time off for a scan, oh I feel sick every day and I might just throw up over my desk, the baby could arrive at any time, and then I must have a nice big chunk of maternity leave while the rest of you do all the work.'

'Well, seeing as I've never had children, this sort of chat is wasted on me,' said Janet, wondering how on earth they had managed to reach such a thorny subject so quickly. She thought of all the women, like Liz and Nina, with so much to offer, who'd give up everything to become a mum if they got half a chance.

'Excuse me, but where do the chaps stand in all this?' she enquired. 'I seem to recall Loopy Liam taking absolutely yonks off because his girlfriend had left him.'

'Exactly my point,' said Harry, thumping the desk as he always did to emphasize a point. 'Liam had a breakdown, perfectly understandable.'

'Crystal clear to me,' Janet muttered, half under her breath. 'So your girlfriend pushing off ranks higher than the trauma of bringing a new life into the world.'

As she walked back to her office, she realized that Harry hadn't even mentioned the Hartford tourism video, let alone thanked her and Liz for all the work they'd put in.

Liz had meant what she said. She'd gone home for the day. Janet's chat with her about her role in the new Hot Breaks series would have to wait until tomorrow.

Janet went back to her desk, where the e-mails were piling up thick and fast. She was still wading through the morning's post when Sue called up from reception.

'Don't forget we're going out with Val on Friday,' said Sue. 'She's booked some new Mexican place down on the waterfront. It's had fantastic reviews.'

'In that case, let's enjoy it for the first and last time,' said Janet. 'Once they've seen Val in action, you can be certain there won't be a reprise.'

'Talking of which,' Sue lowered her voice conspiratorially, 'have you thought any more about keeping a file on Harry? I think you should, you know, just dates and times and short accounts of each horror story.'

'Oh, I dunno,' replied Janet. 'A bit of me knows that I should, but there's another bit of me that's ridiculously loyal to Val and therefore Harry. Crazy though it sounds, I don't like all that scurrying-behind-your-back stuff. I'd rather be upfront. If I'm going to be unpleasant to Harry, then I'd rather do it to his face.'

'I'd like to do something to his face,' said Sue ruefully.

It was eleven o'clock and Val was still in bed, contemplating the empty hours ahead. A fashion preview at Ginette, an exclusive boutique in Hartford, was proving very tempting. Val liked to be ahead of the game in the fashion stakes. Her wardrobe bore the battle scars of that particular illness. Pashminas in every colour, quilted Chanel bags, Fendi baguettes and bowling bags, Jimmy Choo spiky heels; anything that had a waiting list was on Val's wanted list. She had to have that cachet of leading where others followed. And that included ruthlessly marching it all down to the charity shop the moment it was copied on the high street. Val thought of it as merely recycling. No wonder the boutiques always invited her to their previews; she was such a good customer. Val didn't do sales, and couldn't understand why anyone would want to. 'End of the season', 'reduced', 'special purchase', these were alien concepts.

She picked up the phone and rang an old school friend, Charlotte.

'Is Mummy there?' she asked the small voice who answered the phone. After a long pause, a very harassed Charlotte came to the phone.

'Hi, Charlie, it's Val. Listen, I'm going to a preview at Ginette today. Fancy coming out to play?'

'I'd adore to but I've got Henry down with chicken pox, the nanny's just given in her notice and a man's coming to repair the tumble dryer.'

'Oh, bugger,' said Val, wincing at the screams of small children in the background. 'I really felt like a girlies' day out. Never mind, I'll give Susie a call.'

Susie was another old school chum. She'd recently married a chap who did something whizzy in the City and so far was a kids-free zone. She might be available.

Susie's answering machine immediately diverted to her mobile.

'Hi, it's Val. Where are you?'

'Working, darling.'

'Working?'

'Yes, working, sweetie. You know, that thing where you do stuff and they pay you. I'm in this really, really boring office answering the phone and causing chaos.'

'I thought George had promised to love, honour and keep you in Vivienne Westwood?'

'Yeah, so did I,' said Susie. 'Didn't last long, did it? It's not going so well for George at the moment. He didn't get the bonus he'd hoped for. So I've got to work. Dreary, isn't it?' She paused, and Val could hear the click of a lighter and then Susie taking the first big drag.

'Shame, darling. I'd hoped you'd come to a preview at Ginette. We could have had such fun—'

'Oh, for fuck's sake, what kind of place is this!' Susie had suddenly turned her attention away from the phone and was now talking to someone in the office. Voices were raised. 'I didn't realize I'd boarded the ark. No-smoking policy? How can anyone manage that? How totally bloody ridiculous. Oh, Val, are you still there? Did you hear that? Ridiculous, I have to go outside for a fag. Anyway, hon, can't come to the preview. Joined the working bloody classes. Might as well go and put a flat cap on and join them for a fag break.'

Val tried two more old school friends without success. One was away in Italy, according to her housekeeper, and the other was apparently being induced with her third child.

She felt a familiar wave of loneliness sweep over her. Why couldn't she rustle anyone up to go to the preview? What a sad person she'd become. She went downstairs to the kitchen and opened the fridge. A glass of chilled white wine, just to cheer me up, because I deserve it, she thought. And then perhaps another.

Most of the bottle and a packet of cigarettes later, she climbed into her MR2 and drove to Ginette for the preview.

'I know you can do this,' Janet was telling Liz. 'You're long overdue to take more control on a project, and I think this is the perfect one. Especially as you're on a roll after the HOT tourism video. It was a great piece of work.'

Liz sat at her desk, stony-faced.

'Hey, listen, this is a promotion,' pursued Janet. 'You're supposed to be leaping about in excitement. I might be able to get you a decent pay rise after this.'

Still Liz said nothing.

'It's Harry, isn't it?' said Janet. 'Well, whether we like it or not, he's part of the deal here. We go to interesting places, meet interesting people and flog ourselves making interesting videos. The offices aren't bad, the crews know some good jokes, and even the canteen's pasta is sometimes al dente. The only down side is Harry. Every silver lining has a cloud, you know, and ours is the Fat Führer.'

'Look,' said Liz at long last, her voice wavering. 'I'd like to produce the series. I really would. But I'd have to do it without him knowing, if you understand. I don't want any dealings, or any hassle, with him. So could I produce the series but we not tell him? Just pretend that you're doing it.'

'That's the oddest request I've ever heard,' replied Janet, completely flummoxed. 'But if it makes you happy, then fine. You make the programmes, I'll deal with Harry. But sooner or later he'll find out. Sooner or later you'll have to deal with him, unless by chance he leaves the company.'

'Huh! There's about as much chance of Harry leaving as a one-legged man winning an arse-kicking competition.'

'True, but it's a gorgeous thought, though,' Janet grinned. 'Also, if Harry left, we wouldn't have ordeals like Friday night to put up with either.'

'Friday?' asked Liz.

'Our night out with Val. Sue keeps reminding me. We're all booked in at the new Mexican place on the waterfront. It's supposed to be wonderful.'

'No evening's ever wonderful with Val,' said Liz, cheering up visibly as the conversation veered away from Harry. 'Merely eventful. Anyway, one last query. Did you put me on the holiday series in the faint hope I'd meet some new man?'

'Never crossed my mind,' said Janet, unconvincingly.

'Hmm, just as I thought,' replied Liz, laughing. 'I don't hold out much hope of meeting Mr Right at a line-dancing seminar or a patchwork sesh.'

'Keep an open mind. At least he'd be good on his feet or handy with his fingers.'

Another fashion mission safely accomplished, Val left the Ginette boutique laden down with carrier bags containing two shift dresses, a fantastic sparkly cocktail number and all the shoes and bags to match. She'd wear one of the dresses when she took the girls out the following night. Pity they weren't in the right pay league for Ginette's fabulous stuff.

Back home, Val threw open the front door and chucked her bags down in the huge polished oak hallway. Plenty of time to hide them away before Harry came back from work. He was away so much these days, or working late, he never noticed what she wore anyway, so why worry. If she'd answered the door naked he'd still have shouted about the importance of having his dinner on the table. The jolly effect of the champagne at Ginette had now worn off. Time for a top-up, she thought, heading for the kitchen to grab a glass of wine. Also, while the coast was clear, she could put some of the empties and the Ginette carrier bags into black bin liners.

Thursday blurred into Friday. Val awoke with a hangover, trying to focus on the alarm clock. Shit, it was past midday. Loads to do.

She crawled out of bed to run a bath. There was the gym, her reflexologist, a manicure and then the hairdresser's, and she had to get them all done by six o'clock. Good job I can organize myself, she mused, unlike the silly HOT girls, who never made the best of themselves.

Damn her old school friends for being too busy to turn out for the fashion show. Damn the HOT girls for being too poor to turn out for the fashion show. And damn everyone for her having to go alone. It wasn't quite such fun on your own. Nobody to swank to.

Still, she'd give the girls a treat tonight at the new Mexican restaurant. They'd probably been looking forward to it all week, whereas for her it was just another meal she didn't have the bother of cooking. Better have a glance through the papers to find out what was happening in the world, so she could at least follow what they'd all inevitably be rabbiting on about.

Val couldn't admit, even to herself, that the girls from HOT were now increasingly the only company she had.

'How much longer do we have to endure this?' said Nina to the assembled group in the canteen. 'When will it dawn on her that we only go because she asks us and because she pays and because she's the boss's wife?'

'If it was going to dawn on her, it would have done so quite a few mornings ago,' said Liz. 'I personally hate these evenings so much I wish I could wriggle out of them, but I feel I'd be letting you lot down if I didn't go.'

'God, we are all a pathetic lot,' said Janet. 'Let's call this thing what it really is. It's not guilt, pity or sticking up for each other; it's job preservation. And there's nothing wrong with that. Or put it another way, an evening out in a decent restaurant, leaving aside the spectacle and the insults, is another way of making up our salaries. And keeping our jobs.'

'You're right,' chipped in Sue, bringing a tray of coffee over to their table. 'But I think it's time we started to make subtle changes to the way we behave towards her. Instead of taking all the drunken insults on the chin, or listening to fictitious accounts of each other's love lives every time someone goes to the loo, I think we should bite back a little. Just give as good as you get. If she insults you, then lob one back.'

'Bit difficult when you're two stone overweight with a big bum and no prospect of reducing it, and she's an ex-model with a stick-insect figure plus a monthly clothes allowance that's probably five times my mortgage,' said Nina bitterly.

'She can be Claudia Schiffer, Elizabeth Taylor and Mata Hari all rolled into one for all I care,' said Janet. 'The woman's bloody rude and that ain't pretty.'

'It's time we put up a fight,' said Sue. 'She'd be a better person for it in the long run. If she starts up her nonsense tonight, bite back. See what happens.'

Over coffee, the four women fell into the usual discussion about how long it would take for Val to get drunk, insult the waiters and fall over. Modest bets were placed.

chapter nine

Que Pasa?, the new Mexican restaurant, was heaving. It was so packed with animated diners making huge dents in their pay packets that the relentless salsa music was effectively reduced to a subliminal murmur. The restaurant was lit by a mass of different-coloured Tiffany lamps over the tables, reflected by huge mirrors on the walls. Waiters in long starched white aprons negotiated the tables, holding trays above their heads with dishes balanced precariously.

Val instantly hated it. She liked exclusive places where she could be the centre of attention. This was a mistake.

Janet, on the other hand, breathed a sigh of relief. In a place this busy, this noisy, Val and her antics would be a mere blip on the screen. She sipped a glass of mineral water, grateful that she was wearing a strappy summer dress, because with all those bodies and a rather thundery May night outside, it was steaming. She glanced around the table. Liz and Nina were looking as relieved as she was that there was so much distraction. Sue was politely having a conversation with Val, nodding in all the right places but clearly bored out of her skull. She kept firing 'please rescue me' arrows at the others, but they took no notice and just smiled sweetly back.

'Unusual for you to be showing a bit of cleavage,' said Val, glancing disdainfully at Janet as she lit a cigarette. 'You should think about investing in a minimizer bra. Makes such a difference if you're a bit top-heavy.' Val, of course, being an ex-model and still catwalk-thin, had virtually no boobs at all.

'Actually, I think Janet looks terrific,' interrupted Sue. 'Sorry, Val, but you're a bit off the mark on that one. Cleavage is cool this summer. I read in the *Mail* only today that breasts are being worn big this year. So it must be true.'

'Absolutely,' said Liz. 'If you've got it, flaunt it. I only wish I had it.' Liz, tall and willowy, could eat anything and never put on a pound, much to the mock disgust of the others.

But Val wasn't listening to any of this. Unbeknown to them, she was now well into her second bottle of wine, having already drunk one at home just to get herself in the mood for the evening.

'Of course you really should think about your colour before you display that amount of flesh, Janet,' she ploughed on. 'You should give serious thought to some regular sun-bed sessions. Get rid of that pale skin.'

Janet bristled. Liz and Nina bristled. Sue smiled across at Janet and winked as if to say 'go for it'.

'Absolutely *not* on the agenda,' announced Janet.

Val looked startled. No one ever questioned her advice on clothes, hair or make-up. Ever.

'Don't tell me you're hoping to be pale and interesting,' sighed Val as she began rifling through a very small crocodile clutch bag. 'I must fish out a card from my beauty salon for you. They're not the cheapest in town, but you get what you pay for. A few sessions would really make a difference.'

She handed over a card and snapped the bag shut again.

'On the contrary,' said Janet, taking the card without glancing at it, 'far too risky. I wouldn't touch one of those sun beds with a disinfected barge pole. And apart from the danger of skin cancer, a tan is definitely out. It's really dated. Pale is the new brown.'

It took Val a few seconds to assimilate all this. Suddenly her beauty empire's foundations were beginning to feel decidedly rocky.

'Absolutely right, Janet,' chipped in Nina. 'I love the new look, I'm going for it myself. You can wear so many marvellous colours if you're pale. Also, you don't have to walk around slapping grease on all the time to stop your skin flaking. And of course you don't end up with a hide like an old crocodile handbag.'

'Well, sweetie, this one's hardly old, and it cost more than you probably earn in a month,' hissed Val, tapping her bag. 'Anyway, are you still trying to get it together with that ghastly bloke in Accounts? What's his name, Sam?' The wine was really beginning to hit the spot. She took another enormous gulp.

'Only a question of time,' said Janet promptly, before Nina could reply. 'Sam's mad for Nina. He's just plucking up the courage to ask her out.'

'I very much doubt it,' continued Val, now really riled. 'Nobody'd want to go out with the London Derrière, would they?'

Despite the noise, the music and the frantic bustle of the restaurant, an immediate and dreadful silence descended around the table. Nina, initially puzzled at the nickname, looked quickly around at the others. Their downcast looks made her realize they knew exactly who

Val was referring to. As if the comments about Sam weren't bad enough, to find that her bum was the butt of office jokes was just too much. Tears welling up, she picked up her handbag and fled to the loo.

Val, even in her alcoholic daze, sensed she'd gone too far. She called imperiously to the waiters for dessert menus.

'Hate this place,' she proclaimed in just about everybody's earshot. 'Full of plebs and people who don't wash under their armpits. I expect they all enjoy snooker and Stella Artois. We'll go somewhere decent next time. Get out your diaries, girls.'

Without responding, Sue got up and left the table in search of Nina, while Janet and Liz had an attack of convenient deafness and pretended to be completely preoccupied with the dessert menus. Val was left high and dry, having issued an invitation that had been ignored by all.

'More wine,' she shrieked to a passing waiter. 'And take these ghastly plates away.' The waiter gathered up the plates, aware that a tip was now about as likely as him winning a lottery rollover.

Oh no, here we go again, thought Janet; cue insults about Sue and Nina.

'Of course, Sue's aged,' paused Val, 'so well. Amazing for her age, especially after having those ghastly kids. It's only a question of time, though.'

'Time, though, what?' asked Janet.

'Till she finds out,' said Val, viciously.

'Finds out what?'

'Oh come on, Janet, till she finds out her husband's bored and is having an affair.'

'Don't be ridiculous. Sue's one of the most happily married people I know. And so's her husband. The entire world's dog population would have to stray before it would even cross Jon's mind. Look, Val, it may come as a shock, but some people value what they have and are prepared to work at it.' She just stopped herself from adding 'unlike you' to the end of the sentence.

Val shot her a mutinous look and took another huge slug of wine.

'Well, you mark my words,' she snarled, lighting a cigarette.

'Rubbish, Val. If you haven't anything good to say, shut up.' Janet pulled herself up short. She could be talking herself into getting the sack at this rate if she wasn't careful. She deliberately changed the subject.

'Anyway, Val, have you booked anywhere nice for a holiday this year?' She smiled sweetly. God, she sounded like her own hairdresser.

'No,' said Val, rather abruptly. 'In fact, that subject's a bit of a sore point. Harry has to go away soon to some conference, and I bet it's somewhere interesting. The bastard won't take me. I've got to hang on until September when we go the Maldives again.'

'That'll be nice,' said Janet enviously. 'It'll soon be September. Not long to wait.'

'It bloody is,' said Val, in a rage again. 'And anyway, I'm fed up with the Maldives. I get so bored kicking around at home. And Harry's always bloody working. How many hours do they expect? He's rarely home before nine. Perhaps it's my cooking.'

'I didn't think you did any cooking,' said Janet, mentally starting to take notes.

'Well, I can open packets and use a microwave, just like the next person, but it's not really my thing. Mummy always had a cook, so I never saw the need.'

'You could learn, take classes.'

'Don't be ridiculous,' said Val, tossing her head defiantly. 'Harry married glamour, not a galley slave.'

'Anyway, what's this conference Harry's going to?' Janet probed gently.

'No idea, not interested, but it's coming up soon. I thought I might move back home with Mummy and Daddy for the week. Live in a decent house for a change, with proper staff. Anyway, here comes Nina now. I think I might put her in touch with my personal trainer. Get some exercises sorted to shift that derrière. Do you think she'd be offended?'

'Yes,' said Janet. 'Definitely.'

'Good,' said Val, not listening. 'I'll dig out his phone number for her tomorrow.'

Sue and Nina reached the table through the throng and sat down again.

'No desserts,' bellowed Val at them all. 'Too many calories. Just coffee.' With that, she waved again to a passing waiter. But the wine had taken control. Her flailing arm caught an almost full bottle of red wine, which promptly toppled, spilling its contents all over the table. The wine began trickling into their laps. Val, already on her feet to avoid the drips, stalked off to the loo, leaving the others to mop up as best they could before a posse of waiters bearing towels converged on their table.

'I am *not* doing this again,' said Janet, quietly, white with rage. 'So help me, I am not doing it again. I don't care any more that she's the boss's wife. She's a monster. I give you notice that I will invent excuses, I will enter a convent, I will even appear on *Supermarket Sweep*. But I will not do this again.'

'Agreed,' replied Sue, relieved that an end was in sight. 'Let's meet next week, just the four of us, and work out how to knock this ridiculous scenario on the head.'

'Good idea,' said Nina, her eyes smeared black from sobbing in the loo. Waterproof mascara had claimed another victim. When you want to remove it, you need a chisel. When you don't, it smears everywhere.

Janet fished in her handbag for a pen and paper. As usual, this ended up involving a systematic turnout of kit. Janet, being a practical soul, never went anywhere without her filofax, camera, spare film, sewing kit, superglue and two bunches of keys, most of which she hadn't used for years. Then there was make-up, purse and a plethora of pens, receipts and business cards.

'I swear this handbag's haunted,' she muttered, turfing the contents out on the table. 'I'm sure it's my mother at work.'

'I thought your mum was dead,' said Sue, puzzled.

'She is, but she comes back to haunt me. My mother adored handbags. She'd have happily taken root in the bag department at John Lewis. I'm sure she rearranges things in my bags so I can't find them. I know she's watching over me, because when I can't find something, I think of her. She was exactly the same. Buy my ma one of those organizer bags with lots of handy little pockets, and she'd lose everything. Sadly, this is now my inheritance.'

'Quick, put that away,' said Sue urgently, nodding in the direction of Janet's filofax. Val had emerged from the loo and was heading back to the table, a little unsteady on her feet. Waiters hovered, unsure of what she might do next.

Janet hastily stuffed the filofax back into her bag. She still hadn't found a pen.

'Let's meet this time next week,' whispered Sue. 'And definitely no Val on the agenda.'

'Lovely evening,' slurred Val expansively, flopping back on to her seat. 'I'm sure you must all look forward to our little get-togethers.'

Before any awkward silence could follow, Val conveniently filled in the gap herself, losing her balance on the seat and falling backwards on to the next table, clutching the cloth as she went. Diners ducked for cover as chairs, bottles, glasses and dinner plates went flying, scattering their contents like machine-gun fire in all directions.

For the second time that evening, Janet, Nina, Sue and Liz were mopped down by apologetic waiters, along with the next-door-table diners, who were none too amused to discover that their outfits were now spattered with refried beans and jalapeño peppers.

As usual, Val managed to emerge unscathed. Her new lilac Ginette shift dress did not catch a single drop of the low-flying goo. She tutted loudly as everyone else was sponged down, and then made a huge performance about insisting on picking up the bill for the neighbouring table's dinner. The salsa music was suddenly cranked up several notches to distract attention from the ongoing drama.

'A challenge for Stain Devils then,' said Liz, trying to control her anger. 'This lot'll never come out.' She was wearing a cream linen dress and jacket to match that she'd planned to wear to a wedding later that month. Now patterned with red wine and the remains of someone's nachos, it would have made the perfect outfit for the grand opening of an abattoir.

Janet, Sue, Nina and Liz made their way towards the exit, feeling very conspicuous and very stupid. Val, as usual, strutted along like a peacock, looking as immaculate as ever. However, as she reached the small cloakroom by the exit, she started swaying precariously, before completely losing her balance, only managing to stay upright by pulling down a coat stand, complete with a dozen or so jackets and brollies. Once more, waiters rushed in her direction, now mightily fed up with all the problems she was causing. There hadn't been so much food flying since Hartford Players' last Christmas panto.

chapter ten

Harry was sitting smugly at his desk. He'd had a good weekend, all in all. Val had been compliant for once, and he'd spent Sunday morning giving her a serious shagging. She'd also not hit the roof when he'd again mentioned a conference he might be going to. That was unlike Val, he mused; she normally went berserk if he went anywhere interesting and didn't take her. Instead, she seemed to be relishing the idea of a few days in Hampshire with her parents.

'Geraldine,' he bellowed, 'coffee and the Hot Breaks file. Now.'

Geraldine, now firmly back in beige because it was raining, scuttled in with the file and then out again to fetch the coffee.

Harry leaned back in his seat and lit a cigar. He flipped through the file and had a think. This was a big project and he was determined to get it right.

'Get that Bancroft woman in here,' he demanded, as Geraldine reappeared with a cafetière, cup and saucer.

'Harry, I hope you don't mind me saying, but you're not supposed to smoke,' said Geraldine nervously.

'Yeah,' said Harry, still preoccupied with the file.

'It might set off the smoke detectives,' said Geraldine.

'That should give the girls a thrill!' He roared with laughter.

Mystified at his remark, Geraldine went round the office, opened a window and scuttled out again. Harry smiled to himself. Even he had heard the jokes about Geraldine's famous G-spots. But on the plus side, she was fiercely loyal and kept her mouth firmly shut. That, to Harry, was worth its weight in gold. He was also aware that she wasn't exactly the most popular person within the company, keeping herself very much to herself. He liked that too, because as he saw it, it enhanced his power base.

'Ah, Janet, come in, sit down,' he shouted, stubbing out his cigar with venom. Janet reluctantly took up her usual vantage point opposite Harry's crotch.

'I've been thinking about the Hot Breaks project,' he said. 'Might bring in a big shot on this one. I know your lot have their hearts set on it, but you've got to keep that department running with all the other ongoing jobs. Decided I'm going to put a heavyweight on this one.'

'You mean a bloke,' said Janet, trying to keep the bitterness out of her voice.

'Yep. Had a chat with Steven Byfield last week. He recommended a real hotshot with an impressive track record. Might get him down for a chat.'

Steven Byfield was Janet's predecessor. He'd left HOT to go up north to a plum job back in his home town. He'd gone by the time Janet had joined the company, but she'd got the impression that he was well liked. Since then, staff turnover in the production department had been so great that no one from Steven's era remained.

Harry was relishing this. He loved undermining Janet, and this was a perfect opportunity.

'Steven was a great operator here, well respected, good motivator, great loss to the company. So if he says this guy's good, then he probably is.'

'When are you interviewing him?' said Janet, trying not to sound disappointed.

'I'm meeting him for lunch,' smirked Harry. 'Once I've talked through the project with him and sorted out a contract, I'll introduce you.'

'Sounds like it's done and dusted then,' said Janet.

'Yep, more or less. I've heard what this chap's worked on and it's serious stuff. Give your lot a kick up the backside, won't it?'

'Well, they won't exactly be ecstatic when they hear,' said Janet resignedly. 'More underwhelmed, I'd say. There was a lot of competition over who'd get to work on this one. But we'll give this chap a warm welcome and of course I'll put my best researchers on to it.'

'Good, good.' Harry leered at her. 'Now bugger off and get some work done.'

He sat back in amusement as he watched her leave the office. Yes, it was all going well. His thoughts went back to the weekend and his Sunday-morning session with Val. She'd even managed to cook something half decent, even though he had found the Marks and Spencer cartons in the bin afterwards. Might buy the silly cow some flowers on the way home tonight.

What Harry didn't know, of course, was that Val had had a rare attack of remorse about Friday night's scenario in the Mexican restaurant. She'd woken on Saturday morning with a whopping hangover and realized for once that she had behaved badly. She vaguely recalled colliding with a table and food showering everywhere. Eventually she'd ferreted in her bag and found a Visa receipt for over seven hundred pounds. That confirmed that she'd paid not only for the girls, but also for the table next door. Oh well, an evening to remember, she shrugged. But there was still a nagging doubt, as she stared at the bleary face in the bathroom mirror, that she'd somehow upset someone. So she tried to make it up by being nice to Harry.

While Harry was sitting in his office, relishing the wheeling and dealing he was planning, for Val the week ahead stretched out like an interminable sea of boredom. She'd eventually got up and had a coffee over daytime telly, but now what? She could ring a girlfriend and meet for lunch, but she was still stung by all the rejections last week. Even if any of them were free, the talk was all babies these days. Val didn't know the price of Pampers and had no intention of finding out.

She poured herself a glass of wine and flipped through her address book, trying to find an old school friend who was child-free. Page after page indicated familiar names with new ones scribbled next to them, changes of surname on marriage plus children's names as they arrived. One or two already had husbands' names crossed out. They were the least fun because their sole topic of conversation was custody battles and the cost of their lawyers. It all boiled down to Susie again, the friend whose husband's City job hadn't quite lived up to expectations.

'She's on a fag break, love,' said a cockney voice. 'She'll ring you back.'

At least she hasn't been fired, thought Val, recalling their last conversation. She poured another glass of wine and painted her nails as she waited for the call.

'Val, it's Susie. Brilliant of you to ring, sweetie. Let's meet for lunch. One o'clock. Somewhere nearby. I only get an hour.' She rang off abruptly.

Thank God I don't have to put up with that shit, mused Val as she got ready to go out. She put on one of her new shift dresses from Ginette. Pale blue, with a soft cashmere cardie and suede spiky heels to match.

An hour later she was nursing a large glass of wine in a little French brasserie just round the corner from Susie's office. Susie came in, shaking the rain off her trenchcoat and umbrella.

'You look wonderful as always,' she said, taking in Val's outfit. 'Can tell you don't work, sweetie.'

'How's that?' queried Val, lighting a cigarette.

'You wouldn't be able to walk from the nearest car park to my office in those heels,' she laughed. 'Listen, darling, I've joined the Dark Ages. It's bloody archaic. People ring up, they get stroppy, you have to be nice to them, it's ghastly.'

'What do you do there?' said Val, taking menus from a waiter.

'Market research, you know, that stuff where women in sensible shoes hang around on street corners and pounce on you with questions about custard powder.'

'You don't have to do that, do you?' Val was appalled.

'No, thank God. I just answer the phone and help collate the reports. Anyway, let's order quickly, because I have to be back on the dot of two. Pasta's fine for me,' she added, glancing quickly at the menu.

'God, it sounds like school again,' said Val.

'Not far off. I wish now I'd paid more attention to maths and typing. I was more keen on learning how to arrange flowers and how to get in and out of a sports car. Didn't think I'd ever need all that other stuff.'

'How long are you going to do this for?' asked Val. 'What's happened to George's job?'

'Well, basically he missed out on a big promotion, and then they cut his bonus because he buggered up some deal, so it effectively halved his salary. And we'd just taken out a huge mortgage.'

'So what does that mean?'

'It means, sweetie, that we have to sell the house.'

'But don't your earnings help a bit?'

'Hey, Val, get real. I earn diddly-squat, but it might at least help to pay for the solicitor.'

'Solicitor? For the house sale?'

'No, sweetie, for the divorce.'

Before they could continue, two waiters arrived bearing a huge steaming bowl of pasta, which they proceeded to ladle out with great aplomb. This was followed by a bit of show-biz with a huge phallic pepper mill. They then hovered, topping up wine glasses and hoping to pick up the threads of what sounded like an interesting conversation.

Val had to wave them firmly away before Susie could continue.

'Divorce. Yes, the D-word. Isn't it frightfully grown-up?'

'No, it's awful. I'm really sorry. It only seems last week I was in Jasper Conran, drinking champagne at your wedding.'

'Last summer, actually. After George cocked up at work, I went off him in a big way. We ended up not speaking, just shagging.'

'Bit like me and Harry.'

'Don't tell me yours is on the rocks too. I've got this marvellous solicitor, I'll find you his card.' Susie started to fish in her handbag.

'No, it's not got to that. In fact, I've never even thought about it. No, Harry and me, we're all right really. Probably because he's not there much. In fact, he's off to some conference at the end of the month and I'm quite looking forward to having the place to myself.'

'I've always thought he was a bit of a bully,' said Susie, offering Val a cigarette, then taking one herself and lighting them both. 'But there again, perhaps it's just the age gap. What's the difference between you two?'

'Twelve years.'

'At least he's in a good job. And you're not losing your house.'

The waiters were back, scooping up the hardly touched plates and bringing cappuccinos.

'I'm really sorry it's got to this,' said Val. 'But you don't seem all that upset.'

'No, I'm not, am I?' said Susie, cheerfully. 'I'm having an affair with my boss.'

'Bad news,' said Janet to Liz as they sat down to a coffee in the staff canteen. 'Harry's hiring in some whizz-kid to produce the Hot Breaks series,' she said apologetically. 'I feel awful now because I had hoped you could have had a big role in that. I know you wanted to keep it a bit low-key but you were really ready for this. There will be a next time, I promise, if I have anything to do with it.'

'Honestly, Janet, I'm rather relieved. You know my thoughts on the subject. I just didn't want to be in Harry's firing line. I'd much rather take a more secondary role.'

Janet stirred her coffee thoughtfully. 'I think you'll be the only person on the planet who will look at it that way. Lots of people in the department wanted to have a crack at that. Let's see what this new chap is like. Harry's insistent that I put the best people on to the series under him. So you're still in the frame as associate producer if you don't mind, plus I thought I'd give Bob and Nick a go.'

'Good idea,' said Liz. Bob and Nick were two fairly new researchers who were already making their mark as budding workaholics.

'That's settled then,' said Janet, getting up to go. 'Let the excrement hit the ventilation.'

Janet was right. There was uproar about Harry hiring in a producer on what everyone saw as a prestige project. The whingeing went on all week until she had to call an impromptu meeting and put a stop to it.

'Whether we like it or not,' she announced, 'Harry's the boss and what he says goes. I know we all think it's unfair, but moaning and groaning won't make any difference. I too would like to have played a more key role, but Harry's keeping this one close to his chest. So just accept it and get on with your work. Paul Burns is the new producer/director Harry's hired and he arrives on Monday. So I don't want any rubbish from any of you. We will make him welcome, we will be helpful, we will be cheerful. If he's as good as I'm led to believe, then we will all learn from him. A lot. He has a very impressive CV.

'Now, Liz will be associate producer on this project, and Nick and Bob will be the researchers. Wish them luck and shut up. This isn't *Stars in Their Eyes*, this is real life.'

chapter eleven

Friday night at Janet's was to be the council of war on Val. It was a week on from the disastrous Mexican evening, and the clothes worn that night were still going back and forth to the dry cleaner's in an attempt to shift the stains.

'Come scruffy,' Janet had insisted. 'I'll light candles so you'll all look marvellous if you're too tired to tart up. I'm warning you now, I can't be bothered to cook, so it'll be an Indian takeaway and a pudding out of a box.'

They all sat comfortably around the table, scooping up the last of the lamb korma with chapattis, swished down with cans of Bud.

'We have to find a way of stopping this restaurant lark without inciting anything,' said Sue, opening the bidding. 'We could fob Val off by each of us not being available on different dates, so she could never sort out an evening.'

'But that's only a temporary measure,' said Nina. 'I think we've got to be more brutal than that. I think someone should just tell her to her face.'

'What?' said Janet. 'Something like "We all hate you, Val, your stupid evenings and you falling down drunk." I'm sure she'd appreciate that.'

'Well, I don't appreciate what she called me,' said Nina,

still deeply upset at the discovery of her nickname. 'I've felt a complete berk all week. I think everyone's staring at my bum and laughing. I've lost all confidence and I blame Val.'

'She didn't make it up, though,' pointed out Janet.

'No, but at least I wouldn't have found out about it if she'd kept her stupid gob shut.'

Nina was close to tears again. Sue moved the conversation on swiftly.

'I think we should look at the root of the problem,' she said. 'Now, we could say it's Val's drink problem, we could say it's because she's lonely, and we could say it's because she's spoiled. But I think we have to go further back than that to the real root of the problem. And that's Harry. Harry's the reason she's lonely. He's never there. Harry's the reason she drinks. If he treats her like he treats people at work, then she has every reason to get pissed.'

'But she doesn't have every reason to be rude and insulting to us,' chipped in Nina.

'Well, that's drink talking, but also she's been very protected,' said Sue. 'She's come from a privileged background. Mum and Dad have pots of money, she's been to a posh school, she's done a bit of modelling so she's used to turning heads. But now she's married to Harry and she's met an even bigger ego on a stick.'

The others nodded in agreement. More beer was produced. Several slurps on, Sue continued.

'What we need to do is tackle Harry, and that's difficult, because he's not just her husband, he's our boss.'

'Our problems would be solved overnight if Harry left the company,' said Janet thoughtfully. 'If Harry jumped or was pushed, our lives would be sublime. Well, almost.'

Sue took a deep breath and surveyed the others.

'I don't know whether I should tell you this.' She looked suddenly troubled. 'It's more than my job's worth, but there again my job's not worth much as far as Harry's concerned.'

'Well, go on.' Three pairs of eyes bored into her.

Sue realized there was no turning back. She coughed and fiddled with her beer can, hoping the spotlight would be turned off. The three pairs of eyes continued to bore.

'Okay, I'll tell you. It's only a theory, it's just a suspicion, a gut feeling, but you get a real sense of people's characters when you sit at that reception desk and take their phone calls or pass on their messages. Watch them go in and out of the building.'

'Yes, go on,' the three pairs of eyes urged.

'Well, things don't quite match up,' said Sue, choosing her words carefully. 'Harry's up to something. He leaves the office bang on six, but he doesn't always go straight home. If I work a late shift, I occasionally get a call from Val, usually a bit pissed, surprise, surprise, asking where Harry is. Say nine o'clock. So what does he do in those three hours?'

'He might be going out for dinner with a client,' said Janet. 'That's perfectly feasible.'

'No, wrong body language,' said Sue. 'When you sit at that desk long enough, you spot it. Someone leaving the building *after* work moves in a very different way to someone leaving the building to do *more* work.'

'My God, you could give Desmond Morris a run for his money,' said Liz in awe.

'If he's out late, why doesn't Val just ring him on his mobile?' asked Nina.

'Good question,' said Sue. 'When Val rings the office in the evening, she's already tried him on his mobile and it's

95

switched off. Always. That's why she rings. Now, during the day, Harry's a mobile phone-aholic. He's got the damn thing permanently clamped to his ear. Two rings max and he answers. But not during this mysterious three hours between six and nine. It is always switched off. Out of curiosity I even tried it myself the last time Val rang. I thought she might just be too pissed to get the number punched in, but she was right. It was switched off.'

'So, a secret woman,' mused Janet. 'I must say, I never suspected that. Not with a head-turner like Val in tow.'

'I haven't said that,' grinned Sue, who was now beginning to enjoy the limelight. 'But here's another thing. If his and Geraldine's direct lines are busy or they're both away from their desks, their calls get diverted to the switchboard. And just occasionally a woman phones for Harry. Distinctive voice, slight Italian accent. Again, when you do my job, you tend to pick up on voices.'

'What happens when she rings him?' asked Janet.

'If I can't put her through, she never leaves a message, nor a number to call. Never.'

'So what else do you sense?' asked Janet. 'Come on, Sue, you're on a roll here. Trot it all out.'

'Well, this rumour about the freebie holiday.'

'Yes?' they all chorused, the room now electric with anticipation.

'It's true,' Sue announced.

'For definite?' asked Janet.

'Abso-defo-lutely,' said Sue triumphantly. 'And how do I know? Because his tickets and hotel voucher arrived today, delivered by courier.'

'How do you know that's what they were?' asked Liz, incredulous.

'Quite simple,' said Sue, laughing. 'You don't have to be

Miss Marple to work that one out. It said "Tickets" on the envelope.'

'That could be anything, though,' said Janet. 'Theatre tickets, train tickets, parking tickets. We can't jump to conclusions.'

'Oh yes we can,' said Sue. 'I called through to Harry to say that some tickets were in reception for him. All I got were the usual unpleasant grunts. Then a guy from Hot Breaks For Heartaches rang just to make sure that the courier had delivered the air tickets and hotel voucher for Mr Hampton. In view of Harry's earlier reaction, I didn't bother to pass the message on. There was no need, you see, because he already knew they'd been delivered.'

'Well, well, well,' mused Janet as she eased a coffee and walnut gateau out of a supermarket box and cut it up into slices. 'Slaved for hours over this, so you'd better enjoy it,' she threatened.

They had a short coffee and gateau intermission. Everyone fell silent for a few seconds, as they took a mouthful.

'I think I thawed it out rather beautifully,' said Janet, trying to take some credit. 'Now, back to the plot. It does all tie in with what Ray overheard that morning. At the time I thought he was gossiping, just for a laugh, but I did question him about it quietly and he swears it's what he heard.'

'How Harry thinks he's going to pull that one off, I don't know,' said Sue. 'Unless we've got this very wrong, he's actually taking Val as a surprise and it's totally legit. Well, more or less, as freebies go.'

'I doubt it,' said Janet. 'I've known Harry for too long. If he's up to something, he's usually up to his armpits in it.

Everything Harry does is for one purpose and one purpose only. It's called personal gain.'

'This still doesn't solve the problem of Val,' said Nina. 'I don't want to be in the same room as that woman any longer. She may be the boss's wife, she may look like a supermodel, but she's a superbitch as far as I'm concerned.'

'Agreed, but if we're to solve Val, we probably have to solve Harry as well,' said Sue.

Suddenly Janet thumped the table in triumph. Coffee cups jumped and candles flickered precariously.

'I've got it,' said Janet. 'What makes Harry twitchier than anything? Answer: when he's not in control. When he doesn't have all the trump cards. Or when someone's got something on him.'

'I'd like to get something on him,' said Nina. 'Some of the canteen's disgusting lumpy custard for a start.'

'No, seriously, do you remember when Joe and Simon hinted that there was a secret file being kept on him? Of course it was a hoax, but at the time I thought it was an interesting idea. Well, suppose we take that one stage further. Sue and I half joked about keeping a file on him, dates and times of incidents, that sort of stuff, but let's delve a little deeper. Let's find out what happens between six and nine, for a start. Let's find out about this freebie holiday. Let's find out what he's really up to. It could be much worse than we thought.'

'You mean, snoop?' queried Liz, who'd been remarkably quiet throughout the evening.

'Yep, snoop,' said Janet. 'But let's not risk getting caught. We'll log all incidents, dates, times, et cetera, and put the information in a designated pot in the computer system.'

'Bit risky,' said Sue. 'Harry's been snooping around the offices, hasn't he? And nothing's safe in any part of the computer. Better to write things up and store them somewhere off the premises.'

'I'll take notes,' exclaimed Janet, 'then I'll pop them in my handbag and put them into my computer here at home. Then we run no risk of being found out.'

'Hang on a minute, though,' said Sue. 'I thought your handbag was supposed to be haunted.'

'Yep, it is, but my mother will be watching over it.'

They began to plot. Sue would monitor calls as best she could, noting when Harry left work and the dates and times that Val rang in wondering where he was. Plus she would try to get some sort of handle on the woman with the Italian accent by noting the number she rang in on. Liz, since she was working closely with the people from Hot Breaks, would try to suss out whether Harry had indeed landed a freebie. Nina, as production secretary, would keep an eye on the office. She would make notes of instances where files or belongings had been moved, and monitor any relevant gossip. All notes would be handed to Janet personally and the whole thing would be codenamed Operation Haunted Handbag.

The war council meeting over, Janet got up to make more coffee. The evening had begun on a note of low morale and had ended with a battle plan and a triumphant air. They agreed to reconvene in a fortnight at Sue's house.

'It's kind of weirdly exciting,' said Sue to Nina as they walked back down Janet's path to their respective cars.

'Well, if it shuts that silly cow up, then it's all worth it,' said Nina, who was still seething about Val's remarks. 'So long as it brings the pair of them down, it suits me.'

chapter twelve

The first Monday of June, and the only thing flaming about it was a row breaking out in the production office between the tropical team and the shivery radiator huggers over the temperature of the air-conditioning. In the midst of this, Janet had to go off and meet the new whizz-kid producer, Paul Burns.

Harry sat crowing in his *Mastermind* chair as Janet was introduced to a man in the loudest pinstripe suit she had ever seen. Al Capone would have killed for the pattern alone. Along with the wide lapels, trousers with huge turn-ups, red silk tie and matching handkerchief, Paul Burns had a tan that would have done George Hamilton proud. He looked more like a spiv from *Bugsy Malone* than a programme producer. Suddenly Janet felt too casually dressed in her black and white spotted dress and long black cardigan.

Harry did the honours and then summoned the perennially beige Geraldine in with the coffee. He gave Paul a brief rundown about the company and the proposed campaign for Hot Breaks. The conversation took twenty minutes, punctuated constantly by mobile phones going off. Harry took four calls and Paul Burns five. Bit excessive for your first morning at work, thought Janet. Clearly it didn't bother Harry, who nodded appreciatively at everything Paul said.

To her shame, Janet found herself listening more intently to Harry's calls for clues, following Friday night's war council, rather than to all the discussion about the company and the project. It all seemed harmless enough, except that she found herself wondering why people would ring his mobile when he was more likely to be at his desk during business hours. She was musing on this when she suddenly became aware that Harry had asked her a question and she had no idea what it was. She feigned a coughing fit.

'When my production head has recovered her health, I'll get her to introduce you to the team you'll be working with,' glowered Harry. 'See you for lunch, Paul. I've booked a table at Shiraz.'

Shiraz? I've never been taken out for lunch at Shiraz, thought Janet bitterly. Typical blokes, bond together instantly like Loctite and off they go to spend huge dollops of company cash. If I whacked in a bill for pie and chips with Liz at the GX, I'd get a lecture on saving money. Mustn't get bitter, though, she thought, leading Paul out of Harry's office and down the corridor to her department.

Introductions to Liz, Nick and Bob over, Janet installed Paul at Simon's empty desk and showed him how to use the phone and boot up the computer. She then handed him the Hot Breaks file and left him to it.

She'd hardly settled at her desk to whizz through another fifty e-mails when she was summoned back to Harry's office.

'Burns is top-notch,' he bellowed at her. 'Make sure

your people get their act together. This has got to be good, or else.'

'How much do you want me to get involved?' asked Janet.

'I'm taking personal charge of this one. Just recognize that Paul's a good operator and leave him to it,' said Harry. 'Listen and learn, this chap's dynamite.'

Dynamite or not, Paul Burns spent the morning peering at the Hot Breaks file and then disappeared off without a word for lunch with Harry. Neither returned for work that day.

'Janet? It's Liz. I'm back in the office at lunchtime. Can we meet for lunch? The Groin Exchange? Great.'

Janet replaced the phone in its cradle. Liz sounded really fed up. She'd been on the road for three days, doing a recce and setting up filming for the Hot Breaks series. Perhaps the enforced jollity of line dancing and murder mystery weekends was getting to her.

Janet went back to her current project – a video series and website for a chain of estate agencies. Not quite in the league of Hot Breaks, but a chance to snoop around other people's houses and film them. It was going to be a big money-spinner for HOT, with the bonus that it would be an ongoing earner for at least a year because of the need for constant updates. The properties were being divided up into millionaire bracket, waterside and seaview properties, equestrian, farms, flats, urban, and first-time buyers.

There was keen competition, particularly among the girls in the office, to work on the series.

'Glorified window-shopping,' said Ray, scornfully. 'You girls are only ever a whisper away from a chance to spend money.'

'Not at these prices,' replied Janet. 'Some of them are so wicked, even if the entire office clubbed together we couldn't afford them.'

'Might be cosy, though,' said Ray. 'Bags I bunk up with Veronica.'

Veronica was the current office fantasy girl. Tall and blonde, with endless legs and rumoured-to-be-enhanced boobs, she had just joined the company and was working alongside Nina as a production secretary. Nina lived in fear that Sam might take a pop at Veronica and blow her chances for ever. Despite looking as though she'd stepped from the pages of *FHM*, Veronica was never destined to fit in with the general lunacy and terrible jokes in the department. She kept herself aloof and the blokes soon realized that although she looked like a dead ringer for Caprice, she wasn't much fun. So Nina, for all her angst, was still the most popular production secretary because she told a good joke, could drink a pint and was once spotted in the car park changing the air filter on her car.

Janet made her way to the GX, ordered a spritzer and sat in a corner waiting for Liz. Her mobile went off. Probably Liz, to say she was delayed. She rummaged through her handbag to find her phone. It never mattered which zip pocket she put it in, it was never there when she wanted it. By the time she'd found it, the caller had rung off. The display told her it was HOT reception desk. She pressed last-number redial.

'Don't tell me.' Sue answered immediately. 'You couldn't find the phone in that bloody bag of yours.'

'Yeah, sorry,' replied Janet, bootfaced.

'Well, here's one for Operation Haunted Handbag,' said Sue, triumphantly. 'Two calls yesterday for the Fat Controller from the Italian job, and Val phoned up at nine forty-five last night wondering where Harry was. He'd left at six on the dot, as he's done every night this week.'

'And?'

'And yes, his mobile was switched off. As soon as I'd got rid of Val, I tried his number.' She mimicked the recorded message: '"The number you have dialled has been switched off. Please try later." Have you ever known Harry's mobile to be switched off?'

'Nope,' said Janet. 'Harry has no shame about answering his phone wherever he is. I've even seen him take a call in the middle of one of our press presentations. How was Val, by the way? Did she invite us out again?'

'No, mercifully not. But there again, she sounded rather pissed. Having said that, how would we know? I'm not sure what she'd sound like sober. Is it possible for Val to go out and not fall into other people's dinners?'

'No idea,' replied Janet. 'Anyway, gotta go, Liz is heading this way for a pow-wow. Keep up the good work.'

Liz sat down, distress written large on her face. She might as well have carried a placard.

'Gin and tonic, please,' she said.

'Blimey, you are fed up,' said Janet, scuttling off to the bar to fetch Liz's drink and order a couple of prawn sandwiches.

'Cheers, it's a double,' she said, plonking the glass down in front of Liz who immediately took a huge slug.

'Paul Burns is total crap,' Liz announced. 'Apart from his appalling dress sense, he hasn't a clue what he's doing. He just sits there with his Gucci briefcase full of gizmos, and in between the endless calls and e-mails on his laptop and twiddling with his vast collection of electronic organizers, he comes up with gems like "Oh, you know what you're doing," "I'll just leave you to get on with it" or my personal favourite, "Yeah, whatever." It's almost as if he doesn't know how to do the job.'

'What exactly *has* he done so far?'

'Bugger all,' she spluttered, taking another slug of gin and tonic. 'I've been out on the road, setting up and doing a little bit of pre-filming for the first two videos, but I don't really know what he wants. I assumed that as he was hired to direct the series, that's what he would do, but he seems hell bent on staying out of the fray. I get the distinct impression that I'm going to end up directing them as well. And then I can predict it all: I'll come back with the thing shot one way and he'll say, "No, no, no, I wanted it done another way." I just know that I'll end up taking the blame.'

'Hm, this is serious,' said Janet. 'Tell you what, if he's in the office this afternoon, I'll have a word with him. And if I don't get any joy, I'll go and have a moan to Harry. It would be great to shoot down his new wunderkind.'

'No, don't do that. Don't go to Harry, I mean,' said Liz, that anxious look back in her eyes.

Janet looked at Liz for a moment, taking in the ashen face and frightened gaze.

'What's up with you about Harry? Look, we all know he's a big fat bully, but for you it's something else, isn't it?'

'Yes, well, um . . .' faltered Liz. 'I did have a problem with him a while ago, but it's quite a long time ago and I really can't talk about it.'

'Are you sure that's wise? Whatever it is, it keeps coming back to haunt you. Wouldn't it be better to get it out of your system?'

Tears started to trickle down Liz's face. She took another determined slug of gin and tonic, followed by a deep and purposeful breath.

'Yes, you're right. I should tell someone, and that some-one should be you, because I trust you, Janet. I don't want anyone else to know because . . .'

The tears were rapidly turning from a trickle into a deluge.

'Go on, spit it out. It will make you feel better.'

'This has to be in total secrecy. I don't want anybody to know except you. Understand?' she said, wiping her eyes frantically with a tissue.

Janet nodded.

'It was just after I'd joined the company, about two years ago. I'd only been there about three weeks when Harry turned up on my doorstep late one night.'

'Whaaaat?' Janet wished she'd ordered a large gin too.

'He . . . he . . . foisted himself on me. He'd brought a bottle of something with him. God knows what was in it, but it knocked me almost unconscious.'

Liz stopped to take in the shock on Janet's face. She took another slug and continued: 'It was only a few weeks after my mother died, and I'd been drinking that night because I was so upset. I'd sat in front of the telly, had a good cry and drunk a bottle of wine. So I was very vul-nerable. When he turned up on my doorstep, I couldn't quite take in what was happening.'

'Did he say why he was there?' Janet asked.

'I recall some crap about him fancying me the minute I'd arrived at HOT. Thought I was very special and that he could really help me with my career. That was why he was there, to push my corner, get me up a rung or two, that sort of thing. But – and here's the clever bit – we had to keep it a secret because the others would suspect he was favouring me. Of course, I look back now and it's all bollocks, but at the time I believed what he said. Why

106

shouldn't I? Except that he made me cement our new "relationship" with a drink from this mystery bottle, and next thing I found myself in bed, not a stitch on, with Harry putting on his clothes to leave.'

'Bloody Nora,' said Janet. 'And why on earth did he think you'd keep your mouth shut?'

'Well, the next day I went in to confront him about what he'd done. He accused me point blank of being a liar and said that I must be imagining it. Worse still, he warned me that what I'd said amounted to slander and that if he caught me telling anyone else I'd not only get the sack, but he'd take legal action and refuse to give me a reference.'

'Phew, very clever. But it couldn't have just been a nightmare, could it?' said Janet, her mind racing. 'On your own admission, you were upset about your mum.'

'No,' said Liz, smiling bitterly. 'I knew he'd had sex with me. Apart from the tell-tale signs, I eventually decided to do a pregnancy test just to be sure.'

'And?'

'It was positive.'

chapter thirteen

They ate their prawn sandwiches in silence. Janet went to fetch more drinks from the bar. For once, she was totally speechless. Liz gathered strength from her second gin and continued the tale.

'I'd only just got the job. It was like a dream come true; I felt it was a whole new lease of life that would help me through my grief over Mum. I'd always wanted to get into telly or film and I couldn't believe my luck. Next thing I knew, I was having an abortion.' She started to cry again.

'Liz, I had no idea,' comforted Janet. 'What a truly horrible thing to happen. Forgive me for asking the obvious, but are you sure it was Harry's?'

'Absolutely. I hadn't had sex for months. Mum got ill, I'd been commuting to the hospital to see her. Didn't have time for a boyfriend. So it wouldn't have needed a DNA test.'

'Did you tell Harry?'

'God, no. He'd already threatened me with legal action and the sack. No, I couldn't cope with any more from him, so I went and got sorted out. The trouble is,' she started to break down again, 'now I so desperately want a baby, and maybe that was my only chance. There's always a risk you can't have one, after you've had an abortion.'

'Liz, I'm sure you'll meet someone smashing, have lots of gorgeous babies and live happily ever after,' soothed Janet. 'But I don't think you'd have liked a mini Harry, would you? Besides, to be briefly practical, you'd have had an uphill struggle to get him to recognize the baby as his, let alone stump up some maintenance. No, perhaps it was the best thing to do.'

Liz took another huge slug of gin. 'It's a bit ironic,' she continued with a half-smile through her tears, 'that of all people, Val should pick on me to join her little social outings. That's why this must remain a secret. In a funny way, I feel slightly sorry for her, forking out for all those expensive meals. Buying dinner for a woman who got pregnant by her husband.'

'Well, let's hope we can stop that soon. I think even Val might have recognized that she blew it last time,' said Janet. 'Normally by now she's on the blower arranging another of her ghastly soirées. Anyway, at least I now understand exactly why you so hate going into Harry's office.'

'I've never gone in there on my own, only with one of you lot, and even then I've managed to avoid it where possible,' said Liz, still sniffing. 'But do you know, after we had that meeting about Harry and Val at your place last week, my mind went back to that dreadful night and I remembered some more about what happened.'

'Oh, what in particular?' Janet was trying not to sound too curious.

'Two things. Firstly, I had the distinct impression that he didn't expect me to refuse him. He was arrogant enough to think I must fancy him rotten. And secondly, the stuff about me being so talented and him "helping me" with my career sounded like a very well-worn path.'

'I think it probably is,' sighed Janet.

Back in the production office, a Friday-afternoon atmosphere was in full swing. With the weekend in their sights, everyone was behaving badly. Ray was winding Nina up, claiming Sam had been headhunted by a big multinational. Nick, one of the researchers on the Hot Breaks project, was very publicly chatting up the haughty Veronica, who was wearing a face like fizz, but definitely not of the champagne variety. And there was general outrage because someone had started a rumour that from Monday every member of staff would be charged for coffee.

Against this furore, nobody noticed Liz's recently tear-stained face and swollen eyelids. She sank down behind her desk, grateful to be on home territory. Paul Burns was nowhere to be seen.

'Anyone seen Paul?' enquired Janet.

'Paul who?' came back the general response.

'I hope he Burns in hell,' joked Ray. 'Along with Harry. They seem to be new best friends.'

Janet sat down at her desk and whipped through the e-mails that had arrived since lunchtime. Fifty-three! How did anyone get any work done any more? She decided to devote the rest of the afternoon to the new property series, but the same dilemma kept coming back into her head. Should she go and have a word with Harry about Paul? Should she leave him to dig his own hole and fall into it? Or would Liz, as she predicted, get the blame if Janet didn't say anything? She picked up her phone and dialled the dreaded Geraldine.

110

'Harry Hampton's office,' came the imperious voice.

'Is he there?' asked Janet.

'No, he's having lunch with Paul and the boss of Hot Breaks.'

Janet looked at her watch. It was 4.30.

'Just a quick snack then,' she said, jokingly. Humour was, of course, always lost on Geraldine.

'I think you ought to know, it's a very important project,' Geraldine replied huffily. Janet immediately read the implication in her voice, namely: it's out of your league, luv.

'Pity, I did want to have a chat with him about that very project before it gets too far down the road,' said Janet, trying to sound unruffled.

'I really don't think you should be bothering Harry about it,' bounced back Geraldine, who couldn't resist putting the boot in. 'Remember, he's used to handling top-level projects like this. Been doing it for years. It's all mist to the grill for him.'

Janet paused to unravel what she'd just heard. 'Absolutely, Geraldine,' she agreed. Then she replaced the phone and burst into fits of laughter.

'I claim the best G-spot of the week,' she proclaimed to all those in earshot. They all screamed and applauded, all except Veronica, who everyone was now convinced had had a humour bypass.

Janet was just immersing herself once again in the property file when Sue rang from reception.

'Got time for a quick coffee?' she asked. 'I've another contribution to Operation Haunted Handbag.'

They met in their usual corner. Sue was looking triumphant once again, absolutely bursting to impart some gossip.

'Get a load of this,' she said, eyes gleaming. 'I've only got cover on reception for five minutes so I'll have to tell you quickly.'

Janet nodded, indicating for her to go on.

'Val rang up this afternoon to speak to Harry. Pissed as usual, bit slurry down the phone. I put her through to Geraldine, who must have told her that he was out to lunch with Paul and someone else. Then she rang back to say she'd tried his mobile and it was switched off. Now, we know what that means. It means he might be somewhere or with someone he shouldn't. So I did a bit of detective work.'

'What did you do?'

'I got Geraldine to tell me where they were lunching. Hold on to your hat here, it was at the Grand.'

The Grand in Hartford was so unbelievably grand that even Val didn't take the girls there. Michelin-starred, with the London Met Bar atmosphere and prices to match, it featured in all the 'great restaurants of the galaxy' lists. Lunch for three – Harry, Paul and the Hot Breaks supremo – would come to something in the region of three hundred pounds. And the rest, especially if they went through the vintage wine list and the best port.

Sue continued her tale: 'So I rang the Grand and said I had an urgent message for Mr Hampton, who was with a party having lunch. They put me through to the maître d' and I said that a bit of discretion was required. I had a call from the gentleman's wife, which might be a bit awkward, bearing in mind the company. I sort of hoped that he might just tell me who was at the table. And sure enough, he did! There were four people, not three. Three men and a woman. I asked him if he might help me out

112

by describing the woman. In his words, she was young and dark-haired. Italian-looking? I queried. Yes, he said. We left it that he would discreetly tell Harry to call his wife when he had a moment.'

'Amazing, well done,' replied Janet. 'I hope this isn't going to rebound on you.'

'No, I thought about that,' said Sue. 'My fallback position to Harry is that Val was sounding a little strange, i.e. pissed, on the phone and I felt I had to get a message to him as a matter of urgency. The maître d' sounded delightfully camp and was obviously used to having a restaurant full of people who were with people they shouldn't have been.'

'Interesting,' mused Janet. 'Obviously it could just be a coincidence. She might be the wife of the Hot Breaks guy, or even Paul Burns. Although I can't believe there's a woman in *his* life, not with that ghastly wardrobe. But the clue is the mobile being switched off. It seems that whenever Harry's mobile is off, he's up to something.'

Janet went back to her desk, hand-wrote some notes about their conversation and stuffed the piece of paper in her handbag. Another contribution to the home computer. She also looked up a certain Manchester phone number and resolved to give it a try when she got home.

She'd intended to call a short meeting about the property series but it was now too late. Everyone was packing up, intent on a couple of swift ones in the GX before heading home for the weekend. Normally she'd have gone too, but she was suddenly troubled by the events of the day. What on earth was going on?

She headed home in her battered old Citroën. A supper of easy-cook pasta, a couple of glasses of rouge and the rest of the day's papers suddenly seemed like the best thing in the world. She put her key in the door and opened it with that familiar pang of regret. A whole week-end ahead of her and no one to share it with. Janet knew she'd missed out on relationships. Occasionally, she'd look misty-eyed at couples choosing furniture, pushing supermarket trolleys or going out for a pub meal together. Then the horror of her own marriage would return and she'd always come to her senses. Yes, she was better off single; she knew where she was, how much she had in the bank, and there'd be nobody to moan if she bought a pile of clothes she didn't need.

She put on a pan of water for the pasta and poured the first glass of wine. Val would probably be well into her second or third bottle by now, and giving Harry a hard time. She glanced at the phone. No, she'd make that call after supper. Just unwind from the day before ringing. She put on a favourite pair of jogging bottoms – not that she'd ever jogged in them – took off her make-up and then put the chain on the door.

In the end, curiosity overcame her. She turned off the gas under the pan and dialled. The phone seemed to ring endlessly. Just five more rings and then I'll put it down, she thought. Oh, all right, just another five. Then some-one answered.

'Hi. This is Janet Bancroft from Hartford Optimum Television. I don't suppose Steven Byfield is still on this number, is he?'

'Yeah, I'll get him for you.'

Silence, broken by the sound of clip-clopping up and down uncarpeted stairs. It seemed an eternity.

'Hi, Janet, it's Steven Byfield. You took over my job, if I remember.'

'Yes, got it in one. I'm sorry to bother you, especially as

we've never met, but I wonder if you could do me a favour.'

'Well, I'll try. Ask away.'

'Look, I know it's a lot to ask, but could this conversation be in complete confidence? It's about Harry Hampton. I'm taking a risk here, because you could be his all-time best friend for all I know.'

There was a pause and then Steven started laughing, a real belly laugh.

'Harry? My best friend? Do me a favour. Biggest shit that ever walked the earth.'

Janet heaved a sigh of relief. He really did sound genuine.

'Could I ask why you think that?' she probed gently.

'No secret. I caught him out trying a spot of wheeling and dealing. At first he tried to get me on board, I suppose in the hope that I'd shut up. And then when I refused, he made life very difficult for me.'

'Like how?'

'Oh, all the usual bullying stuff. Not putting me in the picture on things and then giving me grief. Insisting on putting his name on credits when he'd had bugger-all to do with it. I once did a huge motoring project, wrote the pitch, got the job, produced and directed it. And then Harry insisted on putting his name on it, claimed credit, sucked up to the board and got another big fat pay rise. Sound familiar?'

'Absolutely. Carbon copy.'

'Well, leopards don't change their spots. And bastards, just like nuns, don't change their habits. So what's he up to this time?'

'More of the same, actually. But that's not quite why I'm ringing.'

Janet went on to outline the hiring of Paul Burns, how impressed Harry was with his CV and how they were now new best mates, disappearing off for expensive lunches and leaving all the work to everyone else. When she'd finished, Steven burst out laughing again.

'Sorry for all the hilarity,' said Steven, trying to control himself. 'And I'm sorry Burns is giving you all so much grief, but you can blame it all on me.'

'How on earth . . .?'

'I'd always wanted to pay Harry back for what he did to me, but he's a clever sod. I left in the end when a good job came up. I didn't want him messing it up for me with one of his revenge references. Anyway, I recently saw my way to a payback situation. We had Burnsie here on a short-term contract. It was like having another Harry on board, bit of a slippery character, with his nasty suits and bogus CV; short on talent, long on bullshit. Couldn't direct the traffic, let alone a programme. Also, as we discovered after he'd left, prone to fiddling, and I'm not hearing violins in this particular instance. So one day I rang Harry up and recommended Burns to him. I figured they'd be kindred spirits. I was very matey down the phone, asked after everyone and muttered all the right phrases. Harry must have swallowed it. Burns is very plausible and the CV's amazing. It's complete fiction. So you see, this is magic news, Janet. It was a long shot but worth it. You come up to Manchester, petal, and I'll buy you the best dinner in town.'

chapter fourteen

Liz was halfway through watching *When Harry Met Sally* for the umpteenth time. It was her favourite film, except that she wished Billy Crystal's character had been called anything but Harry. She'd just reached the fake orgasm scene in the diner when the phone rang. For one delicious moment she thought, 'Sod it,' then she felt trapped by its urgency. Who could it be this late? What if it was some terrible emergency?

She reached out over the back of her settee for the phone, contemplated it for a few seconds and clicked the green button.

'Hello,' she whispered.

'Liz, it's Janet. You all right? You sound as though you're being stalked.'

'Might as well be, after the sort of day I've had,' she replied.

'Yes, yes, yes,' screamed the television.

'Strewth, Liz, what the hell am I interrupting?'

'Nothing,' said Liz, rather detached.

'Yes, yes, yes,' screamed Meg Ryan, in mock ecstasy.

'What on earth's going on? Are you all right? And for God's sake, don't say, yes, yes, yes.'

'Yes, yes, yes.' Meg was at it again.

'Sorry, Janet, it's that crazy scene in the diner from *When Harry Met Sally*. You know the one.'

'Hm, can't remember back that far. Anyway, I'm surprised you're watching that, with its unfortunate title,' mused Janet. 'Let me tell you the tale of When Harry Met Paul Who'd Met Steven.'

'You just lost me,' yawned Liz, reluctantly turning the sound down on the film. But once Janet had related her chat with Steven Byfield, suddenly Liz was up off her settee and jumping around her tiny flat in delight.

'Fantastic. Best news I've heard all week. Trouble is, it doesn't solve my problem with Paul Burns. I've still got to carry him. Knowing my luck, I'm probably carrying him all the way to the bank too. I bet he earns squillions more than me.'

'Yes, undoubtedly,' said Janet, knowing that Harry liked to reward those who were loyal to him. She'd always suspected that Geraldine was on a fat screw. 'But somehow we've got to let Harry know how ineffectual Paul Burns is.'

'How the hell are we going to that?' asked Liz.

'Easy. We'll pick a day next week, better still two days. And these will be days when you are scheduled to direct sequences he should have been doing himself. You pick the most difficult ones, and let me know in advance.'

'Then what?' asked Liz, tiredness creeping back.

'I will make sure that absolutely everyone in the department is out on a shoot, or up to their armpits in editing, or in meetings that can't be cancelled. I might book leave so I'm out of the frame or there again, I might stay around for the sport.'

'What sport?'

'You're going to phone in sick and leave Burns in the

lurch. That should flush something out. He's either talented and lazy, in which case we'll all finally get to admire his handiwork. Or he's completely useless and lazy and our suspicions will be confirmed. And I must say, that last scenario gets my vote.'

'We're supposed to be shooting the line-dancing Hot Break on Friday and Saturday,' said Liz, flipping through her diary for the next week. She was surprised at her own instant acceptance of the plan. 'That would be perfect because it'll be a bit complicated to shoot and he'll have to juggle with music too. I already know that at least two women on the course don't want to be filmed, so we'll have to make sure we avoid them in all the shots. Also, the woman running the tuition side is unbelievably difficult. A right old diva. Thinks she knows everything about telly because about twenty years ago she was interviewed in the street by Esther Rantzen.'

'Sounds perfect then,' said Janet. 'Don't forget, you must drop out at the very last minute so he can't just cancel the shoot.'

'Yes, yes, yes,' said Liz ecstatically.

By midweek, Janet was so fed up of complaints and whingeing about Paul Burns, she felt like going sick herself. All the moans and groans were the same: his unfortunate manner, his downright rudeness, he didn't seem to know what he was talking about, he expected everything to be done for him. In other words, rude, thick and lazy. The only things that everyone admired were his epic lunch hours, ability to take nonstop mobile phone calls, and endless wardrobe of deeply vulgar flashy pinstripe suits, all double-breasted with wide lapels and turn-ups. He looked more like City Boy than Telly Man.

Liz had been tearing her hair out, producing research and recce notes that just sat unread in ever-growing piles on his desk. Burns just wouldn't or couldn't make a decision. He'd avoid it by suddenly disappearing for one of his mega cigar breaks. When the going got tough, the tough went smoking. Which was most of the time. This meant Liz couldn't firm up any filming because she didn't know exactly what he wanted.

'It's all very well going for a fag break,' observed Ray. 'Most people have a few puffs and come straight back in. But Burns' cigar breaks are something else. He's out there watching the rain drying followed by the grass growing. He's out there so long he could do with another shave. Thanks to all that cigar smoking, he'll end up being the healthiest bloke in this building.'

'How come?' asked Janet.

'Outside in the fresh air all the time, while the rest of us idiots answer his calls, take messages and generally do his dirty work.'

Film crews had begun reporting that they were forever seeing Paul Burns outside the office, cigar in one hand, mobile in the other. It was fast becoming an office joke.

'I've told him about those two women on the line-dancing break who don't want to be filmed,' said Liz. 'He's just not taking this on board at all. I've had to go ahead and book three cameras, extra lights and a steadicam for this shoot. If I waited for a decision, I'd be drawing my pension. And possibly my own teeth.'

'Difficult for me, because Harry's insisting it's Paul's baby,' said Janet. 'I've been told to keep out of it. Sorry, I can't really help you.'

They were having their conversation a couple of decibels up for the benefit of the rest of the office.

120

Bob, one of the researchers, was listening intently.

'Does seem daft,' he said, 'that you're out of this one, Janet. After all, you're head of the department.'

'Boss's orders,' said Janet with a half-smile. 'Not worth crossing Harry. You know what he's like when he's made his mind up. Paul is in charge on this one, and that's that.'

'Well I think that's crap,' retorted Bob. 'The man's a complete super-tosser. I'm trying to set up the murder-mystery weekend break, and the way it's looking, it's still a complete bloody mystery to me. Whatever I ask him, he just says, "Do what you think," or "Up to you." And that's only when I can catch him between calls on his mobile. He's permanently out to lunch.'

Janet smiled to herself. Burns wouldn't be out to lunch any longer if everything went according to plan later in the week.

Harry was busy congratulating himself on hiring Paul Burns. He sat back, gently swivelling in his huge chair as he contemplated his office. Burns' arrival had really shaken up the production department, especially Janet. Although he grudgingly admitted to himself that she did a good job, he'd never dream of telling her so. It was absolutely a non-starter to tell a woman she was good at anything. She'd get far too big for her boots. No, it served Janet right to have the rug pulled from under her from time to time. Nothing like keeping all of them on their toes. Staying in control, that was the name of the game.

Also, Burns was far more likely to keep his mouth shut on the little deal they'd hatched over lunch at the Grand last week. Yes, men were much better at wheeling and dealing than women, who tended to be obsessed with all that moral rubbish about right and wrong.

As Harry flipped through some trade papers, the now familiar niggle began to infiltrate. It was the conversation he'd had with Simon and Joe the day he'd fired them. That secret file they'd mentioned. Some of their accusations had hit home. Did they know something? It was still bothering him. He'd have to have another snoop around the office one evening, check a few drawers, look in some computer files, especially if some of the idiots in there had left their computers on. Or maybe he'd rope in Geraldine to do that. Brilliant idea. She'd do his dirty work and no questions asked. Now that was the sort of woman who got his vote.

'Geraldine,' he barked, 'coffee, in here, now, chop chop.'

Geraldine, looking spectacularly drab in a grey and white striped dress and very mumsy sandals, scuttled in the direction of the coffee machine.

As she reappeared with the coffee, Harry was sitting back in his chair smoking a huge cigar.

'Shut that door and siddown,' he bellowed. 'There's something really important I want you to do . . .'

Zero tolerance of Paul Burns and his behaviour was beginning to creep in. Even Liz, slightly buoyed up by the revelation of how he'd been hired, was beginning to stand up to him. She'd been up to her armpits sorting out locations and interviewees for the next two programmes, while Burns, mobile permanently clamped to his ear, was giving her huge lists of things to do.

'Sorry, Paul, I just can't leave my desk right now. I've got about ten calls out to all sorts of people. If I start rushing around the tape library pulling out rushes, I'll miss the calls and have to start all over again. Sorry, can't do miracles.'

'This place is ridiculous. I'm amazed anything gets done at all,' Burns grumped, looking around the office trying to catch some poor sod's attention to do his dirty work for him. Everyone deliberately avoided his gaze and looked very intently at their screens. Angrily, Burns stalked out of the office in the direction of the tape library. A few minutes later he was back, empty-handed and fuming.

Janet, having observed all this, surreptitiously dialled an internal extension. 'Well, what happened there then?' she whispered quietly to Bill, who ran the library.

'In time-honoured tradition, the peasants are revolting,' he said, chuckling. 'I told him to look up the tape numbers on the computer, just like everyone else. Well, that's not exactly true, of course, because we always help people we like. But this chap's such a pain in the arse, he can paddle his own canoe as far as we're all concerned.'

'How did he react?'

'Put it like this,' said Bill. 'We had a . . . let's call it an exchange. He was so pompous and rude that he must have had one-to-one tuition from the Hampton charm school. So in the end I pointed out that sarcasm was just one of the many services we offered.'

'Ooops, he'll go straight to Harry,' warned Janet.

'He can go straight to hell as far as we're all concerned down here,' replied Bill succinctly. 'And we'll help him with the packing.'

'Funny, a lot of people have chosen that destination for him.'

Janet replaced the receiver, smiling to herself. The peasants really were revolting. In all the years she'd worked at HOT, she'd never known such an unprecedented wave of hatred about someone after such a short time. It was an awesome achievement.

The phone rang immediately. Janet steeled herself, fully expecting it to be Harry ranting about something. But it was Colin, their most popular cameraman, asking for a quiet word with her in the canteen. She left her desk, following a glowering Paul Burns, who was obviously heading for another all-boys-together pow-wow with Harry.

Colin was sitting in the furthermost corner, two coffees already on the table.

'Let me guess, a Burning issue?'

'Got it in one,' said Colin. 'In all my years in this game, I have never come across quite such a pillock. We've done some shooting which, frankly, would have been a fiasco if Liz hadn't been there. The guy has no idea what he's doing. I'd asked him about how he wanted the interviewees framed, what filters he wanted, how he wanted the whole thing to look. And he just kept saying, "Whatever" or "Do what you want." He completely exasperated Ron, the sound recordist, who's the most placid bloke on the planet. In the end, Liz and I had a quick confab during one of his endless phone calls and salvaged what we could. But even after that he managed to walk through several shots, and we lost some more because he wouldn't switch off that bloody phone.'

'You're booked for the line-dancing next weekend, aren't you?' said Janet.

'Yeah, much against my better judgement. Why on earth aren't you involved in this series?'

'Good question. I'd rather not go into that. Can we have an off-the-record discussion? I think there are some things you ought to know.'

'Of course,' Colin assured her. 'We go back a long way, Janet.'

She briefly outlined how Paul Burns had come to be hired and how Harry had deliberately kept her off the series. She also told him of the likelihood that Liz would not be on the line-dancing shoot. She didn't want to compromise Colin when the balloon went up.

'I would just ask you one thing. If it all goes wrong at that shoot, don't bail him out. Just get straight on the phone to Harry. At home if necessary. And if you feel that strongly about it, then make your comments known to anyone from the Hot Breaks company.'

'Janet, I'd be delighted. And if anything does go wrong, I'll call you too, if you don't mind.'

'I insist,' she said.

chapter fifteen

'Janet, it's Val. How are you?'

That last bit nearly sent Janet reeling off her chair. It also sent two files of notes to the floor, scattering their contents. Scrabbling around to pick them up bought Janet a bit of time before she had to reply. Val never, ever asked how anyone was. She always knew exactly how they were and put them right on it in no uncertain terms. There was a brief flashback to the fiasco in the Mexican restaurant: Val falling into a table, refried beans scattering like a turbo muck-spreader; Val bringing down a coat stand; and of course Val managing to leave her usual immaculate and expensively dressed self, while the rest of them looked like extras from *The Godfather IV*.

'Fine, thanks,' she lied. 'How are you?'

'Oh, *comme ci, comme ça*. Bit bored really. Just been shopping, bought some nice clothes, nothing much, just a few cheapies from Ghost, and nowhere to wear them to.'

She's run out of people to do the swank to, thought Janet. I don't feel the need to ring someone up when I've just snapped up a cardie from BHS.

'So I thought I'd phone a friend,' pursued Val.

Why don't you ask the bloody audience instead,

thought Janet. This was a novel approach from Val; she sounded different somehow. Perhaps she was sober for once. Also, being referred to as a 'friend' was slightly unhinging. What was occurring?

'Are you free for lunch today?'

'Sorry, Val, up to my eyes.'

'How about tomorrow then?'

'No good either, I'm afraid,' said Janet, glancing at her wall chart. Not that she needed reminding. Tomorrow was Friday and the first day of the line-dancing shoot. It was also the day Liz was going to phone in sick and leave Burns to get on with things himself. Janet wanted to be there to mind the shop. On the other hand, Val witnessing some of the action might just work to their advantage.

'Tell you what,' she said. 'Let me juggle a few things around and see if I can get out for an hour tomorrow. I'll call you back.'

Janet noted down Val's mobile number and pondered for a few seconds. She called Sue in reception. Five minutes later they were huddled over cappuccinos in the canteen, with Janet outlining the game plan for the next day.

Liz would be ringing in at eight o'clock to say she was sick. Throwing up and diarrhoea had been chosen as suitable-house confining conditions, coupled with 'I could try and struggle in but I might be a bit of a liability.'

'I've made sure that absolutely everyone is either out of the office, editing or doing something unmissable tomorrow so that there is absolutely no back-up. That way Paul Burns has to show us all what a little whizz-kid he really is. Colin's on camera tomorrow, and he's had such a gutful of this pillock that he will not be doing any missionary work to save the shoot. He's furious with him, so I suspect the second call you'll get will be him to speak to Harry.'

'I should imagine you'll get a panic call pretty soon after that from Paul,' said Sue. 'It's brilliant that I'm on early shift tomorrow because I'll get to witness all the action. By the way, the security guys are thinking of reporting him.'

'Oh, why?'

'Apart from the fact that he treats them like dirt, he keeps parking in the visitors' bay because it's nearer and he can't be bothered to walk from the staff spaces. And he's been caught smoking those stupid cigars in the building.'

'He's really picking up Harry's habits then,' said Janet.

'Absolutely.' Sue nodded. 'He positively refuses to dial his own numbers when he's using a land line, so he gets us to look up the number, ring and then have the bother of putting them through to him. Makes him sound important to the people at the other end. He called me a silly cow the other day because he wanted Directory Inquiries and it had the temerity to be engaged.'

'Are you going to complain?'

'We all thought about it,' continued Sue, 'but you know how useless it is going to someone like Harry. No, we'll deal with it in our own way.'

'Now, my final problem is Val. She's rung just now. And don't faint, she asked me how I was.'

'Good grief. Do you think she's given up the drink?'

'Dunno, but she did sound a bit different. Chastened somehow. Anyway, she wants to meet me for lunch.'

'New and dangerous territory, I'd say.'

'Well, she got quite persistent,' continued Janet, 'and in

the end I thought tomorrow could be a good day. She might just get to witness some of the Paul Burns drama first hand. Whaddya think?'

'I'll make sure you get a few crisis calls on your mobile while you're out,' promised Sue with a grin.

Janet went back to her desk, tapped in Val's mobile number and got the answering service. She left a brief message saying that tomorrow for lunch was fine.

Friday dawned, sunny with a cloudless blue sky. 'Expect the unexpected,' said Janet's horoscope. Now there was a clairvoyant's cop-out. 'Be prepared for the twists and turns of a roller-coaster. It might give you high cheek bones temporarily, but by tonight you'll be back to face the music.'

Perhaps we've got this horribly wrong, she thought in panic. Supposing Steven Byfield had been lying about Paul Burns' abilities? What if he really was a hot-shot director, one of those very-creative-but-deeply-unpleasant-with-it characters? What if Harry found out about the plot that was about to unfold? Would this mean her job was on the line?

She picked up the paper again to read her alternative horoscope. Janet had been born on the cusp of Aquarius and Pisces. Although she was really Pisces, if the prediction was depressing she then read Aquarius on the basis of a balance of probabilities. Today Aquarius was no better. 'Ever had that feeling that no matter what you do, it all goes wrong. This is the day, so remember and appreciate the times when it all goes right. Why not write off the day and go back to bed with a large gin?'

If only, if only, she thought, shuddering for a moment

at the prospect of being sacked by Harry, never working again because he'd rubbish her around the industry, and then being condemned to a life of total penury. It was tempting to take her morning tea and toast back up to bed and hide under the duvet for ever.

She opened her kitchen curtains. Lazing in her tiny garden was certainly another tempting option. It was a blaze of colour, with terracotta pots spilling over with blood-red geraniums, blue trailing lobelia and snow-white alyssum. If she phoned in sick too, not only would she distance herself from the drama of the day, but she'd also avoid lunch with Val.

Nope, she said aloud to the kitchen mirror, I promised I'd be there to observe. I can't back out now. Also, she knew deep down that she was far too intrigued to stay at home. No, it had to be done. She marched upstairs purposefully for a shower.

'Liz has just rung in.' Sue spoke with a straight face, as one of the security guards was sitting next to her at the reception desk. 'She sounds terrible.'

'What's the problem?' asked Janet, looking instantly a picture of concern. At this rate she'd get into RADA.

'Been up all night with the trots. She thinks it might be food poisoning. She's been violently sick too. She sounds ghastly.'

'Okay, thanks, Sue, I'll pass that on. What a pity, it's the line-dancing shoot starting today. We were all hoping for a few laughs about that one.'

Janet went into the production department and sat down at her desk to deal with piles of post and e-mails. She looked deliberately at the roster. Yes, everyone was really, really busy today. Apart from Nina and Veronica, she wouldn't be seeing much of anyone else. Perfect, she thought as she dialled Paul Burns' mobile to deliver the terrible news. Predictably, it was busy.

Nina bustled in with a pot of coffee and cups.

'Never known it so empty in here,' she said. 'It's like the blinkin' Rue Morgue. Everyone's out today by the look of it except you, me and her.'

She indicated with a flick of her head the beautiful but snooty Veronica, who, as usual, was trying to type with impossibly long nail extensions.

'Liz has phoned in sick,' said Janet. She'd thought it best to tell only essential people about the plan. 'Eaten a dodgy curry or something.'

'Cor, that'll give Paul Burns the shits then, won't it?' said Nina. 'He'll have to do some work for a change, ha ha. Serves him right. Shall I give her a ring, see if we can do anything?'

'No, she's had a rotten night. I think we should leave her in peace. I'll try Paul again, although I don't know why I'm bothering because his bloody mobile's permanently engaged. I want to be able to tell him myself and then measure the shock waves down the phone line.'

Paul was still engaged. Did he ever get off that phone? How come his brain hadn't fried? Or perhaps it already had. How could anyone tell? Oh well, on with the estate agents' video series, which was shaping up quite nicely.

Half an hour later she finally got through. Paul Burns was clearly beside himself at the news. He shouted so loudly he almost didn't need a phone. Janet had to hold the receiver a good six inches away from her ear.

'I've travelled all this way just to find out that Liz is ill!

131

Bloody women, so bloody unpredictable. And thanks a bunch for letting me know. I've never worked with such a load of amateurs in all my life.'

'Well, thank you for that, Paul,' said Janet smoothly. 'I'll pass on that sentiment to the rest of the team. And I'll give your best wishes to Liz. I'm sure you'll be sending her flowers. I have been trying to ring you for the past half an hour but your phone has been constantly engaged. You really ought to invest in a second mobile, you know.'

'Look, I'm here in the backside of nowhere and I've no idea what's been set up. I'm going to look very stupid.'

No change there then, thought Janet. 'Nonsense, Paul,' she continued briskly. 'Liz left copious notes on everything that needed to be done. Obviously you have your copy, so I know you'll be completely au fait with everything she's set up.'

'I . . . I . . . think I must have left them in the office. Anyway, send one of your people up here immediately so we can get on with things. I demand an assistant director on this shoot and I want one now.'

'Let me look at the roster,' said Janet, pausing to create the effect of searching through a long list of names. 'Oh dear, I haven't got a spare bod at all today. Would you believe it, just about everyone's out of the office on various things. And of course I have to turn around an estate agents' project fairly urgently. Nope, sorry, can't help.'

'Then stuff the estate agents,' shouted Paul. 'I don't care what you or anyone else on the planet's doing, I want an assistant director.'

'I think I heard you the second time. Sorry, but Harry told me very firmly that I was definitely hands-off on this one. He knows a whizz-kid when he sees one. And even I'm aware that you're a very experienced director. It's on everyone's lips. No need to be modest,' she added gushingly. 'Tell you what, just in case you've lost Liz's notes, I'll fax you over a copy at your location. I've got the number here. She's so efficient, that girl. You're lucky to have her on the series. She's one of my best.'

'She's no fucking good if she isn't here,' he shouted.

'Sorry, Paul. Don't get paid enough to hear that sort of language. I'll fax over the notes. Have a good shoot.' As she replaced the receiver, she could still hear him ranting.

'Yeeeeeesssss,' she shrieked in triumph to the phone. Nina scuttled over to her desk.

'This is a set-up, isn't it?' she whispered, suspicious all of a sudden.

'Yep,' replied Janet, grinning. 'Liz isn't sick at all, but we thought it best to keep it quiet so that people would react naturally. Sue knows and so does Colin. I've asked him not to rescue the shoot but just to do what Burns asks him. He's sick to death of him too.'

'Brilliant,' said Nina, clapping her hands in delight. 'And there's nobody free to rush up there either.'

'All part of the plan. Also, I'm having lunch with Val today – God knows why – but I thought I might give her a taster of what goes on here. With a bit of luck I'll get a few more abusive calls from Burns while we're in the wine bar. And I've just had another brilliant idea . . .'

Val arrived on time, immaculate in black Jasper Conran with a pair of her trademark spiky heels. Unfortunately, her earlier mood of conciliation had evaporated, along with the first bottle of wine of the day. Cigarette dangling from red-painted lips and fuming because Sue wouldn't

133

let her stand and smoke in reception, she was waiting in the visitors' bay next to her MR2.

When Janet appeared, in cream chinos and a loose white cotton shirt, a look of undisguised disdain passed across Val's face. They climbed into the car and zoomed off at an alarming rate down to the local wine bar, Plonkers.

'Dreadful name. God, it's ghastly,' shuddered Val, taking in the plain wooden seating and spit-and-sawdust atmosphere.

'Well, we all like it and it's handy when you don't have much time,' said Janet, surreptitiously checking her mobile to make sure there was a good signal. They read the chalkboard menu, Val glancing round to make sure that all the clientele had noticed her.

'This place really is full of Plonkers,' she said, a little too loudly. 'I didn't realize men still wore white sports socks with loafers. Eugh.'

'Each to their own,' said Janet, handing her a menu. 'Don't want to hustle you, Val, but I don't have much time. It's proving a difficult day.'

Val was already too pissed to be listening and didn't pick up on Janet's last remark.

'We'll have a bottle of the Sancerre,' she announced pompously to the waiter. 'I'll have the salade niçoise, and for you, Janet?'

'I think I'll go for the steak-and-ale pie.'

'Far too fattening. You'll never get a man if you don't stop all this junk eating,' said Val, pointing a Rouge Noir-painted talon in Janet's direction. 'Pick something healthier.'

Even the waiter looked appalled. Janet was just about to reply when the shrill of the mobile phone came from the depths of her handbag. She scrabbled to find it.

'Oh God, the haunted handbag strikes again,' she muttered, scattering pieces of paper, her notes from this morning's exchange with Paul Burns. She hastily stuffed them back. They were to be typed up when she got home later that day.

'Haunted, why's it haunted?' said Val sarcastically. She'd picked up on that one all right.

'Oh, things in it vanish and then reappear,' said Janet, still delving for the phone.

'You really shouldn't carry around so much junk. Look,' Val said, producing her small Prada clutch bag. 'Just enough room for my lippy, powder, credit cards, car keys and mobile phone. What else would anyone need?'

'Bit different when you work,' muttered Janet bitterly. 'Oh, bugger, I've missed the call now.'

She dialled 121 to retrieve the message. 'You have one new message,' soothed the voice mail. 'Where the fuck are you?' screamed Harry so loudly that even Val heard.

She dialled his direct line, keeping the phone just a fraction away from her ear so that Val could hear the tone of the conversation. Predictably, he launched straight into a torrent of abuse. It was all Janet's fault, Burns shouldn't have been left in the lurch without Liz, this was an important client, one of HOT's biggest contracts for ages, Janet herself should have left immediately to be on location . . . Janet just let him rant until he ran out of steam. Then she launched calmly into a reply.

'Harry, you hired a top-notch director, you showed me his CV, and you told me very firmly to stay off the case. You brought in a big shot to do this project in order to give my lot, and I quote, "a kick up the backside". I'm sure Paul Burns can do this shoot with his hands tied behind his back. Meanwhile, I am having lunch with your wife.'

As she cut him off, a salade niçoise arrived in front of her. She noticed that Val had already got through most of the Sancerre.

chapter sixteen

'Sorry about that,' said Janet, putting away her mobile. 'Slight problem, nothing to worry about.'

'Does he always shout like that?' said Val.

'Oh, you know Harry! But I never take it personally,' Janet lied, amazed at the calm that had come over her. She must get Val involved next time there was a major cock-up. Normally she'd be shaking like a leaf after that onslaught. She managed a couple of mouthfuls of the salade niçoise before the mobile went off again.

'So sorry, Val,' she apologized, fishing out the phone once more. This time it was Paul Burns, ranting because he'd discovered that two women on the line-dancing break had refused to be filmed and were now giving him grief.

'It was all in Liz's research notes, Paul,' Janet said smoothly. 'Even I knew that and I'm nothing to do with this project. I was told strictly hands-off by Harry. With your experience, I'm sure you'll sort it. Have fun and we'll look forward to you teaching us some of the steps on Monday,' she added triumphantly.

She returned to her salad and the now empty bottle of Sancerre. Val had polished off the rest while she was on the phone.

'More wine,' Val demanded of the hovering waiter.

'Not for me, Val. Afternoon's work ahead of me. Don't you think it's a bit risky driving if you have any more?'

Val was about to launch into one of her tirades, punctuated by the painted-talon-stabbing routine, when she was stopped in her tracks. Into the wine bar came a smiling Nina, followed by Sam from Accounts. Nina half waved to them in acknowledgement before they were guided by a waiter to a table at the far end of the room.

'Good God, the London Derrière out with a man. He must think he's watching the world on widescreen.'

'On the contrary,' said Janet. 'That's Sam from Accounts. He finally plucked up the courage and asked her out. They're very much an item now, despite what you said.'

Val lit a cigarette and took another slug of wine. She loathed being proved wrong.

'Well, it won't last,' she almost spat. 'No man would want to be seen out with a butt that size.'

'Sam clearly doesn't see it as a problem. Anyway, Nina's a popular girl. I gather there's quite a waiting list, but he's the only one for her.' At this rate, thought Janet, not only will I have waltzed through RADA, but I could be straight into the National Theatre.

Sue was hovering at the reception desk, dying to find out what had happened.

'I managed to bat all the calls from Harry and Paul on to your mobile,' she grinned. 'How did it go?'

Janet regaled her with what had happened over lunch.

'Apart from accusing me of wearing junk, eating junk and carrying junk around in my handbag, Val was better behaved than usual. By that, I mean that she didn't fall over, scatter food over people or terrorize waiters, so I guess that was a bonus. However, she sank so much wine that she drove up the middle of the road all the way back from Plonkers. It was so scary that I made a virtual will. I've left you my collection of Russ Conway records, by the way.'

'Oh, thanks heaps,' replied Sue. 'So long as it includes "Side Saddle". I'm just amazed she hasn't been done for drinking and driving before now. But that's Val. She gets away with it all the time, lucky sod. If we did it once, it would be a case of instant fine and ban. It's not fair.'

'My other little bit of mischief has paid off, though,' said Janet. 'I told Nina to set up a lunchtime meeting with Sam to discuss the budgets for the property project and how they were going to code them. I told her to book a table at Plonkers and put the bill on her expenses. I'm hoping it might get them together, but it also gave me the satisfaction of getting back at Val over her bitchy remarks.'

'Did it work?'

'I think something registered, but it might have been merely the Sancerre.'

Nina came back from lunch, flushed and obviously happy. To Janet's delight, and Veronica's scowling, she announced that not only had they sorted out all the budget codes, but Sam had asked her out to dinner on Saturday night. After she'd done a celebratory skip around the office, she went off to make some tea.

'Any calls?' Janet asked Veronica.

'Yeah, plenty,' she replied sullenly. 'Harry, Paul, Harry,

Paul, then Harry, then Paul, oh, and one from Colin but he'll ring you again later.'

'Right, I'll just go and see Harry then,' Janet said, with determination in her voice. I will *not* quiver in my shoes, she told herself as she entered the soft grey hessianed walls of the executive corridor. But the bespectacled Geraldine, clacking away on her keyboard, was minding empty offices. The management, including Harry, had obviously gone home early.

'Harry's having a late lunch,' Geraldine announced imperiously, 'and I don't blame him after all that hassle this morning.'

'What hassle?' beamed Janet innocently.

'Oh, the woman running that dancing course thingy is threatening legal action.'

'Really?' Janet fought an inner battle to keep a broad grin off her face. This was the ghastly woman with the ego problem Liz had mentioned. No doubt Burns had rubbed her up the wrong way. He certainly managed to do it with just about everyone else.

'I'm sure the talented Mr Burns will sort it all out,' she continued. 'After all, that's exactly why Harry brought him in. I must say, he's been an inspiration to us all.'

Geraldine glanced up from beneath her hennaed bob and gave Janet a slightly puzzled look. Watch this space – between my ears – it seemed to say. Then she clicked back into blind loyalty mode.

'Harry only hires the best,' she pronounced, with a look that suggested he might have made a bit of a cock-up in Janet's case.

'Oh well, I'll leave you to it. Have a nice weekend. Doing anything special?' It suddenly occurred to Janet that she'd never before asked Geraldine that type of question.

Geraldine was equally stunned to be asked and at a loss to answer.

'I, er, we, er that is, a friend and I are going to see *Carmina Piranha*.'

'Oh, marvellous,' said Janet, mentally adding the latest G-spot to the already bulging file.

Val arrived home in a temper. She'd been looking for fun, sophisticated chat, a laugh. But instead she'd been dragged to that appalling wine bar, sidelined the entire time by a mobile phone and then given a lecture on drinking and driving. How dare Janet? Who did she think she was? From Val's point of view, Janet's only saving grace was that she always looked like a sack of potatoes, which had the effect of making Val look even more glamorous.

Val went into the kitchen, opened a bottle of white wine and poured herself a large glass. Then she picked up her address book and had another flurry through it. Page after page of friends from school and modelling days, now all unavailable, bogged down by kids and boring husbands. Perhaps if she and Harry had a baby it might improve her social life. She could at least then join in all the nappy chat, it would please her parents, who were now dropping huge hints about being grandparents, and it might make Harry get home a bit earlier.

She flopped on to one of the big cream leather sofas in their sitting room, lit a cigarette and flicked on the television. Channel after channel offered her nothing of interest: reruns of old game shows, vintage episodes of soaps, endless makeovers of people and their ghastly houses and gardens. God, they were all at it. Soon they'd be running out of people and places to be made over. She refilled her glass and lit another cigarette. Life was boring and it was all Harry's fault. Then she remembered that he was going away at the end of the month. Even more boring. The room began to sway, the television lost focus, and soon Val was sound asleep.

By the time Janet left the HOT offices, she was completely drained. All she could think about as she pointed her car in the direction of home was a scented bath, a warm dressing gown, a little microwave something or other to make up for the lunchtime salad she'd hardly touched, and then bed. The strain of the day had suddenly caught up with her.

She walked wearily through the front door, flicked on a couple of lamps, put on some soothing classical guitar music and double-checked that her answering machine was on. Peace and quiet, that was what she needed. She flopped down on her old sofa and gazed around the place. Could do with an overhaul, but at least it was cosy and warm. She wondered for a minute how Geraldine was getting on with *Carmina Piranha*. Perhaps the opera had been re-scored with a snappier beat.

The ping of the microwave coincided with the sound of the phone. There was no contest; the Chinese chicken and cashew won hands down. Except that she heard Colin's voice leaving her a message. He wanted a chat about what had happened during the day. She gobbled down the chicken as fast as she could and pressed the call-back button.

'Well?' she said expectantly.

'Where do I begin?' said Colin. There was no mistaking the exasperation in his voice. 'That man is a complete buffoon. He's done about as much filming as

142

I've undertaken keyhole surgery. Didn't have a clue about what he wanted, walked through shots, refused to switch off his phone, insulted the interviewees. You name it, he did it. He upset the woman running the course big-time. Mind you, that wasn't difficult. She was a complete road accident. Big fat cow with a voice to match.'

'I heard from the dreaded Geraldine that she was making some sort of complaint. I hope it's not against you.'

'No, sweet, of course not. There were two women on the course who didn't want to be filmed. Now that's always a nuisance from my point of view, but it's not insurmountable. But it was all too much for that idiot. He kept on insisting that I film wide shots which included them. Well, they would have been unusable and a complete waste of time. So in the end we had a stand-off. Then the women complained, quite rightly, to Mrs Bossy Boots and war was declared. Tomorrow's shoot's been cancelled because of it.'

'Did you ring Harry to report?'

'Tried during the day but he was busy. The way that weirdo Geraldine protects him, you'd think he was running the bloody Kremlin or planning the next world summit. Mind you, Burns got through on his perennial mobile, of course. God knows what was said but I expect I've been rubbished behind my back. Fortunately I have Ron as my witness. He was equally pissed off. We took one or two other little precautions to cover ourselves.'

'Like what?'

'Oh, you'll find out. I'll keep it up my sleeve for now.'

'Good day all round then,' said Janet. 'I enjoyed a certain

amount of abuse from Paul and Harry. All topped off by lunch with Val.'

'Must have been a bit of a belter, then,' said Colin. 'I've just tried Harry at home to register a formal complaint. Val answered, and to be frank, she sounded blind drunk. What did you girls get up to?'

'Not me, matey. I think Val had had a few before she arrived. I had so many calls on the mobile during lunch that she polished off the best part of two bottles of Sancerre. Then I had a white-knuckle ride back to the office in her car.'

'Well, it sounds as though she carried on, because when I rang this evening, she was well and truly vino collapso.'

'Harry not there?' asked Janet.

'No, apparently not.'

'Interesting. Did you try his mobile?'

'Switched off.'

'Hmm, even more interesting.' She reached for paper and pencil.

Saturday dawned bright and sunny. Even the flowers seemed to be looking skywards to say thank you. A pale pink clematis vied with a deep scarlet rambling rose for prime position on the small garden wall in front of Liz's flat. Janet put down her Sainsbury's carrier bags on the front step and rang the doorbell.

'Supplies for the patient,' she grinned when Liz opened the door. 'Can't have you staggering around a supermarket in your state of health.'

In Liz's tiny galley kitchen they unpacked bags of mixed salad, sirloin steaks, french bread, white wine, plus all the usual basics. Soon the steaks were sizzling under the grill, the salad was dressed and the bread cut up and ready to serve.

'I thought we'd eat in the garden as it's such a lovely day,' said Liz. 'Don't worry, we won't be spotted. For a town flat, it's really secluded.'

'Everyone at the office hopes you'll get better soon,' said Janet sarcastically, taking in Liz's Bermuda shorts and strappy tee-shirt.

'Do you think anyone twigged?' Liz asked anxiously.

'The only people who officially know are Colin, Sue and Nina. I thought it safest to keep the number of people in on it to a minimum.'

Over the steak and salad, washed down by copious amounts of chilled Chardonnay, Janet recounted events at the line-dancing weekend. Liz laughed uproariously when she got to the bit about the woman who ran the course.

'I knew she was trouble, that one, when I was setting it up. Maybe I've had a lucky escape. I do hope she makes a complaint to Harry.'

'Oh it's worse than that. Today's shoot has been cancelled, with everyone citing irreconcilable differences. I wouldn't imagine the people from Hot Breaks For Heartaches are going to be all that bowled over. If I were you, I'd stay off on Monday. Keep out of it.'

'I hope I'm not going to be blamed for what's happened. Harry's bound to be looking for a scapegoat,' said Liz, the old familiar fear creeping across her face.

'No, you won't be blamed. I have a copy of your notes, detailing all the potential problems. Colin and Ron are on your side. They were there, don't forget. They witnessed the whole thing. And Colin hinted that he'd taken a few precautions himself. I think I can guess what.'

'Puts Harry's mystery freebie in jeopardy, doesn't it?' said Liz. 'But mark my words, Harry will wriggle out of this one as usual. Someone else will cop the blame.'

'Not this time. I have a feeling . . .'

chapter seventeen

It was Black Monday in every sense. The weekend sunshine had evaporated and now it was hot and humid, with storm clouds threatening to deposit their contents all over Hartford.

News of the events of the previous week had obviously spread like wildfire. All the production office staff seemed to know about what had happened, even though the vast majority had been out of the office on Friday. Clearly phones had been hot over the weekend. People were openly laughing about tales of Paul Burns' incompetence. Like all good gossip, the tales had grown like Topsy. Now the fat woman had taken on legendary status, apparently kicking Burns into Casualty with her cowboy boots. One joke doing the rounds was that Burns had won the Queen's Award for Industry for single-handedly causing his mobile phone company's shares to rocket. Another joke was that *OK!* magazine were going to cover him unveiling a new phone mast which was to be named after him.

Janet sat at her desk, regretting bitterly that she couldn't join in the revelry. Any minute now the phone would ring and it would be Geraldine summoning her to

Harry's office for one of his legendary blame-storming sessions. At least she knew him well enough not to be wrong-footed.

When the inevitable call came, she picked up a file and made her way slowly and deliberately to Harry's office.

'Siddown,' he bellowed, engrossed in the paperwork on his desk.

Janet sank down into her usual chair. Harry didn't look up for a few seconds, during which time Janet became transfixed by the sight confronting her. She was reminded why some of the girls in the office referred to him as 'No Balls Hampton'. The thought made her grin.

'I don't know why you're smiling,' he barked. 'This is no laughing matter.' He thumped what was obviously the Hot Breaks file on his desk. 'I warn you, Janet, heads will roll.'

'Any particular ones in mind?' She couldn't believe how calm she felt. It must be the under-the-desk discovery.

'Don't be fucking flippant with me. Or yours will be the first,' he hissed at her. 'Let me make myself clear. This is an important project, it's worth a lot of money and it was totally fucked up on Friday.'

'Why are you telling me this?'

'You're head of the bloody production department. The buck stops with you. It's your fault.'

'Sorry, Harry, you can't have it both ways. You hired in Paul Burns; you told me in no uncertain terms that he was the man for the job, and that I was to keep out of it. Which I did.'

But Harry wasn't listening. 'I've had a madwoman on the phone ranting to me about the behaviour of our crew on Friday. As a result, the shoot's been cancelled. Hot

148

Breaks have probably lost customers, we've lost the item and we'll have to reshoot at our own expense. And this company has been made to look incompetent.'

'So who are you going to blame?'

'Well, for a start that stupid cow shouldn't have gone sick.'

'By stupid cow, I gather you mean Liz,' said Janet, still amazed at her own calm.

'Yes, I bloody do. She shouldn't have been ill, she was probably skiving. Anyway, she should have warned Paul about this stupid cow running the course.'

'There seems to be a whole herd of stupid cows in this story, Harry.' She smiled sweetly at him. 'But there's one complete dolt-brain, who stands head and shoulders above the rest, and that's Paul Burns. Liz couldn't help being sick. But Paul Burns could certainly do himself a favour by learning to read. All the pitfalls of this shoot were clearly outlined in Liz's notes.' She patted the file on her lap and then selected a piece of paper from it.

'Let me read you an extract,' she continued. "Confidential Warning", it's headed. Then Liz writes: "I anticipate problems with Mrs Saunders. I have briefed her very thoroughly about the complexities of the filming and how we may ask her to do some things twice or possibly three times for different camera angles. She's very dismissive and pompous, a classic know-it-all. I have undertaken that we will not include in the edited product the two people on the course who did not give their consent. We will endeavour to exclude them during the filming to put their minds at rest." I think that's perfectly clear. Unfortunately, it wasn't for Paul Burns because he obviously didn't bother to read the notes before he went off to the shoot. And before you start disagreeing, Harry,' she pointed a finger at him, Val-fashion, 'Paul phoned me on Friday spitting teeth because of course he hadn't a clue what he was doing.'

Harry sat back, his face contorted with rage. Janet noted with secret amusement that he was wearing one of those incredibly naff shirts, blue and white stripes with a plain white collar. The type spivvy politicians wore with pinstriped suits and clashing ties.

'Where's Paul today anyway?' she continued. 'It's only fair he should be part of this discussion.'

'He phoned in sick this morning,' barked Harry.

'Oh, not skiving then,' said Janet, getting up from her chair. The irony of her remark was wasted on Harry. 'Why don't we have another chat when Paul comes back? After all, if there are another seven of these pieces to shoot, he might as well get it right next time. Perhaps we should give him another chance.'

Janet returned to her office, shaking like a leaf. She'd been so calm and controlled, but now it was over she was suffering delayed shock. She'd given Harry a real shock too, and he knew it. After making a quick call to Colin, she replaced the receiver and smiled. 'Gotcha', she muttered, wishing she could down a really large gin and tonic and then feeling ashamed because it was only 9.20 a.m.

Harry paced around the office, white-faced with anger. That cow would have to go sooner or later. She was getting too smart for her own good. He hated losing control of situations. Clearly Paul Burns had been set up by the pair of them, Janet and Liz. Too miffed to cope when real talent was brought in over their heads. He'd have to speak to the Hot Breaks people and do some damage limitation.

He sipped his coffee, lit a cigar, sat back in his chair

150

and spent a few minutes mentally preparing his speech. Then he shouted at Geraldine to get Hot Breaks on the line.

'David Rawlins? Harry Hampton here. How are you, mate? Good. Good. Spot of bother on Friday but it's been dealt with. As you know, I put a real hot-shot director on to this project and of course he's used to dealing with more able people. One or two of our girls haven't shaped up to the standards he requires. So rest assured, heads will be rolling. We'll obviously reshoot at our expense. And of course the first thing I did this morning was to send flowers and a note of apology to Mrs Saunders. Yes, yes. Absolutely. Now, how about dinner on Friday? Good, I'll get Geraldine to book. Okay, matey, see you then.'

He slammed the phone down and breathed a sigh of relief. Salvaged that one. He glanced around at the paintings on his office wall. Yes, originals certainly did have a certain cachet. And the little deal he'd done with the gallery ensured that quite a few more would be winging their way to his home, all of course paid for by the company.

'Geraldine,' he barked through the open door. 'Get fifty quid's worth of flowers off to that madwoman who phoned this morning. Oh, and book a table for four at Shiraz for Friday night.'

Nobody had ever seen Nina work so hard. She whipped through a pile of electronic filing like a whirling dervish, she jumped up and cheerfully made coffee for up to twenty people at a time and generally skipped around the office with a grin stretching from ear to ear.

'If you didn't get it at the weekend,' said Ray, 'I'd like to

151

know what you did get to make you this bloody happy. Whatever it is, where can I find some?'

Ray, usually the fount of all good gossip, obviously didn't know about Nina's date at the weekend with Sam.

'Mind your own blinkin' business,' smiled Nina, delighted to get one over on him. 'What did you do at the weekend?'

'Don't even ask. I can't believe I'm telling you this, but I got dragged along to see *The Sound of Music*.'

Several people overheard this confession and started to laugh. Choruses of 'Do Re Mi' started up, with the emphasis on the Ray.

'Well, it wasn't quite what it seemed,' said Ray, now horribly aware that everyone was listening. 'It was billed as the ultimate karaoke event. They had all the words of the songs burned into the film so everyone could join in. And loads of people came dressed as nuns, or Nazis, or goatherds, or dressed in curtains. It was quite a scream, actually, because you could boo the Baroness and hiss at the Nazis and cheer during the flaky bits. God, I can't believe I'm confessing this to you lot. I'll never live it down.'

'The funny thing was, though,' Ray lowered his voice to talk to Nina, 'when I saw all those people in costume, I had this weird fantasy of Geraldine dressed up as a nun, complete with wimple.'

'Oh, don't be daft,' Nina laughed, skipping off towards Janet's desk at the other end of the office.

'Can we meet for lunch?' she whispered to Janet. 'I think I may have a contribution to the Haunted Handbag.'

An hour later they were in a favourite corner of the GX, tinkering with penne and arrabiata sauce as Nina gave Janet a blow-by-blow account of her date on

Saturday night. Apparently it had gone well, and she and Sam had now swapped home phone numbers, with another date planned for Wednesday evening.

'Good job you're not seeing him tonight,' said Janet. 'This sauce is loaded with garlic. The GX should open franchises in China. It would sort out their population problem overnight. I'm going to have to keep my distance from everyone this afternoon after this lot, and I don't even have any red-hot bonking on my agenda.'

'Well, it's about time you did,' said Nina, desperate not to monopolize the conversation with her new-found happiness. 'Bleugh. You're right about the garlic. Maybe I'll keep away from Accounts this afternoon.'

'Anyway,' said Janet, scooping up the last of the sauce with some ciabatta, 'what's the latest offering for Operation Haunted Handbag?'

'As Head of Office Snooping,' said Nina, lowering her voice conspiratorially, 'I have to report that the office has been got at again.'

'Whaddya mean? Bugged?'

'Well, I wouldn't put it past them. No, things have been walking again. At least two secretaries told me some of their e-mail had been read when they checked this morning. A couple of the researchers remarked that their stuff had been moved and put it down to the cleaners. But I just know that my desk has been shuffled about a bit.'

'How can you tell?' asked Janet sweetly. Nina was renowned for having the most untidy desk in the building.

'I'll ignore that remark,' Nina grinned. 'My filing trays were all over the place and my drawers had been gone through.'

Janet laughed. 'I occasionally lie in bed and fantasize about someone going through my drawers.'

'Then you would have to cut out the garlic,' said Nina. 'No, seriously, it was just like last time, when the catering college tapes went missing and I copped the blame for it.'

'So Harry's been on the prowl again,' said Janet thoughtfully. 'Perhaps it was Friday night, after the line-dancing fiasco. I was summoned to the bollocking room first thing this morning over that one. All my fault, apparently. Oh, and Liz's for having the temerity to be ill!'

'Oh, shit. That must have been terrible.'

'Oddly enough, after all these years of dealing with Harry, shaking in my boots and dreading those sorts of show-downs, for the first time ever I really did stand my ground. The funny thing is, it was actually easy. For a start, it was very firm ground that I was on. Burns is such a plonker and I had Liz's notes about the shoot. But there were a couple of other things that struck me as I sat there.'

'Like what?'

'Well, Harry was wearing a particularly nasty shirt – you know that stripy sort with the contrasting collar. Always look as though they ran out of material. And there was something else.'

'Like what?'

'No balls. I had to sit in that ridiculous visitor's chair with the eye-level view of his crotch. And there was one other thing.'

Nina raised her eyebrows quizzically.

'I found myself emulating Val with her famous finger-pointing routine. There was a moment when I wagged a finger at him, and do you know, he really flinched.'

'Obviously gets a lot of it at home,' said Nina.

They paid up and went back to the office. Paul Burns' Mercedes was parked in a visitor's space, right in front of the main entrance. So he'd returned to face the music.

'Geraldine? Janet here. As Paul's back now, I'd like to set up a meeting with him and Harry at three. Is Harry free then?' Janet kept her voice loud enough for Paul to hear from his desk. She wasn't going to consult him on the matter. 'Yes, urgent need to discuss the next Hot Breaks programmes. Good, we'll come in at three.'

Paul Burns went momentarily white. It wasn't a colour that went with his outfit today. Sporting a green, red and yellow striped blazer and wide cream trousers with turn-ups, he looked as if he'd have been more at home sipping Pimm's at Henley. And after the weekend fiasco, that was where he'd probably have preferred to be. Suddenly his mobile phone went off. The old confidence instantly returned. He was once again on familiar ground, talking to one of his many callers, who all seemed to go by the name of Nigel. There always seemed to be deals going on.

Janet quietly opened one of her desk drawers. There at the back was what she was looking for. She shut the drawer firmly and watched the clock tick round until three.

chapter eighteen

Harry did all the talking. He ranted, he raved, he shouted, he seethed. It was all directed at Janet. Liz was off the series, she could walk the plank as far as he was concerned. Paul Burns needed and deserved better support; this was a big project for HOT. It could lead to many, many more very prestigious and lucrative contracts, but not if there were any more cock-ups. Harry strode about the office, thumping his desk every time he passed it.

Janet sat impassively as the torrent was unleashed. Beside her, Paul Burns lent silent support to Harry, nodding sagely at appropriate moments.

'I will not have my . . . I mean . . . our reputation fucked up by some stupid fat woman running a line-dance class of all things. That bloody woman has caused so much trouble. She's complained to Hot Breaks, the people in the class have complained. This is jeopardizing the whole project, and future projects to come.'

Not to mention your freebie holiday, thought Janet. Wait until he's finished. Keep calm, say nothing.

Eventually even Harry ran out of steam. Then Paul Burns took up the reins.

'I've never worked with such incompetents in all my

career,' he proclaimed. 'I was promised your best researchers and what do I get? Absolute crap. It just beggars belief. And as for the crew, downright rude, bolshy, uncooperative, didn't seem to know what they were doing. I can't believe I was expected to work with people like that. I really don't know how you run a department with such a lack of talent.'

Janet finally stood up. She shot them a look of utter contempt, then she calmly produced a VHS tape from a file she'd been holding and strolled over to the bank of machines on a wall of Harry's office.

'Guys, I'd like to show you something that you might find quite riveting,' she said, picking up the remote control from Harry's desk. She aimed it at the machine and pressed 'play'. Paul smiled contemptuously; Harry sneered. That was all about to change, she was certain.

It was rather like the fascination of watching security videos on *Crimestoppers*. The line-dancing session was in full swing, with the enormous Mrs Saunders, resplendent in stetson, cowboy boots, a Union Jack-patterned flippy short skirt and suede-fringed top, demonstrating some of the steps. Ludicrous would have been too kind a word, and a decent sports bra wouldn't have gone amiss. Suddenly Paul Burns barged into the shot, stopped the demonstration and demanded that she do it again. Grudgingly she obliged. The demonstration started again, only to be interrupted by Paul off camera obviously taking a very noisy call on his mobile. Mrs Saunders visibly bristled but soldiered on. Several more noisy calls followed, all picked up on the sound track, including one to the ubiquitous Nigel, one to book theatre tickets and another to check a stock price on the Nasdaq. Her patience now in tatters, Mrs

Saunders could be seen striding heavily across the room towards Burns, who was still behind the camera, to demand that he switch off the phone. An argument ensued along the lines of 'We're here to film your silly little line-dancing session and this is a Hollywood director you're talking to. And no, I won't switch off my phone. I'm important.'

The next section included a discussion between Colin, the cameraman, and Ron, the sound recordist, on the shooting of a particular sequence. Colin could be clearly heard having to spell out to Paul that if he continually got into shot and didn't switch off his phone, the film would all be unusable. 'If we shoot it from here, it will be completely uneditable,' Colin was pointing out. 'If we move to the position near the window, it just won't cut. It'll cross the line from here. The lighting's all wrong for a start. The shots won't match.'

By now, both Harry and Paul were surreptitiously looking around for the remote control, which Janet still held firmly in her now rather sweaty hand.

The grand finale was a spectacular row: Paul Burns versus the two women who had asked not to be filmed. Paul's attitude could have been best summed up as 'tough shit'. He pompously told them he knew nothing of this request and thought it was the most ridiculous thing he'd ever heard in his entire and very extensive career. Colin then made a rare appearance in front of his own camera, waving Liz's research notes in front of Paul. 'Well, we knew about it several days ago. It's all in there, mate,' he said. 'It's all in our film briefs too.' He then proceeded to apologize to the two women for Paul's behaviour in the most charming way.

Janet stopped the tape. There was a pause.

'A picture paints a thousand words, as I think you'll both agree,' she declared, unsmiling.

'How dare he film all that,' spluttered Paul, crimson with anger. 'That's outrageous.'

'No, just out in the open. A couple of tips about filming, Paul, that I'm very happy to pass on,' said Janet smoothly. 'Firstly, if that little red light's on at the front of the camera, then he's rolling. And secondly, if you want your cameraman to stop filming, just say, "Cut." I'll leave you two gentlemen to enjoy the rest of the tape.'

She walked out of the office without even glancing at Harry. Standing right outside the door and therefore caught by surprise, was Geraldine, who immediately pretended to be scrabbling around her desk for a pen.

'Why not try a glass up to the wall next time?' said Janet as she swept past. 'Much better sound quality.'

'Hmm, the *Hartford Echo* is starting a campaign about mobile phones,' said Ray, feet up on his desk because Janet was out of the office.

'What about them?' asked Bob, one of the researchers, who was taking a call on his and at the same time trying to have a fag by hanging out of an open window because he couldn't be bothered to go outside to the smokers' hut.

'They want to ban them in public places, bars, restaurants, that sort of thing,' said Ray, skimming the article. 'Good idea, if you ask me. I get really sick of people on trains, answering their phones by shouting, "I'm on the train," to which the rest of the carriage choruses, "So are we".'

'Well, it won't stop Burns, will it?' said Bob, rolling his eyes. 'His phone's actually welded to his ear. I should know, I have the misfortune of working with him on Hot Breaks.'

Janet slipped back into her desk at the other end of the office. For the second time that day, she'd have killed for a large gin and tonic. Perhaps she should keep a minibar in her filing cabinet. Her head was now filled with questions. What would happen now? Would Harry carry on defending Paul, or would he find some reason to get rid of him? The one thing she was sure of was that Harry, as always, would come out of it squeaky clean. She was just starting to think about a treatment for another of the property bulletins when Paul Burns came into the office. Without a word, without a glance, he started to clear his desk. It didn't take long. He'd never spent much time there anyway. Then he picked up his briefcase – Gucci, of course – and walked out without a backward glance.

'Bloody hell, that was a whole five minutes without a call on the old mobile,' remarked Bob. 'Hey, get me the *Guinness Book of Records* on the phone immediately.'

'He looked a bit stroppy,' said Ray. 'Perhaps he's upset that he didn't finish that line-dancing course. I really could see him in a ten-gallon hat, prancing around doing all that yee-haw stuff.'

'God knows what he'll do with the murder-mystery weekend I'm setting up,' said Bob. 'I'm dealing with actors, and you know how stroppy they can be.'

'Maybe you could make him the murder victim.'

'Brilliant idea. Trouble is, everyone would have a motive.'

Janet replaced her phone and walked down to where Bob and Ray were sitting.

'Hanging out of the window smoking doesn't count in a no-smoking office,' she said, trying to keep a straight face.

'Er, I was trying to get a signal on my mobile,' muttered Bob.

'Don't be ridiculous. Paul Burns doesn't have that problem,' said Janet sternly. Then her face broke out in a huge grin.

'Or rather, should I say, Paul Burns *didn't* have that problem. I've just heard that he's left the building for good. Gone, kaput, finito.'

'That's fantastic,' they both chorused, not quite believing their luck. 'Drinks all round in the GX after work!'

Janet went back to her desk and quietly dialled a number.

'Thank you, Colin. That was utterly magnificent. It was far more than you promised . . . Yes, yes, it did the trick . . . Yes, he's gone. Won't be darkening our doorstep again . . . No, I didn't get a chance to view it beforehand, so I took a huge flyer on it . . . No, the office was too busy and also, remember, Burns was here. I had to trust what you said and just shove it in the machine . . . You bet I was shaking. The beauty of it was that everything he denied, all the lies, it was all there on the tape. It was a wonderful moment. I will always savour it . . . The rest of the series? I'm hoping Liz will direct. Just have to sort it with the Fat Controller . . . After today? A pushover, I hope. A huge drink next time I see you . . . Yes, it's a promise.'

She replaced the receiver. The phone rang again immediately.

'Elvis has now left the building,' said Sue. 'Is this what I hope it is?'

'Yep,' said Janet in triumph. 'Did you not detect the smell of burning martyr when he left?'

'I think I probably did,' said Sue. 'This is fantastic news, and I insist on a blow-by-blow account. We must have a Haunted Handbag meeting soon. I've something interesting to report.'

'So has Nina. Stuff's been moving again. How about my place on Friday night?'

'Brilliant. I'll tell Liz and Nina.'

Harry sat back in his *Mastermind* chair and contemplated the fiasco he'd just witnessed. Janet had certainly played a blinder, he had to grudgingly give her that one. As for Burns, he'd had the rug pulled from under his feet.

He went across to the VHS machine and ejected the tape. Then he flipped up the back of the plastic cover with a pen and pulled out yard after yard of tape. Satisfied that it was wrecked beyond repair, he dropped both tape and box in the bin.

Harry did not like being made a fool of. And Janet, being a typical female gasbag, would not keep her mouth shut. Everyone in that production office would know about it by teatime.

'Get me Steven Byfield,' he shouted to Geraldine, who was deliberately keeping a low profile but romping home ahead of the field in the Curiosity Stakes.

'Steven, it's Harry Hampton at Hartford Optimum TV. How are you doing, matey? How's it all going?' Harry had never been particularly friendly with Steven, even before his untimely departure. Steven was too smart and too nosy for his own good. But Harry was never averse to a bit of creeping, especially when it involved personal gain.

'Fine, fine,' replied Steven. 'Just finished a series on after-dinner speakers called *Accustomed As I Am*. Network snapped it up, so watch out for it soon. And you?'

'Oh, ducking and diving, the usual.'

'So, what can I do for you?' said Steven, trying to hide the suspicion in his voice. Any call from Harry was always bad news.

'Paul Burns.' Harry's voice was suddenly cold.

'Oh, Paul Burns. Did you hire him in the end?' said Steven innocently.

'I did.'

'And how's he doing? Has he won you any awards yet? Only a question of time, you know. A unique talent.'

'Unique talent, my arse,' Harry hissed. 'That's precisely why I'm ringing. Had to let him go. I sacked him this afternoon. He was total fucking crap.'

'Let's see. Paul Burns?' pondered Steven theatrically. 'Bullshitter extraordinaire, CV with more holes in it than a colander, inventive references and qualifications. Ability to upset people without even trying. Rude, pompous, lazy. Inability to put a sentence together. Perennially clamped to his mobile phone. Still the same?'

'That's him. So why the fuck did you recommend him?' Harry was now incandescent with anger and thumping his desk so loudly that Geraldine was wondering whether she'd burst an eardrum if she followed Janet's advice and put a glass to the wall.

'I recommended him to return a – well, let's call it a favour. It goes like this, Harry. I work at HOT in charge of the production office. I make wonderful programmes, come up with fabulous ideas, create amazing campaigns, work my butt off. You take the credit. I discover you doing a major fiddle with backhanders all over the place. Bungs to the left of you, bonuses to the right.'

'This has got absolutely nothing to do with Paul Burns,' spluttered Harry.

'Oh yes it has,' contradicted Steven, enjoying himself

hugely. 'Paul Burns was one of the most incompetent oppos I have ever come across. Up here, we endured the over-the–top zoot suits, the wall-to-wall mobile phone calls, the ducking out of doing anything because he couldn't actually do it. And I felt that you deserved this most talented man, plus his unusual wardrobe. Which is why I recommended him to you.'

'You total bastard,' barked Harry, now white-faced and livid.

'So, Harry,' continued Steven, 'it was a bit of a long shot really. You didn't have to hire him. But you did, so I guess that makes us fifteen-all.'

chapter nineteen

Val couldn't understand why Harry was in such a filthy mood. He'd wrong-footed her by coming home early, barging into the house just after five o'clock in a monumental fury. At least it wasn't her fault. He was so angry that he hadn't even shouted at her because he'd found her, feet up on the sofa, watching re-runs of *Dynasty*. He didn't even shout at her when she couldn't come up with any sort of suggestion for dinner.

He poured himself a huge gin and tonic and stomped off round the garden. Thank God he's off on this business trip at the weekend, she thought. Good bloody riddance. She'd go to Hampshire, see her parents and get together with some girlfriends. Then the same old pang hit her. The only girlfriends she seemed to catch up with these days were the four from HOT. Maybe they'd know why Harry was in such a strop. Maybe she'd invite them over to the house while Harry was away. Oh God, that meant cooking. No, she thought, she'd get in a chef. That would impress them. She began to plan.

Harry burst in through the French windows and headed straight for the gin bottle again.

'What's up with you?' she enquired casually. 'Bad day at work?'

''Course it bloody was. Why do you think I'm so angry, you stupid cow? Are you blind or something? Now get off your arse and get some dinner sorted. No, on second thoughts, I can't face another evening of your burnt bloody offerings. We'll go out. You'll have to drive. I'm over the limit now.'

Val went upstairs and changed, pathetically pleased that he wanted to spend a whole evening with her. And even more pleased that it didn't involve cooking. She put on another of the new sparkly cocktail numbers she'd bought from the Ginette fashion show. It was a deep plum-red shift dress with shoestring straps, and she'd managed to get some wonderful Italian patent-leather kitten heels in the same colour. She'd lie about the price, if he bothered to ask. Harry rarely noticed if she was wearing anything new. She swept her blonde hair up into a pleat, painted her nails to match the dress, and she was ready to go.

She came downstairs feeling particularly glamorous and hoping for some sort of compliment from Harry. But he was still in the blackest of moods.

'Oh, you ready? Right, let's go. I've booked Shiraz while you were upstairs tarting up. We'll go in the Merc. I can never get into your bloody stupid Toyota.'

That's because you're too fat, she thought. They set off for the restaurant, which was on the other side of Hartford. During the five-mile journey, Harry harangued her nonstop about her driving. By the time they arrived, they were both in even blacker moods.

'Your usual table, Mr Hampton?' enquired the camp maître d'.

'No, by the window, I think, this time.'

'Oh, you've been here before.' Val shot him an accusing look. She turned to the maître d', flashing a huge smile. 'My husband likes to keep me locked up in a cupboard. Never takes me anywhere.'

With Harry still glowering, they took their seats and were presented with menus.

'So where do you normally sit?' Val enquired. 'In some dark secretive corner, I suppose.'

'Oh, for God's sake, Val, let up. I bring clients here. They don't always want to be on view to all and sundry. Now shut up. I'm hungry and I want a drink.'

He turned to the hovering waiter. 'Large gin and tonic for me and mineral water for the lady. She's driving. Then we'll have the scallops to start, followed by the sea bass. Oh, and get a bottle of Pauillac opened, ready for later on.'

Val knew Harry well enough to know there was no arguing with him, either about the choice of meal or about anything else for that matter.

'So what's wrong, Harry?' She was dying to know.

'Oh, never you mind. I'd like to see that bloody Janet Bancroft swing from the rafters. But other than that, just a normal day.'

'Janet? What's she been up to?'

'None of your business. Don't want to discuss.'

'I bet you're looking forward to the conference, aren't you?' Val was hellbent on making some sort of conversation.

Harry looked blank.

'The conference thingy this weekend; you're going away on business, aren't you?'

'Oh yes, the conference. Yes, yes, of course. And a lot of meetings. For God's sake, Val, shut up. All right?'

They finished the meal in silence, Harry polishing off

all the wine with Val sipping her mineral water and look-ing enviously as the last glass disappeared down his throat.

Liz was still reeling from the news. She caught sight of herself in her hall mirror with a stupid grin plastered from ear to ear. So Paul Burns had finally gone. The plan had paid off. And even Harry had got his comeuppance. Just for once she'd have given anything to be in his office, to see their faces as the tape was played.

Then she shivered at the prospect of being in Harry's office. She shivered some more at Janet's suggestion that she take over the directing of the Hot Breaks series as originally mooted. Janet had been very persuasive.

'I know why you ruled it out last time, and I do under-stand,' Janet had said, 'but the tables have now been turned. Burns made such a monumental cock-up that the only way is up. You can do this standing on your head.'

In the end Liz had reluctantly agreed, but on the basis that she never went into Harry's office alone. Janet said she would put the idea in principle to Harry.

Liz wandered back into her kitchen. The mention of Harry's name always sent shivers down her spine, and she thought back to that terrible night he'd turned up at her flat. And the consequences. At least the Paul Burns episode had gone a little way towards paying him back for what he'd done.

Harry finally lost his temper big-time when they reached the police station.

'It's utterly impossible, it's bloody ridiculous,' he shouted, red-faced with anger. 'She can't possibly be over the limit. She didn't have a drink all evening. The silly cow drank water because she was driving. Your testing kit must be faulty. I demand it be checked. Immediately.'

'Sir, I suggest you calm down. Your wife was breath-alysed at the roadside after the accident. She was found to be well over the limit there. Now she has agreed to be tested here, and I'm afraid the tests show she's two and a half times over the limit. Sorry, sir, it's standard procedure. She'll be summonsed to appear in court later this week.'

Harry thumped the inquiry desk, forgetting he wasn't in his own office.

'Do that again, Mr Hampton, and you might find your-self in trouble,' warned the duty sergeant. 'Have *you* been drinking, by any chance?'

'Yes, of course I have,' snapped Harry. 'But that's why I wasn't driving, you stupid—'

He stopped himself with an effort and his mind went back to his gleaming gold Mercedes, now sporting a com-pletely stoved-in wing. Silly cow, he thought. Women, bloody awful drivers. But how could she have been over the limit?

Much, much later that night, Harry and Val went home in a taxi. The Mercedes was towed to a garage for repair estimates. Val fled upstairs to bed without a word. Harry went into the kitchen, rummaged in the flip-top bin and saw the evidence. Half a dozen empty wine bottles. He poured himself another huge gin and tonic, went into the sitting room and quietly seethed. Then he went upstairs to the spare room, and lay down hoping that Morpheus would sweep away the remnants of possibly the worst day of his life.

It made page three of the *Hartford Echo*: MEDIA BOSS'S WIFE MORE THAN TWICE THE LIMIT. The report carried pictures of Val leaving the police station, dressed in one of her trademark short skirts and high heels, with her blonde hair swept up and dark glasses hiding any facial expression. There was a shot of the Mercedes smashed into a tree, plus an official portrait of Harry, all smiling, cigar-smoking corporate success. Obviously supplied with glee by the PR agency that handled HOT affairs.

The story went round the office like wildfire. Ray photocopied the page and distributed it like hymn sheets.

'Bet Val never expected to be a page three girl,' said Sue, ringing from the reception desk. 'Do you think one of us should ring her, express sympathy, et cetera?'

'I will if you like,' offered Janet. 'I'm feeling a mite more sympathetic to her at the moment, after my little victory over Harry. Mind you, we can hardly be surprised at her getting caught. I'm just amazed she's got away with it for so long. We'll have quite a lot to discuss at our Operation HH meeting on Friday. By the way, I'm planning a film show, so make sure your video hasn't been booked out by the kids.'

Janet sipped her coffee and dialled Val's number. Best get it out of the way early. Also, Val might just be sober.

'Val? It's Janet. So sorry to hear what's happened.'

'Yeah, well. Got caught, didn't I? I'll probably get a year's ban. Having to go around in bloody taxis now. Just too ghastly. Harry was unspeakable. The whole evening was a nightmare. I gather he'd had a bad day. He did a bit of ranting about you too. Is there some sort of problem going on at work?'

'Not now.' Janet smiled to herself. 'All sorted and taken care of.'

'Look, Harry's away next week, so I wondered if you'd all come over for dinner,' said Val. 'It would cheer me up.

I wouldn't cook, sod that. I'd get a chef in. How about Tuesday?'

'I'll ask the girls and let you know.' Janet replaced the phone. Now that would be like entering the lion's den, except that the lion would be playing away somewhere else.

To: Harry Hampton
From: Janet Bancroft
Re: Hot Breaks For Heartaches
In view of the recent difficulties on the above, I'd like to suggest that as it is such an important and prestigious project for the company, it is put into the safest hands. As Liz is now fully recovered from her illness, I'd like her to work on this project as director. She's already across all the subjects in the series so she's an obvious choice. I am very willing to be involved in this project now and will undertake to be project producer. As Liz will be out on the road for most of the time, I suggest that I will be the point of contact with you on day-to-day matters. Your thoughts, please.

To: Janet Bancroft
From: Harry Hampton
Re: Hot Breaks For Heartaches
Agreed.

The Gang of Four met at Sue's house on Friday evening. Sue's husband Jon had taken their children to the cinema to see the latest *Star Wars* film so they could have the house to themselves. The other three were secretly disappointed. Because none of them were parents, they all enjoyed the rough and tumble of Sue's kids, who were well behaved but also spirited. They'd each brought sweets or chocolate for them as well as the usual bottles of wine.

'Don't worry,' said Sue, knowingly, as she stuffed the multi packs of Mars bars, KitKats and Smarties in the fridge. 'They'll be mega-hyper when they come back after the film and a bucket of popcorn. Thanks, girls. Really kind of you. Supper won't take long. And if it's crap, we'll just get stuck into the chocolate.'

She went back to tending the pasta and delegated the wine-pouring to Nina. Soon four huge glasses of Mâcon were poured and three toasts declared.

'To Paul Burns. Good riddance!'

'To Val. Shame about the arrest, but you've had a jolly long run.'

'To Harry. Serves you right for being a complete bastard.'

Then they all sat down in Sue's tiny dining room. Sue emerged from the kitchen with steaming bowls of tagliatelle and a seafood sauce bursting with prawns, mussels, squid and hake and laced with tomatoes, herbs and garlic. Silence descended, punctuated only by exclamations of delight. A raspberry pavlova was greeted by another cheer. When that had been demolished, they went through to the sitting room, and Sue poured coffee while Janet made a brief announcement.

'It gives me great pleasure to show you how Mr Paul Burns met his Waterloo. Watch out for the glamorous Mrs Saunders – line-dancing's answer to Barbara Cartland. In other words, a large pink blancmange wearing ten tons of make-up.'

They all sat transfixed by the tape and burst into applause at the end.

'I have a sneaking feeling that Harry's copy ended up in the bin,' said Janet afterwards. 'Fortunately Colin made two copies, and this is mine to keep. I shall always treasure it as one of the happiest days of my life at HOT. The Day of the C Word.'

'What C word?' Liz asked suspiciously.

'No, not that one. C is for comeuppance,' retorted Janet. 'And not only that, I spoke to Steven Byfield today. Remember him, the chap who did my job before I arrived, and left in a mysterious haze?'

'Yes,' they all clamoured.

'Well, he took a call from Harry after the great Burns departure.'

'And . . .' Sue said impatiently.

'And then Steven called me.'

'Yes . . .' They were now all desperate. Janet paused, glanced round at them theatrically, took a slug of wine and then proceeded to relate Steven's account of the conversation, ending with his remark to Harry about the score being fifteen-all.

'Sorry, Janet, but that's not fifteen-all,' said Nina. 'That's game, set and match to Steven. What a brilliant long shot.'

'Yes, it was,' said Janet. 'And now we need to think about what we do next. I must say, our first strike was a great success, but don't underestimate Harry. He'll wriggle out of this one, just like he's done before. Also, his hackles will be severely up after the business with Val. Talking of which, our about-to-be-banned friend has invited us over to their house on Tuesday.'

'Well, count me out,' said Nina. 'It was bad enough spending evenings getting personal abuse from Val in restaurants without going to their home for a further onslaught from her rotten husband.'

'Ah, but remember, Harry won't be there,' said Sue. 'He's off on the mystery freebie early next week. This is a chance to snoop.'

'I'm not sure either,' said Liz, shooting Janet a knowing look. It was the last thing she needed, to be sitting at Harry's table, drinking Harry's wine. They all looked to Janet for a decision.

'Well, I say we go,' she said firmly. 'If we're going to crack this whole business, we ought to find out what really makes him tick. You know what it's like when you visit someone's home, you learn so much about them so quickly.'

'I hardly think Harry and Val are going to have pink crinoline lady crocheted toilet roll covers,' said Nina. 'Or garage glasses, moquette settees and bubble oil lamps.'

'It's up to you lot,' said Janet. 'But personally, I can't wait to have a good snoop.'

'I'll go,' said Sue, emphatically.

'Not me,' said Liz.

'Count me out,' added Nina.

chapter twenty

They decided to have pre-dinner drinks and a council of war at the GX before driving over to Val's house. Then it was agreed that they'd travel together in Janet's car on the basis that they could arrive and leave en bloc. Blatant curiosity, the chance for revenge, and a certain amount of cajoling had finally overcome the reluctance of Nina and Liz.

'If it's a truly hideous house, then at least we'll dine out on it for a while,' said Sue. 'If it's fantastic, then we'll be able to get even angrier with Harry. See, either way we win.'

'Don't forget, our job tonight is to find out what Val thinks Harry gets up to when he's not with her,' said Janet. 'Any observations, make mental notes and then we'll all compare.'

'We still don't know very much,' Sue reminded them. 'All we know so far is that Harry goes home late on Mondays and Thursdays on a regular basis. His mobile is switched off from six when he leaves the building until about ten o'clock when he gets home. We know an Italian-sounding woman makes fairly regular calls to him but never leaves a message. He's gone on some mystery conference and business trip but we don't know precisely where and his phone was switched off all day today.'

'How do you know?' asked Nina.

'Because I had a message for him. Nothing urgent, but it gave me the excuse to keep trying him rather than speak to the dreaded Geraldine. In the end, even Geraldine said she didn't know why his phone was off.'

'Well, well,' mused Janet. 'That's unusual.'

'The other thing is that Geraldine's been clocked doing a bit of snooping,' said Sue.

'Blimey, how did you know that?'

' 'S easy. I meant to tell you at our last HH meeting but I was overwhelmed by the brilliant video. Also, I've now had a chance to confirm it.'

'What sort of snooping?'

'Oh, spotted in the production office opening drawers, that kind of stuff. Anita told me.' Anita was another of HOT's receptionists, who'd been on late shift the previous week.

'I *told* you things had been moving,' said Nina triumphantly. 'Nice of Harry to get old G-spot doing his dirty work. Just typical.'

'Isn't it time we told Harry subtly that we know what he's up to?' said Janet. 'You know, leave a few messages lying around to show we've rumbled him. How about inventing a few files with provocative titles and see if he opens them? It could be quite fun!'

'Fun?' queried Nina sarcastically.

'Yeah. For example, I might leave my computer on and I might just have a file in there called Harry's Game, or Hassle With Harry, or something that would grab his attention.'

'What would you write in the file?' asked Liz quietly.

'Oh, either leave it blank or write something that looks irresistibly provocative, like "I've had the photos developed."'

'And of course he couldn't say anything because it would be tantamount to owning up,' finished Sue.

'By the way, one other snippet,' said Janet. 'Veronica's resigned. She won't say why but I just have the strangest feeling it's something to do with Harry. She handed in her notice yesterday and wants to leave this Friday. Let's see if we can find out the true story on that one.'

'Drink up, everyone,' said Sue, glancing at her watch. 'Time to visit Hampton Court!'

They rang the doorbell, using the delay to size the place up. They'd already noted with envy the carriage driveway, the leaded windows, the immaculate front gardens and lawns. It was one of those modern mini mansions that screamed, 'We've got loadsamoney!'

'Seeing as it's Hampton Court,' said Nina, grinning, 'do you think there's a maze?'

'Not much point in asking Val,' replied Liz. 'She's in a permanent one herself.'

'It's probably pseudo-*Hello!* magazine,' remarked Janet as they waited. 'Lots of very tidy rooms with large sofas and photogenic dogs.'

'Hmm, not that posh. Answers her own front door,' observed Nina, hearing Val click-clacking across the inevitable parquet flooring towards the front door. She greeted the four of them like long-lost friends and ushered them straight into an enormous sitting room. It was very Harry. Huge cream leather sofas, chrome and glass tables, enormous paintings, elaborate chandeliers and chrome table lights greeted them. Sue asked for the loo and was shown to a room nearly as big as the entire downstairs of her house. The walls were covered with awards and posters connected with HOT. Harry was certainly claiming credit for an awful lot of projects and wanted visitors to his loo to be left in no doubt as to how successful he was.

Val was a surprisingly good hostess. She seemed more relaxed on home ground, buzzing around with exquisite canapés and plying her guests with champagne. This gave her a chance to dot in and out of the kitchen, where she could refill her own glass secretly and take a few surreptitious swigs. She'd decided that after the court case, where she'd been banned from driving for a year, it wasn't good form to be seen drinking at all. At least by having to sneak out into the kitchen, it would ration her intake and she might manage to stay reasonably sober. Val was also smarting from a failure. She'd tried to give up drinking the previous day – and only managed to last for a morning. Given that she'd not got up until eleven o'clock, and had succumbed to a glass of vino by one, it wasn't too impressive an effort. Tonight she'd at least pretend she'd given up.

Twenty minutes in, no one had been insulted, criticized or stabbed in the back. And Val was still upright. Dressed in her favourite fuchsia pink, this time cropped linen trousers and a raw silk top, she seemed rather contrite about losing her licence. Perhaps there was a nicer person trying to get out after all, thought Janet, having a sudden tiny rush of guilt. It didn't last long.

'Hm, interesting outfit, Janet,' remarked Val, sweeping Janet's long black satin jacket to one side and exposing the less than perfect body it was intended to hide. 'You really ought to come to Ginette's next fashion show.'

That nicer person had obviously decided to go back in again, Janet decided. Leopards don't change their spots, she reminded herself, wincing as her flab was displayed for all to behold. She waited for a further onslaught of criticism about her weight, but was mildly surprised when none came.

They were ushered into a dark green dining room, where a mahogany table big enough to seat at least twenty was laid with gilt-edged white plates, gleaming silver cutlery and candelabra, crisp white napkins and bottles of Chablis chilling in ice buckets. Charlie, the chef Val had hired, turned out to be a cheerful cockney who could cook up a storm. He brought in plates of oysters nestling in beds of crushed ice. Nina's face fell immediately. She'd never eaten oysters before, mostly because she didn't like the look of them. Timidly she copied what everyone else did and shovelled one into her mouth.

'Blimey,' she said, making a face. 'Like swallowing snot. Sorry, Val, no offence.' She waited for a torrent of abuse and ridicule from Val, but there was none. Something had definitely changed for the better. Perhaps appearing in court had taken Val down a peg or two.

Over the main course of mixed fish kebabs, lemon couscous and the most delicious salad of rocket and frisee, Val was still very preoccupied. She badly wanted a lot more to drink and not being the centre of attention in some crowded and fashionable eaterie had taken the challenge out of the evening.

'Lovely house, Val,' said Sue appreciatively. 'I adore the paintings in this room. Which one of you's the collector?'

'Oh, not me,' said Val, dismissively. 'They're all Harry's choice. They just turned up one day recently.'

Oh, really? thought Janet, realizing suddenly that they looked suspiciously similar in style to the new paintings that had appeared above and behind the *Mastermind* chair. Probably another of his little freebies. God, he never stopped.

'How did Harry take the news about your driving ban?' enquired Janet, as casually as she could.

'He went berserk,' said Val, shoving her plate aside virtually untouched and lighting a cigarette. 'He hasn't really spoken to me since, which is totally unfair. The police test kit must have been faulty. I certainly wasn't over the limit. But anyway, he's been a total pig, and it's probably just as well that he's off at this telly conference thingy.'

'Where is it exactly?' asked Janet lightly.

'Manchester, I think,' said Val vaguely. 'All I know is he's away for a week. What they all find to talk about, God only knows. It sounds sooooo boring. I'm hoping he might have forgotten about the court case when he comes back. I'll just go and help Charlie bring in the pudding. Back in a mo.'

Val click-clacked off in the direction of the kitchen. She had no intention of helping Charlie do anything. She just wanted a decent-sized glass of wine, and she wanted it double quick.

'If Harry *is* in the Algarve, how's he going to pass off a week's worth of suntan when he's supposed to be in Manchester?' half whispered Janet with a grin.

'Oh, they'll have had a freak heatwave up there,' said Liz, who had finally relaxed a little. She still hated being in Harry's house. It made her flesh creep.

'Val doesn't seem to be drinking at all,' observed Nina.

'Hm, I'm not so sure,' said Janet. 'I think that's what these constant trips to the kitchen are all about. Having made all those excuses about the faulty testing kit, she can't be seen to be knocking it back. I think she's doing a Cleopatra on us.'

'Cleopatra?' they all whispered.

'Yeah, Cleopatra,' grinned Janet. 'Queen of Denial.'

They had to suppress their laughter as Charlie and Val emerged from the kitchen, each carrying a pudding. One was a coffee and walnut gateau decorated with chocolate coffee beans, the other a miraculous meringue affair with spun sugar, raspberries and cream. Silence descended for a while as they plunged into a dessert heaven. Val, of course, had her trademark mouthful, moved the rest around the plate with a fork and then lit a cigarette.

'So, what are you doing for the rest of the week? Going up to join Harry?' asked Janet, still trying to sound casual.

'Omigod, no,' replied Val. 'Far too ghastly. It rains in Manchester and they all wear flat caps and talk like *Coronation Street*. No, I'm going to stay with my parents in Hampshire. Get some serious shopping done. I don't even know where Harry's staying, which suits me fine, because then I have the perfect excuse not to call him.'

'Won't he expect you to ring him on the mobile?' Janet pressed gently.

'Oh, no. He's taken to switching it off a bit lately. At one time it was permanently on and frying his brain. Well, maybe now it's been roasted!' Val laughed uproariously at her own joke and swayed precariously on her chair. The surreptitious swigs in the kitchen had suddenly taken effect.

She now pointed a bright pink nail in Janet's direction. 'By the way, Janet, I hear you're in the doghouse.'

'Really?' said Janet. They all sat up, suddenly more attentive.

'Yeah, the night we went out for that stupid dinner, Harry was in a right old temper and mentioned something about stringing you up. Do tell. I've been dying to know.'

'Hm, last Monday, let me see. Just a normal happy day at the office as far as I can recall,' said Janet sarcastically, noting that her theory about why Val kept disappearing to the kitchen was beginning to stand up.

'Oh, wait a minute, let me think,' she continued, pausing for effect. 'It was Paul Burns' leaving day. That must have been it. Perhaps Harry was upset at him going so early on in the Hot Breaks project. I must say, we were all surprised.'

'No, not that,' said Val, now grappling with her fading memory and the effect of more than two bottles of Chablis in as many hours. 'He was definitely very cross with you.'

'Perhaps Harry knew I wouldn't be able to do half as good a job,' said Janet cynically.

'Yeah, that's probably it,' said Val, now not really listening. 'That chap, whassisname, was shit-hot apparently. Geraldine told me, and she ought to know.'

The others didn't make eye contact in case they laughed openly.

Val half stood up, noticed the room swaying and promptly sat down again. 'There's something really odd about that woman,' she announced, pointing a selection of pink nails around the table.

'Oh,' said everyone in chorus. 'Do tell.'

Val tried to stand again, and this time lurched to one side, dragging the starched white tablecloth with her. The others made a dive to stop the candles, plates, glasses and cutlery heading for the floor. But Val was now too pissed to notice.

'Geraldine has a *big* secret,' she persisted.

'Go on,' they urged.

'You'll never believe it.'

'Of course not,' they chorused, still gripping the table-cloth.

'Guess.'

'Don't know.'

Val lit a cigarette, pausing for effect. Although she was now well gone, she still had a sense of timing. Finally she put down her lighter, exhaled dramatically and propped her elbow on the edge of the table. In her haze, her elbow slipped and she shot forward, narrowly missing falling head first into the remains of her raspberry pudding.

'Geraldine's surname is Taylor, right?'

'Right.'

'Geraldine's middle name is Nancy.'

'Okay.'

'So that makes her initials GNT. G 'n' T, gin and tonic, geddit?'

They all feigned hysterical laughter.

'Bet she never thought of that when she married Mr Taylor,' said Val, stubbing out her hardly smoked cigarette.

'Mr Taylor?' said Sue in surprise. 'We didn't know there was a Mr Taylor.'

'Well, there *was* but he divorced her. Oh, absolutely yonks ago.'

'Poor Geraldine,' said Janet insincerely.

'No, poor Mr Taylor,' retorted Val, attempting another rise from the table. 'Let's leave this lot and chill out.'

They all trooped back into the sitting room and flopped back on to the cream sofas.

'Why poor Mr Taylor?' persisted Sue. 'Why did he divorce her?'

'Ha ha, Harry told me,' said Val, giggling softly. 'You'd never guess, looking at Geraldine. I mean, she's so bloody boring.'

'No we can't guess. We give in. Why was it?' said Sue.

'He divorced her,' Val's words were almost incomprehensible now, 'for too much hoovering and too many demands for sex.'

They all thought they were going to explode. Val, however, was out cold.

chapter twenty-one

The mobile phone campaign in the *Hartford Echo* was gathering momentum. Every week the paper carried more success stories, listing public places where mobiles had been banned.

'I'm surprised there's any mileage in this,' said Ray, feet up on a desk, 'now that our very own Olympic gold medallist in the individual phone event, Paul Burns, has left town. And the current world mobile champion is away on the Costa del Manchester. They'll be tearing down loads of redundant phone masts now that the network has been so freed up.'

Janet was only half listening. She was whipping through her e-mails as fast as she could. She was due to start filming the property project in a few days' time and there was still much to do in the fixing and scripting before she would be happy. There was always a period just before the start of an important project when Janet got really nervous. She'd come to realize this was a good sign, that the stress meant her brain was in gear.

'Sorry, Ray, what did you say?' she said absent-mindedly.

He tapped the paper. 'Just that Don't Fry Your Brain Campaign the *Echo*'s running.'

'Oh, that,' she said, disappointed. 'Thought for a minute you had some good gossip.'

'As a matter of fact I do,' said Ray, immediately lowering his voice and sticking his head between the computer screens for privacy.

'Do you know why snotty totty Veronica's leaving? The real reason?'

Janet shook her head and gave him her full attention. 'I thought it was just a personality thing.'

'I've been sworn to secrecy, but . . .'

'You're going to tell me anyway,' finished Janet. 'And no, I won't give you a reference for that job at MI6.'

'Harry made a pass at her.'

Janet's heart skipped a beat. She could feel herself fingering her handbag, perched on top of her filing cabinet. They adjourned swiftly to the canteen, where, over cappuccinos, Ray told her what he knew, namely that Harry had turned up at Veronica's flat armed with a bottle of champagne and tried to charm his way into her underwear, via the 'Babe, I could help you go places with this company' route.

'All the subtlety of a brick,' said Janet. 'So how did she react?'

'Offered him sex and travel,' grinned Ray. 'In other words, she told him to fuck off.'

'Would you do me a favour?' said Janet on the spur of the moment. 'There's something I'd really like you to do for me.'

Janet and Liz met up in the GX for lunch. Liz was anxious to talk through the next two Hot Breaks episodes as they were her first solo efforts. The worried look in her eyes had made Janet realize it would be a good idea to get her off site for an hour, so they'd decamped with all Liz's files of notes and treatments. They toyed with grilled chicken and Greek salad while they went through the final details of the portrait-painting weekend and the murder-mystery break.

'Talking of mysteries, I think I've discovered another one,' said Janet when they'd finished. She poured Liz the last of the wine they'd had with their meal, then carefully outlined the little she knew about Veronica's encounter with Harry.

'The interesting thing is that Harry got it badly wrong with Veronica,' she continued. 'With you it was totally different, because you were so vulnerable at the time. Veronica's a fairly snotty cow and her heart's not in this business. If Harry had made the threats he made to you, all that "You'll never lunch in this town again" nonsense, Veronica wouldn't have cared less. She's looking for a suitably rich husband, not a future in corporate television. And certainly not a quick hump with old Hampton. If Harry'd muttered about giving her a good reference, she'd probably assume it was something to do with the national grid and a large country estate with shooting rights.'

'He certainly fouled up there.' Liz, who'd been visibly shaken by Janet's revelation, was cheering up a little. 'No wonder he's been in such a vile temper recently, one way and another. And Val's starring role in court didn't help matters much.'

'Anyway, by the time he comes back from Manchester's Portuguese quarter, Veronica will have gone, problem solved,' said Janet. 'Except that I'm thinking of enlisting Ray's help in something. I think we'd better have another meeting of the Haunted Handbag committee later this week.'

Veronica's leaving do on Friday turned into an all-day affair. It was not a reflection of her popularity, more that the production office crowd were in desperate need of a party. There was plenty to celebrate: the departure of Paul Burns, plus the luxury of having had a whole Harry-free week.

It started with people drifting across to the GX for lunch. July had suddenly turned scorching, so an advance party was sent ahead to bag all the outside tables. On guaranteed hot sunny days, the GX staff fired up a big barbecue, and soon about thirty people from HOT were tucking into burgers, hot dogs and salads. There had been a whip-round and Nina had been dispatched to buy a present, but with only fifteen quid extracted from around forty people it was always going to be a challenge. She chose a framed print on the basis that it wouldn't betray how little they'd raised.

By early evening they were all back around the outside tables at the GX, with Veronica insisting on buying champagne for everyone. Egged on by the company, Ray decided to make a speech. Somewhat the worse for wear, he rose to his feet.

'Veronica,' he said, 'sorry you're leaving. I thought you were a stuck-up, snotty cow, but tonight I've realized you're not. Nice champagne, petal. Cheers.'

They all raised their glasses. Veronica, also somewhat the worse for wear, took absolutely no offence, and even began to think they weren't such a dreadful bunch after all and perhaps she shouldn't be leaving. Then she thought back to that slimeball Harry and promptly changed her mind again.

'Speech, speech,' they all cried.

'Thank you, one and all,' she said in her cut-glass accent, sweeping back her blonde mane with one hand and raising her glass with the other. 'And thank you, Ray, for that charming speech. I have to admit I've never been called "petal" before. I think I'll miss you after all. With the exception of one person.'

They all started humming the *Mastermind* theme.

'Here's to Harry, wherever he is tonight,' said Nigel, one of the researchers.

'Up yours, Harry!' the cry went up.

'Is that why you're leaving?' asked Nigel innocently. Veronica went purple with anger, put down her glass and stalked off to the loo.

Silence fell immediately.

'Shit, did I say something wrong? Has Harry humped and dumped her or something?' Nigel looked aghast.

'Nah,' said Ray nonchalantly, giving Janet a sideways wink. 'If anything, it should be the other way round. You know Harry fancies anything, with or without a pulse. Come on, mate, a girl looking like Veronica does, of course he'd want a bit of that. What Harry doesn't know is that she views us all, him included, as some sort of pond life.'

'Yeah, you're right, mate,' replied Nigel, draining his champagne. 'Still, she came up trumps tonight. She's probably like a lot of women, heaps more fun when she's pissed. Do you think he did try to give her one?'

'Don't know, and for God's sake, don't ask,' said Ray, nodding in Veronica's direction. She was heading back to the table. 'Whatever it was, she wasn't having it. Serves Harry right. Living up to his name.'

'How d'ya mean?' asked Nigel.

'Hampton. Hampton Wick,' grinned Ray. 'Cockney rhyming slang. Nuff said.'

Because Janet, Sue and Liz had each drunk a couple of glasses of champagne and Nina hadn't because she was on another of her bum-reducing diet regimes, they piled into Nina's car, heading once again for Sue's house. They'd agreed to have their Haunted Handbag meeting there, but only on condition that they picked up a takeaway to save Sue cooking.

They arrived on Sue's doorstep clutching carrier bags of Chinese food and were greeted by her two children jumping up and down in delight. Not at seeing them; just at the thought of Chinese, which was their favourite.

Half an hour later, with the three carrier bags now stacked up with empty containers, everyone flopped back in their seats, pleasantly full. Even Nina, who'd suffered a temporary loss of will power when she smelt the food.

'Thanks, girls,' said Sue. 'It was a real treat not to cook, especially on such a hot night, and also for the kids. They just love Chinese.'

'Yeah, we noticed,' said Nina. 'They were like locusts. Still, it's good news: the more they eat, the less I do. Got to get another inch off my bum. I've got loads of incentive now.'

Nina's relationship with Sam was going great guns. He'd recently hinted at taking her on holiday to Rhodes later in the summer, which had given Nina an attack of the wobbles.

'Has he booked it yet?' asked Liz.

'Yes, today,' said Nina. 'I'm so excited, but I'm also terrified.'

'Why?'

' 'Cos he'll see my bum. We'll have to go to the beach and all that stuff.'

'Well, that's the whole idea, isn't it?' said Janet, grinning. 'Anyway, you go to bed with the guy; he must know every inch of you by now.'

'He takes his glasses off and I insist on lighting the smallest of night lights because I tell him it turns me on.'

'Oh heck, Nina. You can't go on like that.'

'Well, I've managed so far.'

'But you can't live your whole life making him miss Vision Express appointments and saving the planet by using tea lights.'

'Oh, I'll find a way,' said Nina. 'Anyway, I'm meeting his parents next week.'

'Blimey, this *is* serious,' said Janet. 'Here, save some of that egg-fried rice, we might need it for your wedding.'

'Oh shut up,' said Nina sheepishly. 'But he is just totally scrummy.'

'And talking of sex, what about Geraldine, eh?' said Janet. 'I thought sex and shopping went together, but sex and hoovering. That's a new one. Or maybe it's all to do with being a sucker.'

'I haven't been able to look at her this week in case I laughed,' said Sue. 'With Harry away, my dealings with her have thankfully been minimal. I've managed to avoid any eye contact when she's come through reception.'

'I can't imagine Geraldine having torrid sex, let alone rushing around sensuously with a vacuum,' said Janet. 'Perhaps that's why she's so vacuous.'

'I must say, that's the first time Val's ever made me laugh,' remarked Liz. 'I really didn't want to go to Harry's house, but it was worth it. Anyway, what's this new plan you've got for Operation Haunted Handbag?'

Janet paused and collected her thoughts. The only way they were going to find out what Harry was up to, she explained to them, was to follow him on Monday and Thursday nights. Now, it was impossible for any of them to do it unless they put on some ridiculous disguise and

191

borrowed a different car. But there was someone in the office who could, and who had already agreed to do it.

'Who?' they all chorused.

'Ray,' said Janet. 'This week, while Harry was away, Ray bought himself a motorbike. You know boys and their toys. Well, Ray's got the whole bit, leathers, helmet, et cetera; in other words a disguise and a different vehicle. Ray knows an awful lot of what Harry's up to. Don't forget, he found out about the freebie holiday ages ago, and he found out why Veronica was leaving. There's a budding investigative journalist in there. He's just as intrigued as we are, so I say we should let him have a go.'

'What if he's discovered?' asked Liz.

'I think Ray can wriggle out of that,' replied Janet. 'If for some reason Harry got suspicious, Ray would just abandon the chase. It's as simple as that.'

'Do you think Val suspects anything?' said Sue.

'Nah,' chipped in Nina. 'She's too pissed most of the time for it to cross her mind. And too full of herself.' Nina still hadn't forgotten, and had no intention of forgiving, the London Derrière jibe.

'I'm not so sure now,' mused Janet. 'I think Val's had a bit of a rethink since her presentation at court! She was certainly different at home. I know she passed out eventually, but she wasn't quite as obnoxious as usual and at least she didn't create a scene or fall over.'

'I wonder if she did go to Hampshire. It might be worth a casual call to see if she's heard from him,' said Sue.

'Good idea,' said Janet, reaching for her handbag and beginning the customary five-minute search for her filofax. By the time Sue had made a pot of coffee and brought it in, Janet was finally dialling Val's home number.

'It's diverting to her mobile,' she told them, with her hand over the receiver.

'Val? Hi, it's Janet. Just thought I'd ring to say thanks from all of us for the other night. Great fun . . . No, it was fine you falling asleep. You must have had a hard day . . . No, we all helped Charlie clear up . . . Anyway, just wondered how you are? . . . At your folks'? How lovely. Heard from Harry? . . . Right, right . . . Well, thanks again and have a good weekend, bye.'

Janet switched off the phone. They all looked at her expectantly.

'I can't believe I'm saying this, but she sounded relatively sober. Perhaps she can't get to the wine bottle so easily at her parents' house. Anyway, just the one call from Harry. The conference allegedly goes on over the weekend and he returns on Monday.'

'She doesn't sound remotely curious, by the sound of it,' said Sue.

'Nope,' agreed Janet. 'I think, all in all, she's pleased to see the back of him.'

'Me too,' said Liz.

At that moment, Sue's husband Jon put his head round the door.

'Hi, girls,' he greeted them. 'Cor, something smells nice. Monosodium glutamate! You've had Chinese. Any left?'

'No, sorry, darling,' said Sue grinning. 'How about some sex and hoovering instead?'

They all fell about laughing.

chapter twenty-two

She'd grown up with it, yet, strangely, it came as a shock. Val had been at her parents' house for a couple of days when, on Sunday afternoon, her mother, still glamorous at sixty, said casually, 'Your father and I are going upstairs for a while.'

She'd almost forgotten her parents were still at it like rabbits. It had been so much part of her childhood. When her mother mentioned going upstairs, that meant do not disturb. Unlike most children, for whom the thought of their parents having wild, abandoned sex induced vomiting noises into invisible airline paper bags, Val was used to her parents sloping off for a lovemaking session.

The shock for Val was more a reminder that she and Harry didn't do this. They never had. Harry was always far too busy wheeling and dealing, meeting important people, to be spending an afternoon in bed with her. Their sex life was a brief bump and grind at night if he was in the mood, or an occasional Sunday morning.

Although her parents' Georgian mansion was huge, vast enough to be able to keep well away from the sound of bedposts rocking or springs creaking, Val decided to go out. Because of the ban, she could hardly borrow a car and go shopping. Instead she opted for a walk around the grounds. The gardens always looked fantastic at this time of year.

But before she could go out, she'd need a decent drink. She found a bottle of Sancerre in the fridge and poured herself a glass, then sat down at the huge kitchen table to leaf through an old copy of *Hampshire County Magazine*. She noted two of her old school friends beaming from the social pages, presenting charity cheques and wearing inane grins and ridiculous hats. Very mother-of-the-bride, she thought; they'd managed to make themselves look a good ten years older. She shivered and poured another glass. A sudden feeling of loneliness overwhelmed her. Harry away, all her friends married with kids – or in Susie's case having an affair with her boss – even her parents upstairs shagging. Everyone seemed to be getting it except her. To stave off further misery, she gulped down the rest of the bottle and went out into the sunshine.

The gardens really were looking magnificent. The terrace at the rear of the house looked out over immaculately clipped lawns bordered by sculpted trees and shrubs. Over the stone balustrade from huge urns spilled hundreds of geraniums, petunias and trailing lobelia, in deep pinks, purples and blues. Beyond the gardens rolled the yellowing wheat fields owned by her parents and farmed by tenants. Keith and Sheila actually owned everything they could see from the house, and all thanks to her father's waste-disposal business. He'd worked hard, been incredibly successful but still found time for her mother. So why couldn't Harry be the same?

Val felt in need of another drink but forced herself to keep walking. The more she marvelled at the gardens, watching two swallows racing each other across a perfect blue sky, and noticing the flowers opening up as if in gratitude to the warmth of the sun, the more she realized how empty her life had become.

'I hate Harry,' she proclaimed aloud, and then put a hand to her mouth as if to indicate a slip of the tongue. But the words had been spoken, and spoken aloud. From that moment on, she knew she really did hate him. Suddenly she was stone-cold sober.

By the time she got back to the house, her mother was busily mixing gin and tonics for them all before dinner. Her parents both smiled at her, with that inner glow that comes from a shared intimacy. Lucky sods, thought Val. She smiled for a moment, remembering a woman describing having sex with a famous and very fat politician as being flattened by a huge wardrobe with the key sticking in the lock. It could have been Harry. She shuddered again, realizing she didn't want that any more. Did that mean her marriage was dead, or would the magic return? Had there been any magic in the first place? Should she have an affair? Would that solve things? Even top agony aunts would have their work cut out for them with a slippery bastard like Harry.

'I thought we'd eat in the dining room tonight, instead of the kitchen,' said her mother. 'Eve's cooking something rather special, so we'll do it properly.'

Eve, the housekeeper, was the most brilliant cook, so if she was doing something special then it certainly would be amazing. The dining room was one of the most magnificent places in the house, with French doors opening on to the terrace and a fantastic view of the garden.

'Sounds lovely. In that case I'll go and change.' Val ran up the huge sweeping staircase in the main hallway, two at a time, just like she had as a child. She had a quick shower, redid her make-up, pinned her hair up into a chignon and put on a midnight-blue chiffon shift dress that Harry absolutely hated.

'You look wonderful, darling,' said her father, greeting her with a kiss on the forehead. 'Doesn't she look beautiful?' he added proudly, turning to his wife. 'My goodness, you do take after your mother.'

They both beamed at her lovingly. Val was so overcome with emotion she felt her eyes sting with tears. Get a grip, she told herself, it's only because Harry's not like this.

The meal was well up to Eve's standards. Tiny scallops flash-fried to perfection, followed by John Dory cooked in butter and fresh herbs and served with mounds of baby asparagus, sweetcorn and crispy mangetout.

'Sorry the Sancerre wasn't quite chilled,' said her father deliberately. 'I'm sure I told Eve to put one in the fridge this morning.'

Val looked down hurriedly at her empty plate. They knew, she realized. But what else did they know?

'Mum,' she started, feeling her eyes well up, 'Dad, there's something I want to tell you, ask you. I'm just so confused. Oh, I don't know any more.' She burst into tears and hid her face in her napkin.

When she'd calmed down a little and wiped her eyes, she blinked, looking at them both.

'There's something I have to tell you, something I only realized this afternoon but I know it's true.'

'Yes, darling?' said her mother gently.

'I hate Harry. I loathe him and I don't want him near me any more.'

There were more tears, followed by racking sobs into the napkin. She felt a comforting hand touch her arm.

'We know, dear. We've known for a long time,' said her mother simply.

Janet had left her car in the HOT car park over the weekend, because of Veronica's all-day leaving bash. She'd quite enjoyed being carless for once. It made her walk to the corner shop, stroll to the off-licence, linger in the park. She savoured the fresh air and the prolonged hot spell.

Local news bulletins were already warning of bans on hosepipes, sprinklers and car washes, but Janet didn't care. She was enjoying the feeling of the sun beating down on her face and seeping into her bones. Everyone looked happier; people seemed to stroll rather than scuttle everywhere at top speed. The pubs of Hartford overflowed with customers spilling out on to pavements, clutching cooling pints of lager as the sun continued to beat down.

I wonder what the weather's like in Manchester, Janet thought idly. Scorching, said the *Daily Mail*. And probably that lucky sod Harry would get away with it again. A week in the Algarve with his mystery mistress, return bronzed and rested after a week of sun, sea and probably nonstop bonking, and then pass it off as a week slaving away at a conference. Unless, of course, that was exactly where he was. Perhaps they'd got it all wrong. Maybe they'd imagined all this and it had got seriously out of hand.

No, no, she reasoned with herself, he'd not discussed the conference or any business meetings with her; he hadn't even given Val the name of his hotel. Where was he after work for three or four hours on Mondays and Thursdays, and who was the mysterious Italian-sounding woman? If he was on the straight and narrow, why had he made a pass at Veronica? And why had he done the same to Liz?

'Sorry, Harry, you're a big, fat, randy, arrogant, rapidly-going-to-seed complete and utter shit,' she announced aloud to a row of terracotta pots containing purple fuchsias. She was sitting in her tiny garden enjoying the last of the Sunday-afternoon sun and waiting for Liz to arrive to give her a lift to the car park. This really was bliss: a glass of ice-cold fruit juice, the luxury of the Sunday papers and all the time in the world to read them. No computers, no e-mail, no pagers trilling or vibrating. Also, having ascertained that the neighbours were out, she'd even put on an ancient bikini and slapped on some factor 15. Getting burned would make the flab look ten times worse than it was already. A tan might make her look at least a bit thinner. She must have fallen asleep, because the next thing she knew, the doorbell was ringing.

'Christmas come early here?' remarked Liz, stepping over the doorstep. 'Look at your conk. You'll put Rudolf out of a job.'

'Shit,' said Janet, glancing in the hall mirror. 'Must have forgotten that bit when I slapped on the cream. Just what I need tomorrow. I've got a meeting with a pile of extremely posh estate agents. They're all fraightfully yah.'

'Oh, it'll have calmed down by tomorrow,' said Liz. 'If not, you'll have to tone it down with some slap. Anyway, you might be able to match Harry with his perma-tan all the way from Portu . . . I mean Manchester.'

'Do you know, I've decided I'm going to press him about this conference he supposedly went to,' said Janet. 'Six months ago my confidence, or lack of, would never have allowed me to. But I really am going to quiz him.'

'I'm several light years off that stage of life,' said Liz. 'I think I'll always avoid Harry whenever I can, for obvious reasons. I suppose I'm being far too hopeful, but do you think he'd ever leave HOT?'

'No, I don't.' Janet shook her head. 'I think he's on far too good a number. We've seen the house now; Harry's not exactly down to his last Mercedes, is he?'

'Also, that kind of power base takes a long time to build,' said Liz.

'Exactly,' replied Janet. 'Bullying, cheating, creeping, wheeling and dealing, it all takes years to perfect. No, Harry isn't going anywhere.'

'Not unless he's pushed.'

'Exactly.'

Sunday night's gathering humidity finally broke in the small hours of the morning. The heavens released their torrential load and the temperature dropped dramatically. By Monday morning, everything looked fresher from the downpour but the sun had declined to show up. Grey skies threatened more rain.

Harry stormed into the office in a mood to match the weather. He'd come home late last night to an empty house and an empty fridge. Val was still at her parents' and had left a brief message on the answering machine saying she was staying on in Hampshire for another day or two. Harry had flung down his suitcase full of dirty washing and cursed the fact that he'd dumped at Gatwick all the swimming trunks, shorts and tee-shirts he'd bought on holiday. If he'd known the silly cow wasn't going to be there, he'd have brought them home, run them through the washing machine and passed them off as old stuff. Val would never have noticed, or cared. But even she would have clocked swimming shorts covered in sand and still smelling of the Atlantic if they'd come straight out of his case.

On the other hand, it had suddenly struck him that he'd not a clue how to use the washing machine. No, chucking out the evidence had probably been a wise move.

Despite having had a week of nonstop nookie without a shred of guilt, he'd still found himself absurdly angry that Val wasn't at home. She should have been there, welcoming him with open arms. And legs, he added to himself. There'd be hell to pay when the stupid tart got back. He found himself almost savouring the prospect of a row.

He thought back to the week he'd had with Gina in the Algarve, staying in the finest hotel, in their best suite, with its paradise view over the sea and the spectacular rugged coastline. A week of wining and dining in Portugal's finest restaurants, a couple of rounds of golf on the Algarve's most exclusive courses. It had all been courtesy of the Hot Breaks company, in return for the spot of creative accounting he'd done to give them an apparently sizeable discount on the production costs. Except, of course, that he'd massaged the figures to make it look as though he was offering them a huge undercover saving when in fact he was actually quoting the going rate and more. If Hot Breaks thought they were getting a bargain in return for Harry's luxury trip, then they were happy. And Harry was happy too, because a perk such as this luxury trip was absolutely his due. He sat back and mentally totted up what it would have cost. Limo complete with champagne to and from Gatwick, first-class plane seats natch, a five-hundred-pound-a-night suite, meals, vintage wines and cocktails all signed for. Not much change from ten grand. Now that was what he called a freebie.

It had been fun, of course, especially having sex on tap provided by Gina. And yet, and yet . . . there'd been times when he had to admit he'd got bored. Bored with all the endless luxury, the immaculate service, the hand-picked staff whose brief was to provide for their guests' every whim. There was something missing, and Harry knew exactly what it was. Conflict. There were no rows, no arguments, no desk to thump, no deals to be struck, no one to shout at, no oneupmanship. He didn't even have to chase Gina around the bedroom. There was no sense of conquest; she was there for the taking whenever he fancied it. Instead of their twice-weekly evening quickie sessions, furtive lunches and the odd night in a hotel, they'd had a whole week together, and somehow it had taken the challenge out of it.

And there was another cause for alarm. He sensed Gina might want to change the ground rules after their week away. She might suddenly make demands on him that he couldn't fulfil. She might ask him to leave Val, or worse, she might phone Val and give her all the gory details.

Coming back to an empty house had strangely stimulated Harry. He knew he could have a really good shouting match with Val when she got back and he was already relishing the thought. It would redress the balance of power and put Val firmly in her place, plus it would wipe out any guilt he might have about Gina. Yes, he was looking forward to a good old row.

'So how was Manchester?' Janet's voice broke into his thoughts.

'Oh, fine,' said Harry, snarling at her for interrupting his fantasy.

'You look really, really tanned,' she continued, standing in the doorway of his office. 'If I didn't know you'd been up north, I'd have sworn you'd spent a week in some expensive little European hotspot.' She paused, willing him to answer. Or open mouth and insert foot.

His face never flickered. Harry was the consummate liar.

'Don't be ridiculous,' he snapped.

'Anyway, how's Val?' Janet never asked Harry how Val was. Harry flinched momentarily.

'Whaddya mean?' he snarled suspiciously. 'She's in Hampshire with her parents.'

'Oh, do pass on my best when you speak to her,' said Janet triumphantly, as she noted Harry now watching her with hooded eyes. 'I'm sure she told you, we had a fantastic evening round at your place. Brilliant food, a really good laugh. Best evening we've all had for ages.'

'I am pleased,' he snapped, glaring at her. So why can't the fucking cow be there with a meal on the table when *I* get home? he thought. God, there'd be a row when she came back. 'Now bugger off and do some work.'

'Welcome back then,' Janet added sarcastically. She turned tail and strode off to her office, smiling to herself and wondering with a slight shudder whether Harry's tan was an all-over job.

chapter twenty-three

The *Hartford Echo* had stepped up its anti mobile phone protest. The Don't Fry Your Brain campaign now included an offer to send a reporter/photographer along to any public place where readers thought mobile phones should be banned. The idea would be to confront the users and try to persuade them to take their calls elsewhere or switch off their phones.

'What a pity Paul Burns isn't here,' said Janet, putting her paper down as Ray brought her in a coffee.

'Are you feeling all right?' queried Ray. 'I thought we all loathed the bastard.'

'No, the *Echo* campaign,' she said, tapping the paper. 'They're whipping up opposition to people who use mobiles in stupid places, like cinemas, theatres and so on.'

'Yeah, if you remember, I told you about it when they started it.'

'Well, now they have upped the ante with this new naming and shaming idea,' continued Janet. 'You can nominate places where you don't want mobile phones used, and with the consent of the management, presumably, they'll send a reporter along to confront the suspects.'

'Paul Burns would have looked really good on the front of the *Echo* in one of his zoot suits,' said Ray, relishing the thought.

'Anyway,' said Janet, lowering her voice. 'How's our little arrangement going? Any luck yet?'

'Not so far. I've probably been a bit too careful in following him at a safe distance and then lost him in traffic. But it's Monday, so I'll be having another go tonight.'

'Better to be careful, though,' cautioned Janet. 'What would you say if he clocked you?'

'Oh, I'd say I'd just had my tarot cards read and they'd spookily described a particular pub, and so I was compelled to go there by a mystery force.'

Janet roared with laughter. Ray was certainly resourceful. He promised to ring her at home that evening if he had any luck. She gathered up her file ready for a meeting with the estate agents about the video news releases. She sensed it would be long and tedious.

Val gazed out at the Hampshire countryside from the train window. The chalk landscape of the Hampshire basin gave way to the softer rolling hills of Wiltshire and finally they were drawing into Hartford. She thought back to the conversation she'd had with her mother that morning. She'd never felt as close to Sheila as she had today. They'd had a long heart-to-heart about Harry, marriage and sex – in that order.

Val was simply staggered that her parents had known she was so unhappy, particularly as she had only realized it herself yesterday.

'We couldn't tell you, darling,' her mother had said calmly. 'If we'd told you we thought you were making a mistake, it would have made the flames of passion even more intense. Our only hope was to say nothing and pray you'd see Harry for what he was.'

'But you sat back and watched me marry the sod,' Val had said in amazement. 'Why on earth didn't you stop me?'

'What? A grown woman? And also, what if we were wrong? What if there had been qualities in Harry you'd seen but we hadn't? No, we couldn't interfere. We had to let you make your choice. Just as you are now. Are you really sure it's over?'

'You don't need to ask, do you?' said Val, miserably.

'No, I probably don't,' said her mother.

'God, I'm beginning to realize how much you both must have suffered,' said Val.

'Not as much as you,' replied her mother simply.

Sheila would never have dreamed of telling her daughter how much she'd changed since she'd met and married Harry. How she and Keith had quietly despaired, watching their daughter turn into a monster, demanding, self-centred, irrational, deeply unhappy and often drunk. They'd realized that Val was echoing Harry's nastier habits. They'd also suspected Harry was having affairs and almost hoped Val would do the same. Perhaps that way she'd escape the marriage, or at least meet someone else more worthwhile.

'How come you and Dad have lasted so long? What's your secret?' Val had asked in desperation.

'Hmm,' said Sheila, gazing down at her coffee cup demurely. 'Oh, all right, I'll tell you. Your dad and I made a pact when we got married. We agreed that sex was really important and that we didn't want that side of our marriage to slide. So,' she hesitated again, 'we promised each other we'd have sex every day. Obviously it's a bit of a tall order but that was our aim, and mostly we've stuck to it.'

'Bloody hell,' exclaimed Val, embarrassed because her mother had never before directly discussed her sex life. 'Is that normal? Harry does once a week if I'm lucky, and then only when there's a z in the month. I often wonder if he's playing away.'

The look on her mother's face said it all. Val found herself bursting into tears again. Despite saying it, she hadn't really believed it.

'Only you can decide what to do,' said her mother calmly. 'You'll know when it's the right time.'

'You said when, not if,' replied Val between sobs. She lit a cigarette to calm her nerves.

'My advice, for what it's worth,' said her mother, 'is to bide your time. Don't rush into anything. Take a long hard look at the situation before you do anything.'

And with that, Val had bidden her parents a tearful farewell and been dispatched on a train back to Hartford and Harry.

At the station, her mother had slipped a small parcel into Val's bag and told her to open it at a quiet moment on the journey. When she'd torn the brown wrapping off she'd discovered a thin paperback entitled *So You May Have a Drink Problem*.

'Shit', she said aloud, 'I do and they know.' It was that bloody bottle of Sancerre. She was drawn to a question-naire at the beginning of the book. A quick tot-up of her scores revealed she was well up the 'functional alcoholic' zone, as opposed to 'social drinker' below or the 'complete wino' above. I can't possibly be anything like a tramp swigging meths, she thought to herself, but the quiz certainly threw up the possibility that she was not that far away. Getting violently drunk, throwing up, memory loss, split nails, and drinking in the morning were all signs of impending doom. She must get a grip on this. Bit difficult, though, when you lived with a pig like Harry.

Janet stifled another yawn. Estate agents had their own jargon and their own special speech patterns. Talk about the weather or the state of the monarchy and they could pass for normal. But the minute she mentioned buzz words like 'ensuite' or 'inglenook', the two suits sitting in the HOT boardroom immediately lapsed into smoothy sales pitches. The words 'desirable', 'affordable', 'spacious' peppered every sentence. They forgot that they weren't actually selling properties to Janet. They were supposed to be having a discussion about video newsletters and an interactive website. Janet found herself being lulled into a confused stupor by their patter. One of them, a bumbling ex public school type called Hugh, who had clearly mod- elled himself on Hugh Grant playing a bumbling ex public school type, appeared to know only two other words. These were 'potential' and 'cool'.

Janet was trying to impress upon them the essence of speed when it came to video production.

'If we can shoot on a Monday, log and edit on Tuesday and transfer on Wednesday, by Thursday you'll have sev- eral hundred VHS tapes in your branches ready for the weekend onslaught and your website bang up to date,' she explained.

'Cool, cool,' said Hugh, coming to life again.

His colleague, Ralph, older and even more institution- alized, launched into a speech in clipped pre-war BBC tones speculating about what sort of reach the website would have. Janet had already made a presentation on that very subject, based on some up-to-the-minute research. In her frustration and boredom, she found herself trying to spot a sentence which didn't include Ralph's particular *mot du jour*, which was 'affordable'.

'Most property websites are getting a very respectable number of hits,' she put in. 'By far the most successful, if we believe the figures, are the sites that are easiest to use. People do seem to get put off if the website isn't punter-friendly. There's enormous potential for growth out there.'

'Potential, yeah,' contributed Hugh, reawakening to his favourite word.

'Affordable,' nodded Ralph in agreement.

'If we stick to this routine,' said Janet firmly, 'I can block-book the camera crew and edit suites and then we all know where we are.'

'Cool,' offered Hugh. She began to wonder how he ever managed to sell a hamster's cage, let alone a house.

'Right,' she said, meaningfully gathering up her files. 'I'll get you a final costing and then hopefully we're in business. Thank you for your time, gentlemen.'

'Cool.' Hugh proffered a slim and sweaty hand that was anything but. 'Great potential.'

She saw them out of the building and headed up to Harry's office. Outside, Geraldine sat on her customary guard duty, only today she was surreptitiously reading a magazine.

'Any good celebrity goss?' asked Janet, assuming it would be *Hello!* or *OK!*. Or even possibly *Sex and Hoovering* magazine.

Geraldine shot her a venomous look, mostly because she'd been caught out good and proper.

'Actually, it's *Classic FM* magazine,' she said, salvaging her dignity.

'Didn't know you were a Beethoven buff,' said Janet.

'Well, yes,' winced Geraldine, who hated having to reveal anything about herself to anyone. 'There's a free CD this month of Placebo Domingo. He's got such a lovely voice.'

'Placebo?' said Janet. 'Didn't know you were an opera fan. What's your favourite?'

'Oh, let me think,' said Geraldine, pausing in the hope that Janet would go away. 'Puccini, Mozart, that sort of thing. But I also like general classical music. My all-time favourite is Versace's *Four Seasons*.'

'Me too,' said Janet, trying to contain herself. 'That's the beauty of Versace. A total classic, such lasting appeal. I believe Liz Hurley's a fan.'

'Yes, well, I wouldn't put it past her,' said Geraldine tartly, regretting letting her mask slip and praying for the phone to ring. Harry's angry voice saved her from further conversation.

'Bancroft, in here, now,' came the familiar menacing tone, accompanied by thumping of the desk. 'I want a full update on the property project.'

'Cool, cool,' said Janet. This new confidence in Harry's presence was taking even her by surprise. As she briefly outlined the meeting she'd had with the estate agents, Harry sat back in his chair and lit a cigar.

'Harry,' she pointed out with a small smile, 'you're not supposed to smoke in the building. You'll have the fire brigade out in a minute. Mind you,' she paused for effect, 'that cigar does smell good. Very evocative, reminds me of hot countries and balmy nights.'

She stared blatantly at him for a second, wondering if he had gone the tiniest bit pink under the perma-tan. Thrown by her remark, he quickly stubbed out the cigar.

How very un-Harry-like, she thought. How stupid of me to light up a Portuguese cigar, thought Harry.

'Now, I've had an idea for a new pitch,' she continued. 'There's a chain of restaurants starting up, only half a dozen in the pipeline so far but the whisper is that they have some big investors and plans for lots more. The company's called 3F, which stands for Food From Films, and each restaurant is named after a big movie, with the food and decor to match.'

'Sounds interesting,' said Harry, eyes lighting up like the display on a cash register. 'Go on.'

'For example, Casablanca will serve Moroccan food and be done out like Rick's Bar, Apocalypse Now will be Vietnamese food with all the staff in flying suits, Shakespeare in Love will be all doublets and hose, and venison. And then there's Gigi, all French food and fin du siècle. I think it's a great idea, with loads of visual potential.'

God, she was beginning to sound like Hugh.

'I want it,' slammed Harry. He sat bolt upright in his chair and shouted at Geraldine through the office door: 'Get me everything on 3F. Janet will give you the details. Get moving on it, the pair of you. Now.'

He sat back again, watching Janet's departing back. She was bright, that one, and getting just a bit too bright for her own good, he thought. He mused about the project she'd mentioned. It certainly sounded very promising.

He dialled a number and waited impatiently. Pity about the cigar, he thought, glancing at the ashtray.

'Gina, darling,' he half whispered seductively. 'Can't make our usual tonight. Sorry, honey, too much work, it's all stacking up. They couldn't manage without me last week. I'll make it up to you on Thursday . . . Look, I'm sorry . . . Yes, we had the most brilliant week . . . Yes, yes, of course I love you . . . Bye.'

Trouble brewing there, he thought, scratching his chin. He didn't want a fight on his hands. No, tonight belonged to his row with Val; that was, if the silly tart deigned to turn up.

As Val sat in the taxi home from the station, her mother's words came back to her. Yes, she would bide her time and take some legal advice, and no, she wouldn't have a knee-jerk reaction and run away.

As the cab snaked up the lane to their house, she shuddered from the very depth of her being. Keep calm, she told herself repeatedly, stay calm and just keep a watching brief. A man is presumed innocent until he's found guilty. She'd need to know for sure about any affair he was having before she could do anything. She'd want proof. She suddenly felt very fearful about the future. If she left Harry, what would become of her? She'd be second-hand goods, a woman with a failed past, and now officially a 'functional alcoholic'.

Mercifully Harry wasn't back from work. A riot of summer colour greeted her as she stepped out of the cab and paid her fare. Banks of fuchsias and roses were just reaching their peak. Unlike me, she thought miserably. At thirty-two, it was downhill all the way from now on. Past her prime, she mused, just fitted in between Harry's various conquests. What a fool he'd made of her.

She went through the vast entrance hall, threw her bags down on a scarlet velvet sofa and strode purposefully into the kitchen, heading for the drinks fridge. She had too much on her plate to pack in alcohol just yet. She opened a bottle of chilled white wine and poured herself

212

a huge glass. She needed all the help she could get in facing Harry. Practically downing it in one, she poured another. She felt the cold liquid seeping into her body, giving her an instant lift. She ferreted in her handbag and found her cigarettes and lighter. The first big drag had a calming effect. Curse non-smoking trains and taxis, she muttered to herself, but at least they made you appreciate the first cigarette after your journey.

She was just settling down in the sitting room, shoes kicked off and feet up on one of the settees, watching a travel programme on Spain, when Harry burst in through the door.

'So good of you to turn up,' he snarled.

'Great to see you too,' she retorted. 'You remind me of that bull.' She indicated the animal that had just appeared on the screen. 'The crowd like the aggressive ones best.'

'Stupid tart,' he muttered under his breath. 'Why weren't you here when I got back last night?'

'Because I was being thoroughly spoiled at my parents',' she replied. She knew Harry hated any reference to them. He didn't like to be reminded that they were richer than him. Before he could open his mouth to reply, she was at him again.

'That's a pretty amazing tan for Manchester,' she said accusingly, pointing a deep scarlet nail in his direction. 'I'm surprised you managed to get so brown, seeing as you were stuck in a conference all day long.'

For once, Harry was speechless, his mouth open like a vacant haddock. Val got up from the settee and lurched towards him, with the aim of examining the extent of the amazing tan.

But as usual, luck was on Harry's side. The best part of a bottle of white wine had gone to Val's head and she caught one of her beloved Manolos on the edge of a Persian rug and sprawled at his feet. Harry felt he'd been let off a murder charge.

The shock on both sides instantly defused the situation. Val sheepishly regained her balance and composure while Harry silently thanked his lucky stars for the reprieve.

'Look, let's celebrate my homecoming,' he said more affably. 'Why don't we have a special night out tomorrow?'

Val lit another cigarette and contemplated this new Harry. Her brain was too fuddled with the drink and the fall to make any sense of it. She nodded dumbly in agreement.

'We'll have an early dinner and I'll get tickets for the theatre.'

Harry? Theatre? These were not words that usually went together. Val was now totally confused. Quick flashbacks to the conversations she'd had with her mother now seemed unreal. Had she imagined it all? Either way, she felt threatened by Harry's sudden new tack. Was he on a big guilt trip, or was it to do with the fact that she was now a fully qualified functional alcoholic. Dizzy spells, memory loss, falling over. There'd been big ticks against all those. Had she ticked the box marked 'Husband possibly playing away'? Val couldn't remember.

chapter twenty-four

Geraldine stared at the phone and decided to bite the bullet. She disliked Janet, over what she considered her disloyalty to Harry, but she needed to get something right. She dialled Janet's number.

'Er, Janet, it's Geraldine. I need your help.'

Janet pulled a face at the receiver. Geraldine needing help? Was there a doctor in the house?

'Harry's asked me to book theatre tickets for tonight. Any idea what's on and reasonably good?'

Janet took a swig of coffee and thought quickly. Be nice to the silly cow, she thought. This might lead to some interesting information for Operation Haunted Handbag.

'Well, there's a production of *The Importance of Being Earnest* on at the moment,' she said. 'It's had quite good reviews. The only other thing is some Gilbert and Sullivan; Hartford Amateur Musical Society is doing *The Gondoliers*. It's probably crap, though. They're not known as the HAMS for nothing, you know. Anyway, I thought you'd have been a bit of a theatre buff, Geraldine.'

'No, no,' said Geraldine, retreating back into church-mouse-with-attitude mode. 'I'm not effluent enough to go to the theatre very often.'

Geraldine being effluent. What a waste! Janet struggled for some measure of composure. 'Let me know what Harry decides,' she said at last, 'and I'll fish out the reviews. By the way, who's he taking?'

There was a pause. A most interesting pause.

'Val, of course,' said Geraldine tartly.

'In that case, the Gondoliers might as well ditch their oars. I definitely don't think that would be Val's scene.' Oscar Wilde wouldn't be much better either, unless the costumes were by Jasper Conran and they served unlimited white wine throughout the performance.

Janet replaced the phone and immediately dialled Sue's extension. She related Harry's theatre plans and the latest G-spot.

When Sue finally stopped laughing, she asked how Ray had got on tailing Harry the previous night.

'No dice,' replied Janet. 'Harry changed his pattern and went straight home to Val.'

'Hmm, I can see this whole thing falling down around our ears,' said Sue. 'Without a routine, we can't just keep on following him. There'd be no point.'

'Let's give it another couple of weeks,' said Janet. 'Then we'll all look for other jobs.'

Janet returned to the now bulging estate agents' file, which she'd jokily marked 'Affordable Cool'. She'd better get on with this one, set the wheels in motion. And then at some point later on through the contract, she'd hand it over to one of her producers. Possibly Liz, when she'd finished the Hot Breaks project.

Nina, in a delicious daydream about her forthcoming Greek holiday with Sam, wafted across the office, mentally on the beach on Rhodes and slapping on the coconut oil.

'Sorry to break into your reverie, but any chance of a coffee?' said Janet. 'Also, could you hook out last Tuesday's copy of the *Hartford Echo*? I'm looking for a review of *The Importance of Being Earnest*. It's on for a few weeks. And guess who's going?'

'No idea.'

'Hold on to your hat: Val and Harry.'

'Good grief. Not Val's scene, is it? Nor Harry's, I would have thought. Do you think there's a touch of guilt trip about all this?'

'Yes, I certainly do,' said Janet. 'It sounds from this theatre trip as if Harry's got away with it despite that disgusting tan. Ray's been trailing him on his bike, but last night Harry went straight home.'

'Pity,' said Nina. 'I'll make your coffee extra strong then.'

An hour later, Janet had completed the first scripts for the Affordable Cool project. She relaxed for a few minutes and flipped through the copy of the *Hartford Echo* that Nina had brought her. The play had been given a reasonably good review, and she sauntered around to Harry's office to show it to Geraldine. She shuddered at the sight of Geraldine's choice of outfit: a putrid-green knitted tunic and long skirt, completed with some rather ghastly dung-coloured beads. Very effluent, she thought.

'Bancroft? You, in here, now,' shouted a familiar voice.

'Good morning, Harry.' Janet dropped a mock curtsey. 'I was just giving Geraldine a review of *The Importance of Being Earnest*. I gather you're going tonight. It certainly sounds like a good production.'

'Never you mind,' said Harry ungratefully. 'Siddown.'

Janet sank into her customary position in front of Harry's crotch.

217

'Now,' he leered, 'I've had a great idea. There's a company called 3F. They're opening a chain of themed restaurants based on famous films all around the country. We want that job. I've got Geraldine to hook out all the background. It could be a biggie for us. We could do their news releases on video, manage their website. Cover all the openings. This one's got legs.'

Janet smiled outwardly and seethed within. Here was Harry back to his usual trick of passing off her ideas as his own. And probably getting all the credit and the bonuses from the board as well. He threw a file across to her. A quick flip-through revealed a brief company profile and some phone numbers.

'If you recall, Harry, this was my idea,' she said drily. 'I told you about it yesterday.' But Harry wasn't listening. He was back into his wheeling, dealing and bleeding 'em dry mode.

'I'm having dinner with their managing director later this week,' he continued, unflinching, 'so I want some facts and figures and a treatment from you before then. And it had better be good.'

'Sounds like a job for Paul Burns then, rather than silly old me. After all, it was only my idea,' Janet snapped back. Instantly she regretted it. Harry had gone white with rage. He looked as though he might hurl something at her.

'You do as you're told, or you'll be taking an early bath here, make no mistake.'

Rather like a dying man watching his life pass before him, Janet saw her mortgage, council tax, car HP and all the other bills wafting before her eyes. Jobs like hers were very few and far between. That was why most people stuck it out at HOT, despite Harry.

'And don't think you'd get any sort of reference from this company,' he hissed at her. 'Do that treatment, do it well and do it in two hours, or you're dead in the water.'

Janet stood up, turned on her heel and walked out of his office without saying a word. She shook all the way back to her office. Sinking into her chair, she put her head in her hands in a mixture of despair and exhaustion. It was all a waste of time. Harry was just too powerful for the Haunted Handbag committee.

The phone trilled sharply.

'And another thing,' yelled Harry, 'any developments, any important snippets on this project, you ring me immediately. Day or night. My mobile will be permanently switched on. Geddit?' His conversation was accompanied by audible thumps on his desk.

'Okay,' said Janet wearily. 'I get it.'

She glanced at the file Harry had given her and put it on top of Affordable Cool. Suddenly the estate agents seemed a rather attractive, hassle-free option. She was just throwing away the copy of the *Echo* from which she'd cut the theatre review when she had an idea.

Over hot beef sandwiches and spritzers on the outside terrace of the GX, Janet outlined the morning's events to Sue and Nina. They were horrified to hear that Harry was back in bullying mode.

'I thought we were really getting somewhere,' said Nina. 'What with Val's drink-driving case, and him skipping off to that sun-drenched beach in Manchester, I thought he was losing his grip.'

'So did I,' said Sue. 'Obviously leopards don't change their spots. Or in Harry's case, big fat bastards don't bother to file their claws.'

'I shouldn't think Val's having much of a time,' said Nina. 'And perhaps it serves her right.'

'At least she can drink at home all day now that she can't drive her car,' observed Sue.

'She did that anyway,' replied Nina. 'I probably shouldn't say this, but I bet Harry had a better time on the Mancunian Algarve than he would have done at home. Perhaps that's why he's got all stroppy again now that he's back with Val.'

'Could be,' said Janet, 'but then the theatre stuff wouldn't fit into that scenario. I got the distinct impression he was angry that she was still staying at her parents' place when he got back.'

'It seems to me,' said Sue, 'that Harry not only wants it all, he wants to be boss of everything. Plus, of course, he enjoys a good row.'

They all nodded in agreement, sipping their spritzers.

'So what's this idea you had?' asked Nina, gazing sky-wards in an attempt to top up her tan with the last of the summer sun.

Over cappuccinos, Janet outlined her plan. Back at the office, she made one phone call. Everything was in place.

Val decided to go for it. She put on a pale pink beaded dress with shoestring straps plus a cashmere cardigan in a deeper pink. She slipped into a new pair of fiendishly expensive spiky heels she'd bought in Hampshire, picked up the matching clutch bag and went downstairs.

Harry was doing his best to hide his anger at being kept waiting. He'd left the office especially early for this and here she was still fiddling about upstairs. He strode up and down the hallway, cursing under his breath. When at last Val appeared, they climbed into the Mercedes without exchanging a word and sped off to the restaurant. It was a new French place that had opened on the other side of Hartford. Val had picked it because, being new, at least she hadn't fallen over in it. Also, being French, they allowed smoking. Always a plus factor with Val.

The meal was stunning. Val toyed with a warm salad of bacon and quails' eggs to start and then turbot for her main course. As usual she moved most of it around her plate and then lit a cigarette. Harry stopped himself from telling her off. It always provoked a conversation about money and comparisons between his admittedly comfortable salary and her parents' premier-league lifestyle. Harry wasn't tight but he hated waste. They both avoided mentioning the previous week. Harry did not want to discuss his conference in Manchester with her, nor did he want to hear about the week she'd spent at the family pile. Val didn't want to discuss anything at all with him either, so they lapsed into silence, punctuated by offering each other lights for his cigar and her cigarette.

'How's work?' she eventually asked.

'Busy. Some big projects on the go and one potential biggie in the pipeline,' said Harry. Val didn't pursue it, to Harry's relief. He liked to keep his business dealings to himself. He didn't want her prying into his affairs, in case they led to his affair with Gina. To keep her happy, he'd ordered a bottle of wine with the meal, but only had one glass himself. The publicity about Val's drink-drive charge had been quite enough.

Bill paid, they set off for the theatre, again without much to say. Val found herself lost in thought about the advice her mother had given her last week. She was now thoroughly confused about her feelings for Harry and the state of the marriage. But as her mother had said, there was no rush. She needed to think some more. And get some proof.

They arrived at the theatre with five minutes to spare and were shown to their seats, front row of the dress circle. Geraldine had pulled strings to get the best tickets. The lights dimmed and the play began. The *Echo* reviewer was right, it was a good production and the actress playing the indomitable Lady Bracknell was just that. The audience became immediately caught up in the action, and even Val, who couldn't remember the last time she'd been to the theatre, found to her surprise that she was enjoying it.

The play was just reaching the big scene where Lady Bracknell demands to know about Jack Worthing's parentage. He explains that he was found in a handbag in the cloakroom at Victoria railway station. An air of expectation ran around the audience as they braced themselves for the big line.

'A handbag?' roared Lady Bracknell with sneering disdain.

There was a big theatrical pause while Lady Bracknell gathered herself up to full disgust. In the silence came the trilling of a mobile phone.

'A mobile?' offered a member of the audience in suitably Lady Bracknell-esque tones. Everyone started laughing.

Val looked down at the audience in the stalls below. They were all glaring her way as the mobile carried on its incessant trill. She looked quickly to the right and left of her. All eyes seemed to be on her. She shrank back in horror.

Next thing she knew, Harry was wrenching his phone from his inside pocket, sweat pouring from his brow.

'What?' he raged into it. 'Fuck off. Of course I can't talk. I'm in the theatre.'

People started to tut loudly in Harry's direction. Lady Bracknell assumed control.

'A mobile in a handbag?' she proclaimed imperiously, earning a huge round of applause and gales of laughter. The play carried on and the magic swiftly returned. But not for Harry and Val. They sat there trapped in their front-row circle seats, like prisoners awaiting sentence.

The second the curtain came down for the interval, Harry stood and pulled Val up by the arm.

'Out of here,' he fumed.

'Who was it?' said Val, stumbling in Harry's rush to get out. 'Harry, stop, I've lost my shoe.'

'Oh, shut up, you silly cow. Just let's get out of here.'

As they reached the foyer, Val gave up hobbling along on one four-inch heel and took the shoe off. At that moment, a flashbulb went off and a man rushed up to Harry.

'What the fuck do you want?' said Harry, red-faced with anger.

'I'm from the *Hartford Echo*,' the reporter started. 'We're running a campaign about mobile phones in public places . . .'

But Harry didn't stop. He frogmarched the now barefoot Val out of the building, down the steps and on in the direction of the car park.

chapter twenty-five

THE IMPORTANCE OF BEING HARRY, screamed the front-page headline of the following day's *Hartford Echo*:

> Film supremo Harry Hampton found himself well
> and truly in the frame last night when his mobile
> phone went off during a performance at the Civic
> Theatre. The Hartford Optimum Television chief's
> phone started ringing just as actress Julia
> Sandringham was about to deliver the immortal
> line, 'A handbag?' during a performance of Oscar
> Wilde's *The Importance of Being Earnest*.
>   The *Echo*'s Don't Fry Your Brain Campaign,
> dedicated to restricting the use of mobile phones,
> has been appealing to the public to help ban their
> use in designated areas. Mr Hampton ignored
> recent pleas from theatre staff for members of the
> audience to lodge mobile phones in the foyer
> before entering the auditorium. After being booed
> by the audience, he and his wife Valerie left the
> theatre during the interval and did not return to
> their seats. As he stormed out, Mr Hampton
> refused to comment. His wife, a former model,

appeared to lose one of her shoes in their rush to leave the theatre. It's the second time in recent weeks that Mrs Hampton has hit the headlines. She recently pleaded guilty to driving while more than twice the legal alcohol limit.

After the play, members of the cast said they had heard the phone go off and claimed it had definitely distracted them. All said they completely supported the *Echo's* campaign. A spokesman for the theatre said that forty members of the audience demanded their money back, claiming their enjoyment of the performance was ruined by Mr Hampton's phone.

Meanwhile the *Echo's* campaign grows apace. In the past week, five top restaurants have announced a ban on mobiles. Diners are being invited to leave their phones with the cloakroom attendant . . .

Janet smiled as she reread the front-page article, then folded up the paper and dropped it in the bin. The rest of the production office were far more demonstrative. Several punched the air, and there was brief talk of having an Importance of Being Harry party at the end of the week.

'You could come as Lady Bracknell,' suggested Ray, bowing to Janet in mock deference. 'We could cast Geraldine as a maid. Just a walk-on part, no words to get in a twist. Or perhaps a non-speaking nun. Some of them take vows of silence.'

'With Geraldine's gift of the gab, she'd probably think she was in *The Impotence of Being Ernest*,' observed Janet.

'To appear in the local paper once, Mrs Hampton, may

be regarded as a misfortune,' continued Ray in Lady Bracknell-esque tones, 'but twice in a month looks like carelessness.'

Everyone screamed with laughter.

'I did the bloody play for A level,' said Ray. 'I just knew it would come in useful sometime.'

'Okay, a joke's a joke, now get back to your looms before Harry hears this lot and fires us,' Janet warned. 'Nina, do us a favour. Get in a round of strong coffees. The caffeine might give our brains a boost.' Nina disappeared to the small kitchen at the end of the production office.

'Worked a treat, didn't it?' said Sue, phoning from reception. 'Everyone's been chuckling on their way through here this morning.'

'Harry in?'

'Yeah, crack of dawn, face like thunder.'

'No change there then.'

'The Italian woman phoned just now. Harry must have already been on the phone, so her call got redirected to me.'

'How do you know it was her? What did she say?'

'Just drawing on aeons of experience in this job, darlin',' laughed Sue. 'It was her all right, accent is unmistakable. She never leaves a message but she wanted to know if Harry was in. I detected a very controlled anger in her voice.'

'Not surprising really, when you see the man you're having an affair with plastered all over the front pages with his wife all done up to the nines,' said Janet. 'I must say, to be fair, the photograph of Val was stunning. You can see exactly why she was a model.'

Janet was right. Val did look amazing. The pink

sparkly dress was a knockout, even in a black and white photograph. The fact that Val was barefoot, clutching a bag and one shoe, somehow contrived to look incredibly sexy. It would have done even Liz Hurley proud. No wonder the Italian hackles were up. Harry really did have trouble coming in all directions.

'Let's hope they put on *The Rivals* next week,' said Sue. 'Then Harry could take them both, they could slug it out in the stalls and the *Echo* would have another great photo scoop.'

They both hung up. Janet surveyed the scene in the office. Everyone was now engrossed in their work or on the phone. She'd make one quick call.

'Freddie? It's Janet. Nice picture. Got my timing right, didn't I?'

'Spot on, girl,' came the gravelly Essex voice. 'Couldn't have been better if I'd cued you in. Don't like the look of your boss. Deeply unpleasant specimen. Couldn't have happened to a nicer bloke. We'll do lunch next week.'

'Yeah, somewhere quiet, though.'

'Totally understand,' said Freddie. 'Don't want people putting two and two together.'

'Oh well, wish me luck. I might as well go and face the music now.'

'Good luck, love.'

Janet replaced the phone and marched off to Harry's office, knowing it would not be pleasant. She felt like a convicted prisoner crossing the Bridge of Sighs, allowing herself one lingering look across the Venetian lagoon before being banged up for ever.

Val stirred, vaguely aware that the phone was ringing. For a few seconds, she wasn't sure whether she was at her parents' house or back home in Hartford. Disappointed, she realized it was Hartford, but at least Harry had obviously gone off to work. As she grasped the receiver, she noted with shock that it was just past midday.

'Val? It's Susie. Just seen your picture. You look amazing.'

'What?' mumbled Val, still coming to. 'What are you on about?'

'You're on the front page of the *Echo*,' continued Susie. 'I must say, they're all impressed in this shit-hole that I know you. We must do lunch soon.'

'What's on the front page?' said Val, groping for her cigarettes and lighter.

'Sweetie, it's all about your amazing visit to the theatre. "The Importance of Being Harry",' read Susie. '"Film supremo Harry Hampton found himself well and truly in the frame last night when his mobile phone went off . . ." Sweetie, you could get sponsorship from Vodafone.'

'Stop, stop. Oh, shit,' said Val, becoming alarmingly awake. It all started to flood back, including the late-night silent drinking session she and Harry had embarked on when they'd got home from the theatre.

'Everyone here's dying to meet you,' said Susie, 'especially my boss, but you'd better keep your mitts off him.'

'You still having that affair?' asked Val, getting her brain into gear.

'Absolutely, and he's leaving his wife,' added Susie triumphantly. 'We must meet up soon. Got loads to tell you. Shan't be doing this pigging rotten job for much longer.'

'Okay, hon,' said Val, stubbing out one half-smoked cigarette and immediately lighting another. 'Sorry, I was fast asleep. Rather difficult evening.'

'Time you dumped that fat bastard,' said Susie brightly. 'Lunch next week, yah?'

228

Val staggered to the bathroom and stared at herself in the mirror. She looked anything but amazing. Last night's drinking and all the recent tensions were showing in her face. She bent down and threw up.

Deep breaths, keep calm, Janet told herself as she strode down the corridor in Harry's direction. She had avoided this all morning, until the *Echo* first edition came out, certain that she couldn't have pulled off feigned innocence about her phone call. That would have required too much acting. At least this way there would be two rows for the price of one: row one about the phone call, and then row two about the newspaper coverage about the phone call.

'Ah Harry,' she said, as evenly as her nerves would allow. 'Didn't realize my call last night would cause such a furore. Just seen the *Echo* piece. Sorry, but you did say I was to call any time, day or night, about the Food From Films deal.'

'You stupid fucking cow—'

'And there's really good news. In fact, I got it confirmed this morning.'

'Bloody idiot, I've a mind to have you sacked—'

'It's in the bag, Harry. Providing we get our costings right, it's a deal.'

'What?' At the sound of the magic word 'deal', Harry suddenly looked like a rabbit caught in car headlights.

'Well, after I suggested . . . er, we discussed it on Monday, I wrote a quick treatment and sent it plus a copy of my . . . er, our catering college videos by dispatch rider to their offices straightaway. Just thought it would show that we have a track record in the field, so to speak. I was working here really late last night on the estate agents' scripts, and by pure luck, I got a call from the company's marketing chap.'

She paused, noting Harry's utter astonishment and

229

hoping that her face wouldn't give away the fact that the call had happened much earlier in the day.

'He apparently went overboard on it and rang to say yes, you're on. So I called you to tell you the fantastic news. Having seen the *Echo* piece, I'm really sorry I picked such a bum moment—'

'Yes, you bloody well did—'

'But you did say to ring if there were any developments, so I just did as I was told. Anyway, we had another chat this morning and it's in the bag. I must say, I'm impressed at the speed of their decision-making. They're a young company and they want to expand quickly. It seems they're very keen on our input.'

'Well, I'm sure I'll clinch things properly when I have dinner with their MD later this week,' said Harry loftily, regaining his composure.

'I think that will be a formality.' Janet smiled at Harry's crotch. 'They've asked for a budget to be e-mailed today with a view to me starting filming next week. So it's Thunderbirds Are Go.'

Harry would have loved to have taken ten years off his age immediately by looking puzzled about the reference to *Thunderbirds* but he didn't trust himself. Anyway, Janet didn't wait for a reaction. She got up and left his office. She walked past Geraldine's desk trying to stop the huge grin on her face. She kept walking until she reached her office, where she picked up her bag and headed for lunch in the GX with a waiting Sue and Nina. The champagne was already on ice.

'To the Impotence of Being Harry,' they all toasted.

Having finally resurrected herself, Val went downstairs and flopped down in the sitting room. She didn't bother to open the curtains because she still felt queasy and had a pounding headache. After Susie's call, the phone had gone again. One call was from an *Echo* reporter, hoping for a follow-up, and the other was the boss of a local modelling agency who'd clocked the photograph. She'd told them both to get lost.

She dialled Harry's direct line. It was engaged, so the call was diverted to Geraldine.

'What's all this *Hartford Echo* nonsense?' she demanded. Geraldine meekly explained.

'Well, I don't exactly feel like popping out to my local newsagent's and submitting myself to more embarrassment,' snapped Val. 'Nor can I just jump in a car these days.'

'I'll fax it to you,' offered Geraldine, anxious to appease her. 'Did you enjoy the play?'

'Of course I bloody didn't,' shouted Val, and then regretted it because it made her head hurt even more. She continued more calmly: 'Why on earth Harry wanted us to go in the first place, I don't know. One of his more stupid ideas. And then because of his bloody phone we had to leave at half-time. By the way, where did he stay in Manchester last week?'

Val caught even herself by surprise with the suddenness of the question.

Geraldine panicked. 'Oh, I can't remember,' she spluttered. 'Somewhere in the city centre.'

'You must know, you're his bloody secretary, having to send him faxes and all that sort of stuff you lot do,' said Val, growing more suspicious by the second.

'I've probably thrown away the booking form,' said Geraldine triumphantly. 'Sorry, had a big desk clear-out on Monday. Can't help, I'm afraid.'

231

She knows, thought Val. She knows what Harry's up to.

'Pity,' said Val acidly. 'I'd like to stay there sometime. It must have a fantastic solarium.'

She slammed down the phone, shaking with a mixture of anger and shock, then lit a cigarette and headed for the fridge. Her mother's book and all its good advice would have to wait for another day, or another decade at this stress rate. She knocked back two big glasses of wine and then thought about breakfast.

The phone rang again. She snatched it up and barked, 'Hello!' down the receiver. Silence. After a couple of seconds she slammed down the receiver and dialled 1471 to see who'd called.

'You were called today at thirteen forty-seven. The caller withheld their number.'

She abandoned breakfast and headed upstairs again for a shower. She'd just got shampoo all over her hair when the phone went again. She rushed out, blinking hard as the shampoo stung her eyes. Once again no one spoke. Once again the number had been withheld.

Val flung down the phone and seethed aloud. She sensed someone had been at the other end, waiting for her to speak. Next time I'll give them something to listen to, she vowed. Five minutes later the phone rang again.

'I don't know what sort of game you're playing, but you can fuck off and die!' Val shouted.

'I beg your pardon,' said a familiar voice. It was Janet, ringing after an attack of remorse about the newspaper set-up. She'd felt a tiny bit guilty that Val had copped it in the paper as well as Harry. Val had had her fair share of trouble lately.

'It's all right, Janet,' said Val. 'I suppose I ought to be

getting used to this lark by now, though I never got this sort of coverage even when I was a model.'

'Everyone thinks you look great in the photograph,' said Janet, trying to compensate.

'Everyone except Harry, I should think,' said Val bitterly. 'I didn't see him this morning but I should imagine he's in a pretty foul temper. Well, even more foul than usual.'

Janet apologized for the fact that it was she who had made the fateful call.

'Not your fault, sweetie,' said Val, warming a little. 'God knows why Harry insisted on us going in the first place. We never go to the theatre. I'd rather sit home and watch soaps, frankly. By the way, did you try to ring me just now?'

'No. Anything wrong?'

'No. Nothing really. I had two calls just now from someone, except that no one spoke and they withheld their number.'

'These things happen,' replied Janet. 'Perhaps it was just a wrong number. You know how dopey people are. You'd think they'd just say they'd got the wrong number.'

'No, I got the distinct impression someone was listening to see what I sounded like. By the way, was Harry really in Manchester last week?'

Janet was taken aback at the directness of the question.

'Well, I think so,' she started in reply.

'But can you prove it? Do you know for certain that's where he was last week?' Val was sounding very persistent.

'No, I can't prove anything. I had no reason to ring him, but if I had, I'd have rung his mobile. Sorry, that one's a bit of a moot point. Why? Do you doubt him?'

'Yes. Absolutely.'

chapter twenty-six

Harry sat reflecting in his *Mastermind* chair. He couldn't believe the trouble coming in from all sides. His power base was feeling decidedly threatened.

He'd just put down the phone on a screaming Gina. She'd gone into an Italian crescendo after seeing the picture of Val in the paper, and he knew that some nasty threats involving his marriage were possibly just around the corner. He pondered on how Val would react if she found out about Gina. He never understood quite why women got so worked up about fidelity. After all, the lazy cow was on a bloody good deal. She didn't have to work, she could just sit around all day painting her nails and she clearly did just that. She wasn't famed for her cooking. Gardening and housework were no-go areas because as Val constantly reminded him, she hadn't been brought up to do that. The only area in which she'd excelled recently was a magic act involving the contents of the drinks cabinet. Maybe if she filled her days usefully, she might keep off the pop.

She's just a spoiled cow really, thought Harry, blaming her parents once again. He couldn't, however, deny the frisson of pleasure he'd experienced at seeing the amazing picture of Val in the paper. That was his wife, looking like a supermodel. Desired by many and owned by him. Why couldn't the silly cow just learn to stuff the odd mushroom and stay out of trouble?

As for Janet, he'd have stuck pins in a voodoo doll if he'd had one handy. She'd dropped him in the shit twice in as many months. He was still sore about being outsmarted over the Paul Burns episode, and now the bitch was at it again. Ringing him at the theatre, making him look a fool. Trouble was, she'd also come up with yet another top-class project. At least he could use the Food From Films deal to fend off any hassle from the board about the Hot Breaks project.

He fleetingly considered sacking Janet, dumping Gina and divorcing Val. Now that would be a serious clear-out. Trouble was, he liked having a gorgeous-looking wife, lusted after by other men. Janet seemed to keep striking gold with the deals lately. And there was no greater aphrodisiac than a powerful job and a bit on the side. No, sod it, he'd stick with them. For the time being.

Janet was now on overload. She was working overtime to get the Food From Films treatments and rough scripts together, plus the final setting-up of Affordable Cool. She couldn't lean on Liz because she was still busy on the Hot Breaks series, so she resigned herself to working late every evening this week. Harry, of course, would yet again take all the credit, swanning into dinner with the boss of 3F at the end of the week waving Janet's file of work and passing the whole thing off as his own.

Nina, seeing Janet was under pressure, brought her a strong coffee.

'You all right?' she asked. 'Can I help?'

235

'Not really, Nina, but thanks,' said Janet wearily. 'It's all bearing down on me a bit. I could do with a holiday but I've too much to do. And it's all for the benefit of that fat sod down the corridor.'

'It's time we had another HH meeting,' said Nina. 'Or at the very least a girlies' get-together. You need a bit of cheering up. How about Friday night? Come to my place. I'll fix it with the rest of the girls.'

With that, Nina withdrew. Janet smiled a grateful thank-you and returned to the files. She had until the end of the week – just two days to get everything in place. At least Friday night with the Haunted Handbag committee would be fun.

Janet arrived late, last and full of apologies. They were all crammed into Nina's small but cheerful flat. She didn't have a dining table so they all sat either on the sofa or on the floor of her sitting room. Out of her tiny galley kitchen Nina had produced a huge platter of mozzarella, tomatoes, avocados, parma ham, melon, artichoke hearts and olives, all served up with warm ciabatta bread. They washed it down with copious amounts of Valpolicella.

'Very apt wine in the circumstances,' remarked Sue. 'Let's hear it for Val and the Valpolicella.'

'Good job Val's not here to fall over,' replied Nina. 'My sofa hasn't been Scotchguarded. It wouldn't half stain.'

'Food's apt too,' said Sue. 'Italian flavour to the evening. In honour of Fattie Hampton's mystery bit of Italian skirt.'

'Not quite such a mystery now,' said Janet, revived by a glass of wine and something to eat. She'd been dying to tell them but wanted to pick her moment.

'Go on,' urged Sue. 'You know something, don't you?'

Janet triumphantly described how Ray had at last been successful. Disguised in his motorbike leathers and helmet, he'd followed Harry the previous night as usual, but this time he hadn't lost him. The Mercedes had sped off out of Hartford to a village twelve miles away. There Harry had parked outside a small cottage with, according to Ray, the familiarity of someone who'd been there before. A dark-haired woman had briefly appeared at the door before he'd disappeared inside. Ray had then tried Harry's mobile which had been—

'Switched off,' they all chorused in triumph.

'Oh, and it gets better,' said Janet. 'I did a quick search on the electoral roll. Gina Scarparo. Sounds like our Italian telephonista, doesn't it!'

'What happens now?' asked Nina.

'I'm going to have a word with my friend Freddie from the *Echo*. He's got some very long lenses.'

'You sound a bit less defeatist than you did earlier in the week,' observed Nina.

'Yes, I've been having a rethink. Earlier this week we had the same old scenario of Harry yet again pinching my idea and passing it off as his own. Since then I've done eighteen-hour days to get yet another money-spinner for the company up and running. Tonight, as I was leaving to come here, absolutely on my knees with exhaustion, Harry was off to an expensive restaurant for dinner with the MD of the Food From Films company. Waving my file, my ideas and my efforts. Last night, while I was slogging over a computer, he was cavorting with Signorina Scarparo and probably planning their next foreign jolly.

'Well, I've decided, I've had enough. Either he goes or I do. I can't continue like this. It's wearing me down and

I can't take much more. So I think the fight is really back on.'

The others were clearly impressed at this new resolve as they stacked the plates ready for sticky toffee pudding and coffee.

'I think you should record your next big row with Harry,' said Liz suddenly. 'It's time we collected some of this sort of evidence. Just get it on tape, even if it's only stored for a rainy day.'

'Liz's right,' chipped in Sue. 'If this whole thing was to blow up in Harry's face, he'd wriggle his way out of it, just as he's done before. Don't forget, he's got a PhD in bullshit. We're just signing up for the GCSE course.'

'Imagine being summoned to the chairman's office,' continued Liz. 'And there you are facing Sir Stifferton Crapps, or whatever Geraldine calls him these days, and he demands proof of what's gone on. We'd just look desperately girlie and say, "He shouts a lot and pinches ideas." Then Sir Crapperton Stiffs would reply, "And that's exactly what I pay him to do." Result: Harry ten, Haunted Handbaggers nil.'

'There's one other thing in all this that's tipped the balance for me,' said Janet. 'It's Val. I'm actually beginning to feel sorry for her. I know she's rude, embarrassing and a piss artist, but she suspects something's up with Harry. I had a very interesting chat with her after the mobile phone episode. She didn't seem to mind that it was me who'd made the phone call and caused all the *Echo* coverage. She asked me point blank where Harry had been last week. And of course I genuinely couldn't tell her. There was a note in her voice that told me she knew he was playing away. Also, she said she'd been having silent phone calls with the caller withholding their number.'

'Perhaps Gina trying to railroad the marriage into the divorce court,' said Sue. 'After all, she spent a week with the fat bastard. I know it seems incredible to us, but perhaps she had a good time with him and wants more.'

'One would have thought she'd want to see quite a lot less of Harry,' remarked Janet. 'He seems to have put on more weight since his, er, sun-drenched conference. Rather than having a six pack, he seems to have gone for the Party Seven look. My problem with Val is that I think she's going to keep pestering me about Harry's extra-curricular activities, and I don't really know what to say.'

'It all boils down to the same thing,' said Liz. 'Proof. If we can get proof of what Harry's up to, then we'll all benefit in the end. Even Val.'

'Personally I'd like Val to know what a shit she's married to,' said Nina. 'I still haven't forgiven her for what she said about my bum. Come on, Janet, she's been appallingly rude to all of us.'

'Let's get the proof and let time and opportunity decide,' said Janet. 'Okay, next time I go in and have a row with Harry, I'll get one of the sound engineers to wire me up. It won't be difficult to predict when. Our shouting matches are fairly common these days.'

With that, they delved into seconds of sticky toffee pudding and debated the merits of the latest Next Directory, George Clooney movies and thongs versus big pants.

Val was dreading the weekend. She'd enjoyed the peace of Thursday and Friday nights at home on her own with the soaps and a few bottles of Chardonnay. She'd felt safe and unthreatened. Harry had been working both nights, or so he'd claimed. She'd tried to look faintly disappointed but didn't think she was all that convincing. At least he hadn't come up with any other weirdo suggestions like going to the theatre again.

Val was now becoming suspicious and wondering whether she should start checking credit card bills, or go through his briefcase for evidence. She then realized help-lessly that she couldn't do either, even if she'd wanted to. She had no idea where he put the bills and he kept his briefcase firmly locked in the car. It was probably stuffed with wispy knickers from Agent Provocateur and credit card slips from swanky eateries like Shiraz, she decided petulantly. So how was she going to track him down and find the proof? That dipstick Geraldine wouldn't talk. She was far too blindly loyal. The girls at HOT would know exactly what to do, but could she ask them? It was a ter-rible climb-down, and besides, Harry was their boss. She might try Susie, who seemed to have slipped smoothly from Smug Married to Scarlet Woman World.

She lit a cigarette and stretched out her legs, admiring her new toe ring, a present from Harry after his weekend away in sunny Manchester. Perhaps it was compensation for what he'd really been up to that week. She reached down, wrenched it from her toe and chucked it in a nearby waste-paper basket. That felt better. Next week she'd have another go at persuading Janet to spill the beans on Harry. There didn't seem to be much love lost between them at the moment.

Suddenly she heard the Mercedes' tyres scrunching on the drive. She stubbed out her cigarette, scurried upstairs, leaving the lights and the television on, went straight into their bedroom, dived under the duvet and pretended to be asleep. She heard Harry come in, then his footsteps creak-ing upstairs. She sensed him peering into their room, then heard him going downstairs again. From the kitchen came the clanking of bottles. Oh shit, he must have found the last two nights' worth of empties she'd forgotten to put away in a dark corner of the garage. After a while she heard him speaking in very hushed tones to someone. Who on earth would he be ringing at two in the morning?

Val strained to hear, only catching tantalizing bits of the conversation. It seemed that something had gone well tonight, and there was a reference to Monday. The rest was unintelligible. She'd creep downstairs in the morning and press last-number redial just to see who answered.

Val and Harry spent the weekend managing very cleverly not to speak to each other. If one got up early, the other languished in bed. The newspapers were lingered over, television was completely riveting and each appeared to be reading a new best-seller that they couldn't put down. Behind the steamy pages, however, they were both seething and having an unofficial competition as to who could avoid speaking first.

Harry's Friday-night meeting with the boss of 3F films had gone exceptionally well. He was certain that this deal, with its finance and prestige implications, was going to be the all-time biggie for the company. He was already fantasizing about a massive pay rise that would take him up to the two hundred grand mark, smiling pictures of him in *Broadcast* and *Campaign*, meals in the best restaurants, holidays in the most exclusive resorts, perks of every description. Harry was dying to spill the beans and boast a little. But he wanted to keep Val at arm's-length where business was concerned. Too much information wasn't good for her. And besides, she might stumble upon his other life with Gina.

He was also cross about his discovery of the wine bottles. He thought Val would have learned her lesson when she lost her licence. But he knew full well that she had the higher moral ground at the moment over the still undiscussed newspaper picture. He sensed that picking a fight with her would lead to other awkward questions. No, he'd bide his time.

Val, on the other hand, was fantasizing about being at home with her parents again, safe, cosseted and cuddled. She was also still wondering who Harry'd been ringing at two in the morning. She'd crept down on Saturday morning while he was still snoring to check the phone, but the last-number redial had turned out to be Directory Inquiries. So the bastard had tried to cover his tracks. Clever enough to erase the previous number, but not quite clever enough not to arouse suspicion. Val pondered some more, hidden behind the pages of her book. So this was how it felt to be in that infidelity trap she'd read about in magazine agony columns. It had never occurred to her that her husband wouldn't always be there for her. Let alone playing away. She'd always taken him for granted. Perhaps that was the trouble. But she needed to be certain, not rely on her instincts.

She began to formulate a plan. She'd fix up lunch with Susie on Monday, and start picking Janet's brains face to face, not down the phone. She'd confront her over lunch one day next week. Oh, and she'd give up drinking too.

chapter twenty-seven

'So how do you find out if your husband is having an affair?' demanded Val, abruptly lowering her voice when she realized half the restaurant diners were now riveted.

Susie stirred her coffee and thought for a minute. 'Well,' she said, lighting a cigarette and staring at it thoughtfully while she exhaled, 'there's the traditional approach of checking pockets, bills, car mileage, Visa statements, lipstick on the collar, that sort of stuff. But if they're premier-league liars, they just tell you another whopping porkie so you have to go off and investigate that one.'

'That's exactly Harry,' said Val, sipping her mineral water and desperately wishing she could do that old Bible trick and convert it to wine. 'He just wriggles out of everything, the sod. He knows best about any subject you care to name. And he obviously gets plenty of practice all day at work. No, that one won't work.'

'Hm, you're probably right,' said Susie knowingly. 'He always struck me as incredibly bossy. Couldn't mention it before, obviously. He's the archetypal smooth-talking bastard. That's of course why you married him. So you may need to think about a more brutal route. Confront the sod and see how he reacts. That's worth a stab.'

'No, same problem. Harry'd argue black was white if it suited him. I don't think I'd get anywhere on that route either, except another dreadful row.' Val stared miserably at the bottom of her glass.

'By the way, why are you on the wagon?' asked Susie suddenly.

'Decided to give it up', said Val glumly. 'My parents hinted that I'd been overdoing it. I've got drunk a lot recently, if I think back.'

'Bit difficult to think back if you're drunk, isn't it?' queried Susie, lighting another cigarette from the butt of the previous one.

'Exactly,' confessed Val. 'I've tried to think back and I can't remember the half of it most of the time. Then I wake up in the morning, look in the mirror and realize I look like shit.'

'Hmm, can't imagine that for one moment,' said Susie, who'd always been envious of Val's looks.

'I think I started because I got bored at home, but I wonder now if it was because I was subconsciously so unhappy. Now I'm stuck at home most of the time because of my driving ban. Sure, I could get a cab, but it's not the same. And Harry'd go ballistic if I hired a driver. I think he quite likes the idea of me being chained to the Aga, playing the little woman. I suppose I could learn to make a raised pork pie or pipe cream cheese into mangetout. But I've decided I've got to stay sober, if only to find out what he's up to.'

'Then I think the answer is a jolly good snoop,' said Susie. 'You've got to get someone to follow him, find out once and for all what he's up to and then confront the bastard on the spot.'

A waiter intervened to waft dessert menus in front of

them. 'Crème brûlée twice, and two coffees,' said Susie, taking charge. She looked at her watch.

'Ten minutes then I must scoot,' she said, again lighting a cigarette from the butt of the previous one.

'You're a bit heavy on the ciggies,' remarked Val.

'Remember, I'm a working girl these days,' said Susie, half laughing. 'Got to keep up my nicotine intake before I go back to the wonderful world of the smoke-free work-house. Just remember, too, the downside of all this. Dump Harry and you too could be rushing out for an alfresco fag in all weathers.'

Val smiled in sympathy. 'I thought you were giving up work soon to live with the boss?' she queried.

'Yes, well,' said Susie, suddenly getting all flustered. 'Let's just say something weird must happen to men's willies when they get into positions of power. My lovely boss has left his wife for me – and several others, I believe.'

'Oh, shit,' said Val, shocked. Perhaps it would be better to stay with Harry after all. Better the devil you knew . . .

It might have been Monday, but Janet was still exhausted from the extra hours of the previous week. She'd managed to avoid Harry all day. She knew that in her present state of fatigue she'd be absolutely no match for him if he started ranting. No, distance was the best thing. And she had plenty to get on with. Besides, she didn't really want to look Harry in the eye, knowing that tonight was the Night of the Long Lenses. Ray and Freddie had recce-ed Gina's house, in order to set a position for a snatch picture. Fortunately there was a small car park just a little way up on the opposite side of the road which would give Freddie a perfect oblique angle to the doorstep without, hopefully, being seen.

Janet was confident that if there was a picture to be

had, Freddie would get it. He was one of those typical newspaper photographers in that give him all day, a studio and plenty of lighting and he'd take the world's most ghastly portrait, ranking only with having a bad hair day in a photo booth. But put him up a tree, or have him hanging out of a speeding car, or someone's bedroom window, and he'd deliver great shots. If Harry stuck to his timing of last Thursday, he'd arrive at the house at around seven o'clock, when there was still plenty of light. Ray had promised to ring Janet at home that evening to tell her what happened. She mustn't get too hopeful, she thought, as she watched the hours tick past.

Harry, meanwhile, sitting in his office and admiring his paintings for the umpteenth time that day, was itching to gloat to Janet about his successful Friday-night dinner with the boss of Food From Films. That would put the irritating tart in her place. But there was an alarm bell warning him not to, just as there had been with Val. Better to keep it under wraps for a while. Damn the pair of them. He wanted to tell someone, he had to tell someone, to bask in the glory of a deal well done.

'Geraldine,' he barked in the direction of the open office door. A vision in putrid green scuttled into his office. 'I'll just update you on the 3F project. It's going to be an amazing success . . .'

And Harry was off, swelling with pride and too much weekend claret as he addressed his captive audience. Yes, Geraldine might look dreadful in that outfit, but she was at least a devoted and unquestioning listener.

Janet was just packing up to go home, computer switched off, rubbish bin piled high with the day's newspapers, junk mail and discarded scripts, when the phone rang.

'Operation Haunted Handbag here,' whispered Sue. 'Italian woman has made contact with suspect. I put her through. Perhaps they're discussing tonight's meeting. Also, Val's on the line for you. Do you want to speak to her?'

'Oh Gawd, not after the day I've had,' said Janet. 'Why didn't you talk to her?'

'She asked for you.' Oh dear, thought Janet. More questions that I can't or don't want to answer. 'Oh, go on, put her through . . . Val, you've just caught me. I'm packing up to leave.'

Val went straight into an apology for disturbing her and asked if they could meet for lunch, any day this week to suit.

Janet was staggered at the difference in Val. She couldn't pinpoint what it was exactly, only that it was different. They agreed on Wednesday, with Val saying how much she'd look forward to it.

Janet replaced the receiver thoughtfully. Val apologizing? What was the world coming to? She felt an attack of guilt coming on, knowing that tonight they might get the proof about Harry's extra-office antics. It might ultimately impact on Val, especially if she asked the sort of questions Janet thought she might. It might prove ultimately difficult to lie.

Harry left the HOT office so full of his latest piece of news that he hardly knew how to contain himself. He wanted to burst into song, crow from the rooftops and generally tell the world how pretty bloody clever he was. He eased the Mercedes from his reserved parking space and headed out of Hartford on the half-hour journey to Gina's house. He caught sight of his huge grin in his rear-view mirror and grinned some more. He even found himself singing along to the music system.

Champagne, he thought, swiftly pulling into a parking slot outside Bottoms Up. His snap decision nearly caused Ray, following behind, to swerve into a telegraph pole. Once recovered, Ray wondered whether Harry would clock the black-leather-clad and helmeted figure in his rear-view mirror when he resumed his journey. He needn't have worried.

Harry emerged from the off-licence still grinning from ear to ear and clutching a bottle of Moët wrapped in tissue paper. Oblivious to anything but himself, he climbed back into the Merc and resumed his journey. Ray followed at a discreet distance. A quarter of a mile from Gina's house, Ray pulled in and rang Freddie on his mobile phone.

'Man and Merc approaching in under a minute,' he reported. 'Man carrying pre-shag champagne bought from off-licence.'

'Gotcha,' replied Freddie. 'I can see them now. See you in the pub shortly.'

Forty minutes later, Freddie and Ray were seated in the back bar of one of Hartford's scruffiest pubs, nursing pints of lager and celebrating a victory.

'And you really don't think he noticed you?' asked Ray.

'No, doubt it. Remember, mate, I do a lot of this. You can always tell people's state of mind by the way they get out of a car. That chap was preoccupied and I expect what was going on in his brain was mostly X-certificate stuff. He didn't hang around on the doorstep. He was a man with a mission.'

Ray phoned Janet from the pub to tell her the good news, and much later that night they all met up at the

Echo office, where Freddie processed his film. The office block was mostly in darkness, the reporters having long gone home. It added to the drama and illicitness of it all somehow.

The pictures might not have painted a thousand words but they certainly told the story. Harry was even captured sporting a silly little grin as he got out of his car. The tissue-wrapped bottle was clearly champagne, its foil-wrapped neck visible.

'Wonder what they were celebrating?' Janet enquired.

'Not being rumbled on their sunshine break in Manchester?' offered Ray.

'Prospect of a good shag,' said Freddie. 'But I detected this man had had some good news. And he strikes me as the sort of man who will want to boast about it, whatever it is.'

Harry drove home in a very different mood to the one he'd arrived in. He'd been bursting to tell Gina the news that 3F were in advanced negotiations with a Hollywood star to open their first restaurant. Harry loved the idea of hob-nobbing with household names, especially film stars, and perhaps becoming their latest new best friend. He'd fanta-sized about conversations beginning with 'When I had lunch with Julia Roberts the other day . . .' or 'As I was saying to Brad Pitt . . .' He could imagine himself com-manding Geraldine to 'Get Michael Douglas on the phone.'

Unfortunately, it had all backfired. Gina had got so caught up in his enthusiasm that she had demanded point blank to be invited to the opening party too.

'You can't come.' He'd recoiled in horror. 'People would talk. It would get straight back to Val.'

'But you'll have told her by then,' said Gina defiantly.

'You've said you'll tell her about me. You promised. In Portugal.'

'Well, er, yes,' Harry floundered, 'but I, er, can't guarantee that I'll have told her by the end of the month. It might not be possible.'

'Then I'll tell her,' hissed Gina, in full Italian flow. 'I'll tell her all about it. She'll find it much more interesting from me.'

'No, no.' Harry was beginning to feel invisible lead weights bearing down on his shoulders. His panic eventually evaporated as the champagne took effect and they ended up having a hot and passionate grappling session upstairs. He'd finally won an assurance from Gina that she'd keep her mouth shut if he'd guarantee she'd go to the opening party. Even if they had to pass her off as a casual acquaintance. Harry begged her to understand that he had to find the right moment to tell Val their marriage was over. He hinted that Val might threaten suicide when she heard the terrible news. The prospect of life without him would send her over the edge, he suggested, a concept that Gina could empathize with. Nevertheless Harry drove home a very, very worried man.

chapter twenty-eight

By her normally eye-popping standards, Val was looking decidedly low-key. Admittedly she was in her trademark four-inch heels, black today, with a short black trenchcoat and carrying a Prada bowling bag, but there was something missing. Talons, Janet decided. No long blood-red or shocking-pink nails. Not much jewellery either, by Val's standards. Blonde hair in subdued ponytail. Then there was the body language. Even if she'd worn a paper bag on her head, Val would normally have dominated any room she entered. Yet today Janet almost had to seek her out amongst the dozen or so people milling around in the HOT reception area.

'It's great of you to spare the time,' Val began when she saw Janet. Good grief, thought Janet, what on earth has been going on here? Grateful, subdued, humble, these were not words one normally associated with Val. Nor were three more words, 'sparkling mineral water', either.

That was the next shock, when the waiter in the Ganges Indian restaurant came to take their orders. Why on earth didn't Val scream for a bottle of wine the minute she sat down. Perhaps she was rehearsing being on the wagon for when she got her driving licence back.

'This is a bit of a dive,' said Janet, apologizing for the flock wallpaper and tatty tablecloths, 'but you did say you wanted to go somewhere out of the way. Nobody from HOT ever comes here. It's known locally as the Gunges. Anyway, I'm starving, and by the way, it's my treat, if you can call it that.'

Janet could have sworn Val looked so touched at her offer, her eyes nearly welled up. Something strange had happened to this woman, and that Harry was the cause, Janet had no doubt.

'D'you mind if I smoke?'

'Not at all,' Janet replied. Val had never been known to ask such a question before. And where was the imperious nature, the snapping of the fingers, the pointing and the addressing of the waiters as if they were some kind of low-life?

They made small talk until the first course arrived, onion bhaji for Janet, sheek kebab for Val. Just when they were crunching on some inter-course poppadoms, Val made her move. Except that it wasn't quite what Janet had expected.

'Harry thinks he's being stalked,' said Val, sipping her mineral water and then lighting a cigarette. Janet stalled for a moment, pretending to finish a mouthful of pop-padom.

Val continued: 'Stalked. Followed. Call it what you will.'

Janet prayed she wasn't blushing. Had Harry clocked Freddie the Lens after all? He was so convinced he hadn't been spotted.

'What makes him think this?' she managed, covering her mouth as she finished the last bits of poppadom, and hopefully her embarrassment too.

'He's blaming me,' said Val. 'Thinks I suspect he's playing away. And that I've put a detective or someone on to him.'

Janet's embarrassment turned immediately to guilt. Had Harry given Val a hard time? Had he hit her? Or was this a smart diversionary tactic on his part? Her confusion was mercifully interrupted by the arrival of two waiters, one to remove the starter plates and the other to serve up their main courses from a wooden trolley. The dishing-up of the meat balti, chicken tikka and pillau rice was done with a great deal of aplomb. A triumph of style over substance where the Gunges was concerned. And it gave Janet enough time to gather her thoughts.

Had Harry spotted Freddie or Ray or was he just generally ruffled by recent events? He'd certainly got away with his trip to Manchester's sunny playas by the skin of his teeth. But add on the Paul Burns fiasco, the mobile at the theatre scenario plus the rumour about the secret file, and there probably was a very worried man under the surface.

'Well I haven't,' announced Val emphatically.

'Haven't what?' Janet replied absent-mindedly.

'Haven't put a detective on to him,' said Val. 'But it occurred to me that it's a bloody good idea. I was hoping you could, er, help me organize it.'

'Me?' said Janet, not quite able to make eye contact now with Val. 'Oh, Val, I couldn't do that.'

'I'm not asking you to set up a contract killing, just find me a detective,' pleaded Val.

'I . . . I . . . I'm afraid I just don't know any. Besides, if Harry found out, I'd get the sack.'

Val stubbed out her cigarette defiantly. 'Okay, point taken. But I want to ask you point blank and in confidence: where exactly *was* Harry the week he was away?'

'In Manchester, we were told,' said Janet, realizing she couldn't keep playing the innocent. Val clearly knew that she knew more.

'Do *you* believe he was in Manchester?' asked Val.

'No, Val, I don't,' Janet replied, looking her straight in the eye. 'I have no proof, but no, I don't think he was. Sorry. We all thought he looked a bit too brown.'

'Do you think he's playing away?'

Janet took a deep breath. Should she tell Val what she knew about Gina? It didn't amount to much. Disappearing into someone's house clutching a bottle of champagne was hardly proof of an affair. Should she tell Val that Harry was indeed being stalked? Followed and photographed, anyway. Every instinct in her body told her not to. Val needed to confront the awful truth herself, not rely on the tales of others. Wives were always the last to know. Also, if she told Val of the existence of Freddie's photographs, Harry would bully or beat out of her the names of the guilty. Janet's P45 would be guaranteed in the next post.

Suddenly Janet was overwhelmed by a feeling of deep pity, a feeling that she owed Val something. Despite all the ghastly evenings, the insults and the abuse, there was, seated across the table from her, a very sad woman who'd suffered probably much more at Harry's hands than the entire staff at HOT.

'Yes,' she said slowly, eyes downcast, hands clasped. 'I think he could be playing away. But before you ask, I have absolutely no proof.'

Operation Haunted Handbag held what was becoming their regular Friday-night committee meeting.

'So Val wants us to stalk Harry?' exclaimed Sue. 'Bit ironic, isn't it?'

'Well, strictly speaking she wants us to help her hire a detective,' explained Janet, uncorking bottles of Australian Chardonnay and passing round tortilla chips and dips. 'Sorry, I can't give you ABC.'

'What's ABC?' asked Sue.

'Anything but Chardonnay,' replied Janet. 'Apparently it's now regarded as a nineties drink. So passé, darling. But hey, let's be retro.'

'So are we going to help her?' asked Sue.

'Well, as I see it,' said Janet, 'the fact that we've already done that in a way is something we obviously don't want her to know.'

'But she suspects Harry's Game then?' asked Liz.

'Yes, and I get the feeling she's thinking very seriously of baling out.'

'You mean divorce?' asked Nina.

'Absolutely!' said Janet. 'Just consider for a moment what she's getting out of the relationship. Putting aside the fact that she lives with a complete pig, they don't have kids, he's never there and she's lonely. Val's thirty-two now and she's not getting any younger. Her only friends seem to be us, and we're not exactly her most fanatical devotees. She doesn't need Harry's money, she's got wealthy parents. So there's not even a meal-ticket aspect to it. Her answer up to now has been to drink herself senseless, although she seems to be off the pop at the moment, which I think is a bit symbolic.'

'In what way?' asked Sue as she scooped up some garlic and herb dip with a tortilla chip.

'She's having a rethink and she's sober. At our Gunges lunch, she drank only mineral water. She sounds different too, more polite, actually considerate. I'm going to make a suggestion and I want you all to think about it.'

They all stopped mid sip or mouthful.

'Until now, we've been setting Harry up in the hope that he might leave the company, get sacked, join SMERSH or SPECTRE,' continued Janet. 'But perhaps it's time we helped Val out a bit.'

'Dangerous mission, even for James Bond,' said Sue wisely. 'It could so easily backfire and we'd all be fond memories in old HOT telephone directories.'

'No, I mean indirectly,' explained Janet. 'I'm not suggesting we ring her and recommend a list of reputable detective agencies, or show her pictures of Harry arriving at Gina's house. Because that still doesn't necessarily prove anything. No, we have to come up with something more subtle. Perhaps we could take her somewhere where she might find out. Stumble on the truth herself, so to speak.'

'It would need careful thought,' warned Sue. 'You know how Harry can twist anything to his advantage. If he got the slightest hint it was planned, we'd be out on the street. We have to play the innocent on this one.'

The others nodded in approval. They all agreed to go away and think of a possible scenario.

The weekend seemed to pass as if it were on fast forward. After a flurry of supermarket shopping, mounds of week-end newspapers and piles of dirty coffee cups, it was Monday again. Janet thought about Geraldine for a moment as she eased her car into the HOT car park. Had she managed to get any fantastic sex or fulfilling hoovering in over the weekend?

'Geraldine's on the towpath,' grinned Sue as Janet entered the building.

'Blimey, I can't even get through reception before she's at it,' said Janet, her relaxed mood instantly dispelled.

She reached her desk and grabbed her ringing phone.

'Yes, Geraldine, I'm on my way. Give me ten minutes, for goodness' sake, I've only just arrived.'

Janet knew exactly what this was about. Harry wanted all the treatments on Food From Films. All the work that she'd sweated over for the last couple of weeks was about to be taken, stolen, plagiarised, call it what you will, and passed off as Harry's own. Then it would be big brownie points from the board, a pat on the back from the chairman and another whopping bung at the end of the year.

Janet checked her e-mails and then slowly gathered up all her files on 3F. Ten minutes later she was sitting in Harry's office.

'Hmm, not bad,' he admitted grudgingly, glancing through the work she'd handed him. 'Not bad, except you've got the name wrong, you stupid fucking cow.' He flung one of the files back at her.

'If I'm a silly cow, why do you continue to employ me?' said Janet, trying not to tremble. This was bad, even for Harry, first thing on a Monday morning.

'Start that tack and you might just talk yourself out of a job,' he snarled at her. 'The name of the project changed last week to Movie Munch. You should read your bloody e-mail.'

Janet knew full well that he hadn't sent any such e-mail but thought it wise not to pursue that one.

'Look, Harry, I've put in hours and hours on this, over and above doing my property project. I didn't know the title had changed. That's not a major problem. I can soon alter it, although I'll have to get Graphics to do some new mock-ups. Unless, of course, you yourself told them of the name change.'

Harry leaned forward in his *Mastermind* chair and thumped on the desk.

'You should be more on the ball. You should have told Graphics. I want this done again and I want it done by eleven o'clock. I have a very important meeting with this company and I want everything to be perfect. Geddit?'

'Yes,' nodded Janet, wishing she could throw poisoned darts at the view she had under his desk. 'I'll do my best. By the way, Harry, given the hours I've put in, why can't I attend this meeting?'

'Above your head,' hissed Harry. 'What on earth do you think you'd be able to contribute?'

'Well, I developed the treatments that got the contract, and it was my idea in the first place,' said Janet defiantly.

'Bollocks,' he shouted.

Janet took a deep breath. 'Harry, I'm sick of you getting the credit for everything. I came up with the idea, I wrote the pitch that got the contract, and at the end of the day I suppose I'll be credited just as researcher as usual.'

'At the rate you're going, you stupid cow, you won't even get a name check at your own fucking funeral.' He banged the desk once more.

'Thanks a lot, Harry.'

'And just remember who's the boss around here. What I say goes. Geddit? I have a reputation for coming up with ideas, good ideas, and making them happen.'

'But loads of them are my ideas and my treatments.'

'Just fuck off out of my sight. Get back to your desk. And if I don't have that work here by eleven o' clock, then you can start packing your bags. You're all the same, you bloody women. Ideas above your station. Get a move on or you'll be taking an early bath.'

Janet stood up and left his office without another

word. She went straight to the crew room where Ron, the sound recordist, was waiting.

'Cor, that battery pack got hot,' she grinned as she pulled up her jacket for him to dismantle the equipment. He pulled the sticky tape off her back where the battery pack had been secured, and unclipped the tiny microphone hidden beneath her lapel.

'I'd better get back to the office,' she announced.

'I'll let you know how it's come out and transfer it to ordinary cassette tape for you to enjoy at home,' said Ron. 'And don't worry, I'll put the red light on while I'm doing it so I won't be disturbed.'

Ten minutes later, Ron's voice came down the phone.

'At the rate you're going, you stupid cow, you won't even get a name check at your own fucking funeral,' he mimicked.

'What's it like?' asked Janet anxiously 'Is it clear?'

'For technical merit, straight sixes. But for artistic impression, he's right off the scoreboard. That was the most appalling claptrap I've ever heard. Is he always such a charmer?'

'Yeah, that's pretty standard Harry,' said Janet. 'Anyway, I owe you a pint in the GX after work.'

Liz staggered into the production office, laden with tapes and looking exhausted. It had been the final day of the last Hot Breaks For Heartaches shoot. Everything was now in the can. If they hadn't got the shots, it was too late.

As a small cheer went up, Liz half smiled and slumped behind her desk.

'Paul Burns sends his love,' joked Ray. 'He says he'll be in next week to check the rushes.'

259

'Bugger off,' said Liz, laughing. It felt good to be back in the office. She'd been out on the road for what seemed like an eternity. 'I was going to say that I'd missed you,' she continued, 'but I must be suffering from some sort of temporary self-delusion.'

'How was it?' asked Janet, walking over from her desk. Nina was also homing in with a cup of coffee for Liz.

'Well, the last one was fairly excruciating. Carpentry for the cack-handed. Not my idea of a fun-filled weekend, but the people on the break now think they're just waiting to be the next Chippendales. Stripping pine rather than their clothes, I hasten to add. Anyway, I heard a couple of really top bits of gossip.'

'What's that then?' came a chorus.

'It's a very small world. One of the guys on the course was at school with Harry,' announced Liz proudly, 'and he told me some very interesting things. Not a fan, not surprisingly. I should imagine Harry started his bullying career pretty early on in the playground, because this guy absolutely hated him.'

'Harry's certainly had plenty of practice then,' replied Janet, still smarting from the morning's onslaught. 'No wonder he's so good at it. Anyway, go on, what's this gossip?'

'Well,' paused Liz, savouring the attention, 'for a start Harry was never at Oxford, as he claimed. No, our Harry went to a bog-standard polytechnic somewhere in Oxfordshire apparently. Takes the gilt off the gingerbread a bit, doesn't it?'

'Just a bit!' said Janet. 'What's the other snippet?'

'Ah, that's much more fun. This chap and Harry were in the same class at school. Harry claims to be forty-four, as we all know. In fact he's got to be at least forty-eight.'

They all roared with laughter.

'Well, I suppose if you lie about one thing, you might as well lie about everything else,' said Janet. 'I'd love to see Harry's CV. I bet it would give the Brothers Grimm a run for their money.'

'I wonder if Val knows about the age bit,' said Nina. 'What a shock to find that the monster you married is an even older monster.'

'I think Val's well past being shocked,' said Janet ruefully. 'At the rate she's going, they'll name a trauma ward after her.'

'There is one more bit of gossip,' said Liz shyly. 'And it's about me. I think I have an admirer.'

'Brilliant.' Nina clapped her hands. 'Who, when and how did you meet? Oh shit, I hope it wasn't one of the cack-handed carpenters.'

'No, no,' reassured Liz. 'He's an accountant.'

'Chartered, certified or turf?' asked Ray. Nina immediately kicked him in the shin.

'Ironically, he's an accountant with Hot Breaks.'

'See,' said Nina, delighted. 'The system works. And I can thoroughly recommend accountants. He'll be able to take you on lots of those hot breaks.'

'No thanks, Nina. I think I've had enough of them to last a lifetime.'

'Forty-eight and counting, eh?' muttered Janet to herself. 'Does Harry ever tell the truth?'

chapter twenty-nine

A brand new wobble went around the corridors of Hartford Optimum Television. Harry was at it again. He'd apparently just sacked Jed, one of the graphic artists, amid a flurry of tongue-lashing. Legend had it that Harry could be heard all over Hartford. Certainly his raised voice had reverberated down the executive corridor, and soon rumours had spread to all four corners of the building. Jed had apparently been dispatched to clear out his belongings and go.

The production office was a scene of disbelief. Producers and researchers were standing around looking as stunned as if the canteen had just won a Michelin star. Jed was a popular chap, particularly as he was a soft touch for any private work that people wanted. The speculation was that that had been his downfall. He'd popped names and chapter headings on to wedding videos, provided graphics for show reels and generally been helpful and keen as well as extremely gifted. His only other fault, if it could be described as that, was that he was a bit of a flirt and considered serious totty by most of the women. Even the sexless Geraldine was clocked fluttering unmascaraed eyelashes when Jed swept past.

'I think it's because Harry was jealous,' whispered Nina to a huddled throng in the canteen. 'He thinks he's King Dong around here and Jed was a young pretender to the throne.'

'Harry's always had this idea that he can exercise his right of prima nocta,' said Ray.

'Wassat?' said Nina. 'Sounds like a cocktail.'

'Just an early English form of queue-jumping,' explained Ray. 'In olden times, the local Lord of the Manor got first jump, so to speak. Or droit de seigneur. Basically he could shag new brides before their husbands. Very Harry.'

'Well, I think it's appalling that Jed's been sacked,' said Nina. 'I know he was only on a short-term contract, but he's bloody good and—'

'Drop-dead gorgeous.' Janet had come in on the conversation. 'I can't believe Harry could be so stupid. Does he not realize that Jed's the only one in Graphics this week? If he goes, several projects are in jeopardy.'

With that, Janet stalked off in the direction of Harry's office.

'Directional Inquiries didn't have the number,' she could hear Geraldine apologizing.

'Well, get new bloody directionals, then,' shouted Harry in exasperation from his office.

'Harry's busy,' snapped Geraldine. Janet ignored her and marched past her straight into Harry's office.

'Did I hear right? Did I hear you've sacked Jed?'

'Yep, got it in one,' smirked Harry, loving his new power trip.

'As head of production, I should have been consulted.'

'Well, some things are over your silly little head,' snapped Harry, throwing caution – and the company's insurance policy – to the wind yet again by lighting a huge cigar.

'If you had consulted me,' said Janet tartly, 'I would have told you that not only does Jed do a really good job, but he's the only one in Graphics for the next fortnight. The rest are on leave. We have some very tight deadlines on projects, including your beloved Movie Munch, with its last-minute name change, which are all heavily graphic-dependent. No graphic artist means no graphics, so I suggest you ring around your clients and explain that their projects will be at least two weeks late. Meanwhile I'll go off now and cancel the editing. No point in starting without all the material.'

Harry banged his desk. 'Why am I never told about these things?' he hissed.

'You never bother to ask,' replied Janet as she turned tail and walked out.

Five minutes and a strong coffee later, Janet received an e-mail from Harry stating that he'd asked Jed to stay on until the end of the month, to which Jed had agreed. Whatever had Harry said to make him change his mind? Janet nipped round to the graphics suite and found Jed, feet up on the desk, chuckling over a huge cappuccino.

'I've agreed to do another fortnight,' said Jed with a twinkle in his eye. 'Don't worry, Janet. I was planning to leave at the end of my contract anyway. That's why I enjoyed such a big bust-up with Harry. I've got work lined up so I didn't need a reference from him.'

'Not that he'd have given you one,' said Janet.

'Oh no, that was made perfectly clear, together with mutterings about lousing up my career for ever. That guy's mad. He's power-crazed. Very sad. I gather he's got a rather beautiful wife. Why on earth does she stay with him?'

'Lack of a driving licence. Or something like that. Anyway, what on earth made you back down and agree to do another fortnight?' asked Janet.

'Just you wait and see,' replied Jed, enigmatically.

Top of the bill at Friday night's meeting of Operation Haunted Handbag was the playing of the tape. Tonight's host was Janet. She'd promised them a traditional English themed night. This turned out to be not spit-roasted pig, mead and jesters, but fish and chips from the local chippy plus bottles of beer. After they'd finished and packed up the plates and the remains of all the wrapping paper, Nina, Liz and Sue listened aghast as Janet played back the tape of her row with Harry.

'Bloody hell,' said Sue. 'That's even worse than I thought. Is that the norm?'

'By and large, yeah.'

'What are you going to do with the tape?' queried Sue.

'Save it for a rainy day along with all the rest of the evidence.'

'But when will we get this downpour?' said Nina impatiently. 'I hope we're not going to be meeting up like this in ten years' time, still snooping around Harry and wishing he'd disappear.'

'At least we can console ourselves that in ten years' time Harry might have retired!' said Janet. 'Now we know he's forty-eight, he's not got quite as much ahead of him as we thought.'

'Well, he's certainly ahead of himself in the gut department,' said Liz. 'There's definitely an attack of post-middle-aged spread there. I've really noticed the difference, having been out of the office filming so much recently.'

'Talking of eating,' said Janet, 'we have a new piece of information. Harry meets Gina for lunch nearly every Friday at the same place.'

'How do you know?' asked Sue.

'Silly question. Ray told me. He was chatting to Glenda, one of the cleaners, who told him that Geraldine let slip that she books a table every Friday for Harry. I think Glenda was asking her to recommend somewhere countrified for an anniversary or something. And Geraldine said it must be good because Harry went to this place regularly and she always made the booking.'

'Come to think of it,' Sue chipped in, 'Harry always seems to take a long lunch on Friday and looks a bit flushed when he comes back. Must be all that restrained passion over the willow-patterned plates.'

'Also, it would keep Gina topped up on the old pash-ometer before their weekend separation,' said Janet. 'Of course there's one way to find out for sure. And that's to—'

'Go there ourselves,' chorused the others.

'Well, actually, I've an even better idea,' said Janet. 'Let's make it a bit more public. Jed's bound to have a leaving do. Why don't we all go there for lunch?'

The weekend brought storms and sheeting rain. Autumn was hinting at an early arrival with a vengeance. Janet found herself yet again feeling the strain; it was not just Harry's constant outbursts, but the pressure of all the projects. Affordable Cool was more or less up and running and soon she'd be handing it over to Liz. But the Movie Munch project was weighing on her mind. It represented several months of hard slog.

Janet, still in her dressing gown, sipped a mug of coffee and casually flipped through the Saturday papers. There it was staring at her in the face. The travel pages. She needed a break, some sunshine and some respite from Harry. Somehow the rain now battering against her windows clinched it.

'Some leave,' she announced aloud. 'I need some leave.'

Janet hadn't taken any holiday for well over six months. She found herself feverishly scanning the holiday pages, ads and columns of flights, villas, hotels. Somewhere exotic and hot but not too far, she decided. Half an hour, three phone calls and her credit card details later, it was sorted. In a fit of excitement she picked up her phone again and rang Liz.

'I'm off to Morocco,' she announced. 'I woke up this morning really fed up and decided it was time to take a week off. I feel better already.'

'Brilliant, and about time too,' said Liz. 'You've been working far too hard. Who are you going with?'

'Just me. Don't worry, I've done this before,' trilled Janet. 'Only three and a half hours from Gatwick and I shall be completely transported into another world.'

'You'll be able to pick up lots of cheap haunted handbags in one of the souks,' said Liz. 'Or better still, forget about HOT for a week. When are you off?'

'This Friday,' announced Janet. 'Just time to crash-diet into my swimming costumes.'

'Hey, don't bother. Remember, it's belly-dancing country. They like their women curvy and well covered.'

'Hmm, I think I'm rather well covered already. And not just by my travel insurance. By the way, your voice sounds a bit funny. Or is it my phone?'

'No, it's my voice. It's my Big Date tonight with Tony

the accountant and I've got a face pack on. If I get too animated, it'll start cracking.'

Monday brought both good and bad news. The good news was that Liz's date with Tony had gone well. She was now into the agony zone of wondering if he'd ring again or whether she should ring him.

'Not too keen now,' counselled Sue. 'Let him do the chasing. Just wait a bit.'

'That's the trouble when you're past thirty,' wailed Liz. 'If I'm going to get married and have kids, I've got to get a move on. I've got to find the father and get practising, so to speak.'

'Well hang on, you can't map out your entire destiny on the basis of one evening at Que Pasa?. What was it like, by the way?'

They shuddered at the memory of their recent meal at the same restaurant with Val.

'Eventless, I'm pleased to say. It was a real treat to come out unscathed. No flying tables, no falling coat stands and not even a trip to the dry cleaner's afterwards.'

'How about him?'

'Bit shy. I suppose I expect everyone to be as mad as we are here. But accountants aren't necessarily the whackiest people on the planet. I do like him, though. Do you think he'll ring?'

'Yes of course he will,' said Sue, who was beginning to feel like Liz's mother. 'And if the sod doesn't, better now than six months down the line.'

The bad news, Janet discovered, was that the last day of her holiday clashed with Jed's leaving do. She would be flying back late that night. The others promised to let her know what happened.

Ray was taking charge of organizing Jed's farewell lunch. He was keeping it all low-key because no one wanted Harry to get wind of it. As the Country Cottage Restaurant was about ten miles outside Hartford, not everyone could go, but eventually a party of ten emerged, including Sue and Nina. Liz was secretly relieved that she couldn't go. She was still in the middle of editing the Hot Breaks films and couldn't spare the time. She found dealing with Harry incredibly difficult and was still managing to avoid being on her own in his office.

The next few days flew by as Janet frantically cleared her desk, answered every single letter and e-mail and left copious notes on what to do about Movie Munch during her week's absence. As the flight date drew nearer, she became more and more exhausted. At night she didn't have the energy to sort out her summer clothes, let alone get them washed and ironed.

Eventually it was her last day at work. She went round to see Jed and wish him well. He gallantly kissed her on the lips, and told her she was totally gorgeous and that it had been a pleasure to work with her. Janet fervently wished she could have settled for the pleasure, skipped the work, been twenty years younger and about two stone lighter.

Then, with heavy heart, she set off in the direction of Harry's corridor for a brief handover meeting. She'd prepared notes, too, just in case.

Harry was in ebullient mood and grandiosely welcomed her into the office without getting up from his *Mastermind* chair. Probably looking forward to his Thursday-night champagne shag, she thought mischievously.

They ran through her notes, with Janet emphasizing

that there would be a couple of projects that he would have to view and sign off while she was away: four instructional programmes on landscaping for the new gardening channel and three of the Hot Breaks videos. He nodded and then grudgingly wished her a good holiday.

'Where are you off to?' he enquired, without bothering to feign interest.

'Morocco,' she answered. 'Staying on the coast in Agadir, then having a couple of days in Marrakesh.'

'Well, make sure you don't get lost in some bloody kasbah. I know you women and your bloody shopping.'

chapter thirty

Janet stretched out on the beach in Agadir. Blue sky, pale ivory sand, a light breeze that just took the edge off the heat. It couldn't be more perfect. Having holidayed before on her own, she knew the drill. Loads of riveting books, a capacity for long walks, not too much eye contact with the locals, a pseudo wedding ring and preparation for the slight disappointment of a wonderful experience that she wouldn't be able to share.

One of the great delights of holidaying alone was that it didn't really matter what you wore, how fat you were or how burned you got. Not knowing a soul at the Hotel Agador had distinct advantages. She stretched out on a sunlounger on the hotel's private section of the beach and contemplated her lot. A couple of miles of sand, the Atlantic Ocean gently lapping its edge; this was the life. And she'd already caught up with essential reading. The latest Patricia Cornwell and Harry Potter had already been read, enjoyed and consigned to the chambermaid, who was quite upfront about being tipped. Next, another in her series of classics-she'd-never-got-round-to-reading-at-school, *Jane Eyre*, was waiting to be devoured. Janet suddenly thought of Harry cast as Mr Rochester, the moody monster control-freak, and Val as his mad wife, locked up, blind drunk and burning the house down. She began irritatingly to think of the office and wondered what was going on. Perhaps she should have brought one of those self-help books on how to deal with office bullies – an instructional volume entitled *How to Work With A Difficult Man – And Kill Him.*

Much to her annoyance, Harry was now stuck in her thoughts. She pottered down to the water's edge, making deliberate efforts to put him out of her head. That only made it worse. She watched some local salesmen at work on the beach, pestering tourists with their wares. They reminded her of Harry. Eventually she became so absorbed watching the jet skis that thoughts about HOT and all her projects evaporated. Tomorrow she'd be in Marrakesh after a very early start. Just time now for a brisk swim, then a light supper and an early night. The jet skis looked so powerful, skimming the water, bouncing the waves. She'd have liked to pulverize Harry with . . . Oh hell, there he was again. She must try and forget him.

Val was becoming quite an expert. Searching through Harry's pockets, dialling 1471, checking his discarded clothes for traces of lipstick and perfume, sifting through the waste-paper basket, getting up early to get to the post first, even steaming open then resealing envelopes. But so far nothing. In fact, the only suspicions roused were Harry's. He couldn't for the life of him understand why Val, who normally lounged in bed until at least eleven o'clock, was up with the lark and bringing him cups of tea in bed.

Val was often tempted to ring her mother, but there was always something that held her back. Perhaps she was afraid she'd crack under the strain of the inevitable conversation about the failure of her marriage, fear of the future, or just putting into words how wretched her situation was. No, she'd be stronger fighting this battle alone. Or at least with a little help from the HOT girls. She realized she was putting them, Janet in particular, in a difficult situation because of work, but on the other hand, they understood, more than most, exactly what she had to live with. She also suspected Janet knew much, much more than she was letting on. She had her reasons for that, Val understood, but she wished Janet would just spill the beans and be done with it.

Today she'd discovered that Janet was on holiday in Morocco. It made her shudder thinking that her holiday with Harry in the Maldives was only weeks away. The thought held no appeal at all. It felt more like a prison sentence. She'd have to get out of it somehow. Or perhaps she'd be doing Harry a favour by not going. Then he could take his bit on the side, whoever she was. The marriage might be all over by then, bar the shouting.

Val settled down to watch early-evening television. In the bad old days she'd have been well into her second bottle of wine by this stage of the day. She'd been surprised at her own success in giving up. After a few fairly gruesome days, she'd got used to a routine of mineral water, tea and coffee and was proud of the fact that she was no longer dependent on alcohol. What was Harry doing now? she thought. He never said why he had to work late some nights. She rang his mobile on impulse. Switched off. She rang HOT reception. The late receptionist said he'd left an hour ago. Funny, it had never occurred to her before, but this scenario often happened on Thursday nights. Probably in the past she'd been too slewed to notice. Now she was almost hoping he was being unfaithful. It would resolve things so easily. She'd challenge him when he got home.

Unfortunately the effect of the new routine of early rising to screen the post was catching up on her, and by the time Harry sneaked in at 10.30 after his Thursday-night session with Gina, Val was sound asleep on the sofa.

Friday morning and Janet's last day in Marrakesh. On the agenda, a visit to the Saadian tombs and the souk. Janet had been bowled over not just by the heat, but by the sheer colour and excitement of this gateway to the desert. The dusty pink buildings held a special kind of magic and the huge main square, Djema'a al Fna, was one of the most exciting places Janet had ever seen. By day it was hot, colourful and dusty, with its stalls selling fruit, spices, leather bags and slippers and djellabas, while by night it was a mass of smoke from barbecues as row upon row of food stalls were miraculously set up. Berber musicians, acrobats, fortune-tellers, snake-charmers, story-tellers, water-sellers all crammed into the huge arena, just as they had done for thousands of years. All there to make an honest or dishonest dirham or two.

At lunchtime Janet sat down at the Café Glacier for a cool beer and a ringside view of the square. The snake-charmers were out in full force, wrapping their wriggling companions around unsuspecting tourists who had to stump up fistfuls of dirhams to have them removed. With a jolt, Janet realized the snakes were reminding her of Harry yet again. She checked her watch. They'd all be arriving at the Country Cottage Restaurant around now. Would he be there with Gina? She checked her mobile. Yes, there was a good signal. She'd just have to be patient.

She finished her beer, left some coins on the table and made her way purposefully across the square to the entrance to the souk. Some last-minute shopping, that would take her mind off things.

Ray had hired three cabs so that everyone could have a drink at Jed's farewell lunch without the worry of driving. He also secretly wanted the car park at the Country Cottage Restaurant to be free of cars with HOT windscreen stickers in case it put Harry off. He'd booked the table for twelve fifteen so they'd all be seated when – or if – Harry walked in. Ray, Sue and Nina were in on the secret but the other seven had no idea. Better they didn't know. Three people feigning surprise would be less of a problem than all ten.

Miraculously everyone was ready in reception and the three taxis were on their way to the restaurant on the dot of twelve. Ray glanced at his watch for the hundredth time, watched by Sue.

'Nervous?' she asked.

'No, not really,' he replied. 'I'll just be seriously pissed off if this is the one week he doesn't go there.'

'Not the end of the world,' said Sue philosophically. 'The bottom line is that it's Jed's farewell bash. It's important that he has a good time. And if Harry pitches up, well, that's the icing on the cake.'

Nina rubbed her hands with anticipatory glee.

'I can't wait to see his face,' she chuckled. 'It'll serve the bastard right.'

They were all seated by twelve twenty around a huge circular table near the entrance. Brilliant, thought Ray, looking at his watch again. Couldn't have planned it better. He can't fail to spot us when he walks in.

Everyone consulted menus and a huge blackboard of

specials. There followed a lengthy discussion among the women about the calorie counts of the sauces that came with the sea bass as opposed to turbot or hake.

'Oh, spare me. Women and their bloody dieting,' Ray remarked to Jed and Neil, one of the engineers. They were the only chaps at the table.

'Next thing we'll hear is that they're all short for their weight, or that it shrank in the wardrobe,' replied Neil, who had two teenage daughters. 'It's like being at home.'

Eventually the calorie-counting was done and their orders taken, and a debate started up about the pros and cons of Delia, Jamie, Nigella and the two women from the River Café versus the Two Fat Ladies.

At twelve thirty, Ray began to despair. He's not coming, he's not coming. Drat and double drat. The restaurant was beginning to fill up.

An outrageously camp waiter started laying up the correct cutlery for the orders, swapping fish and steak knives where appropriate. Then he faffed around with butter and rolls and did a great deal of the adjusting of glasses that waiters delight in. At last bottles of wine arrived, everyone taking advantage of the no-driving situation.

By twelve forty, Ray had resigned himself to getting it wrong. He rose to his feet.

'While we're waiting for the grub, I think we should drink a toast to Jed and wish him well in the future,' he said. 'Good on yer, mate, for surviving us all at HOT, and may you come back one day.'

They raised their glasses in unison amid mutterings of 'Speech, speech.' Jed stood up. Two of the girls, desperate for a memory of the best bit of totty to arrive at HOT in many a long month, whipped out cameras to take pictures for posterity.

As flash bulbs popped in all directions, everyone was blinded for a split second. Out of the gloom, behind Jed, appeared Harry's flushed and angry face. He'd come in unseen and got caught in the flashfire.

'What the fuck . . .' he muttered, red-faced with anger. Then he nodded in his woman companion's direction. 'Business. I'll keep away from you bloody lot.'

With that he ushered the woman away to a table at the furthest end of the restaurant.

'Not your usual table, sir?' flapped the camp waiter after him.

Sue and Nina exchanged silent grins. It was Gina all right. Her long dark hair was gleaming and she was dressed provocatively in tight cream leather trousers, a cream silk shirt more unbuttoned than buttoned, a Moschino belt and cream leather kitten-heeled boots. Not quite the normal kit for a business lunch.

Jed was still on his feet, being urged by his female fans to make a farewell speech.

'Well, it's been fun and I'm gonna miss you all,' he said, grinning from ear to ear and a huge glass of wine in hand. 'HOT's a terrific company to work for. Full of big-hearted and generous people. I can't tell you how knocked out I am that Harry's come along today as well. Just shows that you can sack a man and still come to his leaving do. What a top bloke.'

Jed's voice was pitched just loud enough for Harry to hear across the restaurant, except of course that he was busily pretending not to.

'Harry,' Jed turned towards his table and raised his glass, 'thanks for the memory.'

Forced to acknowledge the toast, Harry grudgingly raised his glass and turned back to his companion as fast as he could. The HOT table was now convulsed in barely concealed giggles. Jed sat down, roaring with laughter.

The wine flowed, tongues loosened and diets finally went to the wall. After the main courses had been devoured, a blackboard of puddings well off the Richter calorie scale was greeted with enthusiasm. Having carefully chosen grilled fish for their main courses, the dieters now threw caution to the wind by ordering raspberry pavlova with clotted cream.

'I'll never understand women,' said Ray.

'They're a real mystery, mate, and I'm married to one,' replied Neil.

'What beats me is that some of them fall for bastards like Harry,' replied Ray. 'He's not only got Claudia Schiffer for a wife, but he's got Miss Tagliatelle Tasty Bits over there too.'

Every so often Sue and Nina glanced in the direction of Harry and Gina's table. The body language said it all. Harry looked positively shifty and uncharacteristically tense, while Gina, tossing her dark mane of hair, seemed totally at ease. It soon became apparent that Harry was going to stay put until they'd left. He wasn't going to suffer the embarrassment of having to walk past them all again to get to the exit. Eventually, after a round of coffee, they all felt they ought to get back to work. As taxis were ordered via mobile phones, Harry made no attempt to conceal his relief. He then had to endure a round of loud goodbyes from across the restaurant, much to the bemusement of other diners.

There was much speculation in the taxis going back. 'If Harry was on a business lunch, then I'm an alien,' said Julie, one of the accounts clerks. 'That's obviously his bit of stuff on the side. Fancy us stumbling on that!'

'Well, of all the bars in all the world . . .' growled Ray, adopting a Humphrey Bogart voice.

Sue and Nina exchanged glances. They were desperate not to let on that it was a set-up.

'I'm glad I don't have to work with him,' continued Julie, fuelled by far too much Pinot Noir. 'I think he's a right sod. Really fancies himself. Wonder what that woman sees in him.'

'God knows, but Vision Express should open a new branch around here,' replied Ray.

Sue couldn't wait to ring Janet. She finally caught her waiting for her flight at the airport in Marrakesh.

'Caught like a rat in a trap,' she told her cheerfully. 'You should have seen his face. We all behaved quite badly. Jed gave a speech and paid tribute to Harry. The whole restaurant heard.'

'Probably just as well I wasn't there,' said Janet, relieved. 'It would probably somehow be my fault. The trouble is, Harry's bigger than all of us. He'll just shrug off someone like Jed as if he were yesterday's socks.'

Janet was cross with herself for being defeatist about Harry again. It seemed to come in waves. One minute she'd feel quite confident, the next completely undermined.

'Listen, I hope you've had a good holiday and didn't worry about all this stuff,' said Sue, concerned.

'It was fab. I've done so much shopping, I'm souked out. At the rate I've been spending, I'll probably be turned down for a Sainsbury's reward card. It's the coming back that's the worst bit. I've managed to forget about Harry for most of this week, but he's already looming large again.'

chapter thirty-one

Janet did not want to get out of bed. It was so warm and safe under the duvet she wanted to stay there for ever, fuelled by Radio Four and a stream of comfort food and drink. The second of her three alarm clocks had gone off. She really ought to make a move but she couldn't. She'd wait for the third before getting up. That was the one that made her get out of bed. It had an annoyingly shrill ring and she had placed it intentionally on the other side of her bedroom.

Marrakesh was just a distant memory now. Today it was back to reality, back to HOT gossip and back to the problem of Harry. She showered, got dressed and sprayed herself with her new duty-free perfume. At least there was no need for make-up for a couple of weeks, thanks to her tan. Then she flung her briefcase into the back of the car and headed for work.

As she arrived in the HOT car park, she was overcome with a deep sense of foreboding. She felt like a patient going in for an operation knowing they'd run out of anaesthetic.

Two hundred e-mails and a menacing pile of post greeted her, together with so many Post-it notes stuck all over her computer they could have been entered for the Turner prize. She scrolled down through the e-mails. Amongst the usual flats/car/houses for sale she saw there were several messages from Val asking her to call.

'One would have done,' she said half aloud. What does she think I do on holiday, rush to the nearest cyber café and log on every day? She made a bet with herself on how long it would be before Harry demanded her presence. Half an hour, she reckoned. Wrong. The call came after only five minutes. Nerves a-jangle, she made her way to Harry's corridor. All the therapy of the week swept away by one phone call.

Having guessed where Janet was heading, Ray broke into the HOT rendition of a famous football chant – You'll Never Walk Again. For once, Janet found it physically impossible to smile.

'Have you seen this?' Harry shouted, going purple in the face and waving a tape.

'Have I seen what, Harry? Remember me, I've been on holiday for a week.'

Without a word of explanation, he shoved the tape into one of the machines behind his desk. Janet gazed at the screen in anticipation. It was the closing sequence of one of the series of landscape gardening programmes. The presenter, a ditsy blonde with implants that had clinched her contract, was signing off, clutching a designer trug. As the end credits rolled, there was a reprise of someone's ugly back yard being miraculously transformed into a miniature Japanese garden. The crew names then rolled up the screen, all familiar to Janet. But just as Harry's name appeared as executive producer, he hit the freeze button on the remote control.

'Look at that,' he shouted. 'Look at it. That's already

been delivered to the gardening channel. It's on every fucking episode. And every VHS copy we've had run off for the sponsors.'

He threw the remote control across the office, narrowly missing one of his precious paintings. The plastic case burst open and the batteries rolled away noisily across the polished wooden floor.

'It's just not good enough. I warn you, Janet, heads are going to roll. And yours might just be the first.' He banged his desk for effect.

Janet took a deep breath. Please let this be one of her strong days.

'If you recall our conversation before I went on holiday last week, I told you that you would need to sign off this project, plus three of the Hot Breaks videos. We had a meeting, I produced a list of notes and I also e-mailed them to you.'

'That's not good enough.' Thump on desk. 'These sorts of mistakes shouldn't happen.' Thump on desk. 'That pile of shit goes out tonight. And the whole industry will see it.'

'Well, mistakes do happen, and with respect, Harry,' she paused, wondering if she was issuing her own death warrant here, 'you too have made a mistake by not checking them yourself.'

'It's all that stupid bloody idiot Jed's fault,' continued Harry, ignoring her last remark. 'Thank goodness I had the sense to fire him. All too free and easy. Too much chatting up the women. That man's head was in his underpants.'

Janet smiled inwardly. Harry had obviously convinced himself his outing with Gina had gone unnoticed.

'Perhaps you'd like me to get Computers to check that

you did receive and open my e-mail about all this,' she said smoothly. 'And here's a copy of the notes we discussed before I went away.' She indicated the file she'd placed on his desk.

Harry picked it up, glanced at it as if it were an oily rag and flung it at her in temper. Janet stood up and left the office without a word. As she came out, she noticed Geraldine frantically re-adjusting the pussycat bow of her blouse, C&A circa 1984, in a pretence that she hadn't been listening. The absurdity of it all made Janet burst out laughing as she went back to the production office.

She insisted that Sue and Nina join her in the canteen for a quick coffee.

'You've *got* to watch that new gardening channel tonight,' she said, still shaking with laughter. 'Our landscape gardening series is beginning. And it's also Jed's last revenge. He warned me he was going to do something but he wouldn't say what.'

Janet was seized with another bout of giggles.

'Come on, come on, what?' Sue was in suspense.

'Harry's name on the end credits. Jed deliberately spelled it wrongly. He's up as Executive Producer, Harry Humpton.'

Janet finally got around to ringing Val later that afternoon. She'd waded through all the messages, done all the urgent tasks, but the effect of the first day back was beginning to take its toll, especially after the scene with Harry.

'Val? It's Janet. Got your messages. Been on holiday. How are you?'

'Oh, the usual,' said Val. 'Ghastly.'

'I thought I'd better warn you,' said Janet, picking her

words carefully. 'There's a programme going out on the new gardening channel tonight. I don't think Harry's going to like it very much.'

'Why? What's it about?' Val had a sudden rush of fear. Was this some kind of investigative programme into Harry's secret life? She'd had quite enough of her recent brush with the media.

'Oh, just landscape gardening. But Harry's name has been spelled wrong at the end. They've called him Humpton instead of Hampton.'

To Janet's amazement and relief, Val burst out laughing.

'Humpton! Ha ha, that's brilliant. He's certainly got the hump at the moment, and I'm still certain he's humping someone else. Is that what his filthy mood on Friday night was all about?'

'Er, no, that's what his filthy mood tonight will be about. He only discovered it this morning.'

'Any idea what the Friday rage was about?'

'No, no idea, lied Janet. 'I was coming back from Morocco.'

'Anyway, look, I'm bored witless. Could we have a girlies' night again soon? How about this week? Any night, my treat.'

'I'll see what they're up to and come back to you.' Janet replaced the receiver.

Val couldn't resist it in the end. She rang her mother and told her about the gardening programme. Sheila Mortimer, normally the model of restrained elegance, broke down in fits of giggles.

'I can't wait to tell your father, dear,' she said. 'We'll make sure we watch. By the way, how are things? Are you all right? We do so worry about you.'

Val had known it would happen. She burst into tears, Harry's rage over the weekend having taken its toll.

'I can't go on much longer,' she sobbed. 'It's like living with a monster. I can't remember the last time we did anything remotely exciting. The mobile phone disaster was about as good as it gets. He just comes home and rants.'

'Do you think he's seeing someone else?' said her mother gently.

'Yes, I do. Still no proof, but it suddenly dawned on me that he's always late home on Mondays and Thursdays, and his mobile's switched off on those evenings.'

'How long has this been going on, do you think?'

'I don't know. Months probably. Trouble is, Mum, I was doing a bit of drinking up until recently, as you know, and I sort of lost the plot. But I've stopped now.'

'Good girl, I'm proud of you,' said Sheila. 'You don't necessarily need the proof to leave, you know. If you're unhappy, there's always a place for you here.'

'I know, Mum, but I've got to sort this out myself in my own way.'

Val put down the phone and sobbed. It was at times like this that she desperately missed her friend the wine bottle. She mustn't give in, though. She'd got through the worst. But it was tempting.

She mooched around the house aimlessly, gazing out over the manicured garden. She went into the bedroom, looked at the marital bed and shivered. They hadn't had sex for days, thank goodness. Harry was beginning to repulse her. At first it had been the thought that he was screwing someone else. She didn't want to be near him after that. But now his tempers and insults were becoming worse and worse. She wondered if he'd ever hit her in temper, and how she'd react. She realized then that if Harry struck her, she'd have exactly the impetus she needed to leave. It would make it all so very easy.

She wandered into her dressing room. Row upon row of expensive designer dresses, jackets, coats. Spiky-heeled shoes by the yard. In the past clothes had been her quick fix. With her model figure, she could wear anything. And in the past she had openly mocked those who couldn't quite squeeze into the latest designs. She had an attack of remorse over Nina, the London Derrière. How could she have been so cruel? Now who was the lucky one? Nina seemed to be so happy, and madly in love with Sam, despite having a big bum. Yet here Val was, thin, rich but miserable.

In the cold sober light of day she also remembered vaguely being rude to Janet in the past about her appearance. Again embarrassment pricked her eyes. Even Janet seemed happier than she was. At least she had a challenging job which she obviously did well.

And hadn't she suggested that Sue's husband was having an affair, when she couldn't actually remember whether she'd even met him? How could she have been so utterly callous? Liz, too; she knew she must have insulted her somewhere down the line.

'I must apologize to them,' she told herself aloud. 'I've been a complete super-mare.'

The girls agreed to meet Val on Thursday night. There'd been a wave of sympathy, even from Nina and Liz, over Harry's recent tempers. They actually wondered how Val hadn't cracked under the strain. And they were quietly impressed that Val had found the new spelling of her surname vastly amusing.

They'd arranged to meet at a little French restaurant in

the centre of Hartford. Val, realizing that she'd gain more sympathy by not dressing to kill, opted for a black pencil skirt, simple pink cashmere sweater and minimal jewellery. She couldn't resist a pair of her favourite Manolos, but that was her only concession to her old life, as she saw it.

The new look was instantly clocked by the rest of the girls, but they said nothing. Wine was ordered but Val only sipped mineral water. And when Nina announced her big news, that she and Sam were getting engaged, Val said she couldn't have been more delighted. And meant it. Champagne was produced, but again Val just stuck to her water.

When Liz went to the loo, the others braced themselves for the usual insults. But instead Val remarked: 'Liz looks really terrific. I'm so pleased her new chap is working out. Maybe we'll have another cause for celebration soon.'

Let's hope so, thought Sue, or Liz's baby clock will start ticking so loudly it'll keep half of Hartford awake. She was secretly counselling Liz not to eye up Tony as a potential father or sperm bank, but to simply treat him as a human being.

Val realized with a pang how much she was enjoying the evening. How much she enjoyed their company, their gossip and their happiness. Her remorse at how she'd behaved in the past was making her very ashamed. She realized yet again how empty and cheerless her life was compared to these happy and fulfilled human beings sitting around the table.

With the main courses cleared away and taste buds being tickled once again, this time by the array of puddings, Val indicated that she wanted to say a few words. A hush fell over the table.

'I have something very important to say and I want you to believe that it comes from the heart. I've had a drink problem. God knows you've all known it, but sadly I only came to realize it recently. I could make excuses for why I was always drunk but I won't. It should never have got to that. I also realize that in all the time you've known me, I've been rude, obnoxious and selfish. I don't really know why you've put up with me, but I'm glad you have. I ask you to believe that what you see before you is the real me, not that stupid drunken cow you used to hang around with. I can't ask you to forgive me because I have behaved much too badly in the past. But I ask you to accept the new me, and I hope that we will often meet up, as we have done in the past, but with the new me behaving in a more suitable fashion.'

There was a pause, followed by a ripple of applause. Sue, who was sitting next to Val, put her arm around her and gave her a hug.

'Well done, hon,' she said. 'I think I speak for all of us when I say that we're glad you've sorted out your problem. And I think we all admire you for what you've just said.'

Tears started to trickle down Val's cheeks. She made no attempt to stop them.

'We do know Harry's a bit difficult,' continued Sue, picking her words carefully. 'Don't forget, we work with him. We know what he's like. We do sympathize.'

'He's a complete bastard at home, so God knows how you lot put up with him all day at work.' Val broke down in sobs. 'And now I've loused up a lovely evening. I'm so sorry.'

'No you haven't,' piped up Nina. 'We're having a lovely time, and look, it's okay to cry. We know he's a bastard. I honestly don't know how *you* put up with him.'

'Neither do I,' added Liz, glancing meaningfully at Janet. They had never again spoken of Harry's advances that terrible night.

The arrival of the puddings broke up the conversation. Instead there were oohs and aahs as exquisite mouthfuls were savoured. Over coffee, Val whispered to Janet, who was sitting on her other side, that Harry was out tonight and his phone was mysteriously switched off again. Did Janet know where he was? No, she said untruthfully. Val would still have to find that out for herself.

An hour later, the taxi dropped Val off at home. Harry's Mercedes was in the driveway. She hoped he might be in bed and asleep, but he was pacing up and down the sitting room, glass of whisky in hand.

'Where the hell have you been?' he demanded.

'Out, same as you,' she replied nervously.

'Who with? Where?'

'Perhaps you'd like to start. It's funny, Harry, but I've noticed that you're always late home on Thursday nights. You're not in the office and your phone is always switched off. And sometimes on Mondays too.'

'Who's fed you this claptrap?'

'No one. I worked it out for myself. Anyway, I have no secrets. I've had a very nice evening out with the girls from HOT.'

Harry swore under his breath. Would they have told Val about his lunch last Friday with Gina? No, they wouldn't have worked that out. And anyway, he'd stick to his story of strictly business. But he didn't need those bird-brains filling Val's head with rubbish.

'Oh, and what was their news?' He smirked patronizingly.

'Well, Nina's got engaged. I heard about Janet's holiday. Nice things.'

'And I suppose they slagged me off,' Harry mocked her.

'No, why rot up a good evening?' she replied, and flounced off upstairs to bed.

Harry poured himself another couple of fingers of whisky and paced the sitting room some more. Women, nothing but trouble. Gina had been piling on the pressure again tonight. Oh, to dump the lot of them.

chapter thirty-two

Geraldine was being instructed by one of the computer support guys in the art of using the Internet, and already the e-mail jokes were flying.

```
Guess where Geraldine's going for
her holidays this year? She can't
decide between the Greek island of
Lycos or Alta Vista in Spain.

Geraldine's got her own website.
It's called beige-dot-com.
```

Geraldine, oblivious to it all, was finding her launch on to the information super-highway a bit daunting, to say the least. She'd spent ages searching for the Movie Munch site, only to discover to her horror that she'd tapped in a porn site where a very different type of menu was on offer. Even Harry, who forgave Geraldine everything because of her tight-lipped loyalty, was beginning to get exasperated. Geraldine's life was normally saved by the spell checker but that couldn't spare her the demands of a search engine.

The pressure was on because the first Movie Munch restaurant was opening in under a month. This meant that the first video, together with accompanying website, had to be ready on time. There was to be a huge opening party with full-on celebrity guests. It was such an important night for HOT that they'd taken on a specialist guest booker with a bulging filofax to get the right names, and put the public relations work with an agency.

Janet was reeling under the strain, putting the finishing touches to the video. The first restaurant was to be Casablanca, and designers had flown out to Morocco to scour the souks for authentic lamps, brass pots, tagines and rugs with which to fill the place. Janet's own recent trip to Morocco was also paying dividends. Having fallen in love with the country and its culture, the project had become a labour of love. She'd used some authentic music from CDs she'd bought there, and despite being her own sternest critic, she was pleased with the result.

The video featured some stunning footage of Casablanca and the surrounding countryside that she'd had to buy in from an agency in Morocco. Janet had also filmed a short cookery demonstration from the restaurant's chef, a chat with one of the designers and a mission statement from the Movie Munch chairman, and finished it all off with a clip from the immortal film at vast expense. She'd managed to weave it all together into a seamless whole, making even the chairman sound interesting. Jed's graphics, the last project he'd worked on before leaving, were breathtaking, giving the film a real polish. Needless to say, the only end credit was Harry, billed as executive producer – and spelled correctly this time – plus the HOT and Movie Munch logos. By now, Janet was too exhausted to care.

Harry grudgingly told her he was pleased with the video, which in Harry-speak meant it was practically up for an Oscar – he would have of course collected it, congratulated himself in the winning speech and then displayed it in his 'Hall of Fame' loo. And now off he'll go to claim the credit, drink the opening-night champagne and get the whopping end-of-year bonus, Janet thought grimly. It would be interesting to see who would be invited to the big opening night. Invitations were being dispatched in mini tagines by couriers. She doubted very much she'd be getting a knock on her front door.

Meanwhile Harry was wrestling with a different problem about the opening night. Gina had continued to pressure him for an invite, reasoning that by then Harry would have broken the bad news to Val. Harry had done his usual pleading for a little more time to find the right moment to tell Val. But Gina, with her short Italian fuse, was not to be pacified, and Harry knew the only way to maintain any sort of peace was to take her to the opening night. There'd only be a select few there from HOT: probably the chairman, Sir James Patterson Cripps, and members of the board. In that company Gina would be perfectly acceptable; they probably all had mistresses anyway, he reasoned. If push came to shove, he could easily pass her off as a minor celebrity. Gina had had, after all, two small parts in obscure Italian movies four or five years previously.

Harry sat back in his chair and heaved a sigh of relief. Yes, that was what he would do.

'Someone's been snooping around the office again,' said Nina, bringing Janet a cup of tea. 'At least three people have mentioned this week that things have moved or

293

been found not as they left them. It's either Harry again or Uri Geller's in town.'

'Any bent spoons? Cutlery spotted contorting?' said Janet, looking up from her computer screen.

'None that I've noticed,' replied Nina.

'Then Harry gets my vote,' said Janet, gratefully sipping her tea. 'I wonder what he's up to this time. He's either just trying to rattle us or he's still worried about the mystery file. It's funny how much that myth bothered him. Simon and Joe did a good job on that, didn't they?'

'Except that it means he's still searching through everyone's stuff in the office, and I don't like the thought of that,' said Nina. 'Bit like being burgled. And women often say that's almost like being raped.'

Liz was listening and quickly dropped her head, so that a curtain of dark chestnut hair hid the expression on her face. Fortunately Nina didn't notice.

'Perhaps we should put in a few files with jokey names to throw him off the scent.'

'Such as what?' asked Liz, suspiciously.

'Oh, "Whassap", "Harry's Game",' said Nina airily. 'You've got to make it intriguing, get him overcome with curiosity. If you created a file called "Instruction Manual" or "Map and Directions", no man on earth would bother to open it.'

Nina then launched into an account of the delights of the weekend ahead. She and Sam were off to choose the ring.

'It's so exciting,' she trilled. 'I still can't believe it. I've met his parents and they're lovely. And he's met mine and they really like him. It's all like a dream come true. And we'll be having an engagement party so they can all meet. Sorry, I am going on a bit. What are you doing at the weekend?'

'Don't even ask,' said Janet. 'I've only just caught up with the washing since my holiday. So I guess I'm planning to join the Mile High Ironing Club.'

'You look ever so tired,' said Nina, taking in the bags under Janet's eyes. She did look exhausted. The strain of the Movie Munch project, plus the final handing over of the property project to Liz, were all beginning to take their toll.

'It's a good job we're not having a Haunted Handbag committee meeting tonight,' continued Nina. 'You look done in. Why don't you go home early?'

'Can't. Too much to do. I'm going to work late tonight and then sleep in tomorrow,' said Janet wearily. 'You never know, I might catch Harry snooping round the office.'

'Doubt it,' said Nina. 'Sue told me just now that Harry's still not back from lunch. Don't forget it's Friday-footsie-under-the-table-lunch day. Although I doubt he takes Gina to the Country Cottage Restaurant any more.'

'Knowing Harry, I expect he's found some new little Play Away place for them to lunch. And if he hasn't come back, they've probably turned it into a Have It Away Day.'

Seven o'clock and the production office was deserted, except for Janet, still pounding away at her computer. Another hour should do it, she thought, then a quick Chinese chicken à la microwave, followed by an early night.

The phone rang, echoing shrilly in the empty office. It was Sue, doing the late shift on reception.

'Janet,' she said formally, 'I've got Sir James Patterson Cripps in reception for Harry, but I haven't seen him at all this afternoon and Geraldine's gone home. Would you have a moment?'

'Certainly, Susan,' said Janet, 'and I'm using my phone voice too. I'll come through.'

She wandered rather reluctantly into reception. Whatever the chairman wanted, she probably couldn't help with, and she badly wanted to get her work finished and go home.

'Sir James,' she said warmly, shaking the elderly man by the hand. 'How can I help you?'

Sir James, still ramrod straight from Sandhurst days, was dressed in the typical gentrified mixture of tweed jacket, striped shirt with contrasting collar, and unmatching tie with just a hint of breakfast down it. He always reminded Janet of the Major in *Fawlty Towers*. White-haired, with twinkly blue eyes, he gave the impression of being a kindly, avuncular old character, yet he was still a crack shot, rode regularly to hounds and was as fit as a fiddle, bar a bit of prostate trouble.

Geraldine had rocked the office by letting slip that Sir James had had trouble with his 'prostrate'. 'I must suffer from that because I'm prostrate a lot of the time,' Ray had told her. 'I lie down a lot and then I can't get up again.' It had been the G-spot of the day.

'Had hoped to catch Harry. Silly me for arriving unannounced,' he said briskly. 'Just wanted to have a look at that movie restaurant video. Got to mention it in my next report to the board and thought I'd better watch the bugger first. Then I might know what I'm talking about for a change, what!'

He guffawed at his own joke. 'Got to write the bloody thing over the weekend as I'm away most of next week.'

'No problem,' said Janet. 'Come and watch it in my office.' She ushered him down the corridor and into the huge production office. She suddenly felt embarrassed about of the mess it was in. Every desk seemed to be strewn with old coffee cups, files, tapes and newspapers. She couldn't exactly tell anyone off, though; hers was just as bad.

'Excuse the mess, but we have had an exceptionally busy week,' she said.

'No problem,' said Sir James, plonking himself into a chair while Janet dug out a tape. She could just imagine him at home kicking labradors off a hair-encrusted sofa.

'You can take this copy away with you if you like,' she offered.

'No, happy to watch it now,' he said. 'Don't want the bother of carting it around next week.'

'Bloody good,' he pronounced ten minutes later. 'Bloody excellent. One of the best things Harry's done. And it's going to be good for business in the future too. Delighted with that. Thank you, my dear, for sorting it. I shall give it high praise in my report. Don't get up, you carry on. I'll see myself out.'

After he'd gone, Janet kicked the leg of her desk in sheer frustration. As usual, Harry was getting all the credit. Blokes really did bond together like superglue. The silly old fool couldn't believe that a mere woman was capable of producing anything half decent. She'd been almost tempted to put him right, but he would never have believed her. And anyway, what would she have said?

'Oh by the way, Sir James, my boss Harry's actually an accomplished liar. I did all that, not him. Even though his name's on it.'

It would have made her sound like a petulant school-girl. Why should he take her word for it, without corroboration, late on a Friday night in a deserted office? What was the point?

She mentally added a bottle of wine to the microwave meal before bed.

Harry arrived home around seven, having remembered to switch his mobile back on. He'd had lunch with Gina at a new little restaurant a good twenty miles out of Hartford, to make sure they were undisturbed. In the end, to placate her and hopefully put a stop to her threats about phoning Val, he'd agreed to go back to Gina's house, where over a bottle of champagne they'd indulged in a passionate afternoon's bonking. Satisfied that he'd given her a jolly good seeing-to, he'd checked in by phone to the office. No messages or panics, according to the trusty Geraldine, so he'd gone straight home. To his surprise and relief, the house was in complete darkness. Either Val was in bed with all the lights out, or she'd gone somewhere. With her MR2 locked away in the garage for many months to come, there was no way of knowing whether she was in or out.

He opened the front door, put on the hall lights and called her name. No reply. He hung up his coat and went into the kitchen. There in the middle of the table, propped up against a fruit bowl, was a note. For a few seconds Harry actually wondered if Val had left him. Had she rumbled his affair? Had someone at work squealed about the lunch with Gina? Did he care? Curiously, he wasn't sure. The note certainly gave him a start, though.

He surprised himself by fumbling to open it. Nerves? Surely not. Not Harry. He never fumbled. He was far too much in control.

The contents were, however, a slight surprise.

Dear Harry,
Have gone to Hampshire to stay with my parents
for a few days. Spur-of-the-moment thing. Just fed
up being stuck at home relying on taxis. Know
you're working really long hours and probably
want some peace and quiet.
Love, Val

Curious, thought Harry, instantly suspicious. I wonder
what she's up to. A call to Hampshire later tonight would
ascertain whether or not she was there. But was she planning to see anyone else, apart from her parents? Lord and
Lady Muck would certainly cover up for her. They'd
never liked Harry, despite pretending otherwise. It suddenly dawned on Harry that Val might be dumping him
before he dumped her. Humiliation was not on Harry's
agenda. He had to get in there first. Oh well, a weekend
alone meant he could see more of Gina, although this
afternoon's session had worn him out. He wasn't quite
the man he used to be. No, he decided, he wouldn't ring
either of them tonight. He'd let them both stew. Val would
be expecting him to call to see if she was all right. And
Gina, if she knew he was alone, would be gagging for
another sex session, probably followed by more high
pressure on the marital front. No, he'd have a night in and
a few whiskies in front of the box.

He went upstairs to change out of his suit and into his
favourite dressing gown. He found himself wandering
into Val's dressing room to see what she'd taken with her
to Hampshire. Might give him a few clues as to what she
was up to. He looked along the rails of expensive and
glamorous dresses, not recognizing most of them. He'd no
idea whether she'd taken ball gowns or Barbours. And he

was shocked to discover there were enough shoes in there to stock a decent-sized branch of Russell and Bromley.

By Sunday, Janet was so low she was beginning to wonder how she'd get through the next week. Over the Sunday papers and a large strong coffee, she read of the usual tales of death and destruction, kiss-and-tell girls and another sleaze case involving a politician on the fiddle who was refusing to go quietly. In desperation she turned to Mystic Meg's predictions for the week. She half laughed at the 'could meet the love of your life' stuff, but was caught by the final line: 'Destiny brings a life-changing invitation.' Huh, fat chance of that.

She plunged into another fit of gloom, triggered by the fact that she knew she didn't really have a life, let alone any invitations. Her life revolved around her work and her work unfortunately revolved around a big fat bully called Harry. She knew she was investing too much in HOT, but after the long day at work, she had neither the time nor the inclination to take up yoga, learn Spanish or throw pots, although she could think of a few choice targets for the latter. She thought about Liz too, a decade and more younger and desperate for a husband and babies. She knew Liz was eyeing up poor Tony as marriage material just a few dates into their relationship.

'How on earth do you get a man to become truly committed?' she'd asked the entire production office.

'Ring a mental hospital,' Ray had offered.

In an attempt to snap out of her gloom, Janet rang Liz to see if she'd like to go out for Sunday lunch. No luck. Liz was practising the ancient female art of phone sitting.

'Sorry, hon, got to keep the phone free in case he calls,' she apologized. 'You know how important this is to me.'

In the end, Janet rang Sue and unashamedly invited herself for lunch. Sue and Jon were cooking a leg of lamb and were only too delighted to have an extra mouth to feed, as their children were going through a faddy food stage. Over the gravy-making in the kitchen, Janet told Sue about Sir James Patterson Cripps's visit to the office.

'It'll all change, you mark my words,' said Sue. 'Harry can't go on like this. Here, you get carving.' She handed Janet a knife. 'Imagine it's Harry's head.'

'Yeah, as if. He's managed all these years, he might as well keep going,' sighed Janet. 'The company's making pots of dosh, so if that pleases the board and the share-holders, then why rock the boat? Look, if Harry can survive all the stuff we've found out, then he's invincible. He's ridden out the storm on the Paul Burns saga, he's sur-vived the "Importance of Being Harry" headlines, he sacks people when he feels like it. He's bomb proof.'

'But there's one person who could just bring him down,' said Sue as she tasted the gravy, 'and she probably doesn't realize it yet. In a funny way, Val holds at least some of the trump cards.'

Janet finished carving and laid the slices of lamb neatly on a serving dish. 'Val's making no secret of the fact that she thinks Harry's up to something,' she said. 'Remember, she asked me to set a detective on to him. But even if she left him and then divorced him, what difference would it make? Harry'd still bully on as normal. He'd just have more spare time for his extra-curricular activities.'

'Depends how she did it,' said Sue, grinning. 'Knowing Val, even the new non-drinking Val, I think if she made a scene – and we know how good she is at that – she'd do him a lot of damage. And of course now that she's on the wagon, Harry can no longer pass it all off as her being drunk. She looks and behaves so differently now, even he must be getting suspicious. Mark my words, one day there will be an opportunity and Val will go for it.'

'I wish I could believe you're right,' said Janet mournfully.

'Now, end of subject, grab those plates and let's serve up.'

The rest of the day passed without further mention of Harry and Val. After lunch they all played a noisy game of Pictionary and a kids' version of Trivial Pursuit. Janet went home triumphant because her team, which included the two kids, had beaten their parents hollow.

chapter thirty-three

It was second-cup-of-coffee time before Janet got to the envelope. Long and cream, it was addressed to her in a slightly feathery hand. Inside was a short note from Sir James.

> Thank you, my dear, for organizing the video on Friday evening. You were obviously at the end of a very long week. I hope my request did not delay you too much in getting home for the weekend. Harry is always telling me what a marvellous team he has. In gratitude, I am enclosing some tickets to the restaurant opening for you and some of your team just in case you are free.
> Yours etc.

Janet blinked and reread the letter. 'Harry's always telling me what a marvellous team he has, my arse,' she scowled aloud. 'Pity he never bothers to tell us.'

She picked up the phone and rang Sue. Ten minutes later they were in their usual corner of the canteen, with Sue hurriedly reading Sir James's note.

'Well, well,' she said laughing. 'So are you going?'

'I have decided I am definitely going. Time I had a new frock and a new life,' Janet announced. 'And I suggest we throw the rest of the tickets open to discussion by the HH committee on Friday night, chez moi.'

'Good idea,' said Sue. 'Oh, and by the way, we loved having you yesterday. The kids went off to school to write triumphant essays about winning at Trivvies, and what dopes their parents are.'

'It bucked me up no end too,' said Janet. 'I was having a real Sunday gloom with the papers before I came round. Funnily enough, Mystic Meg predicted something about an invitation changing my life. I wonder if this is it?'

'God, you don't believe in that lark, do you?' said Sue.

'Oh, I hang on to anything with a bit of hope attached.' She was too embarrassed to admit that she'd rung Mystic Meg's phone line for a bit of comfort as well.

To add to the fun of deciding who should go to the bash, the HH committee decided they would each make separate wish lists and then compare notes. Those with the most votes would win.

Amid much giggling, the voting took place before the Chinese takeaway was delivered. Then the slips of paper were collected and put to one side while sweet and sour pork, Singapore noodles and chicken cashew were devoured. Janet refilled their wine glasses and declared the ballot ready for counting.

An interesting pattern emerged. They'd all nominated each other, plus Ray, who'd done such good work shadowing Harry on his bike and helping with the secret photographs. That took care of five tickets, including Janet's. Another five remained. Sue, Nina and Liz had nominated respectively Jon, Sam and Tony. Liz had suggested

Geraldine, 'just in case Placebo Domingo, Glynis Paltroon or Prickley Spears turn up'. Nina had named Paul Burns, 'to make up for the fact that he didn't get a leaving do', and Sue had come up with Joe and Simon, whose sacking had been instrumental in forming the Haunted Handbag committee. But the most interesting shout came from Janet.

'I'd like to invite Jed, because he did all the fantastic graphics on the video.' She paused. 'And Val.'

A shock wave went around the table.

'Why Val?'

'I don't really know, but I'd like to invite her. Perhaps it could be our way of thanking her for some of the better bits of our awful evenings out. Perhaps it could also be our way of acknowledging that we prefer the new Val to the old one. And also, I just wonder if she might take a shine to Jed.'

'Well he is rather gorgeous . . .' started Liz.

'And you're all fixed up,' cut in Janet. 'And before you say anything, he's far too old for me. I don't know, I just think I'd like to see them get together. Talking to Val, the marriage is clearly over, in her head anyway.'

'Surely Harry will be taking her to this bash already,' said Sue.

'I don't think so somehow. I phoned Val earlier this week to sound her out vaguely, but her cleaner answered the phone and said she'd gone to see her parents for a few days and that no one knew when she'd be back. Bit strange, I thought.'

'You don't think Harry will be taking Miss Tortellini instead, do you?' asked Sue. 'Not after that lunch fiasco the other week?'

'I doubt it,' chipped in Liz. 'Not if he's any sense left.'

'Harry thinks he's invincible, but Sue thinks that the

chink in his armour might just be Val,' said Janet. 'Let's see if she's game. I've a feeling she might be.'

In the end it was decided that the guest list should be Janet, Sue and Jon, Nina and Sam, Liz and Tony, Ray, Jed and Val. And it was also agreed that they would not discuss the invitations with anyone else at work. Janet would just accept the ten tickets without giving names.

The rest of the evening was devoted to what to wear and where to buy it. Dress code was the works. Dinner jackets for the chaps, full regalia for the girls.

'This weekend I will shop, this weekend I will not drop,' promised Janet.

As she'd expected, after almost a week of being cosseted at her parents', Val dreaded coming back to Hartford and Harry. It was rather like trying to cool your mouth down with a glass of water during a fiery curry; it just made it worse. Harry had eventually phoned her a couple of times, but they were only brief conversations, with each of them trying to quiz each other subtly about what they were up to. Val had gone for long walks around her parents' estate, been shopping and out to lunch, and generally relaxed. It had made her ever more conscious that life with Harry was like living in a war zone.

Harry meanwhile had spent even more time with Gina, which of course was a double-edged sword. Along with all the extra frenetic sex sessions came even more demands from Gina. At least he was able to smuggle his dinner jacket out of the house. Harry knew Val would start asking awkward questions if she caught him leaving the house all tuxedoed up. He could lie and say it was a blokes-only boxing night or something similar, but Val might just get a hint from the HOT girls that it was the Casablanca restaurant opening. She would then insist on going and he would have to lie about not taking partners. Even if the celebrities got pictured in the national press, the company executives would be of no interest to the paparazzi. No, best not to discuss it at all. That way he'd get away with taking Gina and keeping the peace.

Val's first weekend back passed without event. She and Harry were becoming experts at avoiding each other. If he stayed up late, she yawned and went to bed. If he announced he was going to bed, she found an old movie she just had to watch. Several times she was aware that Harry was on the phone, at the other end of the house, but she didn't quite have the bottle to pick up an extension to listen in. Each time, she dived for the phone when she'd thought he'd hung up, to dial 1471 if it had been an incoming call, or last-number redial if Harry'd made the call. Every 1471 call produced 'the caller withheld their number', while every last-number redial promptly rang HOT's main switchboard number. Harry was obviously pressing a speed-dial button after he'd hung up from his mystery phone call. Eventually the security guard at HOT rang back and asked Harry if he was having difficulty getting through. Harry immediately rumbled what was going on and sarcastically asked Val why she'd been trying to ring HOT when he was so obviously at home. Val muttered something about trying to ring her mother and pressing the wrong speed-dial button. But they both knew the game they were playing.

Sunday night, and Harry was sprawled across their huge leather Chesterfield, smoking a cigar, drinking whisky and watching television.

'Wish I'd created that.' He indicated the screen angrily

with his cigar. 'Would have made a bloody fortune selling that format all over the world.'

He was watching Chris Tarrant presenting *Who Wants To Be a Millionaire*. A contestant was teetering on the £125,000 question without any lifelines left.

'If I'd made that, I could have retired by now. Just imagine, I could go anywhere I felt like, do anything I fancied,' he mused. 'Might have made even more money than your old man. By the way, how are Lord and Lady Muck?'

'If that's my parents you're referring to, they're fine. And don't worry, you'll never be as rich as them,' snapped Val. 'My father worked very hard to achieve his success.'

'There's not much glamour in waste disposal, though,' Harry retorted, his eyes glittering with rage. He hated to feel he wasn't top dog. 'Television is a very creative, very competitive industry. It's about ideas, concepts, not just about wondering where to stick a pile of rubbish.'

'How come you're not filthy loaded then if you're so bloody clever?' Val tossed her blonde hair and glared at him. 'I can't remember the last time *you* had a good idea. I get the impression that everyone else does all the work in that place.'

Harry stubbed out his cigar and glared at her. 'You've been talking to those silly girls again, haven't you? Haven't you?' He raised his voice.

'If it's not true, why are you shouting?' said Val, now regretting that she'd started this. The last thing she wanted was for the girls to get into trouble. She'd compromised them enough already.

'I am the driving force behind that company,' Harry stated without a shred of modesty. 'HOT is successful because of me. Because of my ideas and my management. Now get me another drink, woman.'

He handed her the empty glass and slumped back into the settee to watch the poor contestant still agonizing.

'I know a good question for that programme,' Val said more calmly. 'Why don't men get mad cow disease? Answer? Because they're pigs.'

'Don't get me on to the subject of mad cows. It might upset you,' said Harry patronizingly. 'Now shut up and get me that drink.'

Val stood up and glared at him. 'Ask the bloody audience. Or better still, why not phone *your* friend.'

With that, she went straight upstairs and banged shut the bedroom door.

Harry sat for a minute contemplating Val's departure. Perhaps Janet and her friends had been talking and Val had found out about Gina. Or perhaps her mystery flit to Hampshire hadn't quite worked out. Probably just PMT, he concluded.

'Val? It's Janet. Just a quickie, 'cos it's Monday and I'm up against it. Could you do lunch tomorrow? At that ghastly Indian? Good. Meet you in the Gunges around one. Gotta go. I think I've been mistaken for Heathrow. I've got people actually stacking at my desk.'

Val was ridiculously pleased at the phone call. Somebody had actually rung and invited *her* out to lunch. It was usually her hustling others. God, she must have been a pain when she was drinking. It hadn't been easy giving up, but it was beginning to look worth the effort. On impulse, she rang Susie at work to see how she was faring.

'Trying to plan my escape from this disgustingly smoke-free environment,' said Susie.

'How's it with you and the boss?' Val asked tentatively.

'Oh, I gave him his P45 when I realized he wasn't actually leaving home. And by the look of things here, I'm about to get mine.'

'Oh, Susie, I'm sorry.'

'Don't be. I'm not cut out for this work lark. They put me on the switchboard the other week when someone went sick. I managed to cut everyone off or connect them to each other. Not my thang, as they say.'

'So what are you going to do?'

'I'll probably pack in Hartford for a while,' said Susie airily. 'Go home to Mummy. She won't like it, but she'll have to lump it.'

'I went home last week and it was so gorgeous I didn't want to come back.'

'Ah, that's the difference,' said Susie. 'Your parents are in lurve and still shagging. Mine have split up. Very nasty. Now my mother's on HRT and she's having some second life kick. She's on a mega man hunt. Been on so many blind dates she's almost qualified for a free guide dog.'

'Oh God, how ghastly. Imagine your parents going through the whole dating thing.'

'I don't have to imagine. I've got a seat in the front row. Anyway, have you dumped Fat Bastard yet?'

'Er, no. I will, it's just so daunting and . . .'

'You're scared of him,' finished Susie.

'Yes, I suppose I am. But I'm certain he's got someone else, so that might make it easier. Also, I've given up drinking. Completely.'

'Gosh,' said Susie, shocked. 'What brought that on?'

'Just a realization that I couldn't remember very much,' said Val.

'Like why you married Harry?'

'I must have been bonkers.'

'Believe me, you were. Choose someone younger and thinner next time. Someone who can master the art of switching off his mobile.'

'Point taken,' said Val. 'Let's meet up soon. Before you push off to Mummy.'

'Great,' said Susie, 'but no lunch until you've dumped Harry. Gotta go now. Rostered fag break!'

They were halfway through another of the Gunges specials when Janet delicately broached the subject.

'We've been given a pile of tickets to the big Movie Munch opening night and wondered if you'd like to come,' she said, mopping up some of her rogan josh with a piece of chapatti.

Val's eyes lit up. Another invitation.

'Now before you say yes, I think you need to know a little bit of background,' said Janet cautiously.

She outlined the events surrounding Sir James Patterson Cripps's visit, the surprise note and the tickets.

'We all had a chat, drew up a guest list and wanted to include you.'

Again Val's eyes sparkled with delight.

'But you must understand that Harry doesn't know we're going to turn up. Now presumably he's not mentioned this party to you?'

'All news to me. If he does, then I suppose I'll have to go with him, but so far he's not even hinted at it.'

Janet paused and looked her straight in the eye. 'It boils down to this, then, Val. If he doesn't invite you, are you prepared to turn up with us and give him a shock? Is that what you want?'

'Will it get you all into trouble with Harry if I do?' Val asked, lighting a cigarette.

311

'No, we've thought this one out carefully. We've been invited by the chairman. And if he's invited us then that's good enough reason to be there. Unfortunately, though, from Harry's point of view, I am the last person he wants to be there.'

'Why?' said Val, shocked.

'Well, quite simply, the project is the biggest thing that HOT's ever undertaken. It was my idea, I wrote the pitch and clinched the deal, and now I've produced the video. But you'll only see one name at the end of that video. Harry's. According to him, it was all his own work.'

Val nearly choked on her cigarette.

'That call I made to him that night you were at the theatre,' Janet continued. 'That was to tell him that it was all in the bag.' And no, she thought, I'm not going to let on to Val that the photographer was tipped off. Too much information.

Val stubbed out her cigarette emphatically.

'I don't really know why I should be surprised he's such a pig. Yes, I'd love to go, and do you know what? I hope he doesn't ask me. I'd rather go with you lot and see his face.'

'It's posh frocks, and we've hired a minibus because it's a hundred-and-fifty-mile round trip.'

'Fantastic. That'll be great fun. And thank you all so much for inviting me.'

Six months ago, mused Janet, Val would have never deigned to get into a minibus, let alone describe it as fun.

chapter thirty-four

Val went home ridiculously pleased. She hummed away happily in the back of the taxi and gave the driver an extra large tip. Then she spent a couple of hours trying on various long dresses and cocktail gear, twirling in the mirror to see what effect it would have. Val didn't have the problem of her bum looking big in anything.

She was almost on the point of deciding that she would buy something new and devastating. And then she stopped herself. No, she wasn't going to impress, show off or try to be the centre of attention. She wasn't going to make sure she turned all the heads. She was going to blend in with the crowd. Her crowd, her new friends, her pals who'd invited her. Elegant but understated, that was how she realized she wanted to look. In the end she picked out a simple long black shift dress with spaghetti straps and a modest split up the front. With it she'd wear black patent slender heels and a favourite fuchsia-pink beaded organza stole. Hair up, minimal jewellery and no long nails.

Delighted that she had sorted this, she rang her mother and told her about the invitation.

'Well, well, dear, you will give him a shock,' said her

mother in her usual unruffled way. 'Do you think he'll be there with this other woman you suspect?'

'I don't actually think Harry'd be that stupid, especially as it's a company do,' reasoned Val. 'But he hasn't mentioned it to me and it's the sort of thing you'd expect to take your partner to.'

'Well I disagree,' said Sheila. 'If I know Harry, I think there's a good chance he'd be that stupid. Don't forget, dear, this man had the arrogance to come back from Manchester with a Mediterranean suntan. I think sparks will fly if you turn up. I hope you're prepared for fireworks.'

'Yes, I am. And don't forget I'll have my friends around me for protection,' Val said proudly.

'Well, they sound a very nice bunch,' said her mother warmly. 'I'm glad you have some allies there these days.'

'I don't have anything to lose, do I?' Val was reasoning with herself. 'If Harry does invite me, then I will obviously have to accompany him. If he doesn't mention it at all, then I think that's extremely suspicious. If he does mention it but doesn't invite me, then tough shit, I'm going anyway.'

Sheila smiled to herself. She liked the new resolve in her daughter's voice. She also liked the fact that Val was off the wine. She just hoped that any showdown at the party wouldn't trigger a relapse.

'So what *are* you going to wear?' said Sue on the phone to Janet when there was a quiet moment on reception.

'Gawd knows,' replied Janet. 'My shopping trip was disastrous. I've had a good root through my wardrobe for something suitable – which took all of ten seconds – and there's nothing. It's either much too small or too eighties. Unless *Dallas*-style shoulder pads make a quick comeback,

I don't have a thing. I'm considering joining one of those "short for their weight" classes.'

'Same here. Life's never been the same in the tummy department since I had the kids,' said Sue. 'Shoulder pads were soooo fab, weren't they? Instantly made your hips look thinner.'

'But you look absolutely fine,' exclaimed Janet. 'It's me who's the product of years of junk eating and drinking. The only exercise I do is with my wrists – opening a bottle of wine.'

'Don't kid yourself,' replied Sue. 'There's a roll around my stomach that I practically have to dust on a daily basis. It's just that I conceal it with cardigans and jackets. And good old black, of course. But put me in a long tight dress and you'll see a shelf emerging that you could put your canapés on.'

'Look, why don't we hire? And go together to choose so we can be brutally honest?'

'Good idea.' And with that they assigned Saturday to the task, Sue checking that Jon could look after the kids.

Meanwhile, Nina had been through the private despair of trying on just about everything floor-length in Monsoon only to find that nothing fitted. It was of course the unmentionable problem of the London Derrière. She'd tried everything from Weight Watchers to Rosemary Conley but nothing had really worked for her.

'I don't know about the Hip and Thigh Diet,' she said to one of the assistants. 'For all the good it did me, I might as well have been on the Chip and Pie Diet.'

By now she'd tried on so many dresses that she and the assistants were on first-name terms. Then one of them had a bright idea and disappeared mysteriously into the stockroom.

She emerged with a deep aubergine silk ball skirt and a separate corset-style top in a lighter shade covered in beautiful beading.

Nina disappeared wearily through the curtains once more, muttering to herself that this was absolutely the last time. To her relief, it was perfect. The skirt skimmed her bum, the bodice fitted perfectly. The colour looked great too against her pale skin and blonde hair. She was also certain Sam would approve.

The shop was now closing, and the girls who'd helped were so delighted at their success that they suggested going for a drink in the next-door wine bar to celebrate. Over glasses of chilled Frascati, Nina excitedly told them about Sam and flashed around her engagement ring. She found herself talking about the bash they were going to and surprised herself by describing Val in warm tones as 'a friend who's in a rotten marriage and needs cheering up'.

Liz, being tall and willowy, never had any problems buying clothes. She'd decided to treat herself to something really special to impress Tony, so had headed for a little boutique on the outskirts of Hartford that sold designer labels. She'd soon fallen in love with a beautiful black chiffon number from Ghost and handed over a credit card without looking at the price. She then snatched up the carrier bag with a grin from ear to ear. The dress would knock him sideways. She hoped.

On her way back to the car park, she tried to avoid looking in the Pronuptia window. But she couldn't stop herself. One look at the long ivory silk dresses and dashing morning suits and she was off on another fantasy about marrying Tony, having children and living happily ever after. 'I must stop this,' she told herself aloud when she'd climbed into her car. 'I will frighten him off if I go on like this. He'll think I'm desperate. Which I am. I must pretend I'm not.'

She gazed fondly at the carrier bag, now sitting in pride of place on the passenger seat. This was their first black tie do together, and she wanted to look the biz. That dress, whatever it had cost, was just right.

Sue and Janet made a day of it in the end. They met up early on Saturday morning to get decent parking spaces, slapped all-day tickets on their cars and giggled their way to the first of two dress-hire shops they'd earmarked. The first shop proved very disappointing. The range of dresses was frumpy, to say the least. It would have done for a new small-town mayoress, but there was nothing that had anything like the required glamour. The only dress that actually fitted Janet was made of hideous apricot satin trimmed with black lace, with a gathered waist and off-the-shoulder short sleeves. Sue's only real contender was a black and white number with a scary amount of pleated frills.

'I look like I should be in the audience of *The Good Old Days* and you look as though you're about to do the Ascot scene in *My Fair Lady*,' Janet whispered during yet another session in the changing rooms.

'It's almost tempting to turn up in jeans, head scarves and dark glasses and pretend we thought it was a *Thelma and Louise* party,' said Sue.

They thanked the woman assistant, muttered excuses and left rather depressed.

'Still, good to know it'll be there for us when we're in our eighties, wanting a little je ne sais quoi en Crimplene,' said Sue philosophically.

They went to Café Rouge for a coffee to cheer themselves up. The coffee extended into lunch. A bottle of house red and a plate of pasta later and they realized it was well past two and so far they'd achieved nothing. They paid up and set off to their second quarry. This time they both found several likely contenders, and now the difficulty was having to choose. Janet fell in love with a long black low-necked dress with matching tuxedo-style jacket.

'Perfect.' She twirled in front of the huge mirror. 'I can show a bit of cleavage but I'll spare everyone the sight of my flabby arms.'

Sue found a full-length raw silk coat with a wing collar in the most luscious raspberry. 'Just the job to cover my canapé shelf,' she cried. The coat went over a long plain black dress. The effect was extremely dramatic.

Until now the shop assistant, a well-upholstered woman in her fifties, had been rather sniffy. She'd indicated the rails without offering the slightest bit of help. Too fuelled up by lunch, she'd decided, taking in their rather flushed faces.

But when Janet and Sue started deliberately namedropping the guests at the restaurant opening, she perked up considerably.

'Of course, modom, many of our clothes grace the pages of *Hello!* and *OK!* magazines,' she purred to Sue. 'That coat has been extremely popular.'

Too late to try and be Mrs Nice now, you snotty cow, thought Sue and Janet. Had your chance and blew it. They paid their deposits, did some surreptitious winking, then started name-dropping again.

'Well, Angela Rippon always looks so immaculate,' drawled Janet. 'Wonder if Posh and Becks will go in matching again.'

'I wouldn't put it past them,' Sue chipped in. 'Of course, there is a rumour that Dame Edna's going to—'

'And Arnie, don't forget him.'

They were now out of the shop, out of earshot and giggling like schoolgirls.

'Served her right,' said Janet.

'Absolutely,' replied Sue. 'No help whatsoever until you press the right buttons. If we hadn't found such knockout outfits, we'd have gone elsewhere.'

'I'm quite nervous about it all,' said Janet. 'I know I shouldn't be – not at my age – but it's not often you get invited to something as top-notch as this.'

'And of course there is the small matter of our in-house cabaret,' Sue reminded her. 'We are bringing our own pyrotechnics show, after all. If it's any comfort, I'm quite nervous too.'

Val spent all weekend trying to pick her moment. She'd rehearsed it in her dressing room mirror, a casual question about things at HOT, an off-the-cuff mention of having heard something about a restaurant video. She tried to work on her body language, so that she looked ultra relaxed, as if it was just a 'first thing that came into my head' remark. Having perfected the routine, she couldn't pick up the right cue. Harry'd been short, sharp and fairly bad-tempered, burying himself in the papers for the majority of the weekend, only interspersing it with bouts of watching television where he spent the entire time criticizing the shots, the direction, the artwork and the acting and generally shouting at the screen. Watching television with Harry was not a pleasant experience; it was more like attending an industrial tribunal.

Eventually on Sunday evening, after Val's attempt at

roast lamb with rosemary and all the trimmings, she looked up at Harry and caught his gaze.

'Anything exciting happening at HOT?' she stammered, wondering why her voice had suddenly developed a squeak and her heart had started to pound. She covered her embarrassment by noisily stacking up the plates.

'No, fairly mundane,' said Harry, sitting back and lighting a cigar. 'Why do you ask?'

'Oh, nothing.' There was that squeak again. 'It's just that you seem to be working long hours. I hoped there was some nice little project that was keeping you busy.'

Val stopped plate-stacking and lit a cigarette to calm her sudden nerves.

'We don't have "nice little projects",' replied Harry patronizingly. 'What you girlies forget is that we men have to do battle in the boardroom every day of our working lives. Nothing for your little brain to worry about.' His eyes glittered at her with the sarcasm of the remark.

He's not going to invite me, she thought to herself. He's not going to mention it. He's going alone or with someone else. A bizarre kind of relief swept over her. It was the result she'd wanted. She stubbed out her cigarette defiantly, picked up the pile of plates and serving dishes and headed for the kitchen.

'Yeeessss,' she whispered triumphantly to the hall mirror as she passed. Bit like Cinderella in reverse, she thought. I don't want to be swept off to the ball in a crystal coach; I want to go with my friends, and I'll wear my own dress, thank you very much. And I certainly *don't* want to meet Prince Charming.

Harry sat back in his carver chair, puffing thoughtfully on his cigar. Giving up the drink had made Val go a bit gaga, he concluded. She'd get over it. He sat for a few moments contemplating whether he preferred the old Val, the ranting, flamboyant, pissed Val, or the new, more sober, rather boring version. Even Harry felt mildly ashamed that he didn't much care.

chapter thirty-five

They were all finding it hard to keep the secret. Various national newspapers and trade magazines were running pre-publicity stories on the opening of the restaurant. The name-dropping and rumour-mongering had reached epic proportions. A couple of celebrity magazines were rumoured to be fighting over an exclusive picture deal.

But the girls kept their promise, despite many temptations to boast about their invitations. They each reminded Ray on a daily basis to keep his mouth shut.

'Oi, most of the time you lot can't wait to hear the gossip,' he complained. 'Now I've got to keep my mouth shut or you'll beat me up.'

Ray was only kidding. Why spoil what might turn out to be an epic night of gossip in more ways than one? No, this was a secret he had no difficulty in keeping. The gossip would come later.

As the stories in the press gathered momentum, Janet decided it would be unrealistic of her not to mention the grand opening to Harry.

'I jolly well hope you've been invited,' she said to him at the end of one particularly spiky production meeting.

'I'll have to put in an appearance,' he scowled. 'Subpoenaed by the board.'

'Of course,' said Janet amiably, getting up to leave the meeting room.

What's up with that silly tart? he thought. Normally she'd be whingeing over not going to the opening night. She seemed ridiculously happy. Perhaps she was getting a shag somewhere. Hmm, he very much doubted it. Far too fat to get her kit off.

He hoped Val wouldn't start begging to go to the do. He'd already prepared his speech. No staff, no partners, just those at board level, in between sustaining a mock yawn.

But Val never raised the subject, probably because the dippy tart never read any newspapers, he surmised. It was going to be much easier than he had at first thought. No hassle from Val, and Janet seemed to have her mind elsewhere. He'd be able to take Gina without any problems. And that would keep her bubbling for a while longer while he decided what to do about Val.

As the restaurant opening drew closer, Janet decided that they needed to hold a strategy meeting. So the Haunted Handbag committee gathered briefly at Sue's house two nights before the Big One. This time Ray was included in the meeting because it was felt that he needed to know what was happening.

'Aside from the fact that we are all looking forward to wearing posh frocks and mingling with A-, B- and even C-list celebs, there are three main scenarios here that we need to consider,' announced Janet, as she unashamedly pulled trays of curry out of the microwave. 'Firstly, we have the confrontation with Harry, who will wonder how

323

come we all pitched up. Now this affects us all, so we need to be prepared for that one. Secondly, we have the possible confrontation of Harry plus "mystery" partner. He will of course wriggle out of that one very successfully and pass off his lady friend as an "only just met" or a business acquaintance. But of course, Ray, Sue and Nina, you were all at the Country Cottage Restaurant, so you've seen her before. If it's the same lady, I think it's entirely up to you how you react.'

'Well I'm up for saying something,' piped up Nina. 'I won't be able to resist it.'

'So am I,' chorused Ray and Sue.

'But of course the most interesting plot,' continued Janet, 'will be When Harry Meets Val. Now there certainly won't be any fake orgasms there. It could get nasty and we must make sure that she's not left on her own for even a nanosecond.'

They all nodded in agreement. After the initial excitement over the choosing of outfits, they knew it was going to be a tense evening that might turn out to be retrospective fun. One of those 'Omigod, you were there!!' nights where you'd be guaranteed top score on the gossipometer. They went through the last-minute arrangements as though it were a military operation. Pick-up times were checked and rechecked, plus a rather complicated routine about picking up Val. The plan was that she would ring Janet late afternoon after making certain Harry wasn't suddenly taking her. Then she would travel to Janet's in a taxi and change there to avoid any suspicion or risk of last-minute discovery. Again, all subject to what Harry got up to.

'Just suppose that at the last minute Harry doesn't go,' Janet told Val the following day. 'You can't just go waltzing off with a suitcase in a taxi and him not wonder where you're going. Much better to leave the house in mufti.'

So Val sent her frock, jewellery, shoes and bag round to Janet's house the night before in a taxi. Just in case.

On Thursday night, Harry was late home as usual. Val greeted him with a watery smile and, as casually as she could, asked about weekend arrangements.

'It's just that I'll probably meet up with friends tomorrow night,' she mentioned while loading up the cappuccino machine, 'if that's all right with you.'

'That's fine,' muttered Harry, not quite believing his luck and trying to sound nonchalant. 'Don't bother about little old me tomorrow night, because I've got a business dinner with the board.'

Little old me, thought Val. Who's he kidding. Old, yes; little, no. She stifled her giggles over the noise of the milk frothing.

Excellent, Harry thought to himself. He wouldn't even have to stumble in late to the 'and what time do you call this' greeting. His tuxedo was already hanging in Gina's wardrobe. He would go straight to her house from work, change and go to the function. Then it would be back to her place for the obligatory quickie, after which he'd change back into his ordinary business suit to return home in the wee small hours of the morning, when hopefully Val would be sound asleep. Pity she'd given up drinking; it always guaranteed her being comatose.

Janet paced the floor of the production office. It was Friday afternoon, the day of the grand opening, and she was suddenly attacked by a fit of appalling nerves. Once again her courage was deserting her where Harry was concerned. Inviting Val, and even accepting the tickets from Sir James Patterson Cripps in the first place, now seemed to have been the decisions of a lunatic. Should she spend this afternoon sharpening up her CV for life after HOT? She wasn't sure. Hang on a minute, Val's marriage could well be on the line after tonight. Wasn't that worse?

Well, no, she reasoned. Val more or less wanted the marriage to end. She positively welcomed the idea of confronting the other woman. Val could just retreat to her rich parents and then start all over again, perhaps making a better choice of husband next time. What would happen to Janet if she got the sack? Certainly not a flit back to Mummy and Daddy. They were dead, for a start, and even if they'd been alive, their forty-two-year-old daughter descending on them would have been the last thing they'd have wanted. No, she thought selfishly, she had an awful lot more to lose than Val.

But on the other hand, if Harry finally left HOT . . . No stop it, that was a ridiculous thought. It was never going to happen. This was Harry's Game and Harry always played to win. Janet logged off and shut down her computer, slung a few files and a couple of newspapers into her briefcase and strode purposefully out of the building.

'Don't worry, his eminence grease has already gone,' said Sue in reception. 'Only came back from lunch briefly and then left again. Gone for the day. I checked with Geraldine.'

'Haven't seen her for a day or two, I'm pleased to say,' said Janet. 'I wonder if she got an invite tonight?'

'Doubt it,' said Sue knowingly. 'She'd be out of here by now to get home to tart up, just like I am when my shift ends in precisely ten minutes.'

'How could Geraldine possibly tart up? Tarts don't wear beige.'

'Just remember the divorce – too much hoovering and humping,' replied Sue. 'Maybe our Geraldine is a sex bomb after all. Do you think we could persuade Chris de Burgh to write a follow up song, "Lady in Beige"?'

'I very much doubt it. Perhaps she just sticks to hoovering these days,' said Janet.

The minibus picked up Sue and Jon, then Liz and Tony, followed by Ray. Then it made its way to Nina's flat for her and Sam, followed by Jed and then finally Janet and Val. Every time new party guests boarded, they were greeted with a round of applause. Val, devoid of her usual in-your-face make-up, the massive pink talons and the dressed-to-kill outfit, looked more like a Grace Kelly cool blonde type. Elegant but very restrained. The others nodded approval when Val boarded and Val's grin spread from ear to ear when she heard the applause. It almost dispelled her nerves. Almost.

The minibus driver then set out for the restaurant, and with the sound of the engine, everyone fell into their own silent thoughts. Val, particularly, was convinced that tonight she would be witnessing the end of her marriage. She'd stupidly tried to rehearse her feelings in the bathroom mirror, what she'd say and how she'd react to the inevitable showdown. But what she'd planned to say kept sounding like some gibbering idiot. She knew that whatever she said, Harry would twist it this way or that and make her look a fool. After all, he did it on a regular basis, so he was well up to speed. She was worried that he would shout at her, or hit her. Or would he, in front of the assembled glitterati? Once the deed was done, she knew exactly what Harry's version of events would be when they got home. She'd been mistaken, she was pissed, she was stupid, she was embarrassing. He was important, he was doing his job, he was power.

But there was one thing in Val's armoury that she hadn't possessed before. And that was anger. In her new sobriety, Val had discovered what anger was, and how she felt about it. No, there was no turning back. This was the final conflict.

'We're only a couple of minutes away now.'

Janet clocked the sudden look of fear again in Val's eyes and felt complete empathy with her. The poor girl was going to cause ructions, whoever Harry was with. She must be feeling like a lamb going to the slaughter.

The minibus finally came to a halt in the car park adjoining the restaurant. Several shiny Bentleys, a Rolls-Royce, a smattering of TVRs and a stretch limo were already parked there. Everyone silently clocked Harry's Merc, parked in a discreet corner. As the engine of the minibus died away, Janet indicated she would say a few words.

'Hey, before we go in, just remember two things. Sir James invited "me and friends" so we are just as welcome here as the likes of Liz Hurley and Posh and Becks. But Harry has no idea we're coming, so he may be a little bit surprised.'

They all laughed.

'Val, we're all with you on this one. You will not be left on your own, you will be supported at all times,' continued Janet, glancing at her watch. 'Now we're fashionably slightly late, which is great. Makes the others look as though they smack of desperation. And one last thing, this minibus turns back into a pumpkin at twelve o'clock, so be on it.'

They climbed out of the bus, the men adjusting their bow ties and the women smoothing down their dresses. Then they all linked arms and strode purposefully towards the restaurant entrance.

They were greeted with champagne cocktails in the foyer, served by waiters dressed in traditional Moroccan-style djellabah and fez. Then, rather like a Roman army trained in the art of combat, they moved en masse into the main body of the restaurant. The designers had done a breathtaking job on the place. The characteristic Moorish architecture, with its blue and white mosaic tiling, curves and pillars, was simply stunning. Every niche, every table bore testament to Moroccan art, with beautiful beaten brass plates, massive candlesticks and sculptures. Not much evidence of Rick's Café Americain, apart from a piano whose keys were being caressed by a pianist constantly playing 'As Time Goes By' as if it were on a loop tape. Janet found herself scanning the crowd like a radar system. Her gaze took in hordes of the current tabloid celebs, footballers, page three girls, minor film stars and models, plus the odd television personality. A roomful of people whom you recognized but couldn't quite put a name to. Photographers lurked in every corner, flash guns popping. But so far, no glimpse of Harry.

She looked across at Val, whose fixed smile betrayed everything. A tentative mixture of nerves, determination and shaky elation that she might uncover the truth tonight once and for all.

'Do you want me to have a quiet scout around?' whispered Ray in Janet's left ear.

'Not sure,' she said. 'In a way I'd rather he came upon the whole lot of us. Element of surprise. Plus safety in numbers.'

'It'll be okay, you know.' Jed's voice came reassuringly in her right ear. She wheeled round to speak to him but discovered that his comments weren't meant for her. He was talking to Val.

'We're all here rooting for you,' he continued. 'And by the way, nobody's actually said so, but you look great.'

Janet turned away, as if eavesdropping on a conversation between two lovers.

'Slight change of plan, I think,' she said to Ray, suddenly embarrassed. 'Let's just the two of us do a quick and surreptitious circuit to see who's where.'

They linked arms, nodded to Sue and Jon to take care of things and set off. A five-minute tour of the restaurant, jostling with listed and so far unlisted celebrities, told them what they needed to know. They spied Harry in the furthest corner, in his element, quaffing champagne with a group who looked suspiciously like members of the board. Next to him, and half hidden from view, was a dark-haired woman in a long gold dress.

'That's her,' said Ray. 'That's Gina, our little Italian firecracker.'

'Poor Val,' sighed Janet. 'This is all going to end in tears. Let's go back and warn the others.'

Unnoticed by Harry, who was obviously in grandiose mode, they slipped back to the group and quietly told them what they'd seen. Val went white and took a slight stumble backwards in shock. Jed, Janet noted, caught her by the arm and steadied her. She'd need all the support she could get. Harry wouldn't be all that thrilled to see Jed either, after the 'Humpton' episode. It was likely to be a very bumpy ride.

chapter thirty-six

It took a remarkably long time before Harry made the fateful discovery. Because Janet and her party had arrived rather late, there was only time for a swift glass of champagne before the three hundred or so guests took their seats. Again fate had taken a hand. There'd been no time or opportunity to mingle.

Janet's table was just about as far away from Harry's as it was possible to be. Because all the tables seated ten, the Haunted Handbag committee and guests had one to themselves, and were soon installed on the low cushioned seats, Moroccan fashion, around the circular table.

A huge brass gong was sounded, at which point four giant movie screens were lowered from the ceiling and the immortal scene in *Casablanca* started in which Humphrey Bogart meets Ingrid Bergman for the first time in Rick's Café Americain. The film worked its legendary magic, and three hundred people, now ever so slightly pissed on champagne and exhausted from luvvie shrieking and photographic mayhem, were hushed into silence, hearing the famous exchange between two of Hollywood's finest film actors.

When the scene finished, the gong sounded again.

Suddenly the tables lit up from beneath, and fireworks ignited around the piano to a roar of appreciation and applause. The pianist struck up yet again with 'As Time Goes By' to tumultuous applause, along with some rather off-key singing provided by a few guests who were well into the party mood.

The meal was then served by waiters wearing traditional pale grey striped djellabahs. Candles flickered through silver filigree lamps on all the tables, giving off the most magical dappled light. First came small bowls containing spicy salads of every description. Then chicken tagine, served in the typical Moroccan pots and accompanied by piles of pale yellow fluffy couscous. The drink flowed freely. Waiters flurried around topping up glasses, whisking away bottles and bringing more. Tongues loosened as the wine flowed.

Janet glanced around the table. Sam and Nina were gazing into each other's eyes in that first flush of love. Sue and Jon, the initial excitement gone from their relationship, were loving and supportive in a more lasting way. Liz and Tony, both on their best behaviour, were at that difficult stage of any relationship: on the brink of an initial commitment but not yet able to pluck up the courage to talk about it, in case one discovered the other wasn't so keen and it all went pear-shaped.

Janet then glanced at Jed and Val and immediately averted her gaze. Definite electricity was going on there, sparks being generated. They made a knock-out couple, no doubt about that. Janet had never seen Val looking so serene, and so fascinated by what someone had to say, particularly given the circumstances of the evening. And even more impressive, despite all the alcohol washing around, she was sticking to her sparkling mineral water.

Jed was sitting slightly to one side, his arm resting casually on the back of Val's chair. Slightly tanned, his dark hair swept back and his brown eyes flashing, he had a film-star quality about him. He suddenly moved forward to light Val's cigarette, his eyes not leaving her face. No wonder all the girls at HOT had dumped George Clooney and replaced him with Jed as their Fantasy Shag.

Janet, smiling to herself, realized that Ray was watching her.

'Mutual attraction, I'd say,' he whispered. 'Just hope Harry doesn't go berserk over this.'

'He can hardly do that,' said Janet. 'The hypocrisy would be appalling. Mind you, that's never stopped him in the past. Val was a bag of nerves tonight getting on the minibus, but look at her now. I'd rather hoped they might hit it off. At least he'll help get her through the evening.'

'Harry won't quite see it that way,' replied Ray. 'Men never do. Different rules for them.'

'So what do we do now?' she asked him in desperation.

'Well,' said Ray, pausing as he lit a cigarette, 'when the meal's over, you know better than I do that the fun will begin. People will start to mingle, the photographers will resume, so we must not drop our guard. Those two,' he indicated Val and Jed, 'will need protection. And at the rate they're going, it'll be hammer and tongues even before the coffee gets here.'

During a pudding of magnificent fresh fruit salad, a group of musicians struck up in a small area at the front of the tables, playing some very wild and rhythmic music. They were joined by a belly dancer in long, flowing deep red chiffon trimmed with gold embroidery. As she wiggled her hips and rotated in time to the music, she invited a couple of the men to come up and join her.

Unfortunately the two she picked were somewhat well oiled and thought they were watching a lap dancer. To a roar of approval from the audience, they tried to stuff ten-pound notes down her bra top. Completely unfazed, she just kept on smiling and wiggling, and as the tempo of the music increased, she twirled faster and faster. In a drunken attempt to keep up, the guys tried to follow suit, turning faster as well. But when the music abruptly finished, they lost their balance and fell into a heap at her feet.

A storm of applause broke out while the two men picked themselves up and limped back to their table. Then the gong sounded once again and a rather short man with swept-back grey hair stood up and raised his hand in an appeal for silence.

'I'm Mark Haversham and I'm the chief executive of Movie Munch,' he announced. Silence spread quickly, with people noisily shushing each other. Mr Haversham made a sensibly short speech, giving a little of the company's history – which was also mercifully short, since they'd only been formed earlier in the year – and then, with an eye on the PR opportunity, announcing the opening dates of the next two themed restaurants, Indiana Jones, which would have an Egyptian feel, and Out of Africa, specializing in Kenyan dishes. There were cheers from all the guests, by now gripped with the expectation of at least two more freebies to put into their psions. Then Sir James Patterson Cripps rose to his feet from the HOT table at the far end of the restaurant. Dressed in a dinner jacket that had clearly put in at least fifty years' sturdy service, he was surprisingly witty, Janet decided, given his slightly doddery exchange with her that night in the office.

Sir James thanked Movie Munch for placing their trust

in HOT for all their website and general media requirements.

'We're a small team at HOT, but small can be beautiful,' he announced. 'You get a personal service, a friendly service that's not lost in long corporate corridors, and a first-class product created by first-class committed professionals. When you go home tonight, please click on to the Movie Munch website. But just to give you a flavour now of what we can do, here's a short video about the creation of tonight's restaurant.'

Up on screen came the familiar opening moments of Janet's film. Almost immediately silence fell, broken only by the haunting music of the film and the first breathtaking shots. To Janet's relief, she'd hooked them.

The moment the video finished, a cheer went up, and Sir James rose to his feet once more.

'All I'm going to add is a special thank-you to our head of production, Janet Bancroft, who's here tonight with some of her team. Janet wrote, directed and produced that film. So please, Janet, stand up and take a bow.'

Three hundred guests applauded enthusiastically, looking around to see who they were clapping. Janet stood up uneasily to accept the applause, wondering how on earth she'd actually managed to take the credit for her own work for once. Harry would be livid. Everyone in her party clapped and thumped the table with gusto. Then the pianist struck up for the umpteenth time with 'As Time Goes By'.

'What's it feel like hanging over the parapet then?' Ray whispered in Janet's ear. 'Our cover, what there was of it, has been blown. Can I make a suggestion?'

'Hmm, like what?' said Janet, deeply suspicious and still crimson from the public recognition.

'That we take the bull by the horns. We all go over to the HOT board table and thank Sir James for our invites,' said Ray.

'Bloody good idea,' said Jed, who'd been eavesdropping. He turned to Val. 'Hey, babe, are you up to that?'

Val took a deep drag on her cigarette and thought for a second or two.

'Yes, I am,' she said. 'If he's over there with another woman, I want to see her for myself. With witnesses. I want to catch them red-handed. It's no good chickening out now.'

Everyone immediately agreed. They rose en masse, straightened bow ties, collars, straps and wraps, and then, with Janet and Ray in the lead, wended their way in a crocodile across the restaurant, in and out of the tables, until they reached the HOT board's table.

Janet took a deep breath, offered up a silent prayer and stepped forward.

'Sir James,' she said, keeping her eyes firmly on him, 'we've come over to thank you once again for your kind invitation.'

'The pleasure's all mine,' he beamed, standing up to shake hands. 'Your film is terrific. I hope it didn't come as too much of a surprise that we showed it.'

' Just a bit,' replied Janet. 'I probably wouldn't have come if I'd known.'

'Just as I thought,' said Sir James, nodding sagely.

'If you don't mind, Sir James, I'd like to introduce you to some of my colleagues,' she continued, still resisting the urge to look around the table. 'This is Sue, our head receptionist, and her husband, Jon. Nina, our production secretary, and Sam from the accounts department. Liz, one of my senior producers, and her partner Tony. This is

Ray; we couldn't do without him. He's the production office gopher and a budding producer in the making. And this is Jed, who did all the fantastic graphics on the film you saw tonight.'

They all queued up to shake hands with Sir James. Then Janet finally allowed herself to glance to his right. There was Harry half out of his seat, cigar cast aside and smouldering in an ashtray, straining to catch what was going on. He'd turned a violent shade of crimson and had half turned away from Gina sitting beside him in a sub-conscious effort to pretend she wasn't there.

After being introduced to Sir James, Ray and Jed point-edly waved amiably at Harry, whose crimson was turning more purple by the second.

Janet reached her pièce de resistance. 'And finally, Sir James, I don't know if you've already met, but this is Val, Harry Hampton's wife.'

Val beamed at him, praying her nerves wouldn't let her down, and they shook hands vigorously, which at least disguised the shaking.

'I think we probably met at one of the HOT Christmas parties,' she said with a fixed smile.

'Oh,' said Sir James, now puzzled. He half glanced over at Harry, sensed something wasn't quite right and turned back to Val.

'Delighted to see you again, my dear,' he said. Val, now having reached the end of the greeting line, was directly in Harry's line of fire. She followed Ray and Jed's cue by giving him a small wave, then turned and immediately followed the rest of them back towards their own table.

They were about halfway across the restaurant when Val felt a hand on her shoulder. Not a warm hand of affec-tion, but a grasp of malice. It wheeled her round to face a livid Harry, who was almost spitting out his own teeth in his fury. He'd obviously taken a short cut around some of the tables to catch up with them.

'What the fuck are you doing here, you, the lot of you?' he shouted, now purple with rage.

'Same as you,' replied Val firmly.

Suddenly an audience formed around them. Janet, Jed and Ray were immediately by Val's side, the others forming up behind them.

But Harry was now oblivious of all around him. He'd had far too much to drink and was losing control. Then he spied Janet again.

'I suppose this is all your doing, Bancroft,' he shouted at her. 'Might have guessed. Any kind of scheming and you're usually up to your neck in it. How come you're suddenly taking the credit for the video? And who invited you?' he bellowed, pointing at Jed. 'You're fired. I fired you weeks ago. You've absolutely no fucking right to be here.'

'What ees going on? 'Arry, what ees 'appening?' The dark-haired woman in the gold dress pushed her way into the circle that had now formed.

'You stay out of it,' roared Harry, now so angry that veins were appearing on his forehead and a visible pulse was going in his neck. He pushed her aside.

Nina stepped boldly into the makeshift ring.

'Hi, how are you?' She proffered a hand to Gina. 'How lovely to see you again. We met at the Country Cottage Restaurant, remember?'

Gina looked confused but automatically shook Nina's hand. 'And here's Ray,' continued Nina, indicating him. 'Oh, and you'll remember Sue. She was there too when you were having lunch with Harry.'

There was a moment of stunned silence. Jed grabbed the moment.

'You're absolutely right, Harry, you did fire me,' he said cheerfully, 'but funnily enough, Sir James seemed to love the graphics.'

'You bloody—' Harry was stopped mid sentence as flashguns started to pop, and it seemed that half the room suddenly had a notebook and pen on them. People rapidly started to sober up and take more than a passing interest. But Harry ploughed on. The evening's drinking, some of it to calm his nerves about Gina, was now catching up with him rapidly.

'And you,' he resumed, pointing accusingly at Val. 'What the fuck are you doing here?'

'You didn't invite her, so we did,' said Jed defiantly, indicating the circle round Val. By now they were all grappling with the business of staying upright. Many of the guests had surged forward to get a glimpse of the proceedings, and were pushing for a better view. Even the pianist had stopped, having decided perhaps that the Time really had Gone By.

'Anyway, Harry, aren't you going to make the introductions?' Jed continued. 'Shouldn't you introduce your wife to your, er, lady companion here tonight?'

'Good job I fired you.' Harry glared at Jed. He was completely oblivious of the crowd, who were now oohing and aahing at every outburst. 'One of my better ideas. And as for the rest of you, you can all follow in his footsteps, come Monday morning.'

Janet shivered. This was routine Harry stuff, except that even Harry didn't normally do this sort of turn in front of an audience. She caught sight of Val's stricken face. The poor girl looked absolutely devastated and was

340

rooted to the spot. All the carefully rehearsed phrases had gone straight out of her head.

'Time we left, I think,' Janet announced bravely. There were shouts of 'No, no, no!' from the crowd, some of whom had mysteriously turned into members of the paparazzi. She looked around for support from Ray, but he'd disappeared.

'Hey, Val, give us a smile,' shouted one snapper, waving a camera with flash gun.

'You, in the gold dress, come forward, big smile.'

'Harry, let's have a picture of you with your wife? And your girlfriend? All together?'

Another round of flashbulbs brought Harry to his senses. He realized what a mess he was in. His wife and his mistress confronting each other at the most high-profile event of the year; it was the stuff of nightmares. He decided to pretend neither of them existed, and tried to turn tail and walk through the throng that was now gathered. But he couldn't escape, he was hemmed in tight with Gina next to him. Gina, meanwhile, was now secretly enjoying the fuss and the attention. This might just be the thing to make Harry dump Val and take the leap into commitment. She decided to go for it and was beaming for the cameras, linking arms with a smouldering Harry.

'Now, a big smile from both of you,' coaxed one photographer. 'How about a kiss?'

'Fuck off,' Harry snarled. With that, he hit out at the nearest photographer, sending him and his camera sprawling.

Janet, Val and Nina, who were still in the thick of the action, suddenly found themselves being pulled backwards through the crowd, leaving Harry and Gina at the mercy of the mob.

341

When they managed to turn around, they realized they'd been rescued by Ray, Jed and Sam. With the pack still descending on the drama like foxhounds waiting for the kill, Janet was suddenly aware that the rest of the group had collected the coats and were in the process of boarding the minibus. Soon they were all safely on board and the bus pulled away.

Nobody said anything for a while. They were too shocked to speak. The only sound was Val sobbing quietly into Jed's shoulder.

chapter thirty-seven

About ten minutes into the journey home, Janet broke the silence by suggesting that they stop for a coffee at a motorway service station. There were things to be discussed that couldn't wait until the morning. For example, where was Val going to spend the night? She probably didn't fancy the idea of going home. And in the mood Harry was in, Janet was fearful for her safety.

They all stumbled out of the minibus and into the garish lighting of the coffee shop. They made quite an incongruous sight, ten of them in evening clothes, sitting on bright green plastic chairs around a plastic table, clutching cappuccinos in polystyrene cups.

'A Night to Remember?' said Jed.

'Oh What a Lovely War?' replied Ray.

'Armageddon,' chipped in Janet. 'I suppose it was a bit like *Casablanca*, with a love triangle, except that in the movie they didn't have a punch-up.'

They all laughed. Even Val managed a watery smile. But Janet noted that there was still a real fear in her eyes. She looked completely done in.

'Well,' proclaimed Nina, 'I haven't had so much fun in years. At least not since last weekend.' She glanced cheekily at Sam. 'I actually don't care if I get the sack on Monday. It was worth every penny of this Monsoon gear just to see Harry's face. No offence, Val, but your husband's a piece of complete and utter pond life. A complete waste of DNA.'

'Now, talking of which,' Janet chipped in quickly as she noticed Val's eyes welling up, 'you're not going home tonight, Val, and that's an order. You're staying at my place and no arguments. No, Jed, you're not whisking her off anywhere. Not tonight anyway. But I think we'll have to have a council of war over the weekend prior to Monday.'

'Tell you what, why don't you all come for Sunday lunch and we'll have a bit of a think tank then,' said Sue brightly, Jon nodding in approval.

'That would be great,' said Liz. 'I know I'll feel better if we have a group discussion about it. You know how that man terrifies me.' She glanced knowingly at Janet.

'I don't know what to say,' said Val, tears in her eyes. 'We've had this terrible evening, I've now realized what a pig Harry's been to you all and here you all are being nice to me. Janet's inviting me to stay, Sue's inviting me for Sunday lunch.'

'And I'm inviting you out tomorrow night,' said Jed with a twinkle in his eye.

'Oi, steady on,' said Janet, secretly pleased for Val. 'You can ring tomorrow and ask my permission.'

Val slept for most of Saturday morning, grateful for the peace of Janet's sparse spare room, which, with its rather clashing decor, seemed like heaven after what she'd been through.

'Sorry it's not exactly posh,' apologized Janet, indicating the old bed with its pink padded headboard and purple flowering duvet, circa 1970s M&S, 'but it's not been much of a priority.' Val felt so relieved not to have to go home that she felt as though she'd booked into the Ritz.

Jed rang on Saturday morning enquiring how Val was.

'You're keen on her, aren't you?' said Janet, laughing.

'Yep. Fancied her when I saw that picture of her in the paper,' he confessed. 'Couldn't believe she could be married to such a sod. Totally wiped out when I saw her last night.'

'Well, just take it steady,' warned Janet. 'She's had a rough time, in fact she's still asleep, but I'll tell her you called. Leave her in peace today. Why not come round tomorrow and drive us to Sue's for lunch?'

'You're on,' came the instant reply.

Janet decided to have a quick whip round the house while Val was asleep in an attempt to make it a bit more respectable. As she dusted, tidied, straightened cushions, chucked out old newspapers and loaded up the washing machine, she mused yet again about how different Val was from the monster of several months ago. And also how she and the girls had completely changed their feelings towards her. Val had become one of them, instead of being the one who stood out, the one who made the scene, the grand entrance, the one who fell down drunk. Now she was united with them in their hatred of Harry, united in their need to escape his clutches. Not for the first time Janet considered the prospect of being sacked on Monday. Harry had done it to many others before and he'd certainly do it again without any hesitation. But could he sack quite so many people in one fell swoop? Or would he just pick off one or two of them? They'd probably need legal advice if he tried. At least they could split the costs of a lawyer. Surely it wouldn't get to that. They had been invited to the bash by the chairman after all, and they were entitled to be there. But was introducing your boss's mistress to his wife a sackable offence? Even Hillary Clinton never had to meet and greet Monica.

Janet busied herself with a pile of ironing in an attempt to distract herself, and was appalled to discover clothes at the bottom of the basket that she'd long forgotten about, or worse, didn't even recognize. Then she recalled an article she'd read about decluttering, so she piled all the forgotten items into a black bin bag. Anything you've not worn for three years you will never wear again, so cheerfully wave it goodbye, had been the advice. Perhaps she'd soon be saying goodbye not just to old clothes, but her monthly salary, security and her friends at HOT. She shuddered again as she filled a second black bag with clothes.

'My God, that looks serious.' Val appeared around the kitchen door.

'Just black-bag archiving,' Janet joked. 'It's my new revolutionary and very effective way of tackling the ironing. Fancy some breakfast?'

'Not half,' came the reply.

Soon bacon, tomatoes and sausages were sizzling away in a pan, and the kitchen was filled with the dark aroma of coffee bubbling in an ancient percolator.

'Comfort food,' said Val. 'This is just terrific.'

'Jed phoned, by the way,' said Janet, noting the flicker of interest in her eyes. 'I told him to leave you in peace today. But he'll pick us up tomorrow morning and take us to Sue's for lunch.'

'Oh, fantastic,' Val said. Then her face fell.

'No, Harry hasn't phoned,' said Janet, reading her

346

mind. 'Not as much as a squeak. It wouldn't take the Brain of Britain for him to guess you're here. Listen, do you want to ring your folks or anything? The grub won't be ready for another five minutes.'

'Yes, I would. Do you mind?'

Janet turned the bacon with one hand and gave her the phone with the other.

After five minutes Val came back into the kitchen, a little tearful. She lit a cigarette and took a deep drag on it.

'It's very strange, actually telling someone that your marriage is definitely finally over,' she tried to explain, wiping her eyes with a piece of kitchen roll. 'For a long time it's crap and you don't admit it to yourself. And of course I used to blot it all out with a bottle of wine. But it's only when you start to talk to someone about it that you really mean it. Do you remember in that Indian restaurant that day? The Gunges? When I said I thought Harry was up to something? Well, what a long way we've come since then.'

'Is your mum upset?' asked Janet anxiously.

'No, she's thrilled.' Val managed a small smile. 'She and my father are going to open a bottle of champagne tonight to celebrate. I didn't realize until recently how much they hated Harry.'

'Join the club. It's such a big one they'll be closing the membership soon.' Janet started to dish up the breakfast. Val stubbed out her cigarette.

'After we've had this, could I ask you a huge favour?' she said.

'Whassat?'

'Well,' said Val, lowering her eyes in slight embarrassment, 'I've only got the clothes I'm standing up in. I don't want to go back to the house, so could we go shopping this afternoon? I'll need a few clothes and make-up to tide me over the next couple of days.'

At least the old clothes horse in Val was alive and well and champing at her wallet. They decided to avoid Hartford just in case they bumped into Harry. Or worse, Harry and Gina. Instead they went to an out-of-town shopping mall which had just opened.

Val deliberately avoided the most expensive shops. She dived into Next, dragging Janet in with her, and went round like a whirlwind, picking up a couple of fleece tops, tee shirts, jeans, boots, some underwear and a bag of basic skincare. It took her about five minutes flat. Janet couldn't help but envy her for being able to snap up anything in size 10 and know it would fit, without the bother and ordeal of the changing room. Unlike Janet, whose constant dilemma was, would her bulges squeeze into a size 16 or would she have to smuggle in an 18 just in case? The only thing she could guarantee to get into was the bloody changing room itself.

Janet found herself envying Val at the till as well. What it cost didn't really matter to her, it was more a case of how long it would take for the assistant to process the transaction and wrap the goods. Val didn't agonize over air miles, bonus points or boring old discounts. She just paid up and enjoyed. She was a hedonist shopper.

Over lunch and a bottle of sparkling mineral water in Café Rouge, Val produced another carrier bag from Next.

'This is for you, along with this lunch,' she announced. 'And don't you dare open your mouth in protest.'

Janet was momentarily speechless. Inside the bag was the ice-blue jumper she had secretly admired while they were picking out the weekend gear for Val. Val had also

348

bought her a pretty silver necklace and matching ear-rings.

The waiter interrupted Janet's rapturous thanks with grilled sole and green salad. All the shopping had made them ravenous.

'Do you miss driving?' asked Janet in between mouth-fuls.

'Yes, desperately,' admitted Val. 'I've been stuck at home for months now, at the mercy of Harry and the local taxi firm. Also, if I'd still had my licence, I'm sure I'd have followed Harry on one of his Have It Away days by now and found out the awful truth much sooner.'

'Would it have made that much difference?' queried Janet.

'Well, at least the discovery wouldn't have been quite so public,' said Val. 'The irony is that one night when he was a bit pissed, Harry told me he thought he was being followed. I told you about it, if you recall.'

'He *was* being followed,' Janet confessed, hanging her head sheepishly. 'We were all fed up with the way he treated us, and we were also suspicious that the Manchester Riviera suntan wasn't quite what it seemed, so we got someone to follow him and take photographs.'

'What of?' Val was steeling herself for something explicit.

'Oh, just him going into Gina's house. Gina at the door. We weren't doing a *News of the World* job.'

'Why on earth didn't you say when I asked you?' said Val, visibly agitated and lighting a cigarette.

'We all had a bit of a pow-wow and decided we couldn't. Something to do with not playing God, I suppose. We didn't want the responsibility of ending a marriage, much as we hated Harry. Do you understand?'

'Yeah, I guess so,' said Val, crestfallen.

'It would have been dead easy to say, "Oh sure, Val, your husband's playing away and here are the photographs." But we didn't have photographs of Harry in bed with her, just going into her house. It could have been quite innocent. Except of course there was always a pattern.'

'Mondays and Thursdays. You knew that too?' Val was incredulous. 'It took me a while to cotton on. I suppose I was comatose most of the time.'

'Yes, we did clock that routine,' confessed Janet. 'But I *was* telling you the truth when you asked if he really had been to Manchester that week he returned with the amazing tan. I honestly didn't know where he'd been. We did pick up a rumour that he was in the Algarve, but again, it was all surmise. Just a conversation overheard in a corridor.'

Val stubbed out her cigarette and immediately got another one out of the packet.

'Do you think Geraldine was in on all of it?' she asked.

'Yes, I do,' said Janet. 'Harry'd never have got away with it without her. She's very protective. She must have booked the Country Cottage Restaurant for Harry plus one on a regular basis. I'm sure she knew about the Portuguese trip as well, because he was out of the office for a week and she had to be able to contact him. But then Harry hired her for her loyalty, not her legs.'

'Hmm,' pondered Val. 'Seems he got that right.'

chapter thirty-eight

Jed turned up on Sunday morning in his trademark jeans and designer polo shirt, clutching a bunch of red roses. He presented them to Val with great aplomb. Janet noted enviously that Val turned a giveaway pink on receiving them. She also looked effortlessly wonderful in some of the basics she'd bought in Next the previous day: tight dark denim jeans, black kitten-heeled boots, a white cropped cable sweater and a bright red zipped fleece top. She'd scraped her blonde hair back into a ponytail and even with minimal make-up still looked a million dollars.

They climbed into Jed's battered old Citroën and roared off across Hartford towards Sue and Jon's house. Everyone had brought something to help spread the cost. Janet and Val contributed two types of pâté for a starter, Nina and Sam brought various cheeses and savoury biscuits, Ray breezed in with a bag full of cans of lager, Liz and Tony produced a couple of puddings – a bowl of fresh fruit salad and a chocolate gateau out of a box – and Jed had brought champagne.

'Should we be celebrating?' queried Sue, fishing out some glasses.

'Yeah, absolutely,' said Jed. 'Look, he fired me and I

came back for my little bit of revenge. He can't keep doing this. Harry may have the hump, but Harry Humpton's run out of road.'

They all roared with laughter, but there were also anxious looks.

'How on earth is Harry going to explain his behaviour to the board, let alone fire us?' said Nina. 'It was quite a scene, let's face it, and for a public relations exercise it made an extremely good punch-up. We could have sold tickets.'

'I agree,' said Liz. 'I don't suppose the bosses of Movie Munch will be all that chuffed to find that their launch of a brand-new chain of restaurants was overshadowed by a big fat git slugging it out with the photographers they'd actually invited.'

'What I want to know is how the photographers immediately seemed to know who was who,' said Janet. 'I seem to remember that they were instantly on the scene and aware that Harry was trying to hide his Italian woman away from Val.'

'Ah hem.' Sam coughed shyly. All eyes suddenly fixed on him.

'You can blame that one on me,' he announced. 'I tipped them off. I hadn't planned to, because to be honest, I couldn't believe Harry would actually be daft enough to take her along to a company function. Sorry, Val.'

He nodded apologetically in Val's direction.

'Please don't be,' said Val. 'You must remember that I knew Harry was up to something ages ago. He made my life a complete and utter misery. What I needed was the proof before I could make the changes. I needed this confrontation, honestly.'

Sam continued: 'We were all queueing up to say thanks to Sir James when one of the photographers just quietly asked me what was going on. I'm afraid I couldn't resist it. I just said something along the lines of "Stick around, mate. The big fat bloke on the table up ahead has brought his bird, and his wife's in this queue and about to find out. Watch out for the fireworks display." And the rest, as they say, is history.'

Everyone took another slurp of champagne, while they absorbed this new revelation.

'Go on, tell them why,' said Nina, nudging Sam. 'You might as well now, there's nothing to lose.'

'Guess there's not any more,' said Sam, who was not used to all this attention. 'Well, it was a kind of revenge really. Ages and ages ago, I stumbled on some little, well let's call them irregularities in some of Harry's deals and transactions. In simple terms, because we accountants are always accused of making everything complicated, Harry was not averse to the odd backhander. There were some really quite clever little fiddles.'

'What did you do?' asked Liz, incredulous.

'I had a word with him.'

'And?' they all enquired.

'I was accused of not doing my job properly. He said the error was probably mine and how dare I accuse him,' said Sam. 'He threatened me with the sack. Well, I could have kicked myself afterwards, but before I got around to print-ing off copies of the evidence, they'd been mysteriously wiped from the computer. One whole file completely dis-appeared and crucial bits were deleted from others overnight. Someone got straight on to the case and had managed to penetrate the system.'

'Any idea who?' asked Janet.

'Oh yes, Computer Support did manage to find out. The lovely Geraldine, no less.'

'No doubt on Harry's orders,' said Janet grimly.

'Let's eat,' announced Jon, ushering them all into the dining room, where they crammed elbow to elbow around the small table. After the pâté and melba toast, Sue brought in a huge roast chicken which had been cooked with tarragon and lemon, new potatoes and a platter of roasted Mediterranean vegetables. There was a lot of jostling as plates were passed around, everyone giggling at the lack of space. The champagne now all gone, Jon produced fresh glasses and poured out white Burgundy.

Everyone pretended not to notice Val tipping her glass surreptitiously into Jed's once he'd emptied his, just as she'd done during the rounds of champagne. The conversation lulled as everyone tucked in, trying to avoid each other's elbows in the process.

Suddenly Janet banged the table. All eyes turned in her direction.

'It's suddenly come back to me,' she said, 'why did Sir James make that speech mentioning me?'

'Why shouldn't he?' replied Liz. 'He was quite rightly thanking you for making that fantastic film. It was the best bit of the evening.'

'No, no. You're missing the point. Why did he mention *me*? How did he know that I did it? Normally Harry takes credit for everything.'

'But you said Sir James found you in the office working late one night and watched the tape,' replied Liz.

'But he didn't know I'd made the film.' Janet was emphatic. 'He thought it was all Harry's work. All I did was shove a tape in a machine for him to watch. It could have been made by Alfred Hitchcock for all he cared.'

'I told him,' said a small voice from the other end of the

table. All eyes turned towards Val. 'I rang him and told him,' she repeated quietly.

'You what?' went up the chorus.

With all eyes now firmly rooted on Val, she calmly explained how angry she'd felt with Harry about the lies, the swanking, the bullying and of course the affair. But it was when Janet had hinted that he even stooped so low as to take credit for other people's work that she'd decided to act.

'I phoned up Sir James at home on Thursday,' said Val. 'The night before the big do, the night Harry always sees his bit on the side. We had quite an illuminating little chat. I think he was surprised to hear from me, but he was very interested in what I had to say. I just told him that the staff at HOT were absolutely fed up with not getting the credit or the praise for what they did and here was another classic example. I explained to him that Janet had not only made the film, but she'd actually clinched the deal in the first place. I hope you don't mind, but I sort of hinted that if things didn't improve she might leave, and that it would be disastrous for HOT.'

'Did you mention Harry?' said Janet anxiously.

'Absolutely,' said Val. 'I think that's what clinched it. If it had been anyone else I was accusing, then he'd probably have told me to naff off. But because I was effectively stabbing my husband in the back, he really did take note. I also told him that if he didn't believe me, to check my story with any film crew, or anyone else in the building for that matter.'

'Seems he did,' said a stunned Janet. 'Val, you played a blinder.'

'No wonder Harry looked so mutinous,' said Sue. 'We did even better than we thought. Apart from completely mucking up a very expensive PR evening, apart from probably losing the company future projects and apart from introducing our boss's wife to his mistress, we've managed to let the chairman know that his head honcho treats his staff like peasants and claims the credit for everything.'

'He can't sack us now, he just can't,' said Liz, now looking much happier.

'Trouble is, Harry always comes up smelling of roses,' warned Janet. 'We're the ones who'll be left behind in the shit.'

'We'll find out soon enough tomorrow,' said Ray, who'd been uncharacteristically quiet. 'And I'm more than confident it will be good news.'

'Why, what have you heard?' said Sue.

Ray shot them all a look of mischief. 'It's not what I've heard. It's what Sir James may have heard by now.'

'Blimey, this really is turning into a confession session. What have you been up to this time?' asked Janet suspiciously.

'Well, you remember that time you had a conversation with Harry,' said Ray, 'and you were wired up, and he made all those threats.'

'Yeesss,' said Janet resignedly. She was bracing herself for Ray's next revelation.

'Well, Ron had the tape and he said it was locked away for a rainy day,' said Ray, slightly nervous now of the reaction to his announcement. 'Well, we had a couple of beers round at the GX one night last week and decided that this rainy day of yours was never going to come along unless we created some sort of downpour. So first of all Ron played it to me. Bloody hell, Janet, is he always that brutal?'

'Yeah, mostly,' replied Janet. 'He makes Vlad the Impaler

look like a Monday-night darts player by comparison. What did you do then?'

Ray paled slightly and took a big glug of wine. 'I sent the tape round by courier to Sir James yesterday. Honest, Janet, I'm sorry if you're cross, but what was the point of hanging on to it any longer? There was never going to be a better opportunity.'

'Oh, you're right Ray,' conceded Janet. 'I suppose I've been deluding myself about the rainy-day syndrome. It's now or never, isn't it?'

Janet sat back in her chair, her mind reeling. So other forces had been at work: Sam tipping off the photographers about who was who, Ray sending a tape to Sir James of Harry's threats, and amazingly, Val shopping her own husband. It was all quite a shock.

Over the puddings and coffee, she was still deep in thought, replaying the scenes at the Casablanca launch in her head. There was something still not quite right. One more missing jigsaw piece.

'Aha,' she said, snapping her fingers in delight. 'I've got it. I introduced all of you to Sir James on Friday night. But Val, he didn't seem to know you. Yet you say you spoke to him before the event to tell him what Harry had been up to. So why did you greet each other like a couple of strangers?'

Val looked a bit sheepish for a second or two. Then she grinned broadly.

'We were just acting,' she said simply. 'I told him I was probably going to be there, but not with Harry. That was our little secret. I had to take the risk. You see, Sir James realized two things about Harry on Friday that he didn't approve of. Firstly that he'd turned up with a woman who was not his wife, and secondly that Harry couldn't make tea, let alone television.'

chapter thirty-nine

Sunday had been sunny, all upbeat determination that they would finally outdo Harry, or at least keep their jobs. But Monday morning, with its ominous grey skies and gathering storm clouds, dispelled every last ounce of optimism.

Janet was awake at five. The alarm clock could enjoy another two hours' respite, but not her. She half opened the curtains to greet another grey day. How symbolic, she thought, shivering. She lay in bed wondering what to wear. Magazines never gave you advice on the perfect outfit to wear for getting the sack. Probably the same as the outfit for getting the job. Safe old navy blue, nothing outrageous or overtly sexy. Dignified, subdued, just the thing to pop along to the wake afterwards. The last rites and then the final interment of your last pay cheque.

Liz couldn't remember sleeping at all. She'd tossed and turned, constantly noticing the time on her digital alarm clock: 2.37, 3.15, 4.03, 4.39 – she'd seen them all. Would getting the sack affect her relationship with Tony? Jobs in the media weren't two a penny, so maybe she'd have to move to another area. Would Tony move with her, or beg her to stay? Or would he wave her cheerfully off? Maybe this was the catalyst that would make him come to grips with the C word. Commitment wasn't such a very long word, only three syllables. Neither of them had kids or baggage. Just themselves. If he insisted on staying with his job, should she relinquish her next career move? Yes, yes, yes came the resounding answer in her head. She gasped to herself, rather ashamed at how desperately keen she was.

Nina awoke with a start. She'd been having a particularly vivid dream about lottery winners and woke up in that twilight state when it takes a while to sort out reality from the dream. The reality wasn't all that promising. A lottery winner she was certainly not about to be. The only millions she'd be getting anywhere near were the rest of the country's unwaged. And Sam too. Would Harry lump him into the plot? What a horrible start to their life together, both made redundant by a big fat bully. She made a mental note not to wear any mascara today in case she burst into tears.

Sue stirred next to Jon, enjoying the luxurious warmth of his body. Oh God, D-day, she thought. At least Jon's job was still there. It would be a struggle until she could find another post, but they'd manage. She'd miss the folk at HOT, though. She loved her job there. It certainly wasn't dull, and Friday night's scenario was testament to that.

Val, still luxuriating in Janet's spare room, was having a fantasy dream about a holiday with Jed in Kenya, alternating their days on paradise beaches of pure white sand and swaying palm trees with jeep safaris around magnificent game reserves. She could imagine Jed, his skin tanned and beaded with a mixture of sweat and dust, pointing out giraffes quietly feeding from trees, or a herd of elephants plodding its way across a dusty plain, the calves tucked protectively into the line. The pair of them, impossibly glamorous yet casually dressed in khaki cottons and pith helmets, ballooning across the Masai Mara watching exotic wildlife through binoculars, and then returning at night to a sumptuous safari lodge for a fabulous meal followed by all-night sex.

She awoke with a jolt. The shock of wondering where she was was swiftly followed by the fact that it was Monday morning. The Day of Reckoning. She reached for her cigarettes, lit one and lay back against the propped-up pillows. She didn't normally smoke in bed, but given the tension she'd woken up with, she needed one to relax. A couple of deep puffs didn't make the slightest difference. Today was the day. The day when her friends would probably be sacked by her rotten husband, or soon-to-be-ex rotten husband. It couldn't get much more dreadful, because it was partly her fault.

Val had already resolved to follow the girls into HOT without telling them. She'd give Janet an hour or so start and then take a taxi up to the offices. There she'd find out what the score was, confront Harry about a divorce and then escape to her parents' for a few days.

Shuddering at the scenario ahead, she stubbed out her cigarette, got out of bed and went downstairs to fill the kettle. She was just brewing up a pot of tea when Janet appeared in the kitchen, heavy-eyed and tense.

'Oh well, I don't like Mondays at the best of times,' Janet said resolutely, accepting Val's offer of a cup of tea. 'If the world ends at lunchtime, then at least today will be a day of mourning!'

They both made mock chuckling noises.

'What are your plans, Val?' asked Janet. 'You know you can stay here as long as you wish.'

'That's sweet of you, but I'm going to go down to Hampshire today,' said Val. 'My parents are planning a party.'

'Bit unfortunate in the current circumstances, isn't it?' asked Janet.

'Oh no. They're celebrating not ever having to see Harry again,' said Val. 'They absolutely hate his guts. They think he's a big fat sod.'

'And so say all of us,' said Janet wearily.

'Sorry, that was a bit tactless,' apologized Val. 'It's all right for me, skipping off to Hampshire for a celebration. What will you do if he gives you the chop?'

'Get blind drunk is probably a popular option,' said Janet. 'Yesterday at Sue's I really believed we might be spared the Big Elbow, but in the cold light of day, I just don't know. I've seen this all before. Harry's sacked a lot of people for no reason since he's been at HOT. To be fair, he's jolly good at it. Gets lots of practice and gets away with it.'

Janet, Nina, Sue, Liz, Ray and Sam had agreed to meet in the HOT car park on the dot of nine and all go into the building together. So there they were, huddled together in the sharp early-autumn wind, subdued and pale, hearts thumping.

'Whatever happens this morning, let's all meet up for lunch at the Groin Exchange,' suggested Ray. 'However it goes, let's be there. Then we can either drown our sorrows or celebrate the best news HOT's ever had.'

They all nodded in unison in the biting wind. Then they set off purposefully towards the main entrance. So far so good; no official-looking letters at reception, no overnight security guard barring their way or asking them to return their entry passes or mobile phones. Harry hadn't yet arrived, they ascertained, but Geraldine was already in.

'I hope she's had lots of sex and hoovering over the weekend,' said Nina bitterly, 'because it's going to be downhill all the way for that bag. That's only if we win, of course.'

'I suppose if Harry wins he'll probably give her a whopping great pay rise, or a misplaced loyalty bonus,' replied Liz gloomily. 'Then she'll be able to buy even more beige outfits.'

'Huh, she might actually splash out on something half decent,' said Janet. 'I wonder how Geraldine would cope with Red Or Dead.'

'Not enough beige,' said Liz. 'Let's hope she never ventures out in Issy Miyake. I dread to think what she'd make of that.'

They all trooped through the security door and went to their various departments: Sam upstairs to Accounts; Ray, Nina, Liz and Janet to the production office' while Sue took up her place at the reception desk.

By nine thirty there was still no sign of Harry. Sue was keeping Janet's office abreast of events out on the front desk. Janet noticed that her heart started thumping every time the phone rang. By ten o'clock she'd waded through the post and e-mails. Mercifully she'd seen nothing in the morning papers about Harry's big scene at Casablanca. Newspaper editors faced with yet another pile of photographs of Eastender celebrities at yet another opening, had found better fish to fry. However, the trade press at the end of the week might be another matter. They'd be interested in Harry all right, despite the fact that the incident was relatively minor. It was a PR catastrophe.

She turned her attention to the next Movie Munch projects. Probably not much point now, but she might as well do some work on them anyway. At ten thirty she gave in to the strain and summoned the others to coffee in the canteen. They huddled in a corner, nursing their steaming mugs as though they'd just found a Happy Eater near the North Pole.

'Where's Harry then?' asked Nina. 'There's still no sign of him. Trouble is, none of us wants to ring up boring old Geraldine and find out where he is.'

'Might stir up a hornets' nest,' advised Ray.

'On the other hand,' said Liz, 'suppose we sit here all day sweating it out and then find that Harry's at the dentist, or that he's on leave? We're going to feel a teensy bit silly.'

'Val would have known if he was on holiday, wouldn't she?' queried Nina.

'Heavens no, not necessarily,' said Janet. 'Remember who we're dealing with here. This is the man who got away with a five-star freebie in the Algarve by telling everyone including his wife that he was off on a working trip to Manchester. No, sorry, one of us has to find out from Geraldine and it ought to be me. I'll do it when I go back to my desk.'

The telephone on the canteen wall rang shrilly, almost knocking itself off with the vibration. Ray went over and picked it up.

'That was Sue,' he said grim-faced. 'Apparently Sir James has just arrived.'

'Back to our looms then,' said Janet. They trooped silently back down the corridor to the production office. Janet was just bracing herself to call Geraldine to check out Harry's whereabouts when her phone rang. There was no mistaking the honeyed tones of Fiona Crosbie, Sir James's PA. Janet caught her breath, bracing herself for impact. Do come up to Sir James's office in five minutes' time if it's convenient, was the request.

If it's convenient, thought Janet. That doesn't quite sound like the parting of the ways. Or maybe it was a way of putting you at your ease *before* the parting of the ways, before the body blows were delivered. Before she could go over and tell the others, she realized that they too were receiving the same call. So five minutes later, Janet, Sue, Ray, Nina, Sam and Liz found themselves walking along the executive corridor in silence to Sir James's office. Further up, they could see Geraldine at her desk, tapping away at her computer, head firmly down, trying to hide behind a huge vase of yellow lilies stuck in a pot on her desk.

Fiona Crosbie ushered them into Sir James's office. Please make her offer us coffee, prayed Janet. If she does, then we're off the hook. If she doesn't, it's clear your desks and be out in half an hour. Please offer us coffee, she continued to plead silently. Damn, she thought, as the door clicked shut behind them. We're out, she thought in despair.

Sir James Patterson Cripps sat behind a vast desk, even more vast than Harry's, signing a pile of documents. As he put his pen down and looked up, the door opened again behind them. They all turned involuntarily.

'I'm so sorry,' said Fiona smoothly, 'I can't think what came over me then. Would any of you people like tea? Coffee? Mineral water?'

They all asked for coffee. Janet felt she'd just come out of intensive care.

'Well,' said Sir James, smiling benignly at them all over the top of his bi-focals. Janet noticed that he was wearing

364

another random selection of well-worn aristo clothes: tweed jacket, pink shirt, dark blue tie with orange stripes, all obviously expensive and with another good couple of decades left in them.

'There's something I want to discuss with you,' he said, still smiling. 'It follows on really from Friday night. Which, incidentally, I thoroughly enjoyed, and I hope you did too.'

They all mumbled agreement and renewed thank-yous for the tickets.

'As you know, the opening of Casablanca was a great landmark for HOT, probably the biggest thing we've been involved in to date. And it's a long-term project with a huge profile. You may be pleased to know that Casablanca was the first of many openings. Movie Munch are planning at least twenty themed restaurants around the country. Possibly more.'

They all nodded like robots.

Sir James continued: 'A project like this pushes a company like ours into the premier league, a league in which we might at some stage float the company on the stock market. Capital raised in that way could expand the company swiftly and I believe that HOT has the talent, the expertise, the nerve and the integrity to do just that.'

Now for the drop, thought Janet pessimistically. We can't do it with you lot mucking it up and you've all got to go. She tried to take a sip of coffee but her hand was shaking too much. She replaced the cup in the saucer quickly.

'To put it bluntly,' said Sir James, 'there is one stumbling block to all this. I used the word integrity just now. It might be an old-fashioned word, but I'm an old-fashioned man. In the last few days I have discovered some of the practices that have been going on here, and frankly, I'm appalled.'

They all gasped, wondering if he'd rumbled the plottings of the Haunted Handbag committee. Still no one could speak. They all nodded dumbly again, steeling themselves.

Sir James suddenly smiled at them. 'I don't actually know where to begin to apologize to you all. But apologize I must. I had no idea of the way in which Harry Hampton has been conducting the company's business.'

They all broke into smiles of relief.

'In the last few days I have been collecting evidence, and what I am about to tell you must go no further than these four walls. But I feel I owe it to you, and probably most of the production office as well for that matter. We have discovered financial irregularities in Harry's affairs which I won't go into detail about but which include evidence of large payments to him from some of our contractors going back over a number of years in return for favours, commercial information and so on.

'I have also received a tape of Harry speaking to you, Janet. You know of the existence of this tape, I take it?'

Janet nodded. 'It was a fairly typical exchange with Harry,' she mumbled.

Sir James continued: 'Disgraceful, simply disgraceful, and typifies a man who took credit for everything whether it was his work or not. I now gather that a number of people were either threatened or actually sacked if they didn't toe the line. I don't know if you are all aware, but I had a very illuminating telephone conversation last week with Mrs Hampton, who put me right on a number of matters. Hence my speech on Friday night, Janet, emphasizing that the film had been your work.

'I was then appalled to discover that Harry intended to be at a very high-profile opening with a woman who is clearly not his wife. This was not appropriate. I thought Mrs Hampton very brave to turn up in the circumstances. And on that subject, there is one other piece of information that came to light which I'd rather Mrs Hampton did not hear. I think she should be spared this.'

Oh heck, what's this one going to be? thought Janet.

'I gather that Harry often resorted to, er – how can I put this delicately? – sexual harassment to, er, get his way. I am informed that he actually, er, foisted himself sexually on female members of staff from time to time. This is of course tantamount to rape, and if it had been reported he would undoubtedly have been sacked and ultimately imprisoned. This is an intolerable state of affairs which at least is now over. Although small comfort for the women involved.'

Janet couldn't look at Liz. Had she told him? Liz betrayed nothing, looking stony-faced ahead.

'And finally, the managing director of Movie Munch, whilst being delighted with the way the opening went, and of course with Janet's superb video, did not appreciate the public spectacle of Harry hitting a photographer. An exercise in good public relations it was not.

'So there you have it, in a nutshell,' beamed Sir James, sitting back in his seat.

'What happens now?' asked Nina. 'We've spent all weekend thinking we'll be sacked. Harry threatened to boot us out.'

'Absolutely not,' said Sir James. 'In fact I am thinking of sanctioning a bigger Christmas bonus this year as a tacit way of apologizing to those who have had to put up with Harry's disgraceful behaviour over the years. I must insist, though, that you don't circulate that around the building, or indeed this conversation. I'll be addressing the entire staff this afternoon to announce Harry's demise.'

They all screamed in delight, then immediately tried to cover up the fact that they'd reacted so strongly.

'Yes, Harry's gone. After completing my investigations over the weekend, I visited him at home last night and fired him. He is now officially barred from the building.'

They all gasped with relief. It was almost too much to take in.

'Right then, back to work everyone, and let's put this sorry episode behind us. Oh, Janet, would you stay behind for a moment?'

The others trooped out, trying to restrain themselves from whooping when they reached the corridor.

Janet's heart sank. What on earth was this about?

'Now, Janet,' beamed Sir James, 'this is not a reward for putting up with Harry for so long, although God knows you deserve a gong for it. I am offering you the job. Harry's job.'

Janet gasped, the colour draining completely from her face.

'You have all the qualifications and the experience, and your team deeply respect you. I can't think of a better candidate and neither can the board. We had an emergency meeting about Harry's situation yesterday at which we also discussed offering you the job.'

'I don't know what to say,' said Janet, completely stunned.

'Don't say anything. Think about it, and if you agree, I can announce it at the staff meeting this afternoon,' said Sir James. 'They're going to get one bit of good news, so they might as well have another, if you agree.'

Janet's mind was racing. A promotion like this had never entered her head. She now felt almost guilty that she'd help plot Harry's downfall and now here she was benefiting from it.

'There's one problem in all this, Sir James, which is insurmountable,' she said, trying to keep the wobble out of her voice. 'Geraldine. I'm sorry, but I really couldn't work with her.'

'I'm sure we can sort something out,' said Sir James smoothly. 'Confidentially, we're looking closely at whether Geraldine had any knowledge of, or was involved in Harry's various fiddles. If she was, and it looks likely, then she'll be fired. If not, we'll find a way around this. Don't worry.'

Janet stood up and they shook hands. Janet found herself fighting back tears. Tears of relief that the years of Harry's bullying were finally at an end, tears of emotion that her talents had finally been recognized and valued. I should just make it to the loo before I break down, she thought as she left the office.

Stepping outside, she heard a familiar voice, raised in temper.

'You were in on this all the time, you nasty piece of shit. Covering up for him and all his affairs. You're a marriage-wrecker, that's what you are. Sitting there like Goody Bloody Two Shoes, all prim and proper. Aiding and abetting a criminal, a liar and a serial womanizer. You knew what he was up to, didn't you? You took calls from the mistress, ordered flowers, booked restaurants for them. Covered up for him, lied to me. I suppose he's had you as well, along with all the rest. Well, you're welcome to him.'

Val snatched up the yellow lilies that had been on the

369

desk and started hitting Geraldine around the head with them. Deep orange pollen marks were appearing all over Geraldine's beige jacket. She just sat there motionless, too shocked to speak.

'Well, the bottom line, Geraldine, is that you have done me the most enormous favour,' Val continued. 'Thanks to you, I'm out of my marriage, and Harry's welcome to that Italian slut and all the others for all I care.'

With a flourish, she handed back the bashed-up flowers.

'Here, put these in water, they need a bit of loving care, just like me. On second thoughts, don't bother.' Val promptly picked up the vase and tipped the entire contents over Geraldine's head.

Janet was transfixed. She was so enjoying it, she didn't want the scene to end. Sir James, hearing the commotion, came to the door of the office. Janet turned back to speak to him.

'That problem about Geraldine,' she said. 'I think it's just been resolved.'

chapter forty

Janet sat at her desk, thinking back over the past seven or eight months. She'd got rid of the paintings, the ridiculous *Mastermind* chair and the enormous desk. Instead she'd given the office a softer look, with Japanese paper lanterns, some giant palms, a much smaller desk and some comfortable deep green sofas for more informal discussions.

Nina sat outside at Geraldine's old desk but, given her production experience, in a much enhanced role as Janet's PA. Newly married to Sam, with that radiance all new brides have, she kept pinching herself at the thought of her own happiness.

It hadn't been quite such plain sailing for Liz. Promoted into Janet's old job, she'd grown in confidence now that Harry was off the scene and was giving her new challenge 110 per cent. Unfortunately her relationship with Tony had bitten the dust; all her own making, she knew, because she'd got too heavy with him. So she'd thrown herself wholeheartedly into her new job and resolved not to make the same mistakes again. She'd cancelled her *Mother and Baby* subscription, and recently she'd even been able to walk past Pronuptia and Mothercare without looking in the windows.

Janet gazed around the office. It really had been an eventful few months for them all. Val had managed to get almost the fastest divorce on record. With no children and financially able to walk away from the life she and Harry had shared, Val hadn't even bothered to go back to their house. She'd cheerfully left everything: her clothes, her jewellery, her car and her share of the property. And in a wonderful twist of irony, Jed had gallantly agreed to be named as the guilty party so that Harry could save face and swiftly divorce Val on the grounds of adultery. Harry had communicated only through lawyers, and Val now confidently expected never to have to clap eyes on him again. Jed also hoped his gallant action would score even more brownie points with Val.

She'd held a divorce party at her parents' mansion in Hampshire and invited everyone from HOT who could make the journey. Indicative of the hate and loathing which Harry had inspired, there'd been a massive turnout to mark the end of an era. Crate after crate of champagne had been consumed in celebration. But not by Val. She knew she couldn't venture down that route again. And besides, things were going well with Jed, and she was looking forward to getting her driving licence back, so why risk rotting it all up?

Curiously, no one ever mentioned Harry's name again after the day it was announced he'd left. It was as though he'd never existed. His only legacy had been a trail of deep unhappiness and stress from which everyone wanted to move on as quickly as possible.

Yes, it had been an amazing few months. Thanks to her huge pay rise, Janet was now selling her house and moving up. She'd declined the use of Harry's company

Mercedes on the grounds of too many connotations, and opted instead for a more practical Mazda saloon. And she'd even persuaded Val to accompany her on a shopping mission to London to help her choose some good business suits for her new job. Not that Val needed much cajoling.

Over lunch in Langan's Brasserie, they'd giggled and enthused about their new lives.

'Was I really dreadful when I was drinking?' Val had asked, contemplating her glass of mineral water.

'Worse than that; you were simply appalling,' Janet had replied. 'You were a total bitch, Val, to be briefly honest, a completely different person. But I can understand the reasons why.'

'You're the best friend I could ever have.' Tears had welled up in Val's eyes. 'I could never even begin to apologize for what you all put up with.'

'Actually, as it turned out, you did us the most enormous favour. We all got together through you taking us out for those meals, and then we basically plotted Harry's downfall as a result. Harry's gone, Geraldine's gone, and here we are, the very best of friends.'

'Call for you,' came Nina's voice. 'It's a European filmmaking trust. They say it's confidential, won't discuss what they want to ask. Shall I put them through?'

'Might as well,' said Janet.

A man with a French accent introduced himself and briefly outlined the work of the trust.

'How can I help you then?' asked Janet.

'Well, it's fairly straightforward. We have just created a new post of European director of programmes. It's a really key post and we're drawing up a short list.'

He briefly described the job, which came with a massive salary and perks, a megabuck budget and a large team of producers.

'So you understand now,' the Frenchman continued, 'we have to be sure we make the right appointment. One of our contenders has exactly the right experience and I believe he used to work at HOT. But he hasn't listed anyone from the company for a reference. A Mr Harold Hampton. Do you know him? Could you tell me a bit about him?'

The name still gave Janet a familiar jolt. She paused, drew a deep breath and grinned to herself.

'Hm, bit of a problem, that one. If you have five minutes, I'll put you in the picture . . .'